650
Best Food
Processor
Recipes

650 Best Food Processor Recipes

George Geary & Judith Finlayson

Robert
ROSE

650 Best Food Processor Recipes
Text copyright © 2010 George Geary and Judith Finlayson
Photographs copyright © 2010 Robert Rose Inc.
Cover and text design copyright © 2010 Robert Rose Inc.

Some of the recipes in this book have appeared in other cookbooks by the same authors.

For complete cataloguing information, see page 634.

Disclaimer

The recipes in this book have been carefully tested by our kitchen and our tasters. To the best of our knowledge, they are safe and nutritious for ordinary use and users. For those people with food or other allergies, or who have special food requirements or health issues, please read the suggested contents of each recipe carefully and determine whether or not they may create a problem for you. All recipes are used at the risk of the consumer. Consumers should always consult their food processor manufacturer's manual for recommended procedures and cooking times.

We cannot be responsible for any hazards, loss or damage that may occur as a result of any recipe use.

For those with special needs, allergies, requirements or health problems, in the event of any doubt, please contact your medical adviser prior to the use of any recipe.

Design and Production: Kevin Cockburn/PageWave Graphics Inc.
Editor: Carol Sherman
Recipe Editor: Jennifer MacKenzie
Recipe Tester: Audrey King
Copy Editor: Karen Campbell-Sheviak
Indexer: Gillian Watts
Cover Photography: Colin Erricson
Interior Photography: Colin Erricson and Mark T. Shapiro
Food Styling: Kathryn Robertson and Kate Bush
Prop Styling: Charlene Erricson

Cover image: Traditional Coleslaw (page 390)

We acknowledge the financial support of the Government of Canada through the Book Publishing Industry Development Program (BPIDP) for our publishing activities.

Published by Robert Rose Inc.
120 Eglinton Avenue East, Suite 800, Toronto, Ontario, Canada M4P 1E2
Tel: (416) 322-6552 Fax: (416) 322-6936

Printed and bound in Canada

1 2 3 4 5 6 7 8 9 TCP 18 17 16 15 14 13 12 11 10

Mixed Sources
Product group from well-managed forests and other controlled sources
www.fsc.org Cert no. SW-COC-000952
© 1996 Forest Stewardship Council
FSC

Contents

Acknowledgments

Thanks to my parents for their 100 per cent support, my two sisters Monica and Pattie and their families, Neil for the world. Sephno Systems for all of my computer support. The entire "CRAFT" group for testing, eating and sharing so much information. My United Airline family Robin and Reena and Starbucks Corona Crew. Jonathan for his lifelong friendship. The Danish Cultural Center and Erika and Sara from Holland America Line for letting me share my talents aboard your "DAM" ships. And, finally, thanks to my agent Lisa Ekus, publisher Bob Dees, editor Carol Sherman, recipe editor Jennifer MacKenzie, copy editor Karen Campbell-Sheviak and designers PageWave Graphics for being the best team any author could have.

GG

As always, thanks to Bob for being there and for being consistently supportive. To Marian Jarkovich and Nina McCreath for professional commitment above and beyond the call of duty. To recipe tester Audrey King and recipe editor Jennifer MacKenzie for their due diligence. To the team at PageWave Graphics — Andrew, Joseph, Kevin and Daniella — for making the book look beautiful. And to copy editor Karen Campbell-Sheviak and my long-time editor Carol Sherman, for ensuring top-notch quality control on the paper.

JF

We would also like to jointly thank KitchenAid and Cuisinart for providing us with their state-of-the art food processors, which made the volume of recipes we needed to test seem almost as manageable as those first processors did cheese spreads.

Introduction

When the food processor migrated from commercial kitchens to the domestic market in the mid-1970s, it launched a mini-revolution. Suddenly it became possible for home cooks to prepare many dishes they had previously found too labor-intensive.

Using the metal blade rather than arm power, they could produce elegant puréed soups and fresh rustic pestos in no time at all. The slicing and shredding blades made short work of exotic salsas and salads and even old standbys such as scalloped potatoes and coleslaw. Surprisingly, these seemingly miraculous achievements were accomplished with a machine that didn't even have a switch to turn if off and on and a single work bowl that could accommodate only $2\frac{1}{2}$ cups (625 mL) of watery liquid per batch.

Food processors have come a long way since then. The new generation of these magical appliances comes equipped with space-age keypads, settings for kneading dough and wide feed tubes with thinner inserts to suit all your slicing and shredding needs. They have a full range of attachments, from egg whips to juice extractors and bowls in various sizes to accommodate specific tasks and minimize cleanup.

The food processor is one of any cook's most indispensable assistants. In this book we provide more than 650 recipes to help you get the most out of this terrific appliance. We hope you will actively sample our offerings and in so doing will discover many dishes that over time will become old family favorites.

Judith Finlayson & George Geary

Purchasing a Food Processor

With so many different sizes, types, prices and brands of food processors on the market, it can be difficult to know which one is the best fit for you. Before purchasing a food processor, read up on what's available. You want to make the correct decision. If you buy one that is too small you might have to replace it sooner rather than later. On the other hand, you don't want a huge machine with unused capacity occupying valuable counter space.

Using your Processor Efficiently

Food processors have a lot of different parts so be careful not to toss anything out when you're unpacking your new machine. The first things you should do are: lay out all the parts, fill out any registration forms and watch the instructional video/DVD, if one is provided. Watch it again while you're assembling the machine. Instructional materials are key to all the parts and how they work and they will help you to get the most out of your food processor.

General Description of Machine Sizes

Food Processor

A food processor has interchangeable blades that are used for shredding, blending, chopping or slicing food. Many companies classify small choppers as food processors. However, for the purposes of this book, we have defined a food processor as an appliance that has interchangeable blades that can slice and shred as well as chop. In general terms, the appliance is categorized according to size, based on a cup amount. Food processors fall into the following categories:

Small Choppers

1- to 2-cup capacities

These are great for very small jobs in which you only need to chop. These machines work well on herbs or even coffee beans.

Small Food Processors

4- to 9-cup capacities

These are great for small jobs that may include puréeing, shredding and slicing. They are perfect for one or two or a small family.

Medium Food Processors

12- to 14-cup capacities

This size of processor is the kitchen workhorse. It can do all jobs. Most of the recipes in this book will work with a machine of this size.

Large Food Processors

20-cup or more capacities

Large food processors are for large families or for people who entertain a lot.

3-in-1 Food Processors

Many of the newer models have three bowls that nest in each other. They can be cumbersome to use because all the bowls may need to fit together properly before the machine will run. However, they are convenient in terms of cleanup. You can use the smaller bowls first and then the larger ones, which means you don't have to wash up until you're finished processing. The mini-bowl attachment is a small bowl that works with its own metal blade. It's perfect for chopping dry herbs or garlic cloves. It's also great for processing recipes with smaller yields such as salad dressings, salsas and dips.

Getting to Know your Machine

Basic Parts for All Machines

Base Housing

The base houses the motor and power supply for your machine. Most machines have three main buttons: On, Pulse and Off. "On" is referred to as "Process" throughout the recipes in this book. It keeps the motor running until you push the "Off" button. "Pulse" makes the motor "jump." Watch the ingredients in the work bowl while you "pulse" and you'll see the food jumps in the bowl and the blade will move a full spin. The base is the only part of your food processor that cannot be submerged in water. To clean, wipe it down with a soft cloth.

Work Bowl

This bowl must be attached correctly or your food processor won't work. There is only one way to put the machine together and if one part isn't properly attached the machine will not start. This is a safety feature. Because the blades are so sharp and move at such high speeds, the manufacturers want to make sure you don't injure yourself. Before putting any food in the work bowl, assemble the entire unit. Test it with a pulse to make sure it operates.

Metal Blade

This all-purpose blade is also known as the steel blade. It is the one you'll use most. It's used for processing, pulsing, chopping, puréeing and blending. The blade is very sharp — think of it as two knives side by side — so be very careful when handling it. To remove food from the work bowl, take the bowl off the base of the machine, leaving the blade in place. Put your forefinger in the hole underneath and your thumb on the bottom edge of the bowl and secure the blade in the bowl. Tip the bowl over and dump or pour the ingredients into another receptacle. Then grip the plastic hub of the blade and remove it from the bowl. Use a spatula to carefully scrape food from the blade and any remaining food from the work bowl.

When processing with the metal blade, the blade spins very fast. When you turn the motor off, you want the blade to stop immediately — almost on a dime. This is a good test to try when you're looking to purchase a machine. If the blade keeps spinning after you push the "off" button, your recipes are likely to be overprocessed.

Slicing Blade

Most machines come with one slicing blade. Check your manual for specific instructions on using this blade. Typically, it has a stem that is inserted into the base. Once the blade is in place, you place the cover over it. This prevents your fingers from coming in contact with the spinning blade. Ingredients to be sliced are added to the feed tube and you use the plunger to push them down, making contact with the blade. The result is perfect, even slices.

You can purchase other blades that will create different slice thicknesses (see Extra Blades and Other Accessories, opposite).

Shredding Blade

Most machines come with one shredding blade. Check your manual for how to use this blade. Like the slicing blade, it typically has a stem that is inserted into the base and the cover needs to be in place before it will work. Ingredients are placed in the feed tube and the plunger is used to push them down. This is a very handy tool because it makes short work of shredding, which can be a tedious process, particularly if you're doing a large quantity. You can purchase other blades that will create different shreds (see Extra Blades and Other Accessories, opposite).

Lid/Cover

This covers the work bowl. Some models have a completely flat cover except for the center, where you remove a "plug" to add ingredients. Most have a large feed tube area. Food is pushed through the feed tube with the pusher/plunger when slicing or shredding. For safety, in most models the complete cover, feed tube and pusher must be assembled before the motor will run.

Pusher/Plunger

The pusher/plunger is generally used with the slicing or shredding blades and in some models must be in place for the motor to run. The pusher guides the food through the feed tube onto the blade.

You lift the pusher up out of the feed tube, place the ingredient on top of the blade and reinsert the pusher on top. The pusher then triggers an activating rod that goes through the handle and the work bowl into the base, which causes the motor to start.

Feed Tube

The pusher in the large feed tube often has an insert with a small opening that accommodates a small pusher. This opening is referred to as the "small feed tube." The small pusher can be removed separately from the large pusher to create an opening. This opening is mainly used to add liquids, an egg or small amounts of dry ingredients while the motor is running. Some models have a drip hole in the bottom of the small pusher that allows oils or other liquid ingredients to drizzle into the work bowl. This is a great feature if you're making mayonnaise.

Extra Blades and Other Accessories

All the recipes in this book use the blades and accessories that come with a regular food processor (metal blade, shredding blade and slicing blade). Food processor manufacturers have brought out many extras from time to time. These include:

Slicing blades: An array of different thicknesses.

Crinkle cut slicing blades: If you want a zigzag cut pattern.

Shredding blades: Different shred thicknesses are offered.

Mixer/whip attachment: To whip egg whites and whipped cream.

Juicer: Great if you want to juice citrus fruit.

Check your machine's website to see other options available to purchase.

A to Z Ingredient Guide
for Chopping, Slicing, Shredding, Puréeing and More

Almond Paste

This paste, which is used in baking, comes in a tube or small can and is very pliable, like modeling clay. To integrate it into a recipe, cut it into small chunks, then, using metal blade, pulse with the sugar. If the paste is hard, cut into smaller pieces, then, using metal blade, process with sugar until fine.

Apples

Peel, halve and core. If you are not processing immediately or not using your processed apples right away, place in acidulated water (4 cups/1 L water combined with 2 tbsp/30 mL lemon juice) to prevent browning. Drain before using.

Slicing: Pack prepared apples in feed tube and, using slicing blade, press plunger with firm pressure.

Chopping: Cut apples into chunks. Using metal blade, pulse a few times for a coarse chop, a few more times for a finer chop.

Shredding: Pack apples in feed tube and, using shredding blade, press plunger with firm pressure.

Puréeing: If necessary, cut cooked apples into chunks. Using metal blade, process for 10 to 15 seconds until puréed.

> **Yields**
> 1 lb (500 g) = 3 cups (750 mL) sliced
> 1 medium apple = ¾ cup (175 mL) sliced or puréed

Apricots See Stone Fruit

Asiago Cheese See Cheeses (Hard)

Avocados

Since we tend to only use avocados when they are ripe and, therefore, soft, they don't slice well in the food processor. But it is a great tool to purée them. Peel, pit and cut avocados into chunks. Sprinkle with lemon, lime or orange juice to prevent browning.

Puréeing: Using metal blade, pulse avocado with quick on-and-off pulses until desired texture.

> **Yields**
> 1 medium avocado = 1 cup (250 mL) puréed

Bananas

Peel and sprinkle with lemon juice to prevent browning.

Slicing: Use firm bananas. Pack bananas in feed tube and, using slicing blade, press plunger with medium pressure.

Puréeing: Use ripe bananas. Cut bananas into chunks and using metal blade, process about 20 seconds until desired texture.

> ### Yields
> 1 medium banana = 1 cup (250 mL) sliced = ¾ cup (175 mL) puréed

Basil Leaves See Herbs, Fresh

Beets

Wash, cook, peel and trim beets.

Slicing: Cut beets flat on the side that will be closest to the cutting blade and cut to fit snugly in feed tube. Using slicing blade, press plunger down with firm pressure.

Chopping: Place chunks of cooked beets around work bowl, being careful not to overpack the bowl. Using metal blade, pulse until desired texture.

Shredding: Pack feed tube with cooked beet halves and, using shredding blade, press plunger down with medium pressure.

Puréeing: Place chunks of cooked beets around work bowl, being careful not to overpack the bowl. Using metal blade, process 15 to 20 seconds until puréed.

> ### Yields
> 2 medium beets = 1½ cups (375 mL) sliced = 2 cups (500 mL) shredded

Berries

Blueberries, Raspberries and Strawberries

Wash and stem berries. Refrigerate until ready to use. For every hour the berries are out of the refrigerator you will lose 1 day of freshness.

Slicing: Berries are so small, we suggest using a knife.

Chopping and Puréeing: Using metal blade, pulse 6 to 8 times for a fine chop, 10 to 12 times for a purée.

> ### Yields
> 12 oz (375 g) = 1 cup (250 mL) purée

Blue Cheeses

This is one of the cheeses we never process in the food processor. The high speed of the blade makes the cheese color the other ingredients a very unappetizing shade of gray. When using blue cheese, fold it into the mixture at the end of the recipe.

Crumbles: Use fork tines to crumble.

Blueberries See Berries

Brown Sugar

The food processor is a great tool for redeeming brown sugar that has hardened. Pack a few cups of hard brown sugar into work bowl and, using metal blade, process until fine and powdery.

Butter

When you're using your food processor to make a recipe and adding butter, make sure it is softened. If combining with sugar, you can soften it by cutting into small chunks and incorporating it with the sugar called for. Never place a large piece of hard butter in the work bowl as it may damage the blade and motor.

Creaming: Cut room temperature butter into chunks. Disperse butter around work bowl and, using metal blade, process 8 to 10 times or until creamy.

> **Yields**
> 4 oz (125 g) = ½ cup (125 mL)

Cabbages

The food processor makes easy work of preparing slaws.

Shredding or slicing: Cut cabbage to fit feed tube snugly and, using slicing or shredding blade, press plunger down with medium pressure.

> **Yields**
> 2 lbs (1 kg) cabbage = 11 cups (2.75 L) shredded

Candy Pieces

Sometimes a recipe will call for candy pieces. You can buy these or, using the food processor, easily chop them yourself at a third of the cost. If the candy is round, such as mints or drops, before adding it to the food processor, break it in half. Otherwise, it will spin round and round with the blade, rather than being chopped.

Chopping: If necessary, cut large candies, such as a candy bar, into smaller pieces. Add a few spoonfuls of sugar from the recipe (this will keep it from sticking to itself). Using metal blade, pulse to desired texture. Keep motor running if you want your candy to be dust to be used in cheesecakes or decorating cakes. This does make a lot of noise, so put the ear plugs in!

Cantaloupes See Melons

Carrots

Slicing: Cut peeled carrots crosswise into 3-inch (7.5 cm) pieces. Fit snugly in feed tube. Using slicing blade, press plunger down with medium pressure.

Chopping: Place chunks of peeled carrots around work bowl, being careful not to overpack the bowl. Using metal blade, pulse until desired texture and size is achieved.

Shredding: Pack feed tube with peeled carrot pieces and, using shredding blade, press plunger with medium pressure.

Puréeing: Place chunks of peeled cooked carrots around work bowl, being careful not to overpack the bowl. Using metal blade, process 15 to 20 seconds until puréed.

Yields
1 medium carrot = ½ cup (125 mL) sliced = ½ cup (125 mL) shredded = ¼ cup (60 mL) puréed

Celery

Slicing: Cut celery crosswise into 3-inch (7.5 cm) pieces. Fit snugly in feed tube. Using slicing blade, press plunger with medium pressure.

Chopping: Place pieces of celery around work bowl, being careful not to overpack the bowl. Using metal blade, pulse until desired texture.

Yields
1 stalk = 1 cup (250 mL) sliced = ¾ cup (175 mL) chopped

Celery Root

Always peel celery root before processing. The easiest way to peel the vegetable is to cut a piece off the bottom so it can be firmly anchored on a cutting board. Using a chef's knife and pressing down firmly, cut the skin off the sides and then the top.

Since celery root oxidizes quickly on contact with air, transfer it to a bowl of acidulated water (4 cups/1 L water combined with 2 tbsp/30 mL lemon juice) as soon as you have prepared it to prevent discoloration. Drain thoroughly before using.

Slicing: Cut celery root into chunks to fit snugly in feed tube and, using slicing blade, press plunger firmly.

Shredding: Cut celery root into chunks to fit snugly in feed tube and, using shredding blade, press plunger firmly.

Yields
1 lb (500 g) = 2 cups (500 mL) sliced or shredded

Cheddar Cheese See Cheeses (Semi-Hard)

Cheeses (Hard)
Asiago, Parmesan and Romano
>Cut room temperature cheese into small cubes (about 1 inch/2.5 cm).
>**Grating**: With motor running, drop cheese cubes through feed tube and, using metal blade, process until fine.

>**Yields**
>4 oz (125 g) = 1 cup (250 mL) grated

Cheeses (Semi-Hard)
Cheddar, Gruyère, Monterey Jack, Mozzarella, Provolone and Swiss
>**Slicing**: Use cold cheese, directly from refrigerator. Cut a block of cheese to fit feed tube and, using slicing blade, press plunger with firm pressure.
>**Shredding**: Place cheese in freezer for a few minutes. Place cheese in feed tube and, using shredding blade, press plunger with firm pressure.

>**Yields**
>4 oz (125 g) = 1 cup (250 mL) shredded

Cheeses (Soft)
Cottage Cheese, Cream Cheese, Goat Cheese, Light or Lower-Fat Cream Cheese, Mascarpone, Neufchâtel Cheese
>All soft creamy cheeses need to be cut into smaller pieces and evenly distributed around the work bowl. If you keep the cheese in a block, it will just keep going around the work bowl and not incorporate.

>**Yields**
>8 oz (250 g) = 1 to 1¼ cups (250 to 300 mL)

Chiles
>Most chiles are too small to slice. If using three or more in a recipe with other ingredients, then use the processor, otherwise, just use a knife.
>**Chopping**: First cut in half lengthwise with a knife, then seed with a spoon. If you are using at least three chiles, you can chop them in the food processor. Using metal blade, pulse 6 to 8 times or until desired texture.

>**Yields**
>depends on the size of chiles

Chives See Herbs, Fresh

Cilantro Leaves See Herbs, Fresh

Citrus
Lemon, Lime and Orange

Juicing: Some models have attachments for juicing citrus. Follow the instructions that come with your machine, being aware that using the attachment is not likely to be an efficient use of your time unless you are juicing a large quantity.

Lemons

Zest: When citrus zest is called for in a sweet recipe, you can use your food processor to make the job easy. Cut off the outer part of the peel and discard any white "pith." Using metal blade, process rind with a few spoonfuls of the sugar called for in the recipe. Process until fine, about 20 seconds.

Slicing: Do not peel fruit. Clean outside well and cut ends flat. Place whole fruit in a large feed tube or cut to fit, and, using slicing blade, press plunger with firm pressure.

You can freeze zest and juice. Zest your fruit one day and then juice the next. The walls of the fruit will break down thus creating an easier fruit to juice.

Coconut

Before processing a coconut, make a hole in all three "eyes" to drain the liquid. If it does not drain, poke another hole in the bottom. Place coconut on a baking sheet and place in a preheated (400°F/200°C) oven for 12 to 15 minutes. Wrap heated coconut in a towel and, using a hammer, break it open. This should release the skin from the meat. If not, use a vegetable peeler to remove any remaining brown skin.

Shredding: Fill feed tube with white coconut pieces and, using shredding blade, press plunger down with a firm pressure.

Grating: Place 1-inch (2.5 cm) pieces of white coconut around work bowl and, using metal blade, pulse 10 to 15 times or until desired texture.

> **Yields**
> 1 medium coconut = 4 cups (1 L) grated/shredded

Cottage Cheese See Cheeses (Soft)

Cranberries

Wash and drain. Remove any stems and discard. Discard berries that are overripe.

Chopping: Using metal blade, pulse 6 to 8 times.

> **Yields**
> 12 oz (375 g) = 2 cups (500 mL) chopped

Cream Cheese See Cheeses (Soft)

Cucumbers

Peel cucumber and cut in half lengthwise. With a spoon, scrape out seeds.

Slicing: Cut halved cucumbers crosswise to fit snugly in feed tube. Using slicing blade, press plunger down with medium pressure.

Chopping: Place chunks of cucumbers around work bowl, being careful not to overpack the bowl. Using metal blade, pulse until desired texture.

Puréeing: Place chunks of cucumbers around work bowl, being careful not to overpack the bowl. Using metal blade, process 15 to 20 seconds until puréed.

Yields
1 large cucumber = 1½ cups (375 mL) sliced = 1¾ cups (425 mL) chopped = 2 cups (500 mL) puréed

Dill Fronds See Herbs, Fresh

Eggs

Raw

Whole and egg yolks are normally incorporated into the recipe through the feed tube with the motor running.

Egg Whites: Some processors have whip attachments. Follow the manufacturer's instructions.

Hard-cooked

Chopping: Peel and cut the eggs in half. Place around work bowl and, using metal blade, pulse 5 to 8 times until desired texture. If making egg salad, process until fine.

Yields
4 hard-cooked large eggs = 1 cup (250 mL) chopped

Fennel

Chop off celery-like stems and save for making stock. Cut bulb in half on the vertical and remove the knobby core.

Slicing: Cut pieces on the vertical to fit feed tube, and, using slicing blade, press plunger down with firm pressure.

Chopping: Place chunks of prepared fennel around work bowl, being careful not to overpack the bowl. Using metal blade, pulse for about 5 seconds for medium chop, or 8 seconds for fine.

Yields
1 medium bulb = 2 cups (500 mL) sliced = 1 cup (250 mL) chopped

Garlic

If you are mincing a large quantity of garlic, using your food processor makes light work of the task. Select garlic that is heavy to the feel, firm and tight.

Mincing: Use a very dry work bowl fitted with metal blade and turn motor on. Drop whole unpeeled garlic cloves with ends trimmed through feed tube and process until all the garlic is minced. You can discard peel easily.

Slicing: Pack whole peeled clove into the feed tube densely with other vegetables to be sliced such as carrots. Using slicing blade, press plunger down with firm pressure.

> **Yields**
> 1 clove = ½ tsp (2 mL) minced

Goat Cheese See Cheeses (Soft)

Gruyère Cheese See Cheeses (Semi-Hard)

Herbs, Fresh

Basil Leaves, Chives, Cilantro Leaves, Dill Fronds, Italian Flat-Leaf Parsley, Mint Leaves, Oregano Leaves, Sage Leaves, Tarragon Leaves, Thyme Leaves

Wash herbs by spraying with cool water, place in a herb spinner or dry with paper towels. Herbs need to be well dried to chop properly. Separate leaves/fronds from stems and save stems for another use such as making stock, or discard. The stems tend to give a "woody" taste to your dish.

Chopping or Mincing: Place prepared herbs in work bowl and, using metal blade, pulse about 4 to 6 times to chop, 8 to 10 times to mince.

> **Yields**
> 1 cup (250 mL) loosely packed leaves = ⅓ cup (75 mL) chopped

Honeydew See Melons

Italian Flat-Leaf Parsley See Herbs, Fresh

Jack Cheese See Cheeses (Semi-Hard)

Jicama

Wash and trim jicama.

Slicing: Cut jicama flat on the one side that will be closest to the cutting blade and cut to fit snugly into the feed tube. Using slicing blade, press plunger down with firm pressure.

Shredding: Pack feed tube with jicama and, using shredding blade, press plunger down with medium pressure.

Chopping: Place chunks of jicama around work bowl, being careful not to overpack the bowl. Using metal blade, pulse until desired texture.

Puréeing: Place chunks of jicama around work bowl, being careful not to overpack the bowl. Using metal blade, process 15 to 20 seconds until puréed.

> **Yields**
> 1 medium jicama = ¾ cup (175 mL) sliced = 1 cup (250 mL) shredded

Kiwis

Select firm fruit. Peel carefully with a vegetable peeler. Chill prior to slicing.

Slicing: Place fruit in feed tube and, using slicing blade, press plunger with firm pressure.

Puréeing: Cut fruit into quarters and place around bowl and, using metal blade, pulse 8 to 10 times.

> **Yields**
> 2 kiwis = ¾ cup (175 mL) sliced or ½ cup (125 mL) puréed

Leeks

Select large leeks. Wash by cutting the " bulb" in half lengthwise and submerge in cold water to remove any trapped sand.

Slicing: Cut leeks to fit snugly in feed tube and, using slicing blade, press plunger down with firm pressure.

Chopping: Place leeks around work bowl, being careful not to overpack the bowl. Using metal blade, pulse until desired texture.

> **Yields**
> 2 medium leeks = 1 cup (250 mL) sliced = 1¼ cups (300 mL) chopped

Lemons See Citrus

Lettuces, Firm

When making slaws or shredded lettuce for tacos, nothing is easier then a food processor.

Shredding or slicing: Cut lettuce to fit feed tube snugly and, using shredding or slicing blade, press plunger down with medium pressure.

> **Yields**
> 2 lbs (1 kg) lettuce = 11 cups (2.75 L) shredded

Light or Lower-Fat Cream Cheese See Cheeses (Soft)

Limes See Citrus

Mangos

Select firm yet soft fruit. Halve, seed and peel. Coat with lemon juice to prevent browning.

Slicing: Place fruit in feed tube and, using slicing blade, press plunger with firm pressure.

Shredding: Shredding is not recommended. Because ripe mangos are soft, it will produce a purée.

Puréeing: Cut fruit into chunks and place around bowl. Using metal blade, pulse 8 to 10 times.

> **Yields**
> 1 medium mango = ¾ cup (175 mL) puréed

Mascarpone See Cheeses (Soft)

Meats, Raw

Processing and overgrinding any meat will make it tougher. If you are making a meat loaf, process all of the ingredients separately from the meat. Add it in at the end to ensure it isn't overprocessed.

Melons

Cantaloupes, Honeydew and Watermelon

To select the sweetest cantaloupe take a look at the outer "netting" on the surface of the melon. You want the lines in netting to be farther apart. This is the sure way to know that the melon matured while still on the vine and was picked after the sugars developed. You also want the melons to be heavy for their size. Cut rind off melon and remove seeds.

Slicing: Cut into wedges that will fit in feed tube. Using slicing blade, press plunger with firm pressure.

Chunks: Place small wedges of melon in work bowl and, using metal blade, pulse a few times until desired texture.

Puréeing: Using metal blade, process fruit chunks for 10 to 15 seconds or until puréed.

> **Yields**
> 1 cup (250 mL) chopped melon pieces = ¾ cup (175 mL) puréed

Milk Products

Most dairy products are processed with dry ingredients to prevent leakage. They are poured into the feed tube, mainly while the motor is running. If you process liquids past the "stem" of the work bowl, they will leak out of the machine.

Mint Leaves See Herbs, Fresh

Mozzarella Cheese See Cheeses (Semi-Hard)

Mushrooms

To clean mushrooms use a damp paper towel or a mushroom brush. You can also rinse briefly, being careful not to submerge. Trim ends and cut in half lengthwise for slicing.

Slicing: Place cut mushrooms snugly in feed tube. Using slicing blade, press plunger down with firm pressure.

Chopping: Place mushrooms around work bowl, being careful not to overpack the bowl. Using metal blade, pulse until desired texture and size is achieved.

> **Yields**
> 8 oz (250 g) = 2½ cups (625 mL) sliced = 2¾ cups (675 mL) chopped

Nectarines See Stone Fruit

Neufchâtel Cheese See Cheeses (Soft)

Nuts and Seeds

Most nuts and seeds will become a thick paste if processed too long. If this isn't what you are trying to achieve and if your recipe contains flour, add a few spoonfuls of the flour called for to the work bowl along with the nuts. This will keep them from turning to butter.

To toast nuts: Preheat oven to 350°F (180°C). Spread nuts on a baking sheet and bake, shaking the pan several times, until fragrant and toasted; 5 to 7 minutes for chopped almonds; 6 to 9 minutes for whole almonds, whole hazelnuts, whole macadamia nuts, and pecan and walnut halves; 4 to 7 minutes for chopped, sliced and slivered almonds, chopped hazelnuts, and chopped pecans and walnuts.

Chopping: Using metal blade, pulse 4 to 8 times for a course chop and 10 to 12 times for a fine chop. Process for 5 seconds for nut meal/flour.

> **Yields**
> 2 oz (60 g) = ¼ cup (60 mL) chopped nuts

Olives

These little round gems are hard to slice in a food processor. Just use a knife.

Chopping: Tear each pitted olive in half. Using metal blade, pulse olives 4 to 6 times to chop.

Onions
Red Onions, Scallions, Shallots and Yellow Onions

All of these onions are treated similarly. Remove outer skin. If onion is large, cut into quarters. Trim off root and green stems of scallions.

Slicing: Place prepared onion in feed tube and, using slicing blade, press plunger down with medium pressure. If using scallions, pack densely, root end down, in thin inner feed tube. Press plunger down with medium pressure.

Chopping: Pack onion around work bowl and, using metal blade, pulse until desired texture.

Yields
Red/yellow onions: 1 medium = 1¼ cups (300 mL) sliced
= 1 cup (250 mL) chopped
Scallions: 6 = ½ cup (125 mL) chopped
Shallots: 1 small = ¼ cup (60 mL) chopped

Orange See Citrus

Oregano Leaves See Herbs, Fresh

Parmesan Cheese See Cheeses (Hard)

Peaches See Stone Fruit

Pears

Choose ripe firm fruit without any dark spots. Peel and core (using a melon baller or small spoon). Brush with lemon juice. If not using immediately, after further processing, transfer to a bowl of acidulated water (4 cups/1 L water combined with 2 tbsp/30 mL lemon juice).

Slicing: Place fruit upright in feed tube and, using slicing blade, press plunger with firm pressure.

Chopping: Cut fruit into chunks. Place in work bowl and, using metal blade, pulse about 8 to 10 times.

Puréeing: Cut fruit into chunks. Place in work bowl and, using metal blade, process about 15 to 20 seconds.

Yields
1 lb (500 g) = 3 cups (750 mL) sliced
1 medium pear = ¾ cup (175 mL) sliced or puréed

Pepperoni and Hard Sausages

Slicing: Remove outer casing and cut to fit feed tube. Pack feed tube and, using slicing blade, press plunger with medium pressure.

Chopping: Remove outer casings, cut into small pieces, and, using metal blade, pulse until desired texture.

Pineapples

Using fresh pineapples takes a little time but is well worth the effort. Choose whole fruit that is uniform in shape. The aroma should be sweet, and when you move a stem a bit it should easily come off. Before processing remove outer layer and "eyes" with the point of a sharp knife. Core by cutting fruit in quarters or using a pineapple ring core cutter.

Slicing: Cut pineapple into small wedges, place in feed tube and, using slicing blade, press plunger down with firm pressure.

Chunks: Place small wedges of pineapple in work bowl, and using metal blade, pulse a few times to achieve the size you want.

Crushed: Using metal blade, process for 10 to 15 seconds. Strain off some of the excess juice.

Tip: If you have a recipe calling for crushed pineapple and you only have a can of chunks or slices, drain and process with metal blade for 8 to 10 seconds or until fully crushed. Save any juice that the fruit produces to drink or add to a vinaigrette.

Yields
1 medium pineapple = 4 cups (1 L) sliced = 3$\frac{1}{2}$ cups (875 mL) chopped = 3 cups (750 mL) puréed

Plums See Stone Fruit

Potatoes

Wash, peel (if desired) and cut potatoes.

Slicing: If you are going to make potato chips you will need a thin slicing blade. Place potatoes snugly in feed tube. Using slicing blade, press plunger down with firm pressure.

Chopping: Place potato chunks around work bowl, being careful not to overpack the bowl. Using metal blade, pulse until desired texture and size is achieved.

Shredding: Pack feed tube with potatoes and, using shredding blade, press plunger down with medium pressure.

Yields
1 medium potato = $\frac{3}{4}$ cup (175 mL) sliced = $\frac{1}{2}$ cup (125 mL) chopped/shredded

Poultry, Cooked

The advantage to using the food processor for chopping cooked poultry is that when combined with mayonnaise or other creamy salad dressings it creates great texture. Cut meat into large chunks and place around work bowl, being careful not to overpack the bowl. Add dressing and pulse until desired texture.

Provolone Cheese See Cheeses (Semi-Hard)

Radishes

Wash and cut ends off of radishes.

Slicing: Place radishes snugly in feed tube. Using slicing blade, press plunger down with firm pressure. If you only have a few to slice, do it by hand.

Chopping: Place radishes around work bowl, being careful not to overpack the bowl. Using metal blade, pulse until desired texture.

> **Yields**
> 10 to 12 small radishes = 1 cup (250 mL) sliced = 1¼ cups (300 mL) chopped

Raspberries See Berries

Red Onions See Onions

Rhubarb

Prior to processing, trim and cut rhubarb pieces (about 3 inches/7.5 cm long).

Slicing: Fit pieces snugly into the feed tube and, using slicing blade, press plunger with medium pressure.

Chopping: Place pieces of rhubarb around work bowl, being careful not to overpack the bowl. Using metal blade, pulse until desired texture.

> **Yields**
> 1 stalk rhubarb = 1 cup (250 mL) sliced = ¾ cup (175 mL) chopped.

Romano Cheese See Cheeses (Hard)

Sage Leaves See Herbs, Fresh

Scallions See Onions

Seeds See Nuts and Seeds

Shallots See Onions

Squash

Squash come in a variety of sizes and shapes. There is **summer squash**, such as crookneck, pattypan and zucchini, which is soft and can be sliced and shredded raw. And **winter squash**, such as acorn, buttercup, butternut, hubbard, spaghetti and turban, which lends itself to chopping using the metal blade or puréeing after cooking.

Slicing: Cut peeled summer squash to fit feed tube and, using slicing blade, press plunger down with firm pressure.

Chopping: Place peeled winter squash chunks around work bowl and, using metal blade, pulse until desired texture and size is achieved.

Shredding: Pack feed tube with peeled summer squash and, using shredding blade, press plunger down with medium pressure.

Puréeing: Place cooked peeled winter squash chunks around work bowl and, using metal blade, process 10 to 15 seconds until puréed.

Yields
12 oz (375 g) squash = 2 cups (500 mL) sliced = 1½ cups (375 mL) chopped/shredded = 1¼ cups (300 mL) puréed

Stone Fruit
Apricots, Nectarines, Peaches and Plums

To prepare fruit, peel (if desired), pit, and core the center. Sprinkle with lemon juice to prevent browning.

Slicing: Keep fruit as whole as possible. Cut to fit feed tube and, using slicing blade, press plunger down with light pressure

Mincing or Puréeing: Cut fruit into chunks. Using metal blade, pulse fruit 6 to 8 times for mince. Process for 20 seconds for purée or until desired texture.

Yields
1 medium piece fruit = 1 cup (250 mL) sliced = ¾ cup (175 mL) puréed

Strawberries See Berries

Swiss Cheese See Cheeses (Semi-Hard)

Tarragon Leaves See Herbs, Fresh

Thyme Leaves See Herbs, Fresh

Tomatillos

Choose firm fruit and remove the papery skin. Wash well to remove stickiness. Cut into quarters.

Chopping: Cut tomatillos into quarters. Using metal blade, pulse a few times for a coarse chop, a few more times for a finer chop.

Puréeing: Cut tomatillos into quarters. Using metal blade, process for 10 to 15 seconds or until puréed.

> ### Yields
> 15 medium tomatillos = 1 lb (500 g) puréed

Tomatoes

If you only have one or two tomatoes to slice, you should just use a kitchen knife, but if you have more, use the food processor for ease. Select very firm yet ripe tomatoes. Remove stem and peel, if desired.

Slicing: Place tomatoes in feed tube and, using slicing blade, press plunger down with firm pressure.

Chunks: Place quartered tomatoes around work bowl and, using metal blade, pulse a few times to achieve the chunk size you want.

Crushed: Place quartered tomatoes around work bowl and, using metal blade, process 10 to 15 seconds or until fully crushed.

Tip: You can also use your food processor to purée canned drained whole tomatoes. Drain liquid and save for another use. Using metal blade, pulse a few times to chop, or process for 10 seconds to purée.

> ### Yields
> 3 medium tomatoes = 1 lb (500 g) = 1½ cups (375 mL) puréed

Watermelon See Melons

Yellow Onions See Onions

Zucchini See Squash

Appetizers

Traditional Salsa

Makes 2½ cups (625 mL)

Vegan Friendly

This is an all-purpose salsa. Great with chips, grilled meats or tacos.

Tips

When seeding the chiles wear rubber gloves. If any of the chile juice gets on your fingers and you rub your eyes you will feel it.

Salsa keeps well, covered and refrigerated, for 1 week.

1	onion, cut into quarters	1
1 lb	Roma (plum) tomatoes, cored, cut in half and seeded (7 to 9 tomatoes)	500 g
2	serrano or jalapeño chiles, halved and seeded	2
¼ cup	loosely packed fresh cilantro leaves	60 mL
2 tbsp	freshly squeezed lime juice	30 mL
2 tsp	granulated sugar	10 mL
1 tsp	salt (approx.)	5 mL

1. In work bowl fitted with metal blade, pulse onion until finely chopped, 10 to 12 times. Place in a strainer and rinse with water. Drain well. Transfer to a bowl and set aside.

2. In same work bowl, pulse tomatoes, chiles and cilantro until desired consistency, 15 to 20 times, stopping and scraping down sides of the bowl once or twice.

3. Add tomato mixture to drained onions. Add lime juice, sugar, and salt to taste. Let stand for at least 1 hour before serving.

Tomatillo Onion Avocado Salsa

Makes 2½ cups (625 mL)

Vegan Friendly

For other different-colored salsas to serve with this flavorful green salsa, see Roasted Corn and Pepper Salsa (page 33), Peach Mango Salsa (page 34) or Traditional Salsa (page 32).

Tip

Prior to processing, remove the skins and run the tomatillos under water to wash off the stickiness.

½	red onion, cut into quarters (about ⅓ cup/75 mL)	½
1 lb	tomatillos, husked, rinsed and cut into quarters (about 15) (see Tip, left)	500 g
1	avocado, peeled and pitted, cut in half	1
1	serrano chile	1
1 cup	loosely packed fresh cilantro leaves	250 mL
2 tbsp	freshly squeezed lime juice	30 mL
1 tsp	salt	5 mL
¼ tsp	hot pepper sauce, optional	1 mL

1. In work bowl fitted with metal blade, pulse onion until chunky, about 10 times. Place in a strainer and rinse with water. Drain well. Return to work bowl.

2. Add tomatillos, avocado, serrano chile, cilantro, lime juice and salt and pulse until the desired texture is achieved, about 20 times, stopping and scraping down sides of the bowl once or twice. Some people like it chunky so the salsa can stay on a chip while others prefer it smooth.

Roasted Corn and Pepper Salsa

Makes about 5 cups (1.25 L)

Vegan Friendly

This hot and spicy salsa is made on the grill. Serve with chips or with chicken or fish. It's great served with margaritas.

Tips

Do not run water over the chiles to try to loosen the skins. If the skins do not come off easily, you need to let them steam longer in the plastic bag. If you use water over the chiles, you will wash the flavor off.

Instead of the barbecue, place the corn, tomatoes and chiles under the broiler until the skins bubble and the corn is browned, about 10 minutes.

- Preheat barbecue to medium

6	ears corn	6
2 tbsp	olive oil, divided	30 mL
1 lb	Roma (plum) tomatoes (7 to 9 tomatoes)	500 g
12 oz	New Mexico or Anaheim chiles (10 to 12 chiles)	375 g
1	onion, cut into quarters	1
¼ cup	apple cider vinegar	60 mL
1 tsp	granulated sugar	5 mL
½ tsp	dried oregano	2 mL
¼ tsp	salt	1 mL

1. Remove husks from corn cobs. Brush 1 tbsp (15 mL) olive oil on all sides and place on preheated grill. Brush tomatoes and chiles with remaining oil and place on grill. Grill, turning to brown all sides, about 20 minutes. When the corn starts to brown, remove from heat and let cool. When chiles and tomatoes start to blister, place in a plastic bag to sweat for 20 minutes (see Tips, left).

2. Slice corn from cobs and place in a large bowl. Peel skins from sweated chiles. Cut chiles in half and scrape out seeds and membranes.

3. In work bowl fitted with metal blade, pulse chiles until chunky, about 10 times. Add to corn.

4. Peel skins off sweated tomatoes, remove cores and cut in half. Try removing all of the seeds. Place in same work bowl and pulse until smooth, about 10 times. Add to corn mixture.

5. In same work bowl, pulse onion, vinegar, sugar, oregano and salt until chunky, about 10 times. Add to corn mixture. Stir to combine. Let stand for 30 minutes.

Variations

You can use cherry tomatoes in place of Roma and you won't have to seed them.

Use a combination of 6 oz (175 g) jalapeño or hot banana peppers and 6 oz (175 g) poblano or Cubanelle peppers if you can't find New Mexico chiles.

Red Onion Salsa

**Makes 1½ cups
(375 mL)**

Vegan Friendly

Tangy red onions make up this simple salsa with a kick.

Tip

Taste for heat. If you would like additional spice, add another habanero.

- Mini-bowl attachment

2	red onions, cut into quarters	2
1	habanero chile pepper, seeded and quartered (see Tip, left)	1
1 tsp	salt	5 mL
1 tsp	granulated sugar	5 mL
1 tsp	freshly squeezed lime juice	5 mL

1. In mini bowl fitted with metal blade, pulse red onions, chile pepper, salt, sugar and lime juice, just to coarsely chop, about 10 times. You can process longer for a smoother texture, if desired.

Peach Mango Salsa

**Makes 2 cups
(500 mL)**

Vegan Friendly

As well as with chips for a great-tasting dip, this sweet and fruity salsa can be used on top of fish and chicken.

Tips

If you use thin-skinned peaches you will not need to peel them before serving.

Salsa keeps well, covered and refrigerated, for up to 1 week.

1	piece (½ inch/1 cm) fresh gingerroot	1
2	large peaches, pitted and cut into quarters (see Tips, left)	2
1	large mango, peeled, pitted and cut into quarters	1
1 tbsp	freshly squeezed lime juice	15 mL
½ tsp	cayenne pepper	2 mL
½ tsp	salt	2 mL

1. With a garlic press or ginger grater, press juice from ginger so you have ½ tsp (2 mL). Transfer to a bowl.

2. In work bowl fitted with metal blade, pulse peaches and mango until chunky, 8 to 10 times, stopping and scraping down sides of the bowl once or twice. Transfer to bowl with ginger juice. Add lime juice, cayenne pepper and salt. Toss together.

Variation
If you would like a less spicy salsa, omit the cayenne pepper.

Black Bean and Roasted Corn Salsa

Makes 2 cups (500 mL)

Vegan Friendly

This dip is very easy; everything is mixed in the food processor.

Tip

If you can't find roasted corn, you can roast 2 cups (500 mL) fresh or thawed frozen corn kernels in a single layer in a dry skillet over medium heat, stirring constantly, until lightly browned.

2 cups	drained cooked black beans (see Tips, page 45)	500 mL
12 oz	cream cheese, cubed and softened, or vegan alternative	375 g
1/3 cup	roasted red pepper (about 1 small)	75 mL
2	chipotle peppers in adobo sauce, drained	2
2 tbsp	chopped fresh cilantro leaves	30 mL
1 tbsp	taco seasoning	15 mL
2 tsp	freshly squeezed lime juice	10 mL
1	bag (12 oz/375 g) roasted corn (see Tip, left)	1

1. In work bowl fitted with metal blade, process black beans, cream cheese, red pepper, chipotle peppers, cilantro, taco seasoning and lime juice until smooth, about 3 minutes, stopping and scraping down sides of the bowl once or twice. Transfer to a bowl and fold in roasted corn.

Jalapeño Salsa

Makes 2 cups (500 mL)

Vegan Friendly

This salsa is very spicy with a kick. Use it to top roasted eggplant slices for an all-vegan side dish.

- Preheat oven to 400°F (200°C)
- Roasting pan, lined with parchment paper

3	large Anaheim or Cubanelle chiles, cut in half and seeded	3
10	jalapeño peppers, cut in half and seeded	10
1/2	red onion, sliced	1/2
6	cloves garlic	6
1/4 cup	extra virgin olive oil	60 mL
2 tbsp	freshly squeezed lime juice	30 mL
1 tsp	salt	5 mL

1. Place Anaheim chiles, jalapeños, red onion and garlic on prepared roasting pan. Brush with oil. Roast in preheated oven until skins on Anaheim chiles and jalapeños are darkened, about 20 minutes.

2. In work bowl fitted with metal blade, pulse vegetables 10 times or until desired consistency. Transfer to a bowl. Stir in lime juice and salt. Let stand in covered container in refrigerator for 1 hour or for up to 2 days.

Old World Salsa

3	Roma (plum) tomatoes, cored and quartered	3
½	red onion, quartered	½
½	sweet onion, quartered	½
2	cloves garlic	2
½	green bell pepper, seeded and quartered	½
½	red bell pepper, seeded and quartered	½
4	jalapeño peppers, cut in half and seeded	4
2 tbsp	coarsely chopped fresh cilantro leaves	30 mL
2 tsp	freshly squeezed lime juice	10 mL
2 tsp	freshly squeezed lemon juice	10 mL
¼ tsp	freshly ground black pepper	1 mL
¼ tsp	celery salt	1 mL
¼ tsp	salt	1 mL
1	can (8 oz/227 mL) tomato sauce	1

1. In work bowl fitted with metal blade, process tomatoes, red onion, sweet onion, garlic, green and red bell peppers, jalapeños, cilantro, lime and lemon juices, black pepper, celery salt and salt for 1 minute, stopping and scraping down sides of the bowl once or twice. Transfer to a bowl. Stir in tomato sauce. Let stand in a covered container in the refrigerator for at least 1 hour for flavors to develop or for up to 2 days.

Tahini-Spiked Beet Spread

**Makes about
1½ cups (375 mL)**

Vegetarian Friendly

This Middle-Eastern-inspired spread is delightfully different and extremely nutritious. It's particularly delicious with grilled or toasted whole-grain pita bread, but plain baguette works well, too. It's great for entertaining because you can make it well ahead if you're rationing your time.

Tips

To maintain the bright color of the beets, place 2 tbsp (30 mL) vinegar in a bowl. Roll scrubbed beets in the vinegar before roasting.

Dip keeps, covered and refrigerated, for up to 3 days.

- Preheat oven to 400°F (200°C)
- Rimmed baking sheet or baking dish

4	medium beets, scrubbed (see Tips, left)	4
⅓ cup	plain yogurt, preferably Greek-Style (pressed) (see Tip, page 114)	75 mL
¼ cup	tahini paste	60 mL
¼ cup	fresh dill fronds	60 mL
2 tbsp	freshly squeezed lemon juice	30 mL
2	cloves garlic, coarsely chopped	2
1 tsp	salt	5 mL
	Freshly ground black pepper	

1. Place beets on a rimmed baking sheet or in a baking dish and cover with foil. Roast in preheated oven until tender, about 1 hour. Remove from oven, spoon off 2 tbsp (30 mL) of the cooking juice and set aside. Discard any excess juice. Let beets cool just until they are cool enough to touch, then using a piece of paper towel, rub off skins. Cut into quarters.

2. In work bowl fitted with metal blade, process beets, yogurt, tahini, dill, lemon juice, garlic, salt, pepper to taste, and reserved cooking juice until smooth. Serve at room temperature or cover and refrigerate until cold.

Celery Root Avgolemono

**Makes about
4 cups (1 L)**

Vegetarian Friendly

This might be described
as a North African
version of Celery Root
Remoulade (page 389).
Here the celery root is
cooked and tossed in
an avgolemono sauce.
Serve it thoroughly
chilled, as part of a
selection of mezes.

1	large (about 2 lbs/1 kg) celery root, peeled	1
3 tbsp	freshly squeezed lemon juice, divided	45 mL
	Salt and freshly ground black pepper	
2	egg yolks	2

1. In work bowl fitted with shredding blade, shred celery root. Transfer to saucepan. Add 1 tbsp (15 mL) of the lemon juice and water barely to cover. Season with salt and pepper to taste. Bring to a boil over high heat. Reduce heat and simmer until celery root is tender, about 10 minutes.

2. In a small bowl, beat egg yolks with remaining 2 tbsp (30 mL) of lemon juice. Beat in 2 tbsp (30 mL) of cooking water. Add to pan, stirring. Heat through, stirring constantly, until mixture is thickened, being careful not to boil. Transfer to a serving dish and refrigerate until thoroughly chilled.

Roasted Peppers with Anchovy-Spiked Olive Oil

**Makes about
2 cups (500 mL)**

Anchovies and a hint
of garlic lend pleasant
punch to classic
roasted sweet peppers.
Serve this with sliced
baguette — scooping up
the peppers with a fork.

Tip
You can make this dish
up to 1 day ahead and
refrigerate it. Before
serving let stand at room
temperature for about
20 minutes to allow the
flavors to develop.

- Mini-bowl attachment

6	roasted red peppers, peeled, seeded and cut into strips (see Tips, page 147)	6
½ cup	extra virgin olive oil	125 mL
6	anchovy fillets	6
2	cloves garlic, coarsely chopped	2
¼ cup	Italian flat-leaf parsley or basil leaves	60 mL

1. Place peppers in a serving bowl or small platter. In mini bowl fitted with metal blade, pulse olive oil, anchovies, garlic and parsley until blended and smooth. Pour over peppers. For best results, serve immediately at room temperature (see Tips, left).

Variation
Use half yellow or orange bell peppers for a more colorful result.

Roasted Red Pepper Guacamole Dip

Makes 1½ cups (375 mL)

Vegan Friendly

In addition to being a delicious dip for tortilla chips, this recipe is perfect as a sandwich spread on crusty French bread.

Tip

Make sure you do not overprocess the mixture or you will have soup.

1	red onion, cut into quarters (about ⅔ cup/150 mL)	1
2	jalapeño peppers, cut in half and seeded	2
½ cup	loosely packed fresh cilantro leaves (see Tips, page 76)	125 mL
3	avocados, peeled and pitted, cut in half	3
½ cup	roasted red peppers (see Tips, page 147)	125 mL

1. In work bowl fitted with metal blade, pulse red onion and jalapeño peppers until chopped, about 8 times. Add cilantro and pulse 5 times. Add avocados and red peppers and process until chopped, about 10 seconds, stopping and scraping down sides of the bowl once or twice.
2. Transfer to a bowl. Cover and refrigerate for at least 1 hour or for up to 1 day. Serve chilled.

Orange-Spiked Cucumbers with Mint

Makes about 2 cups (500 mL)

Vegan Friendly

This is good as part of an antipasto platter. It can also serve as a salad.

Tip

If you like the flavor of orange, add up to 1 tsp (5 mL) orange blossom water, which is available in Middle Eastern markets, to the dressing.

1 tbsp	finely grated orange zest	15 mL
2 tbsp	freshly squeezed orange juice	30 mL
1 tsp	salt	5 mL
3 tbsp	extra virgin olive oil	45 mL
1	English cucumber, peeled	1
	Freshly ground black pepper	
1 tbsp	finely chopped fresh mint	15 mL

1. In a small bowl, combine orange zest and juice and salt, stirring until salt is dissolved. Gradually whisk in olive oil. Set aside.
2. In work bowl fitted with shredding blade, shred cucumber. Transfer to a serving dish. Pour vinaigrette over cucumbers and stir well. Season with pepper to taste and sprinkle with mint.

Fried Zucchini Bites
with Savory Dill Sauce

Serves 8

Pair these up with hot wings for your next party.

Tips

If you're using prepared mayonnaise don't confuse it with "mayonnaise-type" salad dressings, which are similar in appearance. Mayonnaise is a combination of egg yolks, vinegar or lemon juice, oil and seasonings. Imitators will contain additional ingredients, such as sugar, flour or milk. Make your own or make sure the label says mayonnaise and check the ingredients.

Use zucchini that are the same diameter so they will fry evenly.

- Preheat oven to 200°F (100°C)
- 16-cup (4 L) saucepan or deep-fryer
- Candy/deep-fry thermometer

Savory Dill Sauce

1 cup	sour cream	250 mL
½ cup	Traditional Mayonnaise (page 437) or store-bought	125 mL
½ cup	buttermilk	125 mL
2 tbsp	freshly squeezed lemon juice	30 mL
2 tbsp	finely chopped fresh dill	30 mL

Zucchini Bites

	Vegetable oil for frying	
1½ cups	biscuit mix	375 mL
1 cup	light-colored beer	250 mL
2 tsp	granulated sugar	10 mL
2 lbs	zucchini, cut into ½-inch (1 cm) rounds	1 kg

1. **Savory Dill Sauce:** In work bowl fitted with metal blade, process sour cream, mayonnaise, buttermilk, lemon juice and dill until smooth, about 20 seconds, stopping and scraping down sides of the bowl once or twice. Set aside.

2. **Zucchini Bites:** In a large saucepan over medium heat, heat about 4 inches (10 cm) of oil until thermometer registers 360°F (185°C).

3. In a large bowl, blend biscuit mix, beer and sugar to make a smooth batter. Let stand for 10 minutes.

4. Dip zucchini pieces, one at a time, into beer mixture, coating all sides. Place in hot oil, 4 at a time, and deep-fry for 15 seconds per side. Place on paper towels to absorb excess oil. Transfer to an ovenproof platter and keep warm in preheated oven. Make sure oil is the correct temperature before adding each batch. Serve with Savory Dill Sauce.

Variation

For a spicy bite, add 1 tsp (5 mL) hot pepper flakes to the batter prior to frying.

Spinach and Artichoke Dip

**Makes about
3 cups (750 mL)**

Vegetarian Friendly

A sumptuous blend
with roots in Provençal
cuisine, where the
vegetables are usually
baked with cheese and
served as a gratin. It's
very simple to make,
yet always draws rave
reviews and disappears
to the very last drop.

Tips

If you prefer to use cheese
that is already shredded,
you'll need about 1 cup
(250 mL).

If you are using fresh
spinach leaves in this
recipe, take care to wash
them thoroughly because
they can be quite gritty.
To wash spinach: Fill a
clean sink with lukewarm
water. Remove the tough
stems and submerge the
tender leaves in the water,
swishing to remove the
grit. Rinse thoroughly
in a colander under cold
running water, checking
carefully to ensure that
no sand remains. If you
are using frozen spinach
in this recipe, thaw
and squeeze the excess
moisture out before
adding to the work bowl.

4 oz	mozzarella cheese (see Tips, left)	125 g
1	can (14 oz/398 mL) artichoke hearts, drained	1
2	cloves garlic, coarsely chopped	2
8 cups	fresh spinach leaves or 1 package 10 oz (300 g) spinach leaves, thawed if frozen (about 8 oz/250 g loosely packed)	2 L
1	package (8 oz/250 g) cream cheese, cubed and softened	1
¼ cup	freshly grated Parmesan cheese	60 mL
2 tbsp	heavy or whipping (35%) cream	30 mL
	Tostadas, tortilla chips or sliced baguette	

1. In work bowl fitted with shredding blade, shred mozzarella. Transfer to a heavy-bottomed saucepan.

2. Replace shredding blade with metal blade. Add artichoke hearts and garlic and pulse until desired consistency is achieved, about 10 times. Add to saucepan.

3. Add spinach to work bowl and pulse until desired degree of consistency is achieved, about 10 times. Add cream cheese, Parmesan and cream and pulse until smooth. Add to artichoke mixture and stir well. Place over low heat and cook, stirring constantly, until cheese is melted and mixture is bubbling. Transfer to a warm serving bowl or a chafing dish and serve hot, with tostadas, tortilla chips or sliced baguette.

Chilly Dilly Eggplant

**Makes about
2 cups (500 mL)**

Vegan Friendly

This is a versatile recipe, delicious as a dip with raw vegetables or on pita triangles, as well as a sandwich spread on crusty French bread. It also makes a wonderful addition to a mezes or tapas-style meal. Although it is tasty warm, the flavor dramatically improves if it is thoroughly chilled before serving.

Tip

Although eggplant is delicious when properly cooked, some varieties tend to be bitter. Since the bitterness is concentrated under the skin, peeling eggplant before using is a good idea. Sprinkling the pieces with salt and leaving them to "sweat" for an hour or two also draws out the bitter juice. If time is short, blanch the pieces for a minute or two in heavily salted water. In either case, rinse thoroughly in fresh cold water and, using your hands, squeeze out the excess moisture. Pat dry with paper towels and it's ready for cooking.

1	large eggplant, peeled, cut into 1-inch (2.5 cm) cubes and drained of excess moisture (see Tip, left)	2
2 to 3 tbsp	olive oil	30 to 45 mL
1	onion, chopped	1
2	cloves garlic, chopped	2
1 tsp	dried oregano	5 mL
1 tsp	salt	5 mL
½ tsp	freshly ground black pepper	2 mL
1 tbsp	balsamic or red wine vinegar	15 mL
½ cup	fresh dill fronds	125 mL
	Salt and freshly ground black pepper	
	Dill sprigs, optional	
	Finely chopped black olives, optional	

1. In a skillet, heat 2 tbsp (30 mL) of the oil over medium-high heat. Add eggplant, in batches, and cook, stirring and tossing, until it begins to brown, about 4 minutes per batch. Transfer to a bowl and set aside.

2. Reduce heat to medium. Add more oil, if necessary, and cook onion, stirring, until softened, about 3 minutes. Add garlic, oregano, salt and pepper and cook, stirring, for 1 minute. Return eggplant to pan. Stir in vinegar. Reduce heat to low. Cover and simmer until eggplant is tender, stirring occasionally, about 20 minutes.

3. Transfer to work bowl fitted with metal blade. Add dill and process until smooth, about 30 seconds, stopping and scraping down sides of the bowl as necessary. Taste for seasoning and adjust. Spoon into a serving bowl and refrigerate until thoroughly chilled or for up to 2 days. Garnish with sprigs of dill and chopped black olives, if using.

Lemon-Laced Butterbean Dip

**Makes about
1 cup (250 mL)**

Vegan Friendly

Delicious and healthful,
this Mediterranean-
inspired dip is very
easy to make. Serve
it with toasted pita,
sliced baguette or
vegetable dippers.

Tip

Bring lima beans to a boil
in 6 cups (1.5 L) water
over medium heat. Boil
rapidly for 3 minutes.
Cover, turn off element
and let stand for 1 hour.
Drain.

1 cup	dried lima beans, soaked (see Tip, left)	250 mL
¼ cup	freshly squeezed lemon juice	60 mL
¼ cup	extra virgin olive oil	60 mL
1 tsp	salt	5 mL
	Freshly ground black pepper	
½ cup	loosely packed Italian flat-leaf parsley leaves	125 mL
4	green onions, white part only, cut into chunks	4

1. In a large pot of water, cook soaked beans until tender, about 30 minutes. Scoop out about 1 cup (250 mL) of the cooking liquid and set aside. Drain beans and pop out of their skins.

2. In work bowl fitted with metal blade, pulse cooked beans, lemon juice, olive oil, salt, and pepper to taste, to blend, about 5 times. Gradually add just enough bean cooking water through the feed tube to make a smooth emulsion, pulsing to blend, about 10 times. Add parsley and green onions and pulse until chopped and integrated, about 5 times. Cover and refrigerate for up to 2 days until ready to use.

Feta and Roasted Red Pepper Dip

**Makes about
1¾ cups (425 mL)**

Vegetarian Friendly

Serve this tasty dip with
crudités or crackers.

Tip

Use creamy feta cheese
(about 26% M.F.). The
lower-fat versions produce
a drier dip. If your results
seem dry, add 1 tsp (5 mL)
or so of extra virgin olive
oil and pulse.

8 oz	feta cheese (see Tips, left)	250 g
2	roasted red peppers, store-bought or homemade (see Tips, page 147)	2
	Hot pepper sauce, optional	

1. In work bowl fitted with metal blade, process feta, roasted peppers, and hot pepper sauce, if using, until smooth, about 30 seconds, stopping and scraping down sides of the bowl, as necessary.

Fresh Herb Tomato Dipping Sauce

Makes 1 cup (250 mL)

Vegan Friendly

Spread this sauce over a French baguette instead of butter.

Tips

Cut the tomatoes in half crosswise and squeeze out all the seeds. This is a fast seeding method.

This recipe works best with ¼ cup (60 mL) chopped shallot. One shallot about 1¾ inches (4.5 cm) in diameter will yield about ¼ cup (60 mL) when chopped. If you have a different size shallot, adjust the amount accordingly.

Sauce keeps well, covered and refrigerated, for up to 1 week.

4	Roma (plum) tomatoes, cored and seeded (about 12 oz/375 g) (see Tips, left)	4
1	shallot (about ¼ cup/60 mL) (see Tips, left)	1
1 tbsp	fresh rosemary leaves	15 mL
1	clove garlic	1
½ tsp	freshly ground black pepper	2 mL
⅔ cup	dry white wine	150 mL
¼ cup	red wine vinegar	60 mL
¼ cup	olive oil	60 mL
½ tsp	salt	2 mL
	Granulated sugar, optional	
1	large fresh baguette	1

1. In work bowl fitted with metal blade, pulse tomatoes, shallot, rosemary, garlic and pepper until chunky, about 20 times.

2. Transfer mixture to a small saucepan over medium heat. Cook, stirring, until onion is softened, about 5 minutes. Add wine, vinegar, olive oil and salt. Reduce heat and boil gently, stirring occasionally, until reduced to a thick sauce, 20 to 25 minutes. If the tomatoes are tart, season with up to 1 tbsp (15 mL) sugar.

3. Cut baguette into 1-inch (2.5 cm) slices. Serve warm spread over baguette or use as a dipping sauce.

Variation
Use an herb such as dill or tarragon in place of rosemary.

Basil and White Bean Spread

**Makes about
3 cups (750 mL)**

Vegan Friendly

Don't tell and no one
will ever guess how
easy it is to make
this delicious and
sophisticated spread.
Serve this with Crostini
(page 157). Make about
24. Sliced baguette and
crackers work well, too.

2 cups	drained cooked white kidney (cannellini) beans (see Tips, below)	500 mL
2 cups	packed Italian flat-leaf parsley leaves (see Tips, page 76)	500 mL
2 tbsp	prepared basil pesto sauce	30 mL
4	cloves garlic, coarsely chopped	4
1 tbsp	freshly squeezed lemon juice	15 mL
	Salt and freshly ground black pepper	

1. In work bowl fitted with metal blade, process beans, parsley, basil pesto, garlic and lemon juice until smooth, about 1 minute. Season with salt and pepper to taste. Serve immediately or cover and refrigerate for up to 2 days. If refrigerated, before serving let stand at room temperature for about 20 minutes to allow the flavors to develop.

Black Bean Chipotle Dip

**Makes 2 to 3 cups
(500 to 750 mL)**

Vegan Friendly

This dip has a south-of-
the-border kick. It gets
even hotter the next
day. Serve with crackers,
chips or toast points.

Tips

For this quantity of beans,
use 1 can (14 to 19 oz/
398 to 540 mL) drained
and rinsed, or cook 1 cup
(250 mL) dried beans.

Dip will keep, covered
and refrigerated, for up
to 1 week. The flavors get
stronger after a day or two.

2 cups	drained cooked black beans (see Tips, left)	500 mL
12 oz	cream cheese, cubed and softened, or vegan alternative	375 g
1/3 cup	roasted red peppers (about 1 small)	75 mL
1/2 to 1	chipotle pepper in adobo sauce, drained	1/2 to 1
1 tbsp	fresh cilantro leaves	15 mL
1 tbsp	taco seasoning	15 mL
1 tsp	freshly squeezed lime juice	5 mL

1. In work bowl fitted with metal blade, process black beans, cream cheese, red peppers, chipotle pepper to taste, cilantro, taco seasoning and lime juice until smooth, about 2 minutes, stopping and scraping down sides of the bowl once or twice. Transfer to a serving dish.

Variation
Substitute pinto beans for the black beans for a lighter looking dip.

Hummus from Scratch

**Makes about
3 cups (750 mL)**

Vegan Friendly

Although it's more work, cooking dried chickpeas rather than using canned chickpeas produces the tastiest hummus. Try this and see if you agree. Serve with warm pita. Although it's a bit unconventional, hummus makes a great sauce for grilled kabobs, particularly lamb. It is also great as a topping for roasted eggplant (see Variation, below).

Tip

If you're in a hurry, instead of setting the chickpeas aside to soak, cover the pot and bring to a boil. Boil for 3 minutes. Turn off heat and soak for 1 hour. Drain and rinse thoroughly with cold water. Then proceed with cooking as in Step 2.

1 cup	dried chickpeas (see Tip, left)	250 mL
	Garlic, bay leaves or bouquet garni, optional	
1/3 cup	tahini paste	75 mL
1/3 cup	extra virgin olive oil	75 mL
1/4 cup	freshly squeezed lemon juice	60 mL
1/4 cup	Italian flat-leaf parsley leaves	60 mL
2	cloves garlic (approx.)	2
1 tsp	ground cumin (see Tips, page 56)	5 mL
1 tsp	salt (approx.)	5 mL
1/2 tsp	freshly ground black pepper	2 mL
1/4 tsp	cayenne pepper, optional	1 mL
	Sweet paprika, optional	

1. In a large saucepan, combine chickpeas and 3 cups (750 mL) cold water. Set aside to soak for at least 6 hours or overnight. Drain and rinse thoroughly with cold water.

2. Return drained chickpeas to saucepan and add 3 cups (750 mL) cold fresh water. If desired, season with garlic, bay leaves or a bouquet garni made from your favorite herbs tied together in a cheesecloth bag. Cover and bring to a boil over medium-high heat. Reduce heat and simmer until chickpeas are tender, about 1 hour. Scoop out about 1 cup (250 mL) of cooking water and set aside. Drain and rinse chickpeas.

3. In a work bowl, fitted with metal blade, process cooked chickpeas, tahini, olive oil, 1/4 cup (60 mL) of the cooking water and lemon juice until smooth, about 30 seconds, stopping and scraping down sides of the bowl as necessary. If necessary, add additional cooking water and pulse to blend. (You want the mixture to be quite creamy.) Add parsley, garlic, cumin, salt, pepper, and cayenne, if using, and process until smooth, about 15 seconds. Taste and adjust garlic, lemon juice and/or salt to suit your taste. Process again, if necessary. Spoon into a serving bowl and dust with paprika, if using.

Variation

Roasted Eggplant with Hummus: Cut 1 eggplant into 1/2-inch (1 cm) thick slices. Brush with olive oil and bake in a 400°F (200°C) oven for about 25 minutes. Top with hummus.

Easy Hummus for a Crowd

Vegan Friendly

If you're making a dip, make enough for a crowd because you'll want to snack on this hummus for days after your party.

Tips

If the hummus is too thick after a few days you can thin it with additional lemon juice before serving.

Tahini paste should be stored in the refrigerator. Taste it before use. It should have a clean nutty taste and not taste like rancid sesame seeds.

Store hummus, covered and refrigerated, for up to 3 days.

2	cans (16 or 19 oz/454 or 540 mL) chickpeas, drained and rinsed	2
2	cloves garlic	2
⅔ cup	tahini paste	150 mL
1 cup	freshly squeezed lemon juice (approx.)	250 mL
2 tbsp	Italian flat-leaf parsley leaves	30 mL
¼ tsp	ground cumin	1 mL
¼ tsp	mild curry powder	1 mL
	Salt	

1. In work bowl fitted with metal blade, process chickpeas, garlic and tahini paste until smooth, about 30 seconds, stopping and scraping down sides of the bowl once or twice. With motor running, drizzle lemon juice through feed tube and process until desired consistency. Add parsley, cumin and curry powder and process until smooth. Season with salt to taste. Serve with cracker bread or flatbreads.

Variation
Add 2 tsp (10 mL) fresh mint leaves with parsley leaves.

Smoked Oyster Hummus

**Makes about
3 cups (750 mL)**

This intriguing spread is a variation on traditional Middle Eastern hummus. It always gets rave reviews. Serve with pita bread, pita toasts or crudités, such as celery sticks, peeled baby carrots or sliced cucumbers.

Tip

Taste the oysters before using to ensure their flavor meets your approval, as it can vary from brand to brand, affecting the result.

2 cups	cooked chickpeas, drained and rinsed (see Tips, page 327)	500 mL
¼ cup	freshly squeezed lemon juice	60 mL
¼ cup	extra virgin olive oil	60 mL
1	large roasted red pepper (see Tips, page 147)	1
4	cloves garlic	4
½ tsp	salt	2 mL
1	can (3 oz/90 g) smoked oysters, drained Freshly ground black pepper	1

1. In work bowl fitted with metal blade, process chickpeas, lemon juice, olive oil, roasted red pepper, garlic and salt until smooth, about 30 seconds, stopping and scraping down sides of the bowl as necessary.

2. Add oysters and pulse just to chop and combine, about 5 times. Season with pepper to taste.

Parsley-Laced Tapenade with Roasted Red Pepper

**Makes about
1¼ (300 mL) cups**

The addition of parsley and a roasted red pepper adds lightness to tapenade, which tends to be heavy. Serve this on sliced baguette or celery sticks or as part of an antipasto table.

Tip

For best results, use olives from the Mediterranean region. Do not use canned black olives, which are completely lacking in taste.

8 oz	pitted drained black olives (see Tip, left)	250 g
2 tbsp	drained capers	30 mL
1 cup	loosely packed parsley leaves	250 mL
2	anchovies	2
1	clove garlic, coarsely chopped	1
1	roasted red bell pepper, seeded and coarsely chopped	1
¼ cup	extra virgin olive oil	60 mL

1. In work bowl fitted with metal blade, pulse olives, capers, parsley, anchovies, garlic and roasted pepper until chopped and combined, about 10 times, stopping and scraping down sides of the bowl as necessary. Add olive oil and pulse until desired texture is achieved. Serve immediately or cover and refrigerate for up to 3 days. If refrigerated, before serving, let stand at room temperature for about 20 minutes to allow the flavors to develop.

Tuna Tapenade

Known as Provençal caviar, tapenade is a flavorful mixture of capers, olives and anchovies, among other ingredients. Here, the addition of tuna lightens up the end result. Serve this with carrot or celery sticks, sliced cucumber, crackers or crostini. It also makes a delicious filling for hard-cooked eggs (see Variation, right).

1	can (6 oz/170 g) tuna, preferably Italian, packed in olive oil, drained	1
4	anchovies	4
2 tbsp	drained capers	30 mL
1 tbsp	freshly squeezed lemon juice	15 mL
1	clove garlic, coarsely chopped	1
10	pitted black olives	10
¼ cup	extra virgin olive oil	60 mL

1. In work bowl fitted with metal blade, pulse tuna, anchovies, capers, lemon juice, garlic and olives until ingredients are combined but still chunky, about 10 times. Add olive oil and pulse until blended, about 5 times. Spoon into a bowl, cover tightly and refrigerate for at least 2 hours or for up to 3 days.

Variation

Tuna Tapenade–Stuffed Eggs: To hard cook eggs, place on the bottom of a saucepan in a single layer and add enough cold water to cover by 1 inch (2.5 cm). Bring to a boil over high heat. Remove from heat and without draining the water, cover and let stand for 10 minutes. With a slotted spoon, carefully place eggs in a large bowl filled with ice water. Let cool completely for 5 minutes. Remove eggshells under cool running water. Let eggs come to room temperature. Cut in half lengthwise. Pop out the yolks and add 1 tsp (5 mL) Tuna Tapenade per yolk. Mash together and use this mixture to fill the whites. Dust with paprika, if desired.

Green Olive Tapenade

**Makes about
1 cup (250 mL)**

Vegan Friendly

If you're looking for something a little different, try this. It is much lighter than the traditional tapenade made with black olives. Served on crackers, crostini or sliced baguette, it makes a wonderful accompaniment to cocktails in the garden on a warm summer night.

1 cup	pitted drained green olives	250 mL
¼ cup	fresh basil leaves	60 mL
2	cloves garlic, coarsely chopped	2
1 tbsp	drained capers	15 mL
¼ cup	extra virgin olive oil	60 mL
1 tbsp	freshly squeezed lemon juice	15 mL

1. In work bowl fitted with metal blade, pulse olives, basil, garlic and capers until finely chopped. With motor running, slowly add olive oil and lemon juice through feed tube and process just until blended. Transfer to a small serving bowl. Cover and refrigerate for at least 2 hours or for up to 3 days.

Olive and Pimento Cheese Spread

**Makes 2 cups
(500 mL)**

Vegetarian Friendly

This makes a tasty spread. Perfect for German dark breads and hearty crackers.

10 oz	goat cheese, softened	300 g
1	package (8 oz/250 g) cream cheese, cubed and softened	1
⅓ cup	green olives with pimento	75 mL
2 tbsp	fresh rosemary	30 mL
½ tsp	sea salt	2 mL

1. In work bowl fitted with metal blade, process goat cheese, cream cheese, olives, rosemary and salt until smooth, about 30 seconds, stopping and scraping down sides of the bowl once or twice.

2. Place in a ramekin, cover and refrigerate for 1 hour before serving.

Light Veggie Herb Cheese Spread

Makes 1½ cups (375 mL)

Vegetarian Friendly

It's win-win! This spread offers full flavor and fewer calories.

Tip

Dried red or green bell peppers are concentrated small diced bell peppers that yield a fresh taste and flavor. They are available in bulk food and spice stores. If you can't find them, use a double amount of diced fresh bell peppers instead.

2 tbsp	dried red and green bell pepper flakes (see Tip, left)	30 mL
1 tbsp	dried oregano	15 mL
1 tbsp	dried tarragon	15 mL
2 tbsp	hot water	30 mL
1	clove garlic	1
8 oz	Neufchâtel cheese, softened, or light cream cheese (not whipped cream cheese)	250 g

1. In a small bowl, combine dried peppers, oregano, tarragon and hot water. Stir until softened, about 2 minutes.

2. In work bowl fitted with metal blade, process garlic until finely chopped. Add Neufchâtel and pulse several times to combine. Add herb mixture and process until smooth, about 30 seconds, stopping and scraping down sides of the bowl once or twice.

3. Place in a ramekin, cover and refrigerate for 1 hour before serving.

Herb and Garlic Cheese Spread

Makes 1½ cups (375 mL)

Vegetarian Friendly

Here's a lighter spread for calorie-watchers who don't want to cut down on flavor.

8 oz	Neufchâtel cheese, softened, or light cream cheese not whipped cream cheese)	250 g
4 oz	feta cheese	125 g
1 tbsp	dried oregano	15 mL
1 tbsp	chopped fresh tarragon	15 mL
1	clove garlic	1

1. In work bowl fitted with metal blade, process Neufchâtel cheese, feta, oregano, tarragon and garlic until smooth, about 30 seconds, stopping and scraping down sides of the bowl once or twice.

2. Place in a ramekin, cover and refrigerate for 1 hour before serving.

Sharp Cheddar Spread

Makes 1½ cups (375 mL)

Vegetarian Friendly

The olives add texture and flavor to this cheese spread.

12 oz	sharp Cheddar cheese, cut into 6 cubes	375 g
¼ cup	green olives with pimentos	60 mL
2 tbsp	fresh dill fronds	30 mL
½ tsp	capers, drained	2 mL
¼ tsp	salt	1 mL

1. In work bowl fitted with metal blade, process Cheddar cheese, olives, dill, capers and salt until smooth, about 20 seconds, stopping and scraping down sides of the bowl once or twice.

2. Place in a ramekin, cover and refrigerate for 1 hour before serving.

Curry Cheese Spread

Makes 1 cup (250 mL)

Vegetarian Friendly

This spicy spread livens up the flavor of sliced root vegetables.

1	package (8 oz/250 g) cream cheese, cubed and softened	1
1 tbsp	dried onion flakes	15 mL
¼ cup	flaked sweetened coconut	60 mL
1 tsp	curry powder	5 mL

1. In work bowl fitted with metal blade, process cream cheese, onion flakes, coconut and curry powder until smooth, about 20 seconds, stopping and scraping down sides of the bowl once or twice.

2. Place in a ramekin, cover and refrigerate for 1 hour before serving.

Dill Goat Cheese Spread

**Makes 2 cups
(500 mL)**

Vegetarian Friendly

People who don't like
goat cheese taste this
spread and change their
minds!

1	package (8 oz/250 g) cream cheese, cubed and softened	1
7 oz	goat cheese, softened	210 g
2 tbsp	Italian flat-leaf parsley leaves	30 mL
1 tbsp	fresh tarragon	15 mL
1 tbsp	fresh dill fronds	15 mL
1 tbsp	chopped fresh chives (about 5 stems)	15 mL
1 tbsp	freshly squeezed lemon juice	15 mL
½ tsp	salt	2 mL
¼ tsp	freshly ground black pepper	1 mL

1. In work bowl fitted with metal blade, process cream cheese, goat cheese, parsley, tarragon, dill, chives, lemon juice, salt and pepper until smooth, about 20 seconds, stopping and scraping down sides of the bowl once or twice.

2. Place in a ramekin, cover and refrigerate for 1 hour before serving.

Pumpkin Cream Cheese Spread

Makes 1 cup (250 mL)

Vegetarian Friendly

Try this spread on
pumpkin bread or on
an apple spice muffin.

1	package (8 oz/250 g) cream cheese, cubed and softened	1
2 tbsp	pumpkin purée (not pumpkin pie filling)	30 mL
1 tbsp	liquid honey	15 mL
½ tsp	ground cinnamon	2 mL
¼ tsp	freshly grated nutmeg	1 mL
¼ tsp	ground cloves	1 mL

1. In work bowl fitted with metal blade, process cream cheese, pumpkin purée, honey, cinnamon, nutmeg and cloves until smooth, about 30 seconds, stopping and scraping down sides of the bowl once or twice.

2. Place in a ramekin, cover and refrigerate for 1 hour before serving.

Pineapple Cream Spread

**Makes 2 cups
(500 mL)**

Vegetarian Friendly

Pair this spread with other creamy spreads for your brunch breads.

- Mini-bowl attachment

8 oz	cream cheese, cubed and softened	250 g
1	can (8 oz/227 mL) crushed pineapple, drained well	1
½ tsp	ground cinnamon	2 mL
¼ tsp	ground nutmeg	1 mL

1. In mini bowl fitted with metal blade, process cream cheese, pineapple, cinnamon and nutmeg for 2 minutes.
2. Transfer to a serving bowl and refrigerate until firm, about 30 minutes or for up to 3 days.

Variation

Add 1 cup (250 mL) toasted macadamia nuts to mixture.

Egg Salad Spread

**Makes 2 cups
(500 mL)**

Vegetarian Friendly

This egg salad is great spread on crostini for appetizers. Also, when you have an abundance of colored eggs after Easter, make this spread so you will have lunch for a few days.

Tips

You can hard-cook the eggs a few days before serving.

Spread keeps, covered and refrigerated, for up to 3 days.

- Large bowl of ice water

8	eggs	8
⅓ cup	Traditional Mayonnaise (page 437) or store-bought	75 mL
4 oz	cooked ham or salami, optional	125 g
1 tsp	prepared mustard	5 mL
1 tsp	loosely packed fresh dill fronds	5 mL
⅛ tsp	ground nutmeg	0.5 mL
Pinch	salt	Pinch

1. Place eggs on the bottom of a saucepan in a single layer and add enough cold water to cover by 1 inch (2.5 cm). Bring to a boil over high heat. Remove from heat and without draining the water, cover and let stand for 10 minutes. With a slotted spoon, carefully place eggs in a large bowl filled with ice water. Let cool completely for 5 minutes. Remove eggshells under cool running water. Let eggs come to room temperature.
2. In work bowl fitted with metal blade, process eggs, mayonnaise, ham, if using, mustard, dill, nutmeg and salt until smooth, about 30 seconds, stopping and scraping down sides of the bowl once or twice. Taste and add more salt, if desired.

Homemade Potato Chips

Vegan Friendly

These are very easy to make. They are delicious with dips such as Caramelized Red Onion Dip (page 71) but they also make good anchors for spreads such as Smoked Trout Spread (page 87), Smoked Salmon Spread (page 88) or Eggplant Caviar (page 76). Place a dollop of spread on each chip and pass as an hors d'oeuvre.

Tips

If you're not using a deep-fryer, a thermometer is the best way to judge the temperature of your oil, but if you don't have one, drop 1 potato slice into the hot oil. If the oil bubbles and the slice rises to the surface, the temperature is fine. If the slice sinks to the bottom with no bubbles, it is not hot enough, and if it stays on the surface surrounded by bubbles, the oil is too hot.

Be sure to cook the chips long enough to ensure they are crisp. They can be browned and cooked through but still a bit soft in the middle. Turning them helps to ensure they cook evenly.

- Candy/deep-fry thermometer or deep-fryer

1½ lbs	potatoes, peeled (about 2 medium)	750 g
2 cups	oil, such as peanut or corn for deep-frying (approx.)	500 mL
	Fine sea salt	

1. In work bowl fitted with slicing blade, slice potatoes. Transfer to a large bowl. Cover with cold salted water and soak for 10 minutes. Drain in a colander and rinse thoroughly under cold running water. Place in a salad spinner and dry thoroughly.

2. In a large deep skillet or Dutch oven, heat oil over medium-high heat. (It should be 350°F/180°C.) Add potato slices, in batches, and fry, stirring frequently to keep them separated and turning once to ensure they brown evenly, until golden, about 5 minutes per batch (see Tips, left). Using a slotted spoon, transfer to a paper-towel lined plate. Sprinkle with salt to taste. Repeat with remaining potatoes.

Indian-Spiced Sweet Potato Chips

Vegan Friendly

If you are fortunate enough to visit Vij's, a fabulous nouveau-Indian restaurant in Vancouver that doesn't take reservations, while you wait for your table, you will likely be served sweet potato or cassava fries, seasoned with Indian spices. That's the inspiration for these tasty tidbits.

Tips

If you don't have a deep-fryer or thermometer, drop 1 potato slice into the hot oil. If the oil bubbles and the slice rises to the surface, the temperature is fine. If the slice sinks to the bottom with no bubbles, it is not hot enough, and if it stays on the surface surrounded by bubbles, the oil is too hot.

For the best flavor, toast and grind cumin and coriander seeds yourself. *To toast seeds:* Place seeds in a dry skillet over medium heat, and cook, stirring, until fragrant, about 3 minutes. Immediately transfer to a mortar or a spice grinder and grind.

- Candy/deep-fry thermometer or deep-fryer (see Tips, left)

1 lb	sweet potatoes (about 2), peeled	500 g
1 tsp	ground cumin (see Tips, left)	5 mL
1 tsp	ground coriander	5 mL
1 tsp	fine sea salt	5 mL
¼ tsp	hot paprika	1 mL
2 cups	oil such as peanut or corn for deep-frying (approx.)	500 mL

1. In work bowl fitted with slicing blade, slice potatoes. Transfer to a large bowl. Cover with cold salted water and soak for 10 minutes. Drain in a colander and rinse thoroughly under cold running water. Place in a salad spinner and dry thoroughly.

2. In a small bowl, combine cumin, coriander, salt and paprika. Stir well and set aside.

3. In a large deep skillet or Dutch oven, heat oil over medium-high heat. (It should be 325°F/160°C.) Add potato slices, in batches, and fry, stirring frequently to keep them separated and turning once, until they start to curl up and are brown around the edges, about 3 minutes per batch. Using a slotted spoon, transfer to a paper-towel lined plate. Sprinkle with spice mix and serve immediately. Repeat with remaining potatoes.

Truffle-Spiked Potato Croquettes

**Makes about
60 ½-inch (1 cm)
croquettes**

Vegetarian Friendly

These croquettes are
very versatile. Because
they are quite rich, you
might like to serve them
as pop-in-your-mouth
one-bite canapés, but
they can also be used as
a vegetable course (see
Tips, below).

Tips

If you want to serve
these as a vegetable, make
them a bit larger (about
1½ inches/4 cm) and
increase the cooking time
to 4 to 5 minutes. This will
yield about 24 croquettes
and you should expect to
serve about 4 per person.

We like the flavor
delivered by truffle salt
but if you can't find it,
substitute fine sea salt
instead and just make
potato croquettes.

• Rimmed baking sheet, lined with parchment paper
or waxed paper

1 lb	potatoes, cooked in their skins and refrigerated overnight	500 g
1 tbsp	melted butter	15 mL
1	egg yolk	1
1	egg	1
1 tsp	truffle salt (see Tips, left)	5 mL
	Freshly ground black pepper	

Coating

¼ cup	all-purpose flour (approx.)	60 mL
2	eggs, beaten	2
1 cup	dry bread crumbs such as panko (approx.)	250 mL
¼ cup	butter, divided	60 mL
¼ cup	olive oil, divided	60 mL

1. Peel potatoes, cut into chunks and place in work bowl
fitted with metal blade. Purée until smooth. Add melted
butter, egg yolk, egg, truffle salt, and pepper to taste.
Pulse until blended. Transfer to a saucepan over low heat
and cook, beating constantly with a wooden spoon until
mixture becomes pliable, about 3 minutes. Spread on
prepared baking sheet. Place a piece of plastic wrap over
top and using a rolling pin, roll out to a rough rectangle,
about ½ inch (1 cm) thick. Refrigerate until thoroughly
chilled, at least 2 hours or overnight.

2. **Coating:** When you're ready to cook, shape into small
balls, about ¾ inch (2 cm) in diameter. Spread flour
on 1 plate. Beat eggs in a shallow bowl and place bread
crumbs on another plate. Roll croquettes in flour, then
eggs, then bread crumbs. Once all croquettes are coated,
discard any excess flour, eggs and bread crumbs.

3. In a large skillet over medium-high heat, melt 2 tbsp
(30 mL) of the butter in 2 tbsp (30 mL) of the oil. Add
croquettes, in batches, and cook, turning carefully, until
crisp and golden, about 3 minutes. As cooked, transfer to a
platter and keep warm. Adjust the heat to prevent burning
and add more butter and oil between batches as necessary.

Indian-Style Potato Fritters

Makes about 12

Vegetarian Friendly

These fritters resemble pakora, without the chickpea batter. They are very easy to make and have wide appeal. Pass your favorite chutney alongside and urge people to put a small dollop on top before consuming.

Tips

Double or triple the recipe to suit your needs.

You'll get the best flavor if you toast and grind cumin and coriander seeds yourself. *To toast cumin and coriander seeds:* Place 1 tsp (5 mL) each seed in a dry skillet over medium heat. Cook, stirring, until fragrant, about 3 minutes. Transfer to a mortar or spice grinder and grind.

For best results, it is important to use floury potatoes, which are usually oblong in shape and do not contain as much water as waxy varieties such as thin-skinned red or white potatoes. The most common floury potatoes are russet (Idaho) potatoes.

1 lb	russet (Idaho) potato (about 1 large), peeled (see Tips, left)	500 g
4	green onions, white part with a bit of green, chopped	4
1	egg	1
1 tsp	salt	5 mL
1 tsp	ground cumin (see Tips, left)	5 mL
1 tsp	ground coriander	5 mL
1/8 tsp	cayenne pepper	0.5 mL
1/4 cup	oil (approx.)	60 mL
	Chutney	

1. In work bowl fitted with shredding blade, shred potato. Using your hands, squeeze out as much liquid as possible. Place in a clean tea towel and squeeze out more. Transfer to a bowl.

2. Replace slicing blade with metal blade. Add green onions, egg, salt, cumin, coriander and cayenne. Pulse until finely chopped, about 3 times, stopping and scraping down sides of the bowl once or twice. Return potatoes to work bowl and pulse to blend, about 5 times.

3. Heat oil in a large pan oven medium-high heat. Scoop out a heaping tbsp (15 mL) of potato mixture and drop into pan. Flatten top with back of spoon. Cook, turning once, until golden, about 3 minutes per side. Repeat until all the mixture is used, adding more oil as necessary and cooking fritters in batches (no more than 6 at a time in a large skillet). Transfer to a paper-towel lined platter as completed. Serve hot with chutney.

Potato Pizza

Makes one 10-inch (25 cm) pizza to serve 6

Vegetarian Friendly

The flavor combinations here — mild potatoes with rosemary, onion and smoked mozzarella — are fabulous. They are not the norm on pizza, but the results are very tasty.

Tips

Peel the potato, if you wish, but we like the visual effect of the brown skin on the white background.

We've also made this on a large piece (about 12 by 6 inches /30 by 15 cm) prepared Middle Eastern-type flatbread and it was delicious.

- Preheat oven to 425°F (220°C)

1	potato (about 8 oz/250 g)	1
1	small red onion, cut to fit feed tube	1
2 tbsp	extra virgin olive oil	30 mL
2	cloves garlic, minced	2
1 tsp	chopped fresh rosemary	5 mL
½ tsp	salt	2 mL
½ tsp	freshly ground black pepper	2 mL
4 oz	smoked mozzarella cheese	125 g
1	herbed flat bread (see Tips, left) or ½ recipe Fast and Easy Pizza Dough (page 473)	1
2 tbsp	freshly grated Parmesan cheese	30 mL

1. Pierce potato all over with a fork. Microwave on High for 2 minutes. Let cool for 2 minutes. In work bowl fitted with slicing blade, slice potato and red onion. Transfer to a large bowl. Add olive oil, garlic, rosemary, salt and pepper. Toss well.

2. Replace slicing blade with shredding blade and shred mozzarella. Set aside.

3. If using pizza dough, roll out on a floured surface to a rectangle, about 11 by 8 inches (28 by 20 cm). Place flatbread or dough on a baking sheet. Arrange potato mixture evenly over top. Sprinkle mozzarella evenly over potatoes.

4. Bake in preheated oven until potatoes are tender and pizza is crisp, 20 to 25 minutes. Sprinkle Parmesan evenly over top and bake until melted and lightly browned, about 2 minutes more. To serve, cut into small rectangles and serve immediately.

Variation

Instead of herbed flat bread, you could also use naan, spreading the topping over 2 or 3 smaller ones, if necessary, or even pita breads. Use your imagination. The cooking time will stay the same.

Indian-Style Potato Roti

Vegan Friendly

Unlike Caribbean roti, which are filled, in India roti are simply a flatbread. Here the dough is made with potatoes and flour seasoned with fresh chiles and curry powder. The results are remarkably tasty. Serve them plain with just a sprinkling of fine sea salt or top with a dollop of your favorite chutney.

Tips

An easy way to cook potatoes in their skins is to microwave them. For this quantity, place scrubbed potatoes in a microwave-safe dish in one layer. Add cold water to a depth of about ½ inch (1 cm), cover and microwave on High for 6 minutes. Leave the lid on and let cool for at least 5 minutes before running under cold water and removing the skins.

For best results, it is important to use floury potatoes, which are usually oblong in shape and do not contain as much water as waxy varieties. The most common are russet (Idaho) potatoes.

- Mini-bowl attachment

1½ lbs	russet (Idaho) potatoes (about 1 extra large), boiled in their skins until fork-tender, cooled and peeled (see Tips, left)	750 g
2	fresh green chile peppers, seeded	2
4	green onions, white part only, cut into chunks	4
¼ cup	fresh cilantro leaves	60 mL
1 tsp	salt	5 mL
1 tsp	curry powder	5 mL
1 cup	all-purpose flour	250 mL
¼ cup	oil, divided (approx.)	60 mL
	Fine sea salt	
	Chutney, optional	

1. In work bowl fitted with shredding blade, shred potatoes. Transfer to a bowl.

2. Replace work bowl with mini bowl. Add chiles, green onions, cilantro, salt and curry powder. Process until chopped and blended. Add to potatoes and stir well. Gradually add flour, mixing until a soft dough forms, and using your hands to knead when the dough becomes too stiff to stir.

3. Pinch off a piece of dough about the size of a walnut and, on a lightly floured surface, roll into a 3-inch (7.5 cm) circle. Repeat until all the dough is used up.

4. In a large heavy skillet, heat 1 tbsp (15 mL) of the oil. Add roti, in batches, and cook, turning once until lightly browned on both sides and slightly puffed, about 2 minutes per side. Place on a warm platter as completed and sprinkle tops lightly with sea salt. Pass with a bowl of chutney, if using.

Greek-Style Garlic and Potato Dip

**Makes about
2 cups (500 mL)**

Vegan Friendly

This variation of the Greek sauce skordalia is made with mashed potatoes rather than bread. It is particularly delicious. Serve with pita or crudités.

Tips

Refrigerating this dip will cause it to congeal and dramatically intensify the flavor of the garlic. It is best made and served at room temperature.

1 lb	russet (Idaho) potatoes, boiled in their skins, cooled, peeled and coarsely chopped (about 2)	500 g
4	cloves garlic, coarsely chopped	4
¼ cup	freshly squeezed lemon juice	60 mL
½ cup	coarsely chopped blanched almonds, toasted (see Tips, page 112)	125 mL
½ cup	extra virgin olive oil	125 mL
	Salt and freshly ground black pepper	
	Finely chopped parsley	

1. In work bowl fitted with metal blade, process garlic until finely chopped, stopping and scraping down sides of the bowl. Add potatoes and pulse to blend, about 10 times. Add lemon juice and almonds and pulse to blend, about 5 times. With motor running, add olive oil through the feed tube and process until mixture is smooth and blended. Season with salt and pepper to taste. When ready to serve, garnish with parsley. Serve at room temperature.

Cucumbers with Feta and Dill

**Makes about
24 hors d'oeuvres**

Vegetarian Friendly

This is a wonderful dish to make when cucumbers are in season.

Tips

This quantity will fill 1 long English cucumber or 2 shorter field cucumbers. Use whatever looks freshest or suits your taste.

A grapefruit spoon with a serrated edge is perfect for scraping out cucumber seeds.

- Mini-bowl attachment

½ cup	crumbed feta	125 mL
¼ cup	fresh dill fronds	60 mL
2 tbsp	Traditional Mayonnaise (page 437) or store-bought (see Tip, page 93)	30 mL
1	clove garlic, coarsely chopped	1
1 to 2	cucumbers, peeled and halved lengthwise (see Tips, left)	1 to 2

1. In mini work bowl, process feta, dill, mayonnaise and garlic until smooth and blended, about 20 seconds, stopping and scraping down sides of the bowl as necessary.
2. Using a spoon, scrape out cucumber seeds and discard. Fill hollow with feta spread. Cut cucumbers horizontally into ½-inch (1 mL) slices and serve.

Cheese and Yogurt Spread

**Makes about
1 cup (250 mL)**

Vegetarian Friendly

Nothing could be simpler to make than this herb-infused spread. A small bowl of olives makes a nice accompaniment. Serve with toasted pita, crisp crackers or crudités.

- Mini-bowl attachment

1 cup	crumbled feta (about 8 oz/250 g)	250 mL
1 cup	plain yogurt, preferably Greek-style (pressed) (see Tip, page 114)	250 mL
½ cup	fresh dill fronds	125 mL
½ cup	snipped chives	125 mL
	Freshly ground black pepper	
	Extra virgin olive oil	

1. In mini work bowl fitted with metal blade, process feta, yogurt, dill, chives and pepper to taste, until smooth, about 30 seconds. Transfer to a serving bowl and drizzle with olive oil.

Pimento Cheese

**Makes about
1½ cups (375 mL)**

Vegetarian Friendly

Pimento cheese is an old favorite in the southern U.S. Serve this with sliced baguette, crackers, cracker bread or celery sticks.

Tip

If you prefer, substitute ¼ cup (60 mL) coarsely chopped sweet onion, such as Vidalia, for the green or red.

8 oz	aged Cheddar cheese (about 3 cups/750 mL)	250 g
1	roasted red bell pepper, seeded (see Tip, page 147)	1
½ cup	Traditional Mayonnaise (page 437) or store-bought (see Tip, page 93)	125 mL
3 tbsp	chopped green or red onion (see Tip, left)	45 mL
	Hot pepper sauce	
	Freshly ground black pepper	

1. In work bowl fitted with shredding blade, shred Cheddar. Replace shredding blade with metal blade. Add roasted pepper, mayonnaise, onion, hot pepper sauce and black pepper to taste and pulse until onion is finely chopped and mixture is blended, about 10 times.

2. Transfer to a small serving bowl, cover and refrigerate for at least 2 hours or for up to 2 days. Before serving let stand at room temperature for about 20 minutes to allow the flavors to bloom.

Tzatziki

**Makes about
2½ cups (625 mL)**

Vegetarian Friendly

Use this as a dip for pita or crudités or as a sauce to accompany grilled meat or chicken, particularly souvlaki.

Tip

Be sure to seed your cucumber. Otherwise your dip is likely to be watery.

2 cups	plain yogurt, preferably Greek-style (pressed) (see Tip, page 114)	500 mL
1	cucumber, peeled, seeded and cut into chunks (see Tip, left)	1
½ cup	loosely packed parsley leaves or fresh dill fronds	125 mL
2	cloves garlic, coarsely chopped	2
2 tbsp	extra virgin olive oil	30 mL
2 tbsp	freshly squeezed lemon juice	30 mL
1 tsp	salt	5 mL

1. In work bowl fitted with metal blade, process yogurt, cucumber, parsley, garlic, olive oil, lemon juice and salt until smooth. Cover and refrigerate until chilled or for up to 3 days.

Potted Cheddar

**Makes about
1 cup (250 mL)**

Vegetarian Friendly

Here's a traditional English technique for turning store-bought cheese into something special.

Tip

When choosing crackers for dips and spreads, look for high-quality versions that don't have strong flavors or too much salt. Pita bread or crisps, flatbreads, thinly sliced pumpernickel and crostini go well with specific recipes. And you can rarely go wrong with a fresh baguette.

8 oz	aged Cheddar cheese	250 g
¼ cup	softened butter	60 mL
2 tbsp	sweet sherry	30 mL
1 tbsp	freshly grated Parmesan cheese	15 mL
⅛ tsp	freshly grated nutmeg	0.5 mL
	Freshly ground white pepper	
	Walnut halves, optional	

1. In work bowl fitted with shredding blade, shred Cheddar. Replace shredding blade with metal blade. Add butter, sherry, Parmesan, nutmeg, and white pepper to taste. Process until smooth and blended, about 20 seconds.

2. Transfer to a serving dish. Flatten top with a spatula and press walnut halves into cheese, if using. Cover and chill until flavors meld, about 2 hours or for up to 1 week.

Quark Claqueret

**Makes about
1½ cups (375 mL)**

Vegetarian Friendly

Quark is a fresh lower-fat cheese, long popular in Europe and gaining traction in North America. Look for it in well-stocked supermarkets and natural food stores. Claqueret is a specialty of Lyons, one of France's gourmet centers. This herb-infused spread is traditionally served with dark rye bread but can also double as a dip for raw vegetables, also known as crudités (see Tip, below).

Tip

Crudités are cut-up vegetables used for dipping. Popular choices are broccoli and cauliflower florets, peeled baby carrots, Belgian endive and cherry tomatoes. And don't forget old standbys such as celery sticks and thinly sliced cucumber. If you're willing to think out of the box, try blanched Brussels sprouts, which are particularly good with strongly flavored dips.

2	shallots, quartered	2
2	cloves garlic, coarsely chopped	2
½ cup	coarsely snipped chives	125 mL
½ cup	Italian flat-leaf parsley leaves	125 mL
2	green onions, white part only, coarsely chopped	2
1 tbsp	fresh tarragon leaves	15 mL
1 cup	quark cheese	250 mL
2 tbsp	dry white wine	30 mL
½ tsp	salt	2 mL
	Freshly ground black pepper	
	Additional fresh herbs for garnishing, optional	

1. In work bowl fitted with metal blade, pulse shallots, garlic, chives, parsley, green onions and tarragon until finely chopped, about 15 times, stopping and scraping down sides of the bowl once or twice. Add quark, wine, salt, and pepper to taste. Process until smooth, about 30 seconds. Spoon into a serving dish, cover and chill overnight or for up to 2 days to allow flavors to meld. Garnish with fresh herbs, if using.

Liptauer

**Makes about
1 cup (250 mL)**

Vegetarian Friendly

This is a classic Austrian/ Hungarian dish, often made with Camembert, combined with a creamy cottage cheese. Here it's made with cream cheese and Emmenthal with lively additions such as hot smoked paprika. It is delicious served with thin slices of dark rye bread.

4 oz	Swiss Emmenthal cheese	125 g
4 oz	cream cheese, cubed and softened	125 g
¼ cup	Traditional Mayonnaise (page 437) or store-bought (see Tip, page 93)	60 mL
1 tbsp	Dijon mustard	15 mL
1	shallot, coarsely chopped	1
2	cornichon or gherkin pickles	2
1 tbsp	drained capers	15 mL
2 tsp	caraway seeds	10 mL
½ tsp	hot smoked paprika	2 mL
	Freshly ground black pepper	

1. In work bowl fitted with shredding blade, shred cheese. Replace shredding blade with metal blade. Add cream cheese, mayonnaise, Dijon mustard, shallot, cornichons, capers, caraway and paprika. Process until smoothly blended, about 20 seconds. Season with pepper to taste.

Kentucky Beer Cheese

**Makes about
2½ cups (625 mL)**

Vegetarian Friendly

In Kentucky, this spread is an indigenous treat — some call it America's answer to Britain's Welsh rarebit. Serve with sliced baguette, rye bread or celery sticks. Or spread it on toast, garnish with sliced tomatoes and run under the broiler for a delicious lunch.

Tip
Use light or dark beer to suit your preference.

8 oz	extra sharp (extra old) Cheddar cheese, cut into 1-inch (2.5 cm) cubes	250 g
8 oz	Monterey Jack, cut into 1-inch (2.5 cm) cubes	250 g
2	cloves garlic, coarsely chopped	2
2 tbsp	coarsely snipped chives	30 mL
1 tbsp	Worcestershire sauce or vegetarian alternative	15 mL
1 tbsp	Dijon mustard	15 mL
	Hot pepper sauce	
	Freshly ground black pepper	
¾ cup	beer, divided (see Tip, left)	175 mL
	Paprika	

1. In work bowl fitted with metal blade, process cheeses, garlic, chives, Worcestershire sauce, mustard, hot pepper sauce, pepper to taste, and ¼ cup (60 mL) of the beer until combined, stopping and scraping down sides of the bowl. Add remaining beer and process until smooth. Spoon into a serving dish, cover and refrigerate for at least 2 hours or for up to 1 week. Dust with paprika before serving.

Spicy Savory Cheesecake

Vegetarian Friendly

This unbaked cheesecake goes a long way. Serve it with celery sticks.

Tips

Parsley must be very dry to chop finely.

This cheesecake can be refrigerated in the pan for up to 2 weeks before serving.

- 9-inch (23 cm) cheesecake pan or springform pan with 3-inch (7.5 cm) sides, lined with parchment paper

Filling

1	package (8 oz/250 g) cream cheese, cubed and softened	1
4 cups	shredded pepper Jack cheese	1 L
1 cup	unsalted butter, softened	250 mL
2	jalapeño peppers, cut in half and seeded	2
1	shallot, minced	1
1/4 tsp	freshly ground white pepper	1 mL
1/4 tsp	hot pepper sauce	1 mL
1 cup	pecans, toasted and chopped (see page 24)	250 mL
1/2 cup	chopped green onions (about 8)	125 mL
1/4 cup	chopped Italian flat-leaf parsley	60 mL

Decoration

1/4 cup	pecans, toasted and chopped	60 mL

1. **Filling:** In work bowl fitted with metal blade, in two batches, if necessary, pulse cream cheese, pepper Jack cheese, butter, jalapeños, shallot, white pepper and hot pepper sauce until smooth, stopping and scraping down sides of the bowl once or twice. Transfer to a bowl and fold in pecans, green onions and parsley by hand.

2. Pour into prepared pan, smoothing out to sides of pan. Cover with plastic wrap and press gently to compact. Refrigerate for at least 6 hours before decorating or serving.

3. **Decoration:** To unmold, place a large plate over top of cake and invert. Take sides of pan off, then the bottom. Peel parchment paper off cake. Pack sides with chopped pecans.

Variation

Use a 6-inch (15 cm) cheesecake pan if you want thick slices.

Blue Cheese Pistachio Cheesecake

Serves 10 to 12

Vegetarian Friendly

This cheesecake is perfect as an appetizer with port or used as a cheese course for an elegant dinner party.

Tips

The blue cheese that is not creamed will crumble more uniformly if it is cold. The portion to be creamed should be at room temperature.

To toast pistachios: Preheat oven to 350°F (180°C). Spread nuts on a baking sheet and bake, shaking the pan several times, until fragrant and toasted, 5 to 6 minutes for whole pistachios, 3 to 5 minutes for chopped.

Parsley must be very dry to chop finely.

This cheesecake can be refrigerated in the pan for up to 2 weeks before serving.

• 9-inch (23 cm) cheesecake pan or springform pan with 3-inch (7.5 cm) sides, lined with parchment paper

Filling

1 cup	unsalted butter, softened	250 mL
1	package (8 oz/250 g) cream cheese, cubed and softened	1
1 lb	blue cheese or Gorgonzola, crumbled, divided	500 g
1	shallot, minced (about 1/4 cup/60 mL)	1
1/4 cup	Madeira wine	60 mL
1/4 tsp	freshly ground white pepper	1 mL
1 cup	pistachios, toasted and chopped, divided (see Tips, left)	250 mL
1/2 cup	chopped green onions (about 8), divided	125 mL
1/4 cup	chopped Italian flat-leaf parsley leaves, divided	60 mL

Decoration

1 cup	pistachios, toasted and chopped	250 mL

1. **Filling:** In work bowl fitted with metal blade, in two batches, if necessary, pulse butter, cream cheese, half the blue cheese, shallot, Madeira and white pepper until smooth, stopping and scraping down sides of the bowl once or twice. Set aside.

2. In prepared pan, sprinkle half the remaining blue cheese and half each of the pistachios, green onions and parsley. Top with half the butter mixture, then layer with the remaining blue cheese, pistachios, green onions and parsley. Finish with the remaining butter mixture. Cover with plastic wrap and press gently to compact the layers. Refrigerate for at least 6 hours before decorating or serving.

3. **Decoration:** To unmold, place a large plate over top of cake and invert. Take sides of pan off, then the bottom. Peel parchment paper off cake. Pack sides with chopped pistachios.

Variation

Use a 6-inch (15 cm) cheesecake pan if you want thick slices.

Pesto Sun-Dried Tomato Cheesecake

Serves 10 to 12

Vegetarian Friendly

This is a great appetizer when the main course is pasta. Serve as a spread with crackers.

Tips

Serve slightly warmed, if desired, to make more spreadable. *To serve as a warm appetizer:* Wrap the cheesecake in foil and place in a preheated 350°F (180°C) oven for 10 minutes to heat through. Do not microwave; it will toughen the cheesecake.

To serve as an appetizer, place a thin slice on a lettuce leaf.

- Preheat oven to 350°F (180°C)
- 9-inch (23 cm) cheesecake pan or springform pan with 3-inch (7.5 cm) sides, lined with parchment paper

1 cup	tightly packed fresh basil	250 mL
3 to 4	sprigs Italian flat-leaf parsley leaves	3 to 4
2	cloves garlic, coarsely chopped	2
¼ cup	olive oil	60 mL
½ cup	freshly grated Parmesan cheese	125 mL
¼ tsp	salt	1 mL
¼ tsp	freshly ground black pepper	1 mL
2	packages (each 8 oz/250 g) cream cheese, cubed and softened	2
2	eggs	2
¼ cup	all-purpose flour	60 mL
½ cup	chopped drained oil-packed sun-dried tomatoes (about 10 halves)	125 mL

1. In work bowl fitted with metal blade, pulse basil, parsley, garlic and olive oil until finely chopped. Stir in Parmesan, salt and pepper. Set aside.

2. In clean work bowl, process cream cheese until very smooth, about 20 seconds. With motor running, add eggs, one at a time, through feed tube. Transfer to a bowl and fold in flour, sun-dried tomatoes and basil mixture by hand.

3. Pour into prepared pan, smoothing out to sides of pan. Bake in preheated oven until top is light brown and center has a slight jiggle to it, 20 to 25 minutes. Let cool in pan on a wire rack for 2 hours. Cover with plastic wrap and refrigerate for at least 6 hours before serving.

Variation

Substitute coarsely chopped pine nuts for the Parmesan.

Parmesan Crisps

Vegetarian Friendly

These bite-size crackers are very easy to make and are great nibblers with pre-dinner drinks. Serve them while still warm from the oven. They are very tasty cooled, as well.

- Preheat oven to 325°F (160°C)

1¼ cups	all-purpose flour	300 mL
½ tsp	salt	2 mL
⅛ tsp	cayenne pepper	0.5 mL
¼ cup	cold butter, cubed	60 mL
1	egg, lightly beaten	1
½ cup	freshly grated Parmesan cheese	125 mL

1. In work bowl fitted with metal blade, pulse flour, salt and cayenne to blend, about 4 times. Sprinkle butter over top of mixture and pulse until butter is the size of oatmeal flakes. Add egg and Parmesan and pulse until dough begins to form a ball, about 8 times. If dough does not come together, add a bit of cold water, pulsing. Remove from work bowl and knead lightly.

2. Dust work surface lightly with flour and roll dough out to about ⅛ inch (3 mm) thick. Using a glass or a cookie cutter, cut into rounds about 1 inch (2.5 cm) in diameter. Place on baking sheets, at least 2 inches (5 cm) apart.

3. Bake in preheated oven, rotating baking sheets partway, until nicely browned and fragrant, 22 to 25 minutes. Let cool for 5 minutes on sheet, then transfer to a serving plate. Store in an airtight container for up to 3 days.

Zesty Cheddar Crisps

Makes about 3 dozen

Vegetarian Friendly

These are great to nibble on pre-dinner with a glass of red wine. Mix up a batch during the holiday season and keep the dough in the refrigerator. Slice, bake and serve fresh from the oven, when guests arrive.

- Baking sheet, lined with parchment paper

8 oz	aged Cheddar cheese	250 g
⅔ cup	all-purpose flour	150 mL
1 tsp	baking powder	5 mL
1 tsp	hot smoked paprika or ¼ tsp (1 mL) cayenne pepper	5 mL
½ tsp	salt	2 mL
¼ cup	butter, cubed	60 mL
¼ cup	finely chopped pecans or walnuts	60 mL

1. In work bowl fitted with shredding blade, shred cheese. Transfer to a bowl. Set aside.

2. Replace shredding blade with metal blade. Add flour, baking powder, paprika and salt and pulse to blend, about 4 times. Add shredded cheese and butter and pulse until mixture resembles coarse crumbs, about 20 times. Turn out on a lightly floured board and knead until dough comes together. Shape into a roll about 1 inch (2.5 cm) in diameter. Spread nuts on a cutting board and roll dough in them until well coated. Wrap in plastic wrap and refrigerate until thoroughly chilled, for at least 3 hours or up to 1 week.

3. When you're ready to bake, preheat oven to 400°F (200°C). Cut dough into slices about ¼ inch (0.5 cm) thick. Arrange on prepared baking sheet, at least 2 inches (5 cm) apart. Bake in preheated oven for 6 minutes. Remove from oven. Using a spatula, turn crisps over and bake until lightly browned, about 6 minutes more. Let cool in pan on rack for 2 minutes. Serve warm.

Caramelized Red Onion Dip

Vegetarian Friendly

Gone are the days when onion dip invariably involved a package of dried soup. Full of sweet red onions, this tasty alternative is very easy to make and the results are more than worth the extra effort. Serve with good-quality packaged potato chips, Homemade Potato Chips (page 55) or spears of Belgian endive.

Tips

If you have a small (approx. 2 quart) slow cooker, it is a very convenient tool for caramelizing onions. For instructions, see Tips, page 72).

You can caramelize the onions up to 2 days ahead of time and refrigerate until ready to use. Reheat gently before continuing with the recipe.

4	red onions, quartered	4
4	cloves garlic	4
2 tbsp	butter	30 mL
4 oz	cream cheese, cubed and softened	125 g
½ cup	sour cream	125 mL
2 tbsp	Worcestershire sauce or vegetarian alternative	30 mL
2 tbsp	fresh thyme leaves	30 mL
	Salt and freshly ground black pepper	
	Finely snipped chives	

1. In work bowl fitted with slicing blade, slice onions and garlic.

2. In a large skillet over medium heat, melt butter. Add onions and garlic and stir well. Cook, stirring, until onions are browned and caramelized, about 25 minutes (see Tips, left).

3. Replace slicing blade with metal blade. Add caramelized onion mixture, cream cheese, sour cream, Worcestershire sauce, thyme, and salt and pepper to taste. Process until well blended, about 30 seconds. Transfer to a serving dish and garnish with chives.

Caramelized Onion Crostini

Makes 32 generous crostini

Vegetarian Friendly

How can you go wrong with the mouthwatering combination of caramelized onions and melted cheese. One friend calls this French Onion Soup to go. This makes a big batch — perfect for a party — but if you're not entertaining a lot of people, feel free to cut the recipe in half.

Tips

If you have a slow cooker, it is a very convenient tool for caramelizing onions. Melt the butter and add to stoneware. Add sliced onions and toss well. Add sugar and toss well. Place a clean tea towel, folded in half (so you will have two layers), over top of stoneware to absorb moisture. Cover and cook on High for 5 hours, stirring two or three times to ensure onions are browning evenly and replacing the towel each time, until onions are nicely caramelized.

You can caramelize the onions up to 2 days ahead of time and refrigerate until ready to use. Reheat gently before continuing with the recipe.

6	onions, cut in half	6
3 tbsp	butter	45 mL
1 tbsp	granulated sugar	15 mL
1 tbsp	fresh thyme leaves	15 mL
1 tsp	salt	5 mL
	Freshly ground black pepper	
1 tsp	balsamic vinegar	5 mL
8 oz	Swiss or Gruyère cheese	250 g
Crostini		
32	slices baguette	32
3 tbsp	extra virgin olive oil	45 mL

1. In work bowl fitted with slicing blade, slice onions.

2. In a large skillet over medium heat, melt butter. Add onions and cook, stirring, until softened, about 5 minutes. Stir in sugar and continue to cook, stirring often, until they are browned and caramelized, about 25 minutes (see Tips, left). Stir in thyme, salt, pepper to taste, and balsamic vinegar and remove from heat.

3. Replace slicing blade with shredding blade and shred cheese. Set aside.

4. Crostini: Preheat broiler. Brush baguette slices on both sides with olive oil and place on a baking sheet. Toast under broiler, turning once.

5. Spread each crostini liberally with onion mixture and sprinkle cheese evenly over top. Place on baking sheet and broil until cheese is melted and browned, 2 to 3 minutes. Serve immediately.

Goat Cheese and Sun-Dried Tomato Crostini

Makes 18 crostini

Vegetarian Friendly

Simple, elegant and delicious, these crostini get any meal off to an excellent start.

- Mini-bowl attachment

4 oz	soft goat cheese	125 g
2	sun-dried tomatoes in olive oil	2
¼ cup	snipped chives	60 mL
1½ tbsp	extra virgin olive oil	22 mL
Crostini		
18	slices baguette	18
2 tbsp	extra virgin olive oil	30 mL

1. In mini bowl fitted with metal blade, process cheese, tomatoes, chives and oil until smooth, about 30 seconds.

2. **Crostini:** Preheat broiler. Brush baguette slices on both sides with olive oil and place on a baking sheet. Toast under broiler, turning once.

3. Spread each crostini liberally with goat cheese mixture. Place under broiler until browned and melted.

Roasted Garlic and Mushroom Pâté

Makes 1 cup (250 mL)

Vegetarian Friendly

This tasty spread is robust and incredibly easy-to-make. Serve with crackers or sliced baguette.

Tips

You'll need about 1¼ lbs (625 g) cremini mushrooms to get 1 lb (500 g) mushroom caps.

If you don't have mascarpone, use an equal quantity of heavy cream.

- Preheat oven to 400°F (200°C)
- Rimmed baking sheet

1 lb	cremini mushroom caps (see Tips, left)	500 g
8	cloves garlic	8
2 tbsp	olive oil	30 mL
1 tbsp	fresh thyme leaves	15 mL
½ tsp	salt	2 mL
	Freshly ground black pepper	
2 tbsp	mascarpone cheese (see Tips, left)	30 mL

1. In a bowl, combine mushrooms and garlic. Add oil and toss to coat. Transfer to sheet and bake in preheated oven, stirring once or twice until mushrooms are wizened and garlic is lightly browned, about 20 minutes. Let cool slightly.

2. Transfer to work bowl fitted with metal blade. Add thyme, salt, pepper to taste, and mascarpone. Pulse until finely chopped and blended, about 6 times. Transfer to a serving bowl. Serve warm or chilled.

Italian Bruschetta

Serves 8

Vegetarian Friendly

This appetizer can be made on crackers or a toasted baguette.

- Preheat oven to 375°F (190°C)
- Baking sheet, lined with parchment paper

1	12 oz (375 g) baguette, sliced into 24 slices on the diagonal	1
2	cloves garlic, cut in half	2
6	Roma (plum) tomatoes, cored and seeded	6
1	medium onion, quartered	1
¾ cup	packed fresh basil leaves	175 mL
1 tsp	sea salt	5 mL
1 tsp	freshly ground black pepper	5 mL
6 oz	feta cheese, crumbled	175 g

1. Rub the surface of each slice of baguette on one side with garlic. Place on prepared baking sheet. Bake in preheated oven until toasted light brown on one side, about 15 minutes. Set aside.

2. In work bowl fitted with metal blade, pulse tomatoes, onion, basil, salt and pepper until finely chopped, about 10 times, stopping and scraping down sides of the bowl as necessary.

3. Divide mixture onto toasted side of baguette slices. Top with crumbled feta cheese. Serve cold.

Variation

For a bit of a stronger flavor, try using blue or Stilton cheese in place of the feta.

Mushroom and Ricotta Phyllo Tartlets

Makes 48 mini tartlets

Vegetarian Friendly

This is a small-bite appetizer packed with lots of flavor. You can even prepare larger tarts and serve as a first course.

Tips

Phyllo dough is really easy to work with as long as your adhere to a few rules. Make sure you store your unwrapped dough in the freezer, then place in the refrigerator at least 6 hours ahead to let it thaw before using. Place the dough on a moist towel to keep it from drying out.

If using salted butter, omit the salt called for in recipe.

- Preheat oven to 350°F (180°C)
- Two 24-cup mini-muffin tins, brushed with melted butter

1	box (16 oz/454 g) phyllo dough (see Tips, left)	1
½ cup	unsalted butter, melted (see Tips, left)	125 mL
8 oz	button mushrooms, stems removed	250 g
4 oz	Gruyère cheese, cut into small pieces	125 g
½	medium onion	½
1 cup	ricotta cheese	250 mL
4	eggs	4
½ cup	heavy or whipping (35%) cream	125 mL
½ tsp	sea salt	2 mL
½ tsp	dry mustard	2 mL

1. Lay the phyllo dough out, in batches, on top of moist tea towels. Cut dough into squares (about 1 inch/2.5 cm) larger than the muffin tin.

2. Line each prepared muffin tin with a phyllo square, brush with butter. Place another square on top then butter. Repeat until you have 4 layers of phyllo dough in each tin.

3. Bake in preheated oven until golden brown, 6 to 8 minutes. Let cool completely on a wire rack.

4. In work bowl fitted with metal blade, pulse mushrooms, Gruyère and onion until finely chopped, about 20 times, stopping and scraping down sides of the bowl once or twice. With motor running, add ricotta cheese, eggs, cream, salt and mustard through feed tube.

5. Divide cheese mixture into prepared phyllo cups. Return to oven and bake until pastry is brown, 18 to 20 minutes. Serve warm.

Eggplant Caviar

Vegan Friendly

This spread/dip is
very easy to make and
delicious. Not only is
it a great entertaining
dish, it's also wonderful
to have on hand for
snacking since it is
loaded with nutrients.
Serve with sliced
baguette, warm pita
bread or sliced veggies.

Tips

We always use Italian
flat-leaf parsley because it
has so much more flavor
than the curly leaf variety.
Unless the stems or sprigs
are specifically called for,
use only the tender leaves.

Make sure you have
thoroughly dried the herbs
(patting between layers of
paper towel or in a salad
spinner) before adding
to the food processor;
otherwise your spread
may be watery.

- Preheat oven to 400°F (200°C)

1	medium eggplant (about 1 lb/500 g)	1
1 cup	cherry tomatoes	250 mL
½ cup	Italian flat-leaf parsley leaves	125 mL
4	cloves garlic	4
4	green onions, white part only	4
3 tbsp	freshly squeezed lemon juice	45 mL
2 tbsp	extra virgin olive oil	30 mL
1 tsp	salt	5 mL
	Freshly ground black pepper	

1. Prick eggplant in several places with a fork. Place on a baking sheet and bake in preheated oven until blackened and softened, about 45 minutes. Set aside until cool enough to handle.

2. Scoop out eggplant flesh and place in work bowl fitted with metal blade. Discard skin and stem. Add tomatoes, parsley, garlic, green onions, lemon juice, olive oil, salt, and pepper to taste. Process until smooth, about 1 minute. Transfer to a serving bowl, cover and refrigerate for at least 3 hours until thoroughly chilled or for up to 2 days.

Smoky Eggplant Dip with Yogurt

Makes about 2½ cups (625 mL)

Vegetarian Friendly

This dip is delicious with raw vegetables or on pita triangles. It is also great spread on crusty French bread. For the most flavorful results, use a smoker (see Tip, below) or grill the eggplant on a charcoal barbecue. If you're using a gas barbecue, place dampened wood chips in a smoke box, following the manufacturer's instructions.

Tip

If you are using a smoker, the eggplant will cook in about 1¼ hours at 200°F (100°C). Because of the low temperature, the skin will not blister as it will on a barbecue.

- Preheat gas or charcoal barbecue to high

1	medium eggplant (about 1 lb/500 g)	1
⅓ cup	plain full-fat yogurt, preferably Greek-style (pressed) (see Tips, page 114)	75 mL
6	cherry tomatoes	6
1	green onion, cut into chunks	1
1	clove garlic, coarsely chopped	1
1 tsp	freshly squeezed lemon juice	5 mL
½ tsp	salt	2 mL
	Freshly ground black pepper	
1 tbsp	finely chopped dill fronds	15 mL
	Finely chopped black olives, optional	

1. Place eggplant on preheated grill. Cook, turning several times, until skin is blackened and blistered, about 30 minutes. Set aside until cool enough to handle.

2. Scoop out eggplant flesh and place in work bowl fitted with metal blade. Discard skin and stem. Add yogurt, tomatoes, green onion, garlic, lemon juice, salt, and pepper to taste. Process until smooth. Transfer to a serving bowl, cover and refrigerate for at least 3 hours until thoroughly chilled or for up to 2 days. To serve, garnish with dill, and olives, if using.

Baba Ghanouj

Vegetarian Friendly

No mezes platter would
be complete without a
bowl of this ambrosial
eggplant dip. We find
some versions a bit
overpowering so we
have tamed the stronger
flavors in ours. Serve with
pita triangles or crudités.
If you have any leftover,
it makes a great spread
for sandwiches and a
fabulous topping for
burgers or meat patties.

Tip

It is usually more
convenient to cook
eggplant for Baba
Ghanouj in the oven.
However, if it is the
season, you may want
to try grilling it on the
barbecue. The smoky taste
adds great flavor to the
dip and is the traditional
cooking method in the
Middle East, where this
dip originates.

- Preheat oven to 400°F (200°C)

1	large eggplant (about 1½ lbs/750 g)	1
½ cup	plain yogurt, preferably Greek-style (pressed) (see Tips, page 114)	125 mL
¼ cup	tahini paste	60 mL
¼ cup	freshly squeezed lemon juice	60 mL
¼ cup	Italian flat-leaf parsley leaves	60 mL
2	cloves garlic, coarsely chopped	2
½ tsp	salt	2 mL
	Finely chopped parsley, optional	

1. Prick eggplant in several places with a fork. Place on a baking sheet and bake in preheated oven until blackened and soft, about 1 hour. Alternately, place on a gas or charcoal grill preheated to high and cook, turning several times, until skin is blackened and blistered and eggplant is very soft, about 40 minutes (see Tip, left). Let cool.

2. Scoop out eggplant flesh and place in work bowl fitted with metal blade. Discard skin and stem. Add yogurt, tahini, lemon juice, parsley, garlic and salt and process until smooth, about 1 minute. Transfer to a serving dish and garnish with additional parsley, if using. Serve at room temperature or cover and refrigerate for up to 2 days.

Greek-Style Eggplant Spread

**Makes about
2 cups (500 mL)**

Vegan Friendly

Just a tad tart and
loaded with nutrition,
this delicious dip is
a regular feature of
mezes platters in its
native Greece. It is
incredibly refreshing,
perfect for the summer
but substantive enough
to transition to colder
seasons. Great on
grilled pita bread or
as a vegetable dipper.

Tip

Crudités are cut-up
vegetables used for
dipping. Today, the
selection of vegetables in
the market — more and
more of which are washed
and precut — makes it
convenient to use these
healthful ingredients
as crudités. Popular
choices are broccoli
and cauliflower florets,
peeled baby carrots,
Belgian endive and cherry
tomatoes. And don't
forget old standbys such
as celery sticks and thinly
sliced cucumber. Another
favorite is blanched
Brussels sprouts, which
are particularly good with
strongly flavored dips.

- Preheat oven to 400°F (200°C)

1	medium eggplant (about 1 lb/500 g)	1
½	small red onion, quartered	½
2	cloves garlic, coarsely chopped	2
1 cup	cherry or grape tomatoes	250 mL
¼ cup	packed Italian flat-leaf parsley leaves	60 mL
¼ cup	extra virgin olive oil	60 mL
2 tbsp	red wine vinegar	30 mL
	Salt and freshly ground black pepper	
	Pita bread or crudités (see Tip, left)	

1. Prick eggplant in several places with a fork. Place on a baking sheet and bake in preheated oven until blackened and softened, about 45 minutes. Set aside until cool enough to handle. Peel, coarsely chop and set aside.

2. In work bowl fitted with metal blade, pulse red onion and garlic until puréed, about 10 times, stopping and scraping down sides of the bowl as necessary. Add reserved eggplant, cherry tomatoes, parsley, olive oil and vinegar. Pulse until blended but still chunky. Season with salt and pepper to taste. Cover and refrigerate for at least 2 hours or for up to 3 days. Serve with pita bread or crudités.

Mushroom Terrine

**Makes 3 cups
(750 mL)**

Vegetarian Friendly

If you feel like enjoying
a nibbly that is on the
hearty side but are
cooking for vegetarians,
here is a perfect solution.
Serve this tasty pâté on
crackers, toast points
or sliced baguette,
surrounded by nicely
acidic pickles such as
gherkins to balance its
inherent sweetness.

- Preheat oven to 325°F (160°C)
- 3-cup (750 mL) terrine or baking dish with lid, greased
- Roasting pan or large baking dish

2 tbsp	butter	30 mL
1 lb	cremini mushrooms, trimmed and quartered	500 g
2	shallots, thinly sliced	2
¼ cup	port wine	60 mL
½ tsp	salt	2 mL
½ tsp	freshly ground black pepper	2 mL
1 tbsp	fresh tarragon leaves	15 mL
¾ cup	heavy or whipping (35%) cream	175 mL
4	egg yolks	4
1 tbsp	cornstarch	15 mL

1. In a skillet over medium-high heat, melt butter. Add mushrooms and shallots and cook, stirring, until mushrooms are softened, about 6 minutes. Remove from heat and let cool for 10 minutes. Transfer cooled mushrooms to work bowl fitted with metal blade, in batches, if necessary. Add port, salt, pepper and tarragon and process until puréed, about 30 seconds. With motor running, add cream and egg yolks through feed tube, processing until smooth. Hold a fine sieve over work bowl and sift in cornstarch. Pulse once or twice to blend.

2. Transfer to prepared dish. Cover and place in roasting pan or large baking dish and add hot water to come half way up the sides of terrine. Bake in preheated oven until a tester comes out clean, about 1 hour. Cover and refrigerate for at least 2 hours or preferably overnight.

3. When you're ready to serve, dip the bottom of the terrine into a pan of very hot water for 30 seconds. Dip a kitchen knife into the hot water and run it around the edge of the terrine. Invert terrine onto a serving plate.

Deviled Eggs with Caviar

Makes 12

Little beads of caviar offset the bright yellow of these stuffed eggs.

Tips

You can make the egg mixture 1 or 2 days prior to your party and pipe the filling into the egg whites the day of the party. Cover with plastic wrap and refrigerate until just before serving. Place the caviar eggs on top right before serving.

Use ½ tsp (2 mL) prepared mustard in place of the dry mustard.

- Large bowl of ice water

6	eggs	6
⅓ cup	Traditional Mayonnaise (page 437) or store-bought (see Tip, page 93)	75 mL
2	strips cooked bacon	2
¼ tsp	dry mustard (see Tips, left)	1 mL
⅛ tsp	curry powder	0.5 mL
Pinch	salt	Pinch
⅛ tsp	caviar	0.5 mL

1. Place eggs on the bottom of a saucepan in a single layer and add enough cold water to cover by 1 inch (2.5 cm). Bring to a boil over high heat. Remove from heat and, without draining the water, cover and let stand for 10 minutes. With a slotted spoon, carefully place eggs in a large bowl filled with ice water. Let cool completely for 5 minutes. Remove eggshells under cool running water. Cut eggs lengthwise and carefully remove yolk, keeping egg white intact. Set egg white halves on a plate.

2. In work bowl fitted with metal blade, process egg yolks, mayonnaise, bacon, dry mustard, curry powder and salt until smooth, about 30 seconds, stopping and scraping down sides of the bowl once or twice. Taste and add more salt, if desired.

3. Using a pastry bag fitted with a star tip or using a spoon, pipe or spoon mixture into egg white halves. Top with a few caviar eggs.

Variation

For an Asian flavor, substitute ⅛ tsp (0.5 mL) Chinese 5-spice powder for the curry powder.

Anchovy Crostini

Makes 16 crostini

Here's an appetizer you can make with ingredients you are likely to have on hand — perfect for unexpected guests. It's tasty but pungent, so spread sparingly on the crostini. It's delicious with a glass of robust red wine.

Tip

Anchovy Spread: Simply process anchovies and cream cheese in work bowl fitted with metal blade until smooth. Use one anchovy fillet per ounce (30 g) of cream cheese.

- Mini-bowl attachment

8	anchovy fillets	8
¼ cup	Italian flat-leaf parsley leaves	60 mL
2	cloves garlic, coarsely chopped	2
2 tbsp	extra virgin olive oil	30 mL
Crostini		
16	slices baguette	16
2 tbsp	olive oil	30 mL

1. In mini bowl fitted with metal blade, pulse anchovies, parsley and garlic to chop, about 8 times, stopping and scraping down sides of the bowl as necessary. Add olive oil and pulse to blend, about 6 times.

2. **Crostini:** Preheat broiler. Brush baguette slices on both sides with olive oil and place on a baking sheet. Toast under broiler, turning once. Spread about ½ tsp (2 mL) of anchovy mixture on each crostini.

Peppery Roasted Squash Pâté

Makes about 1½ cups (375 mL)

Vegetarian Friendly

This intriguingly flavored starter is very tasty and mildly addictive. If you're heat averse, use the smaller quantity of jalapeño. Serve this on sliced baguette or warm wedges of pita.

1 cup	puréed roasted acorn or butternut squash or pumpkin	250 mL
1 cup	black pepper-flavored fresh cream cheese, such as Boursin	250 mL
½ to 1	jalapeño pepper, seeded and coarsely chopped	½ to 1
½ cup	pecan halves	125 mL
	Salt and freshly ground black pepper	

1. In work bowl fitted with metal blade, pulse squash, cream cheese, jalapeño and pecans until pecans are finely chopped and ingredients are blended, about 15 times. Season with salt and pepper to taste. Transfer to a serving dish, cover and refrigerate until chilled for at least 2 hours or for up to 2 days.

Anchoyade on Pita

Makes 6 small pitas

This appetizer is very easy to make yet delicious. Use the size of pita bread you're likely to have on hand.

Tip

For convenience, make the topping ahead of time. Cover and refrigerate until you're ready to use, for up to 2 days.

- Baking sheet, lightly greased

3 tbsp	olive oil, divided	45 mL
1	onion, sliced	1
4	cloves garlic, coarsely chopped	4
1	fresh chile pepper, seeded and chopped, optional	1
1	can (2 oz/60 g) anchovy fillets, drained (about 12)	1
	Cracked black peppercorns	
2 cups	cherry tomatoes, halved	500 mL
6	fresh basil leaves	6
6	small (4½ inch/11 cm) pita breads	6

1. In a skillet, heat 2 tbsp (30 mL) of the oil over medium heat. Add onion and cook, stirring, until softened, about 3 minutes. Add garlic, chile pepper, if using, anchovies and peppercorns and cook, stirring, for 1 minute. Add tomatoes, bring to a boil and cook, stirring, until tomatoes have collapsed and anchovies have disintegrated, about 5 minutes. Transfer to work bowl fitted with metal blade. Add basil and process until smooth, about 30 seconds.

2. Meanwhile, preheat oven to 400°F (200°C). Brush both sides of pita with remaining tbsp (15 mL) of oil and place on prepared baking sheet, concave side up. Spread anchoyade evenly over top. Bake in preheated oven until pita begins to crisp and top is fragrant, about 15 minutes. To serve, cut each pita into 4 to 6 wedges.

Anchoyade de Croze

**Makes about
1½ cups (375 mL)**

This unusual but delicious spread is named after the French cookbook author Austin de Croze, who invented it. It is traditionally spread on country bread brushed with olive oil and baked, but warm crostini or even sliced baguette work well, too.

Tips

Use the chile pepper of your choice. We have also made this using 1½ tbsp (22 mL) drained chopped hot banana peppers, which produces a very nice result.

Orange blossom water is available in specialty stores and Middle Eastern markets. It is very strongly flavored. This quantity produces a nice result, but if you like the taste, add a bit more after the ingredients have been combined and pulse to blend.

4	dried figs	4
1	can (2 oz/60 g) anchovy fillets, drained (about 12)	1
12	blanched almonds	12
2	cloves garlic	2
1	small red onion, quartered	1
1	roasted red pepper (see Tips, page 147)	1
1	bottled chile pepper (see Tips, left)	1
¼ cup	fresh Italian flat-leaf parsley leaves	60 mL
¼ cup	fresh tarragon leaves	60 mL
½ tsp	fennel seeds, crushed	2 mL
2 tbsp	freshly squeezed lemon juice	30 mL
¼ cup	extra virgin olive oil (approx.)	60 mL
½ tsp	orange blossom water (see Tips, left)	2 mL
	Hot pepper sauce, optional	

1. In a bowl of warm water, soak figs until softened, about 15 minutes. Drain, remove tough stem ends and chop coarsely.

2. In work bowl fitted with metal blade, pulse figs, anchovies, almonds, garlic, red onion, red pepper, chile pepper, parsley, tarragon, fennel and lemon juice several times to chop. With motor running, add olive oil through feed tube and process until a smooth paste is formed, about 1 minute. Add orange blossom water and hot pepper sauce to taste, if using. Cover and refrigerate for at least 2 hours or for up to 2 days.

Tuna and Artichoke Spread

**Makes about
2 cups (500 mL)**

Canned tuna and artichokes are great convenience foods. They also taste very good together. Serve this with sliced baguette, crackers or crudités.

2	hard-cooked eggs, yolks and whites separated (see Tips, page 385)	2
1/3 cup	extra virgin olive oil	75 mL
1 tsp	salt	5 mL
1/2 tsp	freshly ground black pepper	2 mL
1 tbsp	white wine vinegar	15 mL
1	can (14 oz/398 mL) artichoke hearts, drained	1
1	can (6 oz/170 g) tuna, drained	1
1	roasted red pepper (see Tips, page 147)	1
1	clove garlic, coarsely chopped	1
2 tbsp	toasted pine nuts	30 mL
2 tbsp	Italian flat-leaf parsley leaves	30 mL

1. Press cooked egg yolks through a fine sieve into a bowl. Gradually whisk in oil until combined. Whisk in salt, pepper and vinegar until combined. Set aside.

2. In work bowl fitted with metal blade, pulse egg whites, artichokes, tuna, roasted pepper, garlic, pine nuts and parsley until chopped, about 10 times. Add egg yolk mixture and pulse until blended, about 5 times. Cover and refrigerate for at least 3 hours or for up to 2 days.

Taramasalata

**Makes about
1 cup (250 mL)**

This delicious spread is a fixture of Greek mezes. Serve with grilled pita bread.

Tips

Tarama (carp roe) is available in stores specializing in Greek provisions.

After soaking and squeezing the bread dry, you should have about 1/2 cup (125 mL).

1/2 cup	tarama, thoroughly rinsed under cold running water and drained	125 mL
1	small red onion, quartered	1
2	thick slices day-old white bread, crusts removed, soaked in water and squeezed dry (see Tips, left)	2
1/4 cup	freshly squeezed lemon juice	60 mL
1/2 cup	extra virgin olive oil	125 mL
	Pita bread, optional	
	Crudités, optional	

1. In work bowl fitted with metal blade, process tarama and red onion for 1 minute. Add bread and process until smooth. Add lemon juice and pulse to blend. With motor running, add oil through feed tube and process until pale pink and very creamy. Cover and refrigerate for at least 2 hours or for up to 2 days.

Oyster and Artichoke Gratin

Serves 6

This recipe was inspired by one that appears in Ralph Brennan's *New Orlean's Seafood Cookbook*. It is a great special occasion starter.

- Preheat broiler
- 6 small (about ½ cup/125 mL) ramekins

1	can (14 oz/398 mL) artichoke hearts, drained	1
½ cup	freshly grated Parmesan cheese	125 mL
1 tbsp	fresh Italian flat-leaf parsley leaves	15 mL
1	clove garlic	1
⅛ tsp	cayenne pepper	0.5 mL
2 tbsp	extra virgin olive oil	30 mL
½ cup	dry bread crumbs, such as panko	125 mL
2 tbsp	butter	30 mL
24	shucked oysters, drained, liquid reserved	24
	Freshly ground black or white pepper	
	Olive oil for drizzling	

1. In work bowl fitted with metal blade, pulse artichokes, Parmesan, parsley, garlic, cayenne and olive oil until artichokes are finely chopped and mixture is blended, about 10 times. Add bread crumbs and pulse twice. Scrape down sides of the bowl and pulse twice. Set aside.

2. In a large skillet, melt butter over medium-high heat. Add oysters in one layer and cook, just until the edges curl, about 1 minute. (Do not overcook.) Remove from heat.

3. Using a slotted spoon, transfer 4 oysters to each ramekin. Add about 3 tbsp (45 mL) oyster liquid (liquor) to each ramekin and spread about 2 tbsp (30 mL) artichoke mixture over top. Season with pepper to taste. Drizzle liberally with butter mixture from pan, and a bit of olive oil. Broil until tops brown and oysters are bubbling, about 5 minutes. Serve immediately.

Smoked Trout Spread

Makes about 2½ cups (625 mL)

Save this spread for special occasions because smoked trout is a bit pricey. On the other hand, it is so easy to make you could serve it any day of the week. It is great on thin wheat crackers (fairly bland so the taste doesn't interfere with the exquisite flavor of the trout) or, if you're feeling celebratory, on thinly sliced roasted potatoes (see Variation, right) or even on Homemade Potato Chips (page 55).

1 lb	smoked trout fillets, skin and bones removed	500 g
4	green onions, white part with just a bit of green, cut into 3-inch (7.5 cm) lengths	4
1	stalk celery, cut into 3-inch (7.5 cm) lengths	1
¼ cup	fresh dill fronds	60 mL
¼ cup	Traditional Mayonnaise (page 437) or store-bought (see Tip, page 93)	60 mL
2 tbsp	extra virgin olive oil	30 mL
1 tbsp	freshly squeezed lemon juice	15 mL
1 tbsp	Dijon mustard	15 mL

1. In work bowl fitted with metal blade, pulse trout, green onions, celery and dill until finely chopped, about 5 times. Add mayonnaise, olive oil, lemon juice and mustard and process until smooth. Transfer to a serving bowl and refrigerate for at least 3 hours or for up to 2 days.

Variation

Trout Topped Potato Crisps: Preheat oven to 400°F (200°C). In work bowl fitted with thin slicing blade, slice 2 potatoes very thinly (about ⅛ inch/3 mm). Transfer to a large bowl. Add 2 tbsp (30 mL) extra virgin olive oil and toss until potatoes are well coated. Place in a single layer on a baking sheet and roast, turning once, until potatoes are crisp and browned, about 20 minutes. To serve, top each crisp with a spoonful (about 2 tsp/10 mL) of the spread.

Salmon Herb Mousse on Stone-Ground Crackers

Makes ¾ cup (175 mL)

This flavorful mousse is fast, easy and elegant on toast points or crackers.

Tips

If the cream cheese is not softened, you can process it first and then add the salmon.

Mousse keeps well, covered and refrigerated, for up to 3 days.

4 oz	smoked salmon	125 g
3 oz	cream cheese, cubed and softened	90 g
1 tsp	loosely packed tarragon	5 mL
½ tsp	capers, divided	2 mL
24 to 36	stone-ground crackers	24 to 36
	Fresh tarragon sprigs	

1. In work bowl fitted with metal blade, process salmon until smooth, about 30 seconds. Add cream cheese and tarragon and process until smooth, about 10 seconds, stopping and scraping down sides of the bowl once or twice. Add ¼ tsp (1 mL) of the capers and pulse 8 times.

2. Place mousse into a pastry bag fitted with a star tip. Pipe onto stone ground crackers or spread with a knife. Top each with a sprig of tarragon and a few capers.

Variation
Pipe the mixture on halved strawberries and serve on a large platter.

Smoked Salmon Spread

Makes about 1½ cups (375 mL)

Serve this with thin slices of dark rye bread, pumpernickel rounds or plain baguette. Or use it as a topping for Potato Crisps (see Variation, page 87) or Homemade Potato Chips (page 55).

Tip

Don't overprocess after adding the salmon. You want it to be chopped, not puréed.

½ cup	sour cream	125 mL
3 oz	cream cheese, softened and cubed	90 g
½	small red onion, halved	½
2 tbsp	drained capers	30 mL
2 tbsp	freshly squeezed lemon juice	30 mL
½ tsp	salt	2 mL
4 oz	smoked salmon	125 g
¼ cup	fresh dill fronds	60 mL
	Freshly ground black pepper	

1. In work bowl fitted with metal blade, process sour cream, cream cheese, red onion, capers, lemon juice and salt until smooth, about 30 seconds, stopping and scraping down side of the bowl as necessary. Add smoked salmon, dill, and pepper to taste. Pulse until chopped and blended, about 10 times (see Tip, left). Serve immediately or cover and refrigerate for up to 3 days.

Smoked Salmon Cheese Spread

Makes 1½ cups (375 mL)

Pipe this spread onto water crackers and top it off with fresh dill fronds.

1	package (8 oz/250 g) cream cheese, cubed and softened	1
3 oz	smoked salmon	90 g
¼ cup	fresh dill fronds	60 mL
2 tbsp	capers, drained	30 mL
½ tsp	ground white pepper	2 mL
¼ tsp	hot pepper flakes	1 mL

1. In work bowl fitted with metal blade, process cream cheese, salmon, dill, capers, white pepper and hot pepper flakes until smooth, about 30 seconds, stopping and scraping down sides of the bowl once or twice.

2. Place in a pastry bag fitted with a star tip to pipe on top of crackers.

Smoked Salmon and Red Caviar Mousse

Makes about 2 cups (500 mL)

Serve this on thinly sliced baguette, plain biscuits or cocktail-size slices of dark rye bread. Or, if you're feeling particularly festive, make up a batch of Crêpes Parmentier (page 362) and use those as a base.

Tip

You may need more cream if using wild salmon, which is likely to have a heavier texture than the farmed variety. The mousse mixture should be light enough to fold in the red caviar without appearing to crush the delicate roe.

8 oz	smoked salmon	250 g
½ to ¾ cup	heavy or whipping (35%) cream (see Tip, left)	125 to 175 mL
1 tbsp	freshly squeezed lemon juice	15 mL
2 tbsp	red lumpfish roe	30 mL
	Freshly ground black pepper	

1. In work bowl fitted with metal blade, process smoked salmon, cream and lemon juice until smooth, about 30 seconds. Fold in lumpfish roe. Season liberally with pepper. Spoon into a serving bowl. Serve immediately or cover and refrigerate for up to 2 hours.

Dill-Spiked Crab

**Makes about
3 cups (750 mL)**

Fresh, light and easy to make, this tasty starter is very festive because crab is a luxury item. Serve it with vegetable sticks, leaves of Belgian endive, baguette or crackers. You can also use it to fill avocado halves (see Variation, below).

Tip

If you are using celery hearts, which produce the best results, add any leaves to the work bowl along with the celery.

½ cup	Traditional Mayonnaise (page 437) or store-bought	125 mL
¼ cup	fresh dill fronds	60 mL
4	green onions, white part with just a hint of green, cut into 3-inch (7.5 cm) chunks	4
1	small shallot, quartered	1
2	stalks celery, cut into 3-inch (7.5 cm) chunks (see Tip, left)	2
2 tbsp	extra virgin olive oil	30 mL
2 tbsp	freshly squeezed lemon juice	30 mL
1 tsp	salt	5 mL
	Freshly ground white pepper	
2 cups	drained cooked crabmeat (about 1 lb/500 g)	500 mL

1. In work bowl fitted with metal blade, pulse mayonnaise, dill, green onions, shallot, celery, olive oil, lemon juice, salt, and white pepper to taste until vegetables are chopped and mixture is blended, about 10 times, stopping and scraping down sides of the bowl as necessary. Add crabmeat and pulse until nicely integrated, about 5 times. Cover and refrigerate for at least 2 hours or overnight.

Variation

Crab-Stuffed Avocado: If you have leftovers, use them to stuff avocado halves. It makes a great lunch or a plated appetizer.

Crab Feta Mushrooms

Serves 6

Hot and sizzling out of the oven, these mushrooms will be the hit of the party.

Tips

You can make the filling 1 day prior to serving. Transfer to a bowl. Cover and refrigerate. Let warm slightly before filling mushrooms.

When removing the stems from the mushrooms, check to see that they are fresh. Look under the cap, if the stem looks like it is becoming unattached or dark, your mushroom is getting old.

- Preheated broiler
- Baking sheet, lined with parchment paper

1 lb	button mushrooms, stems removed and reserved	500 g
6 oz	lump canned crabmeat, drained, or frozen crabmeat, thawed	175 g
3 oz	feta cheese, crumbled	90 g
2	green onions, green part only, cut in half	2
1 tbsp	butter, softened	15 mL
1	clove garlic	1
1/4 tsp	ground white pepper	1 mL
1/4 tsp	salt	1 mL

1. Place mushrooms, caps down, on prepared baking sheet. Set aside.

2. In work bowl fitted with metal blade, process half of the mushroom stems, crabmeat, feta cheese, green onions, butter, garlic, white pepper and salt until smooth, 2 to 3 minutes, stopping and scraping down sides of the bowl once or twice. Discard remaining half of the mushroom stems.

3. Fill mushroom caps with cheese mixture. Broil under preheated broiler until cheese mixture starts to melt and bubble, about 3 minutes. Serve hot.

Variation

Use blue cheese or Stilton in place of the feta to give a sharp yet pleasant flavor to this appetizer.

Creamy Crab Salad Spread

Makes 2½ cups (625 mL)

Use as an appetizer spread on crackers or as a spread for a sandwich.

1	can (10 to 12 oz/300 to 375 g) crabmeat, drained	1
8 oz	cooked salad shrimp	250 g
½	red onion, cut into quarters	½
½	red bell pepper, seeded and quartered	½
1 tbsp	fresh dill fronds	15 mL
½ tsp	hot pepper flakes	2 mL
½ tsp	ground white pepper	2 mL
	Salt	

1. In work bowl fitted with metal blade, process crabmeat, shrimp, red onion, bell pepper, dill, hot pepper flakes and white pepper until smooth, about 20 seconds, stopping and scraping down sides of the bowl once or twice. Season with salt to taste. Serve immediately or cover and refrigerate for up to 2 hours or overnight.

Tuna and Roasted Red Pepper Dip

Makes about 1 cup (250 mL)

This tasty dip is great with crudités, crackers, crostini or even plain old sliced baguette.

Tips

You can use drained bottled roasted peppers or roast and peel them yourself (see Tips, page 147).

Piment d'Espelette is a dried mild chile pepper from the Basque region of France. It adds a nice flavor to this recipe, but if you don't have it, cayenne pepper makes a fine substitute.

1	jar (7 oz/210 g) Italian or Spanish tuna, packed in olive oil, drained	1
⅓ cup	Traditional Mayonnaise (page 437) or store-bought	75 mL
2	roasted red peppers (see Tips, left)	2
2 tbsp	drained capers	30 mL
1 tbsp	freshly squeezed lemon juice	15 mL
¼ tsp	Piment d'Espelette or ⅛ tsp (0.5 mL) cayenne pepper (see Tips, left)	1 mL

1. In work bowl fitted with metal blade, process tuna, mayonnaise, roasted peppers, capers, lemon juice and Piment d'Espelette until smooth, about 15 seconds. Cover and chill for at least 4 hours or overnight.

Tunnato Spread

**Makes about
1½ cups (375 mL)**

Don't be fooled by the simplicity of this recipe: it is a mouthwatering combination. Amazingly versatile, this ambrosial mixture excels as a dip. Make it the centerpiece of a tasting platter, surrounded by celery sticks and cucumber slices or tender leaves of Belgian endive. It also performs well as a sauce for plated appetizers or salade compose (for which the ingredients are arranged on a plate rather than tossed together) (see Variations, right).

Tip

Don't confuse real mayonnaise with "mayonnaise-type" salad dressings, which are similar in appearance. Mayonnaise is a combination of egg yolks, vinegar or lemon juice, olive oil and seasonings. Imitators will contain additional ingredients, such as sugar, flour or milk. Make your own or make sure the label says mayonnaise and check the ingredients.

¾ cup	Traditional Mayonnaise (page 437) or store-bought (see Tip, left)	175 mL
½ cup	Italian flat-leaf parsley leaves	125 mL
2	green onions, white part only, cut into 2-inch (5 cm) lengths	2
1 tbsp	drained capers, optional	15 mL
1	can (6 oz/170 g) tuna, preferably Italian, packed in olive oil, drained	1
	Freshly ground black pepper	
	Crudités (see Tip, page 79)	

1. In work bowl fitted with metal blade, process mayonnaise, parsley, green onions, and capers, if using, until smooth. Add tuna, and pepper to taste. Pulse until chopped and blended, about 15 times.

2. Transfer to a small bowl and serve surrounded by crudités for dipping. If not using immediately, cover and refrigerate for up to 3 days.

Variations

Tunnato-Stuffed Eggs (Serves 6 to 8): Hard cook 4 eggs (see Tips, page 49). Let cool and peel. Cut in half lengthwise. Pop out the yolks and mash with ¼ cup (60 mL) Tunnato Spread. Mound the mixture back into the whites. Dust with 1 tsp (5 mL) paprika, if desired.

If you prefer a plated appetizer, simply cut the peeled cooked eggs in half, arrange them on a platter and spoon the sauce over top.

Asparagus with Tunnato (Serves 4): Arrange 1 can or jar (16 oz/330 g approx.) white asparagus, drained, on a small platter or serving plate. Top with ¼ cup (60 mL) Tunnato Spread. Use cooked fresh green asparagus in season, if desired. You can also turn this into a salad by spreading a layer of salad greens over a large platter. Arrange the asparagus over the greens and top with Tunnato Spread.

Potted Shrimp

Potted shrimp is a traditional English dish. It is a very good way of serving shrimp, not only because it is very tasty, but also because you can make it up to three days ahead of time. This version is nicely flavored with thyme, garlic and mace, the orange covering of the nutmeg shell. Serve on plain crackers or sliced baguette.

Tips

Clarified butter has the milk solids removed, which in this dish gives a fresher taste. *To clarify butter for this recipe:* Place about ⅓ cup (75 mL) butter in a small saucepan and melt over low heat. Using a slotted spoon, scoop off the foam, then carefully pour the clear yellow liquid into a measuring cup, leaving the white solids behind.

Be sure to chill this dish thoroughly before serving. The butter needs to harden in order to hold it together.

8 oz	peeled deveined shrimp	250 g
1 tbsp	fresh thyme leaves	15 mL
1	clove garlic, chopped	1
½ tsp	salt	2 mL
¼ tsp	freshly ground white pepper	1 mL
⅛ tsp	ground mace or freshly grated nutmeg	0.5 mL
¼ cup	clarified butter (see Tips, left)	60 mL
1 tbsp	freshly squeezed lemon juice	15 mL

1. In work bowl fitted with metal blade, process shrimp, thyme, garlic, salt, white pepper and mace until shrimp are finely chopped and mixture is blended, about 15 seconds.

2. In a saucepan over medium heat, bring clarified butter to a simmer. Add shrimp mixture, return to a simmer and cook, stirring, until shrimp are pink and opaque, about 5 minutes. Remove from heat and stir in lemon juice. Transfer to a serving dish, cover and refrigerate until butter solidifies, overnight or for up to 3 days.

Shrimp Pâté with Leeks

This is a great pâté to make for your next party.

Tips

To clean leeks: Fill a sink full of lukewarm water. Split the leeks in half lengthwise and submerge them in the water, swishing them around to remove all traces of dirt. Transfer to a colander and rinse thoroughly under cold water.

Pâté keeps well, covered and refrigerated, for up to 3 days.

2	leeks, white parts only, cut into quarters (about 1/2 cup/125 mL) (see Tips, left)	2
1	package (8 oz/250 g) cream cheese, cubed and softened	1
4 oz	cooked shrimp	125 g
2 tbsp	butter, softened	30 mL
2 tbsp	brandy	30 mL
Pinch	ground white pepper	Pinch
Pinch	salt	Pinch

1. In work bowl fitted with metal blade, add leeks and pulse until coarsely chopped, about 10 times. Transfer to a bowl and set aside.

2. In same work bowl, process cream cheese, shrimp, butter and brandy until smooth, about 2 minutes, stopping and scraping down sides of the bowl once or twice. With motor running, add leeks, white pepper and salt through feed tube and pulse until leeks are loosely incorporated, about 5 times.

Variation
Add 2 cloves minced garlic to the pâté for a simple change in flavor.

Brandade de Morue

Makes about 1½ cups (375 mL)

This is a classic preparation — salt cod blended with potatoes, garlic and olive oil. Serve it on slices of whole-grain baguette for a cornucopia of interesting textures.

Tips

Salt cod is, not surprisingly, very salty. Before using, it needs to be soaked in water to remove the salt. *To soak the cod for this recipe:* Place cod in a large bowl of cold water. Cover and refrigerate for 2 to 3 days, changing the water at least twice daily to remove the salt.

Whether you need to add salt or not depends upon how much salt was removed from the fish during the soaking process.

4 oz	salt cod, soaked and drained (see Tips, left)	125 g
1	potato (about 8 oz/250 g), cooked, peeled and cut into chunks	1
⅓ cup	heavy or whipping (35%) cream	75 mL
3	cloves garlic, coarsely chopped	3
¼ tsp	freshly grated nutmeg	1 mL
¼ tsp	freshly ground white pepper	1 mL
¼ cup	extra virgin olive oil	60 mL
1 tbsp	freshly squeezed lemon juice (approx.)	15 mL
	Salt, optional	

1. In work bowl fitted with shredding blade, shred potato. Transfer to a bowl.

2. Meanwhile, place cod in a saucepan. Cover liberally with water and bring to a boil over medium heat. Cover, reduce heat to low and simmer until tender, about 10 minutes. Drain and transfer to work bowl fitted with metal blade.

3. Meanwhile, in a separate saucepan, combine cream, garlic, nutmeg and white pepper. Bring to a simmer over low heat and simmer slowly until flavors infuse, about 6 minutes. Add to work bowl. Process until mixture is blended but still chunky.

4. With motor running, add olive oil and lemon juice through feed tube. Purée until smooth. Fold into shredded potatoes. Season to taste with salt, if using. Taste and adjust seasoning, adding more lemon juice or pepper as necessary. Transfer to a serving bowl.

Bubbling Bacon and Horseradish Dip

**Makes about
2 cups (500 mL)**

There's nothing like a good dollop of horseradish to add zest to a dish. A bubbling pot of this savory blend is the perfect antidote to a cold winter's day. Open a big bag of potato chips or make your own (page 55). For a more elegant presentation, serve on crisp spears of Belgian endive.

Tip

Don't confuse real mayonnaise with "mayonnaise-type" salad dressings, which are similar in appearance. Mayonnaise is a combination of egg yolks, vinegar or lemon juice, olive oil and seasonings. Imitators will contain additional ingredients, such as sugar, flour or milk. Make your own or make sure the label says mayonnaise and check the ingredients.

2	slices bacon, chopped	2
4 oz	aged Cheddar cheese	125 g
1	package (8 oz/250 g) cream cheese, cubed and softened	1
1/4 cup	sour cream	60 mL
2 tbsp	Traditional Mayonnaise (page 437) or store-bought (see Tip, left)	30 mL
2 tbsp	Homemade Horseradish (page 469) or store-bought	30 mL
2 tbsp	finely chopped green onions	30 mL
1	clove garlic, minced	1
1/4 tsp	freshly ground black pepper	1 mL
	Potato chips, optional	
	Belgian endive, optional	

1. In a skillet over medium-high heat, cook bacon until crisp. Remove with a slotted spoon and drain thoroughly on paper towel. Crumble coarsely.

2. In work bowl fitted with shredding blade, shred cheese. Transfer to a heavy-bottomed saucepan.

3. Replace shredding blade with metal blade. Add cream cheese, sour cream, mayonnaise, horseradish, green onions, garlic, pepper and bacon. Pulse until mixture is chopped and blended, about 5 times. Transfer to saucepan with cheese. Stir well. Place over low heat and cook, stirring constantly, until cheese is melted and mixture is bubbling. Transfer to a serving bowl or chafing dish and serve hot. Serve with potato chips or Belgian endive, if using.

Pork Carnitas with Guacamole

Makes about 36 carnitas

Makes 2 cups (500 mL) guacamole

You won't believe how tasty these bits of deeply browned pork are until you taste them. To serve, place on a small platter. People can spear a carnita with a toothpick or small fork and dip in the guacamole. They will disappear quickly.

Tips

If fresh tomatoes aren't in season, you may want to substitute cherry or grape tomatoes instead. You'll need 10 for this quantity.

If you are a heat seeker, use a second jalapeño. One makes a pleasantly mild guacamole.

If you have leftover guacamole, cover tightly and refrigerate for up to 24 hours. Serve it with tortilla chips or tostadas.

- Large frying pan with lid

3 lbs	boneless pork shoulder blade (butt), cut into 1-inch (2.5 cm) cubes	1.5 kg
1 tsp	kosher salt	5 mL

Guacamole

3	small avocados, such as Haas	3
1	tomato, cored and peeled (see Tips, left)	1
4	green onions, white part only, or 1 slice (about ½ inch/2 cm) red onion	4
1 to 2	jalapeño peppers, seeded and cut in half	1 to 2
½ cup	fresh cilantro leaves	125 mL
3 tbsp	freshly squeezed lime juice	45 mL
	Salt	

1. Place pork in skillet. Add water just to cover and sprinkle with salt. Cover and bring to a boil over medium heat. Reduce heat and simmer until meat is fork tender, about 1 hour. (You want it to be firm, not falling apart.) Remove lid, stir well, and continue cooking, stirring occasionally, until water is evaporated and meat is nicely browned, about 30 minutes. Transfer to a warmed serving platter.

2. **Guacamole:** Just before the pork has finished cooking, in work bowl fitted with metal blade, process avocados, tomato, green onions, jalapeno pepper(s) to taste, cilantro and lime juice until desired consistency is achieved. (We like ours a bit chunky.) Season with salt to taste. Transfer to a serving bowl.

Variation

Serve carnitas with Traditional Salsa (page 32), Tomatillo Onion Avocado Salsa (page 32) or Jalapeño Salsa (page 35) instead of the Guacamole or as a second option.

Mini Chicken Puffs

Perfect for large get-togethers! You only have to make one batch to feed a crowd.

Tips

If you have a smaller package of puff pastry, the pastry may be thinner, but will still work. If the pastry feels too thin to enclose filling, you may need to use a little less chicken mixture for each square.

It's important to always use cooked items, such as the chicken, in puff pastry because the cooking time does not allow raw meats to cook fully.

- Preheat oven to 425°F (220°C)
- 2 baking sheets, lined with parchment paper

1	package (18 oz/540 g) puff pastry, thawed (see Tips, left)	1
	All-purpose flour, for rolling pastry	
4 oz	Cheddar cheese, cut into chunks	125 g
8 oz	cooked chicken (see Tips, left)	250 g
2	green onions, green part only, cut in half	2
¼ cup	Smoked Chili Sauce (page 445) or store-bought	60 mL

1. Working with one half of pastry, on a lightly floured board, roll pastry into a 12-inch (30 cm) square. Using a pizza cutter, cut equally, horizontally and vertically so you end up with 4 strips by 4 strips to make 16 squares. Repeat with second piece of pastry. Set aside.

2. In work bowl fitted with shredding blade, shred cheese. Transfer to a bowl and set aside.

3. Replace shredding blade with metal blade. Add chicken, green onions and chili sauce and pulse until mixture is chunky, 5 to 8 times. Place 1 tbsp (15 mL) of the mixture on center of each square. Top with 1½ tsp (7 mL) of the cheese. Starting with two opposite corners of one square of pastry, fold in toward the center to meet above filling. With remaining corners, fold up to meet in the center and squeeze edges together to seal (like a dim sum dumpling). If pastry seems dry, lightly brush edges with water before folding to ensure a good seal. Place on prepared baking sheets, about 2 inches (5 cm) apart. Repeat with remaining pastry squares and filling to make 32 puffs.

4. Bake in preheated oven until light brown and puffed up, 14 to 18 minutes. Serve warm or cold with Chipotle Mayonnaise (page 439).

Variation

Mini Vegetarian Puffs: Replace the chicken with 8 oz (250 g) portobello mushrooms that have been sliced with the slicing blade.

Crispy Chicken Cakes
with Fresh Dill Mayonnaise

Makes 10 appetizers or 6 entrées

These herbed cakes are packed with so much flavor and pizzazz that whenever you make them as an appetizer don't be surprised if you're asked to make them as a main dish.

Tips

You can form the patties and refrigerate them up to 3 days ahead. Coat with bread crumbs when you are ready to use them. Allow for a few extra minutes on each side when cooking them.

You can purchase cooked chickens at most grocery stores to reduce your preparation time.

12 oz	cooked chicken	375 g
1 cup	Fresh Bread Crumbs (page 468), or store-bought, divided	250 mL
¼ cup	Traditional Mayonnaise (page 437), Fresh Dill Mayonnaise (page 438) or store-bought	60 mL
1	egg	1
2 tsp	prepared mustard	10 mL
⅓ cup	roasted red pepper (about 1 small)	75 mL
½	red onion, cut into quarters (about ⅓ cup/75 mL)	½
2 tbsp	olive oil, divided	30 mL
	Fresh Dill Mayonnaise (page 438)	

1. In work bowl fitted with metal blade, process cooked chicken, ½ cup (125 mL) of the bread crumbs, mayonnaise, egg, mustard, red peppers and red onion until almost smooth, about 30 seconds. Mixture will be tacky. With moistened hands, form into 10 patties if making appetizers or 6 patties if making a main course. Coat with remaining bread crumbs. Discard any excess crumbs.

2. Heat half of the olive oil in a frying pan over medium heat. Add patties, in batches, and fry until light brown, 3 minutes per side, adding more oil as necessary. Serve with Fresh Dill Mayonnaise.

Variation

Herbed Seafood Cakes: Substitute 3 cups (750 mL) chopped cooked or thawed frozen crab for the chicken.

Savory Chicken Cheese Balls

Serves 12

These cheese balls are so creamy and rich. Serve them with crackers or carrot sticks.

Tips

To toast almonds: Place almonds in a dry nonstick skillet over medium heat and toast, stirring constantly, until golden brown, 3 to 4 minutes.

You can use lower-fat cream cheese and sour cream without sacrificing flavor or texture.

½ cup	toasted sliced almonds (see Tips, left)	125 mL
2	packages (each 8 oz/250 g) cream cheese, cubed and softened	2
1 lb	cooked chicken	500 g
1 cup	seedless grapes	250 mL
6	green onions, green part only, cut in half (about ½ cup/125 mL)	6
2 tbsp	sour cream	30 mL
1 tsp	curry powder	5 mL
1 tsp	seasoned salt	5 mL

1. In work bowl fitted with metal blade, pulse almonds until finely ground, about 10 times. Transfer to a small bowl and set aside.

2. In same work bowl, process cream cheese until smooth. Add chicken, grapes, green onions, sour cream, curry powder and seasoned salt and process until smooth, 2 to 3 minutes, stopping and scraping down sides of the bowl once or twice. Divide mixture between 2 pieces of plastic wrap and form each into 2 balls, wrapping to seal. Refrigerate until firm, about 30 minutes or for up to 3 days.

3. Just before serving, remove plastic wrap and roll balls in chopped almonds. Place on a serving dish.

Variation

Use 2 fresh apricots (about 1 cup/250 mL) in place of the grapes.

Mini Meatballs with Garlic Tomato Sauce

Serves 4

Serve these meatballs with little toothpicks as an appetizer for a party. The flavor is intense. You can also serve them as a main dish with a side of pasta.

- Preheat oven to 350°F (180°C)
- 13- by 9-inch (33 by 23 cm) baking dish

1 cup	Fresh Bread Crumbs (page 468) or store-bought	250 mL
½ cup	milk	125 mL
1	onion, cut into quarters	1
8 oz	ground beef	250 g
8 oz	ground pork	250 g
1	egg	1
½ tsp	ground allspice	2 mL
½ tsp	ground ginger	2 mL
⅛ tsp	salt	0.5 mL
1 tbsp	vegetable oil	15 mL
	Basic Garlic Tomato Sauce (page 402)	

1. Place bread crumbs in a large bowl. Add milk and let it absorb.

2. In work bowl fitted with metal blade, add onion and process until chopped, about 10 seconds. Add to bread crumbs with ground beef, ground pork, egg, allspice, ginger and salt. Blend together. Shape mixture into about 24 1-inch (2.5 cm) meatballs.

3. Heat vegetable oil in a frying pan over medium heat. Add meatballs and sauté until light brown, 3 to 4 minutes. Place in baking dish, cover and bake in preheated oven until no longer pink inside, 20 to 25 minutes. Drain off any excess oil. Toss meatballs with warm sauce.

Variation
You can substitute ground turkey for part or all of the pork.

Grande Beef Nachos

When you get a crowd over you need to serve something fast and hearty. This dish can be put together in just a few minutes.

Tips

For this quantity of beans, use 1 can (14 to 19 oz/ 398 to 540 mL) drained and rinsed, or cook 1 cup (250 mL) dried beans.

Do not place the hot meat mixture over the corn chips until you are ready to microwave. It will make your chips soggy.

1	bag (12 oz/375 g) tortilla chips	1
8 oz	Cheddar cheese, cut into chunks	250 g
8 oz	Monterey Jack cheese, cut into chunks	250 g
1	onion, cut into quarters	1
2 cups	drained cooked pinto or black beans (see Tips, left)	500 mL
1 tsp	chili powder	5 mL
1 tsp	paprika	5 mL
¾ tsp	salt	3 mL
¾ tsp	dried onion flakes	3 mL
¼ tsp	cayenne pepper	1 mL
¼ tsp	onion powder	1 mL
⅛ tsp	ground oregano	0.5 mL
8 oz	lean ground beef	250 g
¼ cup	sour cream	60 mL

1. On a microwave-safe platter, place chips in a single layer. Set aside.

2. In work bowl fitted with shredding blade, shred Cheddar and Monterey Jack cheeses. Transfer to a bowl and set aside.

3. Replace shredding blade with metal blade. With motor running, drop onion though feed tube and process until finely chopped. Into the work bowl, add beans, chili powder, paprika, salt, onion flakes, cayenne pepper, onion powder and oregano and process until smooth, 2 to 3 minutes, stopping and scraping down sides of the bowl once or twice.

4. In a large skillet over medium heat, cook ground beef until no longer pink, 10 to 15 minutes. Drain off fat. Add bean mixture and cook, stirring, until hot.

5. Spoon beef mixture over chips. Sprinkle cheese mixture over top. Microwave for 20 seconds or until cheese is bubbling. Garnish with sour cream.

Variations

Use ground sausage (casings removed) in place of the ground beef to add a little zip.

You can also make this in the oven. Place under preheated broiler until cheese melts, 2 to 5 minutes.

Thai Beef Skewers with Peanut Sauce

Finger foods and skewers are great appetizers for a cocktail party where people are eating and mingling.

Tips

Soak the skewers in water for at least 10 minutes prior to threading so they will not catch fire on the grill.

For a main dish, serve the beef skewers over a bed of rice.

Use reduced-sodium soy sauce because the regular kind is too salty.

You should be able to find all of the ingredients in your local grocery store in the international section.

- Preheat grill to medium or oven to 400°F (200°C)
- 13- by 9-inch (33 by 23 cm) baking dish
- 16 wooden skewers (see Tips, left)

1 lb	boneless beef sirloin, sliced into ¼-inch (0.5 cm) strips	500 g
6	green onions, green part only, sliced in half	6
⅓ cup	peanut oil	75 mL
3 tbsp	freshly squeezed lemon juice	45 mL
2 tbsp	granulated sugar	30 mL
1 tbsp	sesame oil	15 mL
1 tbsp	hoisin sauce	15 mL
1 tbsp	reduced-sodium soy sauce (see Tips, left)	15 mL
1 tsp	dry mustard	5 mL
¼ tsp	ground white pepper	1 mL
¼ tsp	Chinese 5-spice powder	1 mL
⅛ tsp	ground ginger	0.5 mL
	Peanut Sauce (page 403)	

1. Thread beef strips onto skewers and place in baking dish side by side in one layer. Set aside.

2. In work bowl fitted with metal blade, process green onions, peanut oil, lemon juice, sugar, sesame oil, hoisin sauce, soy sauce, dry mustard, white pepper, 5-spice powder and ginger until smooth, 2 to 3 minutes. Pour over beef. Cover and marinate in the refrigerator for 2 hours.

3. Grill over medium heat or bake in preheated oven, turning partway through, until light brown, 20 to 25 minutes. Discard any excess marinade. Serve Peanut Sauce on the side for dipping.

Variation

You can use chicken in place of the beef.

Potted Beef

**Makes about
3 cups (750 mL)**

Whenever you serve
roast beef, make extra
so you can prepare
this delicious nibble. It
is spicy and intriguing
and people gobble it
up. It is also a great way
to use up almost any
leftover beef, including
steak. Serve it on toast
points, accompanied by
cornichons, or crackers
and plain baguette.

8	anchovy fillets	8
1	small red onion, quartered	1
2	cloves garlic, coarsely chopped	2
1 tsp	salt	5 mL
½ tsp	cracked black peppercorns	2 mL
1	piece (about 1 by ¼ inches/ 2.5 by 0.5 cm) mace, crumbled, or ¼ tsp (1 mL) freshly grated nutmeg, optional	1
2 cups	cubed (½ inch/1 cm) cooked beef	500 mL
½ cup	melted or clarified butter (see Tip, page 94)	125 mL

1. In work bowl fitted with metal blade, pulse anchovies, red onion, garlic, salt, peppercorns and mace, if using, until finely chopped, about 10 times, stopping and scraping down sides of the bowl once or twice. Add beef and melted butter and process until smooth, about 30 seconds. Cover and refrigerate for up to 3 days.

Instant Pâté

**Makes about
2 cups (500 mL)**

This is a classic because
it's so easy to make and
delicious. Put a small
terrine of this out for
a party and watch it
disappear.

1 lb	chicken livers, trimmed	500 g
6 oz	butter, softened	175 g
¼ cup	coarsely chopped sweet onion, such as Vidalia	60 mL
2	cloves garlic	2
2 tbsp	fresh thyme leaves	30 mL
2 tbsp	cognac or brandy	30 mL
1 tsp	salt	5 mL
1 tsp	cracked black peppercorns	5 mL
	Baguette or crackers	

1. In a pot of boiling water, cook chicken livers until just a hint of pink remains in the center, about 3 minutes. Drain. Transfer to work bowl fitted with metal blade. Add butter, onion and garlic. Purée until smooth. Add thyme, cognac, salt and peppercorns and process until blended. Transfer to a serving dish. Cover and refrigerate for at least 3 hours or for up to 2 days. Serve on sliced baguette or your favorite crackers.

Squash-Spiked Chicken Liver Pâté

Chicken liver pâtés are so easy to make, yet seem so impressive. This version is lightened up with the addition of roasted squash and herb-infused fresh cheese. A splash of eau de vie or cognac completes the flavor profile. Strongly flavored, this is best served on plain crackers or sliced baguette.

Tips

For best results, roast the squash, rather than steaming it. (The flavor will be more intense and the squash will be less watery.) You will need half of a good size acorn or butternut squash. Simply cut the squash in half, scoop out the seeds and cover in foil. Place in preheated oven (400°F/200°C) until flesh is soft, about 45 minutes. Set aside until cool enough to handle. Scoop out flesh, transfer to work bowl fitted with metal blade and purée. Measure out 1 cup (250 mL) of purée and return to work bowl. Complete the recipe.

Use a prepared cheese such as Boursin or leftover Quark Claqueret (page 64.)

1 cup	puréed roasted squash (see Tips, left)	125 mL
1 tbsp	olive oil	15 mL
1	small onion, chopped	1
2	cloves garlic, coarsely chopped	2
8 oz	chicken livers, trimmed and coarsely chopped	250 g
½ cup	herb-infused cream cheese (see Tips, left)	125 mL
1 tbsp	eau de vie, such as kirsch or Poire Williams or cognac, optional	15 mL
½ tsp	salt	2 mL
½ tsp	cracked black peppercorns	2 mL
	Finely chopped parsley	

1. In a skillet, heat oil over medium heat. Add onion and cook, stirring, until softened, about 3 minutes. Add garlic and chicken livers and cook until lightly browned and just a hint of pink remains in center of the livers, about 5 minutes. Let cool slightly.

2. In work bowl fitted with metal blade, process chicken liver mixture, squash, cream cheese, eau de vie, if using, salt and peppercorns until smooth. Transfer to a serving bowl. Garnish with chopped parsley. Cover and refrigerate for at least 3 hours or for up to 2 days.

Country Terrine

Why pay a fortune for prepared pâtés or terrines when you can so easily make your own? This one has a beautiful mild flavor and the dots of green pistachio add great visual appeal. Serve on sliced baguette with thin slices of gherkins or cornichons and/or a small bowl of the best Dijon mustard.

Tip

You can buy pistachios shelled and peeled or peel them yourself. *To peel pistachios:* Drop shelled nuts into a saucepan of rapidly boiling water. Return to a boil and boil for 1 minute. Transfer to a colander and drain. Spread nuts on a clean tea towel and rub until the skins come off.

- 6-cup (1.5 L) loaf pan or crockery terrine, lightly greased
- Instant-read thermometer

4 oz	pancetta, coarsely chopped	125 g
½ cup	whole peeled pistachios (see Tip, left)	125 mL
1 lb	lean ground pork	500 g
1 lb	ground veal	500 g
¼ cup	brandy or cognac	60 mL
2 tbsp	fresh thyme leaves	30 mL
1 tsp	salt	5 mL
1 tsp	cracked black peppercorns	5 mL
2	eggs, beaten	2

1. In work bowl fitted with metal blade, pulse pancetta and pistachios until finely chopped, about 8 times. Add pork, veal, brandy, thyme, salt, peppercorns and eggs and pulse until blended, about 15 times. Transfer to a bowl, cover and refrigerate overnight to allow flavors to blend.

2. Preheat oven to 400°F (200°C). Transfer meat mixture to prepared loaf pan and pack tightly. Place in a larger pan filled with enough boiling water to come halfway up to the top of the dish. Cover tightly with foil.

3. Bake in preheated oven until center is 165°F (74°C) about 1½ hours. Let cool in pan on a rack for 15 minutes then refrigerate for at least 3 hours until thoroughly chilled before serving. Store in refrigerator for up to 3 days.

Soups

Peppery Cucumber Avocado Soup

Serves 4 to 6

Vegan Friendly

This soup is so easy to make, yet surprisingly delicious. Keep some in the fridge for snacks during the dog days of summer — it is remarkably refreshing.

Tip

Use the quantity of jalapeño that suits your taste. If you prefer just a bit of heat, use half of one. If you like the taste of chile, use a whole one.

1	English cucumber, seeded and cut into 3-inch (7.5 cm) chunks	1
2	avocados	2
1 cup	plain yogurt, preferably Greek-style (pressed) (see Tip, page 114) or soy yogurt	250 mL
1 cup	cold water	250 mL
¼ cup	coarsely snipped chives	60 mL
½ to 1	jalapeño pepper, halved and seeded	½ to 1
2 tbsp	freshly squeezed lime juice	30 mL
2 tbsp	fresh cilantro leaves	30 mL
1 tsp	salt	5 mL
	Freshly ground white pepper	

1. In work bowl fitted with metal blade, purée cucumber, avocados, yogurt, water, chives, jalapeño, lime juice, cilantro, salt, and white pepper to taste, until smooth. Taste and adjust seasoning. Cover and chill thoroughly, for at least 3 hours or for up to 3 days.

Sorrel Soup

Serves 4 to 6

Vegetarian Friendly

This soup is extremely simple to make, delivers great flavor and is excellent served hot or cold. Look for sorrel in farmers' markets. If you like it, it will make a great addition to your cupboard of culinary delights.

1 tbsp	butter or oil	15 mL
2	onions, coarsely chopped	2
1	clove garlic, coarsely chopped	1
2	potatoes, peeled and cut into chunks	2
4 cups	chicken or vegetable broth	1 L
½ tsp	salt	2 mL
6 cups	packed sorrel leaves	1.5 L
½ cup	heavy or whipping (35%) cream	125 mL

1. In a large saucepan over medium heat, melt butter. Add onions and garlic and cook, stirring, until softened. Add potatoes, broth and salt and bring to a boil. Cover, reduce heat and simmer until potatoes are tender. Increase heat to medium. Add sorrel, in batches, stirring to submerge each, and cook until wilted, about 2 minutes.

2. Strain soup. Transfer solids to work bowl fitted with metal blade and add 1 cup (250 mL) of the liquid. Purée until smooth. Return puréed solids to saucepan, stir in remaining liquid and cream. If serving cold, cover and chill thoroughly.

Tomato Gazpacho

Serves 6

Vegan Friendly

When you mention gazpacho, a version of this recipe — built around fresh tomatoes, cucumber, olive oil and vinegar — is usually what comes to mind. However, in Spain, its country of origin, gazpacho refers to a soupy salad, thickened with bread, which can be made from a wide variety of ingredients ranging from lettuce to almonds. We love to make this when fresh tomatoes and cucumbers are in season. As with most cold soups, we recommend that you keep extra chilling in the refrigerator for a perfect snack on a hot day.

Tips

Extra virgin olive oil is called for here because of its more complex flavors, which will enhance the soup. Also, the oil is not heated and so will maintain all of its healthful properties.

If you are serving this and other cold soups on a hot day, chilling the serving bowls before adding the soup is a nice touch.

1	slice (about $\frac{1}{2}$ inch/1 cm) day-old country bread, crust removed	1
1	red bell pepper, seeded and quartered	1
$\frac{1}{2}$	small red onion	$\frac{1}{2}$
1 to 2	jalapeño peppers, seeded and quartered	1 to 2
1 to 2	cloves garlic	1 to 2
3	large ripe tomatoes, peeled, cored and quartered	3
1	cucumber, peeled and cut into chunks (1 inch/2.5 cm)	1
2 tbsp	sherry or red wine vinegar	30 mL
1 tsp	salt	5 mL
$\frac{1}{2}$ cup	extra virgin olive oil (see Tips, left)	125 mL
	Freshly ground black pepper	

1. Soak bread in $\frac{1}{2}$ cup (125 mL) water. Squeeze dry and set aside.

2. In work bowl fitted with metal blade, pulse bell pepper, red onion, and jalapeño and garlic to taste until chopped, about 15 times, stopping and scraping down sides of the bowl once or twice. Add tomatoes, cucumber, vinegar and salt and pulse until coarsely chopped, about 10 times. Add bread and pulse to blend, about 5 times. With motor running, add olive oil through feed tube. Season with black pepper to taste. Transfer to a serving bowl, cover and chill thoroughly, for at least 3 hours or for up to 3 days.

Almond Gazpacho with Green Grapes

Serves 4

Vegan Friendly

Serve this soup very cold for a refreshing treat on a hot summer's day. This makes a small quantity, but small servings are appropriate and the recipe can easily be doubled. It's a great way to use up leftover baguette.

Tips

For the best flavor, buy almonds with the skin on and blanch them yourself. *To blanch almonds:* Drop almonds in a pot of rapidly boiling water and boil until the skins start to pucker. Transfer to a colander and rinse well under cold running water. Using your hands, pop the almonds out of their skins. Place on paper towels and let dry for at least 10 minutes, changing the paper towels, if necessary.

Although it may seem like a lot of work, it is important to press the liquid out of the solids until they are virtually dry. Otherwise your gazpacho will lack the rich almond flavor that makes this soup so delicious.

1	piece (about 3 inches/7.5 cm) stale baguette, crust removed	1
1 cup	blanched almonds (see Tips, left)	250 mL
1	clove garlic	1
2 tbsp	best-quality sherry vinegar (approx.)	30 mL
2 cups	ice water, divided	500 mL
2 tbsp	extra virgin olive oil (see Tips, page 111) plus additional for drizzling	30 mL
	Salt and freshly ground white pepper	
12	seedless green grapes, halved	12

1. Soak bread in 1/2 cup (125 mL) water and squeeze dry. Set aside.

2. In work bowl fitted with metal blade, process almonds until quite fine, about 20 seconds, stopping and scraping down sides of the bowl once or twice. Add garlic, vinegar, reserved bread and 1/2 cup (125 mL) of the ice water and process until smooth, about 10 seconds. Add olive oil, remaining 1 1/2 cups (375 mL) of water, and salt and white pepper to taste, and process until blended.

3. Place a fine sieve over a bowl and strain soup. Using a wooden spoon, press against solids to extract as much liquid as possible (see Tips, left). Cover and chill thoroughly, for at least 3 hours or for up to 3 days. Before serving taste and adjust seasoning. You may need to add a bit more vinegar as well as salt and pepper. To serve, ladle into bowls and garnish with grapes. Drizzle with olive oil.

Tipsy Tomato Shooters

Vegetarian Friendly

Serve this soup as an appetizer in shot-type glasses. It looks beautiful and lends an air of elegance and fun to a very simple dish. A garnish of minced jalapeño pepper adds a zesty finish, but if you don't like heat, dill works well, too.

Tip

We like to use Italian San Marzano tomatoes when making this soup. They are reputedly the best tomatoes in the world and are very flavorful. If you're using domestic tomatoes, you may want to add 1 tsp (5 mL) or so tomato paste and a pinch of sugar before simmering the soup.

2 tbsp	butter	30 mL
1	onion, chopped	1
1	carrot, peeled and chopped	1
2	cloves garlic, chopped	2
½ tsp	salt	2 mL
½ tsp	freshly ground pepper, preferably white	2 mL
1	can (14 oz/398 mL) tomatoes with juice (see Tip, left)	1
2 cups	chicken or vegetable broth	500 mL
½ cup	half-and-half (10%) cream	125 mL
¼ cup	gin	60 mL
	Finely chopped dill or minced jalapeño pepper	

1. In a large saucepan or stockpot over medium heat, melt butter. Add onion and carrot and cook, stirring, until softened, about 5 minutes. Add garlic, salt, and freshly ground pepper to taste, and cook, stirring, for 1 minute. Add tomatoes with juice and broth and bring to a boil. Cover, reduce heat to low and simmer until flavors meld, about 25 minutes.

2. Place a strainer over a large bowl and strain soup. Transfer solids and 1 cup (250 mL) of the liquid to work bowl fitted with metal blade. Purée until smooth. Return to bowl and stir well. Cover and chill thoroughly, for at least 3 hours or for up to 3 days. When you're ready to serve, stir in cream and gin. Taste and adjust seasoning. Pour into glasses and garnish with dill.

Summer Borscht

Vegan Friendly

On a hot summer day there are few things more refreshing than a cold soup. Here is a particularly delicious and visually attractive variation on the theme. Serve small quantities in crystal cocktail or martini glasses. It makes a very elegant presentation and will get any garden party off to a great start.

Tip

Make an effort to get Greek-style yogurt, also known as "pressed." It is lusciously thick and adds beautiful depth to this and many other dishes. Greek yogurt is available in well-stocked supermarkets and specialty stores. If you can't find it, you can make your own. *To make Greek-style yogurt:* Line a sieve with a double layer of cheesecloth or paper towels. Add plain yogurt, cover and refrigerate overnight. The watery component will have drained out and you will be left with lovely thick yogurt.

1 tbsp	butter	15 mL
1	shallot, sliced	1
2	cloves garlic, chopped	2
2	whole cloves	2
2	whole allspice	2
	Salt and freshly ground black pepper	
2	medium beets, peeled and quartered (8 oz/250 g)	2
2 cups	chicken or vegetable broth	500 mL
1 tbsp	liquid honey, optional	15 mL
1 cup	plain yogurt, preferably Greek-style (pressed) (see Tip, left), or soy yogurt	250 mL
¼ cup	minced seeded cucumber	60 mL
¼ cup	minced red onion	60 mL
1 tbsp	finely chopped fresh dill fronds	15 mL

1. In a saucepan, melt butter over medium heat. Add shallot and garlic and cook, stirring, until softened, about 3 minutes. Add cloves, allspice, and salt and pepper to taste, and cook, stirring, for 1 minute. Add beets and broth and bring to a boil. Cover, reduce heat to low and simmer until beets are tender, about 20 minutes. Remove and discard cloves and allspice. Stir in honey, if using.

2. Place a strainer over a large bowl and strain soup. Transfer solids and 1 cup (250 mL) of the liquid to work bowl fitted with metal blade. Purée until smooth. Return to bowl and stir well. Cover and chill thoroughly, for at least 3 hours or for up to 3 days. When you're ready to serve, whisk in yogurt. Taste and adjust seasoning.

3. In a small bowl, combine cucumber, red onion and dill. Stir to combine. To serve, ladle soup into glasses and garnish with cucumber mixture.

Beet Soup with Lemongrass and Lime

Vegan Friendly

This Thai-inspired soup is elegant and refreshing. Its jewel-like appearance and intriguing flavors make it a perfect prelude to any meal. It's especially wonderful served at summer dinners in the garden.

Tip

For a change, try using coconut oil when making this soup. Its pleasantly nutty taste complements the Thai flavors.

1 tbsp	oil or coconut oil (see Tip, left)	15 mL
1	onion, chopped	1
4	cloves garlic, chopped	4
2 tbsp	minced gingerroot	30 mL
2	stalks lemongrass, trimmed, and cut in half crosswise	2
2 tsp	cracked black peppercorns	10 mL
6	medium beets, peeled and quartered (about 2½ lbs/1.25 kg)	6
6 cups	chicken or vegetable broth	1.5 L
1	red bell pepper, seeded and quartered	1
1	long red chile pepper, seeded and quartered, optional	1
	Grated zest and juice of 1 lime	
	Salt, optional	
	Coconut cream, optional	
	Finely chopped cilantro	

1. In a large saucepan or stockpot, heat oil over medium heat. Add onion and cook, stirring, until softened, about 3 minutes. Add garlic, ginger, lemongrass and peppercorns and cook, stirring, for 1 minute. Add beets and broth and bring to a boil. Cover, reduce heat to low and simmer until beets are tender, about 45 minutes.

2. Place a strainer over a large bowl and strain soup. Remove lemongrass and discard. Transfer solids to work bowl fitted with metal blade and add 1 cup (250 mL) of the liquid. Purée until smooth. Return to saucepan and add remaining liquid. Add red bell pepper, and chile pepper, if using, to work bowl. Pulse until finely chopped, about 10 times, stopping and scraping down sides of the bowl once or twice. Add to saucepan. Cover and simmer until peppers are tender, about 15 minutes. Stir in lime zest and juice. Season to taste with salt, if using. Cover and chill thoroughly, for at least 3 hours or for up to 3 days.

3. When ready to serve, spoon into individual bowls, drizzle with coconut cream, if using, and garnish with cilantro.

Watercress Vichyssoise

Serves 8 to 10

Vegan Friendly

In the dog days of summer, a big bowl of vichyssoise chilling in the fridge makes a great pick-me-up snack, as well as a fabulous starter for even the most elegant meal. The addition of peppery watercress takes this version uptown while adding valuable nutrients.

Tips

Because leeks can be gritty, it is customary to slice and rinse them before using. *To clean leeks:* Fill a sink full of lukewarm water. Split the leeks in half lengthwise and submerge in the water, swishing them around to remove all traces of dirt. Transfer to a colander and rinse thoroughly under cold water.

Place shallots and garlic in the feed tube together so the shallots can stabilize the garlic for slicing.

When preparing the watercress for this soup, use only the leaves and tender stems. Break off the thicker base stem and discard. Save some from the bunch to use as a garnish.

3	leeks, white part with a bit of green, cut to fit feed tube (see Tips, left)	3
2	shallots	2
2 tbsp	butter or oil	30 mL
2	cloves garlic	2
1 tsp	salt	5 mL
½ tsp	cracked white peppercorns	2 mL
4	potatoes, peeled and quartered	4
6 cups	chicken or vegetable broth	1.5 L
1	bunch watercress (leaves and tender stems, about 4 cups/1 L) (see Tips, left)	1
1 cup	heavy or whipping (35%) cream or soy creamer	250 mL

1. In work bowl fitted with slicing blade, slice leeks, then shallots and garlic (see Tips, left).

2. In a large saucepan or stockpot over medium heat, melt butter. Add sliced leeks, shallots and garlic and cook, stirring, until leeks are softened, about 5 minutes. Add salt and peppercorns and cook, stirring, for 1 minute. Add potatoes and broth. Cover and bring to a boil. Reduce heat and simmer until potatoes are tender, about 25 minutes.

3. Place a strainer over a large bowl and strain soup. Transfer solids to work bowl fitted with metal blade and add 1 cup (250 mL) of the liquid. Purée until smooth. Add watercress (set aside about ¼ cup/60 mL for garnish) and pulse until chopped and blended, about 10 times. Return puréed solids to bowl and stir in cream. Cover and chill thoroughly, for at least 3 hours or for up to 3 days. Before serving, taste and adjust seasoning. Garnish with additional watercress.

Variation

Classic Vichyssoise: Omit watercress. Garnish with finely chopped chives

Vichyssoise with Celery Root and Watercress

Serves 8

Vegan Friendly

This refreshing soup is delicious, easy to make and can be a prelude to the most sophisticated meal. Using celery root rather than traditional potatoes, gives it a pleasing nutty flavor that may be enhanced with a garnish of chopped toasted walnuts.

Tips

Since celery root oxidizes quickly on contact with air, transfer it to a bowl of acidulated water (4 cups/ 1 L water combined with 2 tbsp/30 mL lemon juice) as soon as you have sliced it to prevent discoloration. Drain thoroughly before using.

Because leeks can be gritty, it is customary to slice and rinse them before using. *To clean leeks:* Fill a sink full of lukewarm water. Split the leeks in half lengthwise and submerge in the water, swishing them around to remove all traces of dirt. Transfer to a colander and rinse thoroughly under cold water.

1	large celery root, peeled and cut to fit feed tube (see Tips, left)	1
3	leeks, white part with a bit of green, cut to fit feed tube (see Tips, left)	3
2	cloves garlic	2
1 tbsp	oil	15 mL
1 tsp	salt	5 mL
½ tsp	cracked black peppercorns	2 mL
6 cups	chicken or vegetable broth	1.5 L
2	bunches watercress (leaves and tender stems, about 8 cups/2 L) watercress, tough parts of the stems removed	2
½ cup	heavy or whipping (35%) cream or soy milk	125 mL
	Toasted chopped walnuts, optional	
	Watercress sprigs, optional	

1. In work bowl fitted with slicing blade, slice celery root. Transfer to a bowl of acidulated water and set aside (see Tips, left). Add leeks, then garlic to feed tube and slice.

2. In a large saucepan or stockpot, heat oil over medium heat. Add leeks and garlic and cook, stirring, until softened, about 5 minutes. Add salt and peppercorns and cook, stirring, for 1 minute. Add broth and reserved drained celery root and bring to a boil. Cover, reduce heat to low and simmer until celery root is tender, about 25 minutes. Stir in watercress until wilted.

3. Place a strainer over a large bowl and strain soup. Transfer solids to work bowl fitted with metal blade and add 1 cup (250 mL) of the liquid. Purée until smooth. Return puréed solids to bowl and stir in cream. Taste and season with salt, if needed. Cover and chill thoroughly, for at least 3 hours. Before serving, taste and adjust seasoning. To serve, ladle into bowls and garnish with toasted walnuts and/or watercress sprigs, if using.

Cream of Corn Soup

Vegetarian Friendly

This soup is very easy to make, yet light and elegant. It makes a perfect starter to a special meal but is equally at home with family-style dining.

1 tbsp	butter	15 mL
1	onion, coarsely chopped	1
1	dried red chile pepper	1
2 cups	corn kernels, thawed if frozen	500 mL
½ tsp	salt	2 mL
½ tsp	freshly ground black pepper	2 mL
4	sprigs parsley	4
Pinch	granulated sugar	Pinch
2 cups	chicken or vegetable broth	500 mL
1 cup	whole milk	250 mL
	Heavy or whipping (35%) cream	
	Finely snipped chives	

1. In a large saucepan over medium heat, melt butter. Add onion and chile pepper and cook, stirring, until onion is softened, about 3 minutes. Add corn, salt, freshly ground pepper, parsley and sugar and stir well. Add broth and milk. Cover, reduce heat to low and cook until corn is very tender, about 20 minutes. Remove and discard chile pepper.

2. Place a strainer over a bowl and strain soup. Transfer solids and 1 cup (250 mL) of the liquid to work bowl fitted with metal blade. Purée until smooth. Return strainer to bowl and add puréed soup. Push against solids to extract as much liquid as possible. Return liquid to saucepan and discard solids. Taste and adjust seasoning. To serve, ladle into warm bowls, drizzle with cream and garnish with chives.

Cucumber Soup Avgolemono

Serves 6 to 8

Vegetarian Friendly

When cucumbers are used in soup, we usually think of chilled soups. This warm, delicately flavored version is delightfully different and quite delicious. Avgolemono is a Greek term used to describe dishes that combine eggs and lemon.

Tips

Because leeks can be gritty, it is customary to slice and rinse them before using. *To clean leeks:* Fill a sink full of lukewarm water. Split the leeks in half lengthwise and submerge in the water, swishing them around to remove all traces of dirt. Transfer to a colander and rinse thoroughly under cold water.

Once you've added the egg mixture to the soup, watch carefully to be sure it doesn't boil. Otherwise, you'll have curdled eggs in your soup.

2 tbsp	butter	30 mL
1	leek, white part with a bit of green, sliced (see Tips, left)	1
1 tsp	paprika	5 mL
1 tsp	salt	5 mL
	Freshly ground black or white pepper	
2	cucumbers, peeled, seeded and chopped	2
6 cups	chicken or vegetable broth	1.5 L
½ cup	fresh dill fronds	125 mL
1 tbsp	freshly squeezed lemon juice	15 mL
2	egg yolks	2
3 tbsp	heavy or whipping (35%) cream	45 mL

1. In a large saucepan over medium heat, melt butter. Add leek and cook, stirring, until softened, about 5 minutes. Add paprika, salt, and pepper to taste, and cook, stirring, for 1 minute. Stir in cucumbers. Add broth and bring to a boil. Cover, reduce heat to low and simmer for 20 minutes until vegetables are tender. Stir in dill.

2. Place a strainer over a large bowl and strain soup. Transfer solids to work bowl fitted with metal blade and add 1 cup (250 mL) of the liquid. Purée until smooth. Return puréed solids to saucepan and stir in remaining liquid.

3. In a small bowl, whisk together lemon juice, egg yolks and cream. Gradually beat in 1 cup (250 mL) of the hot broth, whisking constantly. Add to saucepan and cook over medium heat, stirring, until mixture is thickened slightly, about 1 minute (see Tips, left). Remove from heat, taste and adjust seasoning.

Tomato and Rice Soup Avgolemono

Serves 4

Vegetarian Friendly

This is a great recipe to have on hand for those times when unexpected guests drop by. It can be easily made from ingredients you're likely to have on hand and is very flexible in terms of quantities. We've made a 4-serving batch here, but it can easily be doubled.

Tip

Once you've added the egg mixture to the soup, watch carefully to be sure it doesn't boil. Otherwise, you'll have curdled eggs in your soup.

½ cup	cooked white or brown long-grain rice	125 mL
1	can (14 oz/398 mL) tomatoes with juice	1
1 tsp	granulated sugar	5 mL
¼ tsp	ground cinnamon	1 mL
2 cups	chicken or vegetable broth	500 mL
	Salt and freshly ground black pepper	
2 tbsp	finely chopped dill plus additional for garnish	30 mL
1	egg	1
1 tbsp	freshly squeezed lemon juice	15 mL

1. In work bowl fitted with metal blade, process tomatoes with juice, sugar and cinnamon until smooth. Transfer to a large saucepan and add broth and rice. Season with salt and pepper to taste. Bring to a boil, reduce heat and simmer for 10 minutes to blend flavors. Stir in dill.

2. In a small bowl, whisk together egg and lemon juice. Gradually beat in 1 cup (250 mL) of the hot broth, whisking constantly. Add to saucepan and cook over low heat, stirring, for 1 minute (see Tip, left). Remove from heat, taste and adjust seasoning. To serve, ladle into bowls and garnish with additional dill.

Jump-Start Tomato Soup

Serves 4

Vegan Friendly

This soup is delicious and not much more difficult to make than one straight out of the can.

1 tbsp	butter or oil	15 mL
1	onion, coarsely chopped	1
Pinch	ground allspice	Pinch
Pinch	cayenne pepper	Pinch
1 tbsp	all-purpose flour	15 mL
2 cups	chicken or vegetable broth	500 mL
1	can (28 oz/796 mL) tomatoes with juice, coarsely chopped	1
½ cup	heavy or whipping (35%) cream or soy creamer	125 mL
	Salt and freshly ground black pepper	
	Finely chopped Italian flat-leaf parsley or dill	

1. In a large saucepan or stockpot over medium heat, melt butter. Add onion and cook, stirring, until softened, about 3 minutes. Stir in allspice and cayenne. Add flour and cook, stirring, for 1 minute. Add broth and tomatoes with juice. Bring to a boil. Reduce heat to low and simmer, stirring occasionally, for 10 minutes.

2. Place a strainer over a large bowl and strain soup. Transfer solids to work bowl fitted with metal blade and add 1 cup (250 mL) of the liquid. Purée until smooth.

3. Return puréed solids to saucepan over low heat and add remaining liquid. Stir in cream and heat through but do not boil. Add salt and pepper to taste. Ladle into warm bowls, garnish liberally with parsley and serve immediately.

Easy Borscht

Vegan Friendly

Borscht is one of those hearty peasant soups that has transcended its origins. Here's an easy-to-make version that eliminates the need to peel beets. The baby spinach adds a pleasant note of freshness, which is sometimes provided by the addition of beet leaves in traditional recipes. Serve hot or cold with plenty of dark rye bread.

Tip

You can also use prepared or homemade beef, chicken or vegetable broth in this recipe. If it is not concentrated, use 2 cups (500 mL) broth and omit the water.

1 tbsp	oil	15 mL
1	onion, coarsely chopped	1
1 tbsp	minced garlic	15 mL
1	can (14 oz/398 mL) beets with juice	1
1	can (10 oz/284 mL) condensed beef, chicken or vegetable broth (see Tip, left)	1
½ cup	water	125 mL
½	bag (10 oz/300 g) baby spinach or 2 cups (500 mL) tightly packed baby spinach	½
2 tbsp	freshly squeezed lemon juice	30 mL
	Salt and freshly ground black pepper	
	Sour cream or vegan alternative	
	Finely chopped fresh dill	

1. In a large saucepan, heat oil over medium heat. Add onion and cook, stirring, until softened, about 3 minutes. Add garlic and cook, stirring, for 1 minute.

2. Add beets with juice, broth and water. Bring to a boil. Reduce heat to low and simmer for 10 minutes to combine flavors. Add spinach and cook, stirring, just until wilted. Stir in lemon juice. Season with salt and pepper to taste.

3. Place a strainer over a large bowl and strain soup. Transfer solids to work bowl fitted with metal blade and add 1 cup (250 mL) of the liquid. Purée until smooth. Return puréed solids to saucepan and stir in remaining liquid. Reheat and serve hot or cover and chill thoroughly for at least 3 hours or for up to 3 days. Top individual servings with a dollop of sour cream and/or finely chopped dill.

Ginger-Laced Beet Soup with Orange

Vegan Friendly

The robust flavors in this soup — a strong hit of ginger and the very pleasant orange finish — are delicious. The cranberries add delightful fruitiness. This is a great soup to make in the fall when vegetable aisles and farmers' markets are brimming over with beautiful fresh beets. It is equally good hot or cold.

2	onions, quartered	2
2	stalks celery, cut into 3-inch (7.5 cm) lengths	2
¼ cup	chopped gingerroot	60 mL
4	cloves garlic, chopped	4
1 tbsp	oil	15 mL
1 tbsp	finely grated orange zest	15 mL
	Salt and freshly ground black pepper	
4	large beets, peeled and quartered	4
4 cups	chicken or vegetable broth	1 L
1 cup	freshly squeezed orange juice	250 mL
½ cup	dried cranberries	125 mL
	Plain yogurt, optional	

1. In work bowl fitted with metal blade, pulse onions, celery, ginger and garlic until finely chopped, about 15 times, stopping and scraping down sides of the bowl once or twice.

2. In a large saucepan or stockpot, heat oil over medium heat. Add onion mixture and cook, stirring, until softened, about 5 minutes. Add orange zest, and salt and pepper to taste. Cook, stirring, for 1 minute. Add beets and broth and bring to a boil. Reduce heat and simmer until beets are tender, about 30 minutes. Remove from heat. Stir in orange juice and cranberries. Taste and adjust seasoning.

3. Place a strainer over a large bowl and strain soup. Transfer solids to work bowl fitted with metal blade and add 1 cup (250 mL) of the liquid. Purée until smooth. If serving hot, return puréed solids to saucepan and stir in remaining liquid. If serving cold, add puréed solids to bowl, cover and refrigerate for at least 3 hours or for up to 3 days. To serve, ladle into bowls and top with a dollop of yogurt, if using.

Cranberry Borscht

Serves 6 to 8

Vegan Friendly

Served cold in chilled bowls, this fresh, fruity soup is a perfect prelude to an outdoor dinner on a warm night. It's a summer borscht because it uses the leaves of the beet root, which resemble Swiss chard in texture and taste. The fruity tang of the cranberries provides just enough tartness to round out the flavors. This soup is also good served hot.

6	medium beets, peeled and quartered	6
	Leaves from the beets, coarsely chopped and set aside in refrigerator	
4	cloves garlic, chopped	4
5 cups	beef or vegetable broth	1.5 L
1 tsp	salt	5 mL
½ tsp	freshly ground black pepper	2 mL
1 cup	cranberries	250 mL
2 tbsp	granulated sugar	30 mL
	Grated zest and juice of 1 orange	
	Sour cream or vegan alternative	

1. In a large saucepan or stockpot over medium heat, combine beets, garlic, broth, salt and pepper. Bring to a boil. Cover, reduce heat to low and simmer until beets are tender, about 45 minutes. Add cranberries, sugar, orange zest and juice and beet leaves. Cover and cook until cranberries are popping from their skins, about 10 minutes.

2. Place a strainer over a large bowl and strain soup. Transfer solids to work bowl fitted with metal blade and add 1 cup (250 mL) of the liquid. Purée until smooth. If serving hot, return puréed solids to saucepan, stir in remaining liquid and reheat. If serving cold, add puréed solids to bowl, cover and chill thoroughly, for at least 3 hours or for up to 3 days.

3. When ready to serve, ladle into individual bowls and top with a dollop of sour cream.

Sweet Green Pea Soup

Serves 6

Vegan Friendly

This is an elegant light soup that is perfect as a prelude to dinner. It is good hot or cold. Cooking lettuce with peas is a French technique. It adds flavor and balance to the peas and is a good way to use up lettuce that is about to pass its peak. However, this soup is quite tasty without that addition. The flavor can easily be varied by using different herbal accents. Mint is the most common, but tarragon, parsley and chives work well, too.

2 tbsp	butter or oil	30 mL
1	onion, chopped	1
½ tsp	dried tarragon or thyme	2 mL
½ tsp	salt	2 mL
	Freshly ground black pepper	
10	Boston or romaine lettuce leaves, shredded, optional	10
4 cups	chicken or vegetable broth	1 L
1	package (12 oz/375 g) frozen sweet green peas	1
Pinch	granulated sugar	Pinch
½ cup	heavy or whipping (35%) cream or soy creamer, optional	125 mL
	Finely chopped parsley or chives	

1. In a large saucepan or stockpot, melt butter over medium heat. Add onion and cook, stirring, until softened, about 3 minutes. Add tarragon, salt, and pepper to taste, and cook, stirring, for 1 minute. Add lettuce, if using, and stir until wilted.

2. Add broth, green peas and sugar. Bring to a boil. Reduce heat to low and simmer until peas are tender, about 7 minutes.

3. Using a slotted spoon, remove about ¼ cup (60 mL) of the whole peas from the saucepan and set aside. Place a strainer over a large bowl and strain soup. Transfer solids to work bowl fitted with metal blade and add 1 cup (250 mL) of the liquid. Purée until smooth. Return puréed solids to saucepan and stir in remaining liquid. Stir in cream, if using. To serve, ladle into warm bowls and garnish with reserved peas and parsley.

Variation
Sweet Green Pea Soup with Mint: Omit tarragon or thyme. Garnish soup with ¼ cup (60 mL) finely chopped mint, along with the whole peas.

Split Green Pea Soup with Mint Cream

Serves 6 to 8

Vegetarian Friendly

Not only is this soup delicious and elegant, it's extremely easy to make. If you grow mint in your garden, or on your windowsill, it can be made from pantry ingredients. The addition of Mint Cream provides a nice finish, and if you prefer a richer soup, you can add additional cream to taste, before serving.

1 cup	dried split green peas	250 mL
1 tbsp	oil	15 mL
1	large onion, chopped	1
3	stalks celery, thinly sliced	3
2	cloves garlic, chopped	2
4	sprigs mint	4
1 tsp	salt	5 mL
½ tsp	cracked black peppercorns	2 mL
6 cups	chicken or vegetable broth	1.5 L

Mint Cream

¼ cup	heavy or whipping (35%) cream	60 mL
¼ cup	sour cream	60 mL
2 tbsp	finely chopped mint	30 mL
1½ cups	hot cooked green peas	375 mL

1. In a saucepan, combine peas with 3 cups (750 mL) water. Cover and bring to a boil. Boil for 3 minutes. Turn off heat and let soak for 1 hour. Drain and rinse thoroughly under cold water.

2. In a saucepan or stockpot, heat oil over medium heat. Add onion and celery and cook, stirring, until celery is softened, about 5 minutes. Add garlic, mint, salt and peppercorns and cook, stirring, for 1 minute. Stir in soaked split green peas and broth and bring to a boil. Cover, reduce heat to low and simmer until peas are tender, about 40 minutes.

3. **Mint Cream:** Meanwhile, in a bowl, whisk cream until thick. Add sour cream and mint and blend well. Refrigerate until ready to use.

4. Place a strainer over a large bowl and strain soup. Transfer solids to work bowl fitted with metal blade and add 1 cup (250 mL) of the liquid. Purée until smooth. Return puréed solids to saucepan and stir in remaining liquid. Stir in cooked green peas. Ladle into warm bowls and garnish with Mint Cream.

Variation

Split Green Pea Soup with Tarragon Cream: Substitute fresh tarragon for the mint in both the soup and the cream.

Creamy Cauliflower Soup

Serves 6

Vegan Friendly

This soup is very versatile. It is delicious in its basic version but can easily be dressed up for special occasions (if you're not a vegetarian try the Mulligatawny or Smoked Salmon variations, below).

Tips

For a hint of celery flavor, add ¼ tsp (1 mL) celery seeds along with the black pepper.

If you prefer, substitute Two-Tomato Coulis (page 409) for the pesto.

2 tbsp	butter	30 mL
1	onion, coarsely chopped	1
1 tsp	salt	5 mL
	Freshly ground black pepper	
2	potatoes, peeled and quartered	2
4 cups	cauliflower florets	1 L
6 cups	chicken or vegetable broth	1.5 L
½ cup	heavy or whipping (35%) cream or soy creamer	125 mL
2 tbsp	prepared sun-dried tomato pesto (see Tips, left)	30 mL

1. In a large saucepan or stockpot, melt butter over medium heat. Add onion and cook, stirring, until softened, about 3 minutes. Add salt, and pepper to taste, and cook, stirring, for 1 minute.

2. Add potatoes, cauliflower and broth. Bring to a boil. Cover, reduce heat to low and simmer until potatoes are tender, about 20 minutes.

3. Place a strainer over a large bowl and strain soup. Transfer solids to work bowl fitted with metal blade and add 1 cup (250 mL) of the liquid. Purée until smooth. Return puréed solids to saucepan over low heat and stir in remaining liquid. Add cream and pesto and heat gently until mixture almost reaches a simmer. Ladle into warm bowls and serve immediately.

Variations

Mulligatawny Soup: Add 1 tbsp (15 mL) curry powder along with the salt. Omit the pesto and stir in 2 cups (500 mL) chopped cooked chicken and/or ¼ cup (60 mL) mango chutney along with the cream.

Creamy Cauliflower Soup with Smoked Salmon: Garnish the finished soup with 2 oz (60 g) chopped smoked salmon and, if desired, 2 tbsp (30 mL) chopped green onion, chives or dill.

Hearty Cauliflower and Asparagus Soup

Vegan Friendly

Your guests will think you laced this soup with cream because of the rich flavor, but it all comes from the vegetables.

Tips

If the soup seems a little thick, add additional broth or wine.

To store leftover soup, cool first to room temperature and place in an airtight container in the refrigerator for up to 4 days.

1	onion, quartered	1
2 tbsp	butter or oil	30 mL
6	cloves garlic, minced	6
2½ cups	cauliflower florets	625 mL
2 tbsp	dry white wine	30 mL
1	large bunch asparagus (about 1 lb/500 g), divided	1
3 cups	chicken or vegetable broth, divided	750 mL
2 tbsp	all-purpose flour	30 mL
1 tsp	salt	5 mL
½ tsp	ground white pepper	2 mL
Pinch	ground nutmeg	Pinch
¼ cup	loosely packed fresh basil	60 mL

1. In work bowl fitted with slicing blade, slice onion.

2. In a large saucepan over medium heat, melt butter. Add onion and garlic and cook, stirring, until onion is translucent, 5 to 7 minutes. Add cauliflower and wine. Cook for 2 minutes. Reduce heat to low and simmer while continuing with the recipe.

3. Replace slicing blade with metal blade. Add half of the asparagus and purée until smooth. If it seems a bit dry, add a few tablespoons (30 mL) of the broth through feed tube. Transfer to saucepan.

4. Trim ¼ inch (0.5 cm) from the ends of remaining asparagus. Discard ends. Slice stems on a diagonal into ¼- to ½-inch (0.5 to 1 cm) pieces. Add to saucepan.

5. Pour 2 cups (500 mL) of the broth into the pot and bring to a simmer. Meanwhile, pour ½ cup (125 mL) of the broth into a small bowl. Add flour, salt, white pepper and nutmeg and whisk until smooth. Add to the saucepan and cook, stirring, until thickened, 3 to 5 minutes. Add remaining broth.

6. In same work bowl fitted with metal blade, add basil and pulse just until chopped slightly, about 5 times. Stir into soup.

Variation
For an all-green soup for St. Patrick's Day substitute broccoli for the cauliflower.

Old-Fashioned Cream of Mushroom Soup

Vegetarian Friendly

The ultimate comfort food, this soup makes a wonderful lunch, great snack or a perfect prelude to even the most elegant meal. We like to use cremini mushrooms for their robust flavor, but white mushrooms will work well, too.

Tip

Because leeks can be gritty, it is customary to slice and rinse them before using. *To clean leeks:* Fill a sink full of lukewarm water. Split the leeks in half lengthwise and submerge in the water, swishing them around to remove all traces of dirt. Transfer to a colander and rinse thoroughly under cold water.

2	leeks, white part with a bit of green, cut to fit feed tube (see Tip, left)	2
1½ lbs	cremini mushrooms, trimmed	750 g
2 tbsp	butter	30 mL
1 tsp	salt	5 mL
½ tsp	dried tarragon	2 mL
1	bay leaf	1
	Freshly ground black or white pepper	
1 tbsp	all-purpose flour	15 mL
6 cups	chicken or mushroom broth	1.5 L
½ cup	heavy or whipping (35%) cream	125 mL
	Snipped chives	

1. In work bowl fitted with slicing blade, slice leeks, then mushrooms.

2. In a large saucepan or stockpot over medium-high heat, melt butter. Add leeks and cook, stirring, for 1 minute. Add mushrooms and cook, stirring, until they release liquid, about 5 minutes. Add salt, tarragon, bay leaf, and pepper to taste, and cook, stirring, for 1 minute. Add flour and cook, stirring, for 1 minute. Stir in broth. Cover, reduce heat to low and simmer until mushrooms are very tender, about 30 minutes. Remove and discard bay leaf.

3. Place a strainer over a large bowl and strain soup. Transfer solids to work bowl fitted with meal blade and add 1 cup (250 mL) of the liquid. Purée until smooth. Return purée to saucepan and stir in remaining liquid. Stir in cream and simmer until heated through. To serve, ladle into warm bowls and garnish with chives.

Caramelized Onion and Mushroom Soup

Serves 6

Vegetarian Friendly

On a cool fall evening this soup will warm your insides fast!

Tips

Using an array of different mushrooms deepens the flavor of this soup.

Unsalted or "sweet" butter is manufactured without adding salt to preserve the butter, thus creating a fresher product. The amount of salt added varies between brands so you don't have as much control over the amount of salt in your dish. Both butters are interchangeable, but taste for salt before adding any to your recipe.

To store leftover soup, cool first to room temperature and place in an airtight container in the refrigerator for up to 4 days.

2 lbs	assorted mushrooms, such as button, chanterelles, morels or shiitake, trimmed (see Tips, left)	1 kg
½	onion, quartered	½
3	cloves garlic	3
¼ cup	butter (see Tips, left)	60 mL
¼ cup	all-purpose flour	60 mL
1 cup	hot chicken or vegetable broth	250 mL
6 cups	milk, at room temperature	1.5 L
½ tsp	salt	2 mL
½ tsp	ground white pepper	2 mL
¼ cup	loosely packed Italian flat-leaf parsley leaves	60 mL
2 tbsp	brandy	30 mL
1 cup	sour cream	250 mL

1. In work bowl fitted with slicing blade, slice mushrooms. Transfer to a bowl. Set aside.

2. Replace slicing blade with metal blade. Add onion and garlic and pulse until minced, about 15 times, stopping and scraping down sides of the bowl once or twice.

3. In a large saucepan over medium heat, melt butter. Add onion mixture and cook, stirring, until just starting to caramelize, 12 to 15 minutes. Add mushrooms and cook, stirring, until mushrooms are softened, 2 to 4 minutes. Sprinkle with flour and cook, stirring, for 3 minutes. Add broth, stirring vigorously. Stir in milk, salt and white pepper. Bring to a simmer, stirring frequently to be sure the soup is not burning on the bottom of the pan, for 10 minutes. Add parsley and simmer, stirring occasionally, for 10 minutes.

4. Stir in brandy and sour cream until heated through (do not let boil).

Variation

Try using 1 cup (250 mL) chopped leeks in place of the onion for a lighter flavor.

Sumptuous Celery Soup

Vegan Friendly

Celeriac, or celery root, is a type of celery, with crispy white flesh that is slightly peppery. Since it will keep for a week or longer in the refrigerator, it makes an excellent winter vegetable. This simple cream soup has a lovely sweet, yet piquant flavor, which is complemented with the addition of dill. Serve it as a starter to an elegant dinner or as a weekday meal with crusty bread and salad.

Tip

Since celery root and to some extent potatoes, oxidize quickly on contact with air, transfer them to a bowl of acidulated water (4 cups/1 L water combined with 2 tbsp/ 30 mL lemon juice) as soon as they have been sliced to prevent discoloration. Drain before adding to pot.

1	large celery root, peeled and cut to fit feed tube (see Tip, left)	1
1	large potato, peeled and cut to fit feed tube	1
1	medium onion, cut to fit feed tube	1
1	clove garlic	1
1 tbsp	butter or oil	15 mL
1/2 tsp	salt	2 mL
1/4 tsp	freshly ground black pepper	1 mL
4 cups	chicken or vegetable broth	1 L
1/2 cup	heavy or whipping (35%) cream or soy creamer	125 mL
Pinch	freshly grated nutmeg	Pinch
1/4 cup	chopped fresh dill fronds	60 mL

1. In work bowl fitted with slicing blade, slice celery root and potato. Transfer to a bowl of acidulated water and set aside. Add onion and garlic to feed tube and slice.

2. In a large saucepan or stockpot over medium heat, melt butter. Add onion and garlic and cook, stirring, until softened, about 3 minutes. Add salt and pepper and cook for 1 minute. Add drained celery root, potato and broth and bring to a boil. Cover, reduce heat to low and simmer until vegetables are tender, about 25 minutes.

3. Place a strainer over a large bowl and strain soup. Transfer solids to work bowl fitted with metal blade and add 1 cup (250 mL) of the liquid. Purée until smooth. Return puréed solids to saucepan and stir in remaining liquid. Stir in cream and nutmeg and reheat. Ladle soup into warm bowls and garnish with dill.

Orange-Spiked Carrot Soup

The hit of ginger and chile in this classic soup is particularly enticing. It is equally at home as a starter to an elegant meal or as the centerpiece of a soup and salad dinner.

Tips

Because leeks can be gritty, it is customary to slice and rinse them before using. *To clean leeks:* Fill a sink full of lukewarm water. Split the leeks in half lengthwise and submerge in the water, swishing them around to remove all traces of dirt. Transfer to a colander and rinse thoroughly under cold water.

For the best flavor, toast and grind cumin yourself. *To toast cumin:* Place seeds in a dry skillet over medium heat, and cook, stirring, until fragrant, about 3 minutes. Immediately transfer to a mortar or a spice grinder and grind.

2	leeks, white part with a bit of green, cut to fit feed tube (see Tips, left)	2
4	stalks celery, cut to fit feed tube	4
8	carrots, peeled (about 1½ lbs/750 g)	8
1 tbsp	oil	15 mL
2	cloves garlic, chopped	2
2 tbsp	finely chopped gingerroot	30 mL
1 tbsp	ground cumin (see Tips, left)	15 mL
1 tbsp	ground coriander	15 mL
1 tbsp	grated orange zest	15 mL
1 tsp	salt	5 mL
2	dried red chile peppers	2
	Freshly ground black pepper	
4 cups	chicken or vegetable broth	1 L
½ cup	freshly squeezed orange juice	125 mL
	Finely chopped cilantro or parsley	

1. In work bowl fitted with slicing blade, slice leeks, then celery. Transfer to a bowl. Slice carrots. Set aside.

2. In a large saucepan or stockpot, heat oil over medium heat. Add leeks and celery and cook, stirring, until softened, about 5 minutes. Add garlic, ginger, cumin, coriander, orange zest, salt, chiles, and pepper to taste, and cook, stirring, for 1 minute. Add reserved carrots and broth. Cover and bring to a boil. Reduce heat and simmer until carrots are tender, about 25 minutes.

3. Place a strainer over a large bowl and strain soup. Remove and discard chiles. Transfer solids to work bowl fitted with metal blade and add 1 cup (250 mL) of the liquid. Purée until smooth. Return puréed solids to saucepan and stir in remaining liquid. Reheat. Remove from heat and stir in orange juice. To serve, ladle into warm bowls and garnish with cilantro.

Variation

Instead of garnishing the soup with cilantro, top with a dollop of Parsley Walnut Pesto (page 404).

Soup à la Crécy

Vegan Friendly

In French cooking, *crécy* is a term for certain dishes containing carrots. In our books, this soup, which may be thickened with potatoes or rice, is one of the tastiest. This classic soup makes a nice centerpiece for a light soup and salad dinner accompanied with dark rye bread. It also makes an elegant first course for a more sophisticated meal.

Tip

We like to use brown rice when making this soup because it is the most nutritious form of the grain but white rice works well, too. If you are using white rice reduce the cooking time to 25 minutes. If using brown rice, be sure to store it in the refrigerator or use it within a few weeks of purchase. The bran layer contains oil, which although healthy, becomes rancid when kept at room temperature for a long period.

2	leeks, white part with a bit of green, cut to fit feed tube (see Tips, page 132)	2
6	carrots, peeled and cut to fit feed tube (about 1 lb/500 g)	6
1 tbsp	oil	15 mL
2 tsp	dried thyme, crumbled	10 mL
1 tsp	cracked black peppercorns	5 mL
2	bay leaves	2
6 cups	chicken or vegetable broth	1.5 L
1/2 cup	brown rice (see Tip, left)	125 mL
	Salt, optional	
	Heavy or whipping (35%) cream or soy creamer, optional	
1/2 cup	finely chopped parsley or snipped chives	125 mL
1/2 cup	Garlic Croutons (page 138)	125 mL

1. In work bowl fitted with slicing blade, slice leeks, then carrots.

2. In a large saucepan or stockpot, heat oil over medium heat. Add leeks and carrots and cook, stirring, until carrots are softened, about 7 minutes. Add thyme, peppercorns and bay leaves and cook, stirring, for 1 minute. Add broth and rice and bring to a boil. Cover, reduce heat to low and simmer until rice is tender, 25 to 50 minutes, depending upon whether you are using brown or white rice. Remove and discard bay leaves.

3. Place a strainer over a large bowl and strain soup. Transfer solids to work bowl fitted with metal blade and add 1 cup (250 mL) of the liquid. Purée until smooth. Return puréed solids to saucepan and stir in remaining liquid. Reheat and season to taste with salt, if using. To serve, ladle into warm serving bowls and drizzle with cream, if using. Garnish with parsley and croutons. Serve hot.

Gingery Carrot Soup with Orange and Parsley

Serves 8

Vegan Friendly

Carrots and ginger always make a superlative combination. Here, they are enhanced with zesty orange and a hit of earthy parsley to produce a delicious and versatile soup. Serve this with whole-grain bread and a tossed green salad for a light but nourishing supper or as a first course to a more substantial meal. If you prefer a creamy soup and a hint of exotic coconut flavor, add a drizzle of coconut milk and use coconut oil to soften the onions.

Tips

If you find ginger a bit assertive, use the smaller amount. If you like its flavor go for the larger quantity.

Because you are using the skin of the fruit to add flavor to this soup, we recommend buying organically grown oranges for use in this recipe.

Always use flat-leaf rather than curly parsley because it has more flavor.

6	large carrots, peeled and cut to fit feed tube	6
2	onions, cut to fit feed tube	2
1 tbsp	oil or coconut oil	15 mL
2 to 3 tbsp	minced gingerroot (see Tips, left)	30 to 45 mL
1 tbsp	finely grated orange zest (see Tips, left)	15 mL
1 tsp	salt	5 mL
1 tsp	cracked black peppercorns	5 mL
2	bay leaves	2
4 cups	chicken or vegetable broth	1 L
1 cup	packed Italian flat-leaf parsley leaves (see Tips, left)	250 mL
1½ cups	freshly squeezed orange juice	375 mL
	Coconut cream, optional	

1. In work bowl fitted with slicing blade, slice carrots. Transfer to a bowl and set aside. Add onions to feed tube and slice.

2. In a large saucepan or stockpot, heat oil over medium heat. Add onions and cook, stirring, until softened, about 3 minutes. Add ginger, orange zest, salt, peppercorns and bay leaves and cook, stirring, for 1 minute. Add reserved carrots and broth and bring to a boil. Cover, reduce heat to low and simmer until carrots are tender, about 25 minutes. Stir in parsley.

3. Place a strainer over a large bowl and strain soup. Remove and discard bay leaves. Transfer solids to work bowl fitted with metal blade and add 1 cup (250 mL) of the liquid. Purée until smooth. Return puréed solids to saucepan and stir in remaining liquid. Stir in orange juice. Reheat until almost at a simmer. To serve, ladle into warm bowls and drizzle with coconut cream, if using.

Carrot-and-Coriander-Spiked Sunchoke Soup

Vegan Friendly

Make this delicious soup in autumn, when sunchokes (also known as Jerusalem artichokes) are at their peak. With the addition of carrots and a good hit of coriander, these nutty tasting tubers are puréed into a hearty soup that is equally at home as the centerpiece of a light supper or as a starter to an elegant meal. If you like the taste (many people don't) finish with a liberal garnish of fresh cilantro (the leaves of the coriander plant). If not, drizzle with cream and dust with parsley.

Tip

For the best flavor, toast and grind coriander yourself. *To toast coriander:* Place seeds in a dry skillet over medium heat and cook, stirring, until fragrant, about 3 minutes. Immediately transfer to a mortar or a spice grinder and grind.

2	onions, cut to fit feed tube	2
4	cloves garlic	4
2 lbs	sunchokes, scrubbed and cut to fit feed tube	1 kg
2	carrots, peeled and cut to fit feed tube	2
1 tbsp	oil	15 mL
1 tbsp	ground coriander (see Tips, left)	15 mL
½ tsp	salt	2 mL
½ tsp	cracked black or white peppercorns	2 mL
6 cups	chicken or vegetable broth	1.5 L
	Heavy or whipping (35%) cream or soy creamer, optional	
	Finely chopped cilantro or parsley	

1. In work bowl fitted with slicing blade, slice onions and garlic. Transfer to a bowl and set aside. Add sunchokes and carrots to feed tube and slice. Set aside.

2. In a large saucepan or stockpot, heat oil over medium heat. Add onions and garlic and cook, stirring, until softened, about 3 minutes. Add coriander, salt and peppercorns and cook, stirring, for 1 minute. Add sunchokes, carrots and broth and bring to a boil. Cover, reduce heat to low and simmer until chokes and carrots are tender, about 25 minutes.

3. Place a strainer over a large bowl and strain soup. Transfer solids to work bowl fitted with metal blade and add 1 cup (250 mL) of the liquid. Purée until smooth. Return puréed solids to saucepan and stir in remaining liquid. Reheat. To serve, ladle into warm bowls, drizzle with cream, if using, and garnish with cilantro.

Leek and Celery Soup with Stilton

Serves 6

Vegetarian Friendly

This is an elegant soup with a delicate celery flavor. The in-your-face finish — robust Stilton cheese — makes a wonderful combination. This is a special occasion soup and the recipe can easily be doubled or tripled.

Tips

Because leeks can be gritty, it is customary to slice and rinse them before using. *To clean leeks:* Fill a sink full of lukewarm water. Split the leeks in half lengthwise and submerge in the water, swishing them around to remove all traces of dirt. Transfer to a colander and rinse thoroughly under cold water.

It's important that the soup be very hot when serving — almost at the boiling point — so the cheese will melt easily when added.

2	leeks, white part with a bit of green, cut to fit feed tube (see Tips, left)	2
8	stalks celery, cut to fit feed tube	8
2 tbsp	butter	30 mL
2 tbsp	all-purpose flour	30 mL
½ tsp	salt	2 mL
¼ tsp	freshly ground white pepper	1 mL
4 cups	chicken or vegetable broth	1 L
½ cup	heavy or whipping (35%) cream	125 mL
4 oz	Stilton, crumbled	125 g

1. In work bowl fitted with slicing blade, slice leeks and celery.

2. In a large saucepan or stockpot over medium heat, melt butter. Add leeks and celery and cook, stirring, until softened, about 5 minutes. Add flour and cook, stirring, for 1 minute. Stir in salt and white pepper. Add broth and cook, stirring, until mixture comes to a boil and thickens slightly. Reduce heat and simmer, stirring occasionally, until vegetables are tender, about 25 minutes.

3. Place a strainer over a large bowl and strain soup. Transfer solids and 1 cup (250 mL) of the liquid to work bowl fitted with metal blade. Purée until smooth. Return strainer to bowl and add puréed solids. Using a wooden spoon, push against solids to extract as much liquid as possible. Return liquid to saucepan and discard solids. Add cream and reheat (see Tips, left). Taste and adjust seasoning.

4. To serve, ladle soup into warm bowls. Divide Stilton equally among bowls and serve immediately.

Creamy Leek Soup with Blue Cheese

Serves 6 to 8

Vegetarian Friendly

This English version of a classic French soup is a quintessential winter dish.

Tip

Because leeks can be gritty, it is customary to slice and rinse them before using. *To clean leeks:* Fill a sink full of lukewarm water. Split the leeks in half lengthwise and submerge in the water, swishing them around to remove all traces of dirt. Transfer to a colander and rinse thoroughly under cold water.

5	leeks, white part with a bit of green, cut to fit feed tube (see Tip, left)	5
1	onion, cut to fit feed tube	1
4	cloves garlic	4
2 tbsp	butter	30 mL
1 tsp	salt	5 mL
¼ tsp	freshly ground black pepper	1 mL
6 cups	chicken or vegetable broth	1.5 L
3 cups	cubed (½ inch/1 cm) peeled potatoes	750 mL
	Heavy or whipping (35%) cream	
8 oz	good blue cheese, such as Gorgonzola, Roquefort, Stilton or Maytag, crumbled	250 g

1. In work bowl fitted with slicing blade, slice leeks, then onion and garlic.

2. In a large saucepan or stockpot over medium heat, melt butter. Add leeks, onion, garlic, salt and pepper and cook, stirring, until vegetables are softened, about 5 minutes. Add broth and potatoes and bring to a boil. Cover, reduce heat to low and simmer until potatoes are tender, about 20 minutes.

3. Place a strainer over a large bowl and strain soup. Transfer solids to work bowl fitted with metal blade and add 1 cup (250 mL) of the liquid. Purée until smooth. Return purée to saucepan and stir in remaining liquid. Reheat. To serve, ladle into warm bowls. Drizzle with cream and top each serving with about 2 heaping tbsp (30 mL) blue cheese. Serve immediately.

Peppery Cream of Turnip Soup

Serves 6 to 8

Vegetarian Friendly

This soup must be made with white turnips — the more pungent yellow rutabagas, although delicious in their own right, would be overwhelming. This amount of hot pepper sauce makes a nicely piquant version — vary the quantity to suit your preference. For an added touch, sprinkle with Garlic Croutons (see below).

Tips

To make acidulated water combine 4 cups (1 L) water with 2 tbsp (30 mL) lemon juice. Drain turnips and potatoes before adding to soup.

Garlic Croutons: Preheat oven to 375°F (190°C). In a small bowl, combine 2 tbsp (30 mL) olive oil and 1 clove finely minced garlic. Place 2 cups (500 mL) cubed (¼ inch/0.5 cm) crustless white bread in a large bowl. Pour olive-oil mixture over cubes and toss to combine. Arrange bread on a baking sheet in a single layer. Toast until golden, turning once, about 10 minutes.

2	onions, cut to fit feed tube	2
2	carrots, peeled and cut to fit feed tube	2
8	small white turnips, peeled and cut to fit feed tube (about 6 cups/1.5 L)	8
2	potatoes, peeled and cut to fit feed tube	2
1 tbsp	butter	15 mL
1 tsp	salt	5 mL
½ tsp	freshly grated nutmeg	2 mL
½ tsp	granulated sugar	2 mL
¼ tsp	freshly ground black pepper	1 mL
6 cups	chicken or vegetable broth	1.5 L
1 cup	heavy or whipping (35%) cream	250 mL
1 tsp	hot pepper sauce, such as Tabasco	5 mL
	Finely chopped parsley or chives	
	Garlic Croutons, optional (see Tips, left)	

1. In work bowl fitted with slicing blade, slice onions and carrots. Transfer to a bowl and set aside. Add turnips and potatoes and slice. Transfer to a bowl of acidulated water (see Tips, left).

2. In a large saucepan or stockpot over medium heat, melt butter. Add onions and carrots and cook, stirring, until softened, about 5 minutes. Add salt, nutmeg, sugar and pepper and cook, stirring, for 1 minute. Add drained turnips and potatoes and broth and bring to a boil. Cover, reduce heat to low and simmer until vegetables are tender, about 25 minutes.

3. Place a strainer over a large bowl and strain soup. Transfer solids to work bowl fitted with metal blade and add 1 cup (250 mL) of the liquid. Purée until smooth. Return puréed solids to saucepan and stir in remaining liquid. Stir in cream and hot pepper sauce. Reheat.

4. Ladle soup into warm bowls and garnish with parsley and garlic croutons, if using.

Curried Parsnip Soup with Green Peas

Serves 8

Vegan Friendly

This soup is flavorful and elegant. Complete it with a drizzle of cream, which gives a smooth and sophisticated finish, but if you're averse to that much dairy fat, substitute coconut milk, plain yogurt or a bit of soy creamer.

Tips

To enhance the Asian flavors and expand the range of nutrients you consume, use extra virgin coconut oil for the oil. Its flavors blend very well with the others in this recipe.

For the best flavor, toast and grind cumin and coriander seeds yourself. *To toast cumin and coriander seeds:* In a dry skillet over medium heat, place seeds. Cook, stirring, until fragrant, about 3 minutes. Immediately transfer to a mortar or a spice grinder and grind. Set aside.

If you are using large parsnips in this recipe, cut away the woody core and discard.

1 tbsp	oil (see Tips, left)	15 mL
2	onions, coarsely chopped	2
4	cloves garlic, coarsely chopped	4
2 tsp	curry powder	10 mL
2 tsp	ground cumin (see Tips, left)	10 mL
1 tsp	ground coriander	5 mL
1 tsp	salt	5 mL
½ tsp	cracked black peppercorns	2 mL
1	piece (1 inch/2.5 cm) cinnamon stick	1
1	bay leaf	1
6 cups	chicken or vegetable broth	1.5 L
4 cups	sliced peeled parsnips (about 1 lb/500 g) (see Tips, left)	1 L
2 cups	sweet green peas, thawed if frozen	500 mL
4 tsp	freshly squeezed lemon juice	20 mL
⅓ cup	heavy or whipping (35%) cream or coconut milk, optional	75 mL

1. In a large saucepan or stockpot, heat oil over medium heat. Add onions and cook, stirring, until softened, about 3 minutes. Add garlic, curry powder, cumin, coriander, salt, peppercorns, cinnamon stick and bay leaf and cook, stirring, for 1 minute. Add broth and parsnips and bring to a boil. Cover, reduce heat to low and simmer until parsnips are tender, about 25 minutes. Discard cinnamon stick and bay leaf.

2. Place a strainer over a large bowl and strain soup. Transfer solids to work bowl fitted with metal blade and add 1 cup (250 mL) of the liquid. Purée until smooth. Return puréed solids to saucepan and stir in remaining liquid. Stir in peas and lemon juice. Return to a boil and cook until peas are tender, about 2 minutes. To serve, ladle into warm bowls and drizzle with cream, if using.

Cucumber-Spiked Bean and Potato Soup

Serves 8

Vegan Friendly

With the combination of white beans and potatoes, this soup is quite hearty. Yet the addition of cucumbers and dill add summery lightness. It is equally good hot or cold.

Tip

To prepare the dried beans for this recipe: Bring beans to a boil in 6 cups (1.5 L) water over medium heat. Boil rapidly for 3 minutes. Cover, turn off element and let stand for 1 hour. Drain in a colander placed over a sink and rinse thoroughly under cold running water. Using your hand, pop the beans out of their skins. Discard skins and add beans to recipe.

¾ cup	dried lima beans, soaked and popped out of their skins (see Tip, left)	175 mL
2 tbsp	oil	30 mL
2	onions, coarsely chopped	2
4	cloves garlic, chopped	4
1 tsp	salt	5 mL
½ tsp	cracked white peppercorns	2 mL
2	potatoes, peeled and quartered	2
5 cups	chicken or vegetable broth	1.25 L
2	cucumbers, peeled, seeded and cut into chunks	2
½ cup	fresh dill fronds	125 mL
½ cup	plain yogurt, preferably Greek-style (pressed) or soy yogurt (see Tip, page 114)	125 mL
	Extra virgin olive oil	

1. In a large saucepan, heat oil over medium heat. Add onions and cook, stirring, until softened, about 3 minutes. Add garlic, salt and peppercorns and cook, stirring, for 1 minute. Add beans, potatoes and broth and bring to a boil. Cover, reduce heat to low and simmer until potatoes and beans are tender, about 30 minutes.

2. In work bowl fitted with metal blade, combine cucumbers and dill. Place a strainer over a large bowl and strain soup. Transfer solids to work bowl containing cucumbers and dill and add 1 cup (250 mL) of the liquid. Purée until smooth. Return puréed solids to saucepan and stir in remaining liquid. Simmer over medium heat to blend flavors, about 5 minutes. Taste and adjust seasoning. Serve hot or chill thoroughly, for at least 3 hours or for up to 3 days. To serve, ladle into bowls, top with yogurt and drizzle with olive oil.

Creamy Onion Soup with Kale

**Vegan Friendly
(see Tips, below)**

There is no cream in this delicious soup — unless you decide to drizzle a bit over individual servings. The creaminess is achieved with the addition of potatoes, which are puréed into the soup, providing it with a velvety texture.

Tips

If you are making this soup for vegans, omit bacon and heat 1 tbsp (15 mL) vegetable oil in a large saucepan or stockpot over medium heat for 30 seconds. Add onions and garlic and continue with the recipe.

You can use any kind of paprika in this recipe: Regular, hot, which produces a nicely peppery version, or smoked, which adds a delicious note of smokiness to the soup. If you have regular paprika and would like a bit a heat, dissolve ¼ tsp (1 mL) cayenne pepper in the lemon juice along with the paprika.

4	onions, cut to fit feed tube	4
2	cloves garlic	2
4	slices bacon, optional (see Tips, left)	4
1 tsp	grated lemon zest	5 mL
½ tsp	cracked black peppercorns	2 mL
1	bay leaf	1
4	whole allspice	4
5 cups	chicken or vegetable broth	1.25 L
3	medium potatoes, peeled and quartered	3
1 tsp	paprika, dissolved in 2 tbsp (25 mL) lemon juice (see Tips, left)	5 mL
4 cups	chopped kale	1 L

1. In work bowl fitted with slicing blade, slice onions and garlic. Set aside.

2. In a skillet, cook bacon, if using, over medium-high heat until crisp. Drain on paper towel and crumble. Cover and refrigerate until ready to use. Scoop out 2 tbsp (30 mL) fat from pan and transfer to a large saucepan or stockpot.

3. Place saucepan over medium heat. Add onions and garlic to saucepan and cook, stirring, until softened, about 5 minutes. Add lemon zest, peppercorns, bay leaf and allspice and cook, stirring, for 1 minute. Add broth and potatoes and stir well. Cover and bring to a boil. Reduce heat and simmer until potatoes are tender, about 20 minutes. Discard bay leaf and allspice. Stir in paprika solution and kale. Cover and cook until kale is tender, about 10 minutes.

4. Place a strainer over a large bowl and strain soup. Transfer solids to work bowl fitted with metal blade and add 1 cup (250 mL) of the liquid. Purée until smooth. Return puréed solids to saucepan and stir in remaining liquid. Add reserved bacon, if using. Reheat. To serve, ladle into warm bowls.

Ginger Chile Sweet Potato Soup

Vegetarian Friendly

This delicious soup features an intriguing combination of flavors. Hearty yet elegant, it makes a great prelude to a meal or a light dinner accompanied by salad.

Tips

Use the chile powder you prefer. This recipe was tested with Mexican chile powder, which is blended with other spices such as cumin and oregano. But you could use a pure ground chile powder made from New Mexico or ancho chiles for a slightly different result. All will be delicious.

Use a drained bottled roasted red pepper or roast and peel your own (see Tips, page 143).

1 tbsp	oil	15 mL
1	onion, coarsely chopped	1
4	cloves garlic, chopped	4
1 tbsp	minced gingerroot	15 mL
1 tbsp	chile powder (see Tips, left)	15 mL
½ tsp	salt	2 mL
	Freshly ground black pepper	
4 cups	chicken or vegetable broth	1 L
1	large sweet potato, peeled and cubed	1
1 cup	corn kernels or thawed if frozen	250 mL
1	roasted red pepper, chopped (see Tips, page 147)	1
1 tbsp	freshly squeezed lemon juice	15 mL

1. In a large saucepan or stockpot, heat oil over medium heat. Add onion and cook, stirring, until softened, about 3 minutes. Add garlic, ginger, chili powder, salt, and pepper to taste, and cook, stirring, for 1 minute. Add broth and sweet potato. Bring to a boil. Reduce heat to low and simmer until sweet potato is almost tender, about 15 minutes. Add corn and simmer until potatoes are tender, about 10 minutes. Stir in red pepper.

2. Place a strainer over a large bowl and strain soup. Transfer solids to work bowl fitted with metal blade and add 1 cup (250 mL) of the liquid. Purée until smooth. Return puréed solids to saucepan and stir in lemon juice. Reheat. Ladle into warm bowls and serve immediately.

Santa Fe Sweet Potato Soup

Vegetarian Friendly

Here's a flavorful, rib-sticking soup with lots of pizzazz and universal appeal. New Mexico chiles add an enticing, slightly smoky flavor, but ancho or guajillo chiles also work well. The lime, roasted red pepper and cilantro finish provides a nice balance to the sweet potatoes. If you are a heat seeker, add the jalapeño pepper.

Tips

Use drained bottled roasted red peppers or roast your own.

To roast peppers: Preheat oven to 400°F (200°C). Place pepper(s) on a baking sheet and roast, turning two or three times, until skin on all sides is blackened, about 25 minutes. Transfer pepper(s) to a heatproof bowl. Cover with a plate and let stand until cool. Remove and, using a sharp knife, lift skins off. Discard skins and slice according to recipe instructions.

2	dried New Mexico, ancho or guajillo chile peppers	2
2 cups	boiling water	500 mL
1 tbsp	oil	15 mL
2	onions, coarsely chopped	2
4	cloves garlic, chopped	4
1 tsp	salt	5 mL
1 tsp	dried oregano	5 mL
6 cups	chicken or vegetable broth	1.5 L
4 cups	cubed (about $\frac{1}{2}$ inch/1 cm) peeled sweet potatoes	1 L
1	jalapeño pepper, finely chopped, optional	1
2 cups	corn kernels, thawed if frozen	500 mL
1 tsp	grated lime zest	5 mL
2 tbsp	freshly squeezed lime juice	30 mL
2	roasted red peppers, cut into thin strips (see Tip, left)	2
	Finely chopped cilantro	

1. In a heatproof bowl, soak dried chile peppers in boiling water for 30 minutes, weighing down with a cup to ensure they remain submerged. Drain, discarding soaking liquid and stems. Pat dry, chop coarsely and set aside.

2. In a large saucepan or stockpot, heat oil over medium heat. Add onions and cook, stirring, until softened, about 3 minutes. Add garlic, salt and oregano and cook, stirring, for 1 minute. Add broth, sweet potatoes and reserved chile peppers and bring to a boil. Cover, reduce heat to low and simmer until sweet potatoes are tender, about 20 minutes. Add jalapeño pepper, if using.

3. Place a strainer over a large bowl and strain soup. Transfer solids and 1 cup (250 mL) of the liquid to work bowl fitted with metal blade. Purée until smooth. Return puréed solids to saucepan over medium heat and stir in remaining liquid. Add corn and lime zest and juice. Cover and cook until corn is tender, about 10 minutes. When ready to serve, ladle soup into warm bowls and garnish with red pepper strips and cilantro.

Potato Leek Cheese Soup

Vegetarian Friendly

We like to serve this soup in a bread bowl made from the Honey Whole Wheat Sunflower Bread (page 495).

Tips

To store leftover soup, cool first to room temperature and place in an airtight container in the refrigerator for up to 4 days.

Because leeks can be gritty, it is customary to slice and rinse them before using. *To clean leeks:* Fill a sink full of lukewarm water. Split the leeks in half lengthwise and submerge in the water, swishing them around to remove all traces of dirt. Transfer to a colander and rinse thoroughly under cold water.

If you forgot to warm cream prior to use, place in microwave for a few seconds and then use. If the cream is cold and you add it to the hot liquid it may curdle the soup.

8 oz	Monterey Jack cheese, cut into chunks	250 g
2	russet potatoes, peeled and quartered (about 8 oz/250 g)	2
4	leeks, white part with a bit of green, cut to fit feed tube (see Tips, left)	4
1	onion, quartered	1
2	cloves garlic	2
2 tbsp	unsalted butter	30 mL
4 cups	chicken or vegetable broth	1 L
1 cup	heavy or whipping (35%) cream, at room temperature (see Tips, left)	250 mL
¼ tsp	salt	1 mL
¼ tsp	ground white pepper	1 mL

1. In work bowl fitted with shredding blade, shred cheese. Transfer to a bowl. Set aside.

2. Replace shredding blade with slicing blade and slice potatoes. Transfer to another bowl. Set aside.

3. Replace slicing blade with metal blade. Add leeks, onion and garlic and process until finely chopped, about 30 seconds.

4. In a large saucepan over medium heat, melt butter. Add onion mixture and cook, stirring until onion is translucent and leeks are wilted, 8 to 10 minutes. Add broth and bring to a gentle boil. Add cream and stir for a few minutes. Add potatoes and cook until potatoes are fork tender, 15 to 20 minutes. Stir in reserved cheese. Season with salt and white pepper.

Variation

If leeks are out of season or too expensive use 1 large diced sweet onion instead.

Peach Mango Salsa (page 34)

Old World Salsa (page 36)

Spinach and Artichoke Dip (page 41)

Chilli Dilly Eggplant (page 42)

Tuna Tapenade (page 49)

Hearty Cauliflower and
Asparagus Soup (page 128)

Leafy Greens Soup (page 158)

Cabbage Borscht (page 166)

New World Leek and Potato Soup

Serves 8

Vegan Friendly

This soup was christened "new world" because it's a variation on the classic French leek and potato soup, using sweet potatoes and peppers, two ingredients that Christopher Columbus introduced to Europe during his explorations of the Americas. Serve small quantities as a prelude to a celebratory meal, or add whole-grain bread and a tossed green salad for a light supper.

Tips

For the best flavor, toast and grind cumin yourself. *To toast cumin:* In a dry skillet over medium heat, cook cumin seeds, stirring, until fragrant and they just begin to brown, about 3 minutes. Immediately transfer to a mortar or a spice grinder and grind.

If you prefer, use one red and one green bell pepper.

2 lbs	sweet potatoes, peeled and cut to fit feed tube (about 3 potatoes)	1 kg
4	large leeks, white part with a bit of green, cut to fit feed tube (see Tips, page 144)	4
4	cloves garlic	4
1 tbsp	olive oil	15 mL
1 tbsp	ground cumin (see Tips, left)	15 mL
1 tsp	salt	5 mL
1/2 tsp	cracked black peppercorns	2 mL
6 cups	chicken or vegetable broth	1.5 L
2	green bell peppers, seeded and quartered (see Tips, left)	2
1	long red chile pepper, coarsely chopped, optional	1
	Salt, optional	
1/2 cup	heavy or whipping (35%) cream or soy creamer	125 mL
	Roasted red pepper strips, optional	
	Finely snipped chives	

1. In work bowl fitted with slicing blade, slice sweet potatoes. Transfer to a bowl and set aside. Slice leeks and garlic.

2. In a large saucepan or stockpot, heat oil over medium heat. Add leeks and garlic and cook, stirring, until softened, about 5 minutes. Add cumin, salt and peppercorns and cook, stirring, for 1 minute. Add sweet potatoes and broth and bring to a boil. Cover, reduce heat to low and simmer until sweet potatoes are almost tender, about 20 minutes.

3. Meanwhile, replace slicing blade with metal blade. Add green peppers, and chile pepper, if using, to work bowl. Pulse until finely chopped, about 15 times, stopping and scraping down sides of the bowl once or twice. Add to soup. Cover and cook until peppers are tender, about 10 minutes. Add salt to taste, if using.

4. Place a strainer over a large bowl and strain soup. Transfer solids to work bowl fitted with metal blade and add 1 cup (250 mL) of the liquid. Purée until smooth. Return puréed solids to saucepan and stir in remaining liquid. Reheat. To serve, ladle soup into warm bowls, drizzle with cream and garnish with roasted red pepper strips, if using, and chives.

Chipotle-Spiked Butternut Soup with Coconut

Vegan Friendly

Lusciously rich and intriguingly flavored, this soup makes a great starter or the centerpiece of a soup and salad meal.

Tip

For the best flavor, toast and grind cumin yourself. *To toast cumin:* In a dry skillet over medium heat, cook cumin seeds, stirring, until fragrant and they just begin to brown, about 3 minutes. Immediately transfer to a mortar or a spice grinder and grind.

2	onions, cut to fit feed tube	2
2	stalks celery, cut to fit feed tube	2
1	carrot, peeled and cut to fit feed tube	1
4	cloves garlic	4
1 tbsp	oil	15 mL
1 tbsp	ground cumin (see Tip, left)	15 mL
1 tsp	salt	5 mL
½ tsp	cracked black peppercorns	2 mL
½ tsp	ground allspice	2 mL
4 cups	cubed (½ inch/1 cm) butternut squash (about 1 small)	1 L
4 cups	chicken or vegetable broth	1 L
1	chipotle chile in adobo sauce	1
1	can (14 oz/400 mL) coconut milk	1
	Finely chopped parsley or cilantro	

1. In work bowl fitted with slicing blade, slice onions, celery, carrot and garlic.

2. In a large saucepan or stockpot, heat oil over medium heat. Add onions, celery, carrot and garlic and stir well. Cover, reduce heat to low and cook until vegetables are softened, about 10 minutes. Increase heat to medium. Add cumin, salt, peppercorns and allspice and cook, stirring, for 1 minute. Add squash and broth and bring to a boil. Cover, reduce heat to low and simmer until squash is tender, about 25 minutes. Add chipotle pepper.

3. Place a strainer over a large bowl and strain soup. Transfer solids to work bowl fitted with metal blade and add 1 cup (250 mL) of the liquid. Purée until smooth. Return puréed solids to saucepan and stir in remaining liquid. Stir in coconut milk and return to a simmer over low heat. Simmer for 5 minutes to meld flavors. Ladle into warm bowls and garnish with parsley.

Southwestern Corn and Roasted Red Pepper Soup

Vegan Friendly

Although the roots of this soup lie deep in the heart of Tex-Mex cuisine, it is elegant enough for even the most gracious occasion. Hot sourdough bread makes a perfect accompaniment.

Tips

If you don't have fresh rosemary, use an equal quantity of dried.

To roast peppers: Preheat oven to 400°F (200°C). Place pepper(s) on a baking sheet and roast, turning two or three times, until skin on all sides is blackened, about 25 minutes. Transfer pepper(s) to a heatproof bowl. Cover with a plate and let stand until cool. Remove and, using a sharp knife, lift skins off. Discard skins and slice according to recipe instructions.

1	dried New Mexico, ancho or guajillo chile pepper	1
1 cup	boiling water	250 mL
1	jalapeño pepper, seeded	1
6 cups	chicken or vegetable broth, divided	1.5 L
1	large onion	1
6	cloves garlic	6
1 tbsp	oil	15 mL
1 tbsp	ground cumin (see Tip, page 146)	15 mL
1 tbsp	chopped fresh rosemary leaves	15 mL
1	bay leaf	1
1 tsp	salt	5 mL
½ tsp	cracked black peppercorns	2 mL
4 cups	corn kernels, thawed if frozen	1 L
2	roasted red peppers, cut into ½-inch (1 cm) cubes (see Tips, left)	2
½ cup	heavy or whipping (35%) cream or soy creamer	125 mL
	Finely chopped parsley or cilantro	

1. In a heatproof bowl, soak chile pepper in boiling water for 30 minutes, weighing down with a cup to ensure it remains submerged. Drain, discarding soaking liquid and stem and chop coarsely. Transfer to work bowl fitted with metal blade. Add jalapeño pepper and 1 cup (250 mL) of the broth. Purée until smooth. Transfer to a bowl and set aside. In clean work bowl fitted with metal blade, process onion and garlic until finely chopped, about 15 times.

2. In a large saucepan or stockpot, heat oil over medium heat. Add onion and garlic and cook, stirring, until softened, about 3 minutes. Add cumin, rosemary, bay leaf, salt and peppercorns and cook, stirring, for 1 minute. Add corn and remaining 5 cups (1.25 L) broth and bring to a boil. Stir in reconstituted chile mixture. Cover, reduce heat to low and simmer until corn is tender and flavors meld, about 20 minutes.

3. Stir in roasted red peppers and cream. Cover and cook until heated through, about 5 minutes. Discard bay leaf. Spoon into warm bowls and garnish with parsley.

Butternut Apple Soup with Swiss Cheese

Vegan Friendly

Topped with melted cheese, this creamy and delicious soup is an ideal antidote to a blustery day. Serve it as a light main course, accompanied by a green salad and whole-grain bread or as a starter to a more substantial meal.

Tip

If you prefer to use cheese that is already shredded, you'll need 1 cup (250 mL).

1 tbsp	olive oil	15 mL
2	onions, coarsely chopped	2
4	cloves garlic, coarsely chopped	4
2 tsp	dried rosemary, crumbled, or 1 tbsp (15 mL) chopped fresh rosemary leaves	10 mL
½ tsp	cracked black peppercorns	2 mL
5 cups	chicken or vegetable broth	1.25 L
1	butternut squash, peeled and cut into 1-inch (2.5 cm) cubes (about 2½ lbs/1.25 kg)	1
2	tart apples, such as Granny Smith, cored, peeled and coarsely chopped	2
	Salt, optional	
4 oz	Swiss cheese or vegan alternative	125 g
½ cup	finely chopped walnuts, optional	125 mL

1. In a large saucepan or stockpot, heat oil over medium heat. Add onions and cook, stirring, until softened, about 3 minutes. Add garlic, rosemary and peppercorns and cook, stirring, for 1 minute. Add broth, squash and apples and bring to a boil. Cover, reduce heat to low and simmer until squash is tender, about 35 minutes.

2. Preheat broiler. Place a strainer over a large bowl and strain soup. Transfer solids to work bowl fitted with metal blade and add 1 cup (250 mL) of the liquid. Purée until smooth. Return puréed solids to saucepan and stir in remaining liquid. Season to taste with salt, if using.

3. In clean work bowl fitted with shredding blade, shred cheese. Ladle soup into ovenproof bowls. Sprinkle with cheese and broil until cheese is melted, about 2 minutes. (You can also do this in a microwave oven, in batches, on High, about 1 minute per batch.) Sprinkle with walnuts, if using.

New England Clam Chowder

Serves 8

We see so many mixes for clam chowder but it's so easy to make yourself. During the cold months enjoy soup parties. You can serve this and a few other soups with the breads starting on page 482.

Tips

If you can't find salt pork use the same amount of bacon instead.

To store leftover soup, cool first to room temperature and place in an airtight container in the refrigerator for up to 4 days.

6 oz	salt pork, cut into 4 chunks (see Tips, left)	175 g
1	large onion, quartered	1
3	stalks celery, cut to fit feed tube	3
1	large leek, white part with a bit of light green, cut to fit feed tube (see Tips, page 144)	1
2 tbsp	all-purpose flour	30 mL
4 cups	hot water	1 L
1/4 tsp	salt	1 mL
1/4 tsp	ground white pepper	1 mL
1/8 tsp	ground nutmeg	0.5 mL
4 to 6	russet (Idaho) potatoes, peeled (about 1 lb/500 g)	4 to 6
5 cups	milk, at room temperature	1.25 L
1	can (16 oz/454 g) clams, drained	1

1. In work bowl fitted with metal blade, process pork and onion until minced, about 45 seconds. Transfer to a heavy-bottomed saucepan over medium heat. Cook onion mixture, stirring, until softened, about 10 minutes. Skim the fat off the top.

2. Replace metal blade with slicing blade and slice celery and leek. Add to mixture in saucepan and cook, stirring, until softened, 12 to 15 minutes. Sprinkle with flour and cook, stirring to coat vegetables evenly, creating a golden roux, about 3 minutes. Gradually add hot water, stirring well to prevent lumps. Reduce heat to low. Add salt, white pepper and nutmeg and simmer, stirring occasionally, until thickened, about 30 minutes.

3. Meanwhile, in same work bowl, slice potatoes. Add to saucepan and simmer, stirring often, until potatoes are almost tender, about 15 minutes. Add milk and heat thoroughly, 10 to 12 minutes. Do not scorch or let boil. Add clams and heat through. Taste and adjust seasonings.

Variation

Try adding 1 1/2 cups (375 mL) chopped tomatoes (about 8 oz/250 g) and 2 1/2 cups (625 mL) sliced mushrooms (about 8 oz/250 g) to the chowder when you add the clams in Step 3.

Chanterelle Oyster Bisque Soup

The fresh taste of the chanterelle mushrooms and the flavorful oysters in this rich soup will warm you on a cool fall day.

Tips

Make sure your mushrooms are fresh. Purchasing them at your local farmer's market is a good idea.

If chanterelle mushrooms are unavailable or too pricey, use button mushrooms instead.

To store leftover soup, cool first to room temperature and place in an airtight container in the refrigerator for up to 4 days.

½	shallot	½
1	stalk celery, cut into 3-inch (7.5 cm) lengths	1
1 lb	chanterelle mushrooms, trimmed (see Tips, left)	500 g
2 tbsp	olive oil	30 mL
1 tsp	dried oregano	5 mL
1 tsp	dried basil	5 mL
1 tsp	dried thyme	5 mL
2 cups	chicken broth	500 mL
2 cups	heavy or whipping (35%) cream, at room temperature	500 mL
1	can (12 oz/375 g) chopped oysters, drained	1
Pinch	salt	Pinch
Pinch	ground white pepper	Pinch

1. In work bowl fitted with metal blade, process shallot and celery until finely chopped. Add mushrooms and pulse until coarsely chopped, about 15 times, stopping and scraping down sides of the bowl once or twice.

2. In a saucepan, heat oil over medium heat. Add mushroom mixture and cook, stirring, until mushrooms are tender, 6 to 8 minutes. Add oregano, basil and thyme and cook, stirring for 10 minutes. Add chicken broth and simmer for 3 minutes.

3. Place a strainer over a large bowl and strain soup. Transfer solids to work bowl fitted with metal blade and add 1 cup (250 mL) of the liquid. Purée until smooth. Return purée to the saucepan over medium heat and stir in remaining liquid. Stir in cream and oysters and heat through. Add salt and white pepper. Serve hot.

Pumpkin Soup with Shrimp and Lime

Serves 6 to 8

This soup, which is delicious hot or cold, has its origins in both French provincial and Latin American cuisine. If pumpkin is unavailable, substitute any orange-fleshed squash, such as acorn or butternut.

Tips

Because leeks can be gritty, it is customary to slice and rinse them before using. *To clean leeks:* Fill a sink full of lukewarm water. Split the leeks in half lengthwise and submerge in the water, swishing them around to remove all traces of dirt. Transfer to a colander and rinse thoroughly under cold water.

If you prefer, use drained canned shrimp. You'll need 2 cans (each 3¾ oz/106 g), rinsed and drained.

If using pumpkin seeds, pan-fry in a dry, hot skillet over medium heat until they are lightly browned and puffed. When purchasing pumpkin seeds, taste first because they tend to go rancid quickly. Store in the freezer until ready to use.

3	leeks, white part only, with a bit of green, cut to fit feed tube (see Tips, left)	3
1 tbsp	oil	15 mL
1 tsp	salt	5 mL
½ tsp	cracked black peppercorns	2 mL
6 cups	cubed (2 inch/5 cm) peeled pie pumpkin	1.5 L
5 cups	chicken or vegetable broth	1.25 L
	Grated zest and juice of 1 lime	
⅛ tsp	cayenne pepper	0.5 mL
½ cup	heavy or whipping (35%) cream	125 mL
8 oz	cooked salad shrimp (see Tips, left)	250 g
6 to 8	cherry tomatoes, halved	6 to 8
2 tbsp	toasted pumpkin seeds, optional (see Tips, left)	30 mL
	Finely chopped chives or cilantro	

1. In work bowl fitted with slicing blade, slice leeks.

2. In a large saucepan or stockpot, heat oil over medium heat. Add leeks and cook, stirring, until softened, about 5 minutes. Add salt and peppercorns and cook, stirring, for 1 minute. Add pumpkin and broth and bring to a boil. Cover, reduce heat to low and simmer until pumpkin is tender, about 35 minutes.

3. Place a strainer over a large bowl and strain soup. Transfer solids to work bowl fitted with metal blade and add 1 cup (250 mL) of the liquid. Purée until smooth.

4. If serving hot, return puréed solids to saucepan over low heat and stir in remaining liquid. Stir in lime zest and juice, cayenne, cream and shrimp and simmer for 5 minutes, or until shrimp are heated through. If serving cold, add purée to liquid in bowl along with lime zest and juice, cayenne, cream and shrimp and chill thoroughly, for at least 3 hours.

5. When ready to serve, ladle soup into individual bowls and garnish with cherry tomatoes, pumpkin seeds, if using, and chives.

Thai-Style Pumpkin Soup

Serves 8

Vegan Friendly

This soup is both versatile and delicious. It has an exotic combination of flavors and works well as a prelude to a meal. If you prefer a more substantial soup, top each serving with cooked shrimp or scallops, or add some brown rice (see Variations, below).

Tips

Coconut cream is the thick part of the liquid that accumulates on the top of canned coconut milk. Scoop out the required quantity, then stir the remainder well for use in the soup.

For the best flavor, toast and grind cumin yourself. *To toast cumin:* In a dry skillet over medium heat, cook cumin seeds, stirring, until fragrant and they just begin to brown, about 3 minutes. Immediately transfer to a mortar or a spice grinder and grind.

1 tbsp	oil or coconut oil	15 mL
2	onions, chopped	2
4	cloves garlic, chopped	4
2 tbsp	minced gingerroot	30 mL
1 tbsp	ground cumin (see Tips, left)	15 mL
1 tsp	cracked black peppercorns	5 mL
2	stalks lemongrass, trimmed, smashed and cut in half crosswise	2
8 cups	cubed (2 inch/5 cm) peeled pie pumpkin or other orange squash	2 L
6 cups	chicken or vegetable broth	1.5 L
1 cup	coconut milk	250 mL
1 tsp	Thai red curry paste	5 mL
	Finely grated zest and juice of 1 lime	
¼ cup	toasted pumpkin seeds, optional	60 mL
	Finely chopped cilantro	

1. In a large saucepan or stockpot, heat oil over medium heat. Add onions and cook, stirring, until softened, about 3 minutes. Add garlic, ginger, cumin, peppercorns and lemongrass and cook, stirring, for 1 minute. Add pumpkin and broth and bring to a boil. Cover, reduce heat to low and simmer until pumpkin is fork-tender, about 20 minutes

2. Skim off 1 tbsp (15 mL) of the coconut cream (see Tip, left). In a small bowl, combine with curry paste and blend well. Add to saucepan along with remaining coconut milk and lime zest and juice. Cover and cook until flavors meld, about 20 minutes. Remove and discard lemongrass.

3. Place a strainer over a large bowl and strain soup. Transfer solids and 1 cup (250 mL) of liquid to work bowl fitted with metal blade. Purée until smooth. Return to saucepan and stir in remaining liquid. Reheat. Ladle into warm bowls, and garnish with pumpkin seeds, if using, and cilantro.

Variation

Add ½ cup (125 mL) brown rice, rinsed, along with the pumpkin. Increase cooking time in Step 1 by 20 minutes. Finish soup with a topping of cooked salad shrimp or scallops (about 1 pound/500 g). Pat scallops dry, cut into quarters and dust with 1 tsp (5 mL) of your favorite chili powder. Sauté in 1 tbsp (15 mL) oil, in 2 batches, for about 1½ minutes per side.

Roasted Pecan Pumpkin Soup

Vegetarian Friendly

When you have too much fresh pumpkin leftover and are tired of making pies, try this creamy and nutty soup.

Tips

If cream is not at room temperature it may curdle when you add it to the soup.

To store leftover soup, cool first to room temperature and place in an airtight container in the refrigerator for up to 4 days.

1	onion, quartered	1
½ cup	pecan halves	125 mL
1	clove garlic	1
6 cups	chicken or vegetable broth	1.5 L
2¼ cups	Pumpkin Purée (page 472) or canned pumpkin purée (not pie filling)	550 mL
1½ tsp	salt	7 mL
½ tsp	dried thyme	2 mL
½ tsp	ground white pepper	2 mL
½ cup	heavy or whipping (35%) cream, at room temperature (see Tips, left)	125 mL
8	Italian flat-leaf parsley sprigs	8

1. In work bowl fitted with metal blade, process onion, pecans and garlic until finely chopped.

2. Transfer mixture to a large saucepan over medium heat and cook, stirring, until onions are translucent and pecans are light brown, 5 to 8 minutes. Add broth, pumpkin purée, salt, thyme and white pepper. Bring to a simmer. Reduce heat to low and simmer for 20 minutes. Stir in cream. Ladle into warm bowls and garnish with parsley sprigs.

Variation

Use pine nuts in place of pecans but keep them whole and don't process.

Ribollita

Serves 6 as a main course or 8 as a starter

Vegetarian Friendly

Originally intended as a method for using up leftover minestrone — hence the name *ribollita*, which means "twice cooked" — this hearty Italian soup has acquired an illustrious reputation of its own. The distinguishing ingredient is country-style bread, which is added to the soup and cooked in the broth. Drizzled with olive oil and sprinkled with grated Parmesan cheese, this makes a satisfying light meal or tasty starter to an Italian-themed dinner.

Tips

For this quantity of beans, use 1 can (14 to 19 oz/398 to 540 mL) white kidney (cannellini) beans, drained and rinsed, or cook 1 cup (250 mL) dried beans.

If you can't find Swiss chard, use an equal quantity of spinach. Be sure to wash Swiss chard thoroughly like spinach (see Tips, page 158).

2	onions, quartered	2
2	carrots, peeled and cut into 3-inch (7.5 cm) lengths	2
2	stalks celery, cut into 3-inch (7.5 cm) lengths	2
4	cloves garlic, chopped	4
1/2 cup	Italian flat-leaf parsley leaves	125 mL
2 cups	drained cooked white kidney (cannellini) beans (see Tips, left)	500 mL
5 cups	chicken or vegetable broth, divided	1.25 L
1 tbsp	oil	15 mL
1 tbsp	grated lemon zest	15 mL
1 tsp	finely chopped fresh rosemary leaves or dried rosemary, crumbled	5 mL
1 tsp	salt	5 mL
1/2 tsp	cracked black peppercorns	2 mL
2	potatoes, peeled and cut into 1/2-inch (1 cm) cubes	2
4 cups	packed torn Swiss chard leaves (about 1 bunch) (see Tips, left)	1 L
1	long red chile pepper, minced, optional	1
3	thick slices day-old country-style bread	3
	Extra virgin olive oil	
	Freshly grated Parmesan cheese	

1. In work bowl fitted with metal blade, pulse onions, carrots, celery, garlic and parsley until finely chopped, about 15 times, stopping and scraping down sides of the bowl once. Transfer to a bowl and set aside.

2. In same work bowl, purée beans with 1 cup (250 mL) of the broth until smooth. Set aside.

3. In a large saucepan or stockpot, heat oil over medium heat. Add onion mixture and cook, stirring, until carrots are softened, about 7 minutes. Add lemon zest, rosemary, salt and peppercorns and cook, stirring, for 1 minute. Add bean mixture, potatoes and remaining 4 cups (1 L) broth and bring to a boil. Cover, reduce heat to low and simmer until potatoes are tender, about 25 minutes.

4. Stir in Swiss chard, chile pepper, if using, and bread. Cover and cook until chard is tender, about 8 minutes.

5. Ladle into warm bowls, breaking bread into pieces over top. Drizzle with olive oil and sprinkle with Parmesan.

Caldo Verde

Serves 8

Vegan Friendly

This soup, which is Portuguese in origin, is usually made with white beans and kale. This version, which uses chickpeas and collard greens, is equally delicious and also lends itself to many adaptations. If you can't find collards, use kale, and feel free to substitute white beans for the chickpeas.

Tips

For this quantity of chickpeas, use 1 can (14 to 19 oz/398 to 540 mL) drained and rinsed or cook 1 cup (250 mL) dried chickpeas.

Shred collard greens as if you were making a chiffonade of basil leaves. Remove the stems, including the thick vein that runs up the bottom of the leaf and thoroughly wash the leaves by swishing them around in a sink full of warm water. On a cutting board, stack the leaves, 2 or 3 at a time. Roll them into a cigar shape and slice as thinly as you can.

2	onions, quartered	2
2	carrots, peeled and cut into 3-inch (7.5 cm) lengths	2
2	cloves garlic, minced	2
1 tbsp	olive oil	15 mL
1 tsp	ground cumin (see Tips, page 152)	5 mL
1 tsp	salt	5 mL
½ tsp	cracked black peppercorns	2 mL
2 cups	cooked chickpeas, drained and rinsed (see Tips, left)	500 mL
2	potatoes, peeled and cut into cubes	2
6 cups	chicken or vegetable broth	1.5 L
2 tsp	paprika, dissolved in 2 tbsp (30 mL) lemon juice	10 mL
4 cups	shredded collard greens (about one 12 oz/375 g bunch) (see Tips, left)	1 L
4 oz	cooked smoked sausage, such as cured chorizo or kielbasa, sliced and chopped into bite-size pieces, optional	125 g
	Red wine vinegar, optional	

1. In work bowl fitted with metal blade, pulse onions, carrots and garlic until finely chopped, about 15 times, stopping and scraping down sides of the bowl once or twice.

2. In a large saucepan or stockpot, heat oil over medium heat. Add onion mixture and cook, stirring, until carrots are softened, about 7 minutes. Add cumin, salt and peppercorns and cook, stirring, for 1 minute. Add chickpeas, potatoes and broth and bring to a boil. Cover, reduce heat to low and simmer until potatoes are tender, about 20 minutes.

3. Place a strainer over a large bowl and strain soup. Transfer solids to work bowl fitted with metal blade and add 1 cup (250 mL) of the liquid. Purée until smooth. Return puréed solids to saucepan over medium heat and stir in remaining liquid. Stir in paprika mixture. Add collards, in batches, stirring each to submerge before adding the next batch. Add sausage, if using. Cover and bring to a boil. Reduce heat and simmer until collards are tender, about 20 minutes. Season with vinegar to taste, if using.

Pasta e Fagioli

Serves 8

This delicious Italian soup is great winter fare. For a stick-to-your ribs meal, serve with hot whole-grain rolls.

Tips

For this quantity of beans, soak and cook 1 cup (250 mL) dried beans or use 1 can (14 to 19 oz/398 to 540 mL) white kidney (cannellini) beans, drained and rinsed.

If you have a leftover boot (the tough outer rind) of Parmesan in the fridge add it to the soup along with the stock. It will add pleasant creaminess.

Three chiles add a pleasant hint of heat to the soup. Use more if you are a heat seeker.

If you don't have fresh rosemary, use ½ tsp (5 mL) dried.

2 cups	drained cooked white kidney (cannellini) beans, divided	500 mL
4 oz	chunk pancetta, coarsely chopped	125 g
2	onions, quartered	2
2	each carrots and celery stalks, peeled and cut into 3-inch (7.5 cm) lengths	2
2	cloves garlic, coarsely chopped	2
1 tbsp	olive oil	15 mL
1	sprig fresh rosemary	1
1 tsp	dried oregano	5 mL
½ tsp	cracked black peppercorns	2 mL
3	dried red chile peppers (approx.)	3
2	bay leaves	2
6 cups	chicken broth	1.5 L
1	can (28 oz/796 mL) diced tomatoes with juice	1
1 cup	tiny pasta, such as ditalini or orzo	250 mL
1 tbsp	butter, optional	15 mL
½ cup	finely chopped parsley leaves	125 mL
	Freshly grated Parmesan cheese	
	Extra virgin olive oil	

1. In work bowl fitted with metal blade, pulse 1 cup (250 mL) of the beans until mashed, about 5 times. Transfer to a bowl and set aside. In same work bowl, pulse pancetta, onions, carrots, celery and garlic until finely chopped, about 15 times.

2. In a stockpot or large saucepan, heat oil over medium heat. Add pancetta mixture and stir well. Cover, reduce heat to low and cook until vegetables are soft and pancetta has rendered most of its fat, about 10 minutes. Add rosemary, oregano, peppercorns, chile peppers and bay leaves and cook, stirring, for 1 minute. Add broth, tomatoes with juice, remaining 1 cup (250 mL) whole beans and mashed beans and bring to a boil. Cover, reduce heat to low and simmer until vegetables are tender and flavors meld, about 20 minutes.

3. Meanwhile, in a large pot of boiling salted water, cook pasta until al dente. Drain well, toss with butter, if using, and stir into soup. Remove and discard bay leaves and chile peppers. To serve, ladle into warm bowls, garnish with parsley, Parmesan and a drizzle of olive oil.

Wheat Berry Minestrone

Serves 6

Vegan Friendly

Here's a hearty meal-in-a-bowl that makes a delicious lunch or light supper any time of the year. Serve this soup for supper, accompanied by whole-grain bread and a simple green salad.

Tips

Puréeing the beans with some of the broth gives this soup a creamy texture without the addition of cream.

For this quantity of beans, use 1 can (14 to 19 oz/ 398 to 540 mL) drained and rinsed, or cook 1 cup (250 mL) dried beans.

For enhanced flavor, if you have a boot of Parmesan, the tough rind that is left over from a whole piece, add it to the soup along with the tomatoes.

To make crostini: Brush 8 to 10 baguette slices with olive oil on both sides. Toast under preheated broiler, turning once, until golden, about 2 minutes per side.

2	onions, quartered	2
4	stalks celery, cut into 3-inch (7.5 cm) lengths	4
4	cloves garlic, chopped	4
1 tbsp	oil	15 mL
2 tsp	dried Italian seasoning	10 mL
1 tsp	salt	5 mL
¼ tsp	cayenne pepper	1 mL
2 cups	drained cooked white kidney beans (see Tips, left)	500 mL
4 cups	chicken or vegetable broth, divided	1 L
1 cup	wheat, spelt or Kamut berries, rinsed and drained	250 mL
1	can (14 oz/398 mL) diced tomatoes with juice	1
8 cups	coarsely chopped trimmed kale or Swiss chard (see Tips, page 158)	2 L
	Salt and freshly ground black pepper	
	Crostini, optional (see Tips, left)	
	Freshly grated Parmesan cheese or vegan alternative, optional	
	Extra virgin olive oil	

1. In work bowl fitted with metal blade, pulse onions, celery and garlic until finely chopped, about 15 times. In a large saucepan or stockpot, heat oil over medium heat. Add onion mixture and cook, stirring, until vegetables are softened, about 5 minutes. Add Italian seasoning, salt and cayenne and cook, stirring, for 1 minute.

2. Meanwhile, in same work bowl, purée beans with 1 cup (250 mL) of the broth until smooth. Add to saucepan along with wheat berries, tomatoes with juice, 2 cups (500 mL) water and remaining 3 cups (750 mL) of the broth and bring to a boil.

3. Cover, reduce heat to low and simmer until wheat berries are almost tender, about 1 hour. Stir in kale. Cover and cook until kale and wheat berries are tender, about 15 minutes. Season with salt and pepper to taste.

4. When ready to serve, ladle soup into warm bowls. Float 1 or 2 crostini in each bowl, if using. Sprinkle liberally with Parmesan, if using, and drizzle with olive oil.

Leafy Greens Soup

Serves 8

Vegan Friendly

This delicious country-style soup is French in origin and based on the classic combination of leeks and potatoes, with the addition of healthful leafy greens.

Tips

Sorrel is available from specialty greengrocers or at farmers' markets during the summer, but if you're unsuccessful in locating it, arugula or parsley also work well in this recipe.

When using leafy greens, such as kale or Swiss chard, be sure to remove the tough stems before chopping. Also, since they can be quite gritty, pay extra attention when washing. Swish the leaves around in a basin of lukewarm water to remove any grit, then rinse thoroughly under cold running water before using.

6	small leeks, white with a bit of green, cut to fit feed tube (see Tips, page 160)	6
4	cloves garlic	4
1 tbsp	butter or olive oil	15 mL
1 tbsp	olive oil	15 mL
1 tsp	salt	5 mL
1 tsp	dried tarragon	5 mL
½ tsp	cracked black peppercorns	2 mL
6 cups	chicken or vegetable broth	1.5 L
3	medium potatoes, peeled and cut into ½-inch (1 cm) cubes	3
4 cups	packed torn Swiss chard leaves (about 1 bunch) (see Tips, left)	1 L
1 cup	packed torn sorrel, arugula or parsley leaves	250 mL
	Heavy or whipping (35%) cream, optional	
	Garlic Croutons (page 138), optional	

1. In work bowl fitted with slicing blade, slice leeks, then garlic.

2. In a large saucepan or stockpot over medium heat, melt butter and olive oil. Add leeks and cook, stirring, until softened, about 5 minutes. Add garlic, salt, tarragon and peppercorns and cook, stirring, for 1 minute. Add broth and potatoes and bring to a boil.

3. Cover, reduce heat to low and simmer until potatoes are tender, about 20 minutes. Add Swiss chard and sorrel, in batches, stirring after each to submerge the leaves in the liquid. Cover and cook until greens are tender, about 10 minutes.

4. Place a strainer over a large bowl and strain soup. Transfer solids to work bowl fitted with metal blade and add 1 cup (250 mL) of the liquid. Purée until smooth. Return puréed solids to saucepan and stir in remaining liquid. Reheat. Ladle into warm bowls and drizzle with cream and/or top with croutons, if using.

Roasted Tomato Parmesan Soup

Vegetarian Friendly

The fresh flavors of ripe tomatoes and rich Parmesan cheese will make you feel as though you are in the hills of Tuscany.

Tips

Make sure the tomatoes are fully blistered and steamed so you can remove the skins easily.

To store leftover soup, cool first to room temperature and place in an airtight container in the refrigerator for up to 4 days.

- Preheat broiler
- Baking sheet, lined with parchment paper

6 oz	Parmesan cheese, cut into chunks	175 g
½ cup	loosely packed fresh basil	125 mL
1½ lbs	Roma (plum) tomatoes (10 to 14 tomatoes)	750 g
2 tbsp	unsalted butter	30 mL
2 tbsp	all-purpose flour	30 mL
2 cups	milk, at room temperature, divided	500 mL
2 cups	heavy or whipping (35%) cream, at room temperature	500 mL
¼ tsp	ground white pepper	1 mL
Pinch	salt	Pinch

1. In work bowl fitted with metal blade, with motor running, add Parmesan cheese through feed tube and process until finely grated. Transfer to a small bowl. Set aside.

2. In same work bowl, pulse basil until finally chopped, 8 to 10 times. Transfer to another bowl. Set aside.

3. Cut tomatoes in half crosswise and core. Squeeze seeds and membranes out. Place on prepared baking sheet, skin side up. Broil in preheated oven until skins blister, about 10 minutes. Transfer to a plastic bag and let stand to steam, about 10 minutes. Peel off charred skins and discard. Set tomatoes aside.

4. In a large saucepan over medium heat, melt butter. Add flour and cook, stirring, until a thick paste forms but does not brown. Whisk in ¼ cup (60 mL) of the milk and cook, whisking constantly, until thickened, about 3 minutes. Whisk in remaining milk and cream. Add tomatoes, basil and half of the Parmesan cheese and heat through. Season with white pepper and salt. Ladle into warm bowls and garnish each bowl with remaining cheese.

Variation
Try using heirloom tomatoes for a different look and taste.

Savory Cheddar Cheese Soup

This hearty meal-in-a-bowl makes a great weeknight dinner or doubles as a starter to a traditional dinner such as roast beef with Yorkshire pudding.

Tips

If you prefer to use cheese that is already shredded, you'll need 3 cups (750 mL).

Because leeks can be gritty, it is customary to slice and rinse them before using. *To clean leeks:* Fill a sink full of lukewarm water. Split the leeks in half lengthwise and submerge in the water, swishing them around to remove all traces of dirt. Transfer to a colander and rinse thoroughly under cold water.

12 oz	Cheddar cheese (see Tips, left)	375 g
1	leek, white part with a bit of green, cleaned and cut into 3-inch (7.5 cm) lengths (see Tips, left)	1
2	medium carrots, peeled and cut into 3-inch (7.5 cm) lengths	2
3	stalks celery, cut into 3-inch (7.5 cm) lengths	3
1 tbsp	butter	15 mL
1 tsp	dry mustard	5 mL
½ tsp	salt	2 mL
½ tsp	freshly ground black pepper	2 mL
2 tbsp	all-purpose flour	30 mL
2	cans (each 10 oz/284 mL) condensed beef consommé (undiluted)	2
3 cups	water	750 mL
1 tbsp	Worcestershire sauce	15 mL
1	bay leaf	1
½ cup	heavy or whipping (35%) cream	125 mL
	Hot pepper sauce to taste, optional	

1. In work bowl fitted with shredding blade, shred cheese. Transfer to a bowl and set aside.

2. Replace shredding blade with metal blade. Add leek, carrots and celery. Pulse until finely chopped, stopping and scraping down sides of the bowl once or twice.

3. In a large saucepan or stockpot over medium heat, melt butter. Add leek, carrots and celery. Reduce heat to low, cover and cook until vegetables are softened, about 10 minutes. Add dry mustard, salt, pepper and flour and cook, stirring, for 1 minute. Increase heat to medium. Stir in consommé, water, Worcestershire sauce and bay leaf and bring to a boil. Cover, reduce heat to low and simmer until vegetables are very tender and flavors have melded, about 20 minutes. Discard bay leaf.

4. Place a strainer over a large bowl and strain soup. Transfer solids and 1 cup (250 mL) of the liquid to clean work bowl fitted with metal blade. Purée until smooth. Return puréed solids to saucepan over low heat and stir in remaining liquid. Stir in cream. Add cheese, ½ cup (125 mL) at a time, stirring until each batch is melted, being sure not to let the mixture boil. To serve, ladle into warm bowls and pass the hot pepper sauce.

Broccoli and Cheddar Cheese Soup

Serves 4

Vegetarian Friendly

We love the rich Cheddar taste of this hearty soup. Serve smaller portions as a prelude to a traditional roast beef dinner or add a salad and crusty bread for a nutritious light meal.

Tip

If you prefer to use cheese that is already shredded, you'll need 2 cups (500 mL).

1	onion, quartered	1
4	cloves garlic	4
1 tbsp	oil	15 mL
Pinch	cayenne pepper	Pinch
	Freshly ground black pepper	
1	can (10 oz/284 mL) condensed Cheddar cheese soup, undiluted	1
1 tbsp	Dijon mustard	15 mL
3 cups	chicken or vegetable broth	750 mL
4 cups	broccoli florets	1 L
8 oz	Cheddar cheese (see Tip, left)	250 g

1. In work bowl fitted with metal blade, pulse onion and garlic until finely chopped, about 10 times, stopping and scraping down sides of the bowl as necessary.

2. In a large saucepan or stockpot, heat oil over medium heat. Add onion and garlic and cook, stirring, until softened, about 3 minutes. Add cayenne, and black pepper to taste, and cook, stirring, for 1 minute.

3. Add soup and mustard, stirring, until smooth. Gradually stir in broth. Add broccoli and bring to a boil. Reduce heat to low and simmer until broccoli is tender, about 10 minutes.

4. Meanwhile, in clean work bowl fitted with shredding blade, shred cheese. Transfer to a bowl and set aside.

5. Replace shredding blade with metal blade. Place a strainer over a large bowl and strain soup. Transfer solids to work bowl and add 1 cup (250 mL) of the liquid. Purée until smooth. Return puréed solids to saucepan over low heat and stir in remaining liquid. Add reserved cheese, ½ cup (125 mL) at a time, and stir until smooth, being careful not to let the mixture boil. Taste and adjust seasoning. Ladle into warm bowls. Serve piping hot.

Chile Cheddar Soup

Vegetarian Friendly

This delicious and hearty soup is a meal in a bowl. It makes a light weeknight dinner, accompanied by hot crusty rolls and a simple green salad.

Tip

If you prefer to use cheese that is already shredded, you'll need 1 cup (250 mL).

4 oz	Cheddar cheese (see Tip, left)	125 g
2	onions, quartered	2
2	carrots, peeled and cut into 3-inch (7.5 cm) lengths	2
1 tbsp	butter	15 mL
	Freshly ground black pepper	
1	can (10 oz/284 mL) condensed Cheddar cheese soup, undiluted	1
4 cups	chicken or vegetable broth	1 L
1	potato, peeled and cut into chunks	1
1	can (4½ oz/127 mL) mild green chiles, drained	1

1. In work bowl fitted with shredding blade, shred cheese. Transfer to a bowl and set aside.

2. Replace shredding blade with metal blade. Add onions and carrots and pulse until finely chopped, about 15 times, stopping and scraping down sides of the bowl once or twice.

3. In a large saucepan, melt butter over medium heat. Add onion mixture and cook, stirring, until softened, about 5 minutes. Add pepper to taste. Stir in soup until smooth. Gradually add broth, stirring until smooth. Add potato and bring to a boil. Cover, reduce heat to low and simmer until potato is almost tender, about 20 minutes. Add chiles, cover and simmer for 10 minutes to meld flavors.

4. Place a strainer over a large bowl and strain soup. Transfer solids to work bowl and add 1 cup (250 mL) of the liquid. Purée until smooth. Return puréed solids to saucepan over low heat and stir in remaining liquid. Add cheese and cook, stirring, until melted, being careful not to let the mixture boil. Ladle into warm bowls.

French Onion Soup

Serves 6

Vegetarian Friendly

This is a simple soup to make, yet it always seems to cost a great deal in a restaurant.

Tips

You can use a torch similar to one used for crème brûlée instead of the broiler to brown the cheese.

To store leftover soup, after Step 3 cool first to room temperature and place in an airtight container in the refrigerator for up to 4 days. Reheat until steaming before proceeding with Step 4.

12 oz	Monterey Jack cheese, cut into chunks	375 g
3	large sweet onions, quartered	3
¼ cup	unsalted butter	60 mL
2 tbsp	granulated sugar	30 mL
1 tbsp	all-purpose flour	15 mL
2⅔ cups	beef or vegetable broth, divided	650 mL
2 cups	warm water	500 mL
1 tsp	Worcestershire sauce, optional	5 mL
3	drops hot pepper sauce	3
6	slices baguette, toasted	6

1. In work bowl fitted with shredding blade, shred cheese. Transfer to a bowl. Set aside.

2. Replace shredding blade with slicing blade and slice onions. Transfer to another bowl. Set aside.

3. In a saucepan over medium heat, sauté butter and sugar until melted, about 3 minutes. Add onions and cook, stirring occasionally, until tender and just beginning to brown and caramelize, 12 to 18 minutes. Stir in flour. Gradually stir in half of the broth. Bring to a boil, stirring constantly. Stir in remaining broth, water, Worcestershire sauce and hot pepper sauce and bring to a gentle boil. Boil gently for 12 minutes. Reduce heat to low and simmer for 5 minutes. Meanwhile, preheat broiler.

4. Place 1 slice baguette in each of 6 heatproof bowls and pour soup over top. Sprinkle with cheese. Place bowls under preheated boiler until cheese is melted and light brown, 4 to 5 minutes. Serve immediately.

Variation

To make soup spicier, add 1 tsp (5 mL) hot pepper sauce just before serving.

Fennel-Laced Roasted Red Onion Soup with Cheesy Toasts

Serves 6

Vegan Friendly

If you enjoy the taste and textures of French onion soup baked in a blanket of cheese, but prefer something lighter, try this. It has the same onion flavor complemented by a hit of fennel, and offers a nice hit of cheese mitigated by a crostini base.

Tip

Herbes de Provence is a robust mixture of dried herbs such as thyme, fennel and lavender, among others. You can buy it prepackaged, often in pretty little pottery crocks and it is worth having because it is a very flavorful addition to certain recipes. However, if you can't find it you can substitute equal parts dried thyme and lavender with half that amount of fennel seeds.

- Preheat oven to 400°F (200°C)

4	red onions, quartered	4
1	bulb fennel, trimmed, cored and thinly sliced on the vertical	1
6	cloves garlic	6
1 tsp	herbes de Provence (see Tip, left)	5 mL
3 tbsp	olive oil	45 mL
1 tsp	salt	5 mL
	Freshly ground black pepper	
4 cups	chicken or vegetable broth	1 L
1	can (28 oz/796 mL) tomatoes with juice	1
12	slices baguette	12
	Thinly sliced Fontina or vegan melting cheese	

1. In a large bowl, combine red onions, fennel, garlic and herbes de Provence. Add olive oil and toss well. Spread out on baking sheet and roast in preheated oven, stirring once or twice, until lightly browned, about 45 minutes. Sprinkle with salt, and pepper to taste. Transfer to a large saucepan or stockpot.

2. Add broth and tomatoes with juice. Bring to a boil over medium heat. Cover, reduce heat to low and simmer until vegetables are tender, about 20 minutes.

3. Place a strainer over a large bowl and strain soup. Transfer solids to work bowl fitted with metal blade and add 1 cup (250 mL) of the liquid. Purée until smooth. Return puréed solids to saucepan over low heat, stir in remaining liquid and keep warm.

4. Meanwhile, preheat broiler. To make crostini, place baguette slices on a baking sheet and toast under broiler, turning once. Lay cheese slices over top of each and run under broiler until melted. To serve, ladle soup into warm bowls and float 2 crostini on each serving.

Navy Bean Soup

Serves 8

Try making this soup with your leftover ham from a holiday dinner.

Tips

To soak the beans for this recipe: Rinse beans in a colander and sort, discarding any that are blemished. Place in a large saucepan and add 6 cups (1.5 L) fresh cold water. Cover and let stand overnight or bring to a boil over high heat and boil for 3 minutes. Turn off heat and soak for 1 hour. In either case, drain and rinse soaked beans before using.

To store leftover soup, cool first to room temperature and place in an airtight container in the refrigerator for up to 4 days.

2 cups	dried navy beans, soaked and drained (see Tips, left)	500 mL
3	large carrots, peeled and cut into 3-inch (7.5 cm) lengths	3
2	stalks celery, cut into 3-inch (7.5 cm) lengths	2
1	large onion, quartered	1
6 cups	water	1.5 L
8 oz	sliced ham or bacon	250 g
2 tbsp	granulated sugar (approx.)	30 mL
1 tsp	salt	5 mL
1 tsp	ground white pepper	5 mL

1. In work bowl fitted with slicing blade, slice carrots, celery and onion.

2. In a large saucepan over high heat, combine carrot mixture, drained beans and 6 cups (1.5 L) water and bring to a simmer.

3. Replace slicing blade with metal blade. Add ham and pulse until chopped, about 10 times. Add to saucepan. Cover, reduce heat to low and simmer, stirring occasionally, until beans are very tender, about 1½ hours. Add sugar to taste, salt and white pepper.

Variation
Purée half of the cooked beans with the metal blade and then add them back to the stew to create a richer-tasting broth.

Cabbage Borscht

Served with dark rye bread this hearty soup makes a soul-satisfying meal. It has the best flavor when it's made with a combination of beef and vegetable broth, but if you're a vegetarian, vegetable broth works well, too.

Tip

If you're not a vegetarian, you can substitute 2 cups (500 mL) beef broth for an equal quantity of the vegetable broth. You might also like to add chopped kielbasa to the soup bowls before adding the garnishes.

2	onions, quartered	2
4	stalks celery, cut into chunks	4
2	carrots, peeled and cut into chunks	2
4	cloves garlic, chopped	4
1 tbsp	oil	15 mL
1 tsp	caraway seeds	5 mL
1 tsp	salt	5 mL
½ tsp	cracked black peppercorns	2 mL
1	can (28 oz/796 mL) tomatoes with juice, coarsely chopped	1
3	medium beets, peeled and quartered	3
1	potato, peeled and quartered	1
4 cups	vegetable broth (see Tips, left)	1 L
1 tbsp	brown sugar	15 mL
½	head cabbage, cored and cut into wedges	½
1 tbsp	red wine vinegar	15 mL
	Sour cream, optional	
	Finely chopped dill	

1. In work bowl fitted with metal blade, pulse onions, celery, carrots and garlic until finely chopped, about 15 times, stopping and scraping down sides of the bowl once.

2. In a large saucepan or stockpot, heat oil over medium heat. Add onion mixture and cook, stirring, until carrots are softened, about 7 minutes. Add caraway seeds, salt and peppercorns and cook, stirring, for 1 minute. Add tomatoes with juice, beets, potato, broth and brown sugar and bring to a boil. Cover, reduce heat to low and simmer until vegetables are tender, about 40 minutes.

3. Meanwhile, in work bowl fitted with slicing blade, slice cabbage. Set aside.

4. Replace slicing blade with metal blade. Place a strainer over a large bowl and strain soup. Transfer solids to work bowl fitted with metal blade and add 1 cup (250 mL) of the liquid. Purée until smooth. Return purée to saucepan over medium heat and stir in remaining liquid. Add vinegar and cabbage and stir well. Return to a boil. Cover and cook until cabbage is tender, about 10 minutes. To serve, ladle into warm bowls, add a dollop of sour cream, if using, and garnish with dill.

Congee with Chinese Greens and Barbecued Pork

If you live near a Chinatown, where freshly cooked barbecued pork is readily available, this delicious soup is a snap to make. It makes a great weekend lunch. Put the rice on in the morning and it's done by the time you're ready to eat. Just add the pork and Chinese greens and purée the soup.

Tips

Chinese broccoli, also known as *gai lan*, is available in Asian markets. If you can't find it, substitute an equal quantity of shredded bok choy.

Unless you have a stove with a true simmer, after reducing the heat to low we recommend placing a heat diffuser under the pot to prevent the mixture from boiling. This device also helps to ensure the grains will cook evenly and prevents hot spots, which might cause scorching, from forming.

Heat diffusers are available at kitchen supply and hardware stores and are made to work on gas or electric stoves.

4 cups	chicken broth	1 L
4 cups	water	1 L
¾ cup	short-grain brown rice, rinsed and drained	175 mL
4 cups	shredded Chinese broccoli (see Tips, left)	1 L
4 oz	shredded boneless Chinese barbecued pork	125 g
¼ cup	thinly sliced green onions, white part with a bit of green	60 mL
	Chopped fresh chile pepper, optional	
	Soy sauce, optional	

1. In a saucepan, combine broth, water and rice. Bring to a boil over medium-high heat. Reduce heat to low and simmer until rice has almost dissolved and is creamy, about 2½ hours.

2. Add broccoli and cook, stirring, until greens are wilted, about 5 minutes. Place a strainer over a large bowl and strain soup. Transfer solids to work bowl fitted with metal blade and add 1 cup (250 mL) of the liquid. Purée until smooth. Return purée to saucepan over medium heat and stir in remaining liquid. Stir in pork and cook until heated through, about 5 minutes. Garnish with green onions, and chile pepper, if using. Season to taste with soy sauce, if using.

Variation
Duck Congee: Substitute an equal quantity of Chinese barbecued duck for the pork.

Mushroom-Scented Quinoa Congee with Zucchini

Vegan Friendly

Congee is usually a bland rice porridge traditionally served for breakfast in Asia. However, there are many very flavorful versions, which this recipe tries to capture. Serve this congee for Sunday lunch or as a great snack any time of the day.

Tip

We like to use dried portobello, porcini or mixed wild mushrooms in this soup. Although white mushrooms work well, cremini or portobello mushrooms provide a stronger mushroom taste.

1	package (½ oz/14 g) dried mushrooms (see Tip, left)	1
1 cup	hot water	250 mL
1 tbsp	oil	15 mL
2	onions, chopped	2
2	cloves garlic, minced	2
1 tsp	dried oregano leaves, crumbled	5 mL
½ tsp	salt	2 mL
½ tsp	freshly ground black pepper	2 mL
8 oz	fresh mushrooms, chopped (see Tips, left)	250 g
¾ cup	quinoa, rinsed and drained	175 mL
4 cups	cubed (½ inch/1 cm) zucchini	1 L
6 cups	chicken or vegetable broth	1.5 L

1. In a heatproof bowl, soak mushrooms in hot water for 30 minutes. Strain through a coffee filter or a sieve lined with a damp paper towel, reserving liquid. Pat mushrooms dry and chop finely. Set mushrooms and liquid aside separately.

2. In a stockpot or large saucepan, heat oil over medium heat. Add onions and cook, stirring, until softened, about 3 minutes. Add garlic, oregano, salt, pepper and reserved dried mushrooms and cook, stirring, for 1 minute. Add fresh mushrooms and cook, stirring, until well coated with mixture. Add quinoa and cook, stirring until coated. Add zucchini, broth and reserved mushroom soaking liquid and bring to a boil.

3. Reduce heat to low. Cover loosely and simmer until zucchini is tender and quinoa is cooked, about 15 minutes. Remove from heat. Place a strainer over a large bowl and strain soup. Transfer solids to work bowl fitted with metal blade and add 1 cup (250 mL) of the liquid. Purée until smooth. Return puréed solids to saucepan and stir in remaining liquid. Reheat. Serve immediately.

Variation
Mushroom-Scented Millet Congee with Zucchini: Substitute an equal quantity of toasted millet for the quinoa. Cook a bit longer, about 25 minutes.

South American Black Bean Soup

**Serves 4 to 6 as a
main course or
6 to 8 as a starter**

This mouthwatering
combination of black
beans, lime juice and
cilantro with just a
hint of hot pepper is a
favorite one-dish meal.
To jack up the heat, add
a chopped jalapeño
along with the cayenne.
The flavor of this soup
actually improves if it is
allowed to sit overnight
and then reheated.
Garnish with finely
chopped cilantro,
sour cream or salsa.

Tips

For the best flavor,
toast and grind cumin
yourself. *To toast cumin:*
Place seeds in a dry
skillet over medium heat
and cook, stirring, until
fragrant, about 3 minutes.
Immediately transfer to a
mortar or a spice grinder
and grind.

For this quantity of beans,
use 2 cans (each 14 to
19 oz/398 to 540 mL)
drained and rinsed, or
cook 2 cups (500 mL)
dried beans.

6	slices bacon, chopped	6
2	onions, quartered	2
2	stalks celery, cut into chunks	2
2	carrots, peeled and cut into chunks	2
2	cloves garlic, coarsely chopped	2
2 tbsp	ground cumin (see Tips, left)	30 mL
1 tbsp	dried oregano	15 mL
1 tsp	dried thyme	5 mL
1 tsp	salt	5 mL
1 tsp	cracked black peppercorns	5 mL
2 tbsp	tomato paste	30 mL
6 cups	chicken broth	1.5 L
4 cups	drained cooked black beans	1 L
1/3 cup	freshly squeezed lime juice	75 mL
1/4 tsp	cayenne pepper	1 mL
1	jalapeño pepper, chopped, optional	1
	Finely chopped cilantro	
	Sour cream, optional	
	Salsa, optional	

1. In a large saucepan or stockpot, cook bacon over
   medium-high heat until crisp. Drain thoroughly on paper
   towel. Cover and refrigerate until ready to use. Remove
   pot from heat and drain off all but 1 tbsp (15 mL) fat.

2. In work bowl fitted with metal blade, pulse onions, celery,
   carrots and garlic until finely chopped, about 15 times.

3. Return pot to medium heat. Add onion mixture and cook,
   stirring, until vegetables are softened, about 7 minutes.
   Add cumin, oregano, thyme, salt and peppercorns and
   cook, stirring, for 1 minute. Add tomato paste and stir
   to combine thoroughly. Add broth, beans and reserved
   bacon and stir well. Bring to a boil. Cover, reduce heat
   to low and simmer until vegetables are tender, about
   20 minutes. Stir in lime juice, cayenne, and jalapeño, if
   using. Cover and cook until heated through and flavors
   meld, about 10 minutes.

4. Place a strainer over a large bowl and strain soup. Transfer
   solids to work bowl fitted with metal blade and add
   1 cup (250 mL) of the liquid. Purée until smooth. Return
   puréed solids to saucepan and stir in remaining liquid.
   Reheat. To serve, ladle into warm bowls and garnish with
   cilantro, and/or sour cream and/or salsa, if using.

Luscious Avgolemono Soup with Wheat Berries

Serves 6

Vegetarian Friendly

This classic Greek soup, usually made with orzo or white rice, takes on a whole new spin when made with nutrient-packed wheat berries.

Tips

To cook wheat berries: Bring 2½ cups (625 mL) water to a boil in a heavy pot with a tight-fitting lid. Stir in 1 cup (250 mL) rinsed wheat berries and return to a rapid boil over high heat. Reduce heat to low. Cover tightly and simmer until the berries are tender but still a bit chewy, 45 minutes to 1 hour. Remove from heat and let stand, covered, for 5 minutes. Drain off any excess water.

Vary the quantity of lemon juice to suit your taste. The smaller quantity produces a nicely lemony soup. If you really enjoy a strong lemon flavor, choose the larger amount.

Once you've added the egg mixture to the soup, watch carefully to be sure it doesn't boil. Otherwise, you'll have curdled eggs in your soup.

2½ cups	cooked wheat, spelt or Kamut berries (see Tips, left)	625 mL
3	leeks, white with a bit of green, cut to fit feed tube (see Tips, page 160)	3
1 tbsp	olive oil	15 mL
1 tsp	paprika	5 mL
8 cups	chicken or vegetable broth	2 L
½ cup	chopped fresh dill fronds	125 mL
	Shredded cooked chicken, optional	
⅓ to ½ cup	freshly squeezed lemon juice (see Tips, left)	75 to 125 mL
4	egg yolks	4
	Salt and freshly ground black pepper	

1. In work bowl fitted with slicing blade, slice leeks.

2. In a large saucepan or stockpot, heat oil over medium heat. Add leeks and cook, stirring, until softened, about 5 minutes. Add paprika and cook, stirring, for 1 minute. Add cooked wheat berries and broth and bring to a boil. Reduce heat and simmer for 10 minutes to blend flavors.

3. Stir in dill. Place a strainer over a large bowl and strain soup. Transfer solids to work bowl fitted with metal blade and add 1 cup (250 mL) of the liquid. Purée until smooth. Return purée to saucepan over low heat and stir in remaining liquid. Add chicken, if using, and heat until warm.

4. In a small bowl, whisk lemon juice and egg yolks. Gradually beat in 1 cup (250 mL) of the hot broth, whisking constantly. Return to pot and cook, stirring, for 1 minute. Remove from heat (see Tips, left). Season with salt and pepper to taste.

Fennel-Scented Tomato and Wild Rice Soup

Vegan Friendly

If you get cravings for tomatoes, this soup is for you. It's especially welcome in the winter when delicious fresh tomatoes are hard to find. The fennel brings intriguing licorice flavor, which complements the tomatoes, and the wild rice adds texture and nutrients such as dietary fiber.

Tips

Toasting fennel seeds intensifies their flavor. *To toast fennel seeds:* Stir seeds in a dry skillet over medium heat until fragrant, about 3 minutes. Transfer to a mortar or spice grinder and grind.

For a slightly more intense tomato flavor, substitute 2 cans (each 14 oz/398 mL) fire-roasted tomatoes with juice for the crushed tomatoes.

Cooking times for wild rice vary. Expect your grains to be cooked anywhere between 50 minutes to more than 1 hour.

2	leeks, white part with a bit of green, cut to fit feed tube (see Tips, page 160)	2
1	bulb fennel, core and leafy stems discarded, cut to fit feed tube	1
3	cloves garlic	3
1 tbsp	olive oil	15 mL
1 tsp	fennel seeds, toasted and ground (see Tips, left)	5 mL
½ tsp	salt, optional	2 mL
½ tsp	freshly ground black pepper	2 mL
5 cups	chicken or vegetable broth, divided	1.25 L
1	can (28 oz/796 mL) crushed tomatoes (see Tips, left)	1
¾ cup	wild rice, rinsed and drained	175 mL
	Heavy or whipping (35%) cream or soy creamer, optional	
	Finely chopped parsley leaves	

1. In work bowl fitted with slicing blade, slice leeks, then fennel and garlic.

2. In a large saucepan or stockpot, heat oil over medium heat. Add leeks and fennel and cook, stirring, until vegetables are softened, about 7 minutes. Add garlic, fennel seeds, salt, if using, and pepper and cook, stirring, for 1 minute. Stir in 2 cups (500 mL) of the broth and tomatoes.

3. Transfer to work bowl fitted with metal blade. Purée until smooth. Return puréed solids to saucepan over medium heat and stir in remaining liquid, remaining 3 cups (750 mL) of the broth and the wild rice. Bring to a boil. Cover, reduce heat to low and cook until rice is tender and grains have begun to split, about 1 hour. Ladle into bowls, drizzle with cream, if using, and garnish with parsley.

Thai-Inspired Peanut and Wild Rice Soup

Serves 6

Vegetarian Friendly

If your taste buds have grown tired of the same old thing, here's a delightfully different soup to wake them up. With basic flavors that are reminiscent of Thai peanut sauce and the addition of classic North American wild rice, this soup qualifies as fusion cooking. It makes a great lunch, or even a light dinner accompanied by a platter of stir-fried bok choy.

Tip

To cook this quantity of rice: Bring 2 cups (500 mL) of water to a boil. Add ⅔ cup (150 mL) rinsed drained wild rice and return to a boil. Reduce heat to low. Cover and simmer until the kernels begin to burst, 45 to 65 minutes. Remove from heat and let stand, covered, for 10 minutes. Fluff with a fork.

2 cups	cooked wild rice (see Tip, left)	500 mL
2	stalks lemongrass, cut into 3-inch (7.5 cm) lengths	2
4	cloves garlic	4
1	piece (2 inches/5 cm) peeled gingerroot, quartered	1
3	dried red chile peppers	3
2 tbsp	tomato paste	30 mL
6 cups	chicken or vegetable broth, divided	1.5 L
2 cups	unsalted roasted peanuts	500 mL
3 tbsp	rice vinegar	45 mL
2 tbsp	soy sauce	30 mL
1 tbsp	liquid honey	15 mL
	Finely grated zest and juice of 1 lime	
	Finely chopped cilantro	
	Finely chopped fresh chile peppers, optional	

1. In work bowl fitted with metal blade, pulse lemongrass, garlic, ginger, dried chile peppers, tomato paste and 2 cups (500 mL) of broth until finely chopped, about 15 times. Transfer to a large saucepan or stockpot and add remaining broth. Bring to a boil over medium heat. Reduce heat to low. Cover and simmer for 30 minutes. Strain, discarding solids. Return liquid to pot.

2. In clean work bowl fitted with metal blade, process peanuts, rice vinegar, soy sauce, honey and lime zest until mixture is the consistency of chunky peanut butter. Stir into liquid. Add wild rice and bring to a boil over medium heat. Reduce heat to low. Cover and simmer to allow flavors to meld, about 20 minutes. Stir in lime juice. Ladle into warm bowls and garnish with cilantro, and chile peppers, if using.

Poultry

Chicken in Buttermilk Onion Gravy

If you're looking for some down-home comfort food, try this tasty chicken. Served with a mound of steaming mashed potatoes, it's positively divine. For something a little different, try Crêpes Parmentier (page 362) as an accompaniment. Place the chicken and gravy in a deep platter and surround the rim with crêpes.

Tip

We always use Italian flat-leaf parsley because it has so much more flavor than the curly leaf variety. Unless the stems or sprigs are specifically called for, use only the tender leaves.

- Large deep skillet with lid

4	onions, quartered	4
1 tbsp	butter	15 mL
1 tbsp	olive oil	15 mL
3 lbs	skin-on bone-in chicken breasts	1.5 kg
2	cloves garlic, minced	2
1 tsp	salt	5 mL
	Freshly ground black pepper	
1 tsp	dried thyme	5 mL
1	bay leaf	1
¼ cup	all-purpose flour	60 mL
2 cups	chicken broth	500 mL
1 cup	buttermilk	250 mL
½ cup	Italian flat-leaf parsley leaves	125 mL

1. In work bowl fitted with slicing blade, slice onions. Set aside.

2. In a large skillet, heat butter and oil over medium heat. Add chicken, in batches, skin side down, and brown on one side, about 4 minutes per batch. Transfer to a plate as completed and set aside.

3. Add onions and garlic to pan and cook, stirring, until softened and just beginning to turn golden, about 5 minutes. Add salt, pepper to taste, thyme and bay leaf and cook, stirring, for 1 minute. Add flour and cook, stirring, for 1 minute. Add chicken broth, bring to a boil and cook, stirring, until mixture is thickened, about 5 minutes. Return chicken to pan, skin side up. Cover, reduce heat to low and cook until chicken is no longer pink inside, about 40 minutes. Transfer chicken to a warm platter and keep warm.

4. In work bowl fitted with metal blade, pulse buttermilk and parsley until parsley is very finely chopped, about 5 times. Stir into pan and bring to a simmer. Pour over chicken. Serve immediately.

New Orleans Bourbon Chicken

The French quarter of New Orleans is filled with great restaurants. Here's a dish that's served in a few of the older establishments.

Tips

To peel fresh ginger, use a large spoon and scrape off the outer peeling.

Use reduced-sodium soy sauce because the regular kind is too salty.

- Preheat oven to 400°F (200°C)
- 13- by 9-inch (33 by 23 cm) shallow baking dish, buttered

6	skinless boneless chicken breasts (about 2 lbs/1 kg)	6
8	cloves garlic	8
1	piece (about 1½ inches/4 cm long) fresh gingerroot, peeled and cut into 3 chunks (see Tips, left)	1
6	green onions, cut in half	6
1	small onion, quartered	1
1 cup	reduced-sodium soy sauce (see Tips, left)	250 mL
½ cup	lightly packed brown sugar	125 mL
½ cup	bourbon	125 mL
¼ cup	olive oil	60 mL

1. In prepared baking dish, place chicken breasts in a single layer. Set aside.

2. In work bowl fitted with metal blade, pulse garlic, ginger, green onions and onion until coarsely chopped, about 20 times. With motor running, add soy sauce, brown sugar and bourbon through feed tube. Drizzle olive oil through feed tube until incorporated. Pour mixture over chicken breasts and turn to coat underside.

3. Bake in preheated oven until chicken is no longer pink inside, 20 to 25 minutes. Spoon some of the sauce over cooked chicken for presentation.

Variation

You can also use this to make flavorful wings. Just substitute 2 lbs (1 kg) wings for the chicken breasts and serve as an appetizer.

Smoky Sesame Chicken

Crispy baked chicken with a twist — flavorful sesame seeds and a hint of smoke. This is delicious hot or cold. The recipe can easily be doubled if you're serving more people.

Tips

Use hot or sweet smoked paprika, whichever you prefer. If you like the flavor of smoked paprika, use the larger quantity. Otherwise, err on the side of caution because smoked paprika does have a strong taste.

You can use skin-on bone-in or skinless boneless chicken breasts, whichever you prefer. If using skinless boneless breasts, bake at 400°F (200°C) about 10 minutes per side, turning once, until no longer pink inside.

- Preheat oven to 400°F (200°C)
- Long shallow dish
- Rimmed baking sheet

18	soda crackers	18
½ to 1 tsp	smoked paprika (see Tips, left)	2 to 5 mL
	Freshly ground black pepper	
½ cup	sesame seeds	125 mL
2 tbsp	freshly grated Parmesan cheese	30 mL
2	eggs	2
4	chicken breasts (see Tips, left)	4
2 tbsp	olive oil, divided (approx.)	30 mL

1. In work bowl fitted with metal blade, process crackers, smoked paprika, and pepper to taste, until crackers are the consistency of fine crumbs, about 30 seconds. Add sesame seeds and Parmesan and pulse once or twice to blend. Transfer to a large plate.

2. Beat eggs in long shallow dish. Brush chicken with 1 tbsp (15 mL) of the olive oil, then dip in eggs. Dredge in sesame mixture, coating well. Place on baking sheet. Drizzle with remaining olive oil. Discard any egg and sesame mixture.

3. Bake in preheated oven, skin side up, for 10 minutes. Reduce heat to 350°F (180°C) and bake, basting occasionally with pan juices or additional olive oil, until golden brown and chicken is no longer pink inside, about 35 minutes.

Mushroom-Crusted Chicken

Serves 6

This recipe is adapted from one by Kathie Alex, who conducts food tours in the south of France in the former home of Julia Child.

Tip

To make an even layer of mushroom filling, press the filling first on plastic wrap and then transfer it to the chicken.

- Preheat oven to 400°F (200°C)
- 13- by 9-inch (33 by 23 cm) shallow baking dish, lined with parchment paper

6	skinless boneless chicken breasts (about 2 lbs/1 kg)	6
2 tbsp	olive oil	30 mL
8 oz	button mushrooms, stems removed	250 g
2 tbsp	Dijon mustard	30 mL
1 tbsp	herbes de Provence	15 mL
2 tsp	freshly ground black pepper	10 mL
1 tsp	salt	5 mL

1. In a shallow baking dish, coat chicken with olive oil. Arrange in a single layer. Set aside.

2. In work bowl fitted with metal blade, pulse mushrooms until smooth with a few large pieces left. Transfer to a bowl. Add mustard, herbes de Provence, pepper and salt until well combined.

3. Press a thin layer of mushroom filling over top of each chicken breast (see Tip, left).

4. Bake in preheated oven until chicken is no longer pink inside, 20 to 25 minutes.

Variation

You can use the same amount of fresh herbs, such as dill or tarragon, in place of the herbes de Provence.

Potato Chip Chicken

Serves 6

The potato chips create a crunchy texture that seals in the juicy chicken meat.

Tip

Make sure the potato chips are fresh. If they are stale you can crisp them up in a preheated 400°F (200°C) oven for 5 minutes before processing.

- Preheat oven to 400°F (200°C)
- 13- by 9-inch (33 by 23 cm) shallow baking dish, lined with parchment paper

1	bag (2 oz/60 g) potato chips (about 2 cups/500 mL)	1
2	cloves garlic	2
1 tsp	paprika	5 mL
2 tbsp	olive oil	30 mL
6	skinless boneless chicken breasts (about 2 lbs/1 kg)	6

1. In work bowl fitted with metal blade, process potato chips, garlic and paprika until finely ground, about 30 seconds. Transfer to a shallow dish.

2. Rub oil over chicken breasts. Dredge breasts in potato chip mixture. Arrange in a single layer in prepared baking dish. Discard any extra mixture.

3. Bake in preheated oven until chicken is no longer pink inside, 20 to 25 minutes.

Variation

Use flavored potato chips, such as barbecue.

Creamed Chicken Puffs

Makes 32 puffs

Serves 8

Make sure to have napkins nearby because the sauce from this one-bite puff makes it so creamy. Serve four per person as a main dish.

Tips

If you have a smaller package of puff pastry, the pastry may be thinner, but will still work. If the pastry feels too thin to enclose filling, you may need to use a little less chicken mixture for each square.

Thaw puff pastry according to package directions. To make sure it is thawed, take dough out of packaging and pick up one side of dough to make sure it is limp and not still frozen.

It's important to always use cooked items, such as chicken, in puff pastry because the cooking time does not allow raw meats to cook fully.

- Preheat oven 425°F (220°C)
- 2 baking sheets, lines with parchment paper

1	package (18 oz/540 g) puff party, thawed (see Tips, left)	1
	All-purpose flour	
4 oz	Gruyère cheese, cut into chunks	125 g
8 oz	cooked boneless chicken (see Tips, left)	250 g
4 oz	mushrooms, stems removed	125 g
2	green onions, green part only, cut in half	2
2	garlic cloves	2
¼ cup	Creamy Herb Dressing (page 414)	60 mL

1. Working with one half of pastry, on a lightly floured board, roll pastry into a 12-inch (30 cm) square. Using a pizza cutter, cut into 4 strips. Cut crosswise to make 16 squares. Set aside. Repeat with second piece of pastry.

2. In work bowl fitted with shredding blade, shred cheese. Transfer to a bowl and set aside.

3. Replace shredding blade with metal blade. Add chicken, mushroom caps, green onions, garlic and dressing and pulse until mixture is chunky, 5 to 8 times, stopping and scraping down sides of the bowl as necessary. Place 1 tbsp (15 mL) of the mixture on center of each square. Top with 1½ tsp (7 mL) of the cheese. Starting with two opposite corners of one square of pastry, fold in toward the center to meet above filling. With remaining corners, fold up so all points meet in the center, pressing to seal (like a dim sum dumpling). If pastry seems dry, lightly brush edges with water before folding to ensure a good seal. Place on prepared baking sheets, about 2 inches (5 cm) apart. Repeat with remaining pastry squares and filling to make 32 puffs.

4. Bake, in batches, as necessary, in preheated oven until light brown and puffed up, 15 to 18 minutes. Serve warm or cold.

Variation

If you have any filling mixture leftover, place on sliced baguette or crackers and place under boiler for a few minutes to heat and melt cheese.

Chicken Pot Pie with Mushrooms and Leeks

Serves 6

Another traditional Sunday dinner, this is comfort food par excellence. Serve it with a tossed green salad.

Tips

Leeks can be quite gritty so be sure to clean them thoroughly before using. *To wash leeks:* Fill a basin full of lukewarm water. Split leeks in half lengthwise to within ½ inch (1 cm) of the root end and submerge in water, swishing them around to remove all traces of dirt. Transfer to a colander and rinse under cold water. Drain well.

The wine lends a pleasant sharpness to the sauce, but if you prefer, substitute ½ cup (125 mL) of additional chicken broth.

- Preheat oven to 375°F (190°C)
- 10-inch (25 cm) deep-dish pie plate or baking dish
- Rimmed baking sheet

8 oz	mushroom caps	250 g
3	leeks, white part with a bit of green, cleaned and cut in lengths to fit feed tube (see Tips, left)	3
2	carrots, peeled and cut into 3-inch (7.5 cm) lengths	2
2	stalks celery, cut into 3-inch (7.5 cm) lengths	2
¼ cup	all-purpose flour	60 mL
¼ tsp	cayenne pepper	1 mL
1 lb	skinless boneless chicken breasts, cut into ½-inch (1 cm) cubes	500 g
1 tbsp	oil	15 mL
2 tbsp	butter	30 mL
2	cloves garlic, minced	2
2 tsp	dried tarragon	10 mL
½ cup	dry white wine (see Tips, left)	125 mL
1 cup	chicken broth	250 mL
½ cup	heavy or whipping (35%) cream	125 mL
¼ cup	finely chopped parsley	60 mL
1	sheet frozen puff pastry (about 8 oz/250 g), thawed	1
1	egg yolk	1

1. In work bowl fitted with slicing blade, working in batches, place mushroom caps in feed tube on their sides, all facing in the same direction and slice. Repeat until all mushrooms are sliced. Set aside. Slice leeks, carrots and celery. Set aside.

2. On a plate or in a plastic bag, combine flour and cayenne. Add chicken and dredge or toss until well coated. Set any excess flour mixture aside.

3. In a skillet, heat oil over medium heat. Add chicken, in batches, and cook, stirring, until lightly browned, 3 minutes per batch. (You do not want it to be cooked through.) Remove from pan and set aside.

4. Add butter to pan and reduce heat to medium-low. Add leeks, carrots, celery and mushrooms and stir well. Cover and cook on low for 8 minutes or until leeks are softened. Increase heat to medium. Add garlic and tarragon and stir well. Sprinkle excess flour mixture over vegetables, and cook, stirring, for 1 minute. Add wine, bring to a boil and cook until liquid reduces by half, about 3 minutes. Return chicken to pan. Add chicken broth and cream and cook, stirring, until mixture is slightly thickened, about 2 minutes. Stir in parsley and transfer mixture to pie plate.

5. On a lightly floured surface, roll out pastry into a circle about 11 inches (28 cm) in diameter and place over pie. Tuck and overlap under the edge and flute. Place pie plate on baking sheet.

6. In a small bowl, beat egg yolk with 1 tsp (5 mL) water. Brush crust with mixture and pierce with a sharp knife to make several steam vents. Bake in preheated oven until top is golden brown, about 35 minutes.

Chicken with Roasted Red Pepper Sauce

This is a great dish to make when peppers are in season and abundant. It is very fresh tasting and, once you have roasted the peppers, a snap to make.

Tip

Use the type of chicken you prefer. If using skin-on bone-in chicken breasts, we prefer to cook them on the barbecue. Broiling works best for the skinless boneless variety.

- Preheat oven to 400°F (200°C)
- Preheat grill to medium-high or preheat broiler
- Baking sheet

2	red bell peppers	2
2	cloves garlic	2
2 tbsp	extra virgin olive oil	30 mL
1 tbsp	freshly squeezed lemon juice	15 mL
½ cup	loosely packed Italian flat-leaf parsley leaves	125 mL
½ tsp	salt	2 mL
	Freshly ground black pepper	
4	chicken breasts, patted dry (see Tip, left)	4
	Olive oil	

1. Place peppers on a baking sheet and roast in preheated oven, turning two or three times, until the skin on all sides is blackened, about 25 minutes. Transfer peppers to a heatproof bowl. Cover with a plate and let stand until cool. Remove from bowl and, using a sharp knife, lift skins off. Discard skins, stems and seeds.

2. Transfer peppers to work bowl fitted with metal blade. Add garlic, olive oil, lemon juice, parsley, salt, and pepper to taste. Process until smooth. Transfer to a sauce boat.

3. Meanwhile, prepare chicken. To grill bone-in skin on chicken breasts, brush with olive oil. Place on preheated grill and cook, turning once, until skin is crispy and chicken is no longer pink inside, about 20 minutes. If using boneless chicken, preheat broiler. Brush chicken with olive oil. Broil until chicken is no longer pink inside, about 5 minutes per side. To serve, place 1 chicken breast on each plate and spoon sauce over.

Stuffed Chicken Breasts

This recipe originated from using leftovers in the refrigerator.

Tips

To toast pine nuts: Place nuts in a dry skillet over medium heat and cook, stirring, until they begin to brown, 3 to 4 minutes.

If the ham is very salty, omit the salt in the recipe.

- Preheat oven to 400°F (200°C)
- 13- by 9-inch (33 by 23 cm) baking dish, buttered

6	skinless boneless chicken breasts (about 2 lbs/1 kg)	6
2 tbsp	olive oil	30 mL
Filling		
3 oz	feta cheese, crumbled	90 g
3 oz	salami or cured ham	90 g
2 tsp	loosely packed fresh tarragon	10 mL
1/4 cup	toasted pine nuts (see Tips, left)	60 mL
1/2 tsp	ground white pepper	2 mL
1/4 tsp	onion powder	1 mL
1/4 tsp	salt (see Tips, left)	1 mL

1. Slice a 2-inch (5 cm) slit horizontally into each chicken breast to form a pocket. Rub chicken breasts with olive oil. Set aside.

2. **Filling:** In work bowl fitted with metal blade, process feta cheese, salami and tarragon until smooth, about 3 minutes. Transfer to a bowl. Fold in pine nuts, white pepper, onion powder and salt.

3. Fill pockets of chicken breasts with cheese mixture. Arrange in prepared baking dish in a single layer. Bake in preheated oven until chicken is no longer pink inside, 25 to 30 minutes.

Variation

Use gorgonzola or blue cheese in place of the feta.

Chicken Tonnato

Vitello tonnato, an Italian dish of thinly sliced cold veal in a tuna sauce, is a real treat. But poaching a roast of veal can be a bit daunting for many cooks. That's why we love this simplified version, which uses poached chicken breasts instead. It's a wonderful dish for a buffet or for dining al fresco on a warm summer's night.

Tips

Use the smallest skillet that will comfortably accommodate the chicken in order to use the least amount of chicken broth. Ours just fit in a 10-inch (25 cm) skillet.

We specify pasteurized egg yolks because raw eggs are likely to contain salmonella. If you have access to free-range eggs that you are certain are salmonella-free, you can use raw egg yolks in this recipe. If you are not sure of your eggs and do not have pasteurized egg yolks, substitute ¼ cup (60 mL) prepared mayonnaise for the yolks.

- Preheat oven to 325°F (160°C)
- 10-inch (25 cm) ovenproof skillet

4	skinless boneless chicken breasts	4
2 cups	chicken broth (approx.) (see Tips, left)	500 mL
1	jar (about 7 oz/210 g) Italian tuna in olive oil	1
1	clove garlic	1
2 tsp	finely grated lemon zest	10 mL
¼ cup	freshly squeezed lemon juice	60 mL
2	anchovy fillets	2
2	pasteurized egg yolks (see Tips, left)	2
2 tbsp	drained capers	30 mL
⅔ cup	extra virgin olive oil	150 mL
	Salt and freshly ground black pepper	

1. In ovenproof skillet (see Tips, left), place chicken. Add chicken broth to cover and bring to a boil over medium heat. Cover with foil and transfer to preheated oven. Bake until chicken is no longer pink inside, about 20 minutes. (If you're using an instant-read thermometer, the temperature should read 165°F/74°C.) Remove from oven and let cool slightly. Transfer chicken and liquid to a bowl, cover and refrigerate until thoroughly chilled.

2. When chicken is cold, in work bowl fitted with metal blade, process tuna, garlic, lemon zest and juice, anchovies, egg yolks and capers until blended. With motor running, gradually add olive oil through feed tube, until mixture has the consistency of mayonnaise. Season with salt and pepper to taste.

3. Slice chicken thinly. Spread a layer of tonnato over bottom of a deep platter or serving dish. Add a layer of chicken slices and spread with tonnato. Repeat until all chicken and sauce is used up, finishing with a layer of tunnato. (How many layers you have will depend upon the size of your serving dish.) Cover with plastic and refrigerate for at least 8 hours. Remove from fridge about 20 minutes before serving to allow flavors to bloom.

Basque-Style Chicken

Serves 6

This robust chicken dish is perfect for a chilly day. It's easy to make and the addition of prosciutto adds an element of grandeur to a simple peasant-style dish. Serve it over hot orzo or a simple rice pilaf and add a bottle of hearty red wine if you're feeling festive.

Tips

Use 1 red pepper and 1 green pepper for the most visual appeal.

If you're cooking chicken legs and thighs, cook until juices run clear; for breasts the test is until no longer pink inside.

Espelette pepper (Piment d'Espelette) is a mild chile pepper grown in the Basque town of Espelette. It has a mild, slightly smoky flavor and is widely used in Basque cooking. You can find it in specialty stores.

- Large deep skillet with lid

6	pieces skin-on bone-in chicken	6
2 tbsp	freshly squeezed lemon juice	30 mL
1/4 cup	all-purpose flour	60 mL
2 tsp	Piment d'Espelette or 1/4 tsp (1 mL) cayenne pepper (see Tips, left)	10 mL
1/2 tsp	salt	2 mL
2 tbsp	olive oil (approx.)	30 mL
2	bell peppers, seeded and halved	2
2	onions, quartered	2
2	anchovy fillets	2
4	cloves garlic	4
1/2 tsp	salt	2 mL
	Freshly ground black pepper	
1/2 cup	dry white wine	125 mL
1	can (28 oz/796 mL) tomatoes with juice, coarsely chopped	1
6	slices prosciutto, sliced into thin strips	6

1. Rub chicken with lemon juice. On a plate or a sheet of waxed paper, combine flour, Piment d'Espelette and salt. Dredge chicken in mixture, coating on all sides. Discard any excess flour mixture.

2. In a skillet, heat oil over medium-high heat. Add chicken, in batches, and brown well on both sides, turning once, about 6 minutes per batch. Return all chicken to pan. Reduce heat to low. Cover and cook for 30 minutes (see Tips, left). Transfer to an ovenproof serving dish and keep warm. Set skillet aside.

3. Meanwhile, in work bowl fitted with slicing blade, slice bell peppers. Set aside. Replace slicing blade with metal blade. Add onions, anchovies and garlic. Pulse until finely chopped, about 10 times, stopping and scraping down sides of the bowl once.

4. Return skillet to medium-high heat and add more oil, if necessary. Add onion mixture and sliced peppers and cook, stirring, until softened, about 7 minutes. Add salt, and black pepper to taste. Add wine, stir well and boil rapidly for 2 minutes, scraping up brown bits from bottom of pan. Add tomatoes with juice and bring to a boil. Reduce heat and simmer until thickened, about 10 minutes. Pour over chicken and garnish with prosciutto.

Chicken Rockefeller

Serves 4

This recipe is a variation of the famous 1890s' recipe for oysters Rockefeller, originally made in New Orleans and named after John D. Rockefeller (because it was so rich) and created with chicken.

Tips

If you have frozen spinach, just thaw and drain a 12 oz (375 g) package and use like the fresh.

Cover any leftovers and refrigerate for up to 4 days. Reheat in a preheated 350°F (180°C) oven until hot in the center, 18 to 20 minutes.

- Preheat oven to 400°F (200°C)
- 13- by 9-inch (33 by 23 cm) baking dish, buttered

4	skinless boneless chicken breasts (about 1½ lbs/750 g)	4
2 tsp	olive oil	10 mL
½ cup	Fresh Bread Crumbs (page 468) or store-bought	125 mL
4 oz	provolone cheese, cut into chunks	125 g
1	bunch fresh spinach, trimmed (about 12 oz/375 g) (see Tips, left)	1
1	onion, quartered	1
2 tsp	butter, melted	10 mL
1 tsp	anise-flavored liqueur, such as Pernod	5 mL
¼ cup	loosely packed Italian flat-leaf parsley sprigs	60 mL

1. Coat both sides of chicken breasts with olive oil and dredge in bread crumbs. Arrange in prepared baking dish in a single layer. Set aside. Discard any excess crumbs.

2. In work bowl fitted with shredding blade, shred provolone cheese. Transfer to a small bowl.

3. Replace shredding blade with metal blade and pulse spinach and onion until finely chopped, about 20 times. Transfer to another bowl. Stir in butter and liqueur until combined.

4. Spoon one-quarter of the mixture over each chicken breast. Top with grated cheese and parsley sprigs.

5. Bake in preheated oven until chicken is no longer pink inside, about 20 minutes. Transfer chicken to serving plates and spoon remaining sauce over top.

Variation

Try the same amount of fresh basil in place of the spinach.

Five-Alarm Chicken

This chicken is very easy to make and tastes deliciously intriguing. Leftovers are great eaten cold or sliced for sandwiches.

Tips

Use whatever fresh chile peppers you have easy access to. Habanero will produce the hottest result, but a long red or green chile or 2 or 3 tiny Thai chiles work well, too.

Cut off the outer part of the lemon peel and discard any white "pith." It will become fine zest when processed.

Hot smoked paprika gives this dish wonderful flavor, but the sweet smoked version will be good, too, although the result will not be as incendiary.

- Mini-bowl attachment
- 13- by 9-inch (33 by 23 cm) shallow baking dish

½ cup	Easy Ketchup (page 442), Homemade Ketchup (page 443) or store-bought	125 mL
4	green onions, white part only	4
4	cloves garlic	4
1	chile pepper, seeded and cut in half (see Tips, left)	1
1	strip lemon peel (see Tips, left)	1
2 tbsp	freshly squeezed lemon juice	30 mL
2 tbsp	soy sauce	30 mL
1 tsp	smoked paprika (see Tips, left)	5 mL
4 lbs	skin-on bone-in chicken pieces	2 kg
1 tbsp	olive oil	15 mL
	Sea salt, such as fleur de sel or Maldon	

1. In mini bowl fitted with metal blade, process ketchup, green onions, garlic, chile pepper, lemon peel and juice, soy sauce and smoked paprika until smooth, about 30 seconds.

2. In a large bowl, combine chicken and ketchup mixture, mixing to ensure chicken is evenly coated. Cover and refrigerate overnight or for up to 2 days.

3. Preheat oven to 350°F (180°C). Remove chicken from marinade, discarding excess marinade, and place, skin side up, in a single layer in baking dish. Drizzle with olive oil. Bake until juices run clear when pierced for legs or thighs and no longer pink inside for breasts, about 30 minutes. Remove from oven and sprinkle with sea salt.

Buffalo Chicken Wings

What would a major sports event be without a big bowl of this American classic? Traditionally, Buffalo wings are deep-fried. Cooked on the barbecue, these are mouthwatering, with far less fat than the norm.

Tips

To purée garlic: Use a fine, sharp-toothed grater, such as those made by Microplane, or put the garlic through a garlic press.

If you prefer, roast the wings in a 375°F (190°C) oven for about 40 minutes, turning once.

These wings are moderately spicy; if you prefer a five-alarm version, add more hot pepper sauce.

- Preheat grill to medium-high

1 tbsp	paprika	15 mL
1 tsp	puréed garlic (see Tips, left)	5 mL
½ tsp	cayenne pepper	2 mL
½ tsp	hot pepper sauce, or to taste	2 mL
	Freshly ground black pepper	
¼ cup	oil or melted butter	60 mL
3 lbs	chicken wings, tips removed and patted dry, about 12 wings	1.5 kg
	Coarsely ground sea salt, optional	

Blue Cheese Sauce

½ cup	Traditional Mayonnaise (page 437) or store-bought	125 mL
2 tsp	freshly squeezed lemon juice	10 mL
2	cloves garlic, quartered	2
½ tsp	Worcestershire sauce	2 mL
¼ cup	crumbled blue cheese, about 2 oz (60 g)	60 mL
	Freshly ground black pepper	
	Celery sticks	

1. In a bowl large enough to accommodate the wings, combine paprika, garlic, cayenne, hot pepper sauce, and pepper to taste. Stir well. Gradually stir in oil until combined. Add chicken wings and toss until they are well coated.

2. On preheated barbecue (see Tips, left), grill wings, turning frequently, until skin is crisp and browned and juices run clear when the meat is pierced, about 20 minutes. Transfer wings to a warm platter. Sprinkle lightly with sea salt, if using.

3. Blue Cheese Sauce: Meanwhile, in work bowl fitted with metal blade, process mayonnaise, lemon juice, garlic, Worcestershire sauce and blue cheese until smooth, about 30 seconds, stopping and scraping down sides of the bowl as necessary. Season with pepper to taste. Transfer to a small serving bowl.

4. Serve wings with Blue Cheese Sauce and celery sticks for dipping.

Chicken in Ancho-Laced Pepita Sauce

Serves 4

If you're feeling bored with what you've been eating, this Mexican-inspired dish is a refreshing change. Serve it over brown rice and add a tossed green salad with sliced avocado for a delicious meal.

Tip

Ancho chiles are among the mildest chile peppers. If you have heat seekers in your group, add a coarsely chopped jalapeño (or two) to the work bowl along with the tomatoes.

- Large deep skillet with lid

6	dried ancho chiles (see Tip, left)	6
3 cups	boiling water	750 mL
2	onions, quartered	2
4	stalks celery, cut into 3-inch (7.5 cm) lengths	4
4	cloves garlic, coarsely chopped	4
1 tbsp	oil	15 mL
3 lbs	skin-on bone-in chicken breasts, patted dry	1.5 kg
2 tsp	dried oregano	10 mL
1 tsp	salt	5 mL
½ tsp	freshly ground black pepper	2 mL
1	can (28 oz/796 mL) tomatoes with juice	1
1 cup	green pumpkin seeds (pepitas)	250 mL
1 cup	chicken broth	250 mL
	Finely chopped cilantro	

1. In a heatproof bowl, combine ancho chiles and boiling water. Weigh down with a cup to ensure they remain submerged and set aside for 30 minutes. Drain, discarding soaking liquid and stems. Pat dry, chop coarsely and set aside.

2. Meanwhile, in work bowl fitted with metal blade, pulse onions, celery and garlic until finely chopped, about 10 times, stopping and scraping down sides of the bowl, once or twice.

3. In a large skillet, heat oil over medium-high heat. Add chicken, in batches, and brown, turning once, about 6 minutes per batch. Transfer to a plate and set aside. Reduce heat to medium.

4. Add onion mixture to pan and cook, stirring, until softened, about 5 minutes. Add oregano, salt and pepper and cook, stirring, for 1 minute.

5. Meanwhile, add tomatoes with juice, pepitas and reserved ancho chiles to work bowl fitted with metal blade. Purée. Add to skillet along with chicken broth. Return browned chicken to pan and bring to a boil. Cover, reduce heat to low and cook until chicken is no longer pink inside, about 40 minutes. To serve, transfer to a warm serving dish and garnish with cilantro.

Southwestern-Style Chile Chicken with Wehani Rice

Bathed in a luscious sauce and served on a bed of robust red rice, perfectly braised chicken is home cooking at its finest. Complete this meal with warm tortillas and a tossed green salad.

Tips

Wehani rice, which is grown by Lundberg Family Farms, is a favorite variety of rice. It is robust and chewy and is widely available in well-stocked supermarkets or natural foods stores. Bhutanese, Thai or Camargue red rice can be substituted, although the cooking times vary. If you prefer, cook the rice in a rice cooker.

For the best flavor, toast and grind cumin yourself. *To toast cumin:* Place seeds in a dry skillet over medium heat and cook, stirring, until fragrant, about 3 minutes. Immediately transfer to a mortar or a spice grinder and grind.

3 cups	chicken broth, divided	750 mL
1 cup	Wehani rice, rinsed and drained (see Tips, left)	250 mL
4	dried ancho, mild New Mexico or guajillo chiles	4
2 cups	boiling water	500 mL
2	onions, quartered	2
4	cloves garlic, coarsely chopped	4
1 cup	packed coarsely chopped cilantro (leaves and stems)	250 mL
2 tbsp	red wine vinegar	30 mL
1 tbsp	olive oil (approx.)	15 mL
3 lbs	skin-on bone-in chicken breasts, cut into serving-size pieces, patted dry	1.5 kg
1 tbsp	ground cumin (see Tips, left)	15 mL
1 tsp	dried oregano leaves, preferably Mexican	5 mL
½ tsp	cracked black peppercorns	2 mL
	Salt	
	Finely chopped cilantro	

1. In a saucepan with a tight-fitting lid over medium-high heat, bring 2 cups (500 mL) of the broth to a boil. Add rice and stir well. Return to a rapid boil. Reduce heat to low. Cover and cook until liquid is absorbed and rice is tender, about 45 minutes.

2. Meanwhile, in a heatproof bowl, combine dried chiles and boiling water. Weigh down with a cup to ensure they remain submerged and set aside for 30 minutes. Drain, discarding soaking liquid and stems. Pat dry, chop finely and set aside.

3. In work bowl fitted with metal blade, pulse onions and garlic until finely chopped, about 10 times, stopping and scraping down sides of the bowl once. Transfer to a bowl and set aside.

4. Add reconstituted chiles to work bowl fitted with metal blade. Add remaining 1 cup (250 mL) of broth, cilantro and vinegar. Purée and set aside.

5. Meanwhile, in a Dutch oven, heat oil over medium-high heat. Add chicken, in batches, and cook, turning once, until skin is browned and crispy, about 10 minutes per batch, adding more oil, if necessary. Transfer to a plate and set aside. Drain off all but 1 tbsp (15 mL) fat from pan. Reduce heat to medium.

6. Add onion mixture to pan and cook, stirring, until softened, about 3 minutes. Add cumin, oregano and peppercorns and cook, stirring, for 1 minute. Stir in reserved chile mixture. Add salt to taste. Return chicken to pan, skin side up, and spoon a little sauce over each piece. Reduce heat to low. Cover and simmer until chicken is no longer pink inside, about 30 minutes, turning the chicken over to cook in the sauce for the last 5 minutes of cooking.

7. To serve, arrange rice in a ring around the edge on a deep platter, leaving the center hollow. Spoon chicken and sauce into the center and garnish with additional cilantro.

Mexican-Style Chicken with Chorizo

Serves 4

The robust in-your-face flavors of this delicious chicken are very appealing. It is fabulous served with a bowl of Mexican-style rice and beans.

Tip

Make an effort to find chorizo, which is available at Portuguese or Latin American markets. Sometimes you can find it at good butchers or delis specializing in a wide range of charcuterie. If you can't find it, substitute an equal quantity of hot Italian sausage.

3 to 4	mild dried chile peppers, such as pasilla, ancho or guajillo	3 to 4
3 cups	boiling water	750 mL
2	onions, quartered	2
4	cloves garlic, coarsely chopped	4
¾ cup	blanched almonds (see Tips, page 112)	175 mL
1 tbsp	oil	15 mL
3 lbs	skin-on bone-in chicken breasts, patted dry	1.5 kg
2	fresh chorizo sausages, removed from casings (see Tip, left)	2
1	piece (2 inches/5 cm) cinnamon stick	1
1 tsp	salt	5 mL
	Freshly ground black pepper	
1	can (14 oz/398 mL) diced tomatoes with juice	1
2 cups	chicken broth	500 mL
	Finely chopped cilantro leaves	

1. In a heatproof bowl, combine chiles and boiling water. Weigh down with a cup to ensure they remain submerged and set aside for 30 minutes. Drain, discarding soaking liquid and stems. Pat dry, chop coarsely and set aside.

2. Meanwhile, in work bowl fitted with metal blade, pulse onions and garlic until finely chopped, about 7 times. Transfer to a bowl and set aside. Add almonds and reconstituted chiles to work bowl and pulse until very finely chopped, about 15 times.

3. In a skillet, heat oil over medium-high heat. Add chicken, in batches, and brown, turning once, about 6 minutes per batch. Transfer to a plate and set aside.

4. Add chorizo and onion mixture to pan and cook, stirring and breaking up with a spoon, until lightly browned and cooked through, about 5 minutes. Add almond mixture along with cinnamon stick, salt, and pepper to taste, and cook, stirring, for 2 minutes. Add tomatoes with juice and chicken broth and bring to a boil. Return browned chicken to pan and bring to a boil. Cover, reduce heat to low and cook until chicken is no longer pink inside, about 40 minutes. To serve, transfer to a warm serving dish and garnish with cilantro.

Mexican-Style Chicken with Cilantro and Lemon

With a sauce of pumpkin seeds, cumin seeds, oregano and cilantro, this dish is reminiscent of evening dinners in the courtyard of a Mexican hacienda. Mexicans have been thickening sauces with pumpkin seeds long before the Spanish arrived and, today, every cook has their own recipes for mole, one of the world's great culinary concoctions. Serve this with rice and fresh corn on the cob.

Tip

Buy seeds and nuts at a natural foods or bulk food store with high turnover, as they are likely to be much fresher than those in packages.

- Preheat oven to 350°F (180°C)
- Dutch oven or large deep skillet with lid

¼ cup	raw green pumpkin seeds (pepitas)	60 mL
2 tsp	cumin seeds	10 mL
1 tbsp	oil	15 mL
2	onions, coarsely chopped	2
4	cloves garlic, chopped	4
2 tbsp	tomato paste	30 mL
1 tsp	salt	5 mL
1 tsp	cracked black peppercorns	5 mL
1 tsp	dried oregano	5 mL
¼ tsp	ground cinnamon	1 mL
1 cup	coarsely chopped cilantro (stems and leaves)	250 mL
1 to 2	jalapeño peppers	1 to 2
1 tbsp	grated lemon zest	15 mL
2 tbsp	freshly squeezed lemon juice	30 mL
½ cup	chicken broth	125 mL
3 lbs	skinless bone-in chicken thighs (about 12 thighs)	1.5 kg
	Finely chopped cilantro and green onion	
	Grated lemon zest	

1. In a Dutch oven over medium-high heat, toast pumpkin and cumin seeds, stirring constantly, until pumpkin seeds are popping and cumin is fragrant, about 3 minutes. Transfer to a small bowl and set aside.

2. In the same pan, heat oil over medium heat. Add onions and cook, stirring, until softened, about 3 minutes. Add garlic, tomato paste, salt, peppercorns, oregano and cinnamon and cook, stirring, for 1 minute. Transfer contents of pan to work bowl fitted with metal blade. Add cilantro, jalapeno pepper(s), lemon zest and juice, broth and reserved pumpkin and cumin seeds and process until smooth, about 1 minute.

3. Arrange chicken over bottom of Dutch oven and cover with vegetable mixture. Bring to boil. Cover and transfer to preheated oven. Bake until juices run clear when chicken is pierced, about 40 minutes. When you're ready to serve, garnish with cilantro, green onion and lemon zest.

Indian-Style Chicken with Puréed Spinach

This mouthwatering dish is an adaptation of a recipe from Suneeta Vaswani's terrific book *Easy Indian Cooking*. It is a great centerpiece for a meal, accompanied by rice and/or whole wheat chapati.

Tips

If you don't have a 14 oz (398 mL) can of diced tomatoes, use 2 cups (500 mL) canned tomatoes with juice, coarsely chopped.

If using fresh spinach, be sure to remove the stems, and if it has not been prewashed, rinse it thoroughly in a basin of lukewarm water. You will need to push it well down in the food processor before puréeing in batches. If using frozen spinach, thaw it first and squeeze the water out.

One chile produces a medium-hot result. Add a second chile only if you're a true heat seeker.

- Large deep skillet with lid

4 lbs	skinless bone-in chicken thighs (about 16 thighs)	2 kg
1/4 cup	freshly squeezed lemon juice	60 mL
2	onions, cut to fit feed tube	2
2 tbsp	oil	30 mL
1 tbsp	ground cumin (see Tips, page 195)	15 mL
2 tsp	ground coriander	10 mL
1 tbsp	minced peeled gingerroot	15 mL
1 tbsp	minced garlic	15 mL
1 tsp	ground turmeric	5 mL
1 tsp	cracked black peppercorns	5 mL
1 tsp	salt, or to taste	5 mL
1	can (14 oz/398 mL) diced tomatoes with juice (see Tips, left)	1
2	packages (each 10 oz/300 g) fresh or frozen spinach (see Tips, left)	2
1 to 2	long red or green chiles, chopped	1 to 2
1 cup	chicken broth	250 mL
	Juice of 1 lime or lemon	

1. In a bowl, combine chicken and lemon juice. Toss well and set aside for 20 to 30 minutes. In work bowl with slicing blade, slice onions. Set aside.

2. In a skillet, heat oil over medium-high heat. Add onions and cook, stirring, until they begin to color, about 5 minutes. Reduce heat to medium and cook, stirring, until golden, about 12 minutes. Add cumin, coriander, ginger, garlic, turmeric, peppercorns and salt and cook, stirring, for 1 minute. Stir in tomatoes and bring to a boil. Remove from heat.

3. Arrange marinated chicken over tomato mixture and spoon sauce over it. Cover and cook on low heat for 20 minutes.

4. In work bowl fitted with metal blade, pulse spinach, chile(s) and chicken broth until spinach is puréed. Add to chicken and stir well. Cover and simmer until juices run clear when chicken is pierced, about 15 minutes. Remove from heat and stir in lime juice.

Indian-Style Cashew Chicken

Serves 6 to 8

This rich, comforting mélange is called Indian-Style to distinguish it from Thai Cashew Chicken, which is a very different dish, although equally delicious. Serve this over brown basmati rice with zesty mango chutney, but other robust fruit chutneys work well, too. Add a green vegetable, such as steamed broccoli, to round out the color palette.

Tips

If you're buying cashews in bulk and planning to purée them, buy cashew pieces because they are much less costly. Reduce the quantity by about 1 tbsp (15 mL).

If you don't have a long red chile and would still like a bit of heat in this recipe, blend ¼ tsp (1 mL) cayenne pepper, or to taste, with the cashew mixture.

To toast cumin seeds: Place seeds in a dry skillet over medium heat, and cook, stirring, until fragrant, about 3 minutes. Immediately transfer to a mortar or a spice grinder and grind.

- Dutch oven or large deep skillet with lid

2	onions, quartered	2
4	cloves garlic, coarsely chopped	4
1	piece (about 2 inches/5 cm) peeled gingerroot, quartered	1
1 tbsp	oil	15 mL
1 tbsp	ground cumin (see Tips, left)	15 mL
1 tsp	ground turmeric	5 mL
1 tsp	salt	5 mL
½ tsp	cracked black peppercorns	2 mL
1	can (14 to 19 oz/398 to 540 mL) diced tomatoes with juice	1
3 lbs	skinless bone-in chicken thighs (about 12 thighs)	1.5 kg
½ cup	dry roasted cashews or cashew pieces (see Tips, left)	125 mL
½ cup	coconut milk	125 mL
1	long red chile pepper, optional (see Tips, left)	1

1. In work bowl fitted with metal blade, pulse onions, garlic and ginger until finely chopped, about 15 times, stopping and scraping down sides of the bowl once or twice.

2. In Dutch oven, heat oil over medium heat. Add onion mixture and cook, stirring, until softened, about 3 minutes. Add cumin, turmeric, salt and peppercorns and cook, stirring, for 1 minute. Add tomatoes with juice and bring to a boil.

3. Add chicken to pan, covering with the sauce. Bring to a boil. Cover, reduce heat and simmer until juices run clear when chicken is pierced, about 40 minutes.

4. In work bowl fitted with metal blade, process cashews, coconut milk and chile pepper, if using, until smooth. Add to chicken and stir to combine. Cover and cook, until mixture is hot and bubbling and flavors meld, about 5 minutes.

Lemongrass Roasted Chicken

Serves 4

The combination of lemongrass with chicken is a match made in heaven. Lemongrass adds a wonderfully earthy yet fresh flavor to dishes from soups to desserts.

Tips

Making sure the marinade mixture is well-puréed helps to extract liquid from the lemongrass, which encourages the flavors to permeate the chicken.

Ask your butcher to cut the chicken or do it yourself. *To cut a chicken in half for roasting:* Place breast side down on a cutting board. Using poultry shears and beginning at the neck, cut lengthwise down one side of the backbone. Repeat on other side. Remove and discard backbone. Turn chicken over and open up like a book. Place in dish and complete Step 2.

Normally we don't use the stems of herbs such as cilantro because, although flavorful, they are too tough for the finishing stage of dishes. In this recipe, though, they add welcome robustness to the marinade.

- Roasting pan with rack

2	stalks lemongrass, tough outer layers peeled off and cut into 2-inch (5 cm) lengths	2
1	piece (about 2 inches/5 cm) peeled gingerroot	1
4	cloves garlic	4
2	shallots	2
2	long red or 4 Thai chiles	2
4	sprigs cilantro (stems and leaves)	4
1 tsp	grated lime zest	5 mL
1/4 cup	freshly squeezed lime juice	60 mL
2 tbsp	fish sauce	30 mL
2 tbsp	olive oil	30 mL
1	roasting chicken, halved (see Tips, left)	1
	Olive oil for basting	

1. In work bowl fitted with metal blade, process lemongrass, ginger, garlic, shallots, chiles, cilantro, lime zest and juice, fish sauce and oil until lemongrass is finely puréed, about 1 minute, stopping and scraping down sides of the bowl once or twice.

2. Pat chicken dry and coat with lemongrass mixture. Cover and refrigerate overnight or for up to 2 days.

3. When you're ready to cook, preheat oven to 350°F (180°C). Scrape most of the marinade off the skin-side of the chicken and discard. Place chicken, skin side up, on a rack in roasting pan and rub olive oil liberally into the skin. Roast until juices run clear when meat is pierced in legs and thighs and no longer pink inside in breasts, basting frequently with pan juices, about 45 minutes.

Jerk Chicken

Jerk is a Caribbean spice mixture that is very popular in Jamaica and is used most often as a rub or marinade for chicken or pork. You can vary the intensity of the heat by increasing or decreasing the marinating time (see Tips, below).

Tips

If you don't want so much heat, reduce the chiles to 3.

Use reduced-sodium soy sauce because the regular kind is too salty.

If you like just a little kick, marinate the chicken for only 10 minutes. For the full effect, marinate for the entire 45 minutes.

- Preheat oven to 375°F (190°C)
- Roasting pan, greased
- Instant-read thermometer

1	roasting chicken (about 3 to 4 lbs/1.5 to 2 kg), cut into pieces	1
2 tbsp	olive oil	30 mL
6	green onions, white and green parts only, cut in half	6
5	cloves garlic	5
1	onion, quartered	1
6	habanero chiles, stemmed, seeded and cut in half (see Tips, left)	6
2 tbsp	lightly packed brown sugar	30 mL
1½ tbsp	sea salt	22 mL
1 tbsp	loosely packed fresh thyme	15 mL
2 tsp	ground allspice	10 mL
2 tsp	whole black peppercorns	10 mL
¾ tsp	freshly ground nutmeg	3 mL
½ tsp	ground cinnamon	2 mL
¼ tsp	ground ginger	1 mL
¼ cup	freshly squeezed lime juice	60 mL
¼ cup	olive oil	60 mL
3 tbsp	reduced-sodium soy sauce (see Tips, left)	45 mL

1. In prepared roasting pan, coat chicken parts with oil. Arrange in a single layer. Set aside.

2. In work bowl fitted with metal blade, process green onions, garlic, onion and chiles until finely chopped, about 2 minutes. Add brown sugar, sea salt, thyme, allspice, peppercorns, nutmeg, cinnamon and ginger and pulse until blended, about 10 times. With motor running, add lime juice, olive oil and soy sauce through feed tube until incorporated.

3. Pour mixture over chicken pieces. Let marinate in the refrigerator for 45 minutes (see Tips, left). Bake in preheated oven, uncovered, until juices run clear when chicken is pierced and an instant-read thermometer inserted into the thickest part of the thigh registers 165°F (74°C), 35 to 40 minutes.

Grilled Lemongrass Chicken Wings

Serves 4

This recipe, which is Thai in origin, is an adaptation of one developed by Andrew Chase in his *Asian Bistro Cookbook*.

Tip

If you prefer, roast the wings in a 375°F (190°C) oven for 30 minutes, turning once. Brush with glaze and roast for 10 minutes more, turning once.

- Preheat grill to medium-high (see Tips, left)

3	stalks lemongrass, tough outer layers peeled off and cut into 2-inch (5 cm) lengths	3
¼ cup	freshly squeezed lime juice	60 mL
2 tbsp	fish sauce	30 mL
4	cloves garlic, coarsely chopped	4
1	piece (2 inches/5 cm) gingerroot, quartered	1
1 tbsp	oil	15 mL
1 tbsp	granulated sugar	15 mL
2 tsp	Asian chile sauce, such as sambal oelek	10 mL
1 tsp	cracked black peppercorns	5 mL
3 lbs	chicken wings, tips removed, about 12 wings	1.5 kg

Glaze

¼ cup	liquid honey	60 mL
1 to 2	finely chopped fresh Thai chile peppers, optional	1 to 2

1. In work bowl fitted with metal blade, process lemongrass, lime juice, fish sauce, garlic, gingerroot, oil, sugar, chile sauce and peppercorns until lemongrass is finely puréed, stopping and scraping down sides of the bowl once or twice. Place chicken wings in a bowl and pour sauce over top. Cover and refrigerate for at least 4 hours or preferably overnight.

2. Remove wings from marinade. Discard marinade.

3. **Glaze:** In a bowl, combine honey and chiles, if using. Set aside.

4. On preheated barbecue, grill wings, turning frequently, for 15 minutes. Remove from grill and brush with glaze. Return to barbecue and grill turning frequently until the skin is crisp and browned and the juices run clear when meat is pierced, about 5 minutes.

Indonesian Chicken

Serves 6

Although this chicken dish is remarkably easy, its slightly sweet yet spicy coconut-milk sauce gives it an exotic flavor. For a more fiery version, increase the quantity of chile sauce. Serve over fluffy white rice.

Tip

If you prefer, use skinless bone-in chicken thighs when making this recipe. Do not brown (Step 1). Complete Step 2 after heating oil. Place thighs on the bottom of the skillet and complete the recipe.

1 tbsp	oil	15 mL
3 lbs	skin-on bone-in chicken breasts, patted dry (see Tip, left)	1.5 kg
2	onions, sliced	2
4	cloves garlic, coarsely chopped	4
2 tbsp	chopped gingerroot	30 mL
1 tsp	ground coriander	5 mL
1 tsp	ground turmeric	5 mL
8	blanched almonds (see Tips, page 112)	8
1 cup	chicken broth	250 mL
1	stalk lemongrass, tough outer layers peeled off and cut into 2-inch (5 cm) lengths, or 1 tbsp (15 mL) grated lemon zest	1
1 cup	coconut milk	250 mL
1½ tsp	soy sauce, preferably dark	7 mL
1 tbsp	Asian chile sauce, such as sambal oelek	15 mL
1 tsp	brown sugar	5 mL

1. In a Dutch oven or deep skillet with lid, heat oil over medium-high heat. Add chicken and cook, turning, until brown on all sides, about 6 minutes per batch. Transfer to a plate and drain all but 1 tbsp (15 mL) fat from the pan.

2. Reduce heat to medium. Add onions to pan and cook, stirring, until softened, about 3 minutes. Add garlic, ginger, coriander, turmeric and almonds and cook, stirring, for 1 minute. Transfer contents of pan to work bowl fitted with metal blade. Add chicken broth and process until smooth.

3. Return chicken to pan, cover with puréed mixture and add lemongrass. Cover and cook on low for 30 minutes. Remove and discard lemongrass.

4. In a bowl, combine coconut milk, soy sauce, chile sauce and brown sugar. Mix well. Add to chicken. Cover and cook until chicken is no longer pink, about 15 minutes.

Cilantro Chicken Kabobs

Serves 6 to 8

These tasty chicken kabobs are Asian in spirit and pack a rich cilantro flavor. They make a great informal dinner accompanied by fluffy white rice and a simple salad such as sliced cucumbers in an Asian-flavored vinaigrette (see Tips, below).

Tips

Eight sprigs of cilantro yields about 100 cilantro leaves.

Use strong metal skewers to ensure they don't bend under the weight of the chicken.

If you prefer, cook the chicken in the oven under the broiler. Place skewers on broiling pan under preheated broiler and broil, turning once, for about 15 minutes.

Asian Cucumber Salad: Whisk together 2 tbsp (30 mL) rice vinegar, 1 tbsp (15 mL) soy sauce and 1 tbsp (15 mL) olive oil in a serving bowl. Fit work bowl with slicing blade and slice a peeled cucumber. Add to vinaigrette and toss to combine. Season with salt and pepper to taste.

10	sprigs cilantro (stems and leaves)	10
1/4 cup	soy sauce	60 mL
1 tbsp	oil	15 mL
1 tbsp	rice wine vinegar	15 mL
2 tsp	cracked black peppercorns	10 mL
2 tsp	oyster sauce	10 mL
6	cloves garlic, coarsely chopped	6
1/4 tsp	cayenne pepper	1 mL
2 lbs	skinless boneless chicken, cut into 1-inch (2.5 cm) cubes	1 kg

Dipping Sauce

1 cup	water	250 mL
1/2 cup	granulated sugar	125 mL
8	sprigs cilantro (leaves only) (see Tips, left)	8
2	cloves garlic	2
3 tbsp	freshly squeezed lime juice	45 mL
1 tbsp	Asian chile sauce	15 mL
1 tbsp	fish sauce	15 mL
1/2 cup	peanuts, optional	125 mL

1. In work bowl fitted with metal blade, process cilantro, soy sauce, oil, vinegar, peppercorns, oyster sauce, garlic and cayenne until smooth, about 15 seconds.

2. In a resealable plastic bag, combine chicken and marinade. Seal and toss until chicken is coated. Refrigerate for at least 4 hours or overnight.

3. **Dipping Sauce:** In a saucepan, combine water and sugar. Bring to a boil over medium heat and cook until syrupy, about 10 minutes. Let cool. In work bowl fitted with metal blade, combine cilantro, garlic, lime juice, chile sauce, fish sauce, and peanuts, if using. Add cooled syrup and process until smooth, about 30 seconds.

4. Remove chicken from marinade. Discard marinade. Pat dry with paper towel and thread onto skewers (see Tips, left), leaving space between pieces to allow the heat to circulate. Place on preheated barbecue (see Tips, left) and grill, turning several times, until chicken is no longer pink inside, about 15 minutes. Serve immediately accompanied by Dipping Sauce.

Chicken Satay with Peanut Sauce

Satay, a traditional Thai dish served on tiny wooden skewers, has become a fashionable North American party food. This recipe moves it to the table, where, as in Thailand, it is served as a family meal. Fluffy white rice and steamed spinach sprinkled with toasted sesame seeds make great accompaniments.

Tips

If you don't have fresh limes, substitute lemon zest and juice in the chicken marinade.

Use strong metal skewers to ensure they don't bend under the weight of the chicken.

If you prefer, cook the chicken in the oven under the broiler. Place skewers on broiling pan under preheated broiler and broil, turning once, for about 15 minutes.

- Mini-bowl attachment

4	cloves garlic, chopped	4
1	piece (about 2 inches/5 cm) peeled gingerroot, quartered	1
¼ cup	soy sauce	60 mL
½ tsp	grated lime zest	2 mL
2 tbsp	freshly squeezed lime juice	30 mL
1 tbsp	fish sauce	15 mL
1 tbsp	oil	15 mL
1 tsp	granulated sugar	5 mL
1 tsp	Asian chile sauce	5 mL
2 lbs	skinless boneless chicken, cut into 1-inch (2.5 cm) cubes	1 kg
	Peanut Sauce (page 403)	

1. In mini bowl fitted with metal blade, process garlic, ginger, soy sauce, lime zest and juice, fish sauce, oil, sugar and chile sauce until smooth, about 30 seconds. Place chicken in a large bowl. Add puréed mixture and toss to coat. Set aside to marinate at room temperature for 30 minutes.

2. When you're ready to cook, preheat grill to medium-high or preheat broiler (see Tips, left). Remove chicken from marinade. Discard marinade. Pat dry with paper towel and thread onto skewers (see Tips, left), leaving space between pieces to allow the heat to circulate. Place on preheated barbecue and grill, turning several times, until chicken is no longer pink inside, about 15 minutes. Serve immediately accompanied by Peanut Sauce.

Thai-Style Baked Chicken

Serves 6

This dish uses a peanut sauce as a basis for baking chicken. Try it with jasmine rice and steamed vegetables for a complete meal.

Tip

You will get a stronger flavor if you prepare the dish the evening before; add sauce to chicken, cover and refrigerate for up to 1 day. Bake just before serving.

- Preheat oven to 425°F (220°C)
- 13- by 9-inch (33 by 23 cm) baking dish

2 lbs	skinless boneless chicken breasts (5 or 6), cut into 2-inch (5 cm) strips	1 kg
1/2 cup	chunky peanut butter	125 mL
1/2 cup	peanut oil	125 mL
1/4 cup	biscuit mix	60 mL
1/4 cup	white wine vinegar	60 mL
1/4 cup	soy sauce	60 mL
1/4 cup	freshly squeezed lemon juice	60 mL
4	cloves garlic, minced	4
2 tbsp	cayenne pepper	30 mL
2 tsp	chopped gingerroot	10 mL

1. Place chicken strips in baking dish and set aside.

2. In work bowl fitted with metal blade, process peanut butter, oil, biscuit mix, vinegar, soy sauce, lemon juice, garlic, cayenne pepper and ginger until smooth. Add a few drops of water if the sauce is too thick.

3. Pour peanut sauce over chicken. Bake in preheated oven until chicken is no longer pink inside, 22 to 28 minutes. Spoon some of the sauce over chicken pieces partway through.

Variation

Pork or beef strips also work well with this dish.

Chicken and Wheat Berry Salad with Avocado

Serves 6

This is a simple main-course salad, yet very tasty and nutritious. It's also a great way to use up leftover chicken. For a special treat, or if company is coming, use freshly grilled chicken breasts (see Variation, below right) and garden-fresh arugula for the greens.

Tips

To cook this quantity of wheat berries: Combine 1 cup (250) rinsed wheat berries and 2½ cups (625 mL) water. Bring to a rolling boil in a heavy pot with a tight-fitting lid. (You can also cook these in a rice cooker with a brown rice setting.) Reduce heat to low and cook, covered, until berries are tender but still a bit chewy, 45 minutes to 1 hour. Remove from heat and let stand, covered, for 5 minutes. Drain off any excess water.

Use leftover chicken or, for convenience, a cut-up rotisserie chicken.

- Mini-bowl attachment

2 cups	cooked wheat, spelt or Kamut berries, cooled (see Tips, left)	500 mL

Dressing

½ cup	Italian flat-leaf parsley leaves	125 mL
3 tbsp	red wine vinegar	45 mL
1 tsp	salt	5 mL
	Freshly ground black pepper	
½ cup	extra virgin olive oil	125 mL
2½ cups	diced cooked chicken (see Tips, left)	625 mL
2	stalks celery, diced	2
4	green onions, white part only, thinly sliced	4
1	tomato, peeled, seeded and diced	1
1	avocado, cubed	1
5 cups	torn salad greens	1.25 L

1. **Dressing:** In mini bowl fitted with metal blade, pulse parsley, vinegar, salt, and pepper to taste, to chop parsley and blend ingredients, about 5 times, stopping and scraping down the sides of the bowl once. With motor running, add olive oil through feed tube.

2. In a bowl, combine wheat berries, chicken, celery, green onions, tomato and avocado. Add dressing and toss well.

3. Line a serving bowl with salad greens. Cover with wheat berry mixture.

Variation

Grilled Chicken and Wheat Berry Salad with Avocado: To dress this salad up, substitute the cooked chicken with about 2 lbs (1 kg) skin-on bone-in chicken breasts. Grill them using your favorite method. Let cool slightly, then slice the meat off the bone in thin strips and set aside, rather than combining with wheat berry mixture. Also set 2 tbsp (30 mL) of the dressing aside. Line a deep platter with salad greens, spread wheat berry mixture on top and arrange sliced grilled chicken over that. Drizzle reserved dressing over chicken.

Herbed Chicken Salad

Serves 6

This recipe was created using an entire deli-roasted chicken. If you have part of a chicken, you can adjust the recipe accordingly.

Tip

If you process the chicken spread too much you will get a creamy consistency. Avoid this by pulsing the mixture as described.

½ cup	red onion, sliced	125 mL
3	cloves garlic	3
3 oz	cream cheese, softened	90 g
⅓ cup	Traditional Mayonnaise (page 437)	75 mL
2 tbsp	chopped tarragon, dill or rosemary	30 mL
¼ tsp	freshly ground black pepper	1 mL
¼ tsp	salt	1 mL
3 lbs	deli-roasted chicken, bones and skin removed	1.5 kg
1	large head Boston lettuce	1

1. In work bowl fitted with metal blade, process onion until finely chopped, about 20 seconds. In the last 5 seconds, add garlic to feed tube. Add cream cheese, mayonnaise, tarragon, pepper and salt and pulse about 3 times. Add chicken and pulse 6 times until coarsely chopped.

2. Divide lettuce leaves among 6 plates. Serve salad on top.

Chicken Garlic Salad Sandwiches

Serves 6

You can make this salad with any leftover chicken purchased from the grocery store deli section. This recipe uses an entire chicken, but you can adjust the recipe for your needs.

Tips

Do not overprocess the chicken spread or you'll get a creamy consistency. Avoid this by pulsing the mixture as instructed.

Spread keeps well, covered and refrigerated, for up to 3 days.

2	firm tomatoes	2
½	red onion, cut into quarters	½
3 lbs	deli-roasted chicken, bones and skin removed	1.5 kg
3 oz	cream cheese, cubed and softened	90 g
3	cloves garlic	3
⅓ cup	Fresh Dill Mayonnaise (page 438) or store-bought, adding 2 tbsp (30 mL) fresh dill	75 mL
¼ tsp	each black pepper and salt	1 mL
12	slices whole wheat bread, toasted	12

1. In work bowl fitted with slicing blade, with motor running, add tomatoes through feed tube using the pusher with firm pressure and slice. Set aside.

2. Replace slicing blade with metal blade. Add onion and process until finely chopped. Add chicken, cream cheese and garlic and pulse until coarsely chopped, about 6 times. Add mayonnaise, pepper and salt and pulse about 5 times. Divide spread among six bread slices. Top with tomato slices and remaining bread slices.

Turkey Meatballs in Tomato Sauce

Serves 6

This is great family fare that is tasty enough to serve to guests. It's great served with hot buttered orzo and a tossed green salad. If you're feeling festive, open a bottle of wine.

Tips

Use store-bought bread crumbs or make your own (page 468).

If you want to save a washing up step, chop the vegetables for the sauce (Step 3) before making the meatballs. Set them aside in a bowl, and complete Step 1.

If you have an instant-read thermometer, insert into the center of a meatball. The temperature should read at least 165°F (74°C).

Meatballs

1	small red onion, quartered	1
2 tsp	dried oregano	10 mL
1 tsp	salt	5 mL
	Freshly ground black pepper	
1½ lbs	ground turkey	750 g
½ cup	bread crumbs (see Tips, left)	125 mL
1	egg	1
2 tbsp	oil (approx.)	30 mL

Tomato Sauce

1	onion, quartered	1
2	each celery stalks and carrots, cut into chunks	2
4	cloves garlic	4
2 tsp	dried Italian seasoning	10 mL
1 tsp	each salt and cracked black pepper	5 mL
1 cup	dry white wine or chicken broth	250 mL
1	can (28 oz/796 mL) tomatoes with juice	1

1. **Meatballs:** In work bowl fitted with metal blade, pulse red onion, oregano, salt, and pepper to taste, until finely minced, about 10 times. Add turkey, bread crumbs and egg and pulse just until mixed. Wet your hands and shape into 12 meatballs. Set aside. Clean work bowl and blade.

2. In a large skillet, heat oil over medium-high heat. Add meatballs, in batches and brown well, turning often, about 5 minutes per batch. Set aside as completed.

3. **Tomato Sauce:** Meanwhile, refit work bowl with metal blade. Add onion, celery, carrots and garlic and pulse until finely chopped, about 15 times.

4. Return pan to medium heat; add more oil, if necessary. Add onion mixture and cook, stirring, until softened, about 7 minutes. Add Italian seasoning, salt and peppercorns and cook, stirring, for 1 minute. Add wine, bring to a boil and boil for 2 minutes. Meanwhile, add tomatoes to work bowl and pulse to coarsely chop, about 4 times. Add to pan and return to a boil. Add meatballs, turning to coat lightly with sauce. Return to a boil. Cover, reduce heat and simmer until meatballs are no longer pink inside, about 30 minutes (see Tips, left).

Turkey Mole

Serves 6

In many parts of Mexico, no special occasion is complete without turkey cooked in mole poblano. The authentic dish is quite a production; this simplified version is delicious nonetheless. Serve with hot tortillas, fluffy white rice and creamed corn.

2	dried ancho, New Mexico or guajillo chiles	2
2 cups	boiling water	500 mL
1 tbsp	oil	15 mL
1	skin-on bone-in turkey breast, about 2 to 3 lbs (1 to 1.5 kg), patted dry	1
2	onions, sliced	2
4	cloves garlic, sliced	4
1 tbsp	chili powder	15 mL
1 tsp	salt	5 mL
1 tsp	cracked black peppercorns	5 mL
1	can (28 oz/796 mL) tomatillos, drained	1
1 cup	chicken broth	250 mL
½ cup	coarsely chopped cilantro (stems and leaves)	125 mL
1 to 2	jalapeño peppers, seeded and chopped	1 to 2
½ oz	unsweetened chocolate, broken into pieces	15 g
4	whole cloves	4
1	piece (2 inches/5 cm) cinnamon stick	1
3 tbsp	diced mild green chiles, optional	45 mL

1. In a heatproof bowl, combine dried chiles and boiling water. Weigh down with a cup to ensure they remain submerged and set aside for 30 minutes. Drain, discarding soaking liquid and stems. Chop coarsely and set aside.

2. In a Dutch oven, heat oil over medium-high heat. Add turkey and brown on all sides. Transfer to a plate. Reduce heat to medium. Add onions to pan and cook, stirring, until softened, about 3 minutes. Add garlic, chili powder, salt and peppercorns and cook, stirring, for 1 minute. Transfer mixture to work bowl fitted with metal blade. Add tomatillos, broth, cilantro, jalapeños and chocolate and process until smooth. Add cloves, cinnamon stick, and mild green chiles, if using.

3. Pour sauce over turkey. Cover, return to a boil, reduce heat and simmer until turkey is no longer pink inside or meat thermometer reads 170°F (77°C), about 1 hour.

Not-Too-Corny Turkey Chili with Sausage

Serves 6 to 8

This delicious chili, which is loaded with vegetables and the complex flavors of a variety of hot peppers, is mild enough to be enjoyed by all family members, even with the addition of a chipotle pepper in adobo sauce.

Tips

For convenience, chop vegetables (Step 2) while dried chiles are soaking. Transfer to a bowl and set aside. Then purée chile mixture in same work bowl without rinsing.

Use cilantro stems and leaves.

Use a red or green bell pepper to suit your taste.

For this quantity of beans, use 1 can (14 to 19 oz/398 to 540 mL) drained and rinsed, or cook 1 cup (250 mL) dried beans.

2	dried ancho or New Mexico chiles	2
2 cups	boiling water	500 mL
1 cup	coarsely chopped cilantro	250 mL
1/2 cup	chicken broth	125 mL
1	chipotle chile in adobo sauce	1
2	onions, quartered	2
4	stalks celery, cut into chunks	4
6	cloves garlic, coarsely chopped	6
1	bell pepper, seeded and quartered	1
1 tbsp	oil	15 mL
1 lb	mild Italian sausage, removed from casings	500 g
1 tbsp	ground cumin (see Tips, page 195)	15 mL
1 tbsp	dried oregano	15 mL
2 tsp	chili powder	10 mL
1 tsp	salt	5 mL
1	can (28 oz/796 mL) diced tomatoes with juice	1
1 lb	skinless boneless turkey, cut into 1/2-inch (1 cm) cubes	500 g
2 cups	drained cooked pinto beans	500 mL
2 cups	corn kernels, thawed, if frozen	500 mL

1. In a heatproof bowl, combine dried chiles and boiling water. Weigh down with a cup to ensure they remain submerged and set aside for 30 minutes. Drain, discarding soaking liquid and stems and chop coarsely. Transfer to work bowl fitted with metal blade. Add cilantro, chicken broth and chipotle pepper and purée.

2. Meanwhile, in same work bowl (see Tips, left), combine onions, celery, garlic and bell pepper. Pulse until finely chopped, about 15 times.

3. In a Dutch oven, heat oil over medium heat. Add sausage and onion mixture and cook, stirring, until sausage is no longer pink, about 10 minutes. Add cumin, oregano, chili powder and salt and cook, stirring, for 1 minute. Add tomatoes and bring to a boil. Add turkey and pinto beans and return to a boil. Cover, reduce heat and cook until turkey is no longer pink inside, about 40 minutes. Add corn and simmer until corn is tender, about 10 minutes.

Wheat Berry Salad with Shredded Hearts of Romaine

Serves 4 as a main course or 8 as a side

This is an absolutely delicious combination of ingredients. Serve it on a buffet table or bring it to a potluck and expect that it will quickly disappear.

Tips

To cook this quantity of wheat berries: Combine 1¼ cups (300 mL) rinsed wheat berries and 3 cups (750 mL) water. Bring to a rolling boil in a heavy pot with a tight-fitting lid. Reduce heat to low and cook, covered, until berries are tender but still a bit chewy, 45 minutes to 1 hour. Remove from heat and let stand, covered, for 5 minutes. Drain off any excess water.

We like to use very hot pickled peppers, such as Tabasco, in this salad, but if you're heat averse, milder ones, such as banana peppers, taste good, too.

You will want about 6 cups (1.5 L) shredded lettuce.

- Mini-bowl attachment

3 cups	cooked wheat, spelt or Kamut berries, cooled (see Tips, left)	750 mL

Dressing

2 tbsp	red wine vinegar	30 mL
2 tbsp	chopped drained pickled hot peppers (see Tips, left)	30 mL
1 tbsp	Dijon mustard	15 mL
1	clove garlic, chopped	1
½ tsp	salt	2 mL
	Freshly ground black pepper	
⅓ cup	extra virgin olive oil	75 mL
4 oz	Asiago cheese	125 g
8 oz	turkey or pork kielbasa, tough casing peeled off	250 g
4	stalks celery, cut into 3-inch (7.5 cm) lengths	4
1	small red onion, halved, if necessary to fit feed tube	1
1	large heart of romaine lettuce, cut to fit feed tube	1

1. **Dressing:** In mini bowl, pulse vinegar, hot peppers, mustard, garlic, salt, and pepper to taste, to blend, 2 or 3 times. Scrape down sides of the bowl. With motor running, add olive oil through feed tube, stopping and scraping down sides of the bowl as necessary. Set aside.

2. In work bowl fitted with shredding blade, shred Asiago. Transfer to a serving bowl.

3. Replace shredding blade with slicing blade. Slice kielbasa, celery and red onion. Transfer to serving bowl. Add wheat berries and dressing to bowl and toss well. Add lettuce to feed tube, in batches, and shred. Arrange shredded lettuce on top. Cover and chill thoroughly. When ready to serve, toss well.

Variation

Substitute 3 cups (750 mL) cooked cooled barley or farro for the wheat berries.

Meat

Peppery Filets with Whiskey-Spiked Mushroom Sauce

If you're looking for a special occasion dish that has a Wow! factor but is very easy to make, look no further. This version of that old chestnut *Steak au Poivre* is made with tender filet mignon and uses far less pepper than traditional recipes. Whiskey, rather than cognac, is used for flambéing, and the addition of mushrooms to the sauce adds an elegant finishing touch.

Tip

We recommend the use of a flaky sea salt such as Maldon for its superior taste and texture. It continues the standard of elegance set by this dish. The product known as table salt is highly refined and has an unpleasant acrid taste.

- Instant-read thermometer

1 tbsp	cracked black peppercorns	15 mL
4	filet mignon (thick-cut beef tenderloin)	4
8 oz	cremini mushrooms, stemmed	250 g
1	shallot, peeled	1
½ cup	beef broth	125 mL
¼ cup	Italian flat-leaf parsley leaves	60 mL
1	clove garlic, coarsely chopped	1
2 tbsp	butter	30 mL
	Sea salt (see Tip, left)	
2 tbsp	peanut or corn oil	30 mL
⅓ cup	whiskey	75 mL
½ cup	heavy or whipping (35%) cream	125 mL

1. Divide peppercorns into 4 batches and press each into one side of a filet. Set aside.

2. In work bowl fitted with slicing disk, working in batches, place mushroom caps in feed tube on their sides, all facing in the same direction and slice. Add shallot to feed tube and slice. Set mushrooms and shallot aside.

3. Replace slicing blade with metal blade. Process broth, parsley and garlic until herbs are finely minced. Set aside.

4. In a large skillet, melt butter over medium-high heat. Immediately add mushrooms and shallot and cook, stirring, until mushrooms lose their liquid and are nicely browned, about 5 minutes. Transfer to a bowl. Season with salt to taste and set aside.

5. Return skillet to medium-high heat. Add oil and steaks pepper side down. Sear, turning once, for 3 minutes per side. Reduce heat to medium and cook, turning once, until desired degree of doneness is reached, about 6 minutes for rare (120°F/49°C). Transfer to a warm platter. Sprinkle with sea salt, tent with foil and set aside.

6. Add whiskey to pan and cook until it reduces by half, about 1 minute. Add broth mixture and cream and bring to a boil. Reduce heat and simmer until thickened, about 3 minutes. Return mushroom mixture to pan and cook, stirring, for 1 minute. Add any accumulated juices from steaks on the platter and stir well. Pour sauce over steaks.

Thai-Style Beef Salad

Serves 4

This is an elegant salad with intriguing flavors, perfect for lunch or dinner. It is a great way to use up leftover steak, but for a real treat, grill steak and serve it warm on top of the salad, pouring any accumulated juices over the salad before adding the dressing.

Tip

Use cold leftover steak or for a real treat, freshly grill and slice it.

1 lb	grilled sirloin steak, thinly sliced (see Tip, left)	500 g
1	English cucumber, peeled and seeded, cut into 3-inch (7.5 cm) chunks to fit feed tube	1
1	small red onion, quartered	1
1/4 cup	freshly squeezed lime juice	60 mL
3 tbsp	fish sauce	45 mL
1	piece (1/2 inch/1 cm) peeled gingerroot, cut into quarters	1
1 tsp	Asian chile sauce, such as sambal oelek or Sriracha	5 mL
1/2 cup	fresh cilantro leaves	125 mL
1/4 cup	fresh mint leaves	60 mL
4 cups	arugula leaves	1 L
12	cherry tomatoes, halved	12

1. In work bowl fitted with slicing blade, slice cucumber and red onion. Transfer to a bowl and set aside.

2. Replace slicing blade with metal blade. Add lime juice, fish sauce, gingerroot, chile sauce, cilantro and mint to work bowl and process until herbs are finely minced.

3. Spread arugula evenly over a deep platter. Arrange sliced cucumber and onion evenly over top. Arrange sliced meat over vegetables and surround with cherry tomatoes. Pour dressing evenly over dish. Serve immediately.

Beef Fajitas with Guacamole

Serves 4

This is a great family dinner that has a celebratory air when made with good steak. Freshly made corn tortillas produce the best results, but prepared supermarket versions work well, too. Place the garnishes and guacamole in nice serving bowls and add a big tossed salad. If you prefer, serve a fresh salsa instead of guacamole, (see Variations, below) and add sliced avocado tossed in freshly squeezed lime juice to the garnishes.

- Preheat oven to 300°F (150°C)
- Instant-read thermometer

1	recipe Guacamole (page 98)	1
8	tortillas (8 inch/20 cm)	8
1	small head iceberg lettuce, quartered	1
1	small red onion, quartered	1
4 oz	medium or aged (old) Cheddar cheese	125 g
	Sour cream, optional	
2 tbsp	oil	30 mL
1½ lbs	boneless beef striploin	750 g
2 tbsp	oil	30 mL
	Fine sea salt	

1. Wrap tortillas in foil and place in preheated oven to keep warm.

2. In work bowl fitted with slicing blade, slice lettuce. Transfer to a serving bowl. Slice red onion and transfer to a small serving bowl. Replace slicing blade with shredding blade and shred cheese. Transfer to a small serving bowl. Place guacamole, and sour cream, if using, in separate serving bowls.

3. In a large skillet, heat oil over medium-high heat. Add steak and cook for 5 minutes. Turn and cook for approximately 5 minutes more, until desired degree of doneness is achieved (145°F/63°C for medium). Transfer to a warm platter and sprinkle liberally with sea salt. When you're ready to serve, slice steak thinly across the grain and return to platter. Allow people to assemble their own fajitas.

Variations

Chicken Fajitas with Guacamole: Substitute skinless boneless chicken breasts for the steak and adjust cooking time accordingly.

Fajitas with Salsa: Use beef or chicken for the meat and substitute a fresh salsa such as Jalapeño Salsa (page 35) or Roasted Corn and Pepper Salsa (page 33) for the Guacamole.

Squash-Laced Curried Beef Patties

Delightfully different, these flavorful patties are one way of getting reluctant kids to eat their vegetables. Since they are quite robust, we like to serve them with a simple rice pilaf.

Tips

Roasting the squash intensifies the flavor and makes the squash less watery. You will need one whole small winter squash or half of a good-sized one for this quantity. Simply cut the squash in half, scoop out the seeds and cover in foil. Roast in preheated oven (400°F/200°C) until flesh is soft, about 45 minutes. Remove from oven and set aside until cool enough to handle. Scoop out flesh, transfer to work bowl fitted with metal blade and purée. Measure out 1 cup (250 mL) of purée and return to work bowl. Reserve any extra for another use.

The patties will not brown well if they are crowded in the skillet. If necessary, use a second skillet to ensure wide spacing among them, adding more oil, if necessary.

1 cup	roasted squash purée (see Tips, left)	250 mL
1	onion, quartered	1
1	green bell pepper, seeded and quartered	1
2	cloves garlic, coarsely chopped	2
1	red chile pepper, coarsely chopped	1
2 tsp	curry powder	10 mL
½ tsp	salt	2 mL
	Freshly ground black pepper	
1 lb	lean ground beef	500 g
1 cup	dry bread crumbs, such as panko	250 mL
3 tbsp	oil (approx.)	45 mL

1. In work bowl fitted with metal blade, pulse squash purée, onion, bell pepper, garlic, chile pepper, curry powder, salt, and pepper to taste until chopped. Add beef and pulse just until blended, about 20 times. Remove from bowl and shape into 6 patties.

2. Spread bread crumbs on a large plate and dredge patties in them, ensuring both sides are well covered. Discard any excess crumbs.

3. In a large skillet (see Tips, left), heat oil over medium-high heat. Add patties and cook, turning once, until browned and no longer pink inside, about 5 minutes per side. Serve hot.

Variation

Pumpkin-Laced Curried Beef Patties: Substitute an equal quantity of Pumpkin Purée (page 472) for the squash.

Fast and Easy Meat Loaf

We love fast and easy dishes that you can prepare days in advance of needing them. This one fits the bill.

Tips

Cooked meat loaf keeps, covered and refrigerated, for up to 2 days. To reheat, place in a preheated 400°F (200°C) oven until warm inside, 10 to 15 minutes for slices.

Make sure the beef broth is hot because it will incorporate more easily.

- Preheat oven to 325°F (160°C)
- 9- by 5-inch (23 by 12.5 cm) loaf pan, lined with parchment paper
- Instant-read thermometer

1 lb	ground beef	500 g
1 lb	ground mild sausage (casings removed)	500 g
3	eggs	3
2 cups	Fresh Bread Crumbs (page 468) or store-bought	500 mL
1	onion, quartered	1
½	red bell pepper, seeded and cut into large pieces	½
½	yellow bell pepper, seeded and cut into large pieces	½
2	cloves garlic	2
1	can (6 oz/175 g) tomato paste (about ¾ cup/175 mL)	1
½ cup	hot beef broth (see Tips, left)	125 mL
1½ tsp	onion powder	7 mL
1 tsp	paprika	5 mL
⅛ tsp	salt	0.5 mL
⅛ tsp	freshly ground black pepper	0.5 mL

1. In a large bowl, combine ground beef, sausage, eggs and bread crumbs. Set aside.

2. In work bowl fitted with metal blade, pulse onion, red and yellow peppers and garlic until chunky, about 20 times. Transfer to bowl with meat mixture. Add tomato paste, beef broth, onion powder, paprika, salt and pepper. Mix well.

3. Transfer to prepared loaf pan, packing firmly. Bake in preheated oven for 30 minutes. Then increase temperature to 375°F (190°C) and bake until firm when pressed on top and an instant-read thermometer inserted in the center of the loaf registers 160°F (71°C), about 45 minutes. Let loaf rest for at least 20 minutes before removing from the pan and slicing.

Variation

You can substitute all ground turkey for the beef and sausage if you like.

Biscuit-Topped Beef Pie

Serves 6

This hearty dish makes a great weekday dinner and is a favorite with teenage boys. Just add a green salad or, when in season, sliced tomatoes vinaigrette.

Tips

You can make the filling ahead of time, without adding the beans, and refrigerate for up to 2 days. When you're ready to bake, cook the beans and add them. Reheat on the stovetop or in a microwave before adding the biscuits.

For a more robust and nutritious crust, substitute ¾ cup (175 mL) whole wheat flour for an equal quantity of all-purpose.

- Preheat oven to 400°F (200°C)
- 10-inch (25 cm) deep-dish pie plate or glass baking dish

1 tbsp	olive oil	15 mL
1 lb	lean ground beef	500 g
1	onion, finely chopped	1
4	cloves garlic, minced	4
½ tsp	dried thyme leaves	2 mL
1 tbsp	all-purpose flour	15 mL
2 tbsp	tomato paste	30 mL
1 cup	beef broth	250 mL
½ cup	dry white wine	125 mL
1 tbsp	Worcestershire sauce	15 mL
	Salt and freshly ground black pepper	
2 cups	cooked sliced green beans	500 mL

Herbed Biscuit Topping

1½ cups	all-purpose flour (see Tips, left)	375 mL
2 tsp	baking powder	10 mL
¼ tsp	salt	1 mL
2 tbsp	cold butter, cubed	30 mL
½ cup	cold buttermilk (approx.)	125 mL
¼ cup	finely chopped parsley or chives	60 mL

1. In a skillet, heat oil over medium heat. Add beef and onion and cook, breaking up meat with a spoon, for 5 minutes or until beef is no longer pink. Add garlic, thyme and flour and cook, stirring, for 1 minute. Stir in tomato paste, beef broth and white wine and bring to boil. Cook, stirring, for 2 minutes or until slightly thickened. Stir in Worcestershire sauce and season with salt and pepper to taste. Stir in green beans. Transfer to pie plate and place on a rimmed baking sheet.

2. **Herbed Biscuit Topping:** In work bowl fitted with metal blade, pulse flour, baking powder and salt to mix. Add butter, pulsing until mixture resembles coarse meal. Add buttermilk and parsley, pulsing just until mixture starts to come together. If mixture seems too crumbly, add a bit more buttermilk.

3. Divide dough into 6 balls. Flatten each into the size of an average biscuit (about 2 inches/5 cm) and arrange over top of pie. Bake in preheated oven until top is golden brown and biscuit is totally cooked through, about 20 minutes.

Tourtière

This meat pie is a tradition in Quebec, where it is often served on Christmas Eve. It is rich and dense. All it needs is a green salad and your favorite chutney or relish.

Tips

Although we've been brainwashed to think of lard as unhealthy, it is actually loaded with heart-healthy fats such as monounsaturates.

Although shredding the potatoes with your food processor may seem like an extra step, it's a snap and the texture is great in this dish. Shredded potatoes almost dissolve into the meat, creating a particularly luscious result.

Your potatoes will shred more easily if you cook them ahead of time and refrigerate overnight.

You can make the pie and freeze it for up to 1 month before baking. Thaw in the refrigerator and bake as directed.

- 10-inch (25 cm) deep-dish pie plate

Crust

2½ cups	all-purpose flour	625 mL
1 tbsp	fresh thyme leaves or 1 tsp (5 mL) dried	15 mL
½ tsp	salt	2 mL
½ cup	cold lard or non-hydrogenated shortening, cubed (see Tips, left)	125 mL
¼ cup	cold butter, cubed	60 mL
¼ cup	ice water	60 mL

Filling

2	potatoes	2
4 oz	salt pork, diced	125 g
3	onions, finely chopped	3
12 oz	ground pork	375 g
12 oz	ground beef	375 g
2	cloves garlic, minced	2
1 tbsp	minced gingerroot	15 mL
1 tsp	ground cinnamon	5 mL
½ tsp	cracked black peppercorns	2 mL
1	can (14 oz/398 mL) diced tomatoes, drained	1
	Chutney or relish	

1. **Crust:** In work bowl fitted with metal blade, pulse flour, thyme and salt to blend. Add lard and butter and pulse until mixture resembles large flake oatmeal. Sprinkle ice water over top and pulse just to blend. Transfer dough to a clean surface and knead well until dough holds together. Divide pastry dough into 2 pieces, one slightly larger than the other. Shape each into a ball, press flat into a disk, wrap in plastic and refrigerate for 1 hour.

2. **Filling:** In a large pot of boiling water, cook unpeeled potatoes until barely tender. Drain, rinse well under cold water and set aside until cool enough to handle. Peel off skins. Replace metal blade with shredding blade and shred potatoes. Set aside.

3. Meanwhile, in a large skillet over medium-high heat, cook salt pork, stirring, until it browns and renders its fat, about 7 minutes. Add onions, pork and beef and cook, stirring and breaking up meat with a spoon, until onions are softened and meat is browned, about 5 minutes. Add garlic, ginger, cinnamon and peppercorns and stir well. Stir in tomatoes and shredded potatoes. Reduce heat to low and simmer until mixture is cooked and flavors have melded, about 45 minutes. Let cool.

4. Meanwhile, on a lightly floured surface, roll out larger piece of dough into a circle large enough to fit pie plate, dusting work surface and dough as necessary to keep the dough from sticking (or roll between 2 pieces of waxed or parchment paper). Press dough into pie plate. Place pie plate in freezer or refrigerator for 15 to 20 minutes to chill while you prepare the filling. Roll out remaining dough for top crust and set aside at room temperature on sheet of parchment paper.

5. Preheat oven to 425°F (220°C). Transfer meat mixture into prepared bottom crust. Lightly brush edge with a little water. Place top crust over filling, trimming and fluting edge.

6. Bake in preheated oven for 15 minutes. Reduce heat to 350°F (180°C) and bake until crust is golden, about 30 minutes more. Let cool for about 20 minutes before serving. Serve with relish or chutney.

Shepherd's Pie

This version of that old classic is a bit of work, but it takes an everyday dish uptown. In fact, it's good enough to serve to guests.

Tips

For best results, it is important to use floury potatoes, which are usually oblong in shape and do not contain as much water as waxy varieties such as Yukon Gold. The most common are russet (Idaho) potatoes. You'll need about 3 for this recipe.

An easy way to cook potatoes in their skins is to microwave them. For this quantity, pierce scrubbed potatoes all over and place in a microwave-safe dish in one layer. Add cold water to a depth of about ½ inch (1 cm), cover and microwave on High for 8 minutes. Leave the lid on and let cool for at least 5 minutes before running under cold water and removing the skins.

Your potatoes will shred more easily if you cook them ahead of time and refrigerate overnight.

- 13- by 9-inch (33 by 23 cm) glass baking dish

2½ lbs	russet (Idaho) potatoes, boiled in their skins	1.25 kg
2	onions, quartered	2
2	each carrots and celery stalks, cut into chunks	2
2	green bell peppers, seeded and quartered	2
4	cloves garlic, coarsely chopped	4
2 tbsp	oil	30 mL
2 lbs	lean ground beef	1 kg
2 tsp	each dried thyme and salt	10 mL
1 tsp	cracked black peppercorns	5 mL
½ cup	all-purpose flour	125 mL
2 cups	beef broth	500 mL
1 cup	dry red wine	250 mL
3 tbsp	steak sauce, such as A1	45 mL
2 tbsp	butter	30 mL
2 tbsp	heavy or whipping (35%) cream	30 mL
2	egg yolks	2
	Salt and freshly ground black pepper	

1. In large capacity work bowl (if your food processor is smaller, do this in batches) fitted with metal blade, pulse onions, carrots, celery, bell peppers and garlic until finely chopped, about 15 times. Rinse out work bowl.

2. In a large skillet, heat oil over medium heat. Add onion mixture and cook, stirring, until softened, about 7 minutes. Add beef and cook, stirring, until no longer pink, about 5 minutes. Add thyme, salt and peppercorns and cook, stirring, for 1 minute. Add flour and cook, stirring, for 2 minutes (mixture will become quite thick). Add broth and wine and stir well. Reduce heat to low and simmer, stirring occasionally from the bottom up to prevent sticking, until sauce is thickened, about 45 minutes. Stir in steak sauce. Transfer to baking dish.

3. Meanwhile, preheat oven to 375°F (190°C). Peel potatoes. Replace metal blade with shredding blade and shred. Transfer to a bowl. Add butter, cream and egg yolks and beat well. Season with salt and pepper to taste. Spoon over beef mixture. Bake in preheated oven until mixture is bubbling and top is lightly browned and crispy, about 30 minutes.

Meatballs in Spinach Sauce

Serve this Middle-Eastern inspired dish on a bed of couscous for a delicious one-dish meal that is intriguingly different.

Tips

To cook couscous for this recipe: Bring 2 cups (500 mL) chicken or vegetable broth or water to a boil. Gradually add 1 cup (250 mL) couscous, stirring well. Season with salt to taste. Remove from heat, cover and let stand for at least 15 minutes. Fluff with a fork before using.

For the best flavor, toast and grind cumin yourself. *To toast cumin:* Place seeds in a dry skillet over medium heat, and cook, stirring, until fragrant, about 3 minutes. Immediately transfer to a mortar or a spice grinder and grind.

- Preheat oven to 350°F (180°C)
- Rimmed baking sheet, lightly greased

Meatballs

½ cup	fine bulgur	125 mL
¾ cup	ice cold water	175 mL
1 lb	lean ground beef	500 g
¼ cup	sun-dried tomato pesto	60 mL
1	egg, beaten	1
	Salt and freshly ground black pepper	

Spinach Sauce

1 lb	fresh spinach, stems removed, or 1 package (10 oz/300 g) spinach leaves, thawed if frozen	500 g
⅓ cup	tahini paste	75 mL
2 tbsp	freshly squeezed lemon juice	30 mL
2	green onions, white part only, chopped	2
2	cloves garlic, minced	2
½ tsp	ground cumin (see Tips, left)	2 mL
	Salt and freshly ground black pepper	
	Cooked couscous (see Tips, left)	

1. **Meatballs:** In a bowl, combine bulgur and ice water. Stir well and set aside for 5 minutes. Drain and squeeze out excess liquid and return to bowl. Add ground beef, pesto, egg and salt and pepper to taste. Using your hands, mix well. Shape into 12 meatballs, each about ¼ cup (60 mL). Place on prepared baking sheet and bake in preheated oven for 15 minutes. Turn and bake until beef is no longer pink, about 15 minutes more.

2. **Spinach Sauce:** Meanwhile, in a large pot, cook spinach until wilted, about 5 minutes (or just until heated through if using frozen). (Drain spinach but don't squeeze the water out. Otherwise, your sauce will not have enough liquid.) Transfer to work bowl fitted with metal blade. Add tahini, lemon juice, green onions, garlic and cumin. Season with salt and pepper to taste. Process until smooth, about 30 seconds.

3. To serve, spoon couscous onto a deep platter and top with spinach sauce. Arrange meatballs over top.

Italian-Style Meatballs in Lemon Sauce

Makes about 36 meatballs

If you've grown tired of meatballs in tomato sauce, try this delightfully different, but equally Italian, approach to cooking ground beef. These are particularly nice served with a simple risotto.

- Large skillet with lid

1	onion, quartered	1
20	sage leaves	20
1 tsp	salt	5 mL
	Freshly ground black pepper	
4	slices stale baguette, soaked in 1/4 cup (60 mL) water	4
1/4 cup	freshly grated Parmesan cheese	60 mL
2 lbs	extra lean ground beef	1 kg
2	eggs	2
1/2 cup	dry bread crumbs	125 mL
2 tbsp	olive oil	30 mL
2 tbsp	butter	30 mL

Lemon Sauce

1 tsp	grated lemon zest	5 mL
1 cup	dry white wine	250 mL
3 tbsp	freshly squeezed lemon juice	45 mL
	Salt and freshly ground black pepper	

1. In work bowl fitted with metal blade, pulse onion, sage, salt, and pepper to taste, until onion is finely chopped. Squeeze water out of bread and add to work bowl along with the Parmesan. Pulse to blend, about 8 times. Add ground beef and eggs and process until blended, about 1 minute. Shape mixture into 36 balls, each about 2 inches (5 cm). Roll in bread crumbs.

2. In a large skillet, heat oil and butter over medium-high heat. Add meatballs, in batches, and brown, turning frequently, about 4 minutes per batch. Return all meatballs to skillet. Cover, reduce heat to medium-low and cook until no longer pink inside, about 20 minutes. Transfer meatballs to a deep platter or serving bowl and keep warm.

3. **Lemon Sauce:** Return pan to medium-high heat. Stir in lemon zest. Add wine, bring to a boil and cook, stirring and scraping up brown bits from bottom of pan, for 2 minutes. Stir in lemon juice. Season with additional salt and pepper to taste. Pour sauce over meatballs and serve.

Butternut Chili

Serves 6

The combination of beef, butternut squash, anchos and cilantro in this chili is a real winner. Don't be afraid to make extra because it's great reheated.

Tips

For the best flavor, toast and grind cumin yourself. *To toast cumin:* Place seeds in a dry skillet over medium heat, and cook, stirring, until fragrant, about 3 minutes. Immediately transfer to a mortar or a spice grinder and grind.

For this quantity of beans, use 1 can (14 to 19 oz/ 398 to 540 mL) drained and rinsed, or cook 1 cup (250 mL) dried beans.

2	onions, quartered	2
4	cloves garlic	4
2	dried New Mexico, ancho or guajillo chile peppers	2
2 cups	boiling water	500 mL
½ cup	coarsely chopped cilantro (stems and leaves)	125 mL
1 tbsp	oil	15 mL
1 lb	lean ground beef	500 g
1 tbsp	ground cumin (see Tips, left)	15 mL
2 tsp	dried oregano	10 mL
1 tsp	salt	5 mL
½ tsp	cracked black peppercorns	2 mL
1	piece (2 inches/5 cm) cinnamon stick	1
1	can (28 oz/796 mL) diced tomatoes with juice	1
3 cups	cubed (1 inch/2.5 cm) peeled butternut squash	750 mL
2 cups	drained cooked red kidney beans (see Tips, left)	500 mL

1. In work bowl fitted with slicing blade, slice onions and garlic. Transfer to a bowl and set aside.

2. Replace slicing blade with metal blade. In a heatproof bowl, soak dried chile peppers in boiling water for 30 minutes, weighing down with a cup to ensure they are submerged. Drain, reserving ½ cup (125 mL) of the soaking liquid. Discard stems and chop coarsely. Add chiles, reserved soaking water and cilantro to work bowl and purée. Set aside.

3. In a Dutch oven, heat oil over medium-high heat. Add beef, sliced onions and garlic and cook, stirring and breaking up beef with a spoon, until beef is no longer pink, about 5 minutes. Add cumin, oregano, salt, peppercorns and cinnamon stick and cook, stirring, for 1 minute. Add diced tomatoes with juice, squash, beans and reserved chile solution and bring to a boil. Cover, reduce heat to low and simmer, stirring occasionally, until chili is thickened slightly and is very flavorful, about 1 hour.

Chunky Black Bean Chili

Serves 8

Here is a great-tasting, stick-to-the-ribs chili that is perfect for a family dinner or casual evening with friends. The combination of milder New Mexico and ancho chile peppers gives the mix unique flavoring, and the optional fresh chile peppers will satisfy any heat seekers in your group. Garnish to suit your taste with any combination of sour cream, finely chopped red or green onion, shredded Monterey Jack cheese and salsa. Serve this with crusty country bread, a big green salad and robust red wine or ice cold beer.

Tip

For this quantity of beans, use 2 cans (14 to 19 oz/398 to 540 mL) black beans, drained and rinsed, or cook 2 cups (500 mL) dried beans.

- Preheat oven to 325°F (160°C)
- Ovenproof Dutch oven

2	onions, cut to fit feed tube	2
4	cloves garlic	4
2	each dried ancho and New Mexico chile peppers	2
1 cup	coarsely chopped cilantro (stems and leaves)	250 mL
1 to 2	jalapeño peppers, chopped, optional	1 to 2
1½ cups	flat beer or beef broth, divided	375 mL
1 tbsp	oil (approx.)	15 mL
2 lbs	stewing beef, trimmed cubed and patted dry	1 kg
1 tbsp	ground cumin (see Tips, page 221)	15 mL
1 tbsp	dried oregano	15 mL
1 tsp	cracked black peppercorns	5 mL
1 tsp	salt	5 mL
1	can (28 oz/796 mL) diced tomatoes with juice	1
4 cups	drained cooked black beans (see Tip, left)	1 L

1. In work bowl fitted with slicing blade, slice onions and garlic. Transfer to a bowl and set aside.

2. Replace slicing blade with metal blade. In a heatproof bowl, soak dried chile peppers in boiling water for 30 minutes, weighing down with a cup to ensure they remain submerged. Drain, discarding soaking liquid and stems and chop coarsely. Transfer to work bowl fitted with metal blade. Add cilantro, jalapeño, if using, and ½ cup (125 mL) of the beer and purée until smooth. Set aside.

3. In a Dutch oven, heat oil over medium-high heat. Add beef, in batches, and cook, stirring, adding oil if necessary, until browned, about 4 minutes per batch. Using a slotted spoon, transfer to a bowl as completed.

4. Reduce heat to medium. Add onions and garlic and cook, stirring, until softened, about 3 minutes. Add cumin, oregano, peppercorns and salt and cook, stirring, for 1 minute. Add tomatoes, remaining beer, beans, reserved beef and chile solution and bring to a boil. Cover and bake in preheated oven until meat is very tender, about 2 hours. To serve, ladle into bowls and garnish as desired.

Red Hot Chili

This is a crowd-pleasing recipe for a tailgate party. You can save the leftovers but we warn you: the chili gets hotter every day!

Tip

Make sure you wear plastic gloves when handling the hot peppers because the hot seeds and oil will stay on your skin and burn your eyes if you rub them.

1	large onion, quartered	1
1	green bell pepper, seeded and quartered	1
2	stalks celery, cut into 3-inch (7.5 cm) pieces	2
2	jalapeño peppers, cut in half and seeded	2
4	cloves garlic	4
2 tbsp	vegetable oil	30 mL
4 lbs	lean ground beef	2 kg
1	can (6 oz/175 mL) tomato paste (about ¾ cup/175 mL)	1
1	can (28 oz/796 mL) stewed tomatoes with juice, coarsely chopped	1
1 tbsp	chili powder	15 mL
1 tbsp	salt	15 mL
1 tbsp	freshly ground black pepper	15 mL
½ tsp	dried oregano	2 mL
½ tsp	garlic salt	2 mL

1. In work bowl fitted with metal blade, pulse onion, green pepper, celery, jalapeño and garlic until finely chopped, about 15 times.

2. Heat oil in a large saucepan over medium heat. Add onion mixture and sauté until onions are translucent, about 10 minutes. Add ground beef and cook, stirring and breaking up beef with a spoon, until no longer pink, 10 to 15 minutes. Stir in tomato paste and stewed tomatoes with juice. Add chili powder, salt, black pepper, oregano and garlic salt. Reduce heat and simmer for 30 minutes. Taste and adjust salt and pepper. Let simmer for 2½ hours, stirring every 10 to 15 minutes.

Variation

For a hotter chili, add additional jalapeño peppers to your heat threshold.

Baked Beef Burgundy

Serves 6 to 8

The flavorful taste of burgundy wine in this dish will warm you up during the cold winter months.

Tips

Always use a good-quality Burgundy or merlot wine that's good enough to drink.

Use reduced-sodium soy sauce because the regular kind is too salty.

- Preheat oven to 325°F (160°C)
- Large ovenproof saucepan

5	large carrots, cut into 3-inch (7.5 cm) lengths (about 12 oz/375 g)	5
6	stalks celery, cut into 3-inch (7.5 cm) lengths	6
3	large onions, quartered (about 1 lb/500 g)	3
12 oz	button mushrooms, stemmed	375 g
¼ cup	all-purpose flour	60 mL
¼ cup	reduced-sodium soy sauce (see Tips, left)	60 mL
4	cloves garlic	4
3 lbs	stewing beef, cut into 3- to 3½-inch (7.5 to 8.5 cm) cubes	1.5 kg
1½ cups	Burgundy wine (see Tip, left)	375 mL
½ tsp	freshly ground black pepper	2 mL
½ tsp	dried thyme	2 mL
	Cooked rice or noodles	

1. In work bowl fitted with slicing blade, slice carrots, celery and onions, in batches if necessary. Transfer to a large ovenproof saucepan.

2. In same work bowl, slice mushrooms. Transfer to a bowl.

3. Replace slicing blade with metal blade and add flour. With motor running, pour soy sauce though feed tube. Add garlic and process until smooth. Transfer to saucepan with carrot mixture. Add beef, wine, pepper and thyme.

4. Cover tightly and bake in preheated oven for 1 hour. Add reserved mushrooms. Bake, covered, until beef is fork-tender, about 1 hour more. Serve over rice or noodles.

Variation

Try using pork cubes in place of the beef.

Chile-Spiced Steak with Mushrooms

Braising is a great way to bring out the best in less tender but more flavorful cuts of meat, and the combination of two different kinds of chile peppers with mushrooms is quite divine. Serve this over steaming mounds of garlic-mashed potatoes. Rice and beans make a good pairing, too.

Tips

Passila, ancho or guajillo chiles all work well in this recipe.

Steaks that are good for braising include round, blade or cross-rib. For this recipe, cut the meat into 4 or 6 steaks, each about ¾-inch (2 cm) thick.

If you prefer, substitute 1 chipotle pepper in adobe sauce for the jalapeño.

- Preheat oven to 325°F (160°C)
- Baking dish

2	dried mild chile peppers	2
2 cups	boiling water	500 mL
8 oz	cremini mushroom caps	250 g
2	onions, cut to fit feed tube	2
2	stalks celery	2
4	cloves garlic	4
2 tbsp	butter	30 mL
2 tbsp	oil	30 mL
2 lbs	braising steak (see Tips, left)	1 kg
1	can (28 oz/796 mL) tomatoes with juice	1
1	jalapeño pepper, quartered or chipotle pepper in adobe sauce	1
1 tbsp	ground cumin (see Tips, page 221)	15 mL
1 tsp	salt	5 mL
	Freshly ground black pepper	

1. In a heatproof bowl, combine dried chiles and boiling water. Weigh down with a cup to ensure they remain submerged and set aside for 30 minutes. Drain, discarding soaking liquid and stems. Chop coarsely.

2. Meanwhile, in work bowl fitted with slicing blade, working in batches, place mushroom caps in feed tube on their sides, all facing in the same direction and slice. Set aside. Slice onions, celery and garlic and set aside.

3. In a large skillet, melt butter over medium-high heat. Add mushrooms and cook, stirring, until they release their liquid, about 5 minutes. Transfer to a bowl and set aside. Add oil to pan. Add steaks, in batches, and cook, turning once, until nicely browned, about 4 minutes per batch. Transfer to baking dish.

4. In work bowl fitted with metal blade, pulse tomatoes, jalapeño and reconstituted dried chiles until finely chopped, about 5 times. Set aside.

5. Add onions, celery and garlic to skillet and cook, stirring, until softened, about 5 minutes. Add cumin, salt, and pepper to taste, and cook, stirring, for 1 minute. Add tomato mixture and mushrooms. Stir well and bring to a boil. Pour over steak. Cover tightly with foil and bake in preheated oven until steak is very tender, about 1½ hours.

Italian-Style Pot Roast

Serves 8

A perfect dish for Sunday dinner, this robust pot roast simmers in the oven all afternoon, creating inviting aromas that waft through the house. Serve it over polenta to complete the Italian theme, but mashed potatoes or a simple risotto work well, too. Don't worry about leftovers — they reheat very well.

- Ovenproof Dutch oven
- Parchment paper

1	onion, quartered	1
3	cloves garlic	3
1	carrot, peeled and cut into 1-inch (2.5 cm) thick slices	1
1	stalk celery, cut into 1-inch (2.5 cm) thick slices	1
1 tsp	salt	5 mL
1/2 tsp	cracked black peppercorns	2 mL
1	boneless bottom round (outside round) or chuck (cross rib) roast, about 4 lbs (2 kg)	1
1	piece (2 inches/5 cm) cinnamon stick	1
2	bay leaves	2
3 cups	dry red wine	750 mL
1/4 cup	all-purpose flour (approx.)	60 mL
2 tbsp	oil	30 mL
2 oz	pancetta or guanciale, chopped	60 g
1/4 cup	grappa or brandy	60 mL

1. In work bowl fitted with metal blade, pulse onion and garlic until coarsely chopped, about 10 times. Add carrot and celery and pulse until mixture is very finely chopped, about 20 times, stopping and scraping down sides of the bowl as necessary. Add salt and peppercorns and pulse to blend. Transfer to a large bowl.

2. Add beef, cinnamon and bay leaves to bowl and cover with wine. Cover and refrigerate overnight or for up to 2 days, turning once or twice.

3. Preheat oven to 325°F (160°C). Remove beef from marinade and pat dry. Drain marinade through a fine sieve, pressing to extract as much liquid as possible. Reserve liquid and vegetable mixture, including bay leaves and cinnamon, separately.

4. Pat beef dry. Spread flour on a large plate and dredge beef in it until evenly covered. Discard any excess flour. In Dutch oven, heat oil over medium-high heat. Add pancetta and cook, stirring until browned about 5 minutes. Add beef and brown on all sides, about 15 minutes. Remove from pot and set aside. Add reserved vegetable mixture and cook, stirring, until vegetables soften, about 5 minutes. Add grappa. Bring to a boil, scraping up brown bits from the bottom of pan, and boil for 2 minutes. Add reserved marinade and bring to a boil. Return beef to pot.

5. Place a large piece of parchment paper over the beef, pressing it down to brush the meat and extending up the sides of the Dutch oven so it overlaps the rim. Cover and bake in preheated oven until meat is falling-apart tender, about 4 hours. Remove and discard parchment, being careful not to spill accumulated liquid into the sauce. Transfer meat to a warm platter, tent with foil and let rest for 10 minutes. Slice thinly. Spoon some sauce over top and pass the remainder in a sauceboat.

Peppery Roast Beef with Chimichurri Sauce

Serves 4 to 6

Chimichurri is a South American green sauce, traditionally served with churrasco-style grilled meats, most often steak. It makes a great accompaniment for roast beef. Its Latin origins inspire dining al fresco on a lazy summer night. Add your favorite salad, a good bottle of Chilean Cabernet and enjoy!

Tip

If you prefer, substitute ½ tsp (2 mL) ground cinnamon for the cinnamon stick. Do not toast. Add to the spice mixture after it has been ground. You could also substitute Chile Pepper Rub (page 448) for the spice rub.

- Roasting pan with rack
- Instant-read thermometer

Chimichurri Sauce

2 cups	packed Italian flat-leaf parsley leaves	500 mL
½	red bell pepper, seeded and coarsely chopped	½
1	long red chile or jalapeño pepper, seeded and coarsely chopped	1
2	cloves garlic, chopped	2
½ tsp	dried oregano or 1 tbsp (15 mL) fresh oregano leaves	2 mL
½ tsp	salt	2 mL
½ tsp	freshly ground black pepper	2 mL
3 tbsp	red wine vinegar	45 mL
⅓ cup	extra virgin olive oil	75 mL

Spice Rub (see Variations, right)

1 tbsp	coarse sea salt or 1 tsp (5 mL) table salt	15 mL
1 tsp	cumin seeds	5 mL
2	dried red chile peppers	2
10	black peppercorns	10
1	piece (¼ inch/0.5 cm) cinnamon stick (see Tip, left)	1
1	boneless beef roast, such as top sirloin prime rib or eye of round, about 3 lbs (1.5 kg)	1
1 tbsp	Asian chile oil or olive oil	15 mL

1. **Chimichurri Sauce:** In work bowl fitted with metal blade, pulse parsley, bell pepper, chile pepper, garlic, oregano, salt, pepper and vinegar until finely chopped, about 10 times, stopping and scraping down sides of the bowl once. With motor running, gradually add olive oil through feed tube, processing until mixture is smooth. Cover and chill for about 2 hours to allow the flavors to blend.

2. **Spice Rub:** In a small dry skillet over medium heat, toast salt, cumin seeds, chiles, peppercorns and cinnamon until the spices release their aroma, about 2 minutes. Transfer to a spice grinder and grind to a fine powder. (You can also do this in a mortar with a pestle or between 2 sheets of waxed paper, using the bottom of a wine bottle or measuring cup.) Set aside.

3. Pat meat dry with paper towel. Rub spice mixture into the meat, covering all surfaces except for the ends. Brush with chile oil, ensuring the surface is entirely covered. Let stand at room temperature for 30 minutes.

4. Preheat oven to 400°F (200°C). Place roast on a rack in a roasting pan. Roast until nicely browned, about 20 minutes. Reduce oven temperature to 300°F (150°C) and continue to roast until an instant-read thermometer inserted into the thickest part of the meat registers the desired degree of doneness, 125°F (52°C) for rare, about 25 minutes. Remove from oven, place on a warm platter, tent with foil and let rest for 10 minutes. Slice thinly across the grain and serve accompanied with the sauce.

Variation

Mixed Peppercorn Crust: If you prefer, rub the beef with a simple mixture of sea salt and peppercorns. Skip the toasting step and combine 1 tbsp (15 mL) coarse sea salt with 1 tbsp (15 mL) each black, white and dried green peppercorns. Grind coarsely. Rub over the meat and brush with olive oil rather than chile oil. Continue as directed.

Roast Beef with Balsamic-Onion Gravy

Serves 8

Sometimes nothing will do but roast beef, which has become a special occasion dish in many households. Go all out and serve it with this luscious gravy, as well as Homemade Horseradish (page 469).

- Preheat oven to 400°F (200°C)
- Ovenproof grill pan
- Instant-read thermometer

Beef

1	boneless top sirloin or prime rib roast with a layer of fat, about 3 lbs (1.5 kg)	1
1 tbsp	olive oil	15 mL
	Coarse flaky sea salt, such as Maldon	

Onion Gravy

3	large white onions, quartered	3
¼ cup	butter, divided	60 mL
¼ cup	all-purpose flour	60 mL
1 tsp	dried thyme	5 mL
1 tsp	salt	5 mL
	Freshly ground black pepper	
2 cups	beef broth	500 mL
2 tbsp	balsamic vinegar	30 mL

1. **Beef:** Rub beef with olive oil. Heat a grill pan over medium-high heat. Add meat, fat side down, and cook until fat renders and is sizzling, about 5 minutes. Transfer to preheated oven. Roast for 25 minutes or until an instant-read thermometer reads 125°F (52°C) for rare or 145°F (63°C) for medium. Remove from oven, sprinkle with sea salt, tent with foil and let rest for 5 minutes.

2. **Onion Gravy:** Meanwhile, in work bowl fitted with slicing blade, slice onions. In a large skillet over medium heat, melt 2 tbsp (30 mL) of the butter. Add onions and cook, stirring, until they begin to turn golden, about 10 minutes. Add flour and cook, stirring, for 2 minutes. Add thyme, salt, and pepper to taste, and cook, stirring, for 1 minute. Add beef broth and vinegar and bring to a boil, stirring and scraping up brown bits from the bottom of the pan, until nicely thickened, about 5 minutes. Taste and adjust seasoning. Pour any accumulated juices from resting meat into gravy and stir well.

3. To serve, slice meat thinly across the grain and arrange on a warm platter. Pass onion gravy at the table.

Brisket in Tomatillo Sauce

This combination of slightly tart tomatillos and robust meat with a finish of cilantro and chipotle peppers in adobo sauce is absolutely delicious. Serve over fluffy mashed potatoes, hot onion buns or, to continue the Mexican theme, a pot full of beans and rice. If it suits your schedule, cook the brisket the day before you intend to serve it (see Tips, page 233)

Tips

If the whole piece of brisket won't fit in your Dutch oven, cut it in half to brown, then lay the two pieces on top of each other when it goes into the oven.

This quantity of chiles produces a nicely spicy result. If you're a heat seeker, increase the quantity.

For the best flavor, toast and grind cumin yourself. *To toast cumin:* Place seeds in a dry skillet over medium heat and cook, stirring, until fragrant, about 3 minutes. Immediately transfer to a mortar or a spice grinder and grind.

- Preheat oven to 325°F (160°C)
- Ovenproof Dutch oven

2	onions	2
4	cloves garlic	4
1 cup	coarsely chopped cilantro (stems and leaves)	250 mL
1 cup	beef broth	250 mL
2	chipotle chile peppers in adobo sauce	2
1 tbsp	oil	15 mL
4 to 5 lbs	double beef brisket, trimmed (see Tips, left)	2 to 2.5 kg
1 tbsp	ground cumin (see Tips, left)	15 mL
1 tsp	dried oregano leaves	5 mL
1 tsp	salt	5 mL
1 tsp	cracked black peppercorns	5 mL
1	can (28 oz/796 mL) tomatillos, drained	1

1. In work bowl fitted with slicing blade, slice onions and garlic. Transfer to a bowl and set aside.

2. Replace slicing blade with metal blade. Add cilantro, beef broth and chipotle chiles in adobo sauce to work bowl and process until smooth, about 30 seconds. Set aside.

3. In a Dutch oven, heat oil over medium-high heat. Add brisket and brown well on both sides. Transfer to a platter and set aside (see Tips, left).

4. Reduce heat to medium. Add onions and garlic to pan and cook, stirring, until onions are softened, about 3 minutes. Add cumin, oregano, salt and peppercorns and cook, stirring, for 1 minute. Add tomatillos and chipotle mixture and stir well. Return brisket to pan and bring to a boil. Cover and bake in preheated oven until meat is very tender, about 2 hours. To serve, slice brisket thinly across the grain and place on a deep platter. Spoon sauce over top.

Southwestern Brisket

Juicy and full of flavor, when properly cooked brisket is tender and delicious and lends itself to a wide variety of sauces and seasonings. This version, which relies on New Mexico chiles for its rich, tangy taste, is mildly piquant and can be enjoyed by all family members. If you prefer a spicier version, add 1 to 2 finely chopped jalapeño peppers, along with the green bell peppers. We like to serve this over piping hot mashed potatoes.

Tips

Be aware that dried New Mexico chiles come in both mild and hot versions. We tested this recipe using the mild variety. Hot ones would produce a very spicy result.

To save washing the work bowl and blade, complete Step 2 immediately after you have set the chiles aside to soak and transfer the mixture to a bowl. Then once the chiles are reconstituted, you can add them to the same work bowl along with the beef broth and vinegar.

- Preheat oven to 325°F (160°C)
- Ovenproof Dutch oven

2	dried mild New Mexico chile peppers (see Tips, left)	2
2 cups	boiling water	500 mL
½ cup	beef broth	125 mL
¼ cup	red wine vinegar	60 mL
2	onions, quartered	2
6	stalks celery, cut into 3-inch (7.5 cm) lengths	6
2	green bell peppers, seeded and quartered	2
6	cloves garlic	6
1 tbsp	oil	15 mL
4 lbs	double beef brisket, trimmed (see Tips, right)	2 kg
1 tbsp	dry mustard	15 mL
1 tbsp	dried oregano	15 mL
1 tbsp	cracked black peppercorns	15 mL
2 tsp	ground cumin (see Tips, right)	10 mL
1 tsp	salt	5 mL
¼ cup	all-purpose flour	60 mL
1	can (28 oz/796 mL) diced tomatoes, drained	1
½ cup	packed brown sugar	125 mL
4	bay leaves	4
½ cup	finely chopped parsley	125 mL

1. In a heatproof bowl, soak dried chile peppers in boiling water for 30 minutes, weighing down with a cup to ensure they remain submerged. Drain, discarding soaking liquid and stems. Transfer to work bowl fitted with metal blade. Add beef broth and vinegar (see Tips, left). Purée and set aside.

2. In clean work bowl fitted with metal blade, pulse onions, celery, bell peppers and garlic until finely chopped, about 30 times, stopping and scraping down sides of the bowl once or twice. Transfer to a bowl.

3. In a Dutch oven, heat oil over medium-high heat. Add brisket and brown well on both sides. Transfer to a platter and set aside.

Tips

For the best flavor, toast and grind cumin yourself. *To toast cumin:* Place seeds in a dry skillet over medium heat, and cook, stirring, until fragrant, about 3 minutes. Immediately transfer to a mortar or a spice grinder and grind.

You can cook the brisket the day before you intend to serve it. Cover and refrigerate in the sauce. When it is cold, spoon off the accumulated fat, which has congealed on top of the dish. Transfer meat to a cutting board, slice it very thinly and place in an ovenproof serving dish. Add remaining sauce. Cover and cook in 350°F (180°C) oven until hot and bubbling, about 30 minutes.

4. Reduce heat to medium. Add onion mixture to pan and cook, stirring, until vegetables are softened, about 7 minutes. Add mustard, oregano, peppercorns, cumin and salt and cook, stirring, for 1 minute. Sprinkle with flour and cook, stirring, for 1 minute.

5. Add tomatoes and reserved chile mixture and cook, stirring, until thickened. Stir in brown sugar and bay leaves. Return brisket to pan and bring to a boil. Cover and bake in preheated oven until meat is very tender, about 2 hours. Discard bay leaf. To serve, slice brisket thinly across the grain and place on a deep platter. Spoon sauce over top and garnish with parsley.

Glazed Osso Buco with Lemon Gremolata

Serves 6 to 8

This is probably one of the all-time great veal dishes and it is a fabulous entertaining dish. The wine-flavored sauce and the succulent meat, enhanced with just a soupçon of gremolata, pungent with fresh garlic and lemon zest is fabulous. But the best of all is eating the marrow from the bones, a rare and delicious treat. Pass coffee spoons to ensure that every mouthwatering morsel is extracted.

Tip

To clean leeks: Fill sink full of lukewarm water. Split leeks in half lengthwise and submerge in water, swishing them around to remove all traces of dirt. Transfer to a colander and rinse under cold water.

- Preheat oven to 325°F (160°C)
- Ovenproof Dutch oven
- Large baking or serving dish

1	package (1/2 oz/14 g) dried porcini mushrooms	1
1 cup	boiling water	250 mL
3	leeks, white part with a bit of green, cleaned and cut into 3-inch (7.5 cm) lengths (see Tips, left)	3
2	carrots, peeled and cut into 3-inch (7.5 cm) lengths	2
2	stalks celery, cut into 3-inch (7.5 cm) lengths	2
2	cloves garlic	2
1/4 cup	all-purpose flour	60 mL
1 tsp	salt	5 mL
1/2 tsp	freshly ground black pepper	2 mL
1/8 tsp	cayenne pepper	0.5 mL
6 to 8	sliced veal shanks	6 to 8
1 tbsp	olive oil	15 mL
1 tbsp	butter	15 mL
1 tsp	dried thyme or 2 sprigs fresh thyme	5 mL
1/2 cup	dry white wine	125 mL

Lemon Gremolata

2	cloves garlic, minced	2
1 cup	finely chopped parsley	250 mL
	Zest of 1 lemon	
1 tbsp	extra virgin olive oil	15 mL

1. In a heatproof bowl, combine porcini mushrooms and boiling water. Let stand for 30 minutes. Drain through a fine sieve, reserving liquid. Pat mushrooms dry with paper towel and chop finely. Set aside.

2. In work bowl fitted with metal blade, pulse leeks, carrots, celery and garlic until finely chopped, about 30 times, stopping and scraping down sides of the bowl once or twice. Set aside.

3. In a bowl, mix together flour, salt, black pepper and cayenne. Lightly coat veal shanks with mixture, shaking off the excess. Set any flour mixture remaining aside.

4. In a Dutch oven, heat olive oil and butter over medium heat. Add veal and cook, turning once, until nicely browned on both sides, about 6 minutes per batch. Transfer to a plate and set aside.

5. Add leeks, carrots, celery and garlic to pan and stir well. Reduce heat to low, cover and cook until vegetables are softened, about 10 minutes. Increase heat to medium. Add thyme and reserved reconstituted mushrooms and cook, stirring, for 1 minute. Add reserved flour mixture, stir and cook for 1 minute. Add wine and reserved mushroom liquid and bring to a boil.

6. Return veal to pan and bring to a boil. Cover and bake in preheated oven until veal is very tender, about 2 hours.

7. When veal has finished cooking, preheat broiler. Transfer the cooked shanks to a baking/serving dish large enough to accommodate them in a single layer. Transfer sauce to a clean work bowl fitted with metal blade and process until smooth. Spoon approximately 2 tbsp (30 mL) puréed sauce over each shank and heat under broiler until the top looks glazed and shiny, about 5 minutes. Transfer remainder of the sauce to a saucepan and heat over medium heat, until slightly reduced. Pass in a sauceboat at the table.

8. **Lemon Gremolata:** In a small serving bowl, combine garlic, parsley, lemon zest and oil and pass around the table, allowing guests to individually garnish.

New Mexico Short Ribs

Serves 4 to 6

These flavorful short ribs are meaty, spicy and delicious. All they really need is a bowl of steaming rice, but the flavors really pop over garlic mashed potatoes or red beans and rice. If you prefer a spicier mixture, add ½ to 1 jalapeño pepper to the food processor mixture and use 4 dried chiles.

Tips

Be aware that dried New Mexico chiles come in both mild and hot versions. We tested this recipe using the mild variety. Hot ones would produce a very spicy result.

To save washing the work bowl and blade, complete Step 3 immediately after you have set the chiles aside to soak and transfer the onion mixture to a bowl. Then once the chiles are reconstituted, you can add them to the same work bowl along with the beef broth and cilantro.

- Preheat broiler
- Ovenproof Dutch oven

4 to 5 lbs	beef short ribs	2 to 2.5 kg
2 to 4	dried mild New Mexico, ancho or guajillo chile peppers	2 to 4
2 cups	boiling water	500 mL
1 cup	beef broth, divided	250 mL
½ cup	coarsely chopped cilantro (stems and leaves)	125 mL
2	onions, cut to fit feed tube	2
4	cloves garlic	4
1 tbsp	oil	15 mL
1 tbsp	ground cumin (see Tip, page 233)	15 mL
2 tsp	dried oregano	10 mL
1 tsp	salt	5 mL
1 tsp	cracked black peppercorns	5 mL
1	piece (4 inches/10 cm) cinnamon stick	1
1	can (14 oz/398 mL) diced tomatoes with juice	1

1. Position broiler rack 6 inches (15 cm) from heat source. Broil ribs on both sides, turning once, until browned, about 10 minutes per side. Drain on paper towels. Separate ribs if in strips and set aside.

2. Meanwhile, in a heatproof bowl, soak dried chile peppers in boiling water for 30 minutes, weighing down with a cup to ensure they remain submerged. Drain, discarding soaking liquid and stems and chop coarsely. Transfer to work bowl fitted with metal blade. Add ½ cup (125 mL) of the beef broth and cilantro and purée. Set aside.

3. In clean work bowl fitted with slicing blade, slice onions and garlic. Set aside.

4. Preheat oven to 325°F (160°C). In a Dutch oven, heat oil over medium heat. Add onions and garlic and cook, stirring, until softened, about 3 minutes. Add cumin, oregano, salt, peppercorns and cinnamon stick and cook, stirring, for 1 minute. Add tomatoes with juice, remaining ½ cup (125 mL) of the beef broth, chile mixture and broiled short ribs and bring to a boil. Cover and bake in preheated oven until very tender, about 2 hours.

Mushroom-Stuffed Pork Chops

Here's the perfect way to serve pork chops, with the vegetable cooked right in!

Tip

If the filling starts to leak during cooking, you can always spoon it over the cooked chops when serving.

6	bone-in pork chops, about 1½ inches (4 cm) thick	6
2 tsp	olive oil	10 mL
Pinch	salt	Pinch
½ cup	button mushrooms, stemmed	125 mL
3 oz	Swiss cheese, cut into chunks	90 g
3	green onions, cut into 3-inch (7.5 cm) lengths	3
4	drops hot pepper sauce	4
1 tsp	unsalted butter, divided	5 mL

1. With a sharp knife, cut a slit horizontally to make a pocket in side of each pork chop opposite bone, working almost but not quite to edges. Rub outside of chops with olive oil and sprinkle with salt.

2. In work bowl fitted with metal blade, pulse mushrooms, cheese, green onions and hot pepper sauce until in small pieces, about 15 times. Fill chops with mushroom mixture, trying not to overstuff the pockets.

3. In a large skillet, melt ½ tsp (2 mL) of the butter over medium heat. Add chops, in batches as necessary to prevent crowding, and cook, turning once, until pork is slightly pink inside, about 8 minutes per side. Add remaining butter in between batches as necessary to prevent sticking.

Variation

Try provolone cheese in place of the Swiss.

Pork Chops with Romesco Sauce

Romesco sauce is Spanish in origin and is traditionally served with poultry or fish, although it goes splendidly with pork as well. This dish is delicious accompanied by whole wheat pasta tossed in a little extra virgin olive oil and a bowl of steaming Swiss chard or collard greens.

Tips

If you don't have a fresh hot red pepper, use 2 dried ones instead. Sauté them for 1 minute in the hot oil before adding the bread to the pan. Remove them from the tomato mixture and discard before transferring the sauce to the food processor.

If you prefer, use 4 bone-in chops.

Do not use "seasoned" pork in recipes that call for brining. It has already been injected with a brine containing salt and sodium phosphate in a water solution, so the product is not recommended for further brining since the meat's cells are already saturated with the solution.

- Instant-read thermometer

Romesco Sauce

¾ cup	extra virgin olive oil, divided	175 mL
1	slice country-style bread, about 1 inch (2.5 cm) thick, crusts removed	1
4	cloves garlic, minced	4
1	red chile pepper (see Tips, left)	1
1 cup	drained chopped tomatoes	250 mL
1	roasted red bell pepper (see Tips, right)	1
½ cup	blanched almonds or pine nuts, toasted (see Tips, page 112)	125 mL
2 tbsp	red wine vinegar	30 mL
	Salt and freshly ground black pepper	

Brine

¼ cup	kosher salt	60 mL
1 cup	boiling water	250 mL
4 cups	cold water (approx.)	1 L
	Ice cubes	
2	large butterflied pork loin chops, about 1 inch (2.5 cm) thick (see Tips, left)	2
2 tsp	paprika	10 mL
1 tsp	ground cumin (see Tips, page 233)	5 mL
1 tsp	coarse sea or Kosher salt, crushed (see Tips, right)	5 mL
Pinch	cayenne pepper	Pinch
2 tbsp	olive oil, divided	30 mL

1. **Romesco Sauce:** In a skillet, heat 2 tbsp (30 mL) of the olive oil over medium heat. Add bread and fry, turning once, until both sides are golden, about 5 minutes. Transfer to work bowl fitted with metal blade.

2. Return skillet to medium heat. Add garlic and chile pepper and cook, stirring, for 1 minute. Add tomatoes and bell pepper and bring to a boil. Add to work bowl. Add almonds and vinegar and process until smooth, about 30 seconds. With motor running, add remaining olive oil in a steady stream through feed tube, processing until smooth. Add salt and black pepper to taste. Transfer to a sauceboat. Cover and refrigerate for at least 4 hours or for up to 2 days to allow the flavors to develop.

Tips

To roast peppers: Preheat oven to 400°F (200°C). Place pepper(s) on a baking sheet and roast, turning two or three times, until the skin on all sides is blackened. (This will take about 25 minutes.) Transfer pepper(s) to a heatproof bowl. Cover with a plate and let stand until cool. Remove and, using a sharp knife, lift off skins. Discard skins, stem and core and slice according to recipe instructions.

To crush coarse sea salt: Use a mortar and a pestle, or place the salt between 2 sheets of waxed paper and crush with a rolling pin or the bottom of a measuring cup. The salt should retain its chunky texture but be fine enough to rub evenly over the meat.

3. **Brine:** In a nonreactive bowl large enough to easily accommodate the pork and brine, combine salt and boiling water. Stir until the salt is thoroughly dissolved. Add cold water and enough ice cubes to cool the solution to room temperature. Add pork chops. Add additional water, if necessary, to cover. Cover and refrigerate for at least 2 hours or for up to 6 hours. Remove chops from brine. Discard brine. Rinse chops under cold running water and pat dry with paper towel.

4. In a small bowl, combine paprika, cumin, salt and cayenne. Rub spice mixture into both sides of meat. Brush with 1 tbsp (15 mL) of the olive oil. In a large sauté pan, heat remaining tbsp (15 mL) of oil over medium-high heat. Add pork and brown, turning once, about 4 minutes per side. Reduce heat to medium-low. Cover and cook until desired degree of doneness is achieved, about 10 minutes. (For medium, until an instant-read thermometer inserted into the thickest part of the chop registers 160°F/71°C). Serve each guest half a chop topped with a dollop of Romesco Sauce and pass the remainder at the table.

Tuscan Pork Chops

Direct from the rolling hills of Tuscany! Try these all-Italian pork chops.

Tip

Try frying capers some time for another use. They pop like popcorn and taste great in a salad.

4 oz	Parmesan cheese, cut into chunks	125 g
1 tbsp	drained capers	15 mL
2 tsp	dried oregano	10 mL
½ tsp	garlic powder	2 mL
6	bone-in pork chops, about 1 inch (2.5 cm) thick	6
2 tsp	olive oil	10 mL
2 tbsp	unsalted butter, divided	30 mL

1. In work bowl fitted with metal blade, with motor running, add Parmesan cheese through feed tube and process until grated. Transfer to a shallow dish.

2. In same work bowl, process capers, oregano and garlic powder until a paste-like consistency, about 30 seconds. Transfer to dish with cheese and combine.

3. Rub both sides of pork chops with olive oil. Dredge pork chops in cheese mixture. Discard any excess mixture.

4. In a large skillet, melt 1 tbsp (15 mL) of the butter over medium heat. Add chops, in batches as necessary to prevent crowding, and cook, turning once, until pork is slightly pink inside, 3 to 4 minutes per side. Add remaining butter in between batches as necessary to prevent sticking.

Variation

You can serve this with canned spaghetti sauce over top for an added touch.

Chicken Rockefeller (page 186)

Indian-Style Cashew Chicken (page 195)

Turkey Mole (page 206)

Southwestern Brisket (page 232)

Butternut Chili (page 221)

Pork Pozole (page 256)

Coconut-Spiked Pork Tenderloin with Quinoa and Peanuts (page 241)

Tourtière (page 216)

Coconut-Spiked Pork Tenderloin with Quinoa and Peanuts

The combination of flavors in this one-dish meal are unusual and delicious. It's easy enough to make for a weeknight dinner and particularly colorful if made with red quinoa.

Tips

To clean leeks: Fill sink full of lukewarm water. Split leeks in half lengthwise and submerge in water, swishing them around to remove all traces of dirt. Transfer to a colander and rinse under cold water.

Use the kind of chile pepper you have on hand. Jalapeño, long red or green or even habanero (if you only use half) will work well in this recipe.

For the best flavor, toast and grind cumin yourself. *To toast cumin:* Place seeds in a dry skillet over medium heat and cook, stirring, until fragrant, about 3 minutes. Immediately transfer to a mortar or a spice grinder and grind.

- Large deep frying pan with lid

2	leeks, white part only, cleaned and cut into 3-inch (7.5 cm) lengths (see Tips, left)	2
4	cloves garlic, quartered	4
1	chile pepper, quartered (see Tips, left)	1
1½ cups	chicken or vegetable broth or water	375 mL
½ cup	coconut milk	125 mL
¼ cup	dry-roasted peanuts	60 mL
1 tbsp	olive oil	15 mL
12 oz	pork tenderloin, thinly sliced	375 g
2 tsp	ground cumin (see Tips, left)	10 mL
½ tsp	salt	2 mL
	Freshly ground black pepper	
1	can (14 oz/398 mL) diced tomatoes with juice	1
1 cup	quinoa, rinsed and drained	250 mL
1 cup	sliced green beans	250 mL

1. In work bowl fitted with metal blade, pulse leeks, garlic and chile pepper until finely chopped, about 15 times, stopping and scraping down sides of the bowl once or twice. Transfer to a bowl and set aside.

2. In same work bowl, process broth, coconut milk and peanuts until smooth, about 30 seconds. Set aside.

3. In a skillet, heat oil over medium-high heat. Add pork, in batches, and cook until lightly browned, about 1 minute per side. Transfer to a plate and set aside.

4. Add leek mixture to pan and cook, stirring, until softened, about 5 minutes. Add cumin, salt, and black pepper to taste and cook, stirring, for 1 minute. Add tomatoes with juice and reserved peanut mixture and bring to a boil. Stir in quinoa and green beans and return to a boil. Reduce heat to low. Stir in pork and any accumulated juices. Cover and simmer until quinoa is tender, about 20 minutes.

Jerked Pork Tenderloin

If you enjoy the flavors
of Jamaican jerk spicing
try this easy-to-make
pork tenderloin. Serve
it with beans and rice
and a green vegetable
or salad make nice
accompaniments. You
can vary the quantity
of habanero peppers
to suit your taste, but
be aware that using
four will produce a
five-alarm result.

- Instant-read thermometer

2	small red onions, quartered	2
4	cloves garlic	4
1 tbsp	coarsely chopped gingerroot	15 mL
2 to 4	habanero or Scotch bonnet peppers	2 to 4
2 tsp	ground allspice	10 mL
1 tsp	dried thyme	5 mL
1 tsp	cracked black peppercorns	5 mL
1 tsp	salt	5 mL
¼ tsp	freshly grated nutmeg	1 mL
1 tbsp	brown sugar, preferably raw cane such as Demerara	15 mL
¼ cup	soy sauce	60 mL
¼ cup	freshly squeezed lime juice	60 mL
2	pork tenderloins	2
	Olive oil	

1. In work bowl fitted with metal blade, process red onions, garlic, ginger, habanero peppers, allspice, thyme, peppercorns, salt, nutmeg, brown sugar, soy sauce and lime juice until smooth and blended, about 1 minute. Place pork in a dish. Cover with marinade, turning to ensure all parts are well coated. Cover and refrigerate overnight or for up to 2 days.

2. When you're ready to cook, preheat oven to 350°F (180°C). Remove pork from marinade, reserving ¼ cup (60 mL) of the marinade. Discard excess marinade. Place pork in a baking dish. Drizzle with olive oil and spoon about 2 tbsp (30 mL) of the marinade over each tenderloin. Cover and bake until just a hint of pink remains (or until an instant-read thermometer inserted into the thickest part of the meat registers 160°F/71°C), about 35 minutes.

Pork and Beans for Gourmands

If you're looking for a tasty and nutritious one-pot meal, this is for you. All you need to add is some crusty rolls.

Tips

To soak the beans for this recipe: Combine beans in a pot with 3 cups (750 mL) cold water. Cover and bring to a boil. Boil for 3 minutes. Turn off heat and soak for 1 hour. If you prefer, soak the beans in cold water for at least 6 hours or overnight. In either case, drain and rinse thoroughly under cold water. Beans are now ready to cook.

For the best flavor, toast and grind cumin yourself. *To toast cumin:* Place seeds in a dry skillet over medium heat and cook, stirring, until fragrant, about 3 minutes. Immediately transfer to a mortar or a spice grinder and grind.

- Preheat oven to 350°F (180°C)
- Ovenproof Dutch oven

1 cup	dried white beans, such as navy or cannellini, soaked, drained and rinsed (see Tips, left)	250 mL
1	onion, quartered	1
2	carrots, peeled and cut into 3-inch (7.5 cm) chunks	2
2	stalks celery, cut into 3-inch (7.5 cm) chunks	2
2	cloves garlic	2
1	jalapeño pepper, seeded and quartered	1
2 tsp	ground cumin (see Tips, left)	10 mL
1 tsp	cracked black peppercorns	5 mL
1 tsp	salt	5 mL
2 tbsp	olive oil	30 mL
1½ lbs	pork spareribs, cut into individual ribs and patted dry	750 g
3 cups	chicken broth	750 mL
1	bunch (about 1 lb/500 g) Swiss chard, stems removed and deveined	1

1. In work bowl fitted with metal blade, pulse onion, carrots, celery, garlic, jalapeño, cumin, peppercorns and salt until finely chopped, about 20 times, stopping and scraping down sides of the bowl once or twice. Set aside.

2. In a Dutch oven, heat oil over medium-high heat. Add ribs, in batches, and cook, turning once, until browned, about 5 minutes. Transfer to a plate as completed. Reduce heat to medium. Add onion mixture to pan and cook, stirring and scraping up brown bits from the bottom of pan, until vegetables are softened, about 7 minutes. Add drained beans and toss until coated. Add broth and bring to a boil.

3. Cover and bake in preheated oven until ribs are falling off the bone, about 1½ hours. Remove from oven, return to element and increase heat to medium high.

4. Using a slotted spoon, scoop out ribs and about ¾ of the bean mixture. Transfer to a serving dish and keep warm. Add chard to pan, stir well, and cook until nicely wilted, about 7 minutes. Transfer mixture to work bowl fitted with metal blade and process until smooth. Add to rib mixture, stir well and serve.

Pancetta-Laced Baked Penne with Roasted Vegetables

Like most baked pastas, this one is a bit of work, but when you bring it to the table, it really delivers on the Wow! factor. All you need to add is a tossed green salad for a great meal.

Tips

This dish can be partially prepared the day before you intend to serve it. Complete Steps 1 through 4. Cover with plastic wrap and refrigerate overnight. When you're ready to serve, complete Step 5, adding about 15 minutes to the cooking time.

If you prefer, substitute 2 tbsp (30 mL) extra virgin olive oil for the melted butter.

When baking pasta, the boiled pasta should not be cooked as long as it would to be tossed in sauce. Because it will continue to cook in the oven it should be firmer than al dente when added to the other ingredients.

- Large rimmed baking sheet
- Preheat oven to 400°F (200°C)
- 13- by 9- by 2-inch (33 by 23 by 5 cm) glass baking dish, lightly greased

2	red onions, quartered	2
2	medium zucchini, trimmed and cut into ½-inch (1 cm) slices	2
1	bulb fennel, trimmed, cored and thinly sliced on the vertical	1
3 cups	cherry tomatoes	750 mL
¼ cup	olive oil	60 mL
1 lb	penne pasta	500 g
4 oz	pancetta, very coarsely chopped	125 g
4	cloves garlic	4
½ cup	fresh parsley leaves	125 mL
8 oz	Fontina cheese	250 g
½ cup	chopped pitted black olives	125 mL
½ cup	Fresh Bread Crumbs (page 468) or store-bought	125 mL
2 tbsp	melted butter (see Tips, left)	30 mL

1. In a large bowl, combine red onions, zucchini, fennel and tomatoes. Add olive oil and toss well. Spread out on baking sheet and roast in preheated oven, stirring once or twice, until lightly browned, about 45 minutes. Set vegetables aside and reduce heat to 375°F (190°C).

2. Meanwhile, in a large pot of boiling salted water over high heat, cook pasta until almost al dente (see Tips, left). Scoop out 1 cup (250 mL) of the pasta water and set aside. Drain pasta.

3. In work bowl fitted with metal blade, pulse pancetta, garlic and parsley until chopped and blended, about 15 times, stopping and scraping down sides of the bowl as necessary. Set pancetta mixture aside. Replace metal blade with shredding blade and shred cheese.

4. In a large bowl, combine roasted vegetables, pancetta paste, hot pasta, cheese and olives. Add about ½ cup (125 mL) of reserved pasta water and toss well. Add more pasta water, if necessary. (You want the mixture to fairly moist.) Transfer to prepared baking dish.

5. In a small bowl, combine bread crumbs and melted butter. Mix well. Sprinkle evenly over top of pasta. Bake in preheated oven until top is nicely browned, about 30 minutes. Serve immediately.

Sausage and Cabbage Casserole

This is classic French family food. It is very easy to make and is particularly delicious made with Savoy cabbage, which comes into North American markets in the fall. Serve with warm whole-grain bread for a hearty and delicious meal.

Tips

Make sure the cabbage is cut small enough to fit through your feed tube.

Any good pork sausage works well in this recipe. If you are using a highly seasoned sausage such as Italian, omit the caraway seeds, which work best with mildly flavored sausages.

- Preheat oven to 325°F (160°C)
- 12-cup (3 L) baking dish with lid, greased
- Parchment paper

1	head (about 3 lbs/1.5 kg) cabbage, cored and cut into wedges (see Tips, left)	1
2	onions, cut to fit feed tube	2
1 tbsp	olive oil	15 mL
1½ lbs	pork sausage, removed from casings (see Tips, left)	750 g
4	cloves garlic, minced	4
2 tsp	caraway seeds, optional (see Tips, left)	10 mL
	Salt and freshly ground black pepper	
1 tbsp	butter, diced	15 mL

1. In work bowl fitted with slicing blade, slice cabbage. Add to a stockpot filled with boiling salted water. Return to a boil and boil for 1 minute. Transfer to a colander and drain. Set aside. Add onions to feed tube and slice.

2. In a skillet, heat oil over medium heat. Add sausage and onions and cook, stirring, breaking up sausage with a spoon, until onions are softened and sausage is starting to brown, about 5 minutes. Add garlic, and caraway seeds, if using, and cook, stirring for 1 minute. Remove from heat.

3. In prepared dish, place ⅓ of the cabbage. Season with salt and pepper to taste, taking into account that the sausage contains salt. Sprinkle with half the sausage mixture. Repeat and finish with a layer of cabbage. Dot with butter. Place a piece of parchment over the cabbage, and cover with lid. Bake in preheated oven until hot and bubbling, about 1½ hours.

Chorizo Cakes

These very tasty cakes make a great weeknight dinner. All you need to add is salad and, if you feel so inclined, a fresh salsa such as Traditional Salsa (page 32) or Roasted Corn and Pepper Salsa (page 33).

Tips

An easy way to cook potatoes in their skins is to microwave them. For this quantity, pierce scrubbed potatoes all over with a fork and place in a microwave-safe dish in one layer, add cold water to a depth of about ½ inch (1 cm), cover and microwave on High for 6 minutes. Leave the lid on and let cool in the liquid for at least 5 minutes before running under cold water and removing the skins.

Your potatoes will shred more easily if you cook them ahead of time and refrigerate overnight.

2	potatoes (each about 6 oz/175 g) boiled in their skins, cooled and peeled (see Tips, left)	2
2	fresh chorizo sausages, removed from casings (each about 6 oz/175 g)	2
2	cloves garlic	2
4	green onions, cut into chunks	4
4 oz	feta cheese	125 g
1	egg	1
	Salt and freshly ground black pepper	
1 cup	dry bread crumbs, such as panko (approx.)	250 mL
¼ cup	oil (approx.)	60 mL
	Salsa	

1. In work bowl fitted with shredding blade, shred potatoes. Transfer to a bowl. Replace shredding blade with metal blade.

2. In a large skillet over medium-high heat, cook chorizo, stirring and breaking up with a spoon, until browned and no hint of pink remains, about 5 minutes. Using a slotted spoon, transfer to work bowl fitted with metal blade. Drain off fat and discard. Set skillet aside.

3. Add garlic, green onions, feta and egg to work bowl. Process until blended, about 15 seconds. Add to potato, season with salt and pepper to taste and mix well. Shape into 8 cakes. Spread bread crumbs on a large plate and dredge cakes liberally on both sides, adding more if necessary to make sure they are well coated.

4. Return skillet to medium-high heat. Add 2 tbsp (30 mL) of the oil. Add cakes, in batches, and cook, turning once, until golden brown, about 5 minutes per side, adding more oil as necessary. Serve with your favorite salsa.

Oregano-Spiked Pork Meatballs

Serves 4 to 6

Dishes made with ground meat are an easy dinner solution, but if you're getting tired of the same old beef dishes, try these tasty meatballs. They are delicious over hot orzo or even a simple rice pilaf. Make them smaller and they can even do double duty as an appetizer.

1	onion, quartered	1
2 tbsp	fresh oregano leaves	30 mL
2 tsp	finely grated lemon zest	10 mL
2 tbsp	oil (approx.)	30 mL
1/4 cup	freshly squeezed lemon juice	60 mL
1 lb	ground pork	500 g
1	egg	1
1 tbsp	sour cream	15 mL
1 tsp	salt	5 mL
	Freshly ground black pepper	
1 cup	dry bread crumbs, such as panko	250 mL
4	cloves garlic, minced	4
1 1/2 cups	dry red wine	375 mL
1	can (28 oz/796 mL) diced tomatoes, drained	1

1. In work bowl fitted with metal blade, pulse onion, oregano and lemon zest until finely chopped, about 8 times, stopping and scraping down sides of the bowl as necessary.

2. In a large skillet, heat oil over medium heat. Add onion mixture and cook, stirring, until softened, about 3 minutes. Add lemon juice and cook until syrupy, about 2 minutes. Remove from heat and let cool slightly.

3. Add onion mixture to work bowl fitted with metal blade. Add pork, egg, sour cream, salt, and pepper to taste, and pulse until blended. Shape into 24 meatballs. Place bread crumbs in a shallow dish. Roll meatballs in bread crumbs. Discard any excess crumbs. Return pan to medium-high heat, adding more oil, if necessary. Add meatballs, in batches, and brown well. Remove from pan as completed and set aside.

4. Add garlic to pan and cook, stirring, until softened. Add wine, bring to a boil and boil for 2 minutes. Add tomatoes and stir well. Return meatballs to pan. Bring to a boil. Cover, reduce heat and simmer until meatballs are no longer pink inside and flavors meld, about 15 minutes. Serve immediately.

Spareribs in Italian Sausage Sauce

Serves 6

This hearty dish is great stick-to-your-ribs winter fare. It's very easy to make and is absolutely delicious served over a mound of steaming soft polenta, mashed potatoes or even Easy White Bean Purée (page 367).

- Preheat oven to 325°F (160°C)
- Ovenproof Dutch oven

1	onion, quartered	1
2	cloves garlic	2
4	fresh sage leaves	4
1 tsp	salt	5 mL
½ tsp	freshly ground black pepper	2 mL
3	sweet Italian sausages, removed from casings	3
2 tbsp	olive oil	30 mL
1 lb	pork spareribs, cut into individual ribs	500 g
1 cup	dry red wine	250 mL
1	can (28 oz/796 mL) tomatoes with juice	1

1. In work bowl fitted with metal blade, pulse onion, garlic, sage, salt and pepper until finely chopped, about 10 times, stopping and scraping down sides of the bowl once or twice. Add sausages and pulse to blend, about 4 times. Set aside.

2. In a Dutch oven, heat oil over medium-high heat. Add ribs, in batches, and cook, turning once, until browned, about 5 minutes per batch. Transfer to a plate as completed. Add sausage mixture to pan and cook, stirring and scraping up brown bits from the bottom, until sausage begins to brown and is no longer pink inside, about 5 minutes. Add wine, bring to a boil and boil for 2 minutes. Add tomatoes with juice and return to a boil, stirring and breaking up tomatoes with a spoon.

3. Return spareribs to pan, cover and return to a boil. Bake in preheated oven until ribs are falling off the bone, about 1½ hours. Remove from oven, return to element and simmer, uncovered, stirring occasionally, for 15 minutes until sauce is thickened.

Ribs in Tablecloth Stainer Sauce

Serve 6

The colorful name of this sauce, which comes from the city of Oaxaca, in Mexico, is a literal translation from the Spanish. It is distinguished by the addition of fruit, such as pineapple and bananas, and you can vary the quantity of chiles to suit your taste. Three produce a pleasantly spicy sauce. Serve this with warm tortillas to soak up the ambrosial liquid.

Tip

To save washing the work bowl and blade, complete Step 3 immediately after you have set the chiles aside to soak. After the onion and garlic have been sliced, transfer them to a bowl. Then once the chiles are reconstituted, you can add them to the same work bowl along with the jalapeños and other ingredients.

- Preheat broiler
- Broiling pan
- Preheat oven to 325°F (160°C)
- Ovenproof Dutch oven

3	dried ancho chile peppers	3
2 cups	boiling water	500 mL
1	jalapeño pepper, coarsely chopped	1
2	bananas, peeled and sliced	2
1 tbsp	apple cider vinegar	15 mL
1 cup	chicken broth, divided	250 mL
4 lbs	pork spareribs	2 kg
2	onions, quartered	2
4	cloves garlic	4
1 tbsp	oil	15 mL
1 tbsp	dried oregano leaves	15 mL
1	piece (2 inches/5 cm) cinnamon stick	1
1 tsp	salt	5 mL
1/2 tsp	cracked black peppercorns	2 mL
6	whole allspice	6
2	apples, peeled, cored and sliced	2
1	can (14 oz/398 mL) diced tomatoes with juice	1
1 cup	pineapple chunks, drained if canned	250 mL

1. In a heatproof bowl, soak dried chile peppers in boiling water for 30 minutes, weighing down with a cup to ensure they remain submerged. Drain, discarding soaking liquid and stems and chop coarsely. Transfer to work bowl fitted with metal blade. Add jalapeño, bananas, vinegar and 1/2 cup (125 mL) of the chicken broth. Purée and set aside.

2. Meanwhile, position broiler rack 6 inches (15 cm) from heat source. Place ribs on broiling pan. Broil ribs on both sides until lightly browned, about 7 minutes per side. Drain on paper towels and cut into individual ribs.

3. Meanwhile, in work bowl fitted with slicing blade, slice onions and garlic.

4. In a Dutch oven, heat oil over medium heat. Add onions and garlic and cook, stirring, until softened, about 3 minutes. Add oregano, cinnamon stick, salt, peppercorns and allspice and cook, stirring, for 1 minute. Add apples, tomatoes with juice and remaining ½ cup (125 mL) of the chicken broth and bring to a boil. Add browned ribs and chile mixture and return to a boil.

5. Cover and bake in preheated oven until ribs are falling off the bone, about 1½ hours. Add pineapple and stir well. Cover and bake until flavors meld, about 10 minutes. Discard allspice and cinnamon stick.

Grilled Five-Spice Asian Ribs

If you're tired of the same ribs on the grill, try these flavorful Asian-style ribs. Don't be afraid of the unusual ingredients — most large grocery stores have an Asian section where you can find everything.

Tip

Chinese 5-spice powder is available in the Asian food section or spice section of many large supermarkets.

- Preheat oven to 300°F (150°C)
- Large rimmed baking sheet

3 lbs	baby back ribs	1.5 kg
3 tbsp	granulated sugar	45 mL
2 tbsp	chopped shallots	30 mL
2 tbsp	all-purpose flour	30 mL
2 tbsp	minced garlic	30 mL
2 tbsp	fish sauce	30 mL
2 tbsp	soy sauce	30 mL
2 tbsp	sesame oil	30 mL
2 tbsp	peanut oil	30 mL
2 tbsp	Chinese 5-spice powder (see Tip, left)	30 mL
1½ tsp	ground coriander	7 mL
1½ tsp	freshly ground black pepper	7 mL
1 tsp	chili bean paste	5 mL
1 tsp	ground cumin	5 mL
1 tsp	hot pepper flakes	5 mL
1 tsp	salt	5 mL

1. Place ribs on a large rimmed baking sheet and pour in enough water to cover bottom of sheet. Cover with foil and bake in preheated oven until fork-tender, about 1 hour and 10 minutes.

2. In work bowl fitted with metal blade, pulse sugar, shallots, flour, garlic, fish sauce, soy sauce, sesame oil, peanut oil, 5-spice powder, coriander, pepper, chili bean paste, cumin, pepper flakes and salt until well blended.

3. Pour mixture into a large bowl. Cut ribs into 3- or 4-rib sections. Add to bowl and rub seasoning mixture all over to coat. Cover and refrigerate for at least 2 hours or for up to 24 hours.

4. Preheat barbecue to medium. Place ribs on barbecue and grill, turning once, until nicely browned, about 7 minutes per side.

Variation

You can use spare, side or sliced short ribs in place of the baby back ribs.

Santa Fe–Style Ribs

If you like Southwestern flavors, you'll love these ribs, which are seasoned with mild New Mexico chiles, toasted cumin seeds and roasted garlic. For a great taste treat, serve this with polenta, cooked with a jalapeño pepper and Monterey Jack cheese.

Tip

For the best flavor, toast and grind cumin yourself. *To toast cumin:* Place seeds in a dry skillet over medium heat and cook, stirring, until fragrant, about 3 minutes. Immediately transfer to a mortar or a spice grinder and grind.

- Preheat broiler
- Broiling pan
- Preheat oven to 325°F (160°C)
- Ovenproof Dutch oven

3	dried mild New Mexico chile peppers	3
2 cups	boiling water	500 mL
1	can (28 oz/796 mL) tomatoes with juice	1
3½ to 4 lbs	pork spareribs	1.75 to 2 kg
2 tbsp	oil	30 mL
8	cloves garlic, slivered	8
1 tbsp	ground cumin (see Tip, left)	15 mL
1 tsp	dried oregano	5 mL
1 tsp	salt	5 mL
½ tsp	cracked black peppercorns	2 mL
2 tbsp	white vinegar	30 mL

1. In a heatproof bowl, soak dried chile peppers in boiling water for 30 minutes, weighing down with a cup to ensure they remain submerged. Drain, reserving ½ cup (125 mL) of the soaking liquid. Discard remaining liquid and stems and chop coarsely. Transfer to work bowl fitted with metal blade. Add reserved soaking liquid and purée. Add tomatoes with juice and pulse to chop, 3 or 4 times.

2. Position broiler rack 6 inches (15 cm) from heat source. Place ribs on broiling pan. Broil ribs on both sides until lightly browned, about 7 minutes per side. Drain on paper towels and cut pork into individual ribs.

3. In a Dutch oven, heat oil over medium heat. Add garlic and cook, stirring often, until golden and softened, about 5 minutes, being careful that the garlic doesn't burn. Add cumin, oregano, salt and peppercorns and cook, stirring, for 1 minute. Stir in tomato mixture and vinegar and bring to a boil. Add ribs and return to a boil.

4. Cover and bake in preheated oven until ribs are falling off the bone, about 1½ hours.

Café au Chile Ribs

This is a recipe for a coffee-flavored barbecue sauce adapted from Mark Miller, the chef-anthropologist who pioneered Southwestern cuisine. It has intriguing flavors that are quite addictive.

Tip

Sea salt has a clean, crisp taste and enhanced mineral content, which is preferable to refined table salt. However, you can use tiny quantities of table salt in its place, if you prefer.

- Roasting pan

Parboiling

12 cups	water	3 L
2	cloves garlic, sliced	2
1 tsp	salt	5 mL
10	whole black peppercorns	10
2	racks pork baby back ribs, about 4 lbs (2 kg)	2

Sauce

3	dried ancho chile peppers, stems removed	3
1	dried chipotle pepper, stem removed, optional	1
1 tbsp	oil	15 mL
1	onion, chopped	1
4	cloves garlic, chopped	4
1 tsp	fine sea salt or table salt (see Tip, left)	5 mL
1 tsp	cracked black peppercorns	5 mL
2 tbsp	apple cider vinegar	30 mL
1	can (28 oz/796 mL) tomatoes, drained and coarsely chopped	1
1 cup	strong brewed coffee	250 mL
¼ cup	fancy (light) molasses	60 mL

1. **Parboiling:** In a stockpot over medium heat, bring water to a boil. Add garlic, salt, peppercorns and ribs. Return to a boil. Reduce heat to low. Cover and simmer for 40 minutes. Remove from heat. Pat ribs dry with paper towel. If you're not roasting the ribs immediately, let cool and cover them tightly. Refrigerate until you're ready to use, up to 1 day.

2. **Sauce:** Preheat oven to 375°F (190°C). Meanwhile, in a dry skillet over medium heat, stir ancho peppers, and chipotle pepper, if using, until they release their aroma, about 3 minutes. Transfer to a cutting board. Let cool and cut into quarters. Set aside.

3. Return skillet to medium heat and heat oil. Add onion and cook, stirring, until softened, about 3 minutes. Add garlic, salt and peppercorns and cook, stirring, for 1 minute. Add vinegar and cook, stirring, until it evaporates, about 2 minutes. Add tomatoes, coffee, molasses and reserved chiles, and bring to a boil. Reduce heat to low and simmer until chiles are soft and sauce is thickened, about 20 minutes.

4. Transfer mixture to work bowl fitted with metal blade and process until smooth, about 1 minute. Place a strainer over a large bowl and add puréed mixture. Using a wooden spoon, press the mixture through the strainer until all the liquid and most of the solids have been extracted.

5. Pour off 1 cup (250 mL) of the sauce to use for basting and set remainder aside. Brush the ribs liberally with the basting sauce and place in roasting pan. Roast in preheated oven for 10 minutes. Turn and roast for 10 minutes more. Serve warm, accompanied by remaining chile-coffee sauce.

Pork Pozole

Serves 6

The robust flavors in this traditional Mexican dish are delicious and perfect for a casual evening with friends. Add the chipotle pepper if you like heat and a bit of smoke. To continue the Mexican theme, serve with a tossed green salad that includes a diced avocado, and warm fresh tortillas.

Tip

Poblano peppers, one of the mildest chile peppers, are becoming increasingly available in markets. Triangular in shape, they are a deep shade of green and have a wonderful hot-fruity flavor that is lovely in this dish. However, if you can't find them, green bell peppers make a more than acceptable substitute. In their dried form, poblano peppers are known as ancho peppers.

4	slices bacon	4
2 lbs	trimmed pork shoulder, cut into 1-inch (2.5 cm) cubes	1 kg
2	onions	2
4	cloves garlic	4
1 tbsp	dried oregano	15 mL
½ tsp	cracked black peppercorns	2 mL
2 tsp	finely grated lime zest	10 mL
1	can (14 oz/398 mL) diced tomatoes with juice	1
2 cups	chicken broth	500 mL
1	can (29 oz/824 mL) hominy, drained and rinsed	1
2	dried ancho or guajillo chile peppers	2
2 cups	boiling water	500 mL
2 tbsp	freshly squeezed lime juice	30 mL
2 tbsp	finely chopped cilantro	30 mL
1	chipotle pepper in adobo sauce, optional	1
2	poblano or green bell peppers, seeded and diced (see Tip, left)	2
	Salt	
	Shredded lettuce, optional	
	Chopped radish, optional	
	Chopped red or green onion, optional	
	Fried tortilla strips, optional	
	Lime wedges	

1. In a Dutch oven, cook bacon over medium-high heat until crisp. Drain on paper towel and crumble. Cover and refrigerate until ready to use. Drain all but 2 tbsp (30 mL) fat from pan. Add pork, in batches, and brown, about 3 minutes per batch. Transfer to a plate. Reduce heat to medium.

2. In work bowl fitted with metal blade, pulse onion and garlic until finely chopped, about 10 times, stopping and scraping down sides of the bowl as necessary.

3. Add onion mixture to pan and cook, stirring, until softened, about 3 minutes. Add oregano, peppercorns and lime zest and cook, stirring, for 1 minute. Add tomatoes with juice, broth, hominy and reserved pork and any accumulated juices and return to a boil. Reduce heat to low. Cover and simmer until pork is almost tender, for 1½ hours.

4. Meanwhile, in a heatproof bowl, soak dried chile peppers in boiling water for 30 minutes, weighing down with a cup to keep submerged. Drain and discard soaking liquid and stems. Chop chiles coarsely. Transfer to work bowl fitted with metal blade. Scoop out ½ cup (125 mL) of the cooking liquid from the pozole and add to work bowl along with lime juice, cilantro and chipotle pepper, if using. Purée and stir into pozole, along with reserved bacon and poblano peppers. Add salt to taste and continue cooking until pork is tender and flavors meld, about 30 minutes.

5. To serve, ladle into soup plates and top with the garnishes of your choice. Season with lime juice to taste.

Pork and Black Bean Chili

Serves 6 to 8

Here's a festive and stick-to-your-ribs chili that is a perfect finish to a day in the chilly outdoors. We like to serve this with hot corn bread, a crisp green salad and a robust red wine or ice cold beer. Olé!

Tips

For this quantity of beans, use 2 cans (14 to 19 oz/398 to 540 mL) drained and rinsed, or cook 2 cups (500 mL) dried beans.

For the best flavor, toast and grind cumin yourself. *To toast cumin:* Place seeds in a dry skillet over medium heat and cook, stirring, until fragrant, about 3 minutes. Immediately transfer to a mortar or a spice grinder and grind.

- Ovenproof Dutch oven
- Preheat oven to 350°F (180°C)

1 tbsp	oil (approx.)	15 mL
2 lbs	trimmed boneless pork shoulder, cut into 1-inch (2.5 cm) cubes, patted dry	1 kg
2	onions, quartered	2
4	cloves garlic	4
1 tbsp	ground cumin (see Tips, left)	15 mL
1 tbsp	dried oregano	15 mL
1 tsp	salt	5 mL
½ tsp	cracked black peppercorns	2 mL
1½ cups	flat beer	375 mL
2 tbsp	tomato paste	30 mL
4 cups	drained cooked black beans (see Tips, left)	1 L
2	dried ancho chile peppers	2
2 cups	boiling water	500 mL
1 cup	coarsely chopped cilantro (stems and leaves)	250 mL
½ cup	chicken broth	125 mL
1	chipotle pepper in adobo sauce	1
	Sour cream, optional	
	Crushed tortilla chips, optional	
	Finely chopped red or green onion, optional	

1. In a Dutch oven, heat oil over medium-high heat. Add pork, in batches, and cook, stirring, adding more oil if necessary, until browned, about 4 minutes per batch. Using a slotted spoon, transfer to a bowl and set aside. Reduce heat to medium.

2. In work bowl fitted with metal blade, pulse onion and garlic until finely chopped, about 10 times, stopping and scraping down sides of the bowl as necessary.

3. Add onion mixture to pan and cook, stirring, until softened, about 3 minutes. Add cumin, oregano, salt and peppercorns and cook, stirring, for 1 minute. Stir in beer and tomato paste. Return pork to pan. Add beans. Stir well and bring to a boil. Cover and bake in preheated oven for 1½ hours.

4. Meanwhile, in a heatproof bowl, soak dried chile peppers in boiling water for 30 minutes, weighing down with a cup to ensure they remain submerged. Drain, discarding soaking liquid and stems and chop coarsely. Transfer to work bowl fitted with metal blade. Add cilantro, broth and chipotle pepper. Purée.

5. After pork has cooked for 1½ hours, add chile mixture to Dutch oven and stir well. Cover and continue to cook until flavors meld and pork is very tender, about 30 minutes. Ladle into bowls and garnish with sour cream, crushed tortilla chips and chopped onion, if using.

Chile-Roasted Loin of Pork with Apricot Chipotle Stuffing

Serves 6 to 8

Although it's a bit of work to untie then retie a rolled pork roast, adding a stuffing is one way of enhancing the preparation for a special meal. This apricot-chipotle combination is delicious. Serve this dish with accompaniments that continue the Southwestern theme, such as sweet potatoes or squash and seasoned black beans.

Tip

To purée gingerroot: Use a fine, sharp-toothed grater, such as those made by Microplane.

- Roasting pan
- Instant-read thermometer

1	boneless pork double-loin roast, about 3 lbs (1.5 kg), trimmed and tied	1
2 tsp	grated orange zest	10 mL
⅔ cup	freshly squeezed orange juice	150 mL
½ tsp	grated lime zest	2 mL
2 tbsp	freshly squeezed lime juice	30 mL
1 tbsp	chili powder	15 mL
2	cloves garlic, minced	2
1 tsp	cracked black peppercorns	5 mL

Apricot Chipotle Stuffing

1 cup	chopped dried apricots	250 mL
2	cloves garlic, chopped	2
2	chipotle peppers in adobo sauce	2
¼ cup	cilantro leaves	60 mL
1 tsp	puréed gingerroot (see Tip, left)	5 mL

1. Cut the string holding the roast together and separate into 2 pieces. On a cutting board, using the flat side of a cleaver, pound each half to flatten it a bit. Set aside.

2. In a long shallow dish large enough to accommodate the pork or in a resealable plastic bag, combine orange zest and juice, lime zest and juice, chili powder, garlic and peppercorns. Add pork and turn to thoroughly coat the meat. Cover and refrigerate for at least 6 hours or overnight, turning several times.

3. Preheat oven to 350°F (180°C). **Apricot Chipotle Stuffing:** In work bowl fitted with metal blade, pulse apricots, garlic, chipotle peppers, cilantro leaves and ginger several times until the mixture is blended but apricots are still a bit chunky, stopping and scraping down sides of the bowl as necessary.

4. Remove pork from marinade and place on a cutting board, flat side up. Discard marinade. Spread flat side of each pork half with the apricot mixture. Press the 2 halves together and, beginning in the middle, retie the roast securely following the butcher's indentations. Also tie once end to end.

5. Place roast in roasting pan and roast in preheated oven until an instant-read thermometer inserted into the thickest part of the meat registers 160°F (71°C), about 1 hour and 20 minutes (depending upon the diameter of your roast). Let rest for 5 minutes before carving.

Rack of Lamb with Greek Stuffing

Serves 4

Here's a recipe that gives you all the élan of a rack of lamb with the benefit of a stuffing. Of course, it's not really stuffing — it's a variation of the Greek sauce *skordalia*, made with bread instead of the more usual mashed potatoes. Serve each piece of lamb with a dollop of the tasty mixture and savor the delicious combination.

Tip

A rack of lamb is a rib roast. We've specified French-cut because the long bones look so elegant, but for the purposes of this recipe, any rack of lamb will do. Just be sure to roast it to the proper internal temperature.

- Preheat oven to 400°F (200°C)
- Instant-read thermometer

1 tsp	coarse sea salt or ½ tsp (2 mL) table salt	5 mL
1 tsp	dried oregano	5 mL
½ tsp	cracked black peppercorns	2 mL
1 tbsp	olive oil	15 mL
1 tsp	grated lemon zest	5 mL
1 tbsp	oil	15 mL
2	racks of lamb (about 10 ribs each) (see Tip, left)	2

Greek Stuffing

2	slices country-style bread, about 1 inch (2.5 cm) thick, crusts removed	2
¼ cup	water	60 mL
¼ cup	coarsely chopped blanched almonds, toasted	60 mL
2	cloves garlic, coarsely chopped	2
2 tbsp	freshly squeezed lemon juice	30 mL
¼ tsp	fine salt, preferably fine sea salt	1 mL
⅓ cup	extra virgin olive oil	75 mL
	Freshly ground black pepper	

1. In a mortar or a spice grinder, combine sea salt, oregano and peppercorns. Lightly grind until oregano is relatively fine and the salt is still chunky but adequately crushed, if using coarse sea salt, so it will adhere to the meat. Transfer to a small bowl. Add olive oil and lemon zest and stir to blend.

2. Pat meat dry with paper towel. Rub salt mixture all over the surface, pressing into the meat. In a large ovenproof skillet, heat oil over medium-high heat. Add lamb racks, fat side down, and sear, about 2 minutes. Turn and repeat. Stand racks on their ends with bones in the air facing each other, balancing them so they support each other. Roast in preheated oven until temperature reaches 130°F (54°C) for rare, about 15 minutes. Transfer to a warm platter and tent with foil. Let rest for 5 minutes.

3. Greek Stuffing: Meanwhile, in a bowl, combine bread and water. Squeeze out water, ensuring the bread is well moistened. Discard water and transfer bread to work bowl fitted with metal blade. Add almonds, garlic, lemon juice and salt and process until relatively smooth, about 15 seconds, stopping and scraping down sides of the bowl as necessary. With motor running, add olive oil in a steady stream through feed tube, processing until smooth. Season with pepper to taste.

4. To serve, slice lamb into individual chops and spoon a dollop of the Greek Stuffing over each one.

Rack of Lamb with Lemon-Mint Sauce

Serves 4

Rack of lamb is a great special occasion dish. Here we've enlisted the help of our food processor to produce a fresh mint sauce laced with fresh lemon flavor. Serve with steaming mashed potatoes and slices of roasted eggplant.

Tip

Use sweet or hot paprika in this recipe: Sweet produces a more delicate flavor and hot adds a nice peppery bite to the sauce. If you just have sweet paprika and would like a bit a heat, dissolve ¼ tsp (1 mL) cayenne pepper in the lemon juice along with the paprika.

- Preheat oven to 400°F (200°C)
- Mini-bowl attachment
- Large ovenproof skillet
- Instant-read thermometer

1 tbsp	oil	15 mL
2	racks of lamb (about 10 ribs each)	2

Lemon-Mint Sauce

1 cup	heavy or whipping (35%) cream	250 mL
50	fresh mint leaves	50
2	shallots, thinly sliced	2
1 tsp	paprika (see Tip, left)	5 mL
½ tsp	salt	2 mL
¼ cup	freshly squeezed lemon juice	60 mL

1. In large ovenproof skillet, heat oil over medium-high heat. Add lamb racks, fat side down, and sear, about 2 minutes. Turn and repeat. Stand racks on their ends with bones in the air facing each other, balancing them so they support each other. Roast in preheated oven until temperature reaches 130°F (54°C) for rare, about 15 minutes.

2. **Lemon-Mint Sauce:** Meanwhile, in mini bowl fitted with metal blade, pulse cream and mint to chop mint, about 3 times. Set aside in the mini bowl.

3. When lamb is cooked, transfer to a warm platter and tent with foil. Pour off all but 1 tbsp (15 mL) of fat from pan and place over medium heat. Add shallots and cook, stirring, until softened, about 3 minutes. Add paprika and salt and stir well. Add lemon juice and stir well. Transfer to a small plate, then add to cream mixture. (You don't want to be wielding the hot frying pan any more than necessary.) Pulse until mixture is smooth, about 15 times. Return to pan. Add accumulated juices from lamb, reduce heat to low and simmer to meld flavors, about 5 minutes. Transfer sauce to a warm sauce boat. To serve, slice lamb into individual chops and pass sauce at the table.

Fish and Seafood

Fish Schnitzel

These tasty fish cakes
are easy to make and
very tasty. They make a
great weeknight dinner
and, if you feel so
inclined, can easily be
turned into fish burgers.
Just add buns, shredded
lettuce, mayo, relish,
pickles — whatever
garnishes strike your
fancy. Serve them
plated, accompanied by
Tartar Sauce (page 442)
or Cherry Tomato Tartar
Sauce (page 441) and
lemon wedges.

Tips

Because of concerns
about the environmental
sustainability of some
fish and seafood,
we recommend that
you check reliable
sites such as www.
montereybayaquarium.
org or the Environmental
Defense Fund at
www.edf.org for the
latest information on
these products before
purchasing.

We always use Italian
flat-leaf parsley because it
has so much more flavor
than the curly leaf variety.
Unless the stems or sprigs
are specifically called for,
use only the tender leaves.

½	small red onion, cut in half	½
¼ cup	Italian flat-leaf parsley leaves	60 mL
1	long red or green chile pepper, seeded	1
1	piece (2 inches/5 cm) baguette, crust removed, soaked in water and squeezed dry	1
1	egg	1
½ tsp	salt	2 mL
	Freshly ground black pepper	
1 lb	skinless firm white fish fillets, such as flounder, halibut or snapper, cut into 4 chunks (see Tips, left)	500 g

Coating

2	eggs, beaten	2
½ tsp	salt	2 mL
	Freshly ground black pepper	
⅛ tsp	cayenne pepper, optional	0.5 mL
½ cup	all-purpose flour	125 mL
¾ cup	dry bread crumbs, such as panko	175 mL
¼ cup	oil	60 mL

1. In work bowl fitted with metal blade, pulse red onion, parsley and chile pepper until finely chopped, about 5 times. Scrape down sides of the bowl. Add bread, egg, salt, and black pepper to taste, and pulse until blended, about 5 times. Add fish and pulse until chopped and blended, about 10 times. Shape into 4 patties, each about ½ inch (1 cm) thick.

2. **Coating:** In a shallow bowl, whisk together eggs, salt, pepper, to taste, and cayenne, if using. Spread flour on one plate and bread crumbs on another. Dip patties into flour, then egg, and finally bread crumbs, coating well. Discard any excess egg, flour and crumbs.

3. In a large skillet, heat oil over medium-high heat. Add patties. Reduce heat to medium and cook, pressing down with a spatula, until golden brown on bottom, about 3 minutes. Turn and cook until other side is golden brown, about 3 minutes. Serve immediately.

Stuffed Fillets of Sole in White Wine with Mushrooms

Serves 4

This is a variation on a classic French recipe, first popularized by Julia Child in *Mastering the Art of French Cooking*. We've added a mascarpone-herb stuffing, which bumps up the result, making it entertaining worthy. It is particularly nice accompanied by a simple pilaf and a green vegetable such as broccoli or steamed green beans.

Tip

A kitchen knife with a sharp point, such as a paring knife, is a good tool for checking fish for doneness. Just insert the knife in the thickest part of the fish. If you encounter resistance it needs more cooking. If it flakes easily or immediately pulls away from the bone, it is done.

- Preheat oven to 400°F (200°C)
- 6-cup (1.5 L) baking dish with lid, large enough to accommodate fish in a single layer, lightly greased

5	skinless sole or flounder fillets, divided	5
¼ cup	mascarpone	60 mL
1 tbsp	fresh tarragon leaves (about 12)	15 mL
1 tbsp	snipped chives	15 mL
	Salt and freshly ground white pepper	
4 tbsp	butter, divided	60 mL
12 oz	white mushrooms, trimmed and sliced	375 g
¾ cup	white wine or chicken broth	175 mL
¾ cup	fish stock or bottled clam juice	175 mL
2 tbsp	all-purpose flour	30 mL
½ cup	heavy or whipping (35%) cream	125 mL
2 tsp	freshly squeezed lemon juice	10 mL

1. In work bowl fitted with metal blade, process 1 sole fillet, mascarpone, tarragon and chives until fish is the texture of ground meat and mixture is blended, about 1 minute. Season with salt and pepper to taste. Divide mixture into 4 equal portions and spoon one portion in the center of each of the remaining fillets. Roll up and secure with a toothpick. Set aside.

2. In a skillet over medium-high heat, melt 2 tbsp (30 mL) of the butter. Add mushrooms and toss until nicely coated and just beginning to cook, about 2 minutes. Arrange evenly over bottom of prepared dish. Arrange fish bundles on top and pour wine and stock over top. Bake in preheated oven until fish flakes easily when pierced with a knife, about 25 minutes.

3. In a small bowl, beat remaining 2 tbsp (30 mL) of butter with flour into a paste. Using a slotted spoon, transfer fish and mushrooms to a serving dish and keep warm. Transfer cooking juices to a skillet and bring to a boil over medium-high heat. Boil for 2 minutes. Remove from heat and whisk in flour-butter paste and cream. Return to heat and cook, stirring, until thickened, about 1 minute. Stir in lemon juice and season with salt and white pepper to taste. Pour over fish bundles and serve immediately.

Pan-Seared Salmon with Dill Cream

Serves 4 to 6

Easy, elegant and delicious, this is a great jack-of-all-trades recipe. It's so simple to prepare that you can make it for a family dinner, yet it's sophisticated enough to serve to guests.

- Preheat oven to 400°F (200°C)
- Mini-bowl attachment
- Large ovenproof skillet

Dill Cream

1	large shallot, quartered	1
½ cup	heavy or whipping (35 %) cream	125 mL
½ cup	fresh dill fronds	125 mL
½ tsp	salt	2 mL
	Freshly ground white pepper	
2 tbsp	butter	30 mL
¼ cup	dry white wine	60 mL
1 tsp	freshly squeezed lemon juice	5 mL
1 tbsp	oil	15 mL
2 lbs	salmon fillets (2 fillets, each about 1 lb/500 g), patted dry	1 kg

1. **Dill Cream:** In mini bowl fitted with metal blade, pulse shallot until finely chopped, about 12 times, stopping and scraping down sides of the bowl. Transfer to a small bowl and using a spatula, scrape mini bowl clean. Add cream, dill, salt, and white pepper to taste, to mini bowl and process until dill is finely chopped and mixture is smoothly blended, about 10 seconds. Set aside.

2. In a saucepan over medium heat, melt butter. Add chopped shallot and cook, stirring, until softened, about 3 minutes. Add wine, bring to a boil and boil for 2 minutes. Stir in cream mixture. Reduce heat and simmer, stirring occasionally, until cream is reduced by half, about 10 minutes. Stir in lemon juice.

3. Meanwhile, in a large ovenproof skillet, heat oil over medium-high heat. Add salmon, skin side down, and cook for 3 minutes. Flip fish over. Transfer to preheated oven and bake until fish flakes easily when pierced with a knife, about 8 minutes. Transfer fish to a warm platter and pass the sauce at the table.

Macadamia-Crusted Salmon

Serves 6

Macadamia nuts are one of the hardest and oiliest nuts, but so flavorful. Here they make a great rub for salmon. Serve with Raspberry Sauce (page 632), if desired.

Tip

If you only can locate salted macadamia nuts, rub them in paper towels to remove as much salt as possible.

- Preheat broiler
- Large baking pan, lined with parchment paper

½ cup	unsalted macadamia nuts (see Tip, left)	125 mL
1 cup	broken pieces stone-ground wheat crackers	250 mL
2 tbsp	all-purpose flour	30 mL
1 tsp	fresh dill fronds	5 mL
3 tbsp	olive oil	45 mL
4	salmon fillets (about 1½ lbs/750 g)	4

1. In work bowl fitted with metal blade, process macadamia nuts, crackers, flour and dill until finely ground. Place in a shallow dish.
2. Rub oil on both sides of fillets. Dredge fillets in nut mixture. Discard any extra mixture.
3. In prepared baking pan, place fillets, skin-side up, at least 2 inches (5 cm) apart. Broil under preheated broiler, turning once, until surface of fish springs back when lightly pressed, 2 to 3 minutes per side.

Variation

You can use whitefish in place of the salmon. Adjust cooking time depending upon thickness.

Salmon Quiche

Serves 4

Here's a delightfully different weekday dinner or a great dish for a brunch or a buffet. Although it cooks for quite a while, it only takes about 15 minutes to prepare.

Tips

The quiche will bake more quickly if you use a glass pie plate.

We like to leave the bones in the salmon because they dissolve into the custard and add calcium.

- Preheat oven to 400°F (200°C)
- 9-inch (23 cm) glass pie plate (see Tips, left)

Crust

30	cheese-flavored crackers, such as Ritz (about half an 8-oz/250 g box)	30
¼ cup	butter, melted	60 mL

Filling

3 oz	cream cheese, cubed and softened	90 g
3	eggs	3
1 cup	milk	250 mL
½ tsp	salt	2 mL
	Freshly ground black pepper	
1	can (7½ oz/213 g) salmon, including juice and bones, skin removed	1
¼ cup	chopped green onion, Italian flat-leaf parsley or fresh dill fronds	60 mL
1	roasted red pepper, coarsely chopped	1

1. **Crust:** In work bowl fitted with metal blade, process crackers until they resemble fine crumbs, about 1 minute. Drizzle melted butter evenly over top and pulse until well blended, about 5 times. Press into pie plate. Bake in preheated oven until golden, about 8 minutes. Reduce heat to 375°F (190°C).

2. **Filling:** In clean work bowl fitted with metal blade, pulse cream cheese and eggs until combined, about 5 times. Add milk, salt, and black pepper to taste and process until blended, about 30 seconds. Add salmon, green onion and roasted pepper and pulse two or three times until combined.

3. Pour salmon mixture into warm crust. Bake in preheated oven until filling is set, 40 to 45 minutes.

Variation
Add ¼ cup (60 mL) chopped celery along with the salmon.

Salmon and Wild Rice Cakes with Avocado-Chile Topping

**Serves 4
(see Tips, below)**

With the addition of a big salad or an abundance of veggies, these tasty burgers make a light weeknight meal. For convenience, cook the rice ahead. The salmon mixture is quickly assembled.

Tips

With additions such as salad, one burger makes a light meal for most people. However, hungry people might want an extra half or whole one.

We prefer to leave the salmon bones in because they add calcium, but if you prefer, remove them.

When mixed, the cakes are very wet and not easily shaped into patties. However, they dry out and solidify quickly on cooking.

If you have a mini-bowl attachment use it to make the topping. Cut the avocado into quarters, add the remaining ingredients and process until smooth.

1½ cups	cooked brown and wild rice mixture, cooled	375 mL
1	can (7½ oz/213 g) salmon, drained (see Tips, left)	1
1	egg	1
4	green onions, white part only with a bit of green, coarsely chopped	4
¼ cup	all-purpose flour	60 mL
1 tbsp	soy sauce	15 mL
	Freshly ground black pepper	
1 tbsp	olive oil	15 mL

Avocado-Chile Topping (see Tips, left)

1	avocado, mashed	1
1 tbsp	freshly squeezed lemon juice	15 mL
¼ tsp	salt	1 mL
	Freshly ground black pepper	
½ tsp	Asian chile sauce, such as sambal oelek or Sriracha	2 mL

1. In work bowl fitted with metal blade, process salmon, egg, green onions, flour, soy sauce, and pepper to taste, until chopped and blended, about 15 seconds. Add rice and pulse to blend, about 5 times.

2. In a skillet, heat oil over medium heat. Using a large spoon, drop salmon mixture into the pan in 4 blobs (see Tips, left). Cook, pressing down with a spatula or the back of a spoon, until crispy outside and hot in the center, about 5 minutes per side.

3. **Avocado-Chile Topping:** Meanwhile, in a bowl, combine avocado, lemon juice, salt, pepper to taste, and Asian chile sauce. Mix well.

4. Serve burgers warm with a large dollop of Avocado-Chile Topping.

Creamy Salmon Lasagna

This is the richest lasagna known. Serve smaller portions than the normal size because it is so filling.

Tips

Let guests salt the lasagna because it tends to have enough salt for most tastes with the salmon and cheeses.

Unsalted or "sweet" butter is manufactured without adding salt to preserve the butter, thus creating a fresher product. The amount of salt added varies between brands so you don't have as much control over the amount of salt in your dish. Both butters are interchangeable, but taste for salt before adding any to your recipe.

- Preheat oven to 375°F (190°C)
- 13- by 9-inch (33 by 23 cm) metal baking pan, at least 2½ inches (6 cm) deep, buttered

12 oz	provolone cheese, cut into chunks	375 g
4 oz	Parmesan cheese, cut into chunks	125 g
1	package (16 oz/500 g) frozen spinach, thawed and drained, divided	1
1 lb	skinless salmon fillet, cut into chunks	500 g
2 tbsp	fresh dill fronds	30 mL
1 lb	ricotta cheese, divided	500 g
1 tbsp	unsalted butter, softened (see Tips, left)	15 mL
½	onion, sliced	½
3 tbsp	all-purpose flour	45 mL
4 cups	heavy or whipping (35%) cream, at room temperature	1 L
1	package (8 oz/250 g) oven-ready lasagna noodles, divided	1

1. In work bowl with shredding blade, shred provolone cheese. Transfer to a bowl. Set aside.

2. Replace shredding blade with metal blade. With motor running, add Parmesan cheese through feed tube and process until finely grated. Transfer to another bowl. Set aside.

3. In work bowl with metal blade, pulse spinach, salmon and dill until finely chopped, about 10 times. Remove lid and add 12 oz (375 g) ricotta cheese and process until smooth and creamy about 10 seconds, stopping and scraping down the sides of the bowl as necessary.

4. In a skillet, melt butter over medium heat. Add onion and sauté until translucent, about 5 minutes. Sprinkle with flour and cook, stirring, for 2 minutes. Gradually whisk in cream and cook, whisking constantly, until mixture starts to thicken, about 5 minutes. Set aside.

5. Place one-third of the noodles in a single layer to line the bottom of the prepared baking pan, trimming to fit if necessary. Spread half of the salmon-spinach mixture evenly over noodles. Then spread one-third of the Parmesan and provolone cheeses and one-third of the cream mixture on top. Add half of the remaining noodles on top, trimming to fit if necessary. Repeat again with salmon, cheese and cream. Top with the remaining noodles, cheese and cream. Dollop remaining ricotta by spoonfuls on top.

6. Cover and bake in preheated oven until noodles are tender, about 45 minutes. Uncover and bake until hot and bubbling and top is browned, about 10 minutes more. Let lasagna stand for 15 minutes prior to serving. Serve hot.

Dill-Spiked Salmon Cakes

If you're cooking salmon, make extra so you'll have leftovers for these tasty cakes. With a green vegetable, such as beans, they make an easy yet elegant dinner that may even call for a bottle of crisp white wine. Tartar Sauce (page 442) or Cherry Tomato Tartar Sauce (page 441) provide a finishing touch.

Tips

An easy way to cook potatoes in their skins is to microwave them. For this quantity, place the scrubbed potatoes in a microwave-safe dish in one layer, add cold water to a depth of about ½ inch (1 cm), cover and microwave on High for 6 minutes. Leave the lid on and let cool in liquid for at least 5 minutes before running under cold water and removing the skins.

Your potatoes will shred more easily if you cook them ahead of time and refrigerate.

For best results, use floury potatoes, such as russets, which aren't as moist as some other varieties.

2	potatoes (each about 6 oz/175 g), boiled in their skins, cooled and peeled (see Tips, left)	2
½	red onion, halved	½
½ cup	fresh dill fronds	125 mL
1	egg, beaten	1
12 oz	cooked salmon, skin removed if necessary	375 g
1 tsp	salt	5 mL
	Freshly ground black pepper	
1 cup	dry bread crumbs, such as panko	250 mL
2 tbsp	oil (approx.)	30 mL

1. In work bowl fitted with shredding blade, shred potatoes. Replace shredding blade with metal blade. Add red onion and dill to work bowl and pulse until chopped, about 3 times, stopping and scraping down sides of the bowl. Add egg and pulse once to blend. Add salmon and pulse until mixture is blended, about 5 times. Be careful not to overprocess — you want the salmon to have some texture and you don't want the potato to be gluey. Season with salt, and pepper to taste. Shape into 4 equal patties.

2. Spread bread crumbs on a large plate and dredge patties liberally with crumbs. Discard any excess crumbs.

3. In a skillet, heat oil over medium heat. Add salmon cakes, in batches, if necessary, and cook, pressing down with a spatula or the back of a spoon, turning once, until golden brown, about 3 minutes per side, adding more oil, if necessary.

Almond-Crusted Fresh Fish

Enjoy the crunchy nutty crust that is encasing the flaky fresh fish.

Tip

If crumbs have cooled, you can place in the microwave for 20 seconds.

- Preheat oven to 350°F (180°C)
- Baking sheet, lined with parchment paper

½ cup	Fresh Bread Crumbs (page 468)	125 mL
½ cup	honey-roasted sliced almonds	125 mL
½ tsp	fresh Italian flat-leaf parsley leaves	2 mL
½ cup	butter, melted	125 mL
2 tsp	freshly squeezed lemon juice	10 mL
4	fresh fish fillets, such as salmon, snapper or firm white fish (about 1½ lbs/750 g)	4
	Salt and freshly ground black pepper	
3 tbsp	extra virgin olive oil	45 mL

1. In work bowl fitted with metal blade, process bread crumbs, almonds and parsley until ground, about 10 seconds. With motor running, pour butter and lemon juice through feed tube, stopping and scraping down sides of the bowl as necessary. Spread out in an even layer on prepared baking sheet. Bake in preheated oven until light brown, 4 to 6 minutes. Set aside.

2. Lightly season fish on both sides with salt and pepper to taste. In a skillet, heat olive oil over medium heat. Add fish and cook, turning once, just until it flakes easily when pierced with a knife, 2 to 3 minutes per side. Transfer to a plate. Top with warm almond mixture.

Whole Roasted Snapper
with Caper-Parsley Sauce

Serves 4

Elegant yet easy to make, this tasty fish makes a nice dish for many occasions.

Tips

Because of concerns about the environmental sustainability of some fish and seafood, we recommend that you check reliable sites such as www.montereybayaquarium.org or the Environmental Defense Fund at www.edf.org for the latest information on these products before purchasing.

We always use Italian flat-leaf parsley because it has so much more flavor than the curly leaf variety. Unless the stems or sprigs are specifically called for, use only the tender leaves.

- Preheat oven to 400°F (200°C)
- Baking dish large enough to accommodate fish or rimmed baking sheet
- Mini-bowl attachment

1	whole snapper, cleaned and scaled (about 2 lbs/1 kg) (see Tips, left)	1
	Salt and freshly ground black or white pepper	
	Thin slices of lemon (½ lemon)	

Sauce

1 cup	Italian flat-leaf parsley leaves	250 mL
2 tbsp	drained capers	30 mL
2	anchovy fillets	2
1	clove garlic	1
1 tbsp	Dijon mustard	15 mL
1 tbsp	freshly squeezed lemon juice	15 mL
⅓ cup	extra virgin olive oil	75 mL
	Salt and freshly ground black or white pepper	

1. Pat fish dry and season with salt and pepper to taste. Place lemon slices in cavity. Place in baking dish and bake in preheated oven until fish flakes easily when pierced with a knife, about 30 minutes.

2. **Sauce:** Meanwhile, in mini bowl fitted with metal blade, pulse parsley, capers, anchovies and garlic until finely chopped and blended, about 15 times, stopping and scraping down sides of the bowl once or twice. Add mustard, lemon juice and olive oil and pulse to blend, 2 or 3 times. Season with salt and pepper to taste. Transfer to a small serving bowl.

3. When fish is cooked, transfer to a clean cutting board and remove the skin. Remove top fillet and place on a warm platter. Remove backbone and remove bottom fillet and place on platter. Serve immediately with sauce.

Snapper in Mexican Green Sauce

If you're trying to increase your consumption of fish but are bored with traditional presentations, try this Mexican-inspired treatment for snapper. We like to serve this with hot fluffy rice.

Tip

For the best flavor, toast and grind cumin yourself. *To toast cumin:* Place seeds in a dry skillet over medium heat and cook, stirring, until fragrant, about 3 minutes. Immediately transfer to a mortar or a spice grinder and grind.

- Preheat oven to 400°F (200°C)
- 6-cup (1.5 L) shallow baking dish with lid, lightly greased

1	onion, quartered	1
1 cup	packed Italian flat-leaf parsley leaves	250 mL
1/4 cup	fresh cilantro leaves	60 mL
2	cloves garlic, coarsely chopped	2
1	jalapeño pepper, seeded and quartered	1
1 tsp	ground cumin (see Tip, left)	5 mL
1 tsp	salt	5 mL
1/2 tsp	freshly ground black pepper	2 mL
1	can (11 oz/312 g) tomatillos, drained	1
1/4 cup	freshly squeezed lime juice	60 mL
2	large snapper fillets (about 1 1/4 lbs/625 g) (see Tips, page 276)	2

1. In work bowl fitted with metal blade, pulse onion, parsley, cilantro, garlic, jalapeño, cumin, salt and pepper until chopped, about 5 times. Add drained tomatillos and lime juice and purée until almost smooth, about 30 seconds.

2. Spread half the sauce in prepared baking dish. Add fish and top with remaining sauce. Cover and bake in preheated oven until fish flakes easily when pierced with a knife, about 15 minutes.

Variation

Substitute any firm white fish for the snapper.

Trout with Shiitake Mushroom Sauce

Serves 6

Trout and shiitake mushrooms make a delicious combination. We like to serve this with oven-baked fries (see Tip, below), which go particularly well with the luscious sauce.

Tip

To make oven-baked fries: Preheat oven to 375°F (190°C). Peel potatoes and slice (about ¼ inch/0.5 cm thick). Brush both sides with olive oil and place on a rimmed baking sheet. Bake in preheated oven, turning once, until brown and crispy, about 40 minutes. Sprinkle with fine sea salt and serve immediately.

- Large baking pan, lined with parchment paper

Mushroom Sauce

2 tbsp	butter	30 mL
2	shallots, sliced	2
2	cloves garlic, coarsely chopped	2
2 cups	coarsely chopped shiitake mushroom caps	500 mL
½ cup	dry white wine	125 mL
½ cup	heavy or whipping (35%) cream	125 mL
½ cup	fresh basil leaves	125 mL
½ tsp	salt	2 mL
	Freshly ground white pepper	
3	trout fillets (each about 12 oz/375 g), cut in half	3

1. **Mushroom Sauce:** In a large skillet, melt butter over medium heat. Add shallots and garlic and cook, stirring, until shallots are softened, about 2 minutes. Add mushrooms and cook, stirring, until they begin to soften, about 3 minutes. Add white wine, bring to a boil and boil for 2 minutes. Transfer mixture to work bowl fitted with metal blade. Add cream, basil and salt. Pulse until mushrooms are chopped and mixture is blended, about 15 times. Season with white pepper to taste. Return to skillet and keep warm while you prepare the fish.

2. Preheat broiler. In prepared baking pan, place fillet pieces, skin-side up, at least 2 inches (5 cm) apart. Broil, turning once, until fish flakes easily when pierced with a knife, about 3 minutes per side. To serve, place trout on a plate and top with a dollop of sauce. Pass additional sauce at the table.

Halibut with Cilantro Chile Butter

Serves 4 to 6

Pacific halibut is a delicious and versatile fish, that is environmentally sustainable. A large fish with glistening white fillets, it is mildly flavored and responds well to a wide variety of seasonings. Here, it's paired with the Latin American combination of chiles, cilantro and lime.

Tips

If you are using unsalted butter, you may want to add a bit of salt, preferably fine sea salt, to taste, to the Cilantro Chile Butter.

We tested this using an especially thick halibut fillet. If you're using smaller pieces of halibut or fillets of a different but smaller fish, such as snapper, reduce the cooking time by 5 to 10 minutes, depending upon the size.

Thick fillets of any firm white fish, such as red snapper, haddock or grouper, also work well in this recipe.

This recipe presents best when the fish is cooked in one piece. But you will get more even cooking if you cut the fish into 2 pieces and reduce the cooking time to about 20 minutes. The choice is yours.

- Preheat oven to 400°F (200°C)
- Mini-bowl attachment
- Rimmed baking sheet, lined with parchment

2 lbs	Pacific halibut fillet	1 kg
½ cup	olive oil	125 mL
¼ cup	freshly squeezed lime juice	60 mL
2	dried red chile peppers, crumbled	2
½ tsp	salt	2 mL

Cilantro Chile Butter

½ cup	butter, softened	125 mL
1 or 2	long red or green chile or jalapeño peppers, seeded and quartered	1 or 2
¼ cup	fresh cilantro leaves	60 mL
1	green onion, white part only, finely chopped	1
2 tsp	finely grated lime zest	10 mL
1 tbsp	freshly squeezed lime juice (approx.)	15 mL
	Salt, optional (see Tips, left)	

1. Rinse halibut thoroughly under cold running water and pat dry with paper towel. In a dish large enough to accommodate the fish in a single layer or in a resealable plastic bag, combine olive oil, lime juice, chiles and salt. Add fish and turn to coat thoroughly. Let stand at room temperature for 30 minutes.

2. **Cilantro Chile Butter:** Meanwhile, in mini bowl fitted with metal blade, process butter, chile pepper(s), cilantro, green onion, lime zest and juice, and salt to taste, if using until smooth, stopping and scraping down sides of the bowl as necessary. Add additional lime juice, if desired, and pulse to blend. Spoon into a ramekin or small bowl and chill until firm, about 30 minutes, or cover and refrigerate until ready to use, for up to 2 days.

3. Remove halibut from the marinade. Discard marinade. Bake in preheated oven until fish flakes easily when pierced with a knife, about 30 minutes. Transfer to a warm platter. Dot with 2 or 3 pats of Cilantro Chile Butter and serve additional butter alongside.

Chile-Baked Halibut

Serves 6

If you're looking for a fish recipe that is a little bit different but still easy to make, look no further: a halibut fillet brushed with a chile-infused mayonnaise and covered in panko crumbs. It's delicious and elegant enough to serve to guests.

Tips

Use whatever chile pepper you prefer: long red or green, jalapeño or habanero and in a quantity to suit your tolerance for heat.

This recipe presents best when the fish is cooked in one piece. But you will get more even cooking if you cut the fish into 2 pieces and reduce the cooking time to about 20 minutes. The choice is yours.

Don't confuse real mayonnaise with "mayonnaise-type" salad dressings. Mayonnaise is a combination of egg yolks, vinegar or lemon juice, olive oil and seasonings. Imitators will contain additional ingredients, such as sugar, flour or milk. Make your own or make sure the label says mayonnaise and check the ingredients.

- Preheat oven to 400°F (200°C)
- Rimmed baking sheet, lined with parchment
- Mini-bowl attachment

½ cup	Traditional Mayonnaise (page 437) or store-bought	125 mL
2 tbsp	freshly squeezed lemon juice	30 mL
1 tbsp	olive oil	15 mL
1 to 2	chile peppers, seeded and halved (see Tips, left)	1 to 2
1	clove garlic	1
½ tsp	salt	2 mL
2 lbs	Pacific halibut fillet (see Tips, left)	1 kg
½ cup	dry bread crumbs, such as panko	125 mL

1. In mini bowl fitted with metal blade, process mayonnaise, lemon juice, olive oil, chile pepper(s), garlic and salt until smooth, about 30 seconds.

2. Pat fish dry and place on prepared sheet. Slather top and sides with mayonnaise mixture. Sprinkle bread crumbs over top. Bake in preheated oven until fish flakes easily when pierced with a knife, about 30 minutes.

Italian-Style Swordfish

Serves 4 to 6

This is a classic Italian way of preparing swordfish that is particularly delicious.

Tips

If you're concerned about swordfish being overfished, ask your fishmonger for harpooned, which is more sustainable, rather than pelagic longline- or net-caught fish.

If you prefer to broil the fish, see Step 3, page 286.

A kitchen knife with a sharp point, such as a paring knife, is a good tool for checking fish for doneness. Just insert the knife in the thickest part of the fish. If you encounter resistance it needs more cooking. If it flakes easily or immediately pulls away from the bone, it is done.

1 cup	extra virgin olive oil	250 mL
1 tbsp	grated lemon zest	15 mL
1 cup	freshly squeezed lemon juice	250 mL
1 cup	loosely packed Italian flat-leaf parsley leaves	250 mL
$\frac{1}{2}$ cup	hot water	125 mL
4	cloves garlic, coarsely chopped	4
1 tsp	dried oregano	5 mL
1 tsp	coarse sea salt or $\frac{1}{2}$ tsp (2 mL) table salt	5 mL
2	dried red chile peppers	2
1	swordfish steak, about 2 lbs (1 kg) (see Tips, left)	1
1 tbsp	drained capers	15 mL

1. In work bowl fitted with metal blade, process olive oil, lemon zest and juice, parsley, hot water, garlic, oregano and salt until parsley is finely chopped, about 30 seconds. Pour off 1 cup (250 mL) of the mixture, cover and refrigerate until the fish is cooked. Add chile peppers to the remainder and process until blended, about 30 seconds.

2. Rinse swordfish under cold running water and pat dry with paper towel. In a dish large enough to accommodate fish in a single layer or in a resealable plastic bag, combine swordfish and olive oil-chile mixture. Let stand at room temperature for 30 minutes or in the refrigerator, covered, for up to 2 hours.

3. Preheat barbecue (see Tips, left). Remove swordfish from marinade. Discard marinade. Arrange on grill and cook, turning once, until fish flakes easily when pierced with a knife, about 12 minutes, depending upon the thickness of the fish.

4. Add capers to refrigerated olive oil mixture. Stir well and pour over hot fish. Serve immediately.

Saucy Halibut on a Bed of Lentils

Serves 4

Thanks to English chef Simon Hopkinson, whose recipe we've adapted here. Hearty yet light and nutritious, this is a perfect dish for entertaining. (Double the quantity if you're serving more people.) It is so easy to make that you can also serve it for a family meal.

Tips

For best results (or if you're serving this to guests) use Puy lentils, a French green lentil with robust flavor that holds its shape during cooking.

We always use Italian flat-leaf parsley because it has so much more flavor than the curly leaf variety. Unless the stems or sprigs are specifically called for, use only the tender leaves.

Lentils

1 tbsp	butter or olive oil	15 mL
1	onion, finely chopped	1
2	cloves garlic, minced	2
1	bay leaf	1
	Salt and freshly ground black pepper	
1 cup	dried brown or green lentils, rinsed and drained (see Tips, left)	250 mL
2½ cups	chicken or vegetable broth	625 mL

Parsley Sauce

4 cups	Italian flat-leaf parsley leaves	1 L
10	basil leaves	10
15	mint leaves	15
2	cloves garlic, coarsely chopped	2
1 tbsp	Dijon mustard	15 mL
4	anchovy fillets	4
1 tbsp	drained capers	15 mL
⅓ cup	extra virgin olive oil	75 mL
	Salt and freshly ground black pepper	

Halibut

3 tbsp	freshly squeezed lemon juice	45 mL
1 tsp	salt	5 mL
1½ lbs	Pacific halibut fillet, cut into 4 pieces	750 g

1. **Lentils:** In a large heavy saucepan over medium heat, melt butter. Add onion and cook, stirring, until softened, about 3 minutes. Add garlic, bay leaf, and salt and black pepper to taste, and cook, stirring, for 1 minute. Add lentils and toss until coated with mixture. Add broth and bring to a boil. Reduce heat and simmer until lentils are tender and liquid is absorbed, about 40 minutes.

2. **Parsley Sauce:** Meanwhile, in work bowl fitted with metal blade, pulse parsley, basil, mint, garlic, mustard, anchovies and capers to chop, about 15 times, stopping and scraping down sides of the bowl as necessary. With motor running, slowly add oil through feed tube until oil is well integrated. Season with salt and black pepper to taste, and set aside.

You may need a bit more or less water, depending upon the configuration of the pan you are using to poach the fish. You want the fish to just be covered with the liquid.

3. **Halibut:** Bring 8 cups (2 L) water (see Tip, left) to a boil in a large covered skillet or fish poacher. Add lemon juice and salt. Add fish and return to a boil. Cover and turn off heat. Set aside for 5 minutes until fish is cooked through.

4. To serve, spread lentils on a serving dish or deep platter. Remove skin from fish, if necessary, and arrange on top of lentils. Spoon a good dollop of sauce over each piece of fish and pass the remainder in a sauceboat at the table. Serve immediately.

Swordfish with Anchovies and Olives

Swordfish is one of the few fish that can stand up to the powerful, but delectable, combination of anchovies and olives. This tangy sauce provides a perfect finish for the fish. Serve this with sliced tomatoes drizzled with extra virgin olive oil and a hint of good balsamic vinegar to complete the Mediterranean flavors.

Tips

If you prefer to broil the fish, see Step 3, page 286.

We always use Italian flat-leaf parsley because it has so much more flavor than the curly leaf variety. Unless the stems or sprigs are specifically called for, use only the tender leaves.

Anchovy and Olive Sauce

2 cups	packed Italian flat-leaf parsley leaves	500 mL
20	pitted black olives	20
2	anchovy fillets, chopped	2
2	cloves garlic, chopped	2
2 tbsp	freshly squeezed lemon juice	30 mL
¼ cup	olive oil	60 mL

Swordfish

1	swordfish steak, about 2 lbs (1 kg) (see Tips, page 281)	1
½ cup	olive oil	125 mL
¼ cup	freshly squeezed lemon juice	60 mL
2	dried red chile peppers, crushed	2
½ tsp	salt	2 mL
½ tsp	cracked black peppercorns	2 mL

1. **Anchovy and Olive Sauce:** In work bowl fitted with metal blade, pulse parsley, olives, anchovies, garlic and lemon juice until olives are coarsely chopped, about 5 times, stopping and scraping down sides of the bowl once. With motor running, gradually add olive oil through feed tube, until the mixture is smooth and blended. Refrigerate for at least 1 hour to allow flavors to blend, or for up to 2 days.

2. **Swordfish:** Rinse swordfish under cold running water and pat dry with paper towel. In a shallow dish large enough to accommodate the fish in a single layer or in a resealable plastic bag, combine olive oil, lemon juice, chile peppers, salt and peppercorns. Add swordfish and coat with mixture. Let stand at room temperature for 30 minutes or in refrigerator, covered, for up to 2 hours.

3. Preheat barbecue (see Tips, left). Remove swordfish from the marinade. Discard marinade. Arrange fish on grill and cook, turning once, until fish flakes easily when pierced with a knife, about 12 minutes, depending upon the thickness of the fish. Serve immediately with the Anchovy and Olive Sauce alongside.

Curry-Spiked Fish Cakes

These tasty fish cakes are a great way to use up leftover fish. They are very versatile. Make them large (4 to 6 to a batch) and add a tossed salad for dinner or make them small and serve them as appetizers. Serve with your favorite chutney or chili sauce.

Tip

We always use Italian flat-leaf parsley because it has so much more flavor than the curly leaf variety. Unless the stems or sprigs are specifically called for, use only the tender leaves.

Your potato will shred more easily if you cook it ahead of time and refrigerate overnight.

1	potato, boiled in its skin, cooled and peeled	1
2 tbsp	butter	30 mL
1	onion, sliced	1
1 to 2	chile peppers, seeded and sliced	1 to 2
1 tsp	curry powder	5 mL
1 tsp	salt	5 mL
1/2 tsp	freshly ground black pepper	2 mL
8 oz	cooked fish, such as cod, salmon or snapper, skin removed if necessary	250 g
1	egg	1
1/4 cup	Italian flat-leaf parsley leaves	60 mL
1/2 cup	dry bread crumbs, such as panko (approx.)	125 mL
2 tbsp	oil (approx.)	30 mL

1. In work bowl fitted with shredding blade, shred potato. Transfer to a bowl and set aside. Replace shredding blade with metal blade and set aside.

2. In a skillet, melt butter over medium heat. Add onion and chile pepper(s) and cook, stirring, until onion is softened, about 3 minutes. Add curry powder, salt and black pepper and cook, stirring, for 1 minute. Remove from heat.

3. In work bowl fitted with metal blade, pulse fish, egg and parsley to chop and blend, 5 times, stopping and scraping down sides of bowl as necessary. Add onion mixture and pulse to blend, about 5 times, stopping and scraping down sides of bowl as necessary. Add shredded potato and pulse to blend, 2 to 3 times. With wet hands, shape mixture into desired number of patties.

4. Spread bread crumbs on a plate. Add patties, in batches, and coat well with crumbs on both sides. Discard any excess crumbs.

5. In a skillet, heat oil over medium-high heat. Add patties, in batches, and cook, turning once and pushing down with a spatula to flatten, until golden, about 2 minutes per side.

Swordfish with Creamy Sun-Dried Tomato Pesto

Serves 4 to 6

The intense flavors of sun-dried tomatoes and tarragon are a perfect finish for swordfish. All you need to add is a tossed green salad and some chilled white wine.

Tips

If you don't have tarragon vinegar, substitute an equal quantity of white wine or champagne vinegar and increase the amount of chopped tarragon by 1 tsp (5 mL).

If you don't like the taste of tarragon, you can make this sauce using white wine or champagne vinegar instead of tarragon vinegar, substituting an equal quantity of fresh thyme, parsley leaves or finely snipped chives for the tarragon.

If you prefer to barbecue the fish, see Step 3, page 284.

• Rimmed baking sheet, lined with parchment

½ cup	olive oil	125 mL
¼ cup	freshly squeezed lemon juice	60 mL
2	dried red chile peppers, crushed	2
½ tsp	salt	2 mL
½ tsp	cracked black peppercorns	2 mL
1	swordfish steak, about 2 lbs (1 kg) rinsed and patted dry (see Tips, page 281)	1

Sun-Dried Tomato Pesto

1 cup	chicken or vegetable broth	250 mL
1 cup	dry white wine	250 mL
¼ cup	white wine vinegar with tarragon (see Tips, left)	60 mL
½ cup	drained oil-packed sun-dried tomatoes	125 mL
1 tbsp	chopped fresh tarragon leaves	15 mL
2 tbsp	heavy or whipping (35%) cream	30 mL
	Salt and freshly ground black pepper	

1. In a shallow dish large enough to accommodate the fish in a single layer or in a resealable plastic bag, combine olive oil, lemon juice, chile peppers, salt and peppercorns. Add swordfish and coat with mixture. Let stand at room temperature, covered, for 30 minutes or in refrigerator for up to 2 hours.

2. **Sun-Dried Tomato Pesto:** Meanwhile, in a saucepan over medium heat, combine broth, wine and vinegar. Bring to a boil and cook until reduced to 1 cup (250 mL), about 10 minutes. Transfer to work bowl fitted with metal blade. Add sun-dried tomatoes and process until smooth, about 30 seconds. Add tarragon and cream and pulse to blend, 2 or 3 times. Season with salt and pepper to taste. Set aside.

3. Preheat broiler (see Tips, left). Remove swordfish from marinade. Discard marinade. Broil fish under preheated broiler, turning once, until fish flakes easily when pierced with a knife, about 12 minutes, depending upon the thickness of the fish. Transfer to a warm platter. Serve the pesto on the side.

Sesame-Dusted Beer-Battered Shrimp with Roasted Pepper and Salt

Serves 4 to 6

Shrimp fried in batter are a classic simply because they taste so good. Here, we've added beer to the batter, which adds depth and a pleasant hint of bitterness, and dusted the cooked shrimp with sesame seeds, roasted salt and peppercorns. Serve them as is or add a small bowl of shrimp cocktail sauce for dipping (see Tips, below).

Tips

The number of shrimp you can cook per batch depends upon the size of your shrimp and the diameter of the cooking vessel. When testing this recipe, we used large shrimp and a Dutch oven that is 10½ inches (26 cm) in diameter.

One of the tastiest and easiest sauces for shrimp cocktail is simply a blend of ketchup and horseradish. Just combine 1 cup (250 mL) ketchup with 1 tbsp (15 mL) prepared horseradish and stir well.

- Candy/deep-fry thermometer

1 cup	all-purpose flour	250 mL
1 tsp	salt	5 mL
1 tsp	hot paprika	5 mL
1 tsp	baking powder	5 mL
1	egg	1
1 cup	beer	250 mL
2 tbsp	coarse sea salt	30 mL
1 tsp	white peppercorns	5 mL
2 cups	vegetable oil, such as peanut or corn (approx.)	500 mL
1½ lbs	shrimp, peeled and deveined	750 g
2 tbsp	sesame seeds	30 mL

1. In work bowl fitted with metal blade, pulse flour, 1 tsp (5 mL) salt, paprika and baking powder to combine, 2 or 3 times. Add egg and beer and process until smooth, about 30 seconds. Cover and chill thoroughly, for 2 hours.

2. Meanwhile, in a small dry skillet over medium heat, toast salt and peppercorns, stirring, until fragrant and pepper begins to pop, about 3 minutes. Immediately remove from heat, transfer to a mortar or spice grinder and grind. Set aside.

3. When you're ready to cook, place oil in a large saucepan or Dutch oven and heat over medium heat until temperature reaches 375°F (190°C). (You can also use a deep fryer; follow the manufacturers instructions.) Pat shrimp dry with paper towel, dip in batter until well coated and drop in hot oil. Repeat until all shrimp are used up, cooking in batches that allow adequate space between the shrimp. (This will depend on the size of both your shrimp and the cooking vessel.) When shrimp are golden (about 2 minutes) remove from oil and drain on paper towels. Discard any excess batter. Immediately sprinkle fried shrimp with sesame seeds and salt mixture.

Crab Cakes

Serves 4 as a main course

Makes 8 crab cakes

These are delicious with just a squeeze of lemon juice but if you prefer, dress them up with Tartar Sauce (page 442), Cherry Tomato Tartar Sauce (page 441) or Sauce Vierge (page 407). They are so easy to make, you can serve them as a treat for a weekday dinner but so special they can double as an appetizer for an elegant meal.

Tips

In order for the cakes to hold together, your crabmeat should be as dry as possible. We recommend placing it in a strainer and draining as much liquid out as possible, then if necessary, using your hands to squeeze out the remainder.

If you prefer, substitute half a fresh chile pepper for the cayenne. Add along with the bell pepper.

1 lb	crabmeat (see Tips, left)	500 g
1	red bell pepper, seeded and quartered	1
3 tbsp	Italian flat-leaf parsley leaves	45 mL
1/3 cup	Traditional Mayonnaise (page 437) or store-bought	75 mL
1	egg	1
1 tsp	freshly squeezed lemon juice	5 mL
1/8 tsp	cayenne pepper (see Tips, left)	0.5 mL
	Salt and freshly ground black pepper	
1 cup	dry bread crumbs, such as panko, divided	250 mL
3 tbsp	oil	45 mL
	Lemon wedges	

1. In work bowl fitted with metal blade, pulse red pepper and parsley until chopped, about 5 times, stopping and scraping down sides of bowl as necessary. Add mayonnaise, egg, lemon juice, cayenne, and salt and black pepper to taste, and process until blended. Add crab and ½ cup (125 mL) of the bread crumbs and pulse to blend, about 8 times.

2. Shape crab mixture into 8 equal patties. Spread remaining ½ cup (125 mL) of bread crumbs on a plate and dredge patties in crumbs on both sides. Discard any excess crumbs.

3. In a large skillet, heat oil over medium-high heat. Add crab cakes and cook until nicely browned on bottom, turning once, about 4 minutes per side. Serve immediately accompanied by lemon wedges.

Seafood Pâté

Serves 8

Serve this pâté cold on a bed of greens drizzled with a light vinaigrette for a summer brunch.

Tips

Purchase shrimp on sale. Use the cooked salad shrimp because it will be chopped up anyway.

Pâté keeps well, wrapped in plastic wrap and refrigerated, for up to 2 days.

- Preheat oven to 325°F (160°C)
- Place a large pan filled with hot water on the lower rack
- 11- by 7-inch (28 by 18 cm) baking dish, lined with plastic wrap

1	bunch fresh spinach (about 12 oz/375 g)	1
1	bunch fresh Italian flat-leaf parsley leaves (about 6 oz/175 g)	1
4	green onions, cut in half	4
2 tsp	butter	10 mL
6 oz	skinless white fish fillets	175 g
1	egg white	1
2 tbsp	heavy or whipping (35%) cream	30 mL
8 oz	cooked peeled shrimp, cut into small pieces (see Tips, left)	250 g
2 tsp	chopped fresh tarragon	10 mL
1/8 tsp	ground white pepper	0.5 mL
1/8 tsp	freshly ground nutmeg	0.5 mL

1. Discard stems from spinach and parsley. Wash leaves and place in a salad spinner to dry.

2. In work bowl fitted with metal blade, pulse spinach, parsley and green onions until coarsely chopped, about 10 times.

3. In a skillet over medium heat, melt butter. Add spinach mixture and sauté until greens start to wilt, about 3 minutes. Transfer to a bowl and refrigerate until cold, about 30 minutes.

4. In same work bowl, add whitefish and purée for 30 seconds. Add egg white and process for 30 seconds. With motor running, add cream through feed tube. Add to bowl with spinach mixture and combine. Add shrimp, tarragon, white pepper and nutmeg.

5. Scoop into prepared baking dish, smoothing top. Cover with foil. Place in preheated oven on rack above pan of water and bake until set, about 25 minutes. Let stand to firm up completely and cool. Remove from pan and remove foil. Slice with a sharp knife. Serve.

Variation

Try scallops in place of shrimp if you find a bargain at the market.

Seafood Pie with Rösti Topping

Serves 6

This is a great dish to serve if you're entertaining guests who avoid meat but will eat fish and seafood, or for a special family dinner. Serve it with a tossed green salad or garden fresh tomatoes drizzled with olive oil. Open a bottle of crisp cold wine.

Tips

If you have a fresh chile pepper on hand, you can substitute it for the cayenne. Seed it, mince finely and cook with the mushrooms and shallots (Step 4).

For best results, it is important to use floury potatoes, which are usually oblong in shape and do not contain as much water as waxy varieties such as thin-skinned red or white potatoes. The most common are russet (Idaho) potatoes. If you have time, cook them ahead and refrigerate until you're ready to peel. They will be easier to shred. You want the potatoes to be a bit firm for this recipe, so err on the side of undercooking.

- 10-inch (25 cm) deep-dish pie plate
- Rimmed baking sheet

8 oz	medium shrimp, shells on	250 g
2 tbsp	freshly squeezed lemon juice, divided	30 mL
1 tsp	paprika	5 mL
1 cup	dry white wine	250 mL
8 oz	white mushroom caps	250 g
3 tbsp	butter, divided	45 mL
1 tbsp	olive oil	15 mL
2	shallots, minced	2
1 tsp	grated lemon zest	5 mL
8 oz	scallops, cut into bite-size pieces	250 g
1/4 cup	all-purpose flour	60 mL
1/2 cup	heavy or whipping (35%) cream	125 mL
1/4 tsp	cayenne pepper (see Tips, left)	1 mL
	Salt and freshly ground black pepper	
1 lb	skinless firm white fish fillets, cut into 1-inch (2.5 cm) squares	500 g
1/4 cup	finely chopped fresh dill fronds or Italian flat-leaf parsley leaves	60 mL

Rösti Topping

3	russet (Idaho) potatoes, boiled in their skins until fork-tender, cooled and peeled (see Tips, left)	3
	Salt and freshly ground black or white pepper	
2 tbsp	melted butter	30 mL

1. Peel and devein shrimp, reserving shells. In a bowl, combine 1 tbsp (15 mL) of the lemon juice and paprika. Stir well to dissolve paprika. Add shrimp and toss well. Set aside in refrigerator.

2. In a saucepan, combine white wine, 1/2 cup (125 mL) water and reserved shrimp shells. Bring to a boil over medium heat. Cover, reduce heat to low and simmer for 15 minutes. Strain, pushing against solids to extract as much liquid as possible. Set liquid aside and discard shells.

3. In work bowl fitted with slicing blade, slice mushrooms. Set aside. Meanwhile, preheat oven to 400°F (200°C).

4. In a skillet, melt 1 tbsp (15 mL) of the butter with the oil over medium-high heat. Add mushrooms and shallots and cook, stirring, until shallots are softened and mushrooms begin to brown, about 5 minutes. Stir in lemon zest and remaining tbsp (15 mL) of lemon juice. Transfer to a bowl and set aside. Add reserved shrimp and scallops to skillet and cook, stirring, just until seared (they should not be cooked through), about 2 minutes. Transfer to bowl with mushrooms and set aside.

5. Reduce heat to low. Melt remaining 2 tbsp (30 mL) of butter to skillet. Add flour and cook, whisking, for 5 minutes. Add reserved shrimp liquid, cream, cayenne and any juices that have collected from mushrooms and seared seafood and cook, stirring, until thickened, about 2 minutes. Season with salt and black pepper to taste. Stir in reserved mushrooms and seafood, fish and dill and transfer to pie plate. Place pie plate on baking sheet.

6. Rösti Topping: Meanwhile, in work bowl fitted with shredding blade, shred potatoes. Spread evenly over top of pie and season with salt and pepper to taste. Drizzle with melted butter. Bake in preheated oven until top is golden brown, about 25 minutes.

Three Herb–Crusted Scallops

Fresh herbs make the flavor in these scallops pop. Serve with Roasted Red Pepper Sauce (page 409), if desired.

Tip

Make sure you purchase sea scallops because bay scallops are smaller and less flavorful.

2 cups	broken pieces stone-ground wheat crackers	500 mL
2 tbsp	all-purpose flour	30 mL
1 tsp	fresh tarragon	5 mL
1 tsp	fresh rosemary	5 mL
1 tsp	loosely packed fresh dill fronds	5 mL
3 tbsp	olive oil	45 mL
12 oz	sea scallops (about 16)	375 g
1 tbsp	unsalted butter	15 mL

1. In work bowl fitted with metal blade, process crackers, flour, tarragon, rosemary and dill until finely ground. Transfer to a shallow dish.

2. Rub oil on both sides of scallops. Dredge scallops in herb mixture. Discard any extra mixture.

3. In a large skillet over medium heat, melt butter. Add scallops, in batches to prevent crowding, and cook, turning once, until light brown and surface springs back when lightly pressed, about 4 minutes per side.

Variation
To add more spice to the scallops, add 1 tsp (5 mL) hot pepper sauce to the herb mixture.

Shrimp in Tomatillo-Pepita Sauce

Serves 4 to 6

This dish is a cornucopia of enticing flavors. In fact, there is so much going on, keep the accompaniments very simple. Serve it with just a bowl of fluffy steamed rice.

½ cup	green pumpkin seeds (pepitas)	125 mL
1 tsp	coriander seeds	5 mL
1 tsp	cumin seeds	5 mL
1	small onion, quartered	1
2	cloves garlic	2
6	sprigs cilantro (stems and leaves)	6
1 to 2	jalapeño peppers, seeded and coarsely chopped	1 to 2
1	can (11 oz/312 g) tomatillos, drained	1
1 cup	chicken broth	250 mL
1 tsp	salt	5 mL
1 tbsp	oil	15 mL
2 lbs	shrimp, peeled and deveined	1 kg
1 tbsp	freshly squeezed lime juice	15 mL

1. In a large skillet over medium-high heat, toast pumpkin, coriander and cumin seeds, stirring constantly, until pumpkin seeds are popping and cumin is fragrant, about 3 minutes. Immediately remove from heat, transfer to a mortar or spice grinder and grind. Set aside.

2. In work bowl fitted with metal blade, pulse onion, garlic, cilantro and jalapeño pepper(s) until finely chopped, about 15 times, stopping and scraping down sides of the bowl once or twice. Add tomatillos, chicken broth and reserved pepita mixture and salt and process until smooth.

3. In same skillet used for toasting pepitas, heat oil over medium-high heat. Add shrimp and cook, stirring, until they curl up, turn pink and are opaque, about 3 minutes. Transfer to a bowl and set aside.

4. Add tomatillo mixture to pan, bring to a boil and cook, stirring for 2 minutes to thicken and blend flavors. Return shrimp to pan and cook, stirring, for 1 minute. Drizzle with lime juice and serve immediately.

Tiger Shrimp with Instant Aïoli

Serves 4

This is a favorite summer meal. Brining the shrimp firms them up and makes them succulent on the barbecue.

Tips

The shrimp used for this recipe are truly colossal, about 7 per pound. If you use smaller shrimp, adjust the cooking time accordingly. Also, because of environmental concerns, we do not recommend buying shrimp that are imported from Asia.

The quantity of garlic depends upon how strong you want the aïoli to taste and the size of the garlic cloves. Four produces a nicely garlicky aïoli. If you love the taste of garlic, use more.

Although plain vegetable oil does the job, you can add a whisper of flavor to the shrimp by brushing them with chili oil or a herb-infused oil such as lemon, garlic or oregano.

2 lbs	tiger shrimp, shells on, about 14 shrimp (see Tips, left)	1 kg
Brine		
¼ cup	kosher salt or 2 tbsp (30 mL) table salt	60 mL
2	dried red chile peppers	2
4	cloves garlic, crushed	4
2 tsp	granulated sugar	10 mL
1 cup	boiling water	250 mL
4 cups	cold water (approx.)	1 L
2 tbsp	rice vinegar	30 mL
	Ice cubes	
Instant Aïoli		
½ cup	Traditional Mayonnaise (page 437) or store-bought (see Tip, right)	125 mL
4 to 6	cloves garlic, coarsely chopped (see Tips, left)	4 to 6
2 tbsp	extra virgin olive oil	30 mL
2 tbsp	freshly squeezed lemon juice	30 mL
1 tsp	Dijon mustard	5 mL
1 tsp	salt	5 mL
½ tsp	freshly ground black pepper	2 mL
Pinch	cayenne pepper, optional	Pinch
¼ cup	oil (see Tips, left)	60 mL

1. Using a knife, slit the shrimp shells along the back, removing the vein but leaving the shells intact. Set aside.

2. **Brine:** In a large heatproof nonreactive bowl, combine salt, chiles, garlic, sugar and boiling water. Stir until salt and sugar are dissolved. Add cold water and vinegar and stir well. Add enough ice cubes to cool the mixture to room temperature.

3. Place shrimp in brining solution, adding additional cold water to cover, if necessary. Cover bowl and refrigerate for 30 minutes to 1 hour.

4. **Instant Aïoli:** Meanwhile, in work bowl fitted with metal blade, process mayonnaise, garlic, 2 tbsp (30 mL) olive oil, lemon juice, mustard, salt, black pepper, and cayenne, if using, until mixture is smooth and well blended, about 1 minute. Cover and chill until ready to use.

Tip

Don't confuse real mayonnaise with "mayonnaise-type" salad dressings, which are similar in appearance. Mayonnaise is a combination of egg yolks, vinegar or lemon juice, olive oil and seasonings. Imitators will contain additional ingredients, such as sugar, flour or milk. Make your own or make sure the label says mayonnaise and check the ingredients.

5. Preheat barbecue. Remove shrimp from brine. Discard brine. Rinse shrimp under cold running water and pat dry with paper towel. Brush liberally with oil. Place on preheated grill and cook, turning once, until shrimp are pink and firm, about 3 minutes per side. Serve hot, in their shells, accompanied by Instant Aïoli.

Variations

Dill Aïoli: Add 2 tbsp (30 mL) chopped dill along with the mayonnaise.

Spicy Aïoli: Add 2 tbsp (30 mL) Asian chile sauce to Instant Aïoli. Pulse to blend.

Cold Shrimp Salad

Serves 4

Here's a refreshing light meal that doesn't require an oven. Perfect for those hot summer months.

Tip

Serve this salad with Whole Wheat Rolls (page 485).

2	sweet pickles, cut in half (about 2 oz/60 g)	2
1 lb	cooked salad shrimp	500 g
½ cup	Traditional Mayonnaise (page 437) or store-bought	125 mL
1 tbsp	loosely packed fresh dill fronds	15 mL
1 tsp	prepared mustard	5 mL
4 cups	salad greens	1 L
4	tomatoes (about 12 oz/375 g)	4
1	avocado, peeled and pitted	1
½ cup	Avocado Tamarind Cashew Dressing (page 413)	125 mL

1. In work bowl fitted with metal blade, add pickles and pulse until finely chopped, about 10 times. Add shrimp, mayonnaise, dill and mustard and pulse until coarsely chopped, about 10 times. Transfer to a small bowl.

2. Divide salad greens evenly among 4 plates. Cut tomatoes and avocado into wedges. Fan over salad greens. Scoop about one-quarter of the shrimp mixture over each salad. Drizzle 2 tbsp (30 mL) of the Avocado Tamarind Cashew Dressing over top.

Variation
Try using cooked scallops in place of the shrimp.

Everyday Tuna and Red Rice Salad

The use of Bhutanese red rice or more delicate brown Kalijira rice, both of which are whole grains that cook in less than 30 minutes, allows you to make this very tasty and nutritious rice salad for a weekday meal. This salad is very flexible. It is designed for convenience, which includes using ingredients you're likely to have on hand.

Tips

Bhutanese red and Kalijira rice are available at specialty stores, Asian grocery stores or Whole Foods. They are often sold under the Lotus Foods label.

To cook the rice for this recipe: In a heavy saucepan with a tight-fitting lid, bring 1½ cups (375 mL) water to a rapid boil. Stir in ¾ cup (175 mL) rice and return to a boil. Reduce heat to low. Cover and simmer until liquid is absorbed and rice is tender, about 25 minutes. (If liquid remains, remove lid and return to element for a few minutes until it evaporates.)

- Mini-bowl attachment

¾ cup	Bhutanese red or Kalijira brown rice, cooked (see Tips, left)	175 mL

Dressing

¼ cup	Italian flat-leaf parsley leaves	60 mL
1	shallot, quartered	1
1	clove garlic, coarsely chopped	1
1 tbsp	white wine vinegar or freshly squeezed lemon juice	15 mL
1 tsp	Dijon mustard	5 mL
½ tsp	salt	2 mL
	Freshly ground black pepper	
¼ cup	extra virgin olive oil	60 mL
1	can (6 oz/170 g) tuna, drained	1
1 cup	cooked sliced green beans, cooled, optional	250 mL
½	red bell pepper, seeded and diced	½
¼ cup	sliced pitted black olives or 1 tbsp (15 mL) diced capers	60 mL
4	green onions, white part only, thinly sliced, or ¼ cup (60 mL) finely chopped red onion	4
1	sun-dried tomato, packed in olive oil, finely chopped, or ½ cup (125 mL) quartered cherry or grape tomatoes	1
	Lettuce leaves or hearts of romaine, optional	

1. **Dressing:** In mini bowl fitted with metal blade, pulse parsley, shallot, garlic, vinegar, mustard, salt, and pepper to taste, to chop and blend, about 5 times With motor running, add olive oil through feed tube, stopping and scraping down sides of the bowl as necessary. Set aside.

2. In a bowl, combine tuna, green beans, if using, bell pepper, olives, green onions and sun-dried tomato. Toss until blended. Add dressing and toss well.

3. To serve, spoon warm rice onto plates and top with tuna mixture. Or, if using lettuce, line a platter with leafy lettuce or hearts of romaine. Spoon rice onto lettuce and top with tuna mixture.

Fish Puff Pockets

Serves 4

Use fish that is in season and fresh. These pockets create a lovely presentation for any brunch or luncheon. Pair it with a vegetable salad for a nice effect.

Tips

Always use cooked meats or fish in puff pastry because cooking time does not allow raw meats or fish to cook fully.

Try an array of shrimp, firm white fish pieces, salmon and/or scallops.

A kitchen knife with a sharp point, such as a paring knife, is a good tool for checking fish for doneness. Just insert the knife in the thickest part of the fish. If you encounter resistance it needs more cooking. If it flakes easily or immediately pulls away from the bone, it is done.

- Preheat oven to 425°F (220°C)
- 2 baking sheets, lined with parchment paper

1	package (18 oz/560 g) puff pastry, thawed (see Tips, left)	1
	All-purpose flour	
4 oz	white Cheddar cheese, cut into chunks	125 g
4 oz	mushrooms, stems removed	125 g
2	green onions, green part only, cut in half	2
2	cloves garlic	2
2 tbsp	extra virgin olive oil	30 mL
1 lb	fresh skinless fish fillets, cut into 4 pieces (see Tips, left)	500 g
½ cup	sour cream	125

1. Working with one half of pastry, on a lightly floured board, roll pastry into a 12-inch (30 cm) square. Using a pizza cutter, cut into 2 equal pieces. Set aside. Repeat with second piece of puff pastry.

2. In work bowl fitted with shredding blade, shred cheese. Transfer to a bowl and set aside.

3. Replace shredding blade with metal blade. Pulse mushroom caps, green onions and garlic until coarsely chopped, for 10 times, stopping and scraping down sides of the bowl as necessary. Set aside.

4. In a skillet, heat oil over medium heat. Add fish pieces and cook, turning once, until fish flakes easily when pierced with a knife, about 3 minutes per side.

5. Divide cheese, mushroom mixture and fish between the 4 pieces of pastry, top with 2 tbsp (30 mL) of sour cream. Fold two opposite sides of pastry toward center over filling then two remaining sides like an envelope. If pastry seems dry, lightly brush edges with water before folding to ensure a good seal. Turn over, seal side down, and place on prepared baking sheet. Bake in preheated oven until light brown and puffed up, 22 to 18 minutes. Serve warm or cold.

Meatless Mains

Tian Provençal

Vegan Friendly

A tian is a kind of French casserole, usually made with layers of vegetables. Here we've combined eggplant, zucchini and onions and cooked them with white wine and tomatoes. This makes a great main course, accompanied by salad, but you can also provide smaller portions and serve it as a vegetable with grilled meat or robustly flavored fish.

Tips

You can peel the eggplant and zucchini or leave the skin on to suit your taste. If you're using the skin, we suggest you purchase organic produce.

To sweat eggplant: Place sliced eggplant in a colander, and sprinkle each slice with salt. Set aside for 30 minutes. Rinse well under cold running water, squeeze out moisture and pat dry.

- Preheat oven to 375°F (190°C)
- Shallow 6-cup (1.5 L) baking dish, lightly greased

1	medium eggplant (about 1 lb/500 g), cut into ½-inch (1 cm) thick slices and sweated (see Tips, left)	1
2	zucchini	2
4	small onions, halved if necessary	4
¼ cup	all-purpose flour	60 mL
¼ cup	olive oil, divided (approx.)	60 mL
4	cloves garlic, minced	4
1 tsp	dried thyme	5 mL
1 tsp	salt	5 mL
	Freshly ground black pepper	
¼ cup	dry white wine	60 mL
1	can (14 oz/398 mL) diced tomatoes with juice	1
1 cup	French-Style Seasoned Bread Crumbs (page 468)	250 mL
2 tbsp	freshly grated Parmesan cheese or vegan alternative	30 mL

1. In work bowl fitted with slicing blade, slice zucchini. Set aside. One at a time, place onions in feed tube and slice. Set aside.

2. Spread flour on a large plate. One at a time, add sweated eggplant slices and dredge. Set aside.

3. In a large skillet, heat 2 tbsp (30 mL) of the oil over medium heat. Add dredged eggplant, in batches, and cook, turning once, until lightly browned, adding more oil as necessary. Transfer to prepared dish. Add zucchini to pan and cook, stirring, just until it begins to brown, about 5 minutes. Layer over eggplant. Add onions to pan and cook, stirring, until softened, about 3 minutes. Add garlic, thyme, salt, and pepper to taste and cook, stirring, for 1 minute. Add wine, bring to a boil and boil for 2 minutes. Add tomatoes with juice and bring to a boil. Pour over zucchini.

4. Spread bread crumbs evenly over top of vegetables. Sprinkle evenly with Parmesan and drizzle with remaining olive oil. Bake in preheated oven until vegetables are tender and top is browned, about 40 minutes.

Roasted Leek, Mushroom and Tomato Clafouti

Serves 4 to 6

Vegetarian Friendly

Clafouti, a French pancake, is usually made with fruit and served as a dessert. Here a savory filling is perfect for lunch or a light dinner.

Tips

The gratin dish this was tested in was a shallow one, measuring 9- by 9-inches (23 by 23 cm). If yours is deeper, adjust the cooking time accordingly.

If you prefer, you can use an equal quantity of ripe Roma (plum) tomatoes. Cut them in half lengthwise and place cut side down on baking sheet.

- Preheat oven to 400°F (200°C)
- Rimmed baking sheet
- 6-cup (1.5 L) gratin dish, buttered (see Tips, left)

1 lb	cherry or grape tomatoes (see Tips, left)	500 g
12	cremini mushroom caps	12
1	leek, white part with a bit of green, cleaned and cut into ½-inch (1 cm) slices (see Tips, page 241)	1
2 tbsp	extra virgin olive oil	30 mL
2	cloves garlic, minced	2
2 tbsp	finely chopped Italian flat-leaf parsley leaves	30 mL
	Freshly ground black pepper	
4	eggs	4
¼ cup	all-purpose flour	60 mL
1 tsp	salt	5 mL
1 cup	whole milk	250 mL
¼ cup	heavy or whipping (35%) cream	60 mL
¼ cup	freshly grated Parmesan cheese	60 mL

1. In a large bowl, combine tomatoes, mushroom caps and leek. Add olive oil and toss well. Spread out on rimmed baking sheet and roast in preheated oven until mushrooms and leek are lightly browned and tomatoes have collapsed, about 30 minutes. Remove from oven and reduce heat to 350°F (180°C). Transfer roasted vegetables to prepared dish and sprinkle with garlic, parsley, and pepper to taste. Set aside.

2. In work bowl fitted with metal blade, pulse eggs, flour, salt, and pepper to taste, to blend, about 5 times. Add milk and cream and process until smooth, about 30 seconds. Pour over vegetables. Bake in preheated oven until edges are set and center is slightly jiggly, about 30 minutes. Remove from oven.

3. Preheat broiler. Sprinkle clafouti with Parmesan and place under boiler until lightly browned. Let cool slightly before serving.

Portobello Mushroom Lasagna

Vegetarian Friendly

You will be rewarded for the cost and time required to make this recipe when you receive all the accolades from your guests.

Tips

Cover and reheat any leftovers in preheated 350°F (180°C) oven until hot throughout, 20 to 25 minutes.

Ask your produce manager how fresh the mushrooms are. Purchase them the day you will use them.

Use a deep baking pan or roasting pan to ensure the assembled lasagna does not fill the pan more than two-thirds full because the noodles will expand while baking.

- Preheat oven to 425°F (220°C)
- 13- by 9-inch (33 by 23 cm) metal baking pan, at least 2½ inches (6 cm) deep, buttered

4 oz	Parmesan cheese, cut into chunks	125 g
12 oz	provolone cheese, cut into chunks	375 g
½	onion, cut in half	½
1 tbsp	olive oil	15 mL
1¼ lbs	portobello mushrooms, stems removed	625 g
1½ tbsp	butter	22 mL
1 tbsp	freshly squeezed lemon juice	15 mL
1½ tbsp	all-purpose flour	22 mL
4 cups	heavy or whipping (35%) cream, at room temperature	1 L
1	package (10 oz/300 g) oven-ready lasagna noodles, divided	1
1	package (10 oz/300 g) frozen spinach, thawed and drained, divided	1
8 oz	ricotta cheese	250 g

1. In work bowl fitted with metal blade, with the motor running, add Parmesan cheese through the feed tube and process until finely grated. Transfer to a bowl. Set aside.

2. Replace metal blade with shredding blade and shred provolone cheese. Transfer to another bowl. Set aside.

3. Replace shredding blade with slicing blade and slice onion. Heat oil in a large pot over medium heat. Add onion and sauté until translucent, about 5 minutes.

4. Meanwhile, in work bowl fitted with slicing blade, slice mushrooms. Add to pot with onion and steam, covered, until tender, for 5 minutes. Transfer mixture to a bowl. Set aside.

5. In same pot over medium heat, cook butter and lemon juice until butter is fully melted, about 1 minute. Whisk in flour and cook, stirring, until light brown and thick, about 2 minutes. Gradually whisk in cream and cook, whisking constantly, until mixture starts to thicken, about 5 minutes. Set aside.

6. Placed one-third of the noodles in a single layer in prepared baking dish, trimming to fit as necessary. Spread half of the spinach evenly over noodles. Then spread half of the mushroom mixture, one-third of the Parmesan cheese, one-third of the provolone cheese and one-third of the cream mixture. Add half of remaining noodles in a layer. Spread with remaining spinach, then mushroom mixture, half of the remaining Parmesan, half of the remaining provolone and half of the remaining cream mixture. Place remaining noodles on top and press down with your hand to even it all out. Add remaining Parmesan, provolone and cream mixture. Dollop ricotta by spoonfuls on top so you have 10 dollops in 5 rows by 2 rows.

7. Bake in preheated oven, covered, for 45 minutes or until noodles are tender. Uncover and bake until hot and bubbling and top is browned, about 10 minutes more. Let lasagna stand for 15 minutes. Serve hot.

Potato Tortilla with Peppers

Vegetarian Friendly

This is a variation on a traditional Spanish tapas dish resembling an omelet, which is usually served cold or at room temperature. But it's also great served hot like an Italian frittata. Add some warm baguette and a salad and enjoy. If you have leftovers, put them in the refrigerator and enjoy them the next day cold, tapas-style.

- Ovenproof skillet

1	potato (about 8 oz/250 g), scrubbed	1
1	red onion, quartered	1
1	red bell pepper, seeded and halved lengthwise	1
1	green bell pepper, seeded and halved lengthwise	1
1	long red chile or jalapeño pepper, seeded	1
2	cloves garlic	2
2 tbsp	extra virgin olive oil	30 mL
4 oz	sharp cheese, such as aged Cheddar or a hard goat cheese	125 g
6	eggs, beaten	6
	Salt and freshly ground black pepper.	

1. Place potato in microwave oven and heat on High for 2 minutes. Remove from oven and let cool for 2 minutes. In work bowl fitted with slicing blade, slice potato. Transfer to a bowl and set aside. Add red onion, red and green bell peppers, chile pepper and garlic to feed tube and slice.

2. In a large skillet, heat oil over medium heat. Add onion, bell peppers, chile pepper and garlic and cook, stirring, until softened, about 5 minutes. Add potato and cook, stirring, until tender, about 8 minutes.

3. Replace slicing blade with shredding blade and shred cheese. Set aside.

4. Preheat broiler. In a bowl, beat eggs with salt and pepper to taste. Pour over onion mixture and sprinkle cheese evenly over top. Reduce heat to low, loosely cover and cook until eggs are set, about 6 minutes. Place under preheated broiler until top is nicely browned. To serve, cut into wedges.

Grilled Portobello Mushrooms with Balsamic Vinegar

Serves 6

Vegan Friendly

These mushrooms are great as a side dish or placed between hamburger buns for a vegetarian main dish.

Tips

Purchase your mushrooms the day you are going to use them.

Make sure the basil is washed and dried. Use a herb spinner to make sure it is as dry as can be.

- Preheat oven to 350°F (180°C)
- 8-cup (2 L) baking dish

10	portobello mushrooms, quartered (about 1½ lbs/750 g) (see Tips, left)	10
¼ cup	packed fresh basil leaves (see Tips, left)	60 mL
2 tbsp	balsamic vinegar	30 mL
2 tsp	salt	10 mL
¼ cup	olive oil	60 mL

1. In work bowl fitted with slicing blade, slice mushrooms. Transfer to baking dish and arrange in layers.

2. Replace slicing blade with metal blade and process basil, vinegar and salt until fairly smooth, about 30 seconds. With the motor running, slowly drizzle oil through feed tube until completely incorporated. Pour over mushrooms. Bake in preheated oven until soft to the touch, 15 to 20 minutes.

Variation

You can sprinkle 8 oz (250 g) freshly grated Parmesan cheese over the mushrooms about 5 minutes before they are done.

Potatoes with Creamy Corn Topping

Vegetarian Friendly

This dish is reminiscent of scalloped potatoes dressed up to become a main course. It's much lighter and more nutritious than that old favorite and has an abundance of interesting flavors. Add a green salad or crisp green beans sprinkled with toasted sesame seeds to complete the meal.

Tips

If you prefer to use already-shredded mozzarella, you'll need 1 cup (250 mL).

Potatoes turn brown on contact with air so be sure to cover them with the tomato mixture as quickly as possible to prevent them from oxidizing.

We always use Italian flat-leaf parsley because it has so much more flavor than the curly leaf variety. Unless the stems or sprigs are specifically called for, use only the tender leaves.

- Preheat oven to 325°F (160°C)
- 13- by 9-inch (33 by 23 cm) baking dish, lightly greased

4 oz	mozzarella cheese	125 g
4	medium potatoes, peeled	4
1	red onion, cut to fit feed tube	1
1	can (28 oz/796 mL) tomatoes with juice	1
½ cup	loosely packed Italian flat-leaf parsley leaves	125 mL
1 tsp	salt	5 mL
4 cups	corn kernels, thawed if frozen	1 L
½ cup	evaporated milk	125 mL
1 tbsp	butter	15 mL
½ tsp	freshly grated nutmeg	2 mL
	Freshly ground black pepper	
	Finely chopped parsley	

1. In work bowl fitted with shredding blade, shred mozzarella. Set aside. Replace shredding blade with slicing blade. Slice potatoes and arrange evenly over bottom of prepared dish. Slice red onion and arrange over top of potatoes.

2. Replace slicing blade with metal blade and process tomatoes with juice, parsley and salt until smooth, about 15 seconds. Pour over potatoes.

3. Rinse out work bowl and metal blade and refit work bowl. Add corn and evaporated milk and process until combined but corn is still a little chunky, about 15 seconds.

4. In a skillet, melt butter over medium-low heat. Add corn mixture and cook, stirring, until thickened, about 5 minutes. Add nutmeg, pepper to taste, and mozzarella and stir until cheese is melted.

5. Spread corn mixture evenly over top of tomato mixture. Bake in preheated oven until potatoes are tender and mixture is hot and bubbling, about 1 hour. Sprinkle liberally with parsley and serve.

Potato Latkes

Vegetarian Friendly

Enjoy latkes as a vegetarian main course, accompanied by applesauce and sour cream or pressed yogurt, but if you're not a vegetarian they are also good topped with a slice of smoked salmon. A tossed green salad makes a great finish.

Tip

You may need to vary the quantity of oil, depending on the size of your pan. You'll want a depth of about ⅛ inch (3 mm).

- Preheat oven to 200°F (100°C)

4	large potatoes, peeled and quartered	4
1	large onion, quartered	1
3	eggs, beaten	3
1 tsp	salt	5 mL
	Freshly ground black pepper	
¾ cup	all-purpose flour, divided	175 mL
¼ cup	vegetable oil (approx.) (see Tip, left)	60 mL
	Applesauce, optional	
	Sour cream, optional	

1. In work bowl fitted with shredding blade, shred potatoes and onion. Transfer to a large bowl. Add eggs, salt, and pepper to taste, and toss well. Sprinkle ¼ cup (60 mL) of the flour evenly over mixture and toss well. Repeat twice until all flour is used up.

2. In a large heavy skillet, heat oil over medium-high heat. Scoop out about 3 tbsp (45 mL) of batter for each latke and place in pan. Flatten with a spatula. Repeat, leaving about 2 inches (5 cm) between latkes and cook until bottom is crisp and golden, about 4 minutes. Turn and repeat. Keep cooked latkes warm in preheated oven until all the batter is used up. Serve hot.

Fried Zucchini Cakes

Makes about 20 cakes

Vegetarian Friendly

Make these yummy treats when zucchini are abundant in local markets. They are particularly delicious served with a dollop of sauce. We like Smoked Chili Sauce (page 445) or Fresh Herb Tomato Dipping Sauce (page 44).

Tip

Peel zucchini or leave the skin on to suit your taste. If you're using the skin, we suggest you purchase organic produce.

• Preheat oven to 200°F (100°C)

4	medium zucchini (see Tip, left)	4
1 tsp	salt	5 mL
1	small red onion, quartered	1
½ cup	Italian flat-leaf parsley leaves	125 mL
4 oz	feta cheese, broken into chunks	125 g
2	eggs, beaten	2
½ cup	dry bread crumbs	125 mL
	Freshly ground black pepper	
¼ cup	all-purpose flour	60 mL
¼ cup	vegetable oil (approx.)	60 mL

1. In work bowl fitted with shredding blade, shred zucchini. Measure out 4 cups (1 L) and save remainder for another use. Sprinkle with salt and transfer to a colander to drain for 30 minutes. Rinse under cold running water and drain. Using your hands, squeeze out as much water as possible. Spread on a clean tea towel and press to soak up as much liquid as possible, using a second tea towel, if necessary.

2. Replace shredding blade with metal blade and pulse red onion and parsley until onion is finely chopped, about 5 times, stopping and scraping down sides of the bowl once or twice. Add feta and pulse just until crumbled and blended, about 7 times. Transfer to a large bowl.

3. Add dry zucchini, eggs, bread crumbs, and pepper to taste, and toss well. Sprinkle flour evenly over mixture and toss well.

4. In a large heavy skillet, heat oil over medium-high heat. Scoop out about 2 tbsp (30 mL) of mixture at a time for each cake and place in pan. Flatten with a spatula, ensuring there is a space of about 2 inches (5 cm) between cakes. Cook, until golden on one side, then flip and repeat, about 4 minutes per side. Drain on a paper towel-lined platter and keep warm in the oven while you complete the frying. Serve hot.

Curry-Spiked Zucchini Galette

Serves 2

Vegetarian Friendly

With the addition of eggs, this dish is like a cross between a galette and a frittata. This makes a small quantity, a perfect dinner for two with the addition of salad. It can also be served in smaller quantities as a vegetable course or even a starter.

Tip

You can peel the zucchini or leave the skin on to suit your taste. If you're using the skin, we suggest you purchase organic produce.

- Preheat oven to 400°F (200°C)
- Small (2 cup/500 mL) shallow gratin or baking dish, greased

1½ lbs	zucchini (about 6 small)	750 g
1 tbsp	olive oil	15 mL
1	sprig fresh thyme or 1 tsp (5 mL) dried thyme	1
2	eggs, beaten	2
½ cup	freshly grated Parmesan cheese	125 mL
1 tsp	curry powder	5 mL
½ tsp	salt	2 mL
	Freshly ground black pepper	
Pinch	freshly grated nutmeg	Pinch

1. In work bowl fitted with slicing blade, slice zucchini.

2. In a large skillet, heat oil over medium-high heat. Add zucchini and thyme and cook, stirring, for 1 minute. Cover, reduce heat to low and cook until zucchini are tender, about 15 minutes. Transfer to a colander and drain.

3. In a large bowl, beat together eggs, Parmesan, curry powder, salt, pepper to taste, and nutmeg. Add zucchini and toss until thoroughly coated.

4. Transfer to dish and, using a spatula, even out the top. Bake in preheated oven until top is slightly puffed and golden about 20 minutes.

Pesto-Stuffed Zucchini

Serves 4

Vegan Friendly

The pesto used here is made from sun-dried tomatoes and drained diced tomatoes, rather than more traditional basil. Use this recipe to provide a hit of tomato flavor when tomatoes aren't in season.

Tips

Do not use tiny zucchini here. They need to be large enough to create a trough that will support the filling. You may want to use 2 large zucchini and give everyone a half.

Sun-dried tomatoes are available in two forms: packed in olive oil or packaged dry. Those packed in olive oil are already reconstituted. If yours are the dry variety, blanche in boiling water for 4 minutes and drain before adding to recipe.

After draining the tomatoes, set the juice aside. If the filling starts to dry out during cooking, sprinkle with reserved tomato juice.

If your pine nuts are becoming very brown and your zucchini aren't tender enough, cover with foil and continue cooking.

- Preheat oven to 375°F (190°C)
- Rimmed baking sheet, greased

4	zucchini (see Tips, left)	4
	Salt and freshly ground black pepper	
4	cloves garlic, coarsely chopped	4
2	reconstituted sun-dried tomato halves, drained if packed in olive oil, coarsely chopped (see Tips, left)	2
1 cup	drained canned diced tomatoes (see Tips, left)	250 mL
1 cup	freshly grated Parmesan cheese or vegan alternative	250 mL
¼ cup	extra virgin olive oil	60 mL
2 tbsp	pine nuts	30 mL

1. Slice zucchini lengthwise and scoop out a trough through the center, leaving enough flesh around the edges to support the stuffing, reserving pulp. Season zucchini with salt and pepper to taste and transfer to prepared baking sheet.

2. Transfer zucchini pulp to work bowl fitted with metal blade. Add garlic, sun-dried tomatoes, and salt and pepper to taste. Process until smooth, about 15 seconds. Add diced tomatoes and Parmesan. With motor running, slowly add olive oil through feed tube until integrated. Spoon mixture evenly into zucchini. Sprinkle with pine nuts.

3. Bake in preheated oven until zucchini are very tender and pine nuts are nicely browned, about 40 minutes.

Mélange of Roasted Vegetables with Chile-Spiked Tahini Sauce

Serves 4

Vegan Friendly

This dish is a bit different from most approaches to platters of roasted vegetables because the vegetables are sliced thinly, which causes them to lose their shape when roasted. Then they are combined so they resemble a dry stew. The dish looks very pretty and a dollop of the sauce provides a very tasty finish.

Tip

If you're not using dairy-free yogurt, make an effort to get pressed, also known as Greek-style yogurt. It is lusciously thick and adds beautiful depth to this and many other dishes. Greek yogurt is available in well-stocked supermarkets and specialty stores. If you can't find it, you can make your own. *To make Greek-style yogurt:* Line a sieve with a double layer of cheesecloth or paper towels. Add plain yogurt, cover and refrigerate overnight. The watery component will have drained out and you will be left with lovely thick yogurt.

- Preheat oven to 400°F (200°C)
- Large rimmed baking sheet
- Mini-bowl attachment

Vegetables

2	eggplants, cut into ½-inch (1 cm) slices	2
¼ cup	olive oil, divided	60 mL
2	red bell peppers, seeded and halved	2
1	large Spanish onion, cut to fit feed tube	1
2 cups	cherry or grape tomatoes	500 mL

Chile-Spiked Tahini Sauce

¼ cup	full-fat or soy plain yogurt (see Tips, left)	60 mL
¼ cup	tahini paste	60 mL
2	cloves garlic	2
½	long red or green chile pepper	½
2 tbsp	freshly squeezed lemon juice	30 mL
2 tbsp	extra virgin olive oil	30 mL
2 tbsp	warm water	30 mL
½ tsp	salt	2 mL
	Freshly ground black pepper	

1. **Vegetables:** Brush eggplant on both sides with 2 tbsp (30 mL) of the olive oil and place on baking sheet.

2. In work bowl fitted with slicing blade, slice bell peppers and onion. Transfer to a large bowl. Add tomatoes and remaining 2 tbsp (30 mL) of oil. Toss well. Transfer to baking sheet and roast in preheated oven, turning eggplant and stirring pepper mixture once, until vegetables are spottily browned, about 40 minutes.

3. **Chile-Spiked Tahini Sauce:** Meanwhile, in mini bowl fitted with metal bade, process yogurt, tahini, garlic, chile, lemon juice, olive oil, water, salt, and pepper to taste, until smoothly blended, about 10 seconds. Transfer to a small serving bowl and pass at the table.

Sweet Potato Gnocchi in Sage-Butter Sauce

Makes about 36 gnocchi

Vegetarian Friendly

Luscious and light, these delectable gnocchi make a great light dinner, accompanied by a tossed green salad. If you're looking for an impressive starter, try them.

Tips

The better the quality of your ricotta, the less water it will contain. It's important to remove as much moisture as possible. Otherwise the mixture will absorb too much flour, making your gnocchi leaden. *To drain ricotta:* Place ricotta in a clean towel, wrap tightly and using your hands, press against the fabric until excess moisture is absorbed.

Baking sweet potatoes, rather than boiling them, not only concentrates their flavor but also produces a starchier result, which is ideal for making gnocchi.

- Preheat oven to 400°F (200°C)
- Baking sheet

Gnocchi

1	medium sweet potato	1
2 cups	fresh ricotta cheese (about 12 oz/ 375 g) drained of excess moisture (see Tips, left)	500 mL
½ cup	freshly grated Parmesan cheese	125 mL
1	egg, beaten	1
½ tsp	freshly grated nutmeg	2 mL
½ tsp	salt	2 mL
½ cup	all-purpose flour (approx.)	125 mL

Sage-Butter Sauce

½ cup	butter	125 mL
20	fresh sage leaves, finely chopped	20
½ cup	freshly grated Parmesan cheese	125 mL
¾ cup	reserved gnocchi water (approx.)	175 mL

1. **Gnocchi:** Pierce top of sweet potato with the tines of a fork and place on baking sheet. Bake in preheated oven until center is soft, about 1 hour (see Tips, left). Let cool slightly, remove from skin, cut into chunks and place in work bowl fitted with metal blade.

2. Add drained ricotta, Parmesan, egg, nutmeg and salt to work bowl and pulse to blend, about 5 times. Sprinkle with flour and pulse just to blend, about 5 times. Transfer to a lightly floured work surface. If necessary, add up to ¼ cup (60 mL) flour, kneading lightly until you have a firm but soft dough. Using 1 tbsp (15 mL), shape dough into small ovals. Press top side of each gnocchi with convex side of a fork (so the tines leave indentations on the top). Place on a lightly floured baking sheet as completed. (If you are not ready to cook the gnocchi, refrigerate, uncovered, for up to 8 hours.)

3. In a large pot of boiling salted water, cook gnocchi, 12 at a time, until they rise to the surface, about 3 minutes. Using a slotted spoon, transfer to a colander to drain. When all gnocchi are cooked, scoop out about 1 cup (250 mL) of the cooking water and set aside. Make sauce.

4. Sage-Butter Sauce: In a large skillet, melt butter over medium heat. Add sage and cook, stirring, just until butter begins to turn golden. Add Parmesan and ¾ cup (175 mL) reserved gnocchi water. Stir well. Add gnocchi and using a wooden spoon, toss very gently until well coated with sauce, adding more gnocchi water, if necessary. Serve immediately.

Spinach Gnocchi with Gorgonzola-Walnut Sauce

**Makes about
36 gnocchi**

Vegetarian Friendly

Decadent and delicious,
these gnocchi are the
perfect solution to a
not-so-good day. They
will make you feel
comforted and reassure
you that the world is
not so awful after all.
Of course, you can
also make them simply
because they taste so
good.

Tips

If your spinach has not
be prewashed, swish the
leaves around in a basin
of lukewarm water before
placing in colander.
Otherwise, it is likely to
be gritty.

The better the quality
of your ricotta, the less
moisture it will have and
the better the texture of
your gnocchi. *To drain
ricotta:* Place ricotta in
a clean tea towel, wrap
tightly and using your
hands, press against
the fabric until excess
moisture is absorbed.

- Baking sheet, lightly dusted with flour

6 cups	fresh spinach leaves (about 1 bunch) (see Tips, left)	1.5 L
2 cups	fresh ricotta cheese (about 12 oz/ 375 g), drained of excess moisture (see Tips, left)	500 mL
½ cup	freshly grated Parmesan cheese	125 mL
1	egg	1
½ tsp	salt	2 mL
	Freshly grated black pepper	
1 cup	all-purpose flour (approx.)	250 mL

Gorgonzola-Walnut Sauce

1 tbsp	butter	15 mL
1	clove garlic, minced	1
½ cup	heavy or whipping (35%) cream	125 mL
4 oz	Gorgonzola cheese, crumbled	125 g
1 cup	reserved gnocchi water (approx.)	250 mL
2 tbsp	chopped walnuts	30 mL

1. In a colander, placed over a sink, thoroughly rinse spinach leaves. Do not drain. Transfer to a large saucepan. Cover and cook over medium heat until wilted, about 4 minutes. Return to colander and drain. Transfer to a clean tea towel and squeeze out liquid. Transfer to work bowl fitted with metal blade.

2. Add drained ricotta, Parmesan, egg, salt, and pepper to taste, to work bowl and pulse to blend, about 5 times. Sprinkle with flour and pulse just to blend, about 5 times. Transfer to a lightly floured work surface. If necessary, add up to ¼ cup (60 mL) flour, kneading lightly until you have a firm but soft dough. Using 1 tbsp (15 mL), shape dough into small ovals. Press top side of each gnocchi with convex side of a fork (so the tines leave indentations on the top). Place on prepared baking sheet as completed. (If you are not ready to cook the gnocchi, refrigerate, uncovered, for up to 8 hours.)

Tip

For light melt-in-your mouth gnocchi, it is important the spinach and ricotta be as dry as possible. Otherwise you will need to add too much flour to get workable dough. The more flour you add, the more leaden your gnocchi will be.

3. In a large pot of boiling salted water, cook gnocchi, 12 at a time, until they rise to the surface, about 3 minutes. Using a slotted spoon, transfer to a colander to drain. When all gnocchi are cooked, scoop out about 1 cup (250 mL) of the cooking water and set aside. Make sauce.

4. **Gorgonzola-Walnut Sauce:** In a large skillet, melt butter. Add garlic and cook, stirring, for 1 minute. Add cream and cook, stirring, for 1 minute. Add Gorgonzola and ½ cup (125 mL) reserved gnocchi water. Stir well. Add gnocchi and using a wooden spoon, toss very gently until well coated with sauce, adding more gnocchi water, if necessary. Transfer to a platter and sprinkle with walnuts. Serve immediately.

Variation

Add about 2 slices finely chopped prosciutto to the sauce along with the Gorgonzola.

Potato Gnocchi

Serves 4 to 6

Vegetarian Friendly

Tossed in tomato sauce, these tiny potato dumplings are a real treat. We usually like to serve gnocchi as simply as possible, but if you're looking to take them uptown (see Variation, below).

Tips

For best results, it is important to use floury potatoes, which are usually oblong in shape and do not contain as much water as waxy varieties such as thin-skinned red or white potatoes. The most common are russet (Idaho) potatoes.

If you have time, cook the potatoes ahead and refrigerate until you're ready to peel. They will be easier to shred. You want the potatoes to be a bit firm for this recipe, so err on the side of undercooking.

1½ lbs	russet (Idaho) potatoes (about 2 large), boiled in their skins, cooled to room temperature and peeled (see Tips, left)	750 g
3	egg yolks, beaten	3
½ cup	freshly grated Parmesan cheese	125 mL
½ tsp	salt	2 mL
	Freshly ground black pepper	
Pinch	freshly grated nutmeg	Pinch
1¼ cups	all-purpose flour (approx.)	300 mL

1. In work bowl fitted with shredding blade, shred potatoes. Transfer to a large bowl. Add egg yolks, Parmesan, salt, pepper to taste, and nutmeg and stir well. Gradually add flour, mixing until a soft dough forms. (You may not need all the flour.) Transfer to a lightly floured work surface and knead several times until dough is firm and pliable. Divide into 4 equal pieces and roll each into a rope about ½ inch (1 cm) wide. Using a knife, cut into ½-inch (1 cm) lengths. Dust lightly with flour and using the tines of a fork, press indentations in each.

2. In a large pot of boiling salted water, cook gnocchi, 12 at a time, until they rise to the surface, about 3 minutes. Using a slotted spoon, transfer to a colander to drain. They are now ready for use in your favorite recipe.

Variation

Toss freshly cooked gnocchi with warm Classic Bolognese Sauce (page 400) in a baking dish. Place a layer of thinly sliced Fontina cheese over top. Bake in a 350°F (180°C) oven until mixture is bubbling and cheese is melted, about 15 minutes.

Pizzoccheri Valtellina

Serves 4 to 6

Vegetarian Friendly

This dish is Northern Italian comfort food — rich and hearty. It is perfect cold weather-cooking.

Tips

You can make your own pizzoccheri (page 464) or purchase it at well-stocked Italian grocers.

You will want about 4 cups (1 L) thinly sliced cabbage for this recipe.

* Large deep skillet with lid

1 lb	pizzoccheri (see Tips, left) or fettuccini	500 g
1	potato, peeled	1
4 oz	Fontina cheese	125 g
½	head cabbage, cored and cut into wedges (see Tips, left)	½
2 tbsp	butter	30 mL
12	fresh sage leaves, minced	12
4	cloves garlic, minced	4
	Salt and freshly ground black pepper	
1 cup	freshly grated Parmesan cheese, divided	250 mL

1. In work bowl fitted with shredding blade, shred potato. Transfer to a bowl of acidulated water and set aside. Add Fontina cheese to feed tube and shred. Set aside.

2. Replace shredding blade with slicing blade and thinly slice cabbage.

3. In a large deep skillet, melt butter over medium heat. Add sage, garlic, and salt and pepper to taste, and cook, stirring, for 1 minute. Add drained shredded potato and cabbage and toss to blend. Add ¼ cup (60 mL) water and bring to a boil. Reduce heat to low, cover and simmer until cabbage and potato are tender, about 6 minutes.

4. Meanwhile, in a large pot of boiling salted water, cook pasta until al dente. Scoop out 1 cup (250 mL) pasta water and set aside. Drain pasta.

5. When vegetables are tender, add drained pasta and ½ cup (125 mL) of the reserved pasta water to pan. Season with additional salt and pepper to taste. Using a wooden spoon, toss to coat evenly, adding more pasta water, if necessary. Cook, stirring, for 1 minute until mixture is well integrated. Add Fontina and half the Parmesan and toss well. Transfer to a large serving bowl and sprinkle with remaining Parmesan. Serve immediately.

Three-Herb Pasta Salad

1	package (8 oz/250 g) cream cheese, cubed and softened	1
½ cup	Traditional Mayonnaise (page 437) or store-bought	125 mL
½ cup	buttermilk	125 mL
2 tbsp	freshly squeezed lemon juice	30 mL
1 tbsp	chopped fresh dill fronds	15 mL
1 tbsp	chopped fresh tarragon	15 mL
1 tbsp	dried onion flakes	15 mL
1 tbsp	freshly ground black pepper	15 mL
1 tsp	chopped fresh rosemary	5 mL
½ tsp	garlic powder	2 mL
1 lb	pasta, cooked (see Tips, left)	500 g

1. In work bowl fitted with metal blade, process cream cheese, mayonnaise, buttermilk and lemon juice until smooth, about 2 minutes. Add dill, tarragon, onion flakes, pepper, rosemary and garlic powder. Process until well blended. Add dressing to cooked pasta and toss. Cover and refrigerate for at least 2 hours prior to serving or for up to 3 days.

Wild Rice Cakes with Red Pepper Coulis

Serves 4 as a main or 8 side servings

Vegetarian Friendly

These make a nice light dinner accompanied by a salad. You can also make the cakes smaller and serve them as a substantial side dish. Enjoy them with the Red Pepper Coulis (see right), but they are also good with Homemade Ketchup (page 443), any of the chile sauces (see pages 445 to 447), tomato sauce, or even a dab of pesto.

Tips

If you prefer to use cheese that is already shredded, you'll need 1½ cups (375 mL).

Be careful when turning the cakes because as they have a tendency to fall apart until they are thoroughly cooked.

The basil adds a nice note to the coulis, but if you can't get fresh leaves, omit it — the coulis will be quite tasty, anyway.

- Preheat oven to 400°F (200°C)
- Large rimmed baking sheet, lightly greased

2½ cups	water	625 mL
1 cup	wild and brown rice mixture, rinsed and drained	250 mL
½ tsp	salt	2 mL
6 oz	Swiss cheese	175 g
½ cup	plain yogurt, preferably pressed (Greek-style) (see Tip, page 311)	125 mL
¼ cup	chopped red or green onion	60 mL
¼ cup	finely chopped Italian flat-leaf parsley	60 mL
2	eggs, beaten	2
	Freshly ground black pepper	

Red Pepper Coulis

2	roasted red peppers (see Tips, page 325)	2
3	drained oil-packed sun-dried tomatoes, chopped	3
2 tbsp	extra virgin olive oil	30 mL
1 tbsp	balsamic vinegar	15 mL
10	fresh basil leaves, optional	10

1. In a large saucepan, bring water to a rolling boil. Add rice and salt. Return to a boil. Reduce heat, cover and simmer until rice is tender and about half of the wild rice grains have split, about 1 hour. Set aside until cool enough to handle, about 20 minutes.

2. In work bowl fitted with shredding blade, shred cheese. In a bowl, combine rice, cheese, yogurt, red onion, parsley, eggs, and pepper to taste. Mix well. Using a large spoon, drop mixture in 8 mounds onto prepared baking sheet. Flatten lightly with a spatula or large spoon.

3. Bake in preheated oven for 15 minutes, then flip and cook until lightly browned and heated through, for 5 minutes. Let cool on pan for 5 minutes before serving. Top with Red Pepper Coulis, if using.

4. **Red Pepper Coulis:** In work bowl fitted with metal blade, process roasted peppers, sun-dried tomatoes, oil, balsamic vinegar, and basil, if using, until smooth, about 30 seconds.

Coconut-Braised Carrots with Cashews

Serves 6 to 8

Vegan Friendly

Here's a recipe that takes a classic combination — peas and carrots — and gives it an exotic twist with the addition of cumin, ginger, cashews, a hint of chile and coconut milk, among other ingredients. The results are deliciously different. Serve this as a main course, over brown basmati rice, accompanied by a tossed green salad. It also makes an excellent side dish.

Tip

To prepare cumin and fennel for this recipe: In a dry skillet over medium heat, toast cumin and fennel seeds, stirring, until fragrant and cumin seeds just begin to brown, about 3 minutes. Immediately transfer to a mortar or a spice grinder and grind.

- Large deep skillet with lid

1 tsp	toasted cumin seeds (see Tip, left)	5 mL
1/2 tsp	toasted fennel seeds	2 mL
6	large carrots, peeled and cut into 3-inch (7.5 cm) lengths	6
1	onion, quartered	1
2	cloves garlic, coarsely chopped	2
1 tbsp	oil	15 mL
1/2 cup	raw cashews	125 mL
2/3 cup	coconut milk	150 mL
2 tsp	minced gingerroot	10 mL
1/2 tsp	ground turmeric	2 mL
1/2 tsp	salt	2 mL
1/2 tsp	cracked black peppercorns	2 mL
2 cups	frozen peas, thawed	500 mL
1	long green or red chile pepper, minced	1
1/4 cup	finely chopped cilantro leaves	60 mL

1. In work bowl fitted with slicing blade, slice carrots. Transfer to a bowl and set aside. Replace slicing blade with metal blade. Add onion and garlic and pulse to chop, about 5 times, stopping and scraping down sides of the bowl once or twice. Transfer to another bowl and set aside.

2. In a large deep skillet, heat oil over medium heat. Add cashews and cook, stirring, until they begin to brown, about 2 minutes. Remove from heat and, using a slotted spoon, transfer to work bowl. Add coconut milk, ginger and turmeric and process until smooth, about 2 minutes.

3. Add onion and garlic to skillet and cook, stirring, until softened, about 3 minutes. Add toasted cumin and fennel, salt and peppercorns and cook, stirring, for 1 minute. Stir in carrots. Spoon cashew mixture into skillet. Add 1/4 cup (60 mL) water to work bowl and process until any remaining mixture falls to the bottom and is well incorporated. Add to skillet and bring to a simmer. Cover, reduce heat to low and cook until carrots are barely tender, about 20 minutes. Stir in peas and chile pepper. Cover and cook for 10 minutes, until peas are tender and flavors meld. Sprinkle with cilantro and serve.

Tomato Basil Tart

• Preheat oven to 375°F (190°C)

½	recipe Savory Buttery Tart Pastry (see Variation, page 477)	½
6 oz	mozzarella cheese, cut into chunks	175 g
3 oz	Romano cheese, cut into chunks	90 g
4	cloves garlic	4
½ cup	Traditional Mayonnaise (page 437) or store-bought	125 mL
⅛ tsp	ground white pepper	0.5 mL
⅛ tsp	salt	0.5 mL
1 cup	loosely packed fresh basil	250 mL
2	Roma (plum) tomatoes, cored	2

1. In work bowl fitted with shredding blade, shred mozzarella. Sprinkle ½ cup (125 mL) cheese over tart shell. Set aside. Transfer remaining cheese to a bowl.

2. Replace shredding blade with metal blade and with motor running, add Romano cheese and garlic through feed tube and process until finely chopped. Transfer to bowl with mozzarella. Add mayonnaise, white pepper and salt. Set aside.

3. In same work bowl, add basil and process until coarsely chopped, about 10 seconds. Transfer to another bowl. Set aside.

4. Replace metal blade with slicing blade and slice tomatoes. Place in a single layer on paper towels and drain for 10 minutes.

5. Arrange tomato slices over cheese in tart shell. Sprinkle basil over tomatoes. Spread cheese mixture evenly over basil to cover. Bake in preheated oven until top is golden and bubbling, 35 to 40 minutes. Serve warm.

Variation

You can try some of the colorful heirloom varieties of tomatoes in place of the Roma varieties.

Sweet Onion Quiche with Potato Pastry

Serves 6 to 8

Vegetarian Friendly

Made with fresh cheese, sweet onions and potato pastry, this quiche is quite different from the norm. Served with salad, it makes a great light dinner or perfect lunch.

Tips

An easy way to cook potatoes in their skins is to microwave them. For this quantity, place the scrubbed potato in a microwave-safe dish, add cold water to a depth of about ½ inch (1 cm), cover and microwave on High for 4 minutes. Leave the lid on and let cool for at least 5 minutes before running under cold water and removing the skin.

If you have a food processor with a bowl that inserts for use with the shredding blade, simply lift it out and set aside and fit the large bowl with the metal blade.

- 10-inch (25 cm) flan pan, preferably nonstick

Pastry

1	small potato (3 oz/90 g), boiled in its skin, cooled and peeled (see Tips, left)	1
1 cup	all-purpose flour (approx.)	250 mL
1 tbsp	fresh thyme leaves or 1 tsp (5 mL) dried	15 mL
½ tsp	salt	2 mL
3 tbsp	cold butter, diced	45 mL
1	egg yolk, beaten	1
1 tsp	ice water (approx.)	5 mL

Filling

4	large onions, peeled and quartered	4
2 tbsp	butter	30 mL
1 tsp	sweet paprika	5 mL
1 tsp	salt	5 mL
	Freshly ground black pepper	
1 tbsp	granulated sugar	15 mL
1 tbsp	all-purpose flour	15 mL
¾ cup	half-and-half (10%) cream or whole milk	175 mL
3	eggs	3
8 oz	quark cheese (about 1 cup/250 mL) (see Tip, right)	250 g
¼ cup	finely chopped fresh dill fronds	60 mL

1. **Pastry:** In work bowl fitted with shredding blade, shred potato. Transfer to a bowl and set aside (see Tips, left). Replace shredding blade with metal blade. Add flour, thyme and salt and pulse to blend. Add butter and pulse until mixture resembles large flake oatmeal, about 8 times. Add shredded potato and egg yolk and pulse to blend about 10 times. Sprinkle ice water over top and pulse just to blend, 2 to 3 times. Dough should look like it will come together with a light kneading. If not, add a bit more ice water and pulse to blend.

2. Transfer dough to a clean surface and knead until it holds together. Shape into a disk, place on a lightly floured surface and roll into a circle large enough to line the flan pan. Transfer to pan. Press dough into the pan and trim around the edges. Refrigerate for 1 hour.

3. **Filling:** In clean work bowl fitted with slicing blade, slice onions. In a large skillet, melt butter over medium heat. Add onions and cook, stirring often, until they begin to brown, about 10 minutes. Add paprika, salt, and pepper to taste, and stir well. Cook, stirring often, for 10 minutes. Sprinkle with sugar, stir well, reduce heat to low and cook until onions begin to caramelize, about 15 minutes. Add flour and cook, stirring, for 1 minute. Add cream and cook, stirring, until mixture becomes very creamy, about 2 minutes. Remove from heat.

4. Meanwhile, preheat oven to 375°F (190°C). In a large bowl, beat eggs. Add cheese and dill and mix well. Add onion mixture and mix well. Transfer to prepared crust. Bake in preheated oven until top is puffed and browned and filling is set, about 40 minutes. Let cool for 10 minutes before serving.

Tomato and Roasted Red Pepper Flan in Potato Pastry Crust

Vegetarian Friendly

Here's a "pie" you can easily make from scratch. The crust is very forgiving and the filling is made from pantry ingredients. It's perfect served at lunch, accompanied by a salad, but it also makes a great light dinner.

Tip

If you have a food processor with a bowl that inserts for use with the shredding blade, simply lift it out and set aside and fit the large bowl with the metal blade.

- 10-inch (25 cm) flan pan, preferably nonstick

Potato Pastry Crust

1	small potato (3 oz/90 g), boiled in its skin, cooled, and peeled (see Tips, page 322)	1
1 cup	all-purpose flour (approx.)	250 mL
1 tbsp	fresh thyme leaves or 1 tsp (5 mL) dried	15 mL
1/2 tsp	salt	2 mL
3 tbsp	cold butter, diced	45 mL
1	egg yolk, beaten	1
1 tsp	ice water (approx.)	5 mL

Filling

3	eggs	3
3/4 cup	heavy or whipping (35%) cream	175 mL
1/2 cup	freshly grated Parmesan cheese	125 mL
1 tsp	salt	5 mL
	Freshly ground black pepper	
1/2 tsp	granulated sugar	2 mL
1	can (14 oz/398 mL) crushed tomatoes	1
2	roasted red peppers (see Tip, right)	2
1/4 cup	fresh Italian flat-leaf parsley leaves	60 mL
2	cloves garlic	2

1. **Potato Pastry Crust:** In work bowl fitted with shredding blade, shred potato. Transfer to a bowl and set aside (see Tips, left). Replace shredding blade with metal blade. Add flour, thyme and salt and pulse to blend. Add butter and pulse until mixture resembles large flake oatmeal, about 8 times. Add shredded potato and egg yolk and pulse to blend about 10 times. Sprinkle ice water over top and pulse just to blend 2 to 3 times. Dough should look like it will come together with a light kneading. If not, add a bit more ice water and pulse to blend.

For convenience, we like to use bottled roasted red peppers, but if you prefer, you can roast your own. *To roast peppers:* Preheat oven to 400°F (200°C). Place peppers on a baking sheet and roast, turning two or three times, until skin on all sides is blackened, about 25 minutes. Transfer peppers to a heatproof bowl. Cover with a plate and let stand until cool. Remove and, using a sharp knife, lift skins off. Discard skins and seeds and cut into strips.

2. Transfer dough to a clean surface and knead until it holds together. Shape into a disk, place on a lightly floured surface and roll into a circle large enough to line the flan pan. Transfer to pan. Press dough into the pan and trim around the edges. Refrigerate for 1 hour. Meanwhile, preheat oven to 375°F (190°C).

3. **Filling:** In clean work bowl fitted with metal blade, pulse eggs, cream, Parmesan, salt, pepper to taste, and sugar to blend, about 3 times. Add tomatoes, roasted peppers, parsley and garlic and process until smoothly blended, about 10 seconds. Pour over crust. Bake in preheated oven until puffed and set, about 40 minutes. Let cool for 10 minutes before serving.

Potato Cheese Soufflé

Serves 8

Vegetarian Friendly

Vegetable soufflés are simple to master. If the soufflé falls before you can serve it, call it a baked vegetable dish instead!

Tips

You can use ½ cup (125 mL) prepared instant potatoes in a pinch. Prepare according to package directions.

If your food processor has a whip attachment, you can use it to whip the egg whites. Make sure the work bowl is clean, free of any grease and dry for the best volume.

- Preheat oven to 375°F (190°C)
- 6-cup (1.5 L) soufflé dish, sprayed with nonstick spray

1	small russet (Idaho) potato, peeled and cut into quarters (see Tips, left)	1
4 oz	Romano cheese, cut into chunks	125 g
2	cloves garlic	2
2½ tbsp	butter	37 mL
¼ cup	all-purpose flour	60 mL
1 cup	milk	250 mL
Pinch	salt	Pinch
Pinch	ground white pepper	Pinch
4	egg yolks	4
5	egg whites	5

1. In a saucepan, cover potato with cold water. Bring to a boil over high heat. Reduce heat and boil gently until tender, about 15 minutes. Drain and set aside to cool.

2. In work bowl fitted with metal blade, with the motor running, add Romano cheese through the feed tube and process until grated. Transfer to a bowl.

3. In same work bowl, add potato and garlic. Process until smooth, about 45 seconds. Set aside.

4. In a clean saucepan over low heat, melt butter. Add flour and cook, stirring, for 1 minute to make a roux. In a steady stream, whisk in milk. Mix in reserved cheese, potato mixture, salt and white pepper. Add egg yolks, one at a time, whisking well between each addition. Transfer to a large bowl.

5. In a large bowl, using an electric mixer, whip egg whites until soft but firm peaks form. Carefully fold egg whites into cheese mixture, trying not to deflate mixture, just until no whites are visible. Do not overmix. Transfer mixture to prepared soufflé dish, smoothing top. Bake in preheated oven until soufflé has risen and browned slightly on top, about 30 minutes. Do not be tempted to open the oven while soufflé is baking or it will fall.

Variation

Try a blue cheese in place of the Romano to add some bite to your soufflé.

Baked Falafel with Tahini Sauce

Serves 4

Makes 8 falafels

Vegan Friendly

These falafels are delicious plated and topped with tahini sauce, but it's more traditional to serve them in pita pockets, spread with tahini sauce and garnished with sliced tomatoes, shredded lettuce and/or sliced cucumber. If you prefer, serve these with Tzatziki (page 63) rather than Tahini Sauce.

Tips

It is important that the fresh herbs be very dry. Otherwise your batter will be too wet. We recommend drying them in a salad spinner.

For this quantity of chickpeas, use 1 can (14 to 19 oz/398 to 540 mL) drained and rinsed, or cook 1 cup (250 mL) dried chickpeas.

If you don't have tahini, substitute an equal quantity of olive oil in the falafel.

- Preheat oven to 375°F (190°C)
- Rimmed baking sheet, lightly greased

Falafel

½	small red onion, halved	½
½ cup	fresh cilantro leaves (see Tips, left)	125 mL
½ cup	fresh Italian flat-leaf parsley leaves	125 mL
2 cups	cooked drained chickpeas (see Tips, left)	500 mL
1	egg	1
2 tbsp	tahini paste (see Tips, left)	30 mL
2 tbsp	all-purpose flour	30 mL
1 tsp	ground cumin (see Tips, page 333)	5 mL
1 tsp	ground coriander	5 mL
	Salt and freshly ground black pepper	
¼ cup	sesame seeds	60 mL

Tahini Sauce

¼ cup	tahini paste	60 mL
2	cloves garlic, minced	2
2 tbsp	freshly squeezed lemon juice	30 mL
4 tbsp	water (approx.)	60 mL

1. **Falafel:** In work bowl fitted with metal blade, pulse red onion, cilantro and parsley until finely chopped, about 5 times, stopping and scraping down sides of the bowl once or twice. Add chickpeas, egg, tahini, flour, cumin, coriander, and salt and pepper to taste. Process until smooth, about 30 seconds, scraping down sides of the bowl once or twice.

2. Wet your hands, divide mixture into 8 equal portions and shape into balls, then flatten into patties. Spread sesame seeds on a large plate and dredge falafels in them. Place on prepared baking sheet and bake in preheated oven for 15 minutes. Turn. Continue baking until both sides are golden, about 15 minutes more.

3. **Tahini Sauce:** In a bowl, combine tahini, garlic and lemon juice. Whisk in 2 tbsp (30 mL) water, gradually adding more until mixture is the consistency of thick cream. Serve over falafel.

Falafel in Pita

Vegan Friendly

These tasty treats are a gift from the Middle East, where they are eaten the way hamburgers are in North America. Liberally garnished, they make a great lunch or light dinner.

Tip

For this quantity of chickpeas, use 1 can (14 to 19 oz/398 to 540 mL) drained and rinsed, or cook 1 cup (250 mL) dried chickpeas.

2 cups	drained cooked chickpeas (see Tip, left)	500 mL
1/2 cup	sliced green onions	125 mL
2 tbsp	freshly squeezed lemon juice	30 mL
1 tbsp	minced garlic	15 mL
1 to 2 tsp	curry powder	5 to 10 mL
1	egg	1
2 tbsp	oil	30 mL
1/2 cup	all-purpose flour	125 mL
4	pita breads	4
	Chopped peeled cucumber	
	Chopped tomato	
	Shredded lettuce	
	Plain yogurt or soy yogurt	

1. In work bowl fitted with metal blade, process chickpeas, green onions, lemon juice, garlic, and curry powder to taste, until blended but chickpeas retain their texture, about 30 seconds. Using your hands, shape into 4 large patties.

2. In a shallow bowl, lightly beat egg. In a skillet, heat oil over medium heat. Dip each patty into the egg, then into the flour, coating both sides well. Fry until golden and heated through, about 2 minutes per side.

3. Fill each pita bread with a falafel and garnish with cucumber, tomato, lettuce and yogurt, as desired.

Variation

Pepper-Spiked Falafel in Pita: Add 1 or 2 roasted red peppers to the chickpeas before processing.

Lentil Shepherd's Pie

Vegetarian Friendly

Here's a flavorful rendition of an old favorite, in which lentils are substituted for the traditional meat.

Tips

Be careful not to overprocess the potato mixture or the topping will be mushy.

An easy way to cook potatoes in their skins is to microwave them. For this quantity, place the scrubbed potatoes in a microwave-safe dish in one layer, add cold water to a depth of about ½ inch (1 cm), cover and microwave on High for 6 minutes. Leave the lid on and let cool for at least 5 minutes before running under cold water and removing the skins.

Your potatoes will shred more easily if you cook them ahead of time and refrigerate overnight.

For this quantity of lentils cook 1 cup (250 mL) dried lentils or use 1 can (14 to 19 oz/ 398 to 540 mL), drained and rinsed.

- Preheat oven to 350°F (180°C)
- 8-cup (2 L) baking dish, lightly greased

Topping

4 oz	Cheddar cheese	125 g
2	potatoes, boiled in their skins and peeled (see Tips, left)	2
½ cup	milk	125 mL
½ cup	dry bread crumbs, such as panko	125 mL
4	green onions (white part only), coarsely chopped	4
1 tbsp	butter, softened	15 mL
½ tsp	salt	2 mL
	Freshly ground black pepper	

Filling

2	onions, quartered	2
2	stalks celery, cut into 3-inch (7.5 cm) lengths	2
1 tbsp	oil	15 mL
1	can (28 oz/796 mL) tomatoes, drained and coarsely chopped	1
2 cups	drained cooked lentils	500 mL
2 tbsp	prepared basil pesto	30 mL
2 tbsp	freshly grated Parmesan cheese	30 mL

1. **Topping:** In work bowl fitted with shredding blade, shred cheese and potatoes. Transfer to a bowl. Replace shredding blade with metal blade. Add milk, bread crumbs, green onions, butter, salt, and pepper to taste, and pulse to blend, about 5 times. Add reserved potatoes and cheese and pulse to blend, about 5 times. Transfer to a bowl and set aside. Rinse out work bowl and blade.

2. **Filling:** In work bowl fitted with metal blade, pulse onions and celery until finely chopped, about 15 times, stopping and scraping down the sides of the bowl once or twice. In a skillet, heat oil over medium heat. Add onions and celery and cook, stirring, until celery is softened, about 5 minutes. Add tomatoes and lentils. Bring to a boil. Stir in pesto and pour into prepared baking dish.

3. Spread reserved potato mixture evenly over lentil mixture. Sprinkle with Parmesan. Bake in preheated oven until top is browned and mixture is bubbling, about 25 minutes.

Sweet Potatoes and Carrots with Chickpea Topping

Serves 4

Vegan Friendly

This tasty and nutritious combination of sweet potatoes, carrots and pineapple, finished with a chickpea topping makes a delightfully different main course. Refrigerate any leftovers and transform them into an interesting side dish. Simply purée in a food processor fitted with metal blade, then reheat in the microwave or over low heat on the stovetop.

Tip

For this quantity of chickpeas, use 1 can (14 to 19 oz/398 to 540 mL) drained and rinsed, or cook 1 cup (250 mL) dried chickpeas.

- Preheat oven to 400°F (200°C)
- 8-cup (2 L) shallow baking dish, greased

2	sweet potatoes (each about 8 oz/250 g), peeled	2
6	carrots, peeled and cut into 3-inch (7.5 cm) lengths	6
1	can (14 oz/398 mL) crushed pineapple with juice	1
2 tbsp	packed brown sugar	30 mL
1/2 tsp	salt	2 mL
	Freshly ground black pepper	

Topping

2 cups	drained cooked chickpeas (see Tips, left)	500 mL
2	cloves garlic, coarsely chopped	2
3/4 cup	vegetable broth or water	175 mL
	Salt and freshly ground pepper	

1. In work bowl fitted with slicing blade, slice sweet potatoes and carrots. Transfer to prepared baking dish. Add pineapple with juice, brown sugar, salt, and pepper to taste, and stir well.

2. **Topping:** In work bowl fitted with metal blade, process chickpeas, garlic and vegetable broth until mixture is well combined but chickpeas are still a little chunky, about 30 seconds, stopping and scraping down sides of bowl once or twice. Season with salt and pepper to taste. Spread mixture evenly over sweet potato mixture. Cover dish with foil and bake in preheated oven for 15 minutes. Remove foil and continue to bake until sweet potatoes are tender and sauce is bubbling, about 25 minutes.

Easy Vegetable Chili

Vegan Friendly

Not only is this chili easy to make, it is also delicious. The mild dried chiles add interesting flavor, along with a nice bit of heat. Only add the jalapeño if you're a heat seeker.

Tips

For this quantity of beans, use 1 can (14 to 19 oz/ 398 to 540 mL) drained and rinsed, or cook 1 cup (250 mL) dried beans.

To save washing the work bowl and blade, complete Step 2 immediately after you have set the chiles aside to soak and transfer the onion mixture to a bowl. Then once the chiles are reconstituted, you can add them to the same work bowl along with the cilantro, broth and jalapeño, if using.

2	dried mild New Mexico, ancho or guajillo chile peppers	2
2 cups	boiling water	500 mL
1 cup	coarsely chopped cilantro (stems and leaves)	250 mL
1 cup	vegetable broth, tomato juice or water	250 mL
1	jalapeño pepper, coarsely chopped, optional	1
2	onions, quartered	2
4	stalks celery, cut into 3-inch (7.5 cm) lengths	4
1	green bell pepper, seeded and quartered	1
4	cloves garlic, chopped	4
1 tbsp	oil	15 mL
2 tsp	ground cumin (see Tips, page 333)	10 mL
2 tsp	dried oregano, crumbled	10 mL
1 tsp	salt	5 mL
1	can (14 oz/398 mL) diced tomatoes with juice	1
2 cups	drained cooked red kidney beans (see Tip, left)	500 mL
2 cups	corn kernels	500 mL

1. In a heatproof bowl, soak dried chile peppers in boiling water for 30 minutes, weighing down with a cup to ensure they remain submerged. Drain, discarding soaking liquid and stems and chop coarsely. Transfer to work bowl fitted with metal blade. Add cilantro, broth, and jalapeño, if using. Purée.

2. In clean work bowl fitted with clean metal blade, pulse onions, celery, bell pepper and garlic until finely chopped, about 20 times, stopping and scraping down sides of the bowl once or twice.

3. In a large saucepan or Dutch oven, heat oil over medium heat. Add onion mixture and cook, stirring, until softened, about 6 minutes. Add cumin, oregano and salt and cook, stirring, for 1 minute. Add tomatoes with juice and bring to a boil. Add beans, corn and reserved chile mixture and stir well. Bring to boil. Cover, reduce heat and simmer until flavors meld, about 30 minutes.

Brown Rice Chili

Serves 6

Vegan Friendly

The reconstituted dried chiles give this chili outstanding flavor. Just be aware that chiles described as New Mexico can range widely in heat. If you are using New Mexico chiles in this recipe, check to make certain that they are not described as "hot." The "mild" variety is called for.

Tip

For this quantity of beans, use 1 can (14 to 19 oz/ 398 to 540 mL) drained and rinsed, or cook 1 cup (250 mL) dried beans.

1 cup	brown rice, rinsed	250 mL
2	dried ancho, mild New Mexico or guajillo chile peppers	2
2 cups	boiling water	500 mL
½ cup	chopped cilantro, stems and leaves	125 mL
1	jalapeño pepper, seeded and diced	1
2	onions, quartered	2
4	stalks celery, cut into 3-inch (7.5 cm) lengths	4
1	green bell pepper, seeded and halved	1
4	cloves garlic, chopped	4
1 tbsp	oil	15 mL
1 tbsp	dried oregano	15 mL
1 tsp	ground cumin (see Tips, page 333)	5 mL
½ tsp	salt	2 mL
½ tsp	cracked black peppercorns	2 mL
1	can (28 oz/796 mL) tomatoes with juice, coarsely chopped	1
2 cups	drained cooked red kidney beans (see Tip, left)	500 mL
2 cups	corn kernels, thawed if frozen	500 mL

1. In a saucepan over medium heat, bring rice and 2 cups (500 mL) water to a boil. Cover, reduce heat and simmer until rice is almost tender, about 35 minutes. Set aside.

2. Meanwhile, in a heatproof bowl, soak dried chile peppers in boiling water for 30 minutes, weighing down with a cup to ensure they remain submerged. Drain, discarding soaking water and stems and chop coarsely. Transfer to work bowl fitted with metal blade. Add 1 cup (250 mL) water, cilantro and jalapeño. Purée and set aside.

3. In work bowl fitted with metal blade, pulse onions, celery, bell pepper and garlic until finely chopped, about 15 times, stopping and scraping down sides of the bowl.

4. In a large saucepan or Dutch oven, heat oil over medium heat. Add onion mixture and cook, stirring, until softened, about 6 minutes. Add oregano, cumin, salt and peppercorns and cook, stirring, for 1 minute. Add tomatoes with juice and bring to a boil. Add beans, corn, rice, including any excess liquid, and chile mixture. Stir well and bring to a boil. Cover, reduce heat and simmer until flavors meld, about 30 minutes.

Savory Chickpea Stew with Coulis

Serves 6 to 8

Vegan Friendly

This mixture of Mediterranean and Indian flavors is delicious. The coulis adds contemporary flair.

Tips

For the best flavor, toast and grind cumin yourself. *To toast cumin:* Place seeds in a dry skillet over medium heat and cook, stirring, until fragrant, about 3 minutes. Immediately transfer to a mortar or a spice grinder and grind.

For this quantity of chickpeas, use 1 can (14 to 19 oz/398 to 540 mL) drained and rinsed, or cook 1 cup (250 mL) dried chickpeas.

Stew

1	large eggplant, peeled, cut into 2-inch (5 cm) cubes and sweated (see Tip, page 300)	1
1	large onion, cut into quarters	1
4	cloves garlic	4
3 tbsp	oil (approx.)	45 mL
2 tsp	ground cumin (see Tips, left)	10 mL
1 tsp	dried oregano	5 mL
1/2 tsp	ground turmeric	2 mL
1 cup	vegetable and chicken broth	250 mL
1	can (28 oz/796 mL) tomatoes with juice, coarsely chopped	1
2	large potatoes, cut into 1/2-inch (1 cm) cubes	2
2 cups	drained cooked chickpeas	500 mL

Onion-Spiked Roasted Red Pepper Coulis

2	roasted red peppers	2
3	oil-packed sun-dried tomatoes, drained	3
1/2	small red onion, quartered	1/2
2 tbsp	extra virgin olive oil	30 mL
1 tbsp	red wine vinegar	15 mL

1. **Stew:** In work bowl fitted with metal blade, pulse onion and garlic until finely chopped, about 6 times. Set aside.

2. In a large saucepan or Dutch oven, heat oil over medium heat. Add sweated eggplant, in batches, and cook, stirring, until lightly browned, about 4 minutes per batch. Transfer to a plate as completed. Add onion mixture and cook, stirring, until softened, about 3 minutes. Add cumin, oregano and turmeric and cook, stirring, for 1 minute. Add broth and tomatoes, stirring and breaking up with a spoon. Bring mixture to a boil and cook, stirring, for 1 minute. Add potatoes, chickpeas and reserved eggplant. Stir well and return to a boil. Cover, reduce heat to low and simmer until eggplant is tender and flavors meld, about 40 minutes.

3. **Coulis:** Meanwhile, rinse out work bowl and metal blade and refit. Add roasted peppers, sun-dried tomatoes, red onion, oil and vinegar and process until smooth. To serve, ladle stew into bowls and top with coulis.

Southwestern Bean and Barley Salad with Roasted Peppers

Vegan Friendly

Ingredients traditionally associated with the American Southwest, such as beans, corn and peppers, combine with hearty barley to produce this deliciously robust salad.

Tips

To cook whole barley (the most nutritious form of the grain), bring 2½ cups (625 mL) water or broth to a boil. Add 1 cup (250 mL) rinsed and drained barley. Return to a rapid boil. Reduce heat to low. Cover and cook until barley is tender, about 1 hour.

For this quantity of beans, soak and cook 1 cup (250 mL) dried beans or use 1 can (14 to 19 oz/ 398 to 540 mL) canned beans, drained and rinsed.

Poblano peppers are a mild chile pepper. If you are a heat seeker, you might want to add an extra one, or even a minced seeded jalapeño pepper for some real punch. The suggested quantity produces a mild result, which most people will enjoy. If you're heat averse, use bell peppers, instead.

3 cups	cooked whole (hulled) barley, cooled (see Tips, left)	750 mL
Dressing		
½ cup	Italian flat-leaf parsley leaves	125 mL
¼ cup	red wine vinegar	60 mL
1	clove garlic, coarsely chopped	1
1 tsp	salt	5 mL
	Freshly ground black pepper	
¾ cup	extra virgin olive oil	175 mL
1	small red onion, cut to fit feed tube, if necessary	1
2 cups	drained cooked red kidney beans (see Tip, left)	500 mL
2 cups	cooked corn kernels	500 mL
2	roasted poblano or roasted red peppers, peeled, seeded and diced (see Tips, left)	2
2	whole sun-dried tomatoes, packed in olive oil, finely chopped	2

1. **Dressing:** In work bowl fitted with metal blade, pulse parsley, vinegar, garlic, salt, and pepper to taste, to chop and blend, about 5 times, stopping and scraping down sides of the bowl once or twice. With motor running, add olive oil through the feed tube, stopping and scraping down sides of the bowl as necessary. Set aside.

2. Replace metal blade with slicing blade and slice red onion. Transfer to serving bowl. Add barley, kidney beans, corn, roasted peppers, sun-dried tomatoes and dressing and toss well. Chill until ready to serve.

Variations

Substitute an equal quantity of cooked wheat, spelt or Kamut berries or farro for the barley.

Puréed Squash–Stuffed Wontons

Makes 36 wontons

Vegetarian Friendly

These crunchy fried wontons are filled with a sweet yet spicy creamy filling.

Tip

To cook squash: Cut the squash into a few small pieces. Remove all the seeds. Brush with melted butter and wrap tightly with foil. Cook in a preheated 400°F (200°C) oven until fork tender, about 1 hour, depending on the thickness of the walls of the squash. Let cool completely before removing skin. In work bowl fitted with metal blade, process cooked squash until smooth, about 10 seconds. Store in containers in freezer for up to 5 months.

- 16-cup (4 L) saucepan or deep-fryer
- Candy/deep-fry thermometer

	Vegetable oil for frying	
2½ cups	squash purée (see Tip, left)	625 mL
4 oz	cream cheese, cubed and softened	125 g
2 tbsp	pure maple syrup	30 mL
1 tbsp	freshly grated gingerroot	15 mL
½ tsp	ground cinnamon	2 mL
¼ tsp	ground nutmeg	1 mL
36	wonton skins	36
1	egg yolk, beaten	1

1. In a large saucepan over medium heat, heat about 4 inches (10 cm) of oil until thermometer registers 360°F (182°C).

2. In work bowl fitted with metal blade, process squash, cream cheese, maple syrup, ginger, cinnamon and nutmeg until smooth, about 10 seconds, stopping and scraping down the sides of the bowl as necessary. Set aside.

3. Working with one wonton skin at a time, place on work surface and spoon 1 tbsp (15 mL) of the squash filling in the center. Brush two adjoining edges with beaten egg yolk. Fold opposite edges over filling to form a triangle, squeezing out air. Prepare all the wontons and then begin to fry.

4. Fry wontons, a few at a time, until golden brown and crispy, 2 to 3 minutes. Adjust heat as necessary between batches to keep the oil at the proper temperature. Drain on paper towels.

California Vegetable Wontons

Makes 36 wontons

Vegetarian Friendly

Try these vegetarian wontons at your next cocktail party.

- 16-cup (4 L) saucepan of deep-fryer
- Candy/deep-fry thermometer

	Vegetable oil for frying	
3	carrots, cut into 3-inch (7.5 cm) lengths	3
1	turnip, quartered	1
¼	head of napa cabbage, cut into smaller pieces	¼
½ cup	drained canned sliced bamboo shoots	125 mL
3 tbsp	reduced-sodium soy sauce	45 mL
8 oz	tofu, cut into small cubes	250 g
36	wonton skins	36
1	egg yolk, beaten	1

1. In work bowl fitted with shredding blade, shred carrots, turnip and cabbage. Place in a bowl and toss with bamboo shoots, soy sauce and tofu.

2. In a large saucepan over medium heat, heat about 4 inches (10 cm) of oil until thermometer registers 360°F (182°C).

3. Working with one wonton skin at a time, place on work surface and spoon 1 tbsp (15 mL) of the filling in the center. Brush two adjoining edges with beaten egg yolk. Fold opposite edges over filling to form a triangle, squeezing out air. Prepare all the wontons and then begin to fry.

4. Fry wontons, a few at a time, until golden brown and crispy, 2 to 3 minutes. Adjust heat as necessary between batches to keep the oil at the proper temperature. Drain on paper towels.

Vegetarian Puffs

Vegetarian Friendly

You can create your own puffs with whatever seasonal vegetables are available at your local farmers' market.

- Baking sheet, lined with parchment paper

1	package (18 oz/540 g) puff pastry, thawed, divided	1
1½ lbs	mixed vegetables, such as carrots, radishes, broccoli and cauliflower	750 g
½	onion, quartered	½
2	cloves garlic	2
4 oz	Parmesan cheese, cut into chunks	125 g
3 tbsp	oil	45 mL
1 tbsp	reduced-sodium soy sauce	15 mL
½ tsp	ground ginger	2 mL
¼ tsp	dry mustard	1 mL
¼ tsp	white pepper	1 mL
	Coarse salt	

1. Working with one half of pastry, on a lightly floured board, roll pastry into a 12-inch (30 cm) square. Using a pizza cutter, cut into 2 equal pieces. Set aside. Repeat with second sheet of pastry.

2. In work bowl fitted with metal blade, pulse mixed vegetables until coarsely chopped, about 10 times, stopping and scraping down the sides of the bowl. Transfer to a bowl and set aside.

3. In same work bowl, pulse onion and garlic until finely chopped, about 10 times. Transfer to a bowl and set aside.

4. In same work bowl, with motor running, drop Parmesan through feed tube and process until grated, about 20 seconds. Transfer to a large bowl and set aside.

5. In a large saucepan, heat oil over medium heat. Add onion and garlic and sauté until onion is translucent, 4 to 6 minutes. Add mixed vegetables and sauté until soft, 8 to 12 minutes. Add to the bowl with Parmesan cheese. Add soy sauce, ginger, mustard and white pepper and toss to combine.

6. Divide mixture between the 4 pieces of pastry. Fold two opposite sides of pastry toward center over filling, then two remaining sides of pastry like an envelope. If pastry seems dry, lightly brush edges with water before folding to ensure a good seal. Place, seal side down, on prepared baking sheet. Bake in preheated oven until light brown and puffed up, 18 to 22 minutes. Sprinkle with a little coarse salt. Serve warm or cold.

Sides and Salads

Sides

Salads

Vegetable Almond Medley

Vegan Friendly

Root vegetables are
perfect for this dish,
which is colorful and
full of flavor.

Tip

Use reduced-sodium soy
sauce because the regular
kind is too salty.

- Preheat oven to 400°F (200°C)
- 8-cup (2 L) baking dish, greased

3 lbs	mixed vegetables, such as carrots, radishes, turnips and broccoli	1.5 kg
1	onion, quartered	1
2	cloves garlic	2
5 tbsp	unsalted butter, divided, or vegan alternative	75 mL
1½ cups	toasted almonds, divided	375 mL
2 cups	vegetable broth, divided	500 mL
3 tbsp	all-purpose flour	45 mL
1 tbsp	reduced-sodium soy sauce (see Tip, left)	15 mL
½ tsp	dry mustard	2 mL
½ cup	Fresh Bread Crumbs (page 468) or store-bought	125 mL

1. In work bowl fitted with slicing blade, slice mixed vegetables in batches. Transfer to a bowl. Set aside.

2. In same work bowl, slice onion. Transfer to another bowl. Set aside.

3. Replace slicing blade with metal blade and pulse garlic until chopped, about 5 times. Transfer to bowl with onion.

4. In a large saucepan, melt 2 tbsp (30 mL) of the butter over medium heat. Add onion and garlic and sauté until onion is translucent, 7 to 12 minutes. Add mixed vegetables and sauté until soft, 8 to 12 minutes. Place in prepared baking dish.

5. In same work bowl fitted with metal blade, process 1 cup (250 mL) of the almonds and ½ cup (125 mL) of the vegetable broth until smooth. Set aside.

6. In same saucepan over medium heat, melt remaining butter. Add flour and cook, whisking until thick, about 1 minute. Gradually whisk in remaining vegetable broth and almond mixture. Add soy sauce and dry mustard and cook, stirring, until thickened, about 10 minutes. Pour over vegetables in baking dish. Sprinkle remaining ½ cup (125 mL) of almonds and bread crumbs over top. Bake in preheated oven until heated through and top is light brown, 15 to 20 minutes.

Roasted Vegetables

Serves 4

Vegan Friendly

This is one of the most flavorful dishes you'll ever serve, and it takes no time to make.

Tips

If any of the vegetables are out of season substitute whatever is in season such as zucchini, yellowneck squash or turnip. Use this recipe as a guide.

This recipe was created for the reddish-orange-skinned, orange-fleshed, long potatoes that are often labeled "yams" but are, in fact, sweet potatoes. True yams are starchy, brown-skinned, white-fleshed subtropical tubers that have a very different flavor and texture and are not interchangeable in recipes designed for sweet potatoes.

- Preheat oven to 400°F (200°C)
- Roasting pan, lined with parchment paper

1	onion, quartered	1
8 oz	new potatoes, quartered, if large (about 3)	250 g
8 oz	sweet potatoes, peeled and quartered, if large (about 2) (see Tips, left)	250 g
2	large carrots, cut into 3-inch (7.5 cm) lengths	2
1 cup	radishes, stems removed (about 8 oz/250 g)	250 mL
1	red bell pepper, seeded and halved	1
2 tbsp	olive oil	30 mL
1 tsp	fresh thyme leaves	5 mL
1 tsp	fresh oregano leaves	5 mL
½ tsp	salt	2 mL
½ tsp	ground white pepper	2 mL

1. In work bowl fitted with slicing blade, one vegetable at a time, slice onion, potatoes, sweet potatoes, carrots, radishes and bell pepper. Transfer to a large bowl and toss with olive oil, thyme, oregano, salt and white pepper.

2. Transfer to prepared roasting pan in a single layer. Roast in preheated oven, stirring every 10 to 15 minutes, until light brown and tender, 45 to 60 minutes. Serve hot.

Pecan Sweet Potatoes

Serves 8

Vegan Friendly

These sweet potatoes will become a staple on your holiday table. To get the kids interested, you could toast a few marshmallows.

- Preheat oven to 350°F (180°C)
- 13- by 9-inch (33 by 23 cm) baking dish, greased

2 lbs	sweet potatoes, peeled and cut to fit feed tube (see Tips, page 341)	1 kg
½ cup	drained crushed pineapple, optional	125 mL
½ cup	unsalted butter or vegan alternative	125 mL
1 cup	lightly packed brown sugar	250 mL
1 tsp	ground cinnamon	5 mL
¼ tsp	freshly grated nutmeg	1 mL
1 cup	pecan halves	250 mL

1. In work bowl fitted with slicing blade, slice sweet potatoes. Transfer to a saucepan over medium heat and fill with cold water to cover. Bring to a boil. Reduce heat and simmer until fork tender, 20 to 25 minutes. Do not let the water boil. Drain well and transfer to prepared baking dish. Stir in pineapple, if using.

2. In same saucepan, melt butter over medium heat. Add brown sugar, cinnamon and nutmeg and heat until melted. Set aside.

3. Replace slicing blade with metal blade and pulse pecans until coarsely chopped. Add to sugar mixture and combine. Pour over sweet potatoes and bake in preheated oven until bubbling, 20 to 25 minutes. Serve hot.

Mustard-Spiked Swiss Chard

Serves 4

Vegan Friendly

This is a great way to serve Swiss chard, which is so loaded with nutrients it is often called a superfood. This purée makes a great accompaniment to just about anything.

1	bunch Swiss chard, deveined and coarsely chopped	1
2	green onions, white part only	2
1 tbsp	butter or olive oil	15 mL
1	clove garlic	1
2 tsp	Dijon mustard	10 mL
½ tsp	salt, or to taste	2 mL
	Freshly ground black pepper	

1. In a saucepan, combine chard and water to cover. Bring to a boil, cover, reduce heat and simmer until tender, about 4 minutes. Drain and transfer to work bowl fitted with metal blade. Add green onions, butter, garlic, mustard, salt, and pepper to taste, and process until smooth.

Eggplant Parmesan

Vegetarian Friendly

Eggplant technically is a fruit like a tomato, but most of us think of it as a vegetable. This dish will be the vegetarian's favorite at a potluck.

- Preheat oven to 400°F (200°C)
- 13- by 9-inch (33 by 23 cm) baking dish, greased

2 oz	Parmesan cheese, cut into chunks	60 g
8 oz	mozzarella cheese, cut into chunks	250 g
1	large eggplant, peeled and cut into ¼-inch (0.5 cm) slices (about 2 lbs/1 kg)	1
¾ cup	vegetable oil	175 mL
2 cups	Basic Garlic Tomato Sauce (page 402) or store-bought	500 mL
½ tsp	dried basil	2 mL
½ tsp	garlic powder	2 mL

1. In work bowl fitted with metal blade, with motor running, add Parmesan cheese through feed tube and process until finely grated. Transfer to a bowl. Set aside.

2. Replace metal blade with shredding blade and shred mozzarella cheese. Transfer to another bowl. Set aside.

3. Replace shredding blade with slicing blade and slice eggplant.

4. In a large skillet, heat oil over medium heat. Add eggplant, in batches, as necessary, and sauté until lightly cooked on both sides, 3 to 4 minutes. Place in a single layer on paper towels and drain.

5. Place one-third of the eggplant in a layer over bottom of prepared baking dish. Spread with one-third each of the tomato sauce, basil, garlic powder, Parmesan cheese and mozzarella. Repeat layering two more times with remaining ingredients, finishing with cheeses on top. Bake in preheated oven, uncovered, until heated through and cheese is melted, 15 to 20 minutes. Serve hot.

Variation

You can also add a layer of 3 sliced Roma (plum) tomatoes on top of the final layer of eggplant.

Saffron-Scented Fennel Gratin

Vegan Friendly

Serve this flavorful gratin as a vegetable side or as a main course sauce over mashed potatoes or polenta or even Easy White Bean Purée (page 367).

Tip

To prepare fennel: Chop off celery-like stems and save for making stock. If you are lucky enough to have some fronds, wash and set aside to use as a garnish on your gratin. Cut bulb in half on the vertical and remove the knobby core. Cut pieces to fit your feed tube and slice.

- Preheat oven to 400°F (200°C)
- 6-cup (1.5 L) shallow baking or gratin dish, lightly greased

3	bulbs fennel, cut to fit feed tube (see Tip, left)	3
1 tbsp	olive oil	15 mL
2 cups	vegetable broth	500 mL
	Salt and freshly ground black pepper, optional	
½ tsp	saffron threads	2 mL
½ cup	coarsely grated Parmesan cheese or vegan alternative	125 mL

1. Bring a large pot of salted water to a rapid boil. Meanwhile, in work bowl fitted with slicing blade, slice fennel. Add to boiling water, return to a boil and blanch until tender-crisp, about 3 minutes. Using a slotted spoon, transfer to prepared dish. Add olive oil and toss well. Add broth. Season with salt and pepper to taste, if using. Bake in preheated oven until fennel is tender, about 20 minutes.

2. Preheat broiler. Pour liquid from baking dish into a saucepan and add saffron. Set dish aside. Bring to a boil over medium heat and cook until reduced by half, about 6 minutes. Pour over fennel. Sprinkle with Parmesan and place under broiler until cheese is melted and brown.

Fennel and Leek Gratin

Serves 6

Vegetarian Friendly

This Mediterranean-inspired dish is like a ray of summer sunshine on a cold winter's day. Serve it with grilled or roasted meat or vegetables. It will complete the meal.

Tips

Leeks can be gritty and it is customary to slice them and rinse them in a basin of water before using. To benefit from the convenience of your food processor for this recipe, slice them first, then transfer to a basin of lukewarm water only if you notice grit that needs to be rinsed off. If your work bowl has acquired some grit, rinse it before slicing the fennel.

To prepare fennel: Chop off celery-like stems and save for making stock. If you are lucky enough to have some fronds, wash and set aside to use as a garnish on your gratin. Cut bulb in half on the vertical and remove the knobby core. Cut pieces to fit your feed tube.

- Preheat oven to 400°F (200°C)
- 6-cup (1.5 L) shallow baking or gratin dish, lightly greased

2	large leeks, white part with just a bit of green (see Tips, left)	2
2	bulbs fennel, cut to fit feed tube (see Tips, left)	2
2 oz	Gruyère cheese	60 g
1	can (14 oz/398 mL) diced tomatoes with juice	1
¼ cup	heavy or whipping (35%) cream	60 mL
½ tsp	salt	2 mL
	Freshly ground black pepper	

1. Bring a large pot of salted water to a rapid boil. Meanwhile, in work bowl fitted with slicing blade, slice leeks and fennel. Add leeks and fennel to boiling water, return to a boil and blanch until tender-crisp, about 3 minutes. Using a slotted spoon, transfer to prepared dish.

2. Meanwhile, replace slicing blade with shredding blade and shred cheese. Set aside.

3. Add tomatoes with juice, cream, salt, and pepper to taste, to leek mixture. Stir to combine. Sprinkle cheese evenly over top and bake in preheated oven until cheese is nicely browned and vegetables are tender, about 20 minutes.

Broccoli and Fennel Purée

Serves 4 to 6

Vegan Friendly

This intriguing combination makes a wonderful accompaniment to roast meats and fish and a great vegetable course all on its own. If you're serving it to guests, have them guess what vegetables it contains.

1	bulb fennel (see Tips, page 345)	1
1	bunch broccoli, florets with a bit of stem, (about 6 cups/1.5 L)	1
2 tbsp	heavy or whipping (35%) cream or soy creamer	30 mL
1 tbsp	butter or olive oil	15 mL
1/4 tsp	ground allspice	1 mL
	Salt and freshly ground black pepper	
	Fennel fronds, optional	

1. Bring a large pot of salted water to a rapid boil. Meanwhile, in work bowl fitted with slicing blade, slice fennel. Add to boiling water. Return to a boil and boil for 1 minute. Add broccoli and cook until vegetables are tender, about 5 minutes. Drain.

2. In work bowl fitted with metal blade, pulse cooked fennel and broccoli until chopped. Add cream, butter, allspice, and salt and pepper to taste. Purée. Transfer to a serving bowl and garnish with fennel fronds, if using. Serve hot.

Fennel Parmigiano

Serves 6

Vegan Friendly

If you're looking for a vegetable dish that is a bit different, try this. Cooking the fennel mellows its licorice flavor and the Parmesan adds pleasant creaminess.

- Preheat broiler
- 6-cup (1.5 L) shallow gratin dish, lightly greased

2	bulbs fennel, cored (see Tips, page 345)	2
2 tbsp	extra virgin olive oil, divided	30 mL
	Salt and freshly ground black pepper	
1/2 cup	freshly grated Parmesan cheese or vegan alternative	125 mL
1/4 cup	dry bread crumbs	50 mL

1. Bring a large pot of salted water to a rapid boil. Meanwhile, in work bowl fitted with slicing blade, slice fennel. Add to boiling water, return to a boil and cook until tender, about 5 minutes. Drain and transfer to prepared dish.

2. Add 1 tbsp (15 mL) of oil and salt and pepper to taste and toss well. Sprinkle Parmesan evenly over top and bread crumbs evenly over Parmesan. Drizzle with remaining tbsp (15 mL) of oil. Place under preheated broiler until cheese is melted and crumbs are nicely browned.

Cheesy Cauliflower Purée

Serves 4

Vegetarian Friendly

This is a quick and easy way of getting all the great flavor of a cauliflower gratin without the work. It makes a great accompaniment to roasted meats or vegetables and can even be the centerpiece of a light meal.

4 oz	Cheddar cheese	125 g
1/3 cup	heavy or whipping (35%) cream	75 mL
1	large head cauliflower (about 2 lbs/1 kg), trimmed and broken into florets	1
1 tbsp	butter	15 mL
1 tsp	salt	5 mL
	Freshly ground black pepper	
Pinch	cayenne pepper, optional	Pinch
	Finely chopped Italian flat-leaf parsley	

1. In work bowl fitted with shredding blade, shred cheese.

2. In a small saucepan, combine cream and cheese. Heat over low heat, stirring occasionally, until cheese is melted, about 2 minutes. Remove from heat.

3. Replace shredding blade with metal blade. In a large pot of boiling salted water, cook cauliflower until tender, about 5 minutes. Drain and transfer to work bowl fitted with metal blade. Add butter and pulse several times to chop cauliflower. Add cheese mixture, salt, pepper to taste, and cayenne, if using. Process until puréed, about 1 minute. Garnish liberally with parsley and serve immediately.

Fresh Vegetable Purée

Vegan Friendly

To gain the optimal flavor you should use only vegetables in season. Check out your local farmers' market.

1	onion, quartered	1
3	carrots, sliced into 3-inch (7.5 cm) lengths	3
1 tbsp	butter or vegan substitute	15 mL
3 lbs	butternut squash, peeled, seeded and cut into ½-inch (1 cm) pieces	1.5 kg
1 cup	unsweetened apple juice	250 mL
2 tbsp	pure maple syrup	30 mL
½ tsp	freshly grated nutmeg	2 mL
¼ tsp	ground coriander	1 mL
	Salt and freshly ground white pepper	

1. In work bowl fitted with metal blade, pulse onion until chopped, about 5 times. Transfer to a bowl. Replace metal blade with slicing blade and slice carrots.

2. In a saucepan, melt butter over medium heat. Add onion and sauté just until tender, about 3 minutes. Add carrots and squash and sauté until softened, 6 to 8 minutes.

3. Pour apple juice over vegetables and cover. Simmer on low until vegetables are softened, about 25 minutes. Stir in maple syrup, nutmeg and coriander.

4. In work bowl fitted with metal blade, working in batches, process mixture until smooth. Season with salt and pepper to taste. Transfer to a serving bowl.

Refried Beans

Serves 8

Vegan Friendly

Beans are a staple for many diets. Try this method for an easy way of preparing refried beans.

Tips

To reheat beans: Bake beans in a covered dish in a 375°F (190°C) oven until hot, 20 to 25 minutes.

When buying lard, ask your butcher if they render their own to be sure it doesn't contain any hydrogenated fat, which is the case with some supermarket brands.

1 lb	pinto beans, rinsed	500 g
1	onion, cut into quarters	1
2 tbsp	lard, bacon fat or olive oil (see Tips, left)	30 mL
	Salt	

1. In a large saucepan, combine pinto beans and cold water. Set aside to soak for at least 6 hours or overnight (see Tips, page 46). Drain and rinse thoroughly with cold water. Return to saucepan and add 3 cups (750 mL) cold fresh water. Cover and bring to a boil over medium-high heat. Reduce heat and simmer until beans are soft and the skin is just beginning to break, about 1 hour. Scoop out about 1 cup (250 mL) of cooking water and set aside. Drain and rinse beans.

2. In work bowl fitted with metal blade, pulse onion until chopped, about 5 times.

3. In a large saucepan, heat lard over medium heat. Add onion and sauté until translucent, about 6 minutes.

4. Transfer onions to work bowl fitted with metal blade and add beans. Pulse about 10 times for a chunky consistency, or process for 10 seconds for a smooth consistency. With motor running, add reserved cooking water through feed tube if consistency is too dry.

Variation

Add 6 oz (175 g) shredded or grated cheese to the top of the hot beans.

Best-Ever Cabbage

Vegan Friendly

When cooked properly, cabbage is delicious. The problem is, most people overcook it, destroying its lovely flavor. Make this in the fall when cabbage is coming into the markets in the Northeast. Sliced thinly in your food processor, it cooks almost in its own juices. Delicious!

- Large skillet with lid

1	head white or Savoy cabbage, cut into wedges to fit feed tube	1
2 tbsp	butter or olive oil	30 mL
1 tbsp	freshly squeezed lemon juice	15 mL
1 tsp	salt	5 mL
	Freshly ground black pepper	

1. In work bowl fitted with slicing blade, slice cabbage.

2. In a large skillet, melt butter over medium heat. Add cabbage and stir to coat. Sprinkle with lemon juice and 3 tbsp (45 mL) water. Reduce heat to low. Cover and cook, stirring 2 or 3 times to ensure even cooking, until cabbage is tender, but still a bit crisp, about 10 minutes. Season with salt, and pepper to taste. Serve immediately.

Braised Red Cabbage

Serves 6 to 8

Vegan Friendly

There is nothing more welcoming than the robust aroma of a big pot of red cabbage wafting through the house. It is particularly enjoyable on a chilly day alongside a pork roast or chops. If you're a vegetarian, try it with mashed potatoes or Buckwheat Pasta (page 464).

1	head red cabbage, cut into wedges to fit feed tube	1
2 tbsp	butter or olive oil	30 mL
1/3 cup	apple cider vinegar	75 mL
1 cup	dry red wine, divided (approx.)	250 mL
2	Granny Smith apples, peeled, cored and chopped	2
3 tbsp	red currant jelly	45 mL
1 tsp	ground allspice	5 mL
	Salt and freshly ground black pepper	

1. In work bowl fitted with slicing blade, slice cabbage.

2. In a large nonreactive saucepan, melt butter over medium heat. Add cabbage and stir to coat. Add vinegar and 1/4 cup (50 mL) of the wine. Cover and cook over low heat until cabbage is quite tender, about 1 hour. Check occasionally, stir well and if cabbage seems to be drying out, add up to 1/4 cup (50 mL) of the red wine.

3. Add apples, 1/2 cup (125 mL) of wine, red currant jelly and allspice. Cover and cook until cabbage is very tender, about 30 minutes. Season with salt and pepper to taste. Serve immediately.

Cabbage Colcannon

Serves 4 to 6

Vegetarian Friendly

This is a traditional Irish dish, a luscious combination of cabbage and mashed potatoes. If you haven't tried it, you won't believe how good it tastes. Many people add finely chopped green onion but we prefer to save that for another well-known potato dish, Champ (below).

1/3	head cabbage, cut into wedges to fit feed tube (about 1 lb/500 g)	1/3
4	russet (Idaho) potatoes (each about 6 oz/175 g), boiled in their skins and peeled (see Tip, below)	4
3/4 cup	whole milk, heated just until bubbles form around the edges	175 mL
2 tbsp	butter	30 mL
1 tsp	salt	5 mL
	Freshly ground black pepper	

1. Bring a large pot of water to a rapid boil. Meanwhile, in work bowl fitted with slicing blade, slice cabbage. Transfer to boiling water. Return to a boil and cook just until tender, about 4 minutes.

2. Meanwhile, replace slicing blade with shredding blade. Add cooked potatoes and shred. Transfer to a warm serving bowl. Add warm milk and mix until well blended. Add hot cabbage, butter, salt, and pepper to taste. Stir well and serve or place in a warm oven (250°F/120°C) for up to 30 minutes.

Champ

Serves 4

Vegetarian Friendly

This traditional Irish potato dish ranks with Colcannon in terms of popularity.

Tip

The potatoes for champ or colcannon should be freshly cooked and hot. After removing them from the cooking water, run under cold water and remove the skins. Shred just as the milk is ready.

4	russet (Idaho) potatoes (each about 6 oz/175 g), cooked in their skins and peeled (see Tip, left)	4
3/4 cup	whole milk	175 mL
3/4 cup	finely chopped green onions, white part with a bit of green	175 mL
1/2 tsp	salt	2 mL
	Freshly ground black pepper	
2 tbsp	butter	30 mL

1. In a saucepan over medium heat, combine milk, green onions, salt, and pepper to taste. Heat until bubbles form around the edges.

2. In work bowl fitted with shredding blade, shred potatoes. Transfer to a warm serving bowl. Add warm milk mixture to potatoes along with butter. Stir well. Serve immediately.

Potatoes Anna

Serves 4

Vegetarian Friendly

With the help of a food processor, which speedily produces thin even slices, this luscious dish is very easy to make. It's like a crisp potato cake and makes a perfect accompaniment to roasted or grilled fish, meat or vegetables. We like to make it using clarified butter because it encourages browning, but plain melted butter works well, too.

Tips

Floury potatoes such as russets (baking potatoes) work best in this recipe because they are not as moist as some other varieties.

If you have an option, use the thinnest slicing blade on your food processor.

If, when unmolding, some of the bottom layer sticks, just remove gently with a spatula and reassemble on top of the potato cake.

- Preheat oven to 400°F (200°C)
- Ovenproof skillet (about 8 inches/20 cm in diameter), well greased

4	potatoes (about 2 lbs/1 kg), peeled and halved (see Tips, left)	4
¼ cup	melted or clarified butter (see Tips, page 94)	60 mL
	Salt	
	Freshly ground black pepper	

1. In work bowl fitted with slicing blade, slice potatoes (see Tips, left). Arrange potato slices in bottom of prepared skillet in a single layer, overlapping as necessary. Drizzle liberally with butter and season with salt and pepper to taste. Repeat until all the potatoes have been used, pressing each layer down with a spatula to make it as compact as possible. Cook over medium-high heat, pressing down with an inverse spatula or the back of the spoon, until sizzling, about 5 minutes.

2. Transfer to preheated oven and bake until potatoes are tender, pressing down with a spatula once or twice, about 35 minutes.

3. Invert a serving plate over the skillet and unmold potatoes onto it (see Tips, left). Cut into wedges and serve immediately.

Potatoes au Gratin

Serves 6

Vegetarian Friendly

We love these potatoes
when their flavors are
allowed to develop.
Don't hesitate to serve
them a few days after
making them.

Tip

If the milk is cold it will
take a lot longer to cook
and thicken the mixture.
Measure the amount
needed and leave on the
counter for at least an
hour prior to making.

- Preheat oven to 400°F (200°C)
- 13- by 9-inch (33 by 23 cm) baking dish, buttered

10 oz	Cheddar cheese, cut into chunks	300 g
6	russet (Idaho) potatoes, peeled and cut in half (about 1½ lbs/750 g)	6
1½	sweet onions, quartered	1½
Pinch	salt	Pinch
Pinch	freshly ground black pepper	Pinch
Pinch	freshly grated nutmeg	Pinch
⅓ cup	unsalted butter	75 mL
¼ cup	all-purpose flour	60 mL
3 cups	milk, at room temperature (see Tip, left)	750 mL

1. In work bowl fitted with shredding blade, shred cheese.
   Transfer to a bowl.

2. Replace shredding blade with slicing blade and slice
   potatoes. Transfer to a small bowl. In same work bowl,
   slice onions.

3. In prepared baking dish, layer half of the potatoes and
   then onion slices. Top with remaining potatoes. Season
   with salt, pepper and nutmeg. Set aside.

4. In a saucepan, melt butter over medium heat. Whisk in
   flour, stirring constantly, for 1 minute. Gradually whisk in
   milk. Cook, stirring constantly, until mixture is thickened,
   about 5 minutes. Remove from heat. Stir in cheese all at
   once and continue stirring until cheese is slightly melted,
   30 to 60 seconds. Pour cheese mixture over potatoes.
   Cover baking dish with foil.

5. Bake in preheated oven until bubbling and potatoes are
   fork-tender, 75 to 90 minutes. If you would like the top
   to have a nice brown look, remove the foil for the last
   5 minutes of baking.

Variation
Try different cheeses, such as Gouda or Edam, in place of
the Cheddar.

Potato Galette

Serves 4

Vegan Friendly

This is another method for making a crisp potato cake, this time seasoned with a hint of garlic.

Tips

Floury potatoes such as russets (baking potatoes) work best in this recipe because they are not as moist as some other varieties.

If you have an option, use the thinnest slicing blade on your food processor.

- Nonstick skillet (about 8 inches/20 cm in diameter), greased

4	potatoes (about 2 lbs/1 kg) (see Tips, left), peeled	4
2 tbsp	olive oil	30 mL
2	cloves garlic, minced	2
1 tsp	salt	5 mL
	Freshly ground black pepper	
2 tbsp	butter or olive oil, divided	30 mL

1. In work bowl fitted with slicing blade, slice potatoes. Transfer to a bowl. Add olive oil, garlic, salt, and pepper to taste, and toss well, ensuring both sides of potatoes are well coated with mixture. Cover and set aside for 30 minutes. Drain off any accumulated liquid from potatoes.

2. In skillet, melt 1 tbsp (15 mL) of the butter over medium heat and remove from heat. (If you're using olive oil, simply place in pan and rotate until bottom is evenly covered with oil.) Arrange potatoes in a single layer, overlapping, as necessary, and pressing down with a spatula to compress as much as possible. Cover with foil and cook over medium heat until potatoes are nicely browned on the bottom, about 15 minutes. Once or twice, while they are cooking, use the back of a spoon or a spatula to compress the potatoes.

3. Invert a dinner plate over the skillet and transfer potatoes onto it. Add remaining butter to pan. Gently slide galette back into the pan, original top side down. Using the back of a spoon or a spatula, flatten. Cover and cook until bottom is nicely browned and potatoes are tender, about 15 minutes. Cut into wedges and serve.

Rösti

Vegan Friendly

If you are a potato lover, rösti is probably one of your favorite dishes. The crisp brown outside and soft interior is a marriage made in heaven.

Tip

If you are using waxy potatoes, which are very wet, after shredding liquid will have accumulated in the work bowl. Discard it.

- Preheat oven to 250°F (120°C)

4	potatoes (about 2 lbs/1 kg), peeled	4
2 tbsp	butter or olive oil, divided	30 mL
2 tbsp	olive oil, divided	30 mL
	Sea salt and freshly ground black pepper	

1. In work bowl fitted with shredding blade, shred potatoes (see Tips, left). Using your hands and working in batches, squeeze to remove water. Transfer to a clean tea towel and squeeze to remove remaining liquid. Divide potatoes into 4 batches. (Leave remaining batches in tea towel, while you cook the first two to prevent oxidation.)

2. In a large skillet over medium-high heat, combine 1 tbsp (15 mL) each butter and olive oil. Add two batches of potatoes and press down with a spatula or the back of a spoon to form a cake about ½ inch (1 cm) thick. Reduce heat to medium and cook until golden brown on the bottom, pressing down occasionally, about 5 minutes. Flip and cook until cooked through, about 5 minutes more. Sprinkle with sea salt and pepper, to taste. Transfer to platter and keep warm in preheated oven, while you cook the second batch.

Bacon-Studded Scalloped Potatoes

If you're feeling a bit indulgent, try this particularly rich and soothing version of scalloped potatoes. It makes an especially good accompaniment to pork, is wonderful on a buffet table and can even function as a main course, along with a simple salad. Although delicious, it is loaded with cream so serve small portions and enjoy every luscious bite.

- Preheat oven to 400°F (200°C)
- 6-cup (1.5 L) gratin or shallow baking dish, buttered

4	potatoes (each about 6 oz/175 g), peeled and cut to fit feed tube	4
2 cups	half-and-half (10%) cream	500 mL
2	cloves garlic, thinly sliced	2
1 tsp	salt	5 mL
Pinch	cayenne pepper	Pinch
	Freshly ground black pepper	
4	slices bacon, cooked crisply and crumbled	4

1. In work bowl fitted with slicing blade, slice potatoes.

2. In a large saucepan over medium heat, combine cream, garlic, salt, cayenne, and pepper to taste. Add potatoes and bring just to a boil. Reduce heat and simmer until potatoes are fork tender, about 10 minutes.

3. Using a slotted spoon, transfer half to prepared dish. Sprinkle crumbed bacon evenly over top. Add remaining potatoes and pour cooking liquid over them. Bake in preheated oven until bubbling and top is nicely browned, about 25 minutes.

Variation

Substitute sliced pancetta or speck, a very flavorful Italian/German pork product that is both cured and smoked, for the bacon. Cook until crisp, then crumble over top of each layer.

Scalloped Potatoes

Serves 6

Vegetarian Friendly

These rich potatoes are a great side dish to any beef or chicken you are cooking.

Tip

For best results, it is important to use floury oblong baking potatoes, such as russets, when making this recipe.

- Preheat oven to 400°F (200°C)
- 13- by 9-inch (33 by 23 cm) baking pan, buttered

6	russet potatoes, peeled and cut in half lengthwise (about 1½ lbs/750 g) (see Tip, left)	6
1½	onions, quartered	1½
3 cups	whole milk	750 mL
Pinch	salt	Pinch
Pinch	black pepper	Pinch
Pinch	ground nutmeg	Pinch

1. In work bowl fitted with slicing blade, slice potatoes and onions. Transfer to a saucepan over medium heat and add milk until milk starts to boil.

2. With a slotted spoon, transfer potatoes and onions to prepared baking pan. Stir salt, pepper and nutmeg into boiled milk. Pour over top of potatoes. Bake in preheated oven until top is light brown, 55 to 60 minutes.

Winter Vegetable Gratin

Serves 6

Vegetarian Friendly

This is a great way to serve winter vegetables. It's easy to make, looks very pretty and can be cooking away while you prepare the rest of the meal.

- Preheat oven to 350°F (180°C)
- 6 cup (1.5 L) baking dish, buttered

3	medium carrots, peeled	3
1	medium rutabaga, peeled and cut in wedges	1
2	potatoes, peeled	2
¼ cup	melted butter	60 mL
1 tsp	salt	5 mL
¼ tsp	freshly grated nutmeg	1 mL
	Freshly ground black pepper	
2 tbsp	heavy or whipping (35%) cream	30 mL

1. In work bowl fitted with slicing blade, slice carrots, rutabaga and potatoes. Transfer, in batches, as necessary to a large bowl.

2. Add butter, salt, nutmeg, and pepper, to taste. Toss well. Transfer to prepared dish. Add 1 cup (250 mL) water. Drizzle cream over top. Bake in preheated oven until vegetables are tender, about 1¼ hours.

Potatoes Boulanger with Caramelized Onions

Vegan Friendly

Although caramelizing the onions is a significant extra step, they produce a lusciously rich dish. Save this for special occasions when you want to impress.

Tip

If you have a slow cooker and plan ahead, you can caramelize the onions for this dish ahead of time. Slice as per Step 1 and transfer to a small (approx. 3 quart) slow cooker. Melt butter, add to onions along with garlic, thyme, salt and pepper and toss well. Place a clean tea towel, folded in half (so you will have 2 layers), over top of stoneware to absorb moisture. Cover and cook on High for 5 hours, stirring once or twice and replacing the towel each time, until onions are nicely caramelized. You can refrigerate the caramelized onions for up to 2 days before using in this recipe. When you're ready to cook, place the onions in the skillet, add the wine and broth and bring to a boil and complete the recipe.

- 6-cup (1.5 L) covered baking dish, lightly greased

4	onions (see Tip, left)	4
3	potatoes	3
2 tbsp	butter or vegan alternative	30 mL
4	cloves garlic, minced	4
1 tsp	dried thyme	5 mL
1 tsp	salt	5 mL
	Freshly ground black pepper	
½ cup	dry white wine	125 mL
½ cup	chicken or vegetable broth	125 mL
½ cup	Fresh Bread Crumbs or French-Style Seasoned Bread Crumbs (pages 468) or store-bought	125 mL
1 tbsp	extra virgin olive oil	15 mL

1. In work bowl fitted with slicing blade, slice onions. Remove from bowl and set aside. In same work bowl, slice potatoes. Transfer potatoes to a large bowl filled with salted water and set aside.

2. In a large skillet, melt butter over medium-low heat. Add onions and toss to coat. Cook, stirring often, until onions are nicely browned, about 45 minutes (see Tips, left). Add garlic, thyme, salt, and pepper to taste, and cook, stirring, for 1 minute. Add wine and broth and bring to a boil. Remove from heat.

3. Meanwhile, preheat oven to 375°F (190°C). When onions are cooked, place half the potatoes in bottom of prepared dish, overlapping as necessary. Using a slotted spoon, layer onions over top. Finish with a layer of potatoes. Pour liquid from skillet over top.

4. Cover and bake in preheated oven until potatoes are tender, about 40 minutes. Remove from oven and preheat broiler. Sprinkle bread crumbs evenly over top. Drizzle with olive oil. Place under broiler until crumbs are nicely browned. Serve hot.

Gratin Dauphinois

Serves 4 to 6

Vegetarian Friendly

What's not to love about this luscious dish? It's basically scalloped potatoes, French-style and it is simply delicious.

Tip

Whether you need to cut potatoes before slicing depends upon their diameter and the size of your feed tube.

- Preheat oven to 375°F (190°C)
- Shallow 12- by 9-inch (30 by 23 cm) baking dish, lightly buttered

4	potatoes (each about 8 oz/250 g), peeled (see Tip, left)	4
4 oz	Gruyère cheese	125 g
	Salt and freshly ground black pepper	
2 cups	whole milk	500 mL
2 tbsp	heavy or whipping (35%) cream	30 mL
2 tbsp	melted butter	30 mL

1. In work bowl fitted with slicing blade, slice potatoes. Set aside. Replace slicing blade with shredding blade and shred cheese. Set aside.

2. Arrange one-third of potatoes over bottom of prepared dish, overlapping as necessary. Sprinkle with one-third of the cheese. Season with salt and pepper to taste. Repeat. Finish with a layer of potatoes and set remaining cheese aside.

3. In a saucepan over low heat, heat milk until bubbles appear around the edges. Pour over potatoes. Bake in preheated oven for 1 hour.

4. In a small bowl, combine cream and butter. Pour over gratin and sprinkle with remaining cheese. Bake until potatoes are tender and top is crisp and golden, about 15 minutes.

Potato and Celery Root Gratin

Serves 4

Vegan Friendly

This is a rich gratin, a perfect accompaniment to roast or grilled meat. If you're a vegetarian, serve it alongside a platter of roasted sliced eggplant or use it as a main course, followed by a large salad.

- Preheat oven to 375°F (190°C)
- Shallow baking or gratin dish (approximately 4 cups/1 L), greased

1	large (or 2 small) celery root (about 1½ lbs/750 g total), peeled	1
2	potatoes, peeled	2
4 oz	Gruyère cheese or vegan alternative	125 g
1½ cups	good-quality tomato sauce	375 mL
¼ cup	heavy or whipping (35%) cream or soy creamer	60 mL

1. Bring a large pot of salted water to a rapid boil. Meanwhile, in work bowl fitted with slicing blade, slice celery root. Transfer to boiling water, return to a boil and boil until tender-crisp, about 2 minutes. Drain well and set aside.

2. Meanwhile, in same work bowl, slice potatoes. Transfer to a bowl and set aside. Replace slicing blade with shredding blade and shred cheese.

3. Layer half the celery root and half the potatoes over bottom of prepared dish. Spread with half the tomato sauce and half of the cheese. Repeat. Drizzle with cream.

4. Bake in preheated oven until top is golden, about 45 minutes. Cut into wedges and serve immediately.

Celery Root and Potato Purée

Serves 4 to 6

Vegan Friendly

Celery root and potatoes have a natural affinity. Here they are combined to produce a delicious purée that is great with roast chicken or meats or as part of a vegetarian meal.

Tips

To ensure the vegetables cook simultaneously, cut potatoes and celery root into chunks that are of similar size.

Since there is quite a bit of wastage when preparing celery root, weigh after it has been trimmed and peeled. For this amount, buy one large root.

1 lb	potatoes, peeled and cut into chunks (see Tips, left)	500 g
1 lb	peeled celery root, cut into chunks (see Tips, left)	500 g
2	cloves garlic	2
2 tbsp	heavy or whipping (35%) cream or soy creamer	30 mL
2 tbsp	butter or vegan alternative	30 mL
2 tbsp	coarsely snipped chives	30 mL
Pinch	freshly grated nutmeg	Pinch
	Salt and freshly ground black pepper	

1. In a saucepan, combine potatoes, celery root and garlic. Add water to cover. Bring to a boil over medium heat. Cover, reduce heat and simmer until vegetables are tender, about 20 minutes. Scoop out 1 cup (250 mL) of the cooking liquid and set aside. Drain. Return vegetables to pot and place over low heat for 1 to 2 minutes to dry.

2. Transfer vegetables to work bowl fitted with metal blade. Add cream, butter, chives, nutmeg, and salt and pepper to taste. Process until mixture begins to come together, about 15 seconds, stopping and scraping down sides of the bowl as necessary. If mixture seems too stiff, add enough reserved cooking water to make a smooth purée, pulsing to combine, about 5 times. Serve hot.

Crêpes Parmentier

**Makes about
24 mini crêpes**

Vegetarian Friendly

In France, these
potato pancakes are
traditionally served
with poached chicken
in a cream sauce.
They are delicious as
a side with Chicken in
Onion Buttermilk Gravy
(page 174), but also
work well like blinis, as
an appetizer base. They
are delicious topped
with smoked salmon and
sour cream or chicken
liver pâté and a dab of
Jalapeño-Spiked Onion
Marmalade (page 467)
or asparagus spears
and a spot of Foolproof
Hollandaise (page 410).

Tip

If you have time, cook
the potatoes ahead and
refrigerate until you're
ready to peel. They will be
easier to shred.

- Preheat oven to 200°F (100°C)

8 oz	potatoes, boiled in their skins, cooled and peeled (see Tip, left)	250 g
2 tbsp	all-purpose flour	30 mL
1 tsp	baking powder	5 mL
½ tsp	salt	2 mL
	Freshly ground black pepper	
4	eggs	4
¼ cup	half-and-half (10%) cream	60 mL
2 tbsp	heavy or whipping (35%) cream	30 mL
2 tbsp	butter, divided	30 mL
2 tbsp	olive oil, divided	30 mL
	Fine sea salt	

1. In work bowl fitted with shredding blade, shred potatoes. Transfer to a bowl and set aside.

2. Replace shredding blade with metal blade, add flour, baking powder, salt, and pepper, to taste, and pulse to blend. Add eggs, half-and-half and heavy creams and process until smoothly blended, about 30 seconds. Add potatoes and pulse to blend, about 5 times.

3. In a large skillet, preferably nonstick, heat half of the butter and half of the oil over medium heat. Working in batches, drop 1 tbsp (15 mL) of batter per crêpe into pan. Cook until top looks set and bottom is browned, about 2 minutes, then flip and cook on the second side. Sprinkle with sea salt. Transfer to a warm plate and keep warm in preheated oven. Repeat until all batter is used up, adding more butter and oil, as necessary.

Parsnip and Carrot Purée with Cumin

Serves 8

Vegan Friendly

The cumin adds a slightly exotic note to this traditional dish, which makes a great accompaniment to many foods.

4 cups	peeled sliced (½ inch/1 cm) parsnips (see Tip, page 364)	1 L
2 cups	thinly sliced peeled carrots	500 mL
2 tbsp	Italian flat-leaf parsley leaves	30 mL
1 tsp	ground cumin (see Tips, page 333)	5 mL
2 tbsp	butter or vegan alternative	30 mL
1 tsp	granulated sugar	5 mL
½ tsp	salt	2 mL
¼ tsp	freshly ground black pepper	1 mL

1. In a large saucepan, combine parsnips and carrots. Add water to cover. Bring to a boil over medium heat. Reduce heat and simmer until vegetables are tender, about 15 minutes. Scoop out ¼ cup (50 mL) cooking water and set aside. Drain. Transfer vegetables to work bowl fitted with metal blade.

2. Add parsley, cumin, butter, sugar, salt, pepper and reserved cooking water. Purée until smooth. Serve immediately.

Fennel-Laced Mashed Potatoes

Serves 4

Vegetarian Friendly

Deliciously rich, with a hint of garlic and the addition of fennel, these potatoes provide a pleasant and intriguing change from the norm.

Tip

The potatoes for this dish should be freshly cooked and hot. After removing them from the cooking water, run under cold water and remove the skins. Shred just as the fennel is cooked.

1	bulb fennel, cored and coarsely chopped (see Tips, page 345)	1
2	cloves garlic, coarsely chopped	2
¾ cup	half-and-half (10%) cream	175 mL
1 tsp	salt	5 mL
	Freshly ground black pepper	
4	small potatoes (about 1½ lbs/750 g), cooked in their skins and peeled (see Tips, left)	4
2 tbsp	butter	30 mL

1. In a saucepan over medium heat, combine fennel, garlic, cream, salt, and pepper to taste. Bring to boil, reduce heat to low and simmer until fennel is tender, about 15 minutes. Remove from heat.

2. Meanwhile, in work bowl fitted with shredding blade, shred potatoes. Transfer to a warm serving bowl. Replace shredding blade with metal blade. Add cooked fennel mixture, with cooking liquid. Purée. Add to potatoes along with butter. Mix well. Serve hot.

Parsnip Cakes

Serves 8

Vegetarian Friendly

Parsnips are a very underutilized vegetable. It's hard to say why because they have a lovely sweet flavor and go well with many things. Here, we've turned them into little patties, which are quite divine with roast poultry and meats as well as a wide variety of vegetables.

Tip

Since parsnips vary so dramatically in size, it is difficult to give a number when calling for them in recipes. However, you would need about 6 medium ones for this recipe. If you are using large parsnips, buy more than you think you'll need because you should cut away and discard the woody core before cooking. The easiest way to do this is to cut parsnip into thirds crosswise and place the flat surface on a cutting board. Using a sharp knife, cut around the core. Discard the core and cut the slices into equal lengths.

1½ lbs	parsnips, peeled and cut into chunks (see Tips, left)	750 g
¼ cup	Italian flat-leaf parsley leaves	60 mL
4 tbsp	butter, divided (approx.)	60 mL
½ tsp	salt	2 mL
	Freshly ground black pepper	
¼ cup	all-purpose flour	60 mL
1	egg, beaten	1
1 cup	dry bread crumbs, such as panko	250 mL
2 tbsp	olive oil, divided (approx.)	30 mL

1. In a pot of salted water, cook parsnips until tender, about 7 minutes, depending upon the thickness of the pieces. Drain. Transfer to work bowl fitted with metal blade. Add parsley, 3 tbsp (45 mL) of the butter, salt, and pepper to taste. Process until smoothly blended, about 15 seconds.

2. With wet hands, shape parsnip mixture into 16 patties. Spread flour on a plate, egg in a shallow bowl and bread crumbs on another plate. Dip each cake into flour, then egg, then bread crumbs. Discard any excess flour, egg and crumbs.

3. In a large skillet, heat remaining 1 tbsp (15 mL) of butter and 1 tbsp (15 mL) of the oil over medium heat. Add cakes, in batches, and cook, turning once, until golden, about 2 minutes per side, adding more butter and oil as necessary. Serve immediately.

Roasted Sweet Potato Squash with Basil Cream

Serves 4

Vegetarian Friendly

Although it used to be relatively unusual, sweet potato squash, also known as delicata, is becoming increasingly common. It is a smallish cream-colored, oblong-shaped squash with green stripes. It has a mild and sweet taste, which is complemented by the relatively robust flavors in this sauce. If you can't find it, substitute medium butternut squash.

- Preheat oven to 375°F (190°C)
- Rimmed baking sheet
- Mini-bowl attachment

2	sweet potato squash (delicata)	2
1 tbsp	olive oil	15 mL

Basil Cream

1 cup	fresh basil leaves	250 mL
2	cloves garlic	2
2 tbsp	freshly squeezed lemon juice	30 mL
¼ tsp	salt	1 mL
	Freshly ground black pepper	
½ cup	heavy or whipping (35%) cream	125 mL

1. Cut squash in half lengthwise and scoop out seeds. Brush cavity and edges with olive oil and wrap each half in foil. Roast in preheated oven until softened, about 40 minutes.

2. **Basil Cream:** In mini bowl fitted with metal blade, combine basil, garlic, lemon juice, salt, and pepper to taste. Purée. Add cream and pulse to blend. Set aside.

3. Remove cooked squash from foil, spoon 1 tbsp (15 mL) of the basil cream into each cavity and place on baking sheet. Bake until basil cream is thickened, about 5 minutes. Pour remaining cream into a small pitcher and pass at the table.

Roasted Squash Purée

This is a delicious dish to accompany any roast meat or even a platter of roasted vegetables. It can easily be doubled or tripled to feed a crowd.

Tip

Substitute butternut or another orange squash for the acorn.

- Preheat oven to 400°F (200°C)

1	acorn squash (see Tip, left)	1
2 tbsp	butter or vegan alternative, divided	30 mL
1 tbsp	brown sugar, divided	15 mL
1/4 cup	coarsely snipped chives	60 mL
1/2 tsp	salt	2 mL
1/8 tsp	cayenne pepper	0.5 mL
	Freshly ground black pepper	

1. Cut squash in half lengthwise and scoop out seeds. Place half the butter and half the brown sugar in each cavity. Wrap each half tightly in foil. Bake in preheated oven until tender, about 45 minutes. Remove foil, scoop out flesh and transfer to work bowl fitted with metal blade, being careful not to lose the melted butter. Discard skins. Add chives, salt, cayenne, and pepper to taste to work bowl. Purée. Serve hot.

Creamy Parsnip Purée

Cooking parsnips in milk is an idea that pops up from time to time. Although it may seem a bit wasteful, the resulting purée uses up most of the cooking liquid and the results are fabulous. Give this a try. We're sure it will become a staple.

4	large parsnips, peeled and cut into chunks (see Tip, page 364)	4
2 cups	whole milk	500 mL
	Salt and freshly ground black pepper	
	Freshly grated nutmeg	

1. In a large saucepan, combine parsnips and milk. Bring almost to a boil over medium heat. Reduce heat and simmer gently until parsnips are tender, about 15 minutes. (Timing will depend upon the size of your chunks.)

2. Using a slotted spoon, transfer parsnips to work bowl fitted with metal blade, reserving cooking liquid. Add half of reserved cooking liquid and process for 30 seconds. Add more liquid, if necessary and process until parsnips are smoothly puréed. Season with salt, pepper and nutmeg to taste.

Easy White Bean Purée

Makes 3 to 4 servings

Vegan Friendly

This is a great solution for days when you don't have time to cook potatoes. Use this purée to complete almost any dish that would benefit from mashed potatoes and double or triple the quantity to meet your needs.

2 cups	drained cooked white beans (see Tips, page 154)	500 mL
½ cup	Italian flat-leaf parsley leaves	125 mL
2	green onions, white part only, coarsely chopped	2
2 tbsp	extra virgin olive oil	30 mL
	Salt and freshly ground black pepper	

1. In a saucepan over medium heat, place beans. Add water to cover. Bring to a boil, reduce heat and simmer until beans are nicely hot. Drain.

2. Meanwhile, in work bowl fitted with metal blade, pulse parsley, green onions and olive oil until chopped, about 5 times, stopping and scraping down sides of the bowl once or twice. Add warm beans and pulse until beans are the consistency you prefer. Season with salt and pepper to taste. Serve hot.

Turnip Gratin

Serves 4

Vegetarian Friendly

This is a great holiday dish — wonderful with turkey or other hearty fare. Add a salad and it can double as a main course for vegetarians.

- Preheat oven to 375°F (190°C)
- 6-cup (1.5 L) shallow baking dish, buttered

2 lbs	white turnips, peeled (about 6 turnips)	1 kg
6 oz	Gruyère cheese, divided	175 g
1½ cups	whole milk, divided (approx.)	375 mL
¼ tsp	freshly grated nutmeg	1 mL
	Salt and freshly ground black pepper	

1. In work bowl fitted with slicing blade, slice turnips. Set aside. Insert shredding blade and shred cheese.

2. Add ½ cup (125 mL) of the milk to prepared baking dish. Layer half the turnips over top, overlapping as necessary. Sprinkle with half each nutmeg and cheese and season with salt and pepper to taste. Repeat. Add remaining milk (more, if necessary to cover turnips). Bake in preheated oven until turnips are tender, about 1½ hours.

Variation

Carrot and Turnip Gratin: Use half carrots and half turnips. Peel the carrots before slicing.

Split Pea Purée

If you're tired of the same old winter vegetables try this for a change. It is particularly good with pork.

Tip

To soak the peas for this recipe: Place peas in 3 cups (750 mL) cold water, cover and set aside overnight. You can also use the quick soak method. Combine peas and water in a saucepan. Cover and bring to a boil. Boil for 3 minutes. Turn off heat and soak for 1 hour. In both cases, drain and rinse thoroughly under cold water before using in recipe.

1 cup	dried split green peas, soaked and drained (see Tip, left)	250 mL
1 tbsp	olive oil	15 mL
2 oz	pancetta, diced	60 g
2	stalks celery, diced	2
2	carrots, peeled and diced	2
1	onion, finely chopped	1
2	cloves garlic, chopped	2
	Salt and freshly ground black pepper	
3 cups	chicken broth	750 mL
2 tbsp	heavy or whipping (35%) cream	30 mL
1/8 tsp	freshly grated nutmeg	0.5 mL
	Finely chopped parsley or snipped chives	

1. In a skillet, heat oil over medium-high heat. Add pancetta and cook, stirring, until it releases fat and begins to brown, about 5 minutes. Add celery, carrots and onion and cook, stirring, until softened, about 7 minutes. Add garlic, and salt and pepper to taste, and cook, stirring, for 1 minute. Add drained peas and toss until coated. Add chicken broth and bring to a boil. Cover, reduce heat to low and simmer until peas are tender, 1 to 1½ hours. (If they haven't absorbed all the liquid, drain.)

2. Transfer to work bowl fitted with metal blade. Add cream and nutmeg and process until puréed. Serve warm, liberally garnished with parsley.

Pepper Pasta Salad

Serves 12

Vegan Friendly

This is a perfect salad for a picnic or a large gathering. You'll have plenty of leftovers for another meal.

Tips

Do not "wash" the cooked pasta with water or it will stick. Coat with the olive oil as directed.

Salad keeps, covered and refrigerated, for up to 1 week.

8 oz	multicolored corkscrew pasta	250 g
⅔ cup	extra virgin olive oil, divided	150 mL
3	green onions, green part only, cut in half	3
½	green bell pepper, seeded and halved	½
½	red bell pepper, seeded and halved	½
½	yellow bell pepper, seeded and halved	½
½ cup	packed fresh basil leaves, stems removed	125 mL
6 oz	Parmesan cheese, cut into chunks, optional	175 g
2 tbsp	balsamic vinegar	30 mL
1½ tsp	Dijon mustard	7 mL
3	cloves garlic	3
½ tsp	granulated sugar	2 mL
Pinch	salt	Pinch
Pinch	hot pepper flakes	Pinch
2	carrots, coarsely chopped	2

1. In a large pot of boiling salted water, cook pasta until al dente, 7 to 12 minutes for dried, 3 to 6 minutes for fresh. Drain well and place in a large bowl. Add ¼ cup (60 mL) of the olive oil and toss to coat. Set aside and let cool to room temperature, occasionally stirring pasta to coat evenly.

2. In work bowl fitted with metal blade, pulse green onions, green, red and yellow peppers and basil 10 times. Add to pasta and toss.

3. In same work bowl, with motor running, add Parmesan cheese, if using, through feed tube and process until grated. Add vinegar, mustard, garlic, sugar, salt and hot pepper flakes and process until smooth, about 2 minutes. With motor running, slowly drizzle remaining olive oil through feed tube until it has been incorporated into the dressing. Pour over pasta salad.

4. In clean work bowl fitted with shredding blade, shred carrots. Add to pasta and toss. Let stand for at least 30 minutes prior to serving for the flavors to develop.

Brown Derby Cobb Salad

The Brown Derby was a celebrated watering hole in Los Angeles, frequented by movie and television stars. This salad was made famous by the restaurant owner, Robert Cobb.

Tip

Store dressing in the refrigerator until ready to use or for up to 1 week. Shake before using.

Dressing

¾ cup	red wine vinegar	175 mL
1 tbsp	Worcestershire sauce	15 mL
2 tsp	freshly squeezed lemon juice	10 mL
1 tsp	granulated sugar	5 mL
1 tsp	freshly ground black pepper	5 mL
1 tsp	Dijon mustard	5 mL
¾ tsp	salt	3 mL
1	clove garlic	1
1 cup	extra virgin olive oil	250 mL
1 cup	vegetable oil	250 mL

Salad

4 cups	finely chopped iceberg lettuce (about ½ head)	1 L
2 cups	finely chopped watercress (about ½ bunch)	500 mL
1 cup	finely chopped chicory (about 1 small bunch)	250 mL
4 cups	finely chopped romaine (about ½ head)	1 L
1	ripe avocado, diced	1
2	Roma (plum) tomatoes, seeded	2
1 lb	cooked skinless boneless chicken breasts, cut into pieces	500 g
8 oz	bacon, crisply cooked	250 g
3	hard-cooked eggs, cut in half	3
2 tbsp	chopped fresh chives	30 mL
½ cup	crumbled Roquefort cheese	125 mL

1. **Dressing:** In work bowl fitted with metal blade, process vinegar, ¼ cup (60 mL) water, Worcestershire, lemon juice, sugar, pepper, mustard, salt and garlic until combined. With motor running, add olive oil and vegetable oil through feed tube. Use immediately or cover tightly.

2. **Salad:** In a large shallow bowl or deep plate, toss together iceberg lettuce, watercress, chicory, romaine and avocado with enough of the dressing to coat. Set aside.

3. In work bowl fitted with metal blade, pulse tomatoes, chicken, bacon, eggs and chives, about 10 times to coarsely chop, stopping and scraping down the sides of the bowl, as necessary. Toss into greens with Roquefort. Serve.

Cabbage Salad with Olives

Serves 6

Vegetarian Friendly

Many cafés in Greece feature salads of cabbage and olives. Here is one for you to try without flying overseas.

1 cup	kalamata olives, pitted	250 mL
1	head cabbage, cut into wedges to fit feed tube	1
½ cup	Roasted Garlic Dressing (page 417) or store-bought	125 mL
	Salt and freshly ground black pepper	

1. In work bowl fitted with metal blade, process olives for about 10 seconds to finely chop. Transfer to a large salad bowl.

2. Replace metal blade with slicing blade and slice cabbage. Add to salad bowl. Toss to coat with dressing. Cover and refrigerate to allow flavors to meld, about 1 hour. Season with salt and pepper to taste.

Carrot and Ginger Salad

Serves 4

Vegan Friendly

This salad is brightly colored and full of flavor. It would make a great addition to any holiday table.

Tip

To peel gingerroot without a vegetable peeler, just use the edge of a large spoon and scrape the skin off.

1 lb	carrots, cut into 3-inch (7.5 cm) lengths	500 g
2 tbsp	extra virgin olive oil	30 mL
1 tbsp	freshly grated gingerroot (see Tip, left)	15 mL
1 tbsp	poppy seeds	15 mL
	Salt and freshly ground black pepper	

1. In work bowl fitted with shredding blade, shred carrots. Transfer to a large salad bowl. Add oil, ginger, poppy seeds, and salt and pepper to taste. Cover and refrigerate to allow flavors to meld, about 30 minutes. Serve at room temperature.

Carrot, Raisin and Dried Apricot Salad

Vegan Friendly

This salad is rich with raisins, flavorful apricots and a creamy dressing.

Tip

If raisins are dried out and not plump, you can soak them in hot water for a few minutes, then drain.

½	head cabbage, cut into wedges to fit feed tube	½
2	carrots, cut into 3-inch (7.5 cm) lengths	2
3	stalks celery, cut to fit feed tube	3
½	red onion, cut to fit feed tube	½
¾ cup	golden raisins	175 mL
½ cup	dried apricots	125 mL
2 tsp	fresh mint leaves	10 mL
½ cup	Traditional Mayonnaise (page 437) or store-bought (vegan or regular)	125 mL
	Salt and freshly ground white pepper	

1. In work bowl fitted with shredding blade, shred cabbage and carrots. Transfer to a salad bowl. Set aside.

2. Replace shredding blade with slicing blade and slice celery and red onion. Add to salad bowl. Set aside.

3. Replace slicing blade with metal blade and pulse raisins, apricots and mint, about 5 times, just to chop. Add to salad bowl. Add mayonnaise to bowl and stir to coat. Season with salt and white pepper to taste.

Chicken Gruyère Salad

Serves 4

Besides eating this as a salad, try placing between toasted bread and enjoy as a sandwich.

Tip

Don't confuse real mayonnaise with "mayonnaise-type" salad dressings, which are similar in appearance. Mayonnaise is a combination of egg yolks, vinegar or lemon juice, olive oil and seasonings. Imitators will contain additional ingredients, such as sugar, flour or milk. Make your own or make sure the label says mayonnaise and check the ingredients.

2 tbsp	Traditional Mayonnaise (page 437) or store-bought (see Tip, left)	30 mL
1 tbsp	Dijon mustard	15 mL
1 tsp	white wine vinegar	5 mL
1 tsp	salt	5 mL
1 tsp	freshly ground black pepper	5 mL
8 oz	Gruyère cheese, cut into chunks	250 g
3	stalks celery, cut into 3-inch (7.5 cm) lengths	3
1	3-lb (1.5 kg) deli-roasted chicken, skin and bones removed, cut into bite-size pieces	1
1	apple, such as Pippin, Granny Smith or Rome, peeled and quartered	1
1 tbsp	sesame seeds	15 mL
2 cups	salad greens	500 mL
	Salt and freshly ground black pepper	

1. In a large salad bowl, combine mayonnaise, mustard, vinegar, salt and pepper. Set aside.

2. In work bowl fitted with shredding blade, shred cheese. Transfer to salad bowl.

3. Replace shredder with slicing blade and slice celery. Add to salad bowl.

4. Replace slicing blade with metal blade and pulse chicken and apple about 10 times to chop, stopping and scraping down sides of the bowl once or twice. Transfer to salad bowl. Add sesame seeds to salad bowl and toss to coat with mayonnaise mixture.

5. Arrange salad greens on a platter and place chicken mixture on top. Season with salt and pepper to taste.

Feta Potato Salad

Serves 4

Vegetarian Friendly

Make potato salads your own. Create new flavors with different cheeses and olives.

Tip

To cook potatoes: Place whole potatoes in a pot of cold salted water; bring to a simmer over medium heat and cook until fork-tender. Do not allow to boil or the skins will burst and allow potato flesh to absorb water. If desired, peel slightly cooled potatoes, then cut into bite-size pieces.

4	stalks green onions	4
½ cup	black olives, pitted	125 mL
¼ cup	Italian flat-leaf parsley leaves	60 mL
1 tbsp	capers, drained	15 mL
1½ lbs	white fingerling potatoes, cooked and cut into bite-size pieces	750 g
½ cup	Traditional Mayonnaise (page 437) or store-bought (see Tip, page 373)	125 mL
6 oz	feta, crumbled	175 mL
	Salt and freshly ground white pepper	

1. In work bowl fitted with metal blade, pulse green onions, olives, parsley and capers, about 10 times, stopping and scraping down the bowl once or twice. Transfer to a large bowl.

2. Add potatoes and mayonnaise. Stir to coat. Add cheese and stir just to blend. Season with salt and white pepper to taste.

Variation
Try using blue cheese or Stilton for a stronger flavor.

Fresh Pear and Blue Cheese Walnut Salad

Serves 6

Vegetarian Friendly

Sweet pears with tart blue cheese and nutty taste of the walnuts create a light salad that will tickle your taste buds. Serve it with a little port wine.

Tip

To toast walnuts: Preheat oven to 350°F (180°C). Spread walnuts on a baking sheet and bake, shaking the pan several times, until fragrant and toasted; 6 to 9 minutes for walnut halves; 4 to 7 minutes for chopped walnuts.

4	carrots, cut into 3-inch (7.5 cm) lengths	4
2	pears, peeled and quartered	2
¾ cup	toasted walnuts (see Tip, left)	175 mL
3 cups	chopped butterhead lettuce	750 mL
1 cup	chopped radicchio	250 mL
1 cup	chopped baby spinach leaves	250 mL
3 tbsp	Blue Cheese Dressing (page 431) or store-bought	45 mL
1 tbsp	crumbled blue cheese	15 mL
½ cup	dried cranberries	125 mL
	Salt and freshly ground black pepper	

1. In work bowl with shredding blade, shred carrots. Transfer to a salad bowl.

2. Replace shredding blade with metal blade and pulse pears and walnuts until chopped, about 10 times. Add to salad bowl. Add lettuce, radicchio, spinach and dressing. Toss to coat fully. Top with blue cheese and cranberries. Season with salt and pepper to taste.

Fruit and Pecan Coleslaw

Serves 6

Vegan Friendly

Adding texture and new flavors to a slaw will also bring new dimension to your meal. Try an array of dried fruits to make this slaw your own.

Tip

To toast pecans: Preheat oven to 350°F (180°C). Spread pecans on a baking sheet and bake, shaking the pan several times, until fragrant and toasted; 6 to 9 minutes for pecan halves; 4 to 7 minutes for chopped pecans.

½ cup	Traditional Mayonnaise (page 437) or store-bought (vegan or regular)	125 mL
1 tsp	freshly squeezed lemon juice	5 mL
Pinch	freshly ground black pepper	Pinch
Pinch	salt	Pinch
Pinch	granulated sugar	Pinch
1	red onion, cut into quarters	1
1	red bell pepper, seeded and quartered	1
1 cup	toasted pecans (see Tip, left)	250 mL
3	large carrots, cut into 3-inch (7.5 cm) lengths	3
½	head cabbage, cut into wedges to fit feed tube	½
1 cup	dried fruit, such as raisins, currants or plums	250 mL

1. In a large salad bowl, whisk together mayonnaise, lemon juice, pepper, salt and sugar until combined. Set aside.

2. In work bowl fitted with metal blade, pulse red onion, bell pepper and pecans until finely chopped, about 20 seconds, stopping and scraping down sides of the bowl once or twice. Transfer to salad bowl.

3. Replace metal blade with shredding blade and shred carrots and cabbage. Add to salad bowl. Add dried fruit. Toss to fully coat.

4. Cover and refrigerate for at least 1 hour to allow flavors to meld prior to serving.

Green Mango Salad

Serves 4

Vegan Friendly

This salad is a little spicy and sweet.

1 lb	green mangos (about 2), peeled and seeded	500 g
½ cup	fresh cilantro leaves	125 mL
1	jalapeño pepper, seeded	1
2 tbsp	granulated sugar	30 mL
2 tsp	grated lime zest	10 mL
2 tsp	freshly squeezed lime juice	10 mL
	Salt	

1. In work bowl fitted with slicing blade, slice mangos. Transfer to a serving platter.
2. Replace slicing blade with metal blade and pulse cilantro, jalapeño, sugar, lime zest and juice, about 10 times, stopping and scraping down sides of the bowl once or twice. Pour on top of mangos. Let stand to allow flavors to meld, about 30 minutes. Season with salt to taste.

Mango and Apple Salad

Serves 4

Vegetarian Friendly

This creamy combination looks terrific on top of a bed of fresh greens.

Salad

3	stalks celery, cut into 3-inch (7.5 cm) lengths	3
2	apples, such as red or Golden Delicious, peeled and quartered	2
2	mangos, peeled, seeded and quartered	2
1 tbsp	fresh dill fronds	15 mL

Dressing

½ cup	plain yogurt	125 mL
2 tsp	fresh dill fronds	10 mL
1 tsp	Homemade Horseradish (page 469) or store-bought	5 mL
	Salt and freshly ground black pepper	

1. **Salad:** In work bowl fitted with slicing blade, slice celery. Transfer to salad bowl.
2. Replace slicing blade with metal blade and pulse apples, mangos and dill, about 10 times to chop. Add to bowl.
3. **Dressing:** In work bowl fitted with metal blade, process yogurt, dill and horseradish until dill is finely chopped, about 10 seconds. Pour into salad bowl. Stir to coat evenly. Season with salt and pepper to taste.

Orange and Chestnut Salad

Serves 6

Vegan Friendly

Try this fresh and easy
salad with a crusty bread
and a hearty soup.

Dressing

½ cup	apple cider vinegar	125 mL
½ cup	granulated sugar	125 mL
1½ tsp	paprika	7 mL
1 tsp	salt	5 mL
1 tsp	celery seeds	5 mL
1 tsp	dry mustard	5 mL
1 tsp	dried onion flakes	5 mL
¼ cup	extra virgin olive oil	60 mL

Salad

½	red onion, quartered	½
½ cup	drained canned chestnuts	125 mL
1	small head butter lettuce	1
2 cups	spinach leaves	50 mL
2	oranges, peeled and segmented	2
	Salt and freshly ground black pepper	

1. **Dressing:** In work bowl fitted with metal blade, process vinegar, sugar, paprika, salt, celery seeds, dry mustard and onion flakes for 10 seconds. With motor running, add oil in a steady stream through feed tube. Transfer to a salad bowl.

2. **Salad:** In work bowl fitted with metal blade, pulse red onion and chestnuts until chopped, about 10 times, stopping and scraping down sides of the bowl once or twice. Add to salad bowl. Add butter lettuce, spinach and oranges to salad bowl. Toss to fully coat. Season with salt and pepper to taste.

Papaya, Tomato and Onion Salad

Serves 6

Vegan Friendly

Serve this colorful salad on a large platter and let guests serve themselves.

Tip

Make this salad only a few hours prior to serving because the vegetables will get mushy if they sit in the vinaigrette for too long.

3	large heirloom tomatoes, seeded	3
2	large papaya, quartered	2
1/2	red onion	1/2
1/2	cucumber, peeled and seeded	1/2
1/2 cup	Italian vinaigrette	125 mL
	Salt and freshly ground black pepper	

1. In work bowl fitted with slicing blade, slice tomatoes, papaya, red onion and cucumber. Transfer to a serving platter. Drizzle vinaigrette on top. Add salt and pepper to taste.

Pesto Coleslaw

Serves 6

Vegan Friendly

A rich basil flavor makes this slaw a new favorite.

Tip

To toast pine nuts: Preheat oven to 350°F (180°C). Spread pine nuts on a baking sheet and bake, shaking the pan several times, until fragrant and toasted, 3 to 4 minutes.

1/2	head cabbage, cut into wedges to fit feed tube	1/2
3	carrots, cut into 3-inch (7.5 cm) lengths	3
1 cup	toasted pine nuts (see Tip, left)	250 mL
6	green onions, white and light green parts	6
2 tbsp	Italian flat-leaf parsley leaves	30 mL
1 cup	Traditional Mayonnaise (page 437) or store-bought (vegan or regular)	250 mL
1/2 cup	lightly packed fresh basil leaves	125 mL
	Salt and freshly ground white pepper	

1. In work bowl fitted with shredding blade, shred cabbage and carrots. Transfer to a salad bowl.

2. Replace shredding blade with metal blade and pulse pine nuts, green onions and parsley until chopped, about 10 times. Add to salad bowl.

3. Process mayonnaise and basil until smooth, about 5 seconds. Toss into salad to coat. Season with salt and white pepper to taste.

Pineapple Ham Salad

Serves 4

Perfect for an island-type party. Bring the tiki torches out and enjoy with rum punch.

Tip

To toast macadamia nuts: Preheat oven to 350°F (180°C). Spread nuts on a baking sheet and bake, shaking the pan several times, until fragrant and toasted; 6 to 9 minutes for whole macadamia nuts; 4 to 7 minutes for chopped.

Salad

8 oz	whole wheat penne pasta, cooked and drained	250 g
3	stalks celery, cut into 3-inch (7.5 cm) lengths	3
½	green bell pepper, seeded and halved	½
4 oz	cooked ham, cut into a few pieces	125 g
½ cup	toasted macadamia nuts (see Tip, left)	125 mL
1	can (8 oz/227 mL) crushed pineapple, drained	1

Dressing

½ cup	plain yogurt	125 mL
1 tbsp	apple cider vinegar	15 mL
1 tsp	Dijon mustard	5 mL
1 tsp	granulated sugar	5 mL
	Salt and freshly ground black pepper	

1. **Salad:** In work bowl fitted with slicing blade, slice celery. Transfer to a salad bowl.

2. Replace slicing blade with metal blade and pulse bell pepper, ham and macadamia nuts until chopped, about 10 times. Add to salad bowl. Add pasta and pineapple.

3. **Dressing:** In same work bowl, process yogurt, vinegar, mustard and sugar, about 10 seconds. Transfer to salad bowl and toss to fully coat. Season with salt and pepper to taste.

Potato Radish Salad

Serves 4

Vegan Friendly

Crunchy radishes with the creamy potatoes make this a delightful summer salad.

1½ cups	radishes	375 mL
¼ cup	extra virgin olive oil	60 mL
2 tbsp	red wine vinegar	30 mL
2 tsp	Dijon mustard	10 mL
2 tbsp	chives	30 mL
1 lb	white fingerling potatoes, cooked and cut into bite-size pieces (see Tips, page 374)	500 g
	Salt and freshly ground white pepper	

1. In work bowl fitted with slicing blade, slice radishes. Transfer to a salad bowl.

2. Replace slicing blade with metal blade and process oil, vinegar, mustard and chives until chives are chopped. Transfer to salad bowl. Add potatoes. Toss to fully coat. Season with salt and pepper to taste.

Roasted Chicken Pecan Salad

Serves 4

You can never have enough ideas for those prepared chickens from the deli.

½ cup	Traditional Mayonnaise (page 437) or store-bought	125 mL
2 tbsp	Dijon mustard	30 mL
2 tbsp	pickle relish	30 mL
1 cup	toasted pecans (see Tip, page 376)	250 mL
2 tbsp	fresh tarragon leaves	30 mL
½ cup	dried cherries or raisins	125 mL
1	3-lb (1.5 kg) deli-roasted chicken, skin and bones removed, cut into bite-size pieces	1
2 cups	salad greens	500 mL

1. In a large bowl, whisk together mayonnaise, mustard and relish. Set aside.

2. In work bowl fitted with metal blade, pulse pecans, tarragon and cherries, about 10 times. Add to bowl. Add chicken and toss to coat. Serve on a bed of greens.

Spicy Chicken Salad

"Dress up" deli chickens
for a fast meal.

1	3-lb (1.5 kg) deli-roasted chicken, skin and bones removed, cut into bite-size pieces	1
8 oz	elbow macaroni, cooked, rinsed and drained	250 g
1	red bell pepper, seeded and quartered	1
2	jalapeño peppers, seeded	2
3	shallots, quartered	3
3	stalks celery, cut into 3-inch (7.5 cm) lengths	3
2 tbsp	liquid honey	30 mL
1 tbsp	Dijon mustard	15 mL
1 tsp	grated lemon zest	5 mL
1 tbsp	freshly squeezed lemon juice	15 mL
2 cups	salad greens	500 mL
	Salt and freshly ground black pepper	

1. In a large salad bowl, combine chicken and pasta. Set aside.

2. In work bowl fitted with metal blade, pulse bell pepper, jalapeños and shallots, about 10 times. Transfer to salad bowl.

3. Replace metal blade with slicing blade and slice celery. Add to salad bowl. Add honey, mustard and lemon zest and juice to salad bowl. Stir to coat fully.

4. Place greens on a large platter. Arrange chicken mixture on top. Season with salt and pepper to taste.

Spinach and Avocado Salad

Serves 4

Vegan Friendly

This colorful salad is eye-appealing with the bright green avocado and red tomatoes.

1	large ripe avocado, diced	1
½ cup	Italian vinaigrette	125 mL
2 cups	radishes	500 mL
4	green onions, cut into 3-inch (7.5 cm) lengths	4
1 cup	cherry tomatoes, cut in half	250 mL
4 cups	baby spinach	1 L
	Salt and freshly ground black pepper	

1. In a salad bowl, coat avocado with vinaigrette. Set aside.

2. In work bowl fitted with slicing blade, slice radishes and green onions. Add to salad bowl. Add tomatoes and baby spinach. Toss to coat. Season with salt and pepper to taste.

Spinach and Mushroom Salad

Serves 4

Vegan Friendly

Here's a colorful salad that can be served for a light lunch or a first course at dinner.

Tip

To roast corn: Place corn in a skillet in a single layer over medium heat and sauté, stirring the entire time, until desired light brown color is achieved, being careful not to burn the corn, 6 to 8 minutes.

2 cups	baby spinach	500 mL
1 cup	roasted corn (see Tip, left)	250 mL
½ cup	Italian vinaigrette	125 mL
2	large heirloom tomatoes, quartered and seeded	2
12 oz	button mushrooms	375 g
½	red onion	½
	Sea salt and freshly ground black pepper	

1. In a salad bowl, toss together spinach, corn and vinaigrette. Set aside.

2. In work bowl fitted with slicing blade, slice tomatoes, mushrooms and red onion. Transfer to salad bowl. Toss to coat fully. Season with salt and pepper to taste.

Waldorf Parma Salad

Serves 4

This is a hybrid of New York and Italian flavors. It's a rendition of the salad made popular from the Waldorf-Astoria Hotel in New York City with the addition of Parma ham.

Tip

To toast walnuts: Preheat oven to 350°F (180°C). Spread walnuts on a baking sheet and bake, shaking the pan several times, until fragrant and toasted; 6 to 9 minutes for walnut halves; 4 to 7 minutes for chopped walnuts.

3	apples, such as Golden Delicious or Jonagold, peeled and quartered	3
8 oz	Parma ham, cut into chunks to fit fed tube	250 g
3	celery stalks, cut into 3-inch (7.5 cm) lengths	3
½	head radicchio, cut to fit feed tube	½
½ cup	toasted walnuts (see Tip, left)	125 mL
2 cups	torn butter lettuce	500 mL
½ cup	Traditional Mayonnaise (page 437) or store-bought	125 mL
	Salt and freshly ground black pepper	

1. In a work bowl fitted with slicing blade, slice apples, ham and celery. Transfer to a salad bowl.

2. Replace slicing blade with shredding blade and shred radicchio. Add to salad bowl.

3. Replace shredding blade with metal blade and pulse walnuts about 10 times. Add to salad bowl. Add butter lettuce and mayonnaise to bowl and toss to coat fully. Season with salt and pepper to taste.

Ribs in Tablecloth-Stainer Sauce (page 250)

Potatoes au Gratin (page 353)

Traditional Coleslaw (page 390)

Thousand Island Dressing (page 416)

Homemade Ketchup (page 443)

Fast and Easy Pizza Dough (page 473)

Sun-Dried Tomato Pesto Bread (page 488)
and Cheddar Cheese Rolls (page 484)

Honey Apple Spice Muffins (page 517)

Wild Mushroom and Ham Salad

Serves 6

Earthy mushrooms and the soft ham pieces make up this salad, which is lightly seasoned with a simple vinaigrette.

Tips

To hard-cook eggs: Place eggs on the bottom of a saucepan in a single layer and add enough cold water to cover by 1 inch (2.5 cm). Bring to a boil over high heat. Remove from heat and, without draining the water, cover and let stand for 10 minutes. With a slotted spoon, carefully place eggs in a large bowl filled with ice water. Let cool completely for 5 minutes. Remove eggshells under cool running water.

Clean mushrooms with a damp towel or a mushroom brush.

Chop the mushrooms with a knife because the wild ones can be fragile and using your food processor can make them into a paste in just a few pulses.

Dressing

1 tbsp	freshly squeezed lime juice	15 mL
1 tbsp	Italian flat-leaf parsley leaves	15 mL
1 tbsp	fresh tarragon leaves	15 mL
1 tbsp	fresh dill fronds	15 mL
1 tsp	Dijon mustard	5 mL
⅓ cup	extra virgin olive oil	75 mL

Salad

6	hard-cooked eggs, cut in half (see Tips, left)	6
8 oz	Parma ham, cut into chunks	250 g
3 cups	wild mushrooms, chopped (see Tips, left)	750 mL
3 cups	salad greens	750 mL
	Salt and freshly ground black pepper	

1. **Dressing:** In work bowl fitted with metal blade, process lime juice, parsley, tarragon, dill and mustard for 10 seconds. With motor running, add oil in a steady stream through feed tube. Transfer to a salad bowl.

2. **Salad:** In work bowl fitted with metal blade, pulse eggs and ham about 10 times just to chop. Add to salad bowl. Add mushrooms and salad greens to salad bowl. Toss to coat fully. Season with salt and pepper to taste.

Citrus Chicken Salad

Here's a salad that's tangy and fresh with citrus flavors. Try serving this with biscuits.

1 tbsp	Traditional Mayonnaise (page 437) or store-bought	15 mL
1 tbsp	liquid honey	15 mL
1 tsp	Dijon mustard	5 mL
2 cups	orange segments	500 mL
½	head napa cabbage, cut into wedges to fit feed tube	½
3	carrots, cut into 3-inch (7.5 cm) lengths	3
2	stalks celery, cut into 3-inch (7.5 cm) lengths	2
3	green onions, green part only, cut in half	3
3 tbsp	fresh tarragon leaves	45 mL
3 cups	shredded cooked chicken	750 mL
	Salt and freshly ground black pepper	

1. In a salad bowl, whisk together mayonnaise, honey and mustard. Add orange segments. Set aside.
2. In work bowl fitted with shredding blade, shred cabbage. Add to salad bowl.
3. Replace shredding blade with slicing blade and slice carrots and celery. Add to salad bowl.
4. Replace slicing blade with metal blade and pulse green onions and tarragon, about 5 times. Add to salad with chicken and toss to coat. Season with salt and pepper to taste.

Curried Chicken Salad

Serves 6

This delicate curry salad has just the right amount of zip without being too strong.

Dressing

½ cup	plain yogurt	125 mL
3 tbsp	fresh cilantro leaves	45 mL
1 tsp	mild curry powder	5 mL
2	cloves garlic, coarsely chopped	2
1	serrano chile pepper, halved and seeded	1

Salad

½	head cabbage, cut into wedges to fit feed tube	½
4	Roma (plum) tomatoes, seeded and cut into quarters	4
2 cups	shredded cooked chicken	500 mL
	Salt and freshly ground black pepper	

1. **Dressing:** In work bowl fitted with metal blade, pulse yogurt, cilantro, curry, garlic and chile until chopped, about 10 times. Transfer to a salad bowl.

2. **Salad:** In work bowl fitted with shredding blade, shred cabbage. Add to salad bowl.

3. Replace shredding blade with metal blade and pulse tomatoes to chop, about 5 times. Add to salad bowl. Add cooked chicken to salad bowl. Toss to coat. Season with salt and pepper to taste.

Dijon Chicken Salad

Serve garlic bread and a hearty soup with this salad to round out a full meal.

¼ cup	Traditional Mayonnaise (page 437) or store-bought	60 mL
2 tbsp	Dijon mustard	30 mL
3	green onions, green part only, cut in half	3
½	red bell pepper, seeded and halved	½
3 tbsp	fresh dill fronds	45 mL
2	cloves garlic, coarsely chopped	2
2 cups	shredded cooked chicken	500 mL
2 cups	salad greens	500 mL
	Salt and freshly ground black pepper	

1. In a salad bowl, whisk together mayonnaise and mustard. Set aside.

2. In work bowl fitted with metal blade, pulse green onions, bell pepper, dill and garlic until chopped, about 10 times. Add to salad bowl. Add chicken and salad greens to salad bowl. Toss to coat. Season with salt and pepper to taste.

Cumin-Spiked Carrot Salad with Cilantro

Serves 4 to 6

Vegan Friendly

This is a classic Moroccan salad, a very pleasant combination of flavors and textures. It works well on a buffet (you can easily double the quantity, if desired) and makes a perfect accompaniment to grilled fish or meat, or if you're cooking Middle Eastern-style, a robust tagine.

6	carrots, peeled (about 1 lb/500 g)	6
2	cloves garlic	2
4 tbsp	oil, divided	60 mL
1 tsp	granulated sugar	5 mL
1 tsp	ground cumin (see Tips, page 333)	5 mL
2 tbsp	freshly squeezed lemon juice	30 mL
½ tsp	salt	2 mL
	Freshly ground black pepper	
	Finely chopped fresh cilantro	

1. In work bowl fitted with shredding blade, shred carrots and garlic. Heat 1 tbsp (15 mL) of the oil in a skillet over medium heat. Add carrots and garlic and cook, stirring, until carrots are slightly softened, about 5 minutes. Add sugar and cumin and toss well. Transfer to a serving dish.

2. In a small bowl, combine lemon juice and salt. Stir until salt is dissolved. Whisk in remaining 3 tbsp (45 mL) of the oil and season with pepper to taste. Pour over carrots. Garnish liberally with cilantro.

Celery Root Remoulade

Vegan Friendly

Celery root is a great winter vegetable because it will keep refrigerated for over a week. However, it is very dense and hard to cut. Thank goodness for the food processor. Its shredding blade makes short work of this earthy root. Serve this tasty salad as a first course, as part of a buffet, or to round out a charcuterie platter.

- Mini-bowl attachment

1	small celery root (about 1 lb/500 g), peeled and halved (see Tips, page 131)	1
1/4 cup	Traditional Mayonnaise (page 437) or store-bought (vegan or regular)	60 mL
1/4 cup	Italian flat-leaf parsley leaves	60 mL
1/4 cup	fresh tarragon leaves	60 mL
2 tbsp	freshly squeezed lemon juice	30 mL
1 tbsp	extra virgin olive oil	15 mL
1 tbsp	drained capers	15 mL
1 tbsp	Dijon mustard	15 mL
2	anchovy fillets, optional	2

1. In work bowl fitted with shredding blade, shred celery root. Transfer to serving bowl.

2. In mini bowl fitted with metal blade, process mayonnaise, parsley, tarragon, lemon juice, olive oil, capers, mustard, and anchovies, if using, until smooth and blended. Add to celery root and mix well. Chill thoroughly before serving.

Peppery Broccoli Slaw

Serves 8

Vegan Friendly

Make this zesty salad in the late summer and early fall when broccoli is abundant in farmers' markets. It is a refreshing change from other salads.

Tip

Use store-bought (vegan or regular) mayonnaise or make Traditional Mayonnaise (page 437).

1/3 cup	mayonnaise (see Tip, left)	75 mL
1/4 cup	plain yogurt or vegan alternative	60 mL
1/2 tsp	salt	2 mL
	Freshly ground black pepper	
8 cups	broccoli florets, with a bit of stalk	2 L
1	small red onion	1
2	carrots, peeled	2
1	jalapeño pepper, seeded and quartered	1
1/4 cup	unsalted roasted sunflower seeds	60 mL

1. In a large salad bowl, whisk together mayonnaise, yogurt, salt, and pepper to taste. Set aside.

2. In work bowl fitted with slicing blade, slice broccoli and red onion. Transfer to salad bowl.

3. Replace slicing blade with shredding blade and shred carrots and jalapeño. Transfer to salad bowl. Add sunflower seeds to salad bowl. Mix well. Cover and refrigerate for at least 1 hour before serving.

Traditional Coleslaw

Serves 8

Vegan Friendly

There is nothing fancy about this coleslaw — it's the kind our mothers used to make. Here we've added some caraway seeds to bump up the flavor and made a jalapeño pepper an option for those who like a bit of heat.

Tips

Grind caraway seeds in a mortar with a pestle or in a clean spice grinder.

Don't confuse real mayonnaise with "mayonnaise-type" salad dressings, which are similar in appearance. Mayonnaise is a combination of egg yolks, vinegar or lemon juice, olive oil and seasonings. Imitators will contain additional ingredients, such as sugar, flour or milk. Make your own or make sure the label says mayonnaise and check the ingredients.

½ cup	Traditional Mayonnaise (page 437) or store-bought (vegan or regular)	125 mL
¼ cup	extra virgin olive oil	60 mL
2 tbsp	apple cider vinegar	30 mL
1 tbsp	caraway seeds, ground (see Tips, left)	15 mL
1 tbsp	Dijon mustard	15 mL
1 tsp	salt	5 mL
	Freshly ground black pepper	
1	red or green bell pepper, seeded and quartered	1
1	small red onion, quartered	1
1	jalapeño pepper, seeded and quartered, optional	1
2	carrots, peeled	2
½	head cabbage, cut into wedges to fit feed tube	½

1. In a large salad bowl, whisk together mayonnaise, olive oil, vinegar, caraway, mustard, salt, and pepper to taste. Set aside.

2. In work bowl fitted with metal blade, pulse bell pepper, red onion, and jalapeño pepper, if using, until finely chopped, about 10 times, stopping and scraping down sides of the bowl once or twice. Transfer to a salad bowl.

3. Replace metal blade with shredding blade and shred carrots. Transfer to salad bowl.

4. Replace shredding blade with slicing blade and slice cabbage. Transfer to salad bowl. Stir all ingredients together. Cover and refrigerate for at least 1 hour before serving.

Blue Cheese Peanut Coleslaw

Serves 6

Vegetarian Friendly

The rich bite of the blue cheese with the creamy peanut dressing makes this coleslaw a picnic favorite.

Tips

To speed up the process of making this salad, have all your vegetables cut and ready.

Salad keeps well, covered and refrigerated, for up to 3 days.

½ cup	Traditional Mayonnaise (page 437) or store-bought	125 mL
1 tsp	freshly squeezed lemon juice	5 mL
Pinch	freshly ground black pepper	Pinch
Pinch	salt	Pinch
Pinch	granulated sugar	Pinch
1	onion, cut into quarters	1
1	green bell pepper, seeded and cut into quarters	1
2	large carrots, cut into 3-inch (7.5 cm) lengths	2
½	cabbage, cut into wedges to fit feed tube (about 12 oz/375 g)	½
4 oz	blue cheese, crumbled	125 g
1¼ cups	unsalted roasted peanuts, crushed (about 8 oz/250 g)	300 mL

1. In a large salad bowl, whisk mayonnaise, lemon juice, pepper, salt and sugar until combined. Set aside.

2. In work bowl fitted with metal blade, process onion and bell pepper until very finely chopped, about 30 seconds. Place in salad bowl.

3. Replace metal blade with shredding blade and shred carrots. Transfer to salad bowl.

4. Replace shredding blade with slicing blade and slice cabbage. Place in salad bowl.

5. Stir all ingredients together. Add blue cheese and roasted peanuts, making sure everything is well coated. Cover and refrigerate for at least 1 hour prior to serving.

Variation

If you have spare garlic on hand add 2 crushed cloves to the onions for added flavor.

Kasha and Beet Salad with Celery and Feta

Serves 6 to 8

Vegan Friendly

In this hearty salad, beets, parsley and feta are the perfect balance for assertive buckwheat. It's a great combination and a wonderful buffet dish, particularly if you're serving to guests who are sensitive to gluten, because buckwheat is gluten-free.

Tips

Buckwheat groats that are already toasted are known as kasha. If you prefer a milder buckwheat flavor, use groats rather than kasha in this dish. Just place them in a dry skillet over medium-high heat and cook, stirring constantly, until they are nicely fragrant, about 4 minutes. In the process they will darken from a light shade of sand to one with a hint of brown. Groats you toast yourself have a milder flavor than store-bought kasha.

Place the celery and green onions in the feed tube together so that the celery provides support to the less rigid onions.

2 cups	chicken or vegetable broth	500 mL
2	cloves garlic, minced	2
1 cup	kasha or buckwheat groats (see Tips, left)	250 mL

Dressing

1 cup	Italian flat-leaf parsley leaves	250 mL
1/4 cup	red wine vinegar	60 mL
1 tsp	Dijon mustard	5 mL
1/2 tsp	salt	2 mL
1/2 tsp	freshly ground black pepper	2 mL
1/4 cup	extra virgin olive oil	60 mL
3	medium beets, cooked, peeled and cut to fit feed tube	3
4	stalks celery, cut to fit feed tube	4
6	green onions, white part only (see Tips, left)	6
3 oz	crumbled feta cheese or vegan alternative	90 g

1. In a saucepan over medium-high heat, bring broth and garlic to a boil. Gradually add kasha, stirring constantly to prevent clumping. Reduce heat to low. Cover and simmer until all the liquid is absorbed and kasha is tender, about 10 minutes. Remove from heat. Fluff up with a fork, transfer to a serving bowl and let cool slightly.

2. **Dressing:** Meanwhile, in work bowl fitted with metal blade, pulse parsley, vinegar, mustard, salt and pepper until parsley is chopped and mixture is blended, about 5 times, stopping and scraping down sides of the bowl once or twice. With motor running, add olive oil through feed tube, stopping and scraping down sides of the bowl as necessary. Pour over kasha.

3. Replace metal blade with slicing blade and slice beets, celery and green onions (see Tips, left). Add to kasha along with the dressing and toss well. Chill until ready to serve. Just before serving, sprinkle feta over top.

Barley Salad with Confetti of Carrot and Dill

Serves 10

Vegetarian Friendly

Here's a refreshing salad with unusual but delicious flavors. It makes a great main course or side salad to accompany grilled chicken, fish or meat. The shredded carrots and dill, which resemble orange and green confetti, will add color to any buffet.

Tips

To cook whole barley (the most nutritious form of the grain), bring 2½ cups (625 mL) water or broth to a boil. Add 1 cup (250 mL) rinsed and drained barley. Return to a rapid boil. Reduce heat to low. Cover and cook until barley is tender, about 1 hour.

For an easy-to-make version of this dressing, combine 6 tbsp (90 mL) of your favorite Italian dressing with 2 tbsp (25 mL) honey Dijon mustard.

You'll want about 2 cups (500 mL) shredded carrots to make this salad.

3 cups	cooked whole (hulled) barley, cooled (see Tips, left)	750 mL
Dressing		
1 tbsp	white wine vinegar	15 mL
½ tsp	salt	2 mL
	Freshly ground black pepper	
1 tbsp	Dijon mustard	15 mL
1 tbsp	liquid honey	15 mL
¼ cup	extra virgin olive oil	60 mL
4	carrots, peeled	4
2 cups	shredded hearts of romaine, optional	500 mL
½ cup	finely chopped dill fronds	125 mL
¼ cup	currants	60 mL
¼ cup	sunflower seeds	60 mL

1. **Dressing:** In a small bowl, combine vinegar, salt, and pepper to taste, stirring until salt is dissolved. Whisk in mustard and honey until blended. Gradually whisk in olive oil until mixture is smooth and creamy. Set aside.

2. In work bowl fitted with shredding blade, shred carrots. If using, shred lettuce.

3. In a serving bowl, combine barley, carrots, dill, currants and sunflower seeds. Add dressing and toss well. Arrange shredded lettuce over top, if using. Cover and chill thoroughly. When ready to serve, toss well.

Variations

Substitute an equal quantity of cooked wheat, spelt, Kamut or rye berries or farro for the barley.

Asian-Style Quinoa Salad with Chili-Orange Dressing

Serves 6

Vegetarian Friendly

Perhaps surprisingly, since quinoa is a "new world" grain, it takes very well to Asian ingredients such as water chestnuts. This is a nice light salad that is perfect for summer dining or a buffet.

Tips

To cook this quantity of quinoa: Rinse 1 cup (250 mL) quinoa under cold running water. Bring 2 cups (500 mL) water to a boil. Add quinoa in a steady stream, stirring to prevent lumps from forming, and return to a boil. Reduce heat to low. Cover and simmer until tender, about 15 minutes. Look for a white line around the seeds — it's the germ and when it bursts out, the grain is cooked.

The chile sauce adds a pleasant bit of zest, but if you're heat averse omit it. Heat seekers can increase the quantity to taste.

Place the red pepper and green onions in the feed tube together so that the pepper provides support to the less rigid onions.

3 cups	cooked quinoa, cooled (see Tips, left)	750 mL

Chili-Orange Dressing

1 tsp	finely grated orange zest	5 mL
¼ cup	freshly squeezed orange juice	60 mL
1 tbsp	reduced-sodium soy sauce	15 mL
1 tbsp	liquid honey	15 mL
2 tsp	sesame oil	10 mL
½ tsp	Asian chile sauce, such as sambal oelek or Sriracha (see Tips, left)	2 mL
	Freshly ground black pepper	
1	can (8 oz/227 g) water chestnuts, drained	1
1	red bell pepper, seeded and halved	1
4	green onions, white part with a bit of green (see Tips, left)	4
1½ cups	chopped snow peas, cooked until tender-crisp and cooled	375 mL

1. **Chile-Orange Dressing:** In a small bowl, whisk together orange zest and juice, soy sauce, honey, sesame oil, chile sauce and pepper to taste. Set aside.

2. In work bowl fitted with slicing blade, slice water chestnuts, bell pepper and green onions.

3. In a serving bowl, combine quinoa, water chestnuts, bell pepper, snow peas and green onions. Add dressing and toss until combined. Chill thoroughly.

Variation

Asian-Style Millet Salad with Chile-Orange Dressing: Substitute 3 cups (750 mL) cooked toasted millet for the quinoa.

Quinoa and Radish Salad with Avocado Dressing

Serves 6

Vegan Friendly

This salad is wonderful to make in summer when tomatoes and radishes are abundant and at their peak.

Tips

To cook this quantity of quinoa: Rinse 1 cup (250 mL) quinoa under cold running water. Bring 2 cups (500 mL) water to a boil. Add quinoa in a steady stream, stirring to prevent lumps from forming, and return to a boil. Reduce heat to low. Cover and simmer until tender, about 15 minutes.

The bit of walnut oil adds appealing but subtle flavor along with beneficial omega-3 fats to this pleasantly mild vinaigrette, but if you don't have it, just use an extra tablespoon (15 mL) olive oil.

You'll want about 2 cups (500 mL) sliced radishes for this salad.

If field tomatoes aren't in season, halved or quartered cherry tomatoes also work well in this salad.

3 cups	cooked quinoa, cooled (see Tips, left)	750 mL

Avocado Dressing

1	avocado, pitted and peeled	1
2 tbsp	extra virgin olive oil	30 mL
2 tbsp	white wine vinegar	30 mL
1 tbsp	walnut oil (see Tips, left)	15 mL
½ tsp	salt	2 mL
	Freshly ground black pepper	
1 lb	trimmed radishes (approx.) (see Tips, left)	500 g
2 cups	diced, cored tomatoes (see Tips, left)	500 mL

1. **Avocado Dressing:** In work bowl fitted with metal blade, process avocado, olive oil, vinegar, walnut oil, salt, and pepper to taste until smooth and blended.

2. Replace metal blade with slicing blade. Add radishes to feed tube and slice. Transfer to serving bowl. Add tomatoes, quinoa and dressing and toss until combined. Chill until ready to serve.

Variations

Millet and Radish Salad with Avocado Dressing: Substitute 3 cups (750 mL) cooked toasted millet for the quinoa.

Quinoa Salad with Lemony Chickpeas and Tomatoes

Vegan Friendly

Although this salad is enjoyable all year round, it is especially nice in winter when its light airy texture and Mediterranean flavors are a reminder that summer will come again. It makes a great addition to a buffet table, an interesting dish for a potluck and is an excellent side served with grilled fish or roast chicken. You can even use it as an appetizer — just put out hearts of romaine to use as dippers.

Tips

You will want about 2 cups (500 mL) thinly sliced radishes.

If field tomatoes are in season, substitute an equal quantity of seeded diced tomatoes for the cherry tomatoes.

For this quantity of chickpeas, soak and cook 1 cup (250 mL) dried chickpeas or use 1 can (14 to 19 oz/398 to 540 mL) chickpeas, drained and rinsed.

- Mini-bowl attachment

2 cups	water or vegetable stock	500 mL
1 cup	quinoa, rinsed	250 mL
Dressing		
½ cup	Italian flat-leaf parsley leaves or fresh dill fronds	125 mL
¼ cup	freshly squeezed lemon juice	60 mL
½ tsp	salt	2 mL
Pinch	cayenne pepper, optional	Pinch
	Freshly ground black pepper	
6 tbsp	extra virgin olive oil	90 mL
1 lb	trimmed radishes (see Tips, left)	500 g
2 cups	halved cherry tomatoes (see Tips, left)	500 mL
2 cups	cooked drained chickpeas (see Tips, left)	500 mL
8	green onions, white part only, finely chopped	8
	Hearts of romaine, optional	

1. In a saucepan over medium heat, bring water to a boil. Add quinoa in a steady stream, stirring to prevent lumps from forming and return to a boil. Reduce heat to low. Cover and simmer until tender, about 15 minutes. (Look for a white line around the seeds.) Remove from heat and let stand, covered, for 10 minutes. Transfer to a serving bowl and fluff with a fork. Set aside and let cool.

2. **Dressing:** In mini bowl fitted with metal blade, pulse parsley, lemon juice, salt, cayenne, if using, and pepper to taste until chopped and blended, about 3 times, stopping and scraping down sides of bowl as necessary. Add olive oil through feed tube, stopping and scraping down sides of the bowl as necessary. Set aside.

3. Replace metal blade with slicing blade and slice radishes. Add to quinoa along with tomatoes, chickpeas and green onions. Add dressing and toss well. Cover and chill. If using lettuce, line a serving bowl with hearts of romaine and add salad. Or serve salad as an appetizer and use romaine as dippers.

Cranberry Pecan Couscous Salad

Vegan Friendly

This salad has a delectable combination of flavors and textures — the slightly tart cranberries and orange are beautifully balanced by the crunchy pecans and mildly nutty flavor of the couscous. It's exotic enough to liven up any buffet and makes a particularly delicious and delightfully different accompaniment to poultry.

Tip

Try other kinds of whole-grain couscous, such as barley or spelt, for a change.

1½ cups	water	375 mL
1 cup	whole wheat couscous	250 mL
	Salt, optional	

Dressing

1 cup	Italian flat-leaf parsley leaves	250 mL
2 tsp	finely grated orange zest	10 mL
⅓ cup	freshly squeezed orange juice	75 mL
1 tsp	balsamic vinegar	5 mL
1 tsp	salt	5 mL
Pinch	freshly grated nutmeg	Pinch
	Freshly ground black pepper	
⅓ cup	extra virgin olive oil	75 mL
1	red bell pepper, seeded and diced	1
½ cup	dried cranberries	125 mL
½ cup	toasted chopped pecans	125 mL

1. In a saucepan with a tight-fitting lid, bring water to a boil. Gradually add couscous, stirring well. Season to taste with salt, if using. Remove from heat and let stand, covered, for at least 15 minutes. Fluff up with fork and break up any clumps, using your hands.

2. **Dressing:** In work bowl fitted with metal blade (preferably a mini bowl) pulse parsley, orange juice, vinegar, salt, nutmeg, and pepper to taste until chopped and blended, about 3 times, stopping and scraping down sides of the bowl, as necessary. With motor running, add olive oil through feed tube, stopping and scraping down sides of the bowl, as necessary.

3. In a serving bowl, combine bell pepper, cranberries, pecans and orange zest. Add fluffed couscous and toss. Add dressing and toss until combined. Chill thoroughly before serving.

Sauces, Dressings, Condiments, Rubs and Seasoned Butters

Condiments

Rubs

Seasoned Butters

Classic Bolognese Sauce

Makes about 8 cups (2 L)

This is a particularly delicious version of the traditional long-simmering Italian sauce. Although it cooks slowly for 2 hours, with the help of your food processor, it is not difficult to prepare and results are worth it. Serve it over fettuccine (either dried or freshly made, see pages 462 to 466) or use as the basic sauce for lasagna, along with béchamel. It is also splendid over fresh-cooked polenta.

Tip

If your grocery store only sells larger (28 oz/796 mL) cans of crushed tomatoes, use 1¾ cups (425 mL) for the quantity in this recipe. Save the remainder for another use.

- Preheat oven to 300°F (150°C)
- Ovenproof Dutch oven with tight-fitting lid

4 oz	pancetta, coarsely chopped	125 g
8 oz	extra lean ground beef	250 g
8 oz	ground pork	250 g
8 oz	ground veal	250 g
1 tbsp	olive oil	15 mL
2 tsp	dried oregano	10 mL
2	bay leaves	2
1 tsp	salt	5 mL
1 tsp	cracked black peppercorns	5 mL
2	onions, quartered	2
2	cloves garlic	2
2	carrots, peeled and cut into 1-inch (2.5 cm) thick slices	2
2	stalks celery, cut into 1-inch (2.5 cm) thick slices	2
1 cup	dry red wine	250 mL
1	can (28 oz/796 mL) Italian tomatoes with juice (see Tip, left)	1
1	can (14 oz/398 mL) crushed tomatoes	1

1. In work bowl fitted with metal blade, pulse pancetta until finely chopped, about 20 times, stopping and scraping down sides of the bowl once or twice. Add beef, pork and veal and pulse until mixture is well blended, but not mushy, about 10 times.

2. In a Dutch oven, heat oil over medium-high heat. Add meat mixture and cook, stirring frequently and breaking up with a wooden spoon, until browned, about 6 minutes. Add oregano, bay leaves, salt and peppercorns and stir well.

3. Meanwhile, add onions and garlic to work bowl and pulse until coarsely chopped, about 20 times, stopping and scraping down sides of the bowl once or twice. Add carrots and celery and pulse until chopped, about 20 times. Add to meat mixture. Reduce heat to medium-low, cover and cook until vegetables are softened, about 10 minutes. Remove cover, increase heat to medium-high and add wine. Bring to a boil and boil, stirring to scrape up brown bits from bottom of pan, for 2 minutes. Add tomatoes with juice and crushed tomatoes and return to a boil.

4. Cover, transfer to preheated oven and bake for 2 hours. Remove from oven, uncover, and simmer over low heat, stirring occasionally, until sauce is very thick, about 20 minutes. Discard bay leaves.

Classic Basil Pesto

Makes about 1½ cups (375 mL)

Vegan Friendly

When people think of pesto, this is usually the one that comes to mind. It makes a delicious seasonal topping for pasta — summer wouldn't be the same without it.

4 cups	medium packed fresh basil leaves	1 L
2 to 4	cloves garlic, coarsely chopped	2 to 4
¼ cup	pine nuts	60 mL
½ tsp	salt	2 mL
½ cup	extra virgin olive oil	125 mL
¼ cup	freshly grated Parmesan cheese or vegan alternative	60 mL

1. In work bowl fitted with metal blade, pulse basil, garlic to taste, pine nuts and salt until basil is coarsely chopped. With motor running, add olive oil in a steady stream through the feed tube until blended. Add Parmesan and pulse to blend.

Basic Garlic Tomato Sauce

Makes 2½ cups (625 mL)

Vegan Friendly

This is a great easy and fast sauce that you can use with the Mini Meatballs (page 102) or on pasta.

Tip

Make sure the basil and parsley are washed and dried. Use a herb spinner to make sure they are as dry as can be.

1 lb	Roma (plum) tomatoes (7 to 9 tomatoes) or 1 can (28 oz/796 mL) whole tomatoes with juice	500 g
6	cloves garlic, coarsely chopped	6
⅓ cup	fresh basil leaves (see Tip, left)	75 mL
2 tbsp	Italian flat-leaf parsley leaves	30 mL
⅓ cup	olive oil	75 mL

1. Cut tomatoes in half, widthwise. Remove cores and squeeze out excess seeds and juices. Transfer to work bowl fitted with metal blade. Add garlic, basil and parsley and pulse until chunky but not smooth, about 10 times. With motor running, gradually add olive oil through feed tube and process until smooth. Transfer sauce to a saucepan over medium heat and bring to a simmer.

Pesto and Tomato Sauce

Makes 2 cups (500 mL)

Vegetarian Friendly

Try dipping Italian bread sticks into this flavorful sauce, as well as eating it with pasta.

Tip

To toast pine nuts: Preheat oven to 350°F (180°C). Spread pine nuts on a baking sheet and bake, shaking the pan several times, until fragrant and toasted, 3 to 4 minutes.

2 cups	lightly packed fresh basil	500 mL
6	cloves garlic, coarsely chopped	6
¼ cup	extra virgin olive oil	60 mL
¼ cup	pine nuts, toasted (see Tip, left)	60 mL
¼ cup	freshly grated Parmesan cheese	60 mL
1	can (28 oz/796 mL) diced tomatoes with juice	1
1 tbsp	granulated sugar	15 mL
1 tbsp	dried onion flakes	15 mL
1 tsp	dried oregano	5 mL

1. In work bowl fitted with metal blade, process basil, garlic and oil until smooth, about 2 minutes. With motor running, add pine nuts and Parmesan through feed tube and process until combined.

2. Transfer mixture to a medium saucepan. Add tomatoes with juice, sugar, onion flakes and oregano and bring to boil over medium heat. Reduce heat and simmer, stirring occasionally, until slightly thickened, for 45 minutes.

Peanut Sauce

Makes about 1 cup (250 mL)

Vegan Friendly

This tasty sauce is very easy to make and is delicious with many dishes. If you're a vegetarian, try it with grilled tofu or vegetable spring rolls. It's traditionally served with satay, Southeast Asian grilled chicken, seafood or meat served on small wooden skewers. Serve in individual bowls for dipping.

½ cup	smooth peanut butter	125 mL
¼ cup	warm water	60 mL
1 tbsp	soy sauce	15 mL
1 tbsp	rice vinegar	15 mL
2 tsp	toasted sesame oil	10 mL
1	piece (about 2 inches/5 cm) peeled gingerroot, cut into quarters	1
2	cloves garlic, coarsely chopped	2
1 tsp	granulated sugar	5 mL
2 tbsp	chopped cilantro, optional	30 mL
1	long red chile pepper, chopped, optional	1
1 tbsp	chopped roasted peanuts, optional	15 mL

1. In mini-bowl fitted with metal blade, process peanut butter, water, soy sauce, vinegar, sesame oil, ginger, garlic, sugar, and cilantro and/or chile pepper, if using, until smooth, about 1 minute. Garnish with peanuts, if using.

Parsley Walnut Pesto

**Makes about
1 cup (250 mL)**

Vegan Friendly

Although pesto is usually paired with pasta, we also like this version as an accompaniment to fish, grilled or roasted. Serve the pesto alongside. If you have leftovers, use them as a finish for soup, spread on crostini or use as a condiment for simple grilled cheese on bread.

4 cups	Italian flat-leaf parsley leaves	1 L
4	green onions, chopped	4
½ cup	walnut halves	125 mL
2 tbsp	freshly squeezed lemon juice	30 mL
¼ cup	extra virgin olive oil	60 mL
1 tbsp	walnut oil or extra virgin olive oil	15 mL
¼ cup	freshly grated Parmesan cheese or vegan alternative, optional	60 mL
	Salt and freshly ground black pepper	

1. In work bowl fitted with metal blade, process parsley, green onions, walnuts and lemon juice, stopping and scraping down sides of the bowl once or twice, until smoothly chopped, about 25 seconds. With motor running, gradually add olive oil then walnut oil through the feed tube, until mixture is smoothly blended. Add Parmesan, if using, and pulse to blend. Season with salt and pepper to taste.

Fresh Watercress Sauce

**Makes about
1 cup (250 mL)**

Vegetarian Friendly

This sauce, which is surprisingly light, is great with fish, chicken or roasted vegetables. It also makes a great dip for cut up vegetables.

Tip

Quark is a fresh lower-fat cheese that has long been popular in Europe. Look for it in well-stocked supermarkets and natural foods stores.

½ cup	quark cheese (see Tip, left)	125 mL
½ cup	Traditional Mayonnaise (page 437) or store-bought	125 mL
1 cup	watercress, leaves and tender parts of stem	250 mL
	Salt and freshly ground black pepper	

1. In work bowl fitted with metal blade, pulse quark and mayonnaise to blend, 4 or 5 times, stopping and scraping down sides of the bowl once or twice. Add watercress and pulse until chopped and blended, 4 or 5 times, stopping and scraping down the sides of the bowl. Season with salt and pepper to taste.

Variations

Substitute arugula for the watercress.

Curry-Spiked Watercress Sauce: Add ½ to 1 tsp (2 to 5 mL) curry powder along with the mayonnaise.

Tomatillo Green Sauce

Makes 4 cups (1 L)

Vegetarian Friendly

Here's a simple flavorful sauce to dress up fish or for use as a dip.

Tip

Don't skip washing the tomatillos after husking them and prior to processing. There is a sticky substance on the skins that you need to remove.

½	onion, quartered	½
1 lb	tomatillos, husked, rinsed and quartered (about 15) (see Tip, left)	500 mL
2	jalapeño peppers, seeded	2
½ cup	fresh cilantro leaves	125 mL
2 tbsp	freshly squeezed lime juice	30 mL
1 tsp	salt	5 mL
1 tsp	dried tarragon	5 mL
¼ tsp	hot pepper sauce	1 mL
½ cup	sour cream	125 mL

1. In work bowl fitted with metal blade, pulse onion until diced, about 10 times. Transfer to a strainer and rinse with cold water. Return onion to food processor and add tomatillos, jalapeños, cilantro, lime juice, salt, tarragon and hot pepper sauce. Pulse 20 times or until the desired texture is achieved. Transfer to a bowl and stir in sour cream.

Green Chile Sauce

Makes 2 cups (500 mL)

Vegan Friendly

This a perfect smooth chile sauce for green enchiladas or for use as a dip with chips.

- **Mini-bowl attachment**

2 tbsp	oil	30 mL
7	Anaheim chile peppers, seeded and chopped	7
½	onion, coarsely chopped	½
2	cloves garlic, coarsely chopped	2
1 cup	water	250 mL
	Salt and freshly ground pepper	

1. In a large skillet, heat oil over medium heat. Add chiles, onion and garlic and sauté until softened, about 6 minutes. Reduce heat to low and simmer for 5 minutes.

2. In mini bowl fitted with metal blade, process cooked vegetables and water until smooth, about 2 minutes.

3. Transfer purée to a saucepan over medium heat and cook, stirring often, until reduced to desired thickness. Season with salt and pepper to taste.

Roasted Red Pepper Vegetable Chili Sauce

Makes 3 cups (750 mL)

Vegetarian Friendly

This satisfying sauce is perfect for any type of pasta.

Tips

To roast peppers: Preheat oven to 400°F (200°C). Place peppers on a baking sheet and roast, turning two or three times, until skin on all sides is blackened, about 25 minutes. Transfer peppers to a heatproof bowl. Cover with a plate and let stand until cool. Remove and, using a sharp knife, lift skins off. Discard skins and seeds and cut into strips.

For this quantity of beans, use 1 can (14 oz/398 mL) drained and rinsed, or cook ¾ cup (175 mL) dried beans.

1	red onion, quartered	1
3	zucchini, cut to fit feed tube	3
1	yellow summer squash, cut to fit feed tube	1
8 oz	button mushrooms, stems removed	250 g
3 tbsp	olive oil	45 mL
1 cup	roasted red peppers, drained (see Tips, left)	250 mL
2	Roma (plum) tomatoes, seeded and quartered	2
½ cup	heavy or whipping (35%) cream, at room temperature	125 mL
¼ tsp	salt	1 mL
¼ cup	Fresh Bread Crumbs or French-Style Seasoned Bread Crumbs (page 468) or store-bought	60 mL
1½ cups	drained cooked kidney beans (see Tips, left)	375 mL

1. In work bowl fitted with slicing blade, slice red onion. Transfer to a bowl. Slice zucchini, squash and mushrooms. Transfer to a large bowl.

2. In a large pot, heat oil over medium heat. Add onion and sauté until softened, about 5 minutes. Add zucchini, squash and mushrooms and sauté until softened, about 15 minutes. Add bell peppers, tomatoes, cream and salt and bring to a boil. Reduce heat and simmer for 30 minutes. Transfer half of the mixture to work bowl fitted with metal blade and process until smooth, about 20 seconds. Return to pot. Add bread crumbs and beans. Stir to combine and heat through.

Italian-Style Salsa Verde

Make this robust sauce throughout the summer when sorrel is in season and available at farmers' markets. It is the perfect finish for grilled chicken breasts or a husky fish, such as grilled tuna. Traditionally, it is served with bollito misto, the Italian dish of boiled mixed meats.

2 cups	packed sorrel leaves	500 mL
1 cup	packed arugula leaves	250 mL
1 cup	packed Italian flat-leaf parsley leaves	250 mL
2 tbsp	drained capers	30 mL
4	anchovy fillets	4
3	cloves garlic	3
½ tsp	salt	2 mL
	Freshly ground black pepper	
2 tbsp	freshly squeezed lemon juice	30 mL
⅓ cup	extra virgin olive oil	75 mL

1. In work bowl fitted with metal blade, pulse sorrel, arugula, parsley, capers, anchovies, garlic, salt, and pepper to taste, until combined, about 8 times, stopping and scraping down sides of the bowl once or twice. With motor running, add lemon juice and olive oil through the feed tube in a slow steady stream until mixture is well blended. Transfer to a small bowl and serve immediately.

Sauce Vierge

Vegan Friendly

This sauce is fresh and light. It is delicious with fish, particularly shellfish. For a great appetizer, sauté peeled shrimp in a little olive oil or, in summer, brush shrimp in shells with olive oil and barbecue, serving the sauce alongside. If you're a vegan, try serving it over some grilled bread drizzled with extra virgin olive oil or your favorite roasted vegetables.

20	fresh basil leaves	20
1	clove garlic, coarsely chopped	1
1 tsp	finely grated lemon zest	5 mL
3 tbsp	freshly squeezed lemon juice	45 mL
½ cup	extra virgin olive oil	125 mL
15	cherry or grape tomatoes	15
15	pitted black olives	15
	Salt and freshly ground black pepper	

1. In work bowl fitted with the metal blade, process basil, garlic, lemon zest and juice and olive oil until basil and garlic are minced. Add tomatoes and olives and pulse to coarsely chop. Season with salt and pepper to taste.

Sorrel Sauce

**Makes about
1 cup (250 mL)**

Vegan Friendly

Throughout the summer, sorrel, a leafy green that looks like spinach but has a very bitter taste — call it spinach with attitude — is available at farmers' markets. This pleasantly acerbic sauce is simply superb over grilled salmon. It is also good with robust fish such as tuna or, if you're a vegetarian, with poached eggs or as a topping for sautéed tofu or roasted squash.

Tips

If your sorrel hasn't been prewashed, swish it around in a basin of lukewarm water until you're sure any grit is removed then rinse in a colander under cold running water. Do not drain after rinsing. This little bit of water is what the leaves will cook in and it goes into the sauce.

Tarragon adds a nice bit of depth to the sauce, but it isn't essential.

4 cups	sorrel leaves (about 4 oz/125 g), rinsed (see Tips, left)	1 L
½ tsp	dried tarragon, optional	2 mL
2	green onions, white part only, coarsely chopped	2
1	clove garlic, coarsely chopped	1
1 tbsp	Dijon mustard	15 mL
1 tbsp	butter or vegan alternative	15 mL
	Salt and freshly ground black pepper	
⅓ cup	heavy or whipping (35 %) cream or soy creamer	75 mL

1. In a heavy saucepan with a tight-fitting lid over low heat, cook sorrel and tarragon, if using, until leaves are wilted, about 4 minutes. Immediately transfer to work bowl fitted with metal blade. Add green onions, garlic, Dijon mustard, butter, and salt and pepper to taste. Purée. With the motor running, add cream through the feed tube until completely incorporated. Transfer to a sauceboat and serve immediately.

Roasted Red Pepper Sauce

Makes 2 cups (500 mL)

Vegetarian Friendly

This sauce is also known as *acquasale*, which means sweet pepper sauce.

3 tbsp	extra virgin olive oil	45 mL
1	medium red onion, thinly sliced	1
1	clove garlic, minced	1
1½ cups	chopped roasted red peppers (about 4) (see Tips, page 406)	375 mL
2	Roma (plum) tomatoes, seeded and diced	2
½ cup	heavy or whipping (35%) cream	125 mL
¼ tsp	salt	1 mL
¼ cup	dry Italian bread crumbs, optional	60 mL

1. In a skillet, heat oil over medium heat. Add red onion and sauté until softened, about 5 minutes. Stir in garlic and red peppers. Cover, reduce heat and sweat vegetables until very soft, 20 to 25 minutes. Add tomatoes, cream and salt. Cook, stirring, for 3 minutes. Let cool to room temperature.

2. In work bowl fitted with metal blade, pulse sauce until finely chopped, about 20 times. Transfer to a saucepan over low heat and reheat until simmering, about 2 minutes. If sauce is too thin for you, add bread crumbs.

Two-Tomato Coulis

Makes about 1 cup (250 mL)

Vegan Friendly

This light fresh-tasting sauce is the perfect finish for a piece of simply cooked fish, slices of baked eggplant or even grilled bread. It can also be used to add flavor to soups (see Creamy Cauliflower Soup, Tips, page 127.)

- Mini-bowl attachment

1 cup	cherry tomatoes	250 mL
2	reconstituted sun-dried tomatoes (see Tips, page 310)	2
¼ cup	chicken or vegetable broth	60 mL
1 tbsp	balsamic vinegar	15 mL
15	fresh tarragon leaves or ¼ cup (60 mL) fresh dill fronds	15
½ tsp	salt	2 mL
	Freshly ground black or white pepper	

1. In mini bowl fitted with metal blade, pulse cherry and sun-dried tomatoes, broth, vinegar, tarragon, salt, and pepper to taste, until chopped and blended, stopping and scraping down sides of the bowl once or twice, about 15 times.

Foolproof Hollandaise

**Makes about
1 cup (250 mL)**

Vegetarian Friendly

When you're feeling celebratory, there is nothing quite like a perfect piece of fish topped with hollandaise. It is also a perfect finish for vegetables such as asparagus.

Tips

Clarified butter is butter from which the milk solids have been removed. When used in hollandaise it produces a thicker sauce. *To make the clarified butter for this recipe:* Heat ⅔ cup (150 mL) butter in a saucepan over medium heat until melted. Remove from heat and, using a small slotted spoon, skim off the foam. Carefully pour off the yellow butterfat and discard the remaining milk solids that sank to the bottom.

Keep a small quantity of boiling water at the side of the stove when making hollandaise. If your eggs start to curdle during the final whisking, add 1 tbsp (15 mL) boiling water to the mixture. Whisk until smooth and thickened, then transfer to work bowl.

3	egg yolks	3
3 tbsp	water	45 mL
1 tbsp	freshly squeezed lemon juice	15 mL
½ cup	warm clarified butter (see Tips, left)	125 mL
½ tsp	salt	2 mL
	Cayenne pepper	

1. In a small saucepan over low heat, combine egg yolks, water and lemon juice. Cook, whisking constantly, until eggs begin to thicken, about 1 minute. Whisk rapidly for about 5 seconds longer to ensure the yolks are cooked, then immediately transfer to small work bowl (see Tip, page 411).

2. With motor running, slowly add clarified butter through the feed tube in a small stream, processing until mixture is smooth and creamy. Add salt and cayenne and process until smooth. Serve immediately.

Variation

Chive Hollandaise: Add ¼ cup (60 mL) coarsely chopped chives along with the salt and process until smoothly blended.

Dill Hollandaise: Add ¼ cup (60 mL) coarsely chopped fresh dill along with the salt and process until smoothly blended.

No-Fail Béarnaise

Makes about ¾ cup (175 mL)

Vegetarian Friendly

A relative of hollandaise, Béarnaise is a deliciously decadent finish for grilled steak, particularly filet. If you're a vegetarian, try it with grilled portobello mushrooms or a platter of roasted root vegetables. Because the butter is added off-heat in this version, it is important that you add the eggs to the wine-vinegar infusion while it is still hot.

Tip

A mini-bowl attachment works best for this recipe, however, a regular-size bowl, up to an 11-cup size, will work.

¼ cup	white wine	60 mL
¼ cup	tarragon or white wine vinegar	60 mL
1	shallot, finely chopped (about 2 tbsp/30 mL)	1
¼ tsp	salt	1 mL
Pinch	freshly ground white pepper	Pinch
2	egg yolks	2
1 tbsp	boiling water	15 mL
½ cup	butter, cubed, softened	125 mL
¼ cup	loosely packed fresh tarragon leaves	60 mL
	Salt and freshly ground white pepper	

1. In a small saucepan, combine wine, vinegar, shallot, salt and pepper. Bring to a boil over medium heat. Reduce heat and simmer until about 1 tbsp (15 mL) of liquid remains. Remove from heat. Add egg yolks and boiling water and beat rapidly until mixture is creamy. Transfer to work bowl fitted with metal blade and pulse 2 or 3 times. With motor running, add butter, 1 tbsp (15 mL) at a time through the feed tube, ensuring each increment is integrated before adding the next. Add tarragon and process until chopped and integrated. Check seasoning and adjust.

Blue Cheese Peppercorn Dressing

**Makes 2 cups
(500 mL)**

Vegetarian Friendly

This rich and peppery
dressing with a hint of
blue cheese goes well
with all types of lettuces.

Tips

If all of the ingredients
are at room temperature
the dressing will be easier
to blend.

Dressing keeps, covered
and refrigerated, for up to
2 weeks.

4 oz	cream cheese, cubed and softened	125 g
4 oz	small curd cottage cheese	125 g
½ cup	sour cream	125 mL
¼ cup	Traditional Mayonnaise (page 437) or store-bought	60 mL
¼ cup	buttermilk	60 mL
1 tbsp	freshly squeezed lemon juice	15 mL
1½ tsp	loosely packed fresh dill	7 mL
1½ tsp	dried onion flakes	7 mL
1½ tsp	whole black peppercorns	7 mL
¼ tsp	garlic powder	1 mL
2 oz	blue cheese, crumbled	60 g

1. In work bowl fitted with metal blade, process cream cheese, cottage cheese, sour cream, mayonnaise, buttermilk and lemon juice until smooth, about 2 minutes. Add dill, onion flakes, peppercorns and garlic powder. Process until well-blended, about 15 seconds.

2. Pour dressing into a medium bowl. Stir in blue cheese until blended. Let dressing stand, covered, in the refrigerator for a few hours to allow the flavors to develop.

Variation

If you would like a lower-fat dressing use low-fat cream cheese and sour cream. You will not sacrifice any flavor whatsoever.

Avocado Tamarind Cashew Dressing

**Makes 2 cups
(500 mL)**

Vegetarian Friendly

Serve this dressing over a cabbage salad while enjoying an Asian meal.

Tips

Tamarind can be found in the international section of most large grocery stores. Use the same amount of paste or seeded pulp if dried is not available.

Dressing keeps in an airtight container in the refrigerator for up to 2 weeks.

1/4 cup	unsalted roasted cashews	60 mL
2/3 cup	packed fresh cilantro leaves	150 mL
2	cloves garlic	2
2	green onions, green parts only, cut in half	2
1/2 cup	liquid honey	125 mL
1 tbsp	granulated sugar	15 mL
1 tbsp	white wine vinegar	15 mL
1 tsp	freshly ground black pepper	5 mL
1 tsp	ground cumin	5 mL
1 tsp	balsamic vinegar	5 mL
1/2 tsp	dried tamarind powder (see Tips, left)	2 mL
1/2 cup	extra virgin olive oil	125 mL
1	avocado	1

1. In work bowl fitted with metal blade, pulse cashews, cilantro, garlic and green onions until mixture is in small pieces, about 12 times.

2. In a microwave-safe container, combine honey, sugar, vinegar, black pepper, cumin, balsamic vinegar and tamarind. Microwave, uncovered, on High until steaming, about 45 seconds.

3. With the motor running, slowly pour honey mixture through the feed tube. Then drizzle olive oil through the feed tube until it has been incorporated into the dressing. Transfer to a covered container and refrigerate for at least 30 minutes to allow the flavors to develop.

4. Peel avocado, slice into small chunks and place in a bowl. Shake dressing and pour over avocado.

Variation

Reduce the olive oil by half and use as a dipping sauce for Mini Chicken Puffs (page 99).

Raspberry Vinaigrette

Vegan Friendly

This dressing may seem
to be a lengthy process
but well worth the efforts
for the fresh flavor.

Tips

Make sure your berries
are free of blemishes and
soft spots.

Dressing keeps in bottle
or cruet in the refrigerator
for up to 3 weeks.

4 cups	loosely packed fresh raspberries	1 L
1¼ cups	white vinegar	300 mL
1½ cups	granulated sugar	375 mL
1 cup	vegetable oil	250 mL

1. Place raspberries in a jar and pour vinegar over top. Let stand in a cool dark place for 6 days, shaking once a day.

2. In work bowl fitted with metal blade, process raspberry mixture until smooth, about 2 minutes.

3. Strain mixture through a fine sieve into a saucepan over high heat. Add sugar and bring to a boil for 2 minutes. Let cool completely. Pour mixture back into work bowl fitted with metal blade. With the motor running, drizzle oil through the feed tube until it is incorporated. Pour dressing into a cruet or empty, cleaned salad dressing bottle.

Variation

Try blueberries or strawberries in place of the raspberries. Reduce sugar if your berries are sweet.

Creamy Herb Dressing

Vegetarian Friendly

Here's a thick dressing
with a light pink color
that goes well with
hearty lettuces, such as
romaine or iceberg.

Tip

Make sure you drain the
cottage cheese or you will
have a watery dressing.

1	red bell pepper, seeded and chopped	1
2 cups	nonfat cottage cheese, drained (see Tip, left)	500 mL
¼ cup	fresh basil leaves	60 mL
3	cloves garlic, coarsely chopped	3
1 tbsp	freshly squeezed lemon juice	15 mL
1 tbsp	chopped fresh chives	15 mL
½ tsp	salt	2 mL
¼ tsp	freshly ground black pepper	1 mL

1. In work bowl fitted with metal blade, process bell pepper, cottage cheese, basil, garlic, lemon juice, chives, salt and pepper until smooth.

Cucumber Dressing

Makes 1¼ cups (300 mL)

Vegan Friendly

Napa cabbage perfectly suits this dressing. Try this dressing as a dip with crackers.

1 cup	plain nonfat yogurt or vegan alternative	250 mL
½	cucumber, peeled, seeded and cut into chunks	½
1 tsp	freshly squeezed lemon juice	5 mL
1 tsp	fresh dill fronds	5 mL
1	clove garlic, coarsely chopped	1
½ tsp	salt	2 mL
½ tsp	ground white pepper	2 mL

1. In work bowl fitted with metal blade, process yogurt, cucumber, lemon juice, dill, garlic, salt and white pepper until smooth, about 1 minute.

Peppercorn Dressing

Makes ⅔ cup (150 mL)

Vegan Friendly

As well as a salad of fresh sliced vegetables, you can also use this dressing as a dipping sauce for crudités.

⅓ cup	Traditional Mayonnaise (page 437) or store-bought (vegan or regular)	75 mL
⅓ cup	plain yogurt or vegan alternative	75 mL
2 tbsp	white wine vinegar	30 mL
1 tsp	whole black peppercorns	5 mL
½ tsp	dried parsley	2 mL
¼ tsp	dried tarragon	1 mL
¼ tsp	salt	1 mL
¼ tsp	freshly ground black pepper	1 mL
¼ tsp	granulated sugar	1 mL
⅛ tsp	garlic powder	0.5 mL

1. In work bowl fitted with metal blade, process mayonnaise, yogurt, vinegar, peppercorns, parsley, tarragon, salt, pepper, sugar and garlic powder until smooth, about 2 minutes. Refrigerate in a sealed container for 2 hours prior to use.

Zesty Tomato Onion Dressing

Makes ½ cup (125 mL)

Vegetarian Friendly

Hearty dishes such as pasta are complemented by this zesty dressing.

Tip

Dried tomato powder is made of the sweetest red tomatoes, dried and ground into a fine powder. It adds a nice fresh tomato flavor without adding moisture to the dressing.

4 oz	cream cheese, cubed and softened	125 g
2 tbsp	Traditional Mayonnaise (page 437) or store-bought	30 mL
2	cloves garlic, minced	2
1 tbsp	dried onion flakes	15 mL
2 tsp	Spicy Chili Sauce (page 446) or store-bought	10 mL
1 tsp	salt	5 mL
1 tsp	dried tomato powder (see Tip, left)	5 mL
½ tsp	Hungarian paprika	2 mL
¼ tsp	freshly ground black pepper	1 mL

1. In work bowl fitted with metal blade, process cream cheese, mayonnaise, garlic, onion flakes, chili sauce, salt, tomato powder, paprika and pepper until smooth, about 2 minutes.

Thousand Island Dressing

Makes 1¾ cups (425 mL)

This is the "secret sauce" that's found on fast food hamburgers or try it on a wedge of iceberg lettuce for a '60s diner feel.

1	hard-cooked egg (see Tips, page 385)	1
1 cup	Traditional Mayonnaise (page 437) or store-bought	250 mL
¼ cup	Bold Chili Sauce (page 447) or store-bought	60 mL
¼ cup	pimento-stuffed olives	60 mL
1	sweet pickle, cut in half	1
1½ tsp	dried onion flakes	7 mL
1½ tsp	freshly squeezed lemon juice	7 mL
1 tsp	dried parsley	5 mL
⅛ tsp	salt	0.5 mL
⅛ tsp	freshly ground black pepper	0.5 mL

1. In work bowl fitted with metal blade, pulse egg, mayonnaise, chili sauce, olives, pickle, onion flakes, lemon juice, parsley, salt and pepper until desired texture. For a chunky dressing, pulse about 10 times; for a smooth dressing, process about 1 minute. Refrigerate for at least 1 hour to allow the flavors to develop.

Tomato Basil Dressing

Makes ¾ cup (175 mL)

Use this dressing with grated cabbages and carrots. Include some nuts or croutons to add a little "crunch."

4 oz	cream cheese, cubed and softened	125 g
2 tbsp	Traditional Mayonnaise (page 437) or store-bought	30 mL
2	cloves garlic, coarsely chopped	2
2 tsp	Bold Chili Sauce (page 447) or store-bought	10 mL
1 tsp	salt	5 mL
1 tsp	dried tomato powder (see Tip, page 416)	5 mL
1 tsp	dried basil	5 mL
½ tsp	Hungarian paprika	2 mL
¼ tsp	freshly ground black pepper	1 mL

1. In work bowl fitted with metal blade, process cream cheese, mayonnaise, garlic, chili sauce, salt, tomato powder, basil, paprika and pepper until smooth, about 2 minutes.

Roasted Garlic Dressing

Makes ¾ cup (175 mL)

Vegetarian Friendly

This dressing is perfect for garlic lovers. Try it with European blends of lettuces such as radicchio or leaf lettuce.

Tip

To roast garlic: Preheat oven to 400°F (200°C). Cut about ¼ inch (0.5 cm) off top of bulb and drizzle with 1 tsp (5 mL) olive oil. Wrap in foil and roast until golden brown and very soft, 30 to 35 minutes. Let cool, turn upside down and press cloves out of bulb.

4 oz	cream cheese, cubed and softened	125 g
¼ cup	Traditional Mayonnaise (page 437) or store-bought	60 mL
8	cloves garlic, roasted (see Tip, left)	8
½ tsp	Hungarian paprika	2 mL
½ tsp	salt	2 mL
¼ tsp	hot pepper flakes	1 mL

1. In work bowl fitted with metal blade, process cream cheese, mayonnaise, garlic, paprika, salt and hot pepper flakes until smooth, about 2 minutes.

Roasted Honey Garlic Dressing

Makes 1 cup (250 mL)

Vegetarian Friendly

As well as on salads this rich creamy dressing also can double as a dip for vegetable sticks.

4 oz	cream cheese, cubed and softened	125 g
¼ cup	sour cream	60 mL
¼ cup	buttermilk	60 mL
8	cloves garlic, roasted (see Tip, page 417)	8
2 tsp	liquid honey	10 mL
1 tsp	dried onion flakes	5 mL
½ tsp	salt	2 mL
¼ tsp	hot pepper flakes	1 mL

1. In work bowl fitted with metal blade, process cream cheese, sour cream, buttermilk, garlic, honey, onion flakes, salt and hot pepper flakes until smooth, about 2 minutes.

Oahu Dressing

Makes about 1½ cups (375 mL)

Vegetarian Friendly

Here is a dressing that is popular served in cafés around Oahu, Hawaii. It goes well with different shredded cabbages.

4 oz	cream cheese, cubed and softened	125 g
½ cup	plain yogurt	125 mL
2 tbsp	unsweetened pineapple juice	30 mL
2 tbsp	liquid honey	30 mL
½ cup	macadamia nuts, toasted and chopped (see Tip, page 380)	125 mL
¼ cup	flaked sweetened coconut	60 mL

1. In work bowl fitted with metal blade, process cream cheese, yogurt, pineapple juice and honey until smooth, about 2 minutes. Transfer to a bowl and fold in macadamia nuts and coconut.

Pecan Pesto Dressing

Makes 1¾ cups (425 mL)

Vegetarian Friendly

Basil and pecans come together to make a very flavorful dressing. Try using hearty lettuces such as romaine or iceberg.

½ cup	packed fresh basil leaves	125 mL
2 tbsp	extra virgin olive oil	30 mL
4 oz	cream cheese, cubed and softened	125 g
½ cup	buttermilk	125 mL
¼ cup	Traditional Mayonnaise (page 437) or store-bought	60 mL
1 tsp	dried onion flakes	5 mL
½ tsp	garlic salt	2 mL
¼ cup	pecans, toasted and finely chopped (see Tip, page 376)	60 mL

1. In work bowl fitted with metal blade, pulse basil and oil about 10 times. Add cream cheese, buttermilk, mayonnaise, onion flakes and garlic salt and process until smooth, about 2 minutes. Transfer to a bowl and fold in pecans.

Louisiana French Dressing

Makes 2 cups (500 mL)

Louisiana has strong French roots, as you can taste in the flavors of many of its recipes, including this one. This dressing goes well with any salad mix that is in season.

1 cup	Traditional Mayonnaise (page 437) or store-bought	250 mL
¾ cup	extra virgin olive oil	175 mL
¼ cup	freshly squeezed lemon juice	60 mL
2	cloves garlic, coarsely chopped	2
2 tsp	Bold Chili Sauce (page 447) or store-bought	10 mL
1 tsp	salt	5 mL
1 tsp	Hungarian paprika	5 mL
½ tsp	dry mustard	2 mL
½ tsp	cayenne pepper	2 mL
¼ tsp	freshly ground black pepper	1 mL

1. In work bowl fitted with metal blade, process mayonnaise, oil, lemon juice, garlic, chili sauce, salt, paprika, mustard, cayenne and black pepper until smooth, about 2 minutes.

Maple Balsamic Dressing

Makes 1 cup (250 mL)

Vegan Friendly

Maple syrup makes a wonderful natural sweetener for salad dressings. Soft blends of lettuce, such as red and oak leaf and arugula, are great with this dressing.

4 oz	cream cheese or vegan alternative, cubed and softened	125 mL
1/4 cup	balsamic vinegar	60 mL
1/4 cup	light olive oil	60 mL
2 tbsp	pure maple syrup	30 mL
1 tbsp	dried basil	15 mL
1 tsp	dried rosemary	5 mL

1. In work bowl fitted with metal blade, process cream cheese, vinegar, oil, maple syrup, basil and rosemary until smooth, about 2 minutes.

Marriott's Creamy Peppercorn Dressing

Makes 4 cups (1 L)

Vegetarian Friendly

This recipe comes from the Chef of the Anaheim Marriott Hotel in California. They now purchase a dressing, but you can make this one just like the original. Try it on mixed salad greens with plenty of vegetables.

Tip

To make onion juice: In a food processor fitted with metal blade, process 1 sweet onion until puréed, about 2 minutes. Press the juice through a fine-mesh strainer, discarding solids.

4 cups	Traditional Mayonnaise (page 437) or store-bought	1 L
1/4 cup	onion juice (see Tip, left)	60 mL
1 1/2 tbsp	apple cider vinegar	22 mL
1 1/2 tbsp	whole black peppercorns	22 mL
1 1/2 tsp	Worcestershire sauce, optional	7 mL
1 1/2 tsp	freshly squeezed lemon juice	7 mL
1 tsp	hot pepper sauce	5 mL
1	clove garlic, coarsely chopped	1
1/3 cup	freshly grated Parmesan cheese	75 mL

1. In work bowl fitted with metal blade, process mayonnaise, onion juice, vinegar, peppercorns, Worcestershire sauce, if using, lemon juice, hot pepper sauce and garlic until peppercorns are ground, for 45 seconds. Transfer to a bowl and fold in Parmesan. Dressing keeps well, covered and refrigerated, for up to 3 weeks.

Variation
Add 4 oz (125 g) crumbled blue cheese when you add the Parmesan.

Crushed Pecan Blue Cheese Dressing

**Makes about
2 cups (500 mL)**

Vegetarian Friendly

Pecans are the perfect
nuts to go with the blue
cheese in this dressing.
A blend of lettuces, such
as romaine, iceberg,
radicchio, endive and
leaf lettuce, are great
with this dressing.

4 oz	cream cheese, cubed and softened	125 g
1/2 cup	buttermilk	125 mL
1/4 cup	Traditional Mayonnaise (page 437) or store-bought	60 mL
1/4 cup	small-curd cottage cheese	60 mL
1 tsp	dried onion flakes	5 mL
1/2 tsp	garlic salt	2 mL
1/2 tsp	hot pepper sauce	2 mL
2 oz	blue cheese, crumbled	60 g
1/4 cup	pecans, toasted and crushed (see Tip, page 376)	60 mL

1. In work bowl fitted with metal blade, process cream cheese, buttermilk, mayonnaise, cottage cheese, onion flakes, garlic salt and hot pepper sauce until smooth, about 2 minutes. Transfer to a bowl and fold in blue cheese and pecans.

Cucumber Garlic Creamy Dressing

**Makes 2 cups
(500 mL)**

Vegan Friendly

Use this creamy
dressing as a dip for
radishes or any other
root vegetables, as well
as salads.

1	cucumber, peeled, seeded and cut into 4 pieces	1
4 oz	cream cheese or vegan alternative, cubed and softened	125 g
1/2 cup	oil	125 mL
1/2 cup	red wine vinegar	125 mL
1/3 cup	Easy Ketchup (page 442), Homemade Ketchup (page 443) or store-bought	75 mL
1/3 cup	granulated sugar	75 mL
2	cloves garlic, coarsely chopped	2
1 tsp	salt	5 mL
1/2 tsp	dried onion flakes	2 mL
1/4 tsp	celery seeds	1 mL
1/8 tsp	Hungarian paprika	0.5 mL

1. In work bowl fitted with metal blade, process cucumber and cream cheese until smooth, about 2 minutes.

2. Add oil, vinegar, ketchup, sugar, garlic, salt, onion flakes, celery seeds and paprika and process until smooth, about 45 seconds.

Feta Cheese Dressing

**Makes 1½ cups
(375 mL)**

Vegetarian Friendly

This fast and easy
dressing has a zip of
feta. Try it as a twist on
a Greek salad or with
sliced cucumbers.

4 oz	cream cheese, cubed and softened	125 g
¼ cup	balsamic vinegar	60 mL
¼ cup	light olive oil	60 mL
2 tsp	Dijon mustard	10 mL
1 tsp	dried rosemary	5 mL
4 oz	feta cheese, crumbled	125 g

1. In work bowl fitted with metal blade, process cream
cheese, vinegar, oil, mustard and rosemary until smooth,
about 2 minutes. Transfer to a bowl and fold in
feta cheese.

French Honey Dressing

**Makes about
1¾ cups (425 mL)**

Lavender makes this
dressing très French.
Use it with soft blends
of lettuce, such as red
leaf lettuce, arugula
and watercress.

¾ cup	extra virgin olive oil	175 mL
4 oz	cream cheese, cubed and softened	125 g
¼ cup	freshly squeezed lemon juice	60 mL
2 tbsp	Traditional Mayonnaise (page 437) or store-bought	30 mL
2 tbsp	liquid honey	30 mL
2	cloves garlic, coarsely chopped	2
2 tsp	Bold Chili Sauce (page 447) or store-bought	10 mL
1 tsp	salt	5 mL
½ tsp	dry mustard	2 mL
½ tsp	Hungarian paprika	2 mL
¼ tsp	freshly ground black pepper	1 mL
¼ tsp	dried lavender	1 mL
⅛ tsp	cayenne pepper	0.5 mL

1. In work bowl fitted with metal blade, process oil, cream
cheese, lemon juice, mayonnaise, honey, garlic, chili sauce,
salt, mustard, paprika, black pepper, lavender and cayenne
until smooth, about 2 minutes.

Lime Cilantro Cream Dressing

Makes 1¼ cups (300 mL)

Vegetarian Friendly

This zippy lime dressing has a touch of cilantro. Use it with spice dishes and soft blends of lettuce, such as arugula, oak leaf or butter lettuce.

4 oz	cream cheese, cubed and softened	125 g
¼ cup	buttermilk	60 mL
¼ cup	Traditional Mayonnaise (page 437) or store-bought	60 mL
¼ cup	plain yogurt	60 mL
½ tsp	grated lime zest	2 mL
¼ cup	freshly squeezed lime juice	60 mL
1 tsp	dried cilantro	5 mL
½ tsp	dried onion flakes	2 mL

1. In work bowl fitted with metal blade, process cream cheese, buttermilk, mayonnaise, yogurt, lime zest and juice, cilantro and onion flakes until smooth, about 2 minutes.

Creamy Dill Dressing

Makes 1 cup (250 mL)

Vegetarian Friendly

Try this dressing on fried fish pieces or sliced cucumbers.

4 oz	cream cheese, cubed and softened	125 g
¼ cup	small-curd cottage cheese	60 mL
¼ cup	buttermilk	60 mL
1 tsp	fresh dill fronds	5 mL
½ tsp	dried onion flakes	2 mL
¼ tsp	freshly ground black pepper	1 mL
¼ tsp	salt	1 mL

1. In work bowl fitted with metal blade, process cream cheese, cottage cheese, buttermilk, dill, onion flakes, pepper and salt until smooth, about 2 minutes.

Creamy Ginger Spice Dressing

Makes 1½ cups (375 mL)

Vegetarian Friendly

Fresh ginger heightens the flavor of this dressing. Try it on napa cabbage the next time you're having an Asian-themed dinner.

8 oz	cream cheese, cubed and softened	250 g
¼ cup	buttermilk	60 mL
¼ cup	small-curd cottage cheese	60 mL
1 tbsp	freshly grated gingerroot	15 mL
½ tsp	tandoori seasoning	2 mL
¼ tsp	salt	1 mL

1. In work bowl fitted with metal blade, process cream cheese, buttermilk, cottage cheese, ginger, tandoori seasoning and salt until smooth, about 2 minutes.

Creamy Poppy Seed Dressing

Makes 1 cup (250 mL)

Vegetarian Friendly

This is a hearty dressing to keep on hand. Use it with bold greens such as radicchio, arugula, endive, even a smattering of sorrel. Spinach works well, too.

Tip
Valued for their color and sweetness, blue poppy seeds aren't always available in stores. If you can't find them, check out online retailers or use regular poppy seeds.

4 oz	cream cheese, cubed and softened	125 g
¼ cup	Traditional Mayonnaise (page 437) or store-bought	60 mL
3 tbsp	white wine vinegar	45 mL
2 tbsp	peanut oil	30 mL
2 tbsp	liquid honey	30 mL
1 tbsp	blue poppy seeds (see Tip, left)	15 mL

1. In work bowl fitted with metal blade, process cream cheese, mayonnaise, vinegar, peanut oil, honey and poppy seeds until smooth, about 2 minutes.

Creamy Two-Cheese Italian Dressing

**Makes 1¼ cups
(300 mL)**

Vegetarian Friendly

This dressing blends two
of our favorite Italian
cheeses — Parmesan
and Romano. Try it with
greens such as iceberg
and romaine.

4 oz	cream cheese, cubed and softened	125 g
¼ cup	Traditional Mayonnaise (page 437) or store-bought	60 mL
1 tbsp	balsamic vinegar	15 mL
1 tbsp	light olive oil	15 mL
1 tbsp	dried basil	15 mL
2 tsp	Dijon mustard	10 mL
1 tsp	dried rosemary	5 mL
¼ cup	freshly grated Parmesan cheese	60 mL
¼ cup	freshly grated Romano cheese	60 mL

1. In work bowl fitted with metal blade, process cream
cheese, mayonnaise, vinegar, oil, basil, mustard and
rosemary until smooth, about 2 minutes. Transfer to a
bowl and fold in Parmesan and Romano cheeses.

Creamy Roma Dressing

**Makes 1½ cups
(375 mL)**

Vegetarian Friendly

Here's a dressing that's
light red with a burst
of flavor. It's great with
greens such as radicchio
and romaine.

4 oz	cream cheese, cubed and softened	125 g
½ cup	Traditional Mayonnaise (page 437) or store-bought	125 mL
¼ cup	buttermilk	60 mL
1 tbsp	freshly squeezed lemon juice	15 mL
½ tsp	hot pepper flakes	2 mL
½ tsp	dried onion flakes	2 mL
¼ cup	diced, seeded Roma (plum) tomatoes	60 mL

1. In work bowl fitted with metal blade, process cream
cheese, mayonnaise, buttermilk, lemon juice, hot pepper
flakes and onion flakes until smooth, about 2 minutes.
Transfer to a bowl and fold in tomatoes.

Creamy Zesty Chipotle Dressing

Makes 1 cup (250 mL)

Vegetarian Friendly

Be forewarned — this is a red-hot dressing. We like to use it for a bold flavor on light leaf blends of lettuce, such as red leaf, arugula and butter lettuce.

4 oz	cream cheese, cubed and softened	125 g
½ cup	Traditional Mayonnaise (page 437) or store-bought	125 mL
¼ cup	plain yogurt	60 mL
½ tsp	hot pepper flakes	2 mL
½ tsp	dried onion flakes	2 mL
2	chipotle peppers in adobo sauce, drained	2
⅛ tsp	salt	0.5 mL
⅛ tsp	freshly ground black pepper	0.5 mL

1. In work bowl fitted with metal blade, process cream cheese, mayonnaise, yogurt, hot pepper flakes, onion flakes, chipotle peppers, salt and black pepper until smooth, about 2 minutes.

Cajun Spice Dressing

Makes 1 cup (250 mL)

Vegetarian Friendly

When you travel to New Orleans, you'll find every restaurant has their version of a Cajun spice dressing. Try dipping boiled crawfish in it or use it as a dressing for a blend of lettuces, such as romaine or iceberg.

4 oz	cream cheese, cubed and softened	125 g
½ cup	Traditional Mayonnaise (page 437) or store-bought	125 mL
¼ cup	buttermilk	60 mL
½ tsp	hot pepper flakes	2 mL
½ tsp	dried onion flakes	2 mL
½ tsp	paprika	2 mL
½ tsp	garlic salt	2 mL
¼ tsp	caraway seeds	1 mL
3	drops hot pepper sauce	3

1. In work bowl fitted with metal blade, process cream cheese, mayonnaise, buttermilk, hot pepper flakes, onion flakes, paprika, garlic salt, caraway seeds and hot pepper sauce until smooth, about 2 minutes.

Celery Seed Dressing

**Makes 2 cups
(500 mL)**

Vegan Friendly

Try this dressing as a
sauce for crab cakes or
roasted eggplant. It's
also good for any salad.

4 oz	cream cheese or vegan alternative, cubed and softened	125 g
½ cup	oil	125 mL
⅓ cup	Easy Ketchup (page 442), Homemade Ketchup (page 443) or store-bought	75 mL
¼ cup	white wine vinegar	60 mL
¼ cup	granulated sugar	60 mL
1 tsp	salt	5 mL
½ tsp	dried onion flakes	2 mL
¼ tsp	celery seeds	1 mL
⅛ tsp	paprika	0.5 mL

1. In work bowl fitted with metal blade, process cream cheese, oil, ketchup, vinegar, sugar, salt, onion flakes, celery seeds and paprika until smooth, about 2 minutes.

Cracked Black Peppercorn Dressing

**Makes 1½ cups
(375 mL)**

Vegetarian Friendly

This peppery dressing
livens up a salad
with lettuces such as
radicchio and romaine.

4 oz	cream cheese, cubed and softened	125 g
½ cup	buttermilk	125 mL
½ cup	Traditional Mayonnaise (page 437) or store-bought	125 mL
1 tsp	whole black peppercorns	5 mL
1 tsp	salt	5 mL
1 tsp	freshly squeezed lemon juice	5 mL
½ tsp	Hungarian paprika	2 mL

1. In work bowl fitted with metal blade, process cream cheese, buttermilk, mayonnaise, black peppercorns, salt, lemon juice and paprika until smooth, about 2 minutes.

Cracked Peppercorn and Parmesan Dressing

Makes 1½ cups (375 mL)

Szechwan peppercorns add a punch to this dressing. Use on any salad or drizzle on fresh fish, such as cod.

Tip
You can replace the Szechwan peppercorns with whole black peppercorns.

4 oz	cream cheese, cubed and softened	125 g
¼ cup	buttermilk	60 mL
¼ cup	Bold Chili Sauce (page 447) or store-bought	60 mL
¼ cup	Traditional Mayonnaise (page 437) or store-bought	60 mL
1 tsp	Szechwan peppercorns	5 mL
½ tsp	dried onion flakes	2 mL
¼ cup	freshly grated Parmesan cheese	60 mL

1. In work bowl fitted with metal blade, process cream cheese, buttermilk, chili sauce, mayonnaise, peppercorns and onion flakes until smooth, about 2 minutes. Transfer to a bowl and fold in Parmesan cheese.

Creamy Asiago Dressing

Makes 1 cup (250 mL)

Vegetarian Friendly

Asiago cheese is an Italian cheese with a flavor that's similar to Cheddar and Romano combined. Use on a salad packed with crunchy vegetables, such as radishes and beets.

3 oz	cream cheese, cubed and softened	90 g
½ cup	Traditional Mayonnaise (page 437) or store-bought	125 mL
¼ cup	half-and-half (10%) cream	60 mL
1 tbsp	Easy Ketchup (page 442), Homemade Ketchup (page 443) or store-bought	15 mL
½ tsp	dried dill	2 mL
½ tsp	garlic powder	2 mL
½ cup	shredded Asiago cheese	125 mL

1. In work bowl fitted with metal blade, process cream cheese, mayonnaise, cream, ketchup, dill and garlic powder until smooth, about 2 minutes. Transfer to a bowl and fold in Asiago cheese.

Creamy California Dressing

Makes 1 cup (250 mL)

Vegetarian Friendly

This dressing was developed using the Hass variety of avocado that was first cultivated in Southern California. It's good for crisp lettuces such as iceberg, radicchio and romaine.

3 oz	cream cheese, cubed and softened	90 g
½ cup	Traditional Mayonnaise (page 437) or store-bought	125 mL
½	ripe avocado	½
2 tsp	olive oil	10 mL
1 tsp	salt	5 mL
½ tsp	hot pepper flakes	2 mL

1. In work bowl fitted with metal blade, process cream cheese, mayonnaise, avocado, oil, salt and hot pepper flakes until smooth, about 2 minutes.

Avocado Chipotle Dressing

Makes 1½ cups (375 mL)

Vegetarian Friendly

This hot, spicy dressing is a good match for a Mexican dinner, and is perfect on a taco salad.

Tip

Make sure your avocado is ripe for the best flavor and texture.

4 oz	cream cheese, cubed and softened	125 g
½ cup	buttermilk	125 mL
½ cup	Traditional Mayonnaise (page 437) or store-bought	125 mL
1	avocado (see Tip, left)	1
2 tsp	fresh dill fronds	10 mL
1 tsp	freshly squeezed lemon juice	5 mL
2	chipotle peppers in adobo sauce, drained	2

1. In work bowl fitted with metal blade, process cream cheese, buttermilk, mayonnaise, avocado, dill, lemon juice and chipotle peppers until smooth, about 45 seconds.

Avocado Dressing

**Makes about
2 cups (500 mL)**

Vegetarian Friendly

Here's a dressing with a light green color that's perfect for St. Patrick's Day. Use it on any salad or as a dip for carrot and celery sticks.

4 oz	cream cheese, cubed and softened	125 g
½ cup	buttermilk	125 mL
½ cup	Traditional Mayonnaise (page 437) or store-bought	125 mL
1	ripe avocado	1
2 tsp	chopped fresh dill fronds	10 mL
1 tsp	freshly squeezed lemon juice	5 mL

1. In work bowl fitted with metal blade, process cream cheese, buttermilk, mayonnaise, avocado, dill and lemon juice until smooth, about 2 minutes.

Baja Dressing

**Makes 1½ cups
(375 mL)**

Vegetarian Friendly

Use this spicy, zippy dressing on salad or as a dip for celery and carrot sticks.

4 oz	cream cheese, cubed and softened	125 g
½ cup	buttermilk	125 mL
½ cup	Traditional Mayonnaise (page 437) or store-bought	125 mL
1 tsp	freshly ground black pepper	5 mL
1 tsp	taco seasoning	5 mL
1	chipotle pepper in adobo sauce, drained	1
1 tsp	freshly squeezed lemon juice	5 mL

1. In work bowl fitted with metal blade, process cream cheese, buttermilk, mayonnaise, black pepper, taco seasoning, chipotle pepper and lemon juice until smooth, about 2 minutes.

Blue Cheese Dressing

**Makes 1½ cups
(375 mL)**

Vegetarian Friendly

Here's a rich and fresh creamy dressing with chunks of blue cheese. Try it on a wedge of iceberg lettuce with a sprinkling of bacon bits.

½ cup	plain yogurt	125 mL
½ cup	buttermilk	125 mL
¼ cup	Traditional Mayonnaise (page 437) or store-bought	60 mL
¼ cup	sour cream	60 mL
1 tsp	dried onion flakes	5 mL
½ tsp	garlic salt	2 mL
2 oz	blue cheese, crumbled	60 g

1. In work bowl fitted with metal blade, process yogurt, buttermilk, mayonnaise, sour cream, onion flakes and garlic salt until smooth, about 2 minutes. Transfer to a small bowl and fold in blue cheese.

Buffalo Blue Cheese Dressing

**Makes 1½ cups
(375 mL)**

Vegetarian Friendly

As well as a classic salad dressing, this is a dandy dipping sauce for Buffalo wings.

4 oz	cream cheese, cubed and softened	125 g
½ cup	buttermilk	125 mL
¼ cup	Traditional Mayonnaise (page 437) or store-bought	60 mL
1 tsp	dried onion flakes	5 mL
½ tsp	garlic salt	2 mL
½ tsp	hot pepper sauce	2 mL
¼ tsp	hot pepper flakes	1 mL
2 oz	blue cheese, crumbled	60 g

1. In work bowl fitted with metal blade, process cream cheese, buttermilk, mayonnaise, onion flakes, garlic salt, hot pepper sauce and hot pepper flakes until smooth, about 2 minutes. Transfer to a small bowl and fold in blue cheese.

English Stilton Dressing

Vegetarian Friendly

A rich cream-based dressing laced with blue cheese, this can be used with iceberg or any other firm lettuce, such as romaine.

4 oz	cream cheese, cubed and softened	125 g
4 oz	small-curd cottage cheese	125 g
½ cup	sour cream	125 mL
¼ cup	Traditional Mayonnaise (page 437) or store-bought	60 mL
1 tbsp	freshly squeezed lemon juice	15 mL
1½ tsp	fresh dill fronds	7 mL
½ tsp	dried onion flakes	2 mL
½ tsp	whole black peppercorns	2 mL
¼ tsp	garlic powder	1 mL
2 oz	Stilton blue cheese, crumbled	60 g

1. In work bowl fitted with metal blade, process cream cheese, cottage cheese, sour cream, mayonnaise, lemon juice, dill, onion flakes, peppercorns and garlic powder until smooth, for 45 seconds. Place in a bowl. Fold in crumbled blue cheese.

Red Pepper Salad Dressing

Makes 2 cups (500 mL)

Vegetarian Friendly

Roasting the red peppers brings out the sugars in the peppers and sweetens the salad dressing naturally. Try using this as a spread on turkey or tofu burgers to liven them up.

- Mini-bowl attachment

4 oz	cream cheese, cubed and softened	125 g
1	roasted red pepper (see Tip, page 406)	1
½ cup	buttermilk	125 mL
½ cup	Traditional Mayonnaise (page 437) or store-bought	125 mL
¼ cup	pickle relish	60 mL
1 tsp	freshly ground black pepper	5 mL
1 tsp	salt	5 mL
1 tsp	dried onion flakes	5 mL

1. In mini bowl fitted with metal blade, process cream cheese, roasted red pepper, buttermilk, mayonnaise, pickle relish, black pepper, salt and onion flakes until smooth, about 2 minutes.

Sweet Caramelized Onion Salad Dressing

Makes 2 cups (500 mL)

Vegetarian Friendly

Roasted garlic and caramelized onions make up this powerful flavor-packed dressing. Use with a hearty lettuce, such as romaine, or cabbage for a picnic.

½	large onion, cut into quarters	½
1 tbsp	butter	15 mL
1 tsp	granulated sugar	5 mL
4	cloves garlic, roasted (see Tips, page 417)	4
4 oz	cream cheese, cubed and softened	125 g
½ cup	sour cream	125 mL
1 tsp	onion powder	5 mL
1 tsp	freshly ground black pepper	5 mL

1. In work bowl fitted with slicing blade, slice onion. Transfer to a bowl. Set aside.

2. In a saucepan, melt butter and sugar over medium heat, stirring until smooth. Add onion and cook, stirring occasionally, until tender and just beginning to brown and caramelize, 8 to 10 minutes. Set aside and let cool to room temperature.

3. Replace slicing blade with metal blade and process onion, garlic, cream cheese, sour cream, onion powder and pepper until smooth, for 2 minutes.

Plum Sauce

Makes 2 cups (500 mL)

Vegan Friendly

Try making your own plum sauce for your next take-out Chinese food.

Tips

Use reduced-sodium soy sauce because the regular kind is too salty.

Sauce keeps well, tightly covered, and refrigerated, for up to 2 weeks.

12 oz	ripe plums, chopped	375 g
¼ cup	minced onion	60 mL
¼ cup	lightly packed brown sugar	60 mL
2 tsp	teriyaki sauce	10 mL
2 tsp	reduced-sodium soy sauce (see Tips, left)	10 mL
1	clove garlic, minced	1
1 tsp	minced gingerroot	5 mL
1 tsp	sesame oil	5 mL
1 tsp	freshly squeezed lemon juice	5 mL
¼ tsp	hot pepper flakes	1 mL
1 tsp	cornstarch	5 mL

1. In a large pot, combine plums, ½ cup (125 mL) water, onion, brown sugar, teriyaki sauce, soy sauce, garlic, ginger, sesame oil, lemon juice and hot pepper flakes and bring to a boil over medium heat. Reduce heat and simmer, stirring often, for 30 minutes.

2. In a small bowl, combine cornstarch and 1 tsp (5 mL) water. Set aside.

3. In work bowl fitted with metal blade, process cooked plum mixture. Add cornstarch mixture and process for 20 seconds.

4. Return to pot and simmer over low heat, stirring, until thickened, about 4 minutes. Serve warm or let cool completely before refrigerating.

Steak Sauce

Makes 2 cups (500 mL)

Bottled steak sauce is full of sugar. Cut down on the sugar and create a sauce that will make your steaks burst with flavor.

Tip

Sauce keeps well, covered and refrigerated, for up to 1 week.

1 cup	Easy Ketchup (page 442), Homemade Ketchup (page 443) or store-bought	250 mL
1	onion, coarsely chopped	1
6	cloves garlic, coarsely chopped	6
1/4 cup	Worcestershire sauce	60 mL
1/4 cup	freshly squeezed lemon juice	60 mL
1/4 cup	white wine vinegar	60 mL
1/4 cup	chopped shallots	60 mL
3 tbsp	lightly packed brown sugar	45 mL
2 tbsp	reduced-sodium soy sauce	30 mL
1 tsp	dry mustard	5 mL
1/2 tsp	dried onion powder	2 mL
1/4 tsp	ground cloves	1 mL
1/4 tsp	ground cinnamon	1 mL

1. In work bowl with metal blade, process ketchup, onion, garlic, 1/4 cup (60 mL) water, Worcestershire sauce, lemon juice, vinegar, shallots, brown sugar, soy sauce, mustard, onion powder, cloves and cinnamon until smooth. Transfer mixture to a medium saucepan over medium heat and bring to a boil. Reduce heat and simmer, stirring occasionally, until thickened, for 20 minutes. Let cool.

Basic Aïoli

Makes 1 cup (250 mL)

Vegetarian Friendly

Aïoli sauces, a kind of mayonnaise, are used most often with fish and seafood dishes to add richness, flavor and spice. The sauce is also great with french fries, green beans or spooned into soups.

Tip

Aïoli keeps well, covered and refrigerated, for up to 3 days.

6	cloves garlic	6
1	egg or ¼ cup (60 mL) pasteurized eggs (liquid or in the shell) (see Tips, page 437)	1
1 cup	extra virgin olive oil, divided	250 mL
1 tbsp	freshly squeezed lemon juice	15 mL
⅛ tsp	salt	0.5 mL
⅛ tsp	freshly ground white pepper	0.5 mL

1. In work bowl fitted with metal blade with motor running, add garlic cloves through feed tube and process until minced. Add egg, ½ cup (125 mL) of the oil, lemon juice, salt and pepper.

2. With the motor running, slowly drizzle remaining oil through the small hole in the feed tube until it has been incorporated into aïoli, about 2 minutes. Use right away or refrigerate.

Citrus Aïoli

Makes 1 cup (250 mL)

Vegetarian Friendly

This aïoli is great spooned over freshly grilled fish and other seafood, french fries, new potatoes and broccoli.

Tip

Aïoli keeps well, covered and refrigerated, for up to 3 days.

6	cloves garlic	6
2	egg yolks, at room temperature, or ¼ cup (60 mL) pasteurized eggs (liquid or in the shell) (see Tips, page 437)	2
1 cup	extra virgin olive oil, divided	250 mL
1 tbsp	freshly squeezed lemon juice	15 mL
½ tsp	grated lime zest	2 mL
1 tsp	freshly squeezed lime juice	5 mL
⅛ tsp	salt	0.5 mL
⅛ tsp	freshly ground white pepper	0.5 mL

1. In work bowl fitted with metal blade with motor running, add garlic cloves through feed tube and process until minced. Add egg yolks, ½ cup (125 mL) of the oil, lemon juice, lime zest and juice, salt and white pepper.

2. With the motor running, slowly drizzle remaining oil through the small hole in the feed tube until it has been incorporated into aïoli, about 2 minutes. Use right away or refrigerate.

Traditional Mayonnaise

Makes 1 cup (250 mL)

Vegetarian Friendly

You can walk down the condiment aisle at the grocery store and see many brands and varieties, in jar after jar. We can't even pronounce many of the ingredients in these jars, let alone understand how they can last for months — or years — in the refrigerator. When you make your own condiments you know exactly what's in each, and how long it will last. Once you make mayonnaise, you will never purchase it again.

Tips

This recipe contains raw egg yolks. If you are concerned about the safety of using raw eggs, use pasteurized eggs in the shell or pasteurized liquid whole eggs, instead.

Mayonnaise keeps well, covered and refrigerated, for up to 5 days. If using pasteurized eggs, it will keep for up to 2 weeks.

If egg yolks are not processed for the full 2 minutes they will not emulsify correctly when the oil is incorporated.

2	egg yolks, at room temperature, or ¼ cup (60 mL) pasteurized eggs (liquid or in the shell) (see Tips, left)	2
2 tbsp	white wine vinegar	30 mL
1 tsp	dry mustard	5 mL
1 tsp	salt	5 mL
1 tsp	granulated sugar	5 mL
½ tsp	ground white pepper	2 mL
1 cup	vegetable oil	250 mL

1. In work bowl fitted with metal blade, process egg yolks, vinegar, mustard, salt, sugar and pepper until smooth, for 2 minutes (see Tips, left). With the processor running, slowly drizzle oil through the small hole in the feed tube until it has been incorporated into the mayonnaise (see Tips, page 438).

2. When all the oil is drizzled into egg mixture, remove processor lid and, with a rubber spatula, scrape down the sides and bottom, which sometimes collect residue, as necessary to incorporate all of the mixture. Replace lid and process for about 15 seconds.

Variation
Try flavored oils in place of the plain vegetable oil to enhance your dishes.

Fresh Dill Mayonnaise

**Makes 1½ cups
(375 mL)**

Vegetarian Friendly

We love using this
spread on roasted
chicken or egg salad
sandwiches.

Tips

Mayonnaise keeps well,
covered and refrigerated,
for up to 5 days. If using
pasteurized eggs, it will
keep for up to 1 week.

We do not advise making
a double batch of this
mayonnaise unless you
use it within a week, since
the dill will turn dark
after that.

If your food processor
has a feed tube with the
drip feature (a small hole
in the bottom of the
tube), fill the tube with
oil and let it drizzle in,
refilling the tube with oil
as it drains until all of
the oil is incorporated.
Alternatively, pour a
thin, steady stream of oil
slowly into the feed tube.
Adding the oil too quickly
can cause the mayonnaise
to separate.

3	egg yolks, at room temperature, or ⅓ cup (75 mL) pasteurized eggs (liquid or in the shell) (see Tips, page 437)	3
3 tbsp	sherry vinegar	45 mL
2 tsp	mustard seeds	10 mL
2 tsp	salt	10 mL
1½ tsp	granulated sugar	7 mL
1 tsp	ground white pepper	5 mL
1 cup	peanut oil	250 mL
2 tbsp	loosely packed fresh dill fronds	30 mL

1. In work bowl fitted with metal blade, process egg yolks, vinegar, mustard seeds, salt, sugar and pepper until smooth, for 2 minutes (see Tips, page 439). With the motor running, slowly drizzle oil through the small hole in the feed tube until it has been incorporated into the mayonnaise (see Tips, left).

2. When all the oil is drizzled into egg mixture, remove processor lid and, with a rubber spatula, scrape down the sides and bottom, which sometimes collect residue, as necessary to incorporate all of the mixture. Add fresh dill. Replace lid and process for about 15 seconds.

Variation
Try the same amount of rosemary in place of the dill.

Chipotle Mayonnaise

Makes 1 cup (250 mL)

Vegetarian Friendly

A dollop of this tasty mayonnaise on the side of any meat or vegetable dish will enhance the flavor.

Tips

If egg yolks are not processed for the full 2 minutes they will not emulsify correctly when the oil is incorporated.

Mayonnaise keeps well, covered and refrigerated, for up to 5 days. If using pasteurized eggs, it will keep for up to 2 weeks.

If you have any of the adobo sauce left from the chiles you can fold it into the mayonnaise to make a great dip for chips.

2	egg yolks, at room temperature, or ¼ cup (60 mL) pasteurized eggs (liquid or in the shell) (see Tips, page 437)	2
2 tbsp	white wine vinegar	30 mL
1 tsp	dry mustard	5 mL
1 tsp	salt	5 mL
1 tsp	granulated sugar	5 mL
½ tsp	ground white pepper	2 mL
¼ tsp	freshly grated nutmeg	1 mL
¾ cup	vegetable oil	175 mL
2	chipotle peppers in adobo sauce, drained and seeded	2

1. In work bowl fitted with metal blade, process egg yolks, vinegar, mustard, salt, sugar, pepper and nutmeg until smooth, for 2 minutes (see Tips, left). With the motor running, slowly drizzle oil through the small hole in the feed tube until it has been incorporated into the mayonnaise (see Tips, page 438).

2. When all the oil is drizzled into egg mixture, remove processor lid and, with a rubber spatula, scrape down the sides and bottom, which sometimes collect residue, as necessary to incorporate all of the mixture. Add chipotle peppers. Replace lid and process for about 10 seconds.

Variation
You can add ⅛ tsp (0.5 mL) cayenne pepper for more heat.

Curry Tarragon Mayonnaise

Makes 1 cup (250 mL)

Vegetarian Friendly

When making chicken or potato salads, use this for added flavor instead of regular mayonnaise.

3	egg yolks, at room temperature, or ⅓ cup (75 mL) pasteurized eggs (liquid or in the shell) (see Tips, page 437)	3
2 tbsp	apple cider vinegar	30 mL
2 tbsp	fresh tarragon leaves	30 mL
1 tsp	hot dry mustard	5 mL
1 tsp	salt	5 mL
1 tsp	mild curry powder	5 mL
1 tsp	lightly packed brown sugar	5 mL
¾ cup	oil	175 mL

1. In work bowl fitted with metal blade, process egg yolks, vinegar, tarragon, mustard, salt, curry and brown sugar until smooth, for 2 minutes. With motor running, slowly drizzle oil through the feed tube until it has been incorporated, stopping and scraping down sides of the bowl once or twice.

Avocado Mayonnaise

Makes 1 cup (250 mL)

Vegan Friendly

Here's a no-egg mayonnaise that we also like to use as a spread.

1	ripe avocado, cut into quarters	1
2 tbsp	freshly squeezed lime juice	30 mL
2 tbsp	fresh cilantro	30 mL
¼ tsp	salt	1 mL
¼ tsp	freshly ground black pepper	1 mL
2 tbsp	extra virgin olive oil	30 mL

1. In work bowl fitted with metal blade, process avocado, lime juice, cilantro, salt and pepper until smooth.

2. With the motor running, slowly drizzle oil through the small hole in the feed tube until it has been incorporated into mayonnaise. Use within a few hours.

Cherry Tomato Tartar Sauce

Makes 1½ cups (375 mL)

Vegan Friendly

Usually plainly cooked fish begs for a dollop of tartar sauce, but sometimes we find ourselves longing for something a little different. Here it is. Like our original version (page 442) this one contains capers and chives, but there the similarity ends. An abundance of cherry tomatoes lightens it up, and if you like heat, you can add a bit of fresh chile. It's great with fish cakes as well as fish or with a vegetarian sandwich on herb-flavored focaccia.

Tip

Sauce keeps well, covered and refrigerated, for up to 5 days.

½ cup	Traditional Mayonnaise (page 437) or store-bought (vegan or regular)	125 mL
1 tbsp	Dijon mustard	15 mL
1 tbsp	drained capers	15 mL
1 tbsp	freshly squeezed lemon juice	15 mL
1	clove garlic, chopped	1
½	long red chile pepper, optional	½
1 cup	cherry or grape tomatoes	250 mL
2 tbsp	coarsely snipped chives	30 mL
	Salt and freshly ground black pepper	

1. In work bowl fitted with metal blade, process mayonnaise, mustard, capers, lemon juice, garlic, and chile pepper, if using, until smooth, about 30 seconds. Add tomatoes and chives and pulse until tomatoes are chopped, but still a bit chunky and mixture is well blended. Season with salt and pepper to taste.

Tartar Sauce

Makes 1¼ cups (300 mL)

Vegetarian Friendly

Kids love this sauce with fish sticks. Grown-ups love it with crab cakes, roasted turnips or even plain boiled potatoes.

Tip

Sauce keeps well, covered and refrigerated, for up to 2 weeks.

1 cup	Traditional Mayonnaise (page 437) or store-bought	250 mL
¼ cup	sour cream	60 mL
1	sweet pickle, cut into pieces	1
2 tbsp	drained capers	30 mL
1 tbsp	white wine vinegar	15 mL
1 tbsp	Italian flat-leaf parsley leaves	15 mL
5	fresh chives	5
2 tsp	fresh tarragon leaves	10 mL
	Salt and freshly ground black pepper	

1. In work bowl fitted with metal blade, process mayonnaise, sour cream, pickle, capers, vinegar, parsley, chives and tarragon until smooth, about 30 seconds. Season with salt and pepper to taste.

Easy Ketchup

Makes 2 cups (500 mL)

Vegan Friendly

Making your own ketchup may seem a bit over-the-top but it's worth it. It's easy to make, and the homemade version is so much more delicious than supermarket varieties, which are loaded with additives.

Tip

Ketchup keeps well, tightly covered and refrigerated, for up to 1 week.

1	can (28 oz/796 mL) crushed tomatoes	1
2 tbsp	extra virgin olive oil	30 mL
1	onion, chopped	1
1 tbsp	tomato paste	15 mL
⅔ cup	lightly packed brown sugar	150 mL
½ cup	apple cider vinegar	125 mL
½ tsp	salt	2 mL

1. In work bowl with metal blade, purée tomatoes.

2. In a heavy saucepan, heat oil over medium heat. Add onion and cook, stirring, until softened and translucent, about 8 minutes.

3. Add puréed tomatoes, tomato paste, brown sugar, vinegar and salt. Simmer, stirring occasionally, until very thick, about 1 hour. (Stir more frequently toward end of cooking to prevent scorching.)

4. Add ketchup to food processor in 2 batches (if you have a smaller food processor) and purée until smooth. Let cool.

Homemade Ketchup

Vegan Friendly

If you've never thought of making your own ketchup, you might when you read the ingredients on the label of a store-bought bottle. You won't even be able to pronounce half of them, so they must be preservatives and stabilizers.

Tips

When seeding the tomatoes, just core them, cut them in half crosswise and squeeze them like a sponge. The seeds extract fast this way.

Store ketchup in a covered container in the refrigerator for up to 2 months.

3	vine-ripened tomatoes (each about 6 oz/175 g), cored, cut in half and seeded (see Tips, left)	3
½	onion, quartered	½
½ cup	tomato paste	125 mL
½ cup	light corn syrup	125 mL
½ cup	apple cider vinegar	125 mL
1 tbsp	granulated sugar	15 mL
1 tsp	salt	5 mL
¼ tsp	onion powder	1 mL
⅛ tsp	garlic powder	0.5 mL

1. In work bowl fitted with metal blade, process tomatoes and onion until smooth, about 2 minutes.

2. Place mixture in a deep saucepan. Add tomato paste, corn syrup, vinegar, sugar, salt, onion powder and garlic powder. Bring to a boil over medium heat. Reduce heat and simmer, stirring occasionally, until thickened, for 20 minutes. Transfer to a bowl or container and let cool, uncovered, to room temperature.

Variation

Combine equal parts Homemade Ketchup and Traditional Mayonnaise (page 437) for a simple salad dressing.

Sweet Red Pepper Relish

**Makes 3 cups
(750 mL)**

Vegan Friendly

Top steak, burgers or
tofu burgers with this
relish for a sweet taste
that's much better than
bottled ketchup.

Tip

Relish keeps well, covered
and refrigerated, for up to
2 weeks.

4	red bell peppers, seeded and quartered	4
3	onions, chopped	3
1 tbsp	salt	15 mL
3 cups	granulated sugar	750 mL
2 cups	white wine vinegar	500 mL

1. In work bowl fitted with metal blade, process peppers, onions and salt until smooth, about 30 seconds.

2. Transfer to a medium saucepan over low heat. Add sugar and vinegar and bring to a boil. Reduce heat and simmer, stirring occasionally, until thickened, about 30 minutes. Let cool.

Pickle Sour Cream Sauce

**Makes 1½ cups
(375 mL)**

Vegetarian Friendly

You will find sauces
similar to this used on
top of white smoked fish
in Russian cuisine.

- Mini-bowl attachment

1 cup	sour cream	250 mL
4 oz	cream cheese, cubed and softened	125 g
2 tbsp	dill pickle juice	30 mL
1	large dill pickle, cut into quarters	1
1 tsp	dried onion flakes	5 mL

1. In mini bowl fitted with metal blade, process sour cream, cream cheese, pickle juice, dill pickle and onion flakes until smooth, about 2 minutes.

Smoked Chili Sauce

Makes about 2 cups (500 mL)

Vegan Friendly

This sauce is so versatile, you can use it as a barbecue sauce or in many of the recipes mentioned in this book.

Tips

Using two types of vinegars prevents a bitter aftertaste.

Sauce keeps well, covered and refrigerated, for up to 3 weeks.

1 cup	natural rice vinegar	250 mL
1 cup	apple cider vinegar	250 mL
2 tsp	ground cloves	10 mL
1 tsp	ground allspice	5 mL
1	onion, cut into quarters	1
10	cloves garlic, coarsely chopped	10
1 cup	lightly packed brown sugar	250 mL
1½ cups	Easy Ketchup (page 442) or store-bought	375 mL
1	can (7 oz/210 mL) chipotle peppers in adobo sauce, drained	1
2 tbsp	fresh cilantro leaves	30 mL
1 tbsp	Worcestershire sauce, optional	15 mL

1. In a deep saucepan over medium heat, combine rice vinegar, cider vinegar, cloves and allspice. Bring to a gentle boil. Set aside.

2. In work bowl fitted with metal blade, process onion, garlic, brown sugar, ketchup, chipotle peppers, cilantro and Worcestershire sauce, if using, until finely chopped, about 30 seconds. Add to vinegar mixture and bring to a gentle boil, stirring occasionally, over medium heat. Reduce heat and boil gently, stirring often, until thickened, about 1 hour. Let cool.

Variation
Omit the chipotle peppers for a basic chili sauce.

Spicy Chili Sauce

Makes 2 cups (500 mL)

Vegan Friendly

Here's a perfect condiment for a hamburger, portobello mushrooms or a beef sandwich.

Tip

Sauce keeps well, covered and refrigerated, for up to 1 week.

1	can (7 oz/210 mL) chipotle peppers in adobo sauce with liquid	1
1	onion, cut into wedges	1
12	cloves garlic, coarsely chopped	12
1 cup	lightly packed brown sugar	250 mL
2 cups	white wine vinegar	500 mL
1 cup	Easy Ketchup (page 442), Country Ketchup (pages 443) or store-bought	250 mL
1/4 cup	extra virgin olive oil	60 mL
1/4 cup	light (fancy) molasses	60 mL
1 tbsp	Worcestershire sauce, optional	15 mL
2 tsp	ground cloves	10 mL
2 tsp	ground coriander	10 mL
1 tsp	ground cinnamon	5 mL
1 tsp	ground allspice	5 mL
1 tsp	hot pepper sauce	5 mL
1/8 tsp	salt	0.5 mL

1. In work bowl fitted with metal blade, process chipotle peppers in adobo sauce, onion and garlic until puréed, about 1 minute. Add brown sugar and purée until smooth. Set aside.

2. In a medium saucepan over medium heat, combine vinegar, ketchup, olive oil, molasses, Worcestershire sauce, if using, cloves, coriander, cinnamon, allspice and hot pepper sauce. Cook, stirring occasionally, until reduced by half, 14 to 16 minutes. Stir in puréed pepper mixture. Reduce heat to low and cook, stirring occasionally, until thickened, for 1 hour. Season with salt. Let cool.

Bold Chili Sauce

**Makes 3 cups
(750 mL)**

This bold and spicy sauce is all you need on hot dogs or steak burgers.

Tip

Sauce keeps well, covered and refrigerated, for up to 1 week.

- Preheat oven to 400°F (200°C)
- Baking sheet, lined with parchment paper

16	dried guajillo chiles	16
2 tbsp	vegetable oil	30 mL
6	cloves garlic, coarsely chopped	6
1½ tbsp	extra virgin olive oil	22 mL
1½ tsp	granulated sugar	7 mL
1 tsp	dried oregano	5 mL
1 tsp	salt	5 mL
¼ tsp	freshly ground black pepper	1 mL
⅛ tsp	ground cumin	0.5 mL
3 cups	beef broth or ready-to-use broth	750 mL

1. Place chiles on prepared baking sheet. Brush with vegetable oil. Roast in preheated oven until soft, about 15 minutes. Split the chiles and remove the seeds. Place in a bowl with enough hot water to cover and let soak for 10 minutes. Drain and transfer to work bowl fitted with metal blade and process until smooth. Add garlic, olive oil, sugar, oregano, salt, pepper and cumin and process for 15 seconds.

2. Transfer mixture to a medium saucepan over medium heat. Add beef broth and simmer, stirring occasionally, until thickened, for 30 minutes. Let cool.

Aztec Spice Rub

**Makes 2 cups
(500 mL)**

This rub feels more like a paste than a traditional rub and is easy to massage into rough cuts of meat such as brisket or butterflied leg of lamb.

½ cup	cumin seeds, toasted (see Tip, page 453)	125 mL
6	cloves garlic, minced	6
3 tbsp	kosher salt	45 mL
2 tbsp	unsweetened cocoa powder	30 mL
1 tbsp	cayenne pepper	15 mL
1 tsp	ground cinnamon	5 mL
1 cup	extra virgin olive oil	250 mL

1. In work bowl fitted with metal blade, process cumin seeds, garlic, salt, cocoa powder, cayenne and cinnamon until powdery, for 1 minute. While motor is running, drizzle in oil through feed tube.

Brown Sugar Rub

Makes ¾ cup (175 mL)

Here's a sweet rub with a hint of pepper. It will caramelize onto the meat to make a sweet yet spicy rub.

½ cup	lightly packed brown sugar	125 mL
2 tbsp	kosher salt	30 mL
1 tsp	cayenne pepper	5 mL
½ tsp	Hungarian paprika	2 mL
½ tsp	onion powder	2 mL

1. In a work bowl fitted with metal blade, process brown sugar, salt, cayenne, paprika and onion powder until fine and powdery, about 20 seconds.

Chile Pepper Rub

Makes 1¾ cups (425 mL)

With a flavor that's intense and strong, this rub even works well with slow smoking of meats.

Tip

Use a mini food processor or a spice grinder to grind the dried jalapeños.

1¼ cups	lightly packed brown sugar	300 mL
½ cup	chili powder	125 mL
2	dried jalapeño peppers (see Tip, left)	2
1 tbsp	cayenne pepper	15 mL
1 tsp	freshly ground black pepper	5 mL

1. In work bowl fitted with metal blade, process brown sugar, chili powder, jalapeños, cayenne and black pepper until powdery, about 1 minute.

Drunken Fresh Herb Marinade

**Makes about
3/4 cup (175 mL)**

This marinade is called drunken because it has tequila in it. See below for the many uses for this flavorful marinade.

Tip
Make sure to use only the leaves of the tarragon and not the stems, which can taste bitter and woody.

3	cloves garlic	3
1/4 cup	sprigs fresh tarragon (see Tip, left)	60 mL
1	serrano chile pepper, seeded and halved	1
1/4 cup	freshly squeezed lime juice	60 mL
3 tbsp	tequila	45 mL
1 tsp	salt	5 mL
1/4 cup	olive oil	60 mL

1. In work bowl fitted with metal blade, process garlic, tarragon and chile until smooth. With the motor running, add lime juice, tequila and salt through the feed tube. Process for 1 minute. With the motor running, slowly drizzle oil through the feed tube until completely incorporated. Transfer to a bowl.

Variation
Use orange or lemon juice in place of the lime.

Uses
Chicken Breasts: Marinate 4 chicken breasts in the mixture in the refrigerator for at least 45 minutes.

Grill on a barbecue preheated to medium or bake in preheated 400°F (200°C) oven until chicken is no longer pink inside, 20 to 25 minutes.

Scallops: Marinate 1 lb (500 g) fresh sea scallops in the mixture for at least 10 minutes or up to 30 minutes. Grill on a barbecue preheated to medium until light brown, 3 to 5 minutes per side.

Jamaican Rub

**Makes ¾ cup
(175 mL)**

This rub is hot and spicy, just like the islands.

- Mini-bowl attachment

¼ cup	unsalted roasted sunflower seeds	60 mL
2 tbsp	ground turmeric	30 mL
2 tbsp	cumin seeds	30 mL
1 tbsp	coriander seeds	15 mL
1 tbsp	ground cinnamon	15 mL
1 tbsp	ground ginger	15 mL
1½ tsp	mustard seeds	7 mL
1½ tsp	whole cloves	7 mL
1½ tsp	hot pepper flakes	7 mL
1 tsp	celery seeds	5 mL

1. In a spice grinder or mini bowl fitted with metal blade, process sunflower seeds, turmeric, cumin seeds, coriander seeds, cinnamon, ginger, mustard seeds, cloves, hot pepper flakes and celery seeds until powdery, about 2 minutes.

Hot and Spicy BBQ Rub

**Makes 2 cups
(500 mL)**

Memphis, Tennessee is known for their dry rub ribs. Here is a similar rub for you to try.

Tips

If the mixture becomes hard and dry, just place in the microwave on Low for 3 minutes and stir.

Rub keeps stored in an airtight container for up to 6 months.

1 cup	lightly packed brown sugar	250 mL
⅔ cup	chili powder	150 mL
¼ cup	paprika	60 mL
2 tbsp	garlic salt	30 mL
2 tbsp	coarse sea salt	30 mL
1 tbsp	whole black peppercorns	15 mL
2 tsp	mustard seeds	10 mL
2 tsp	granulated sugar	10 mL
1 tsp	ground ginger	5 mL
1 tsp	whole cloves	5 mL
¼ tsp	ground turmeric	1 mL
¼ tsp	onion powder	1 mL
¼ tsp	garlic powder	1 mL
¼ tsp	cornstarch	1 mL

1. In work bowl fitted with metal blade, process brown sugar, chili powder, paprika, garlic salt, sea salt, peppercorns, mustard seeds, granulated sugar, ginger, cloves, turmeric, onion powder, garlic powder and cornstarch until finely ground, about 3 minutes.

Kansas City Dry Rub

Makes 2 cups (500 mL)

This Midwestern city is known for ribs and large steaks. Here is a rub that flavors tri-tip or skirt steak perfectly.

1 cup	granulated sugar	250 mL
1/2 cup	Hungarian paprika	125 mL
1/4 cup	celery salt	60 mL
3 tbsp	onion powder	45 mL
3 tbsp	chili powder	45 mL
2 tbsp	ground cumin	30 mL
2 tbsp	whole black peppercorns	30 mL
1 tbsp	kosher salt	15 mL
2 tsp	dry mustard	10 mL
1 tsp	cayenne pepper	5 mL

1. In work bowl fitted with metal blade, process sugar, paprika, celery salt, onion powder, chili powder, cumin, peppercorns, kosher salt, dry mustard and cayenne until powdery, for 1 minute.

Greek Rub

Makes about 1/2 cup (125 mL)

This recipes comes from the Greek island of Rhodes, where they serve this rub on lamb. Happily for us all, the restaurant owner was pleased to share his recipe.

Tip

The capers make this rub a little moist, helping the spices cling to the meat.

1/4 cup	sea salt	60 mL
1/4 cup	drained capers	60 mL
2 tsp	cumin seeds	10 mL
2 tsp	dried dill	10 mL
1 tsp	fennel seeds	5 mL
1 tsp	dried oregano	5 mL
1 tsp	Hungarian paprika	5 mL
1/2 tsp	ground white pepper	2 mL

1. In a spice grinder or food processor fitted with metal blade, process salt, capers, cumin seeds, dill, fennel seeds, oregano, paprika and white pepper until powdery, for 30 seconds.

Herbes de Provence Rub

**Makes about
1½ cups (375 mL)**

Try this rub on lamb shanks. It's just like they make it in the south of France.

Tip

Coat meat, such as lamb, with honey, rubbing all over. Press spice mixture over honey.

1 cup	dry bread crumbs	250 mL
1 tbsp	dried basil	15 mL
2 tsp	dried oregano	10 mL
1 tsp	dried marjoram	5 mL
1 tsp	dried thyme	5 mL
½ tsp	dried sage	2 mL
½ tsp	dried mint	2 mL
½ tsp	dried rosemary	2 mL
½ tsp	fennel seeds	2 mL
½ tsp	dried lavender	2 mL

1. In work bowl fitted with metal blade, process bread crumbs, basil, oregano, marjoram, thyme, sage, mint, rosemary, fennel seeds and lavender until blended, about 20 seconds.

Orange Dill Rub

Makes 1 cup (250 mL)

Try coating jumbo prawns with this zesty rub.

	Zest and juice of 2 oranges	
1	jalapeño pepper	1
5	cloves garlic, coarsely chopped	5
2 tbsp	chili powder	30 mL
1 tbsp	extra virgin olive oil	15 mL
1 tbsp	Hungarian paprika	15 mL
1 tbsp	dried dill	15 mL
1 tsp	ground cumin	5 mL
1 tsp	salt	5 mL
½ tsp	celery seeds	2 mL
½ tsp	dried oregano	2 mL
¼ tsp	ground cinnamon	1 mL

1. In work bowl fitted with metal blade, process orange zest and juice, jalapeño, garlic, chili powder, oil, paprika, dill, cumin, salt, celery seeds, oregano and cinnamon until a paste, about 2 minutes.

Peppery Dry Rub

**Makes about
1/2 cup (125 mL)**

Pat this rub on both
sides of your patted dry
steak before grilling it.

- Mini-bowl attachment

1/4 cup	kosher salt	60 mL
2 tbsp	dried thyme	30 mL
3	bay leaves	3
2 tsp	whole black peppercorns	10 mL
1 tsp	hot pepper flakes	5 mL
1/2 tsp	whole allspice	2 mL

1. In mini bowl fitted with metal blade, process salt, thyme, bay leaves, peppercorns, hot pepper flakes and allspice until a fine powder, about 2 minutes.

Porky Porky Rub

**Makes about
1 cup (250 mL)**

Try this on any types
of pork, pork chops,
roast or loin for a
flavorful meal.

Tip

For the best flavor, toast
and grind cumin yourself.
To toast cumin: Place
seeds in a dry skillet over
medium heat and cook,
stirring, until fragrant,
about 3 minutes.

- Mini-bowl attachment

3 tbsp	kosher salt	45 mL
3 tbsp	whole black peppercorns	45 mL
2 tbsp	cumin seeds, toasted (see Tip, left)	30 mL
2 tbsp	chili powder	30 mL
2 tbsp	lightly packed brown sugar	30 mL
2 tbsp	dried oregano	30 mL
2 tbsp	dried cilantro	30 mL
4	cloves garlic, coarsely chopped	4
1 tsp	grated orange zest	5 mL
1/2 tsp	cayenne pepper	2 mL

1. In mini bowl fitted with metal blade, process salt, peppercorns, cumin seeds, chili powder, brown sugar, oregano, cilantro, garlic, orange zest and cayenne until blended, for 30 seconds.

Tuscan Rub

Makes about ½ cup (125 mL)

This rub has all of the flavors and aromas of Tuscany. Try it on poultry for a zip of Mediterranean flare.

- Mini-bowl attachment

3 tbsp	dried basil	45 mL
1½ tbsp	garlic powder	22 mL
1½ tbsp	kosher salt	22 mL
1 tbsp	dried rosemary	15 mL
1 tbsp	dried oregano	15 mL
1½ tsp	fennel seeds	7 mL
1½ tsp	ground white pepper	7 mL

1. In mini bowl fitted with metal blade, process basil, garlic powder, salt, rosemary, oregano, fennel seeds and white pepper until powdery, for 20 seconds.

Turkey Poultry Rub

Makes about ½ cup (125 mL)

Here's a perfectly flavored seasoned rub for turkey or any poultry.

- Mini-bowl attachment

¼ cup	salt	60 mL
1½ tsp	whole white peppercorns	7 mL
1 tsp	dried tarragon	5 mL
1 tsp	dried oregano	5 mL
1 tsp	grated orange zest	5 mL
1 tsp	grated lemon zest	5 mL
½ tsp	cumin seeds, toasted (see Tip, page 453)	2 mL

1. In mini bowl fitted with metal blade, process salt, white peppercorns, tarragon, oregano, orange zest, lemon zest and cumin seeds until powdery, about 2 minutes.

Austin Dry Rub

Makes 1 cup (250 mL)

Add depth to steaks and meat dishes with this rub from Austin, Texas.

- Mini-bowl attachment

¼ cup	salt	60 mL
3 tbsp	Hungarian paprika	45 mL
2 tbsp	garlic powder	30 mL
2 tbsp	dried onion flakes	30 mL
2 tbsp	dried parsley	30 mL
1 tbsp	dried thyme	15 mL
1 tbsp	black peppercorns	15 mL
1 tbsp	lightly packed brown sugar	15 mL
1 tbsp	dried basil	15 mL
1 tbsp	dry mustard	15 mL

1. In mini bowl fitted with metal blade, process salt, paprika, garlic powder, onion flakes, parsley, thyme, peppercorns, brown sugar, basil and mustard until powdery, about 2 minutes.

Anchovy Butter

Makes about ⅔ cup (150 mL)

This is a very versatile butter. It is great with steak, particularly non-fatty cuts such as filet mignon, roast chicken or grilled fish. Spread it on toast for a quick pick-me-up or rub over lamb before roasting. If you use it as rub for lamb and deglaze the pan juices with some dry white wine and a bit of lemon juice, you will have a gravy that tastes like it was made in heaven.

- Mini-bowl attachment

1	can (2 oz/55 g) anchovy fillets, drained and rinsed (about 12 fillets)	1
1	small shallot, chopped	1
1	clove garlic, chopped	1
1 tsp	finely grated lemon zest	5 mL
½ tsp	cracked black peppercorns	2 mL
½ cup	butter, softened	125 mL

1. In mini bowl fitted with metal blade, process anchovies, shallot, garlic, lemon zest, peppercorns and butter until smooth, stopping and scraping down sides of the bowl once or twice, about 2 minutes. Spoon into a ramekin or small bowl and chill until firm, about 30 minutes. Refrigerate for up to 1 week or freeze in an airtight container for up to 2 months.

Roquefort Butter

Makes about ⅔ cup (150 mL)

Vegetarian Friendly

This is a wonderful accompaniment for grilled steak or, if you're a vegetarian, use it as a spread to enhance sandwiches. It is particularly good with sliced pears. Spread it on toasted baguette and garnish with chopped walnuts for an easy-to-make crostini.

- Mini-bowl attachment

4 oz	Roquefort cheese	125 g
¼ cup	butter, softened	60 mL
1	clove garlic, minced	1
1 tsp	Worcestershire sauce (regular or vegetarian)	5 mL

1. In mini bowl fitted with metal blade, process cheese, butter, garlic and Worcestershire sauce until smooth, stopping and scraping down sides of the bowl as necessary, about 2 minutes. Spoon into a ramekin or small bowl and chill until firm, about 30 minutes. Refrigerate for up to 1 week or freeze in an airtight container for up to 2 months.

Sun-Dried Tomato Butter

Makes about ⅔ cup (150 mL)

Vegetarian Friendly

This butter is great with grilled or roasted fish, poultry or meat. If you're a vegetarian, use it to finish a bowl of warm chickpeas or cannellini beans.

- Mini-bowl attachment

½ cup	butter, softened	125 mL
4	sun-dried tomatoes in oil, drained and chopped	4
1 tbsp	snipped chives	15 mL
	Salt and freshly ground black pepper	

1. In mini bowl fitted with metal blade, process butter, sun-dried tomatoes, chives, and salt and pepper to taste until smooth, stopping and scraping down sides of the bowl as necessary, about 2 minutes. Spoon into a ramekin or small bowl and chill until firm, about 30 minutes. Refrigerate for up to 1 week or freeze in an airtight container for up to 2 months.

Roasted Red Pepper Butter

Makes about 2/3 cup (150 mL)

Vegetarian Friendly

Use this any way you would use Sun-Dried Tomato Butter (page 456).

- Mini-bowl attachment

½ cup	butter, softened	125 mL
1	roasted red pepper, peeled, seeded and diced (see Tips, page 406)	1
1 tsp	grated lemon zest	5 mL
	Salt and freshly ground black pepper	

1. In mini bowl fitted with metal blade, process butter, roasted red pepper, lemon zest, and salt and pepper to taste until smooth, stopping and scraping down sides of the bowl as necessary, about 2 minutes. Spoon into a ramekin or small bowl and chill until firm, about 30 minutes. Refrigerate for up to 1 week or freeze in an airtight container for up to 2 months.

Chipotle Butter

Makes about 2/3 cup (150 mL)

Vegetarian Friendly

This butter adds a zesty finish to grilled or roasted fish, poultry and meat, as well as to a pot of bubbling red beans.

- Mini-bowl attachment

½ cup	butter, softened	125 mL
2	chipotle peppers in adobo sauce	2
½ tsp	grated lime zest	2 mL
1 tsp	freshly squeezed lime juice	5 mL
	Salt and freshly ground black pepper	

1. In mini bowl fitted with metal blade, process butter, chipotle peppers, lime zest and juice, and salt and pepper to taste until smooth, stopping and scraping down sides of the bowl as necessary, about 2 minutes. Spoon into a ramekin or small bowl and chill until firm, about 30 minutes.

Hazelnut Butter

Makes 1 cup (250 mL)

Vegan Friendly

Dark and rich, this butter is perfect on crackers or piped into large strawberries after they've been hulled.

Tip

In some areas hazelnuts are also knows as filberts. *To toast hazelnuts:* Place nuts in a single layer on a baking sheet in a preheated 400°F (200°C) oven until lightly browned, 8 to 12 minutes. Transfer them onto a damp tea towel, then fold over the towel corners and rub the nuts until most of their skins come off.

- Mini-bowl attachment

1½ cups	hazelnuts, toasted with skins removed (see Tip, left)	375 mL
½ tsp	salt	2 mL
½ tsp	lightly packed brown sugar	2 mL

1. In mini bowl fitted with metal blade, process, hazelnuts, salt and brown sugar until smooth, stopping and scraping down sides of the bowl, as necessary. Spoon into a ramekin or small bowl and chill until firm, about 30 minutes. Refrigerate for up to 1 week or freeze in an airtight container for up to 2 months.

Variation

Chocolate Hazelnut Butter: Add 2 tbsp (30 mL) unsweetened Dutch-process cocoa powder when you add the nuts.

Tarragon Dill Butter

Makes 1 cup (250 mL)

Vegan Friendly

When dining in France you'll always get a flavorful butter on top of your vegetables or meats. We like to make this butter for breads and corn muffins.

Tip

Make sure the butter is softened prior to using or it will not blend with the herbs.

- Mini-bowl attachment
- Baking sheet, lined with parchment paper

1 cup	unsalted butter or vegan alternative, softened (see Tip, left)	250 mL
1 tsp	loosely packed fresh tarragon	5 mL
½ tsp	loosely packed fresh dill fronds	2 mL
¼ tsp	salt	1 mL

1. In mini bowl fitted with metal blade, process butter, tarragon, dill and salt until smooth, stopping and scraping down sides of the bowl as necessary, about 3 minutes.

2. Place butter mixture into a pastry bag fitted with a star tip and pipe rosettes onto parchment paper. Or place in small individual ramekins. Refrigerate until firm, about 30 minutes. Remove rosettes from parchment with an offset spatula. Freeze in an airtight container for up to 2 months.

Variation
Substitute ½ tsp (2 mL) loosely packed fresh thyme for the dill for a different flavor.

Garlic Romano Butter

Makes ¾ cup (175 mL)

Vegetarian Friendly

For an added kick, cut a slice of this butter and add to green steamed vegetables or a baked potato.

2 oz	Romano cheese, cut into chunks	60 g
½ cup	butter, softened	125 mL
3	cloves garlic, coarsely chopped	3
1 tsp	freshly squeezed lemon juice	5 mL
1 tsp	fresh tarragon leaves	5 mL

1. In work bowl fitted with metal blade with motor running, add Romano through feed tube and process until fine, about 20 seconds. Add butter, garlic, lemon juice and tarragon and process until smooth, stopping and scraping down sides of the bowl as necessary, about 20 seconds.

2. Place butter on piece of parchment pepper and roll into a log about 4 inches (10 cm) long, twisting ends of paper around butter. Place in freezer to firm up, about 2 hours, or in an airtight container for up to 2 months.

Honey Butter

Makes 1½ cups (375 mL)

Makes 1½ cups (375 mL)

Vegetarian Friendly

Honey butter is synonymous with cornbread. Try using on top of steamed vegetables as well.

Tip

Make sure your butter is unsalted or you will have salty tasting honey butter.

- Mini-bowl attachment

1 cup	unsalted butter, softened (see Tips, left)	250 mL
½ cup	liquid honey	125 mL
1 tsp	ground cinnamon	5 mL
½ tsp	ground nutmeg	2 mL

1. In mini bowl fitted with metal blade, process butter, honey, cinnamon and nutmeg until smooth, stopping and scraping down sides of the bowl as necessary, about 2 minutes. Spoon into a ramekin or small bowl and chill until firm, about 30 minutes. Refrigerate for up to 1 week or freeze in an airtight container for up to 2 months.

Variation

Try using a different-flavored honey such as lavender or clove.

Roasted Garlic Butter

Makes ¾ cup (175 mL)

Vegetarian Friendly

A multi-use compound butter for everything from steaks to crunchy French breads.

Mini-bowl attachment

½ cup	unsalted butter, softened (see Tip, above)	125 mL
6	cloves garlic, roasted (see Tip, page 417)	6
1 tsp	freshly squeezed lemon juice	5 mL
¼ tsp	salt	1 mL
¼ tsp	paprika	1 mL

1. In mini bowl fitted with metal blade, process butter, garlic, lemon juice, salt and paprika, stopping and scraping down sides of the bowl as necessary, for 20 seconds.

2. Place butter on piece of parchment pepper and roll into a log about 4 inches (10 cm) long, twisting ends of paper around butter. Place in freezer to firm up, about 2 hours, or in an airtight container for up to 2 months.

Sundries

Plain Pasta

**Makes about
1 lb (500 g)**

4 to 6 servings

Vegetarian Friendly

This basic recipe is
very easy to make and
is delicious with many
sauces.

Tips

If you are making cut
pasta, let the noodles dry
out a bit before cooking.
If you are making filled
pasta, it's important that
the sheets don't dry out.
Otherwise they will be
difficult to work with.
Work with one sheet
at a time and keep the
remainder tightly wrapped
in plastic wrap.

If you are cooking cut
pasta, bring a large pot of
water to a rapid boil. Add
1 tbsp (15 mL) salt and
fresh pasta. Return to a
boil and cook, uncovered,
until pasta is al dente,
about 6 minutes.

2 cups	all-purpose flour (approx.)	500 mL
1 tsp	salt	5 mL
3	eggs	3
	Water, optional	

1. In work bowl fitted with metal blade, pulse flour and
   salt to blend, 2 to 3 times. Add eggs and pulse until a
   soft dough forms. If dough seems too wet, add more
   flour, 1 tbsp (15 mL) at a time, pulsing to blend with
   each addition. If dough seems too dry, add water, 1 tbsp
   (15 mL) at a time, pulsing to blend after each addition.
   Transfer to a clean work surface and knead until a ball
   forms. Cover with plastic wrap and set aside for 1 hour.
   Knead lightly just before using.

2. When you are ready to roll the pasta out, divide dough
   into 6 pieces and flatten each into a disk. Flour lightly
   on both sides. If you are using a pasta rolling machine,
   follow the manufacturer's instructions. If rolling by hand,
   sprinkle the disk with flour and roll on a floured surface
   into a rectangle about 12 by 8 inches (30 by 20 cm),
   about $\frac{1}{8}$ inch (3 mm) thick. If making pasta sheets, cut
   to desired size and place on lightly floured parchment or
   waxed paper. If you're cutting the pasta, roll the sheet up
   and cut into desired width using a sharp knife. Repeat
   until all the dough is used up.

Whole Wheat Pasta

**Makes about
1 lb (500 g)**

4 to 6 servings

Vegetarian Friendly

This produces a husky pasta, which is a healthier alternative to pasta made exclusively with white flour.

Tips

You can use rolled pasta sheets for baked or filled pasta. Just cut the rectangles to the size you want and place on lightly floured parchment or waxed paper. If cut pasta is your objective, you can cut it yourself or use the appropriate attachment of your rolling machine. To cut by hand, roll the sheet up tightly into a tube and cut into the width you want using a sharp knife.

If you are making cut pasta, let the noodles dry out a bit before cooking. If you are making filled pasta, it's important that the sheets don't dry out. Otherwise, they will be difficult to work with. Work with one sheet at a time and keep the remainder tightly wrapped in plastic wrap.

1½ cups	whole wheat flour	375 mL
1 cup	all-purpose flour (approx.)	250 mL
1 tsp	salt	5 mL
3	eggs	3
3 tbsp	water (approx.)	45 mL
2 tbsp	olive oil	30 mL

1. In work bowl fitted with metal blade, pulse whole wheat flour, all-purpose flour and salt to blend, 2 to 3 times. Add eggs, water and olive oil and pulse until mixture begins to come together, about 20 times. If mixture seems dry, add more water, 1 tbsp (15 mL) at a time, pulsing after each addition. If mixture seems wet, add more all-purpose flour, 1 tbsp (15 mL) at a time, pulsing to blend after each addition. Transfer to a clean work surface and knead until a ball forms. Cover with plastic wrap and set aside for 1 hour. Knead lightly just before using.

2. When you are ready to roll the pasta out, divide dough into 6 portions and flatten each into a disk. Flour lightly on both sides. If you are using a pasta rolling machine, follow the manufacturer's instructions. If rolling by hand, roll on a floured surface into a rectangle about 12 by 8 inches (30 by 20 cm), about ⅛ inch (3 mm) thick. If making pasta sheets, cut to desired size and place on lightly floured parchment or waxed paper. If you're cutting the pasta, roll the sheet up and cut into desired width using a sharp knife. Repeat until all the dough is used up.

Buckwheat Pasta (Pizzoccheri)

Buckwheat, which is not wheat but the seed of a plant related to rhubarb, is a very healthy whole grain. Cut this pasta like fettucine and use it as the Italians do in Pizzoccheri Valtellina (page 317), a rich cabbage and cheese dish, or cut it thin like spaghetti and use it in place of soba noodles in Asian recipes. This version actually has a higher percentage of buckwheat than most supermarket varieties of soba noodles.

Tip

To cook the cut pasta: Bring a large pot of water to a rapid boil. Add 1 tbsp (15 mL) salt and fresh pasta. Return to a boil and cook, uncovered, until pasta is al dente, about 6 minutes.

1¼ cups	buckwheat flour	300 mL
¾ cup	all-purpose flour (approx.)	175 mL
1 tsp	salt	5 mL
3	eggs	3
1 tbsp	warm water (approx.)	15 mL
1 tbsp	extra virgin olive oil	15 mL

1. In work bowl fitted with metal blade, pulse buckwheat flour, all-purpose flour and salt to blend, 2 to 3 times. Add eggs, water and olive oil and pulse until mixture begins to come together, about 20 times. If mixture seems dry, add more water, 1 tbsp (15 mL) at a time, pulsing to blend after each addition. If mixture seems wet, add more all-purpose flour, 1 tbsp (15 mL) at a time, pulsing to blend after each addition. Transfer to a clean work surface and knead until a ball forms. Cover with plastic wrap and set aside for 1 hour. Knead lightly just before using.

2. When you are ready to roll the pasta out, divide dough into 6 portions and flatten each into a disk. Flour lightly on both sides. If you are using a pasta rolling machine, follow the manufacturer's instructions. If rolling by hand, roll on a floured surface into a rectangle about 12 by 8 inches (30 by 20 cm), about ⅛ inch (3 mm) thick. Cut the rolled pasta into strips about ¼ inch (0.5 cm) wide or use the fettuccine attachment of your rolling machine. Repeat until all the dough is used up.

Spinach Pasta

**Makes about
1 lb (500 g)**

4 to 6 servings

Vegetarian Friendly

Use this vibrantly colored pasta on its own or mix and mingle with different-colored pastas such as tomato and whole wheat for a multi-colored pasta dish.

Tips

The addition of spinach introduces a slightly unpredictable variable to the pasta. Be sure to squeeze out all the water before adding to the mixture. Otherwise, your pasta is likely to be quite wet.

You can use rolled pasta sheets for baked or filled pasta. Just cut the rectangles to the size you want and place on lightly floured parchment or waxed paper. If cut pasta is your objective, you can cut it yourself or use the appropriate attachment of your rolling machine. To cut by hand, roll the sheet up tightly into a tube and cut into the width you want using a sharp knife.

2½ cups	all-purpose flour (approx.)	625 mL
1 tsp	salt	5 mL
3	eggs	3
½ cup	finely chopped cooked drained spinach (see Tips, left)	125 mL

1. In work bowl fitted with metal blade, pulse flour and salt to blend, 2 to 3 times. Add eggs and spinach and pulse until mixture begins to come together, about 20 times. If mixture seems wet, add more flour, 1 tbsp (15 mL) at a time, pulsing to blend after each addition. Transfer to a clean work surface and knead until a ball forms. Cover with plastic wrap and set aside for 1 hour. Knead lightly just before using.

2. When you are ready to roll the pasta out, divide dough into 6 portions and flatten each into a disk. Flour lightly on both sides. If you are using a pasta rolling machine, follow the manufacturer's instructions. If rolling by hand, roll on a floured surface into a rectangle about 12 by 8 inches (30 by 20 cm), about ⅛ inch (3 mm) thick. Repeat until all the dough is used up. If making cut pasta, see Tips, left.

Tomato Pasta

Vegetarian Friendly

The hint of tomato and pepper in the pasta makes a particularly nice partner for cheese-based sauces.

Tip

If you are cooking cut pasta, bring a large pot of water to a rapid boil. Add 1 tbsp (15 mL) salt and fresh pasta. Return to a boil and cook, uncovered, until pasta is al dente, about 6 minutes.

2¼ cups	all-purpose flour (approx.)	550 mL
1 tsp	salt	5 mL
½ tsp	freshly ground black pepper	2 mL
3	eggs	3
1 tbsp	tomato paste, preferably double-concentrate	15 mL
	Water, optional	

1. In work bowl fitted with metal blade, pulse flour, salt and pepper to blend, 2 to 3 times. Add eggs and tomato paste and pulse until mixture begins to come together, about 20 times. If mixture seems dry, add water, 1 tbsp (15 mL) at a time, pulsing to blend after each addition. If it seems wet, add more flour, 1 tbsp (15 mL) at a time, pulsing to blend after each addition. Transfer to a clean work surface and knead until a ball forms. Cover with plastic wrap and set aside for 1 hour. Knead lightly just before using.

2. When you are ready to roll the pasta out, divide dough into 6 portions and flatten each into a disk. Flour lightly on both sides. If you are using a pasta rolling machine, follow the manufacturer's instructions. If rolling by hand, roll on a floured surface into a rectangle about 12 by 8 inches (30 by 20 cm), about ⅛ inch (3 mm) thick. Repeat until all the dough is used up. If making cut pasta, see Tips, page 465.

Jalapeño-Spiked Onion Marmalade

**Makes about
1 cup (250 mL)**

Vegan Friendly

This tasty condiment is very easy to make and is an impressive addition to any table. It is very good with roasted and fried meats and with hearty vegetables such as roasted squash. It can also be served as an appetizer, to top Crêpes Parmentier (page 362) or Rösti (page 355).

Tip

After refrigeration the mixture will thicken even more. If yours becomes too solid, before using simply heat it in a microwave oven for 1 minute or over low heat on top of the stove until desired consistency is reached.

2	onions (about 1 lb/500 g total), quartered	2
1½ cups	granulated sugar	375 mL
½ cup	apple cider vinegar	125 mL
2 tsp	caraway seeds	10 mL
1 to 2	jalapeño peppers, seeded and minced	1 to 2
1 tsp	salt	5 mL

1. In work bowl fitted with slicing blade, slice onions very thinly. Set aside.

2. Meanwhile, in a large saucepan, combine sugar and vinegar. Bring to a boil and simmer until sugar is dissolved and mixture begins to become syrupy, about 5 minutes. Add caraway seeds, jalapeño pepper(s) and salt and stir well. Stir in onions and bring to a boil. Reduce heat and simmer, stirring occasionally, until onions are caramelized and mixture is thick, about 1 hour. Transfer to a serving bowl, cover and refrigerate for up to 1 month.

Fresh Bread Crumbs

Vegan Friendly

Many recipes call for bread crumbs, and if you have extra pieces of bread you can make your own.

Tip

Make sure you tear the bread up prior to baking so the bread dries faster and evenly.

- Preheat oven to 300°F (150°C)
- Baking sheet, lined with parchment paper

4	slices French or Italian bread, each 1 inch (2.5 cm) thick, torn into small pieces	4

1. Place bread on prepared baking sheet and toast in preheated oven for 5 minutes. Turn and continue to bake until very light brown and dried, 5 minutes more. Remove and let dry at room temperature for about 1 hour.

2. In work bowl fitted with metal blade, process toasted bread pieces until fine crumbs. If desired, freeze in a resealable plastic freezer bag for up to 3 months.

Variation
Add 1 tsp (5 mL) Italian herb seasonings when processing for Italian bread crumbs.

French-Style Seasoned Bread Crumbs

Vegan Friendly

These seasoned bread crumbs are handy to have on hand as a finish for gratins and other dishes.

Tip

You can make seasoned bread crumbs using frozen Fresh Bread Crumbs. Or make a batch of Fresh Bread Crumbs and instead of freezing them, add the herbs directly to the work bowl and process.

2 cups	Fresh Bread Crumbs (above) (see Tip, left) or store-bought	500 mL
1	shallot, coarsely chopped	1
2	cloves garlic, coarsely chopped	2
2 tbsp	Italian flat-leaf parsley leaves or 1 tbsp (15 mL) fresh thyme leaves	30 mL

1. In work bowl fitted with metal blade, process Fresh Bread Crumbs, shallot, garlic and parsley until herbs are very finely chopped and well integrated. If desired, freeze in a resealable plastic bag for up to 3 months.

Homemade Horseradish

**Makes about
2 cups (500 mL)**

Vegan Friendly

Making your own horseradish is a good idea because it is fresher tasting than prepared versions and you know every ingredient that is in it.

1	small horseradish (about 12 oz/375 g), peeled	1
¼ cup	white wine vinegar	60 mL
¼ cup	water	60 mL
2 tsp	granulated sugar	10 mL
½ tsp	salt	2 mL

1. In work bowl fitted with shredding blade, shred horseradish. (You'll want about 2 cups/500 mL.) Replace shredding blade with metal blade. Add vinegar, water, sugar and salt and pulse until very fine but not puréed, about 15 times, stopping and scraping down sides of the bowl once. Transfer to a bowl or glass preserving jar and refrigerate until ready to use or for up to 2 weeks.

Moroccan-Style Couscous Stuffing

**Makes about
4 cups (1 L)**

Vegan Friendly

This deliciously different stuffing is wonderful with roast chicken or even whole boned fish. Vegans can use it as a stuffing for roasted bell peppers or eggplant.

Tips

If you don't have saffron, substitute 1 tsp (5 mL) turmeric. Add along with the cinnamon.

If you prefer, bake the stuffing at 350°F (180°C) in a greased covered baking dish for 1 hour.

1 cup	chicken or vegetable broth	250 mL
Pinch	saffron threads, crumbled (see Tips, left)	Pinch
¾ cup	whole wheat couscous	175 mL
⅔ cup	toasted coarsely chopped blanched almonds (see Tips, pages 112 and 604)	150 mL
⅔ cup	chopped pitted dates	150 mL
½ cup	dried cherries	125 mL
1 tbsp	grated orange zest, optional	15 mL
1 tsp	ground cinnamon	5 mL
½ tsp	salt	2 mL
½ tsp	freshly ground black pepper	2 mL

1. In a saucepan over medium-high heat, bring broth to a boil. Add saffron and stir until infused. Add couscous in a steady stream, stirring constantly. Cover, remove from heat and let stand for 15 minutes. Fluff with a fork and use your hands to break up any clumps.

2. In work bowl fitted with metal blade, pulse almonds, dates, cherries, orange zest, cinnamon, salt and pepper until chopped and integrated, about 15 times. Add to couscous and stir well. Use as a stuffing or bake on its own (see Tips, left).

Sage and Onion Stuffing

**Makes about
5 cups (1.25 L)
(see Tips, below)**

Vegan Friendly

This is a classic
old-fashioned stuffing
that remains a perennial
favorite. The use of
fresh sage, which chops
beautifully in the food
processor, gives it a
refreshing spin. Vegans
can use this to stuff
small pumpkins and
other kinds of squash,
eggplant, and portobello
mushrooms. Or bake it
separately and use it as
an accompaniment for
grilled tofu.

Tips

If you're using this to stuff
poultry, this recipe makes
enough to stuff a 5- to
6-lb (2.5 to 3 kg) bird.
Using a large spoon, or
your hands, fill neck and
body cavities with stuffing.
just before roasting.

In general terms, allow
¾ to 1 cup (175 to
250 mL) stuffing per
pound of bird. If you are
cooking a large turkey,
triple this recipe.

4	stalks celery, cut into 3-inch (7.5 cm) lengths	4
1	onion, quartered	1
20	fresh sage leaves	20
1 tsp	salt	5 mL
½ tsp	poultry seasoning	2 mL
¼ tsp	freshly ground black pepper	1 mL
4 cups	stale bread cubes	1 L
¼ cup	melted butter or butter substitute	60 mL

1. In work bowl fitted with metal blade, pulse celery, onion and sage until finely chopped, about 15 times. Add salt, poultry seasoning and pepper. Pulse to blend. In a large bowl, place bread. Add celery mixture and melted butter. Using your hands, toss to combine.

Variation

Oven-Baked Stuffing: Preheat oven to 350°F (180°C). Grease a 4-cup (1 L) baking dish and transfer stuffing to prepared dish. Cover loosely with foil and bake in preheated oven until hot, about 1 hour. If you like a crunchy top on the stuffing, remove the foil for the last 10 minutes of baking.

Cornbread Pecan Tarragon Stuffing

Serves 6

Vegetarian Friendly

This is a dressing that you bake in the oven. If you are so inclined, place it into the turkeys' cavity, bake it in the oven first, then place into the cavity for serving presentation.

Tips

To toast macadamia nuts: Preheat oven to 350°F (180°C). Spread nuts on a baking sheet and bake, shaking the pan several times, until fragrant and toasted; 6 to 9 minutes for whole macadamia nuts; 4 to 7 minutes for chopped.

To reheat dressing, cover and place in a 350°F (180°C) oven until hot, about 20 minutes.

- Preheat oven to 350°F (180°C)
- 13- by 9-inch (33 by 23 cm) metal baking pan, buttered

5 cups	cornbread crumbs	1.25 L
3	slices stale bread, torn into pieces	3
½ cup	toasted macadamia nuts (see Tips, left)	125 mL
4	stalks celery, cut into 3-inch (7.5 cm) lengths	4
1	onion, cut into quarters	1
3 tbsp	fresh tarragon leaves	45 mL
3 cups	vegetable or chicken broth	750 mL
3	eggs, beaten	3
2 tsp	butter, melted	10 mL
	Sea salt and freshly ground pepper	

1. In work bowl fitted with metal blade, process about 2 cups (500 mL) of the cornbread crumbs for about 30 seconds to a fine crumb. Transfer to a large bowl. Add remaining bread crumbs to large bowl.

2. In work bowl, process stale bread into a fine crumb, about 30 seconds. Add to large bowl.

3. In work bowl, pulse macadamia nuts, celery, onion and tarragon, until finely chopped, about 10 times. Add to large bowl.

4. Add broth, eggs and butter to large bowl. Stir to coat all the crumbs. Season with salt and pepper to taste.

5. Transfer mixture to prepared pan and bake in preheated oven until firm, 45 to 55 minutes.

Pumpkin Purée

Vegan Friendly

A food processor makes
it so simple to make your
own pumpkin purée.

Tip

Look for a sugar or pie
pumpkin. They are small
and round, less than 2
lbs (1 kg) and have fewer
seeds and more meat.

- Preheat oven to 375°F (190°C)
- Large rimmed baking sheet

6 lbs	sugar or pie pumpkin (see Tip, left)	3 kg
1/4 cup	unsalted butter or vegan alternative, softened	60 mL
1/2 tsp	salt	2 mL

1. Cut pumpkin in half and remove stem. Scoop out seeds and membranes. Discard. Butter inside of pumpkin. Sprinkle with salt. Place skin side up on baking sheet. Bake in preheated oven until fork tender, 1½ to 2 hours.

2. Let pumpkin cool for at least 30 minutes. Scoop out soft flesh and place in work bowl fitted with metal blade. Process until smooth, about 2 minutes. You may have to do this in batches because some pumpkins produce more pulp. Let cool completely. Divide mixture into 2-cup (500 mL) amounts, place in plastic bags and freeze for up to 9 months.

Vanilla Sugar

**Makes 2 cups
(500 mL)**

Vegan Friendly

Put some of this sugar
in your coffee and you'll
feel like you're in Paris!
All of the coffeehouses
serve this. Also, use it in
All-Rich Butter Cookies
(page 571).

Tips

This sugar is used in many
French baked goods in
place of vanilla and sugar.

Vanilla sugar keeps stored
in an airtight container for
up to 1 year.

| 2 | whole vanilla beans | 2 |
| 2 cups | granulated sugar | 500 mL |

1. Cut each vanilla bean in half lengthwise. Cut crosswise into slices.

2. In work bowl fitted with metal blade, process sugar and beans until very smooth, about 2 minutes.

Variation
Add a few drops of almond extract through the feed tube while the motor is running for almond vanilla sugar.

Fast and Easy Pizza Dough

Vegetarian Friendly

Sprinkle this easy dough with your favorite toppings, such as cheeses, cooked chicken, salami and roasted vegetables, to create your very own signature pizzas.

Tip

You can make the dough to the end of Step 2 up to 3 days ahead. Refrigerate until ready to use. Let warm to room temperature before shaping in Step 3.

- Baking sheet, dusted with 2 tsp (10 mL) cornmeal
- Instant-read thermometer

1 cup	milk	250 mL
1 tbsp	unsalted butter, softened	15 mL
3 cups	all-purpose flour, divided (approx.)	750 mL
1 tbsp	granulated sugar	15 mL
1¼ tsp	salt	6 mL
1	package (¼ oz/8 g) quick-rising (instant) dry yeast	1

1. In a saucepan over medium heat, bring milk and butter to a simmer until an instant-read thermometer registers approximately 120° to 130°F (50° to 55°C), about 3 minutes. Do not let boil.

2. Meanwhile, in work bowl fitted with metal blade, process 2 cups (500 mL) of the flour, sugar, salt and yeast until well combined, about 10 seconds. With the motor running, slowly pour hot milk mixture through the feed tube into work bowl. With the motor continuing to run, spoon additional flour through the feed tube, ¼ cup (60 mL) at a time, until dough starts to pull away from sides and begins to gather.

3. Remove from work bowl and place on a floured surface. Knead until dough is smooth and elastic, 3 to 5 minutes. Shape into a ball. Transfer to a large oiled bowl and turn to coat all over. Cover loosely with plastic wrap. Let dough rise in a warm, draft-free place until doubled in volume, about 45 to 90 minutes, depending on humidity and heat factors.

4. Preheat oven to 425°F (220°C). Punch down dough and cut in half. Press each out to about ½ inch (1 cm) thick and 10 inches (25 cm) round. Transfer to prepared baking sheet. Add your favorite toppings. For a thin crust, bake right away; for a thicker crust, let rise for 15 to 20 minutes. Bake in preheated oven until the crust is light brown on bottom, 15 to 20 minutes.

Variation

Replace half of the flour with whole wheat flour for a whole wheat crust. Don't replace all of the flour with whole wheat or you will have a brick.

Whole Wheat Pastry Dough

Makes 1 single 9- to 10-inch (23 to 25 cm) crust

Vegetarian Friendly

This is a very tender and tasty crust that is as tasty as any conventional crust. This quantity makes enough for a single-crust pie. For a two-crust pie, double the quantity.

Tip

For best results, place the cubed butter in the freezer for a few minutes before using.

The crust mixture will be very crumbly. Kneading brings it together.

1 cup	whole wheat pastry flour	250 mL
½ cup	all-purpose flour	125 mL
½ tsp	salt	2 mL
⅓ cup	cold butter, cut into 1-inch (2.5 cm) cubes (see Tip, left)	75 mL
¼ cup	heavy or whipping (35%) cream	60 mL
1 tsp	apple cider vinegar	5 mL

1. In work bowl fitted with metal blade, pulse whole wheat flour, all-purpose flour and salt to blend. Add butter and process until mixture resembles rolled oats, about 10 seconds.

2. In a measuring cup, combine cream and vinegar. Add to work bowl and pulse until mixture is barely combined, about 6 times. Transfer to a floured board and knead until smooth and pliable. Roll out and place in pie plate. Refrigerate until you're ready to fill.

All-Butter Pie Pastry Dough

Makes enough dough for one 9-inch (23 cm) single-crust pie

Vegetarian Friendly

Here is a classic recipe that will suit all of your pie-making needs. With the food processor, you can have a flaky pie crust in less than 5 minutes. Use it with Pumpkin Pecan Pie (page 626) or Apple Spice Pie (page 627).

Tips

If your dough forms a ball in the food processor work bowl, it may be too tough (see Tips, page 476).

Pre-baking is needed when making a pie that does not require the filling to be baked in the pie but the crust needs to be baked prior to adding the filling. *To pre-bake:* Preheat the oven to 350°F (180°C). Prick bottom and sides of pie shell with tines of fork. Bake until light brown, 15 to 20 minutes. Check crust about halfway through to see if crust is puffing up. If it is, prick bottom crust with a fork or pat down with scrunched-up paper towel. Return to oven to finish baking.

¾ cup	cake flour	175 mL
½ cup	all-purpose flour	125 mL
1 tbsp	granulated sugar	15 mL
½ tsp	salt	2 mL
7 tbsp	cold unsalted butter, cut into small chunks	105 mL
3 to 4 tbsp	ice water (approx.)	45 to 60 mL

1. In work bowl fitted with metal blade, process cake flour, all-purpose flour, sugar and salt until combined, about 10 seconds. Remove lid and distribute butter evenly over top. Cover and pulse until mixture resembles coarse crumbs, about 20 times. Place water in a container with a pouring spout and, with motor running, slowly pour through the feed tube in a steady stream just until dough begins to gather. You may not use all the water, which is fine.

2. Turn out dough onto a clean surface and gather into a ball. Flatten into a disk and wrap with plastic wrap. Refrigerate until firm enough to roll out for your pie, about 20 minutes. Roll out the crust ¼ inch (0.5 cm) thick and 1½ inches (4 cm) wider than the pie plate you will be using.

Variations

Flaky Pie Pastry Dough (Vegan Friendly): Replace butter with cold vegetable shortening.

You can double this recipe for a double-crust pie. Just be careful when you add the water because you will not need twice as much as single-crust recipe.

Spiced Pie Pastry Dough

Makes enough dough for two 9-inch (23 cm) single-crust pies or one double-crust pie

Vegetarian Friendly

If you are making a spicy pie, such as Pumpkin Pecan Pie (page 626), Apple Spice Pie (page 627) or a custardy one, you can use this crust.

Tips

If your dough forms a ball in the food processor work bowl, it may be too tough. To save the dough, turn the machine off and sprinkle dough with ¼ cup (60 mL) all-purpose flour. Pulse 5 times, then proceed with Step 2.

Freeze dough in an airtight container for up to 1 month. Thaw in the refrigerator for at least 8 hours or overnight before rolling.

1½ cups	cake flour	375 mL
1½ cups	all-purpose flour	375 mL
2 tsp	ground cinnamon	10 mL
2 tsp	granulated sugar	10 mL
1 tsp	freshly grated nutmeg	5 mL
½ tsp	salt	2 mL
1 cup	cold unsalted butter, cut into small chunks	250 mL
½ cup	ice water	125 mL

1. In work bowl fitted with metal blade, process cake flour, all-purpose flour, cinnamon, sugar, nutmeg and salt until combined, about 10 seconds. Remove lid and distribute butter evenly over top. Cover and pulse until mixture resembles coarse crumbs, about 10 times. Place water in a container with a pouring spout and, with motor running, slowly pour through the feed tube in a steady stream until dough begins to gather. You may not use all the water, which is fine.

2. Turn out dough onto a clean surface and form into 2 balls. Flatten into disks and wrap in plastic wrap. Refrigerate until firm enough to roll out for your pie, 10 to 20 minutes. Roll out the crust ¼ inch (0.5 cm) thick and 1½ inches (4 cm) wider than the pie plate you will be using.

3. For pre-baking instructions, see Tip, page 475, or fill and bake according to recipe directions.

Variations

Vegan Friendly: Replace butter with cold vegetable shortening.

Try using ½ tsp (2 mL) ground cloves or mace in place of the nutmeg.

Buttery Tart Pastry Dough

Vegetarian Friendly

A tart crust, unlike a pie crust, needs to be able to stand on its own outside of a pan. This rich and buttery crust will enhance your tart pastries. Use this crust with Pear Almond Crème Tarts (page 628) or Caramel Chocolate Tarts (page 629).

Tips

You can also use this dough for small individual tart shells.

For small tarts (2-inch/ 5 cm or 3-inch/7.5 cm), press dough into tart shells and prick all over with a fork. Place on a baking sheet and bake in a preheated 375°F (190°C) oven for 14 to 18 minutes or until dry looking.

Freeze unbaked dough in an airtight container for up to 1 month.

- Two 8-inch (20 cm) metal tart pans with removable bottoms

2½ cups	all-purpose flour	625 mL
¼ cup	granulated sugar	60 mL
½ tsp	salt	2 mL
1 cup	cold unsalted butter, cut into small chunks	250 mL
2	egg yolks	2
3 tbsp	cold water	45 mL

1. In work bowl fitted with metal blade, pulse flour, sugar and salt until combined, about 5 times. Remove lid and distribute butter evenly over top. Cover and pulse until mixture resembles coarse crumbs, about 20 times.

2. In a container with a pouring spout, mix together egg yolks and cold water. With motor running, slowly pour mixture through the feed tube in a steady stream until dough begins to gather. Do not overprocess or let a ball form. The dough will be somewhat crumbly at this point. Transfer dough to a board and press lightly with palm of your hand to warm up. It is now ready to press out into tart pans, if desired.

3. Press half of the dough evenly into sides and bottom of each pan. Trim excess dough from top.

4. For pre-baking instructions, see Tip, page 475, or fill and bake according to recipe directions.

Variation

Savory Buttery Tart Pastry: You can make a savory tart shell by omitting the sugar and adding ¼ cup (60 mL) additional all-purpose flour.

Chocolate Tart Dough

Makes 2 tart shells

Vegetarian Friendly

A dark rich chocolate tart crust looks fantastic with a caramel filling (see Caramel Chocolate Tarts, page 629).

Tips

You don't have to use pie weights when blind baking tart shells. Check the tart partway through the baking and then press any bloating down with a fork or scrunched up paper towel.

To bake with filling: Fill crust with your favorite filling and follow recipe directions.

To bake unfilled: Prick bottom and sides of crust. Bake in preheated 425°F (220°C) oven until dry looking, 18 to 22 minutes. Let cool completely.

Freeze unbaked dough in an airtight container in the freezer for up to 1 month.

- Two 8-inch (20 cm) metal tart pans with removable bottoms

2 cups	all-purpose flour	500 mL
1/2 cup	unsweetened Dutch-process cocoa powder	125 mL
1/2 cup	granulated sugar	125 mL
1/2 tsp	salt	2 mL
1 cup	cold unsalted butter, cut into chunks	250 mL
2	egg yolks	2
1/4 cup	cold water	60 mL

1. In work bowl fitted with metal blade, pulse flour, cocoa powder, sugar and salt until combined, about 5 times. Remove lid and distribute butter evenly over top. Cover and pulse until mixture resembles coarse crumbs, about 20 times.

2. In a container with a pouring spout, mix together egg yolks and cold water. With the motor running, slowly pour mixture through the feed tube in a steady stream until dough begins to gather. Do not overprocess or let a ball form. The dough will be somewhat crumbly at this point. Place the dough on a board and press lightly with palm of your hand to warm up, if necessary.

3. Press half of the dough evenly into sides and bottom of each pan. Trim excess dough from top.

Variation
Try adding 1 tsp (5 mL) ground cinnamon to the dough if you are making something that cinnamon will enhance.

Smooth Peanut Butter

Makes 1 cup (250 mL)

Vegan Friendly

A little peanut oil makes this butter smooth.

10 oz	unsalted roasted peanuts	300 g
2 tbsp	peanut oil	30 mL
¼ tsp	salt	1 mL

1. In work bowl fitted with metal blade, process peanuts, peanut oil and salt until smooth, about 2 minutes.
2. Transfer to a container and refrigerate for up to 1 month.

Variation
To make this a crunchy butter, stir ¼ cup (60 mL) chopped peanuts into the finished butter.

Chunky Honey Roasted Peanut Butter

Makes 1 cup (250 mL)

Vegetarian Friendly

The sweet taste of honey makes this butter a hit on toast or crackers. Try using it in your favorite peanut butter cookies instead of regular butter, the next time you bake.

10 oz	honey roasted peanuts, divided	300 g
1 tbsp	peanut oil	15 mL
1 tsp	liquid honey	5 mL

1. In work bowl fitted with metal blade, process 8 oz (250 g) of the peanuts, peanut oil and honey until smooth, about 2 minutes.
2. Coarsely chop remaining 2 oz (60 g) of the peanuts and fold into butter. Transfer to a container and refrigerate for up to 1 month.

Cashew Honey Butter

Makes 1 cup (250 mL)

Vegetarian Friendly

Cashews are very rich and full of flavor. Try using this butter, instead of peanut butter, in cookies.

12 oz	unsalted roasted cashews	375 g
1 tbsp	vegetable oil	15 mL
1 tbsp	liquid honey	15 mL

1. In work bowl fitted with metal blade, process cashews, oil and honey until smooth, about 2 minutes.
2. Transfer to a container and refrigerate for up to 1 month.

Mixed Nut Butter

Makes 1 cup (250 mL)

Vegan Friendly

This mixed nut butter brims with rich flavors.

Tip
If you can find unsalted mixed nuts for this recipe, then skip Step 1.

10 oz	roasted mixed nuts (see Tip, left)	300 g
2 tsp	vegetable oil	10 mL
2 tsp	granulated sugar	10 mL

1. Rub nuts in a tea towel to get as much salt off as possible.
2. In work bowl fitted with metal blade, process nuts, oil and sugar until smooth, about 2 minutes.
3. Transfer to a container and refrigerate for up to 1 month.

Sunflower Seed Butter

Makes 1 cup (250 mL)

Vegan Friendly

Try using this flavorful seed butter with celery sticks.

8 oz	unsalted roasted sunflower seeds	250 g
1 tbsp	vegetable oil	15 mL
1/2 tsp	salt	2 mL

1. In work bowl fitted with metal blade, process sunflower seeds, oil and salt until smooth, about 2 minutes.
2. Transfer to a container and refrigerate for up to 1 month.

White Chocolate Pecan Scones (page 528)

Cashew Butter Cookies (page 545)

Lemon Shortbread Cookies (page 554)

Quadruple Chocolate Chunk Cookies (page 564)

Apple Crisp with Crumb Topping (page 623)

Cherry Clafouti (page 599)

Peaches with Raspberry Coulis and Passion Fruit Sorbet (page 602)

Apple Spice Pie (page 627)

Yeast Breads, Quick Breads, Muffins and Scones

Potato Rolls

Vegetarian Friendly

These rolls add great flavor to any meal. They're perfect for a holiday table.

Tips

If you do not have a potato handy you can use instant potatoes. Prepare according to package directions to make ⅓ cup (75 mL).

In Step 2 when bringing milk, butter and honey to a simmer, check until an instant-read thermometer registers approximately 120° to 130°F (50° to 55°C).

- Baking sheet, lined with parchment paper

½	russet (Idaho) potato, baked and peeled	½
¾ cup	milk	175 mL
2 tbsp	unsalted butter, softened	30 mL
1½ tbsp	liquid honey	22 mL
3 cups	bread flour, divided (approx.)	750 mL
1	package (¼ oz/8 g) quick-rising (instant) dry yeast	1
1 tsp	salt	5 mL

1. In the work bowl fitted with metal blade, process potato until soft and smooth. Measure out ⅓ cup (75 mL). Transfer to a small bowl.

2. In a saucepan over medium heat, bring milk, butter and honey to a simmer, about 3 minutes (see Tips, left). Do not let boil.

3. Meanwhile, in work bowl fitted with metal blade, process 2 cups (500 mL) of the flour, yeast and salt until well combined, about 15 seconds. With the motor running, slowly add hot milk mixture through the feed tube. With the motor continuing to run, add potato, one-third at a time, then spoon additional flour through the feed tube, ¼ cup (60 mL) at a time, until dough starts to pull away from sides and begins to gather and a soft, not sticky, dough forms.

4. Remove dough from work bowl and place on a floured surface. Knead until dough is smooth and elastic, 3 to 5 minutes. Shape into a ball. Transfer to a large oiled bowl and turn to coat all over. Cover loosely with plastic wrap. Let dough rise in a warm, draft-free place until doubled in volume, about 45 to 90 minutes, depending on humidity and heat factors.

5. Preheat oven to 350°F (180°C). Punch down dough and form into 12 round rolls. Transfer to prepared baking sheet touching side by side so they join together when rising. With tips of a pair of kitchen shears, cut a shallow slit in the top of each roll. Dust with additional flour. Cover with a towel and let rest in a warm, draft-free place until they rise slightly, 15 to 20 minutes. Bake in preheated oven until light brown on top, 16 to 20 minutes. Let cool on wire rack. Pull apart to serve.

Potato Cheddar Rolls

Makes 18 rolls

Vegetarian Friendly

These soft yeast rolls have the bite of Cheddar cheese. Many think yeast rolls are difficult to make. Try these and you will be making rolls every week.

Tips

If time is a factor you can prepare the dough through Step 5. Place the oiled bowl in your refrigerator (make sure the fridge does not have any strong odors because the dough will take those on). The next day you can continue with Step 6.

In Step 2 when bringing milk, butter and honey to a simmer, check until an instant-read thermometer registers approximately 120° to 130°F (50° to 55°C).

Dough can take from 45 to 90 minutes to double its volume depending on humidity and heat factors.

- Baking sheet, lined with parchment paper

8 oz	Cheddar cheese, cut into chunks	250 g
½	russet (Idaho) potato, baked and peeled	½
1⅛ cups	whole milk	280 mL
3 tbsp	unsalted butter, softened	45 mL
2 tbsp	liquid honey	30 mL
3 cups	bread flour, divided	750 mL
1½ cups	all-purpose flour, divided	375 mL
2	packages (each ¼ oz/8 g) quick-rising (instant) dry yeast	2
1 tsp	salt	5 mL

1. In a work bowl fitted with shredding blade, shred cheese. Transfer to a small bowl. Set aside. Replace shredding blade with metal blade and process potato until soft and smooth. Measure ½ cup (125 mL) and set aside, discarding or reserving any remaining for another use.

2. In a saucepan over medium heat, bring milk, butter and honey to a simmer, about 3 minutes (see Tips, left). Do not let boil.

3. Meanwhile, in work bowl fitted with metal blade, process 2 cups (500 mL) bread flour, 1 cup (250 mL) all-purpose flour, yeast and salt, about 10 seconds. With motor running, slowly add hot milk mixture through feed tube, then potato and cheese. Spoon additional flour through feed tube, ¼ cup (60 mL) at a time, until dough starts to pull away from sides and begins to gather and a soft, not sticky, dough forms.

4. Turn out onto a floured surface. Knead until dough is smooth and elastic, 2 to 4 minutes. Shape into a ball. Transfer to a large oiled bowl and turn to coat all over. Cover loosely with plastic wrap. Let dough rise in a warm, draft-free place until doubled in volume, 45 to 90 minutes.

5. Preheat oven to 350°F (180°C). Punch down dough and form into 18 round rolls. Transfer to baking sheet touching side by side. Cover with a clean towel and let rest in a warm, draft-free place until they rise slightly, 15 to 20 minutes.

6. Bake in preheated oven until light brown on top, 16 to 20 minutes. Let cool on wire rack. Pull apart to serve.

Cheddar Cheese Rolls

Makes 12 rolls

Vegetarian Friendly

Serve these rich rolls with a hearty chowder. It's a great combo during the winter.

Tips

Sugar adds color to the final baked rolls and salt balances the flavor. Do not omit.

In Step 2 when bringing milk, butter and honey to a simmer, check until an instant-read thermometer registers approximately 120° to 130°F (50° to 55°C).

- Baking sheet, lined with parchment paper

6 oz	Cheddar cheese, cut into chunks	175 g
¾ cup	water	175 mL
1½ tsp	unsalted butter, softened	7 mL
3½ cups	bread flour, divided (approx.)	875 mL
1 tbsp	granulated sugar (see Tips, left)	15 mL
1	package (¼ oz/8 g) quick-rising (instant) dry yeast	1
1 tsp	salt	5 mL
1	egg	1

1. In work bowl fitted with shredding blade, shred cheese. Transfer to a small bowl. Transfer 2 tbsp (30 mL) to a separate bowl, cover and refrigerate. Set remaining cheese aside.

2. In a small saucepan, bring water and butter to a simmer, about 3 minutes (see Tips, left). Do not let boil.

3. Replace shredding blade with metal blade and process 2 cups (500 mL) flour, sugar, yeast and salt, about 15 seconds. With the motor running, slowly add hot water mixture through the feed tube into work bowl. Add egg and all but 2 tbsp (30 mL) cheese and process until incorporated, about 5 seconds. With the motor continuing to run, spoon additional flour through the feed tube, ¼ cup (60 mL) at time, until dough starts to pull away from sides and begins to gather and a soft, not sticky, dough forms.

4. Remove from work bowl and place on a floured surface. Knead until dough is smooth and elastic, 3 to 5 minutes. Shape into a ball. Transfer to a large oiled bowl and turn to coat all over. Cover loosely with plastic wrap. Let dough rise in a warm, draft-free place until doubled in volume, about 45 to 90 minutes, depending on humidity and heat factors.

5. Preheat oven to 375°F (190°C). Punch down dough, form into 12 round rolls and place on prepared baking sheet, about 2 inches (5 cm) apart. Top with grated cheese. Cover with a towel and let rest in a warm, draft-free place until they rise slightly, 15 to 20 minutes. Top with reserved refrigerated grated cheese. Bake in preheated oven until light brown and cheese is bubbling, 12 to 18 minutes. Let cool on wire rack.

Whole Wheat Rolls

Vegetarian Friendly

Pair these rolls with a hearty beef stew, chili or root vegetable soup.

Tip

To create even size rolls, cut the dough in quarters, and then cut those into thirds resulting in 12 rolls.

- Instant-read thermometer
- Baking sheet, lined with parchment paper

1 cup	milk	250 mL
1 tbsp	unsalted butter	15 mL
1½ tbsp	pure maple syrup	22 mL
1¾ cups	all-purpose flour, divided (approx.)	425 mL
1¾ cups	whole wheat flour, divided (approx.)	425 mL
1	package (¼ oz/8 g) quick-rising (instant) dry yeast	1
1 tsp	salt	5 mL

1. In a saucepan over medium heat, bring milk, butter and maple syrup to a simmer until an instant-read thermometer registers approximately 120° to 130°F (50° to 55°C), about 3 minutes. Do not let boil.

2. Meanwhile, in work bowl fitted with metal blade, process 1 cup (250 mL) each of the all-purpose flour, whole wheat flour, yeast and salt until well combined, about 15 seconds. With the motor running, slowly add hot milk mixture through the feed tube into work bowl. With the motor continuing to run, alternately spoon additional all-purpose flour and whole wheat flour through the feed tube, ¼ cup (60 mL) at a time, until dough starts to pull away from sides and begins to gather and a soft, not sticky, dough forms.

3. Remove from work bowl and place on a floured surface. Knead until dough is smooth and elastic, 3 to 5 minutes. Shape into a ball. Transfer to a large oiled bowl and turn to coat all over. Cover loosely with plastic wrap. Let dough rise in a warm, draft-free place until doubled in volume, about 45 to 90 minutes, depending on humidity and heat factors.

4. Preheat oven to 350°F (180°C). Punch down dough and form into 12 rolls. Transfer to prepared baking sheet, about 2 inches (5 cm) apart. Cover with a towel and let rest in a warm, draft-free place until they rise slightly, 20 to 30 minutes. Bake in preheated oven until light brown, 18 to 22 minutes. Let cool on wire rack.

Crusty French Rolls

Makes 12 rolls

Vegetarian Friendly

These rolls are a staple of the French diet. Everyone in France purchases a fresh baguette or roll each day. It's a law that every city and village has to have at least one bakery open every day so everyone has fresh bread.

Tip

Use a misting bottle instead of a pastry brush to avoid flattening the dough.

- Instant-read thermometer
- Baking sheet, lined with parchment paper

1¼ cups	water, divided	300 mL
3½ cups	all-purpose flour, divided (approx.)	875 mL
1	package (¼ oz/8 g) quick-rising (instant) dry yeast	1
1 tbsp	granulated sugar	15 mL
1 tsp	salt	5 mL

1. In a saucepan over medium heat, bring 1 cup (250 mL) of the water to a simmer until an instant-read thermometer registers approximately 120° to 130°F (50° to 55°C). Do not let boil.

2. Meanwhile, in work bowl fitted with metal blade, process 2 cups (500 mL) of the flour, yeast, sugar and salt until well combined, for 10 seconds. With the motor running, slowly add 1 cup (250 mL) warm water through the feed tube into work bowl. With the motor continuing to run, spoon additional flour through the feed tube, ¼ cup (60 mL) at a time, until dough starts to pull away from sides and begins to gather and a soft, not sticky, dough forms.

3. Remove from work bowl and place on a floured surface. Knead until dough is smooth and elastic, 3 to 5 minutes. Shape into a ball. Transfer to a large oiled bowl and turn to coat all over. Cover loosely with plastic wrap. Let dough rise in a warm, draft-free place until doubled in volume, about 45 to 90 minutes, depending on humidity and heat factors.

4. Preheat oven to 400°F (200°C). Punch down dough and form into 12 round rolls. Roll out each ball into logs, like miniature hot dog buns, about 3½ inches (8.5 cm) long. Place on prepared baking sheet, 3 inches (7.5 cm) apart. With the tips of a pair of kitchen shears, cut 3 slits along the top of each roll. Cover with a towel and let rest in a warm, draft-free place until they rise slightly, 20 to 30 minutes. Transfer remaining ¼ cup (60 mL) of the water to a misting bottle and spray dough with a fine mist (see Tip, left). Bake in preheated oven until light brown, 18 to 22 minutes. Let cool on wire rack.

Pesto Herb Bread

Makes 2 loafs or 24 rolls

Vegetarian Friendly

Use fresh garden basil here and serve with an Italian feast of pasta and sauce.

Tip

Unsalted or "sweet" butter is manufactured without adding salt to preserve the butter, thus creating a fresher product. The amount of salt added varies between brands so you don't have as much control over the amount of salt in your dish. Both butters are interchangeable, but taste for salt before adding any to your recipe.

- Instant-read thermometer
- Baking sheet, lined with parchment paper

2 cups	whole milk	500 mL
2 tbsp	unsalted butter (see Tip, left)	30 mL
2 tbsp	fresh basil leaves	30 mL
2	cloves garlic, minced	2
2 tsp	fresh dill fronds	10 mL
5½ to 6 cups	all-purpose flour, divided	1.375 to 1.5 L
2 tbsp	granulated sugar	30 mL
2	packages (each ¼ oz/8 g) quick-rising (instant) dry yeast	2
2½ tsp	salt	12 mL

1. In a saucepan over medium heat, bring milk, butter, basil, garlic and dill to a simmer until an instant-read thermometer registers approximately 120° to 130°F (50 to 55°C), about 3 minutes. Do not let boil.

2. Meanwhile, in work bowl fitted with metal blade, process 4 cups (1 L) of the flour, sugar, yeast and salt until well combined, about 10 seconds. With motor running, slowly add hot milk mixture through feed tube. With motor continuing to run, spoon additional flour through feed tube, ¼ cup (60 mL) at a time, until dough starts to pull away from sides and begins to gather and a soft, not sticky, dough forms.

3. Turn out onto a floured surface. Knead until dough is smooth and elastic, 2 to 4 minutes. Shape into a ball. Transfer to a large oiled bowl and turn to coat all over. Cover loosely with plastic wrap. Let dough rise in a warm, draft-free place until doubled in volume, 45 to 90 minutes.

4. Preheat oven to 350°F (180°C). Punch down dough and form into 2 loaves or 24 round rolls. Transfer to prepared baking sheets; if making bread, place each loaf on a baking sheet; if making rolls, touch side by side so they join together when rising. Cover with a clean towel and let rest in a warm, draft-free place until they rise slightly, 15 to 20 minutes for rolls, 25 to 30 minutes for loaves.

5. Bake in preheated oven until light brown on top, 30 to 40 minutes and an internal temperature of 190°F (88°C) if making loaves, or 16 to 20 minutes if making rolls. Let cool on wire rack.

Sun-Dried Tomato Pesto Bread

Vegetarian Friendly

This is a great bread to have with a big helping of pasta!

Tips

If you can only find sun-dried tomatoes that are not packed in oil, make sure you soften them by placing them in a dish of hot water and soak until softened, about 30 minutes. Drain and pat dry before using.

In Step 2 when bringing milk, butter and honey to a simmer, check until an instant-read thermometer registers approximately 120° to 130°F (50° to 55°C).

- Baking sheet, lined with parchment paper

1/3 cup	oil-packed sun-dried tomatoes, drained (see Tips, left)	75 mL
1/3 cup	packed fresh basil	75 mL
3/4 cup	milk	175 mL
2 tbsp	unsalted butter	30 mL
3 cups	bread flour (approx.)	750 mL
1	package (1/4 oz/8 g) quick-rising (instant) dry yeast	1
1 tsp	granulated sugar	5 mL
1/2 tsp	salt	2 mL
1	egg	1

1. In work bowl fitted with metal blade, process sun-dried tomatoes and basil until smooth, about 2 minutes. Transfer to a bowl.

2. In a small saucepan over medium heat, bring milk and butter to a simmer, about 3 minutes (see Tips, left). Do not let boil.

3. Meanwhile, in clean work bowl fitted with metal dough blade, process 2 cups (500 mL) of the flour, yeast, sugar and salt until well combined, about 15 seconds. With the motor running, slowly pour hot milk mixture through the feed tube into the work bowl. Add egg and process until incorporated, about 20 seconds. With the motor continuing to run, add sun-dried tomato mixture until incorporated. With the motor running, spoon additional flour through the feed tube, 1/4 cup (60 mL) at a time, until dough pulls away from sides and begins to gather, about 90 seconds.

4. Remove dough from work bowl and place on a floured surface. Knead until dough is smooth and elastic, 3 to 5 minutes. Shape into a ball. Transfer to a large oiled bowl and turn to coat all over. Cover loosely with plastic wrap. Let dough rise in a warm, draft-free place until doubled in volume, about 45 to 90 minutes.

5. Preheat the oven to 350°F (180°C). Punch down dough and form into two round loaves. Place on prepared baking sheet, at least 2 inches (5 cm) apart. Cover with a towel and let rest in a warm, draft-free place until they rise slightly, 20 to 30 minutes. Bake in preheated oven until light brown, 30 to 40 minutes. Let cool on wire rack.

California Wine and Cheese Bread

Vegetarian Friendly

The white wine gives this bread a light flavor and great texture.

Tips

Make sure you have plenty of flour on hand. Never try to make a recipe with the exact amount of flour called for in the recipe because most likely you'll end up needing more. If you are making bread in New Orleans, for instance, where the humidity is high, you'll need additional flour to "soak up" the extra moisture, whereas in Phoenix or Edmonton you may need less. This is why the flours are always a variable or an approximation.

Dough can take from 45 to 90 minutes to double its volume depending on humidity and heat factors.

- Instant-read thermometer
- Baking sheet, lined with parchment paper

¼ cup	dry white wine	60 mL
¼ cup	water	60 mL
2 tbsp	unsalted butter	30 mL
4 oz	Monterey Jack cheese, cut into chunks	125 g
2½ cups	bread flour, divided (approx.)	625 mL
1¾ tsp	granulated sugar	8 mL
½ tsp	salt	2 mL
1	package (¼ oz/8 g) quick-rising (instant) dry yeast	1
1	egg	1

1. In a small saucepan over medium heat, bring wine, water and butter to a simmer until an instant-read thermometer registers approximately 120° to 130°F (50° to 55°C), about 3 minutes. Do not let boil.

2. Meanwhile, in work bowl fitted with shredding blade, shred cheese. Transfer to a bowl.

3. Replace shredding blade with metal blade. Add 2 cups (500 mL) of the flour, sugar, salt and yeast and process until well combined, about 15 seconds. With the motor running, slowly pour hot wine mixture through the feed tube into work bowl. Add egg and cheese and process until blended, about 20 seconds. With the motor continuing to run, spoon additional flour through the feed tube into mixture, about ¼ cup (60 mL) at a time, until dough pulls away from sides and begins to gather and a soft, not sticky, dough forms, about 90 seconds.

4. Remove dough from work bowl and place on a floured surface. Knead until dough is smooth and elastic, 3 to 5 minutes. Shape into a ball. Transfer to a large oiled bowl and turn to coat all over. Cover loosely with plastic wrap. Let dough rise in a warm, draft-free place until doubled in volume, about 45 to 90 minutes (see Tips, left).

5. Preheat the oven to 375°F (190°C). Punch down dough and form into a round loaf. Place on baking sheet. Cover with a towel and let rest in a warm, draft-free place until it rises slightly, 20 to 30 minutes. Bake until light brown, 30 to 40 minutes. Let cool on wire rack.

Fresh Tarragon Dill Bread

Makes 2 loaves

Vegetarian Friendly

The taste of fresh herbs in this bread reminds us of the gardens of the south of France.

Tips

The bread will have a green tinge to it because of the herbs. Do not use dry herbs because they will look like specks of black in the dough.

In Step 2 when bringing milk, butter and honey to a simmer, check until an instant-read thermometer registers approximately 120° to 130°F (50° to 55°C).

Dough can take from 45 to 90 minutes to double its volume depending on humidity and heat factors.

- Baking sheet, lined with parchment paper

1¾ cups	milk	425 mL
2 tbsp	unsalted butter	30 mL
½ cup	loosely packed Italian flat-leaf parsley leaves	125 mL
2	cloves garlic	2
2 tsp	fresh dill fronds	10 mL
2 tsp	fresh tarragon leaves	10 mL
4½ cups	all-purpose flour (approx.)	1.125 L
2 tbsp	granulated sugar	30 mL
2	packages (each ¼ oz/8 g) quick-rising (instant) dry yeast	2
2½ tsp	salt	12 mL

1. In a saucepan over medium heat, bring milk and butter to a simmer, about 3 minutes (see Tips, left). Do not let boil.

2. Meanwhile, in work bowl fitted with metal blade, pulse parsley, garlic, dill and tarragon until finely chopped, about 20 times. Transfer to a small bowl.

3. In clean work bowl with metal blade, process 3 cups (750 mL) of the flour, sugar, yeast and salt for 15 seconds. With the motor running, slowly pour hot milk mixture through the feed tube into work bowl. Then add herb mixture, pulsing 10 times. With the motor continuing to run, add additional flour through the feed tube, ¼ cup (60 mL) at a time, until dough pulls away from sides and begins to gather and a soft, not sticky, dough forms, about 90 seconds.

4. Remove dough from work bowl and place on a floured surface. Knead until dough is smooth and elastic, 3 to 5 minutes. Shape into a ball. Transfer to a large oiled bowl and turn to coat all over. Cover loosely with plastic wrap. Let dough rise in a warm, draft-free place until doubled in volume, about 45 to 90 minutes (see Tips, left).

5. Preheat the oven to 350°F (180°C). Punch down dough and form into two round loaves. Place on prepared baking sheet, at least 2 inches (5 cm) apart. Cover with a towel and let rest in a warm, draft-free place until they rise slightly, 20 to 30 minutes. Bake in preheated oven until light brown, 30 to 40 minutes. Let cool on wire rack.

Big Ranch Cornbread

Serves 16

Vegetarian Friendly

This sweet corn bread that goes well with a tossed salad or a cup of soup. Serve with Honey Butter (page 460).

- Preheat oven to 350°F (180°C)
- 13- by 9-inch (33 by 23 cm) metal baking pan, sprayed with nonstick spray

2⅓ cups	all-purpose flour	575 mL
1 cup	cake flour	250 mL
1 cup	granulated sugar	250 mL
2½ tsp	baking powder	12 mL
¼ tsp	salt	1 mL
1¾ cups	whole milk	425 mL
3	eggs	3
½ cup	oil	125 mL
½ tbsp	vanilla extract	7 mL
⅔ cup	yellow cornmeal	150 mL

1. In a bowl, combine all-purpose flour, cake flour, sugar, baking powder and salt. Set aside.

2. In work bowl fitted with metal blade, process milk, eggs, oil and vanilla for 10 seconds. Add flour mixture, process for 10 seconds. Add cornmeal, process for 5 seconds.

3. Transfer to prepared pan, smoothing top. Bake in preheated oven until a toothpick inserted in the center comes out clean, 28 to 35 minutes. Let cool in pan on a wire rack for 15 minutes. Transfer to rack to cool completely.

Variation
Add 2 jalapeño peppers, chopped, to make a spicy cornbread perfect to pair with chowders.

Cheesy Jalapeño Cornbread

Makes 8 servings

Vegetarian Friendly

Slightly spicy, intriguingly savory and deliciously comforting. What more could you want? Serve this cornbread as an accompaniment to dinner or just enjoy it on its own.

Tips

If you are using already shredded cheese, you'll need 1 cup (250 mL).

Be sure to use stone-ground cornmeal. Otherwise the recipe is not likely to work.

Unsalted or "sweet" butter is manufactured without adding salt to preserve the butter, thus creating a fresher product. The amount of salt added varies between brands so you don't have as much control over the amount of salt in your dish. Both butters are interchangeable, but taste for salt before adding any to your recipe.

Not only does pulsing blend the dry ingredients, it also aerates them slightly, contributing to a lighter result.

- Preheat oven to 400°F (200°C)
- 8-inch (20 cm) square baking pan, lightly greased

4 oz	Cheddar cheese, preferably aged	125 g
1 cup	stone-ground yellow cornmeal (see Tips, left)	250 mL
¾ cup	whole wheat flour	175 mL
1 tbsp	granulated sugar	15 mL
2 tsp	baking powder	10 mL
½ tsp	baking soda	2 mL
½ tsp	salt	2 mL
¼ cup	cold unsalted butter, cubed (see Tips, left)	60 mL
1¼ cups	buttermilk	300 mL
2	eggs, separated	2
¼ tsp	baking soda, dissolved in 1 tbsp (15 mL) water	1 mL
1	jalapeño pepper, seeded and minced	1

1. In work bowl fitted with shredding blade, shred cheese. Transfer to a bowl and set aside.

2. Replace shredding blade with metal blade. Add cornmeal, flour, sugar, baking powder, baking soda and salt. Pulse to blend, 2 or 3 times. Add butter and pulse until mixture resembles coarse crumbs. In a measuring cup, combine buttermilk, egg yolks, baking soda and jalapeño pepper and beat well. Pour over cornmeal mixture and pulse just until blended.

3. In a bowl, using an electric mixer on high speed, beat egg whites until stiff peaks form. Fold in cheese. Fold in cornmeal mixture and spoon into prepared pan. Bake in preheated oven until top is golden and springs back, about 25 minutes. Let cool in pan on a wire rack for 5 minutes. Serve warm.

Variation
Cheesy Chipotle Cornbread: Substitute 1 minced chipotle pepper in adobo sauce for the jalapeño.

German Holiday Stollen Bread

Vegetarian Friendly

Christmastime is not the same without a slice of stollen bread — an old-world tradition that originated in Germany. The candied fruit and brandy need to soak overnight. It is always a welcome gift and freezes well.

Tips

You can let fruit soak up to 1 week prior to making this bread.

To freeze: Let cool completely, then wrap in plastic then in foil. Bread keeps for up to 2 months in the freezer.

To toast sliced almonds: Place nuts in a single layer on a baking sheet in a preheated 350°F (180°C) oven, stirring once or twice, for 4 to 7 minutes or until fragrant and golden.

- Instant-read thermometer
- Baking sheet, lined with parchment paper

1½ cups	candied fruit (cherries, pineapple, etc.)	375 mL
¼ cup	brandy	60 mL
1	package (¼ oz/8 g) quick-rising (instant) dry yeast	1
1 tsp	granulated sugar	5 mL
3 tbsp	warm water (110°F/42°C)	45 mL
½ cup	whole milk, warmed to 110°F (42°C)	125 mL
3 cups	all-purpose flour, divided	750 mL
1	egg	1
½ cup	unsalted butter, melted, divided	125 mL
¼ cup	granulated sugar	60 mL
½ tsp	salt	2 mL
½ cup	slivered almonds, lightly toasted	125 mL
	Confectioner's (icing) sugar	

1. In a medium bowl, soak candied fruit and brandy overnight.

2. In a small bowl, combine yeast, 1 tsp (5 mL) sugar and warm water. Stir until yeast is dissolved. Let stand for 5 minutes in a warm place to activate the yeast.

3. In work bowl fitted with metal blade, process milk, 1 cup (250 mL) of the flour and activated yeast mixture for 10 seconds. Let rest for 15 minutes.

4. While motor is running, add egg, 6 tbsp (90 mL) of the butter, ¼ cup (60 mL) sugar and salt through feed tube. Add the remaining 2 cups (500 mL) of flour. Process until dough forms a ball, about 30 seconds.

5. Turn out onto a floured surface. Knead soaked fruit and almonds into dough. Transfer to a large oiled bowl and turn to coat all over. Cover loosely with plastic wrap. Let dough rise in a warm, draft-free place for 45 minutes.

6. Preheat oven to 425°F (220°C). Punch dough down, knead about 12 times. Shape into a loaf. Place on prepared baking sheet.

7. Bake in preheated oven for 10 minutes. Reduce temperature to 350°F (180°C) and bake 45 minutes more or until an instant-read thermometer inserted into center reads 190°F (88°C). Serve with a dusting of icing sugar.

Oatmeal Nutmeg Bread

Makes 2 loafs or 24 rolls

Vegetarian Friendly

This oatmeal bread has a nutty taste and texture. Try it with freshly made nut butter (pages 479 and 480).

- Instant-read thermometer
- Baking sheet, lined with parchment paper

⅔ cup	boiling water	150 mL
⅔ cup	old-fashioned rolled oats	150 mL
1½ tbsp	unsalted butter, softened	22 mL
1½ tbsp	lightly packed brown sugar	22 mL
1½ cups	all-purpose flour, divided	375 mL
1½ cups	whole wheat flour, divided	375 mL
2	packages (each ¼ oz/8 g) quick-rising (instant) dry yeast	2
1 tsp	freshly grated nutmeg	5 mL

1. In a bowl, pour boiling water over oats and let soak for 15 minutes.

2. In a saucepan over medium heat, bring 1 cup (250 mL) water, butter and brown sugar to a simmer until an instant-read thermometer registers approximately 120° to 130°F (50 to 55°C), about 3 minutes. Do not let boil.

3. Meanwhile, in work bowl fitted with metal blade, process 1 cup (250 mL) each of all-purpose flour and whole wheat flour, yeast and nutmeg until well combined, about 10 seconds. With motor running, slowly add hot water mixture and rolled oats through feed tube. With motor continuing to run, add additional all-purpose flour and whole wheat flour through feed tube, ¼ cup (60 mL) at a time, until dough starts to pull away from sides and begins to gather and a soft, not sticky, dough forms.

4. Turn out onto a floured surface. Knead until dough is smooth and elastic, 2 to 4 minutes. Shape into a ball. Transfer to an oiled bowl and turn to coat all over. Cover loosely with plastic wrap. Let dough rise in a warm, draft-free place until doubled in volume, 45 to 90 minutes.

5. Preheat oven to 350°F (180°C). Punch down dough and form into 2 loaves or 24 round rolls. Transfer to prepared baking sheets; if making bread, place each loaf on a separate baking sheet; if making rolls, touch side by side so they join together when rising. Cover with a clean towel and let rest in a warm, draft-free place until they rise slightly, 15 to 20 minutes. Bake in preheated oven until light brown on top, 30 to 40 minutes and an internal temperature of 190°F (88°C), if making loaves, or 16 to 20 minutes, if making rolls. Let cool on wire rack.

Honey Whole Wheat Sunflower Bread

Vegetarian Friendly

Honey makes the texture of this bread so soft and smooth.

Tip

Sometimes the honey sinks to the bottom of the milk mixture. Make sure you use a heatproof spatula to remove it all from the pan.

- Baking sheet, lined with parchment paper

1½ cups	milk	375 mL
1½ tbsp	unsalted butter	22 mL
2 tbsp	liquid honey	30 mL
2 cups	all-purpose flour, divided (approx.)	500 mL
2 cups	whole wheat flour	500 mL
1	package (¼ oz/8 g) quick-rising (instant) dry yeast	1
1 tsp	salt	5 mL
½ cup	roasted unsalted sunflower seeds	125 mL

1. In a small saucepan over medium heat, bring milk, butter and honey to a simmer until an instant-read thermometer registers approximately 120° to 130°F (50° to 55°C), about 3 minutes. Do not let boil.

2. Meanwhile, in work bowl fitted with metal blade, process 1½ cups (375 mL) of the all-purpose flour, the whole wheat flour, yeast and salt until well combined, about 15 seconds. With the motor running, slowly pour hot milk mixture through the feed tube into work bowl. With the motor continuing to run, spoon additional all-purpose flour through the feed tube, about ¼ cup (60 mL) at a time, until dough pulls away from sides and begins to gather and a soft, not sticky, dough forms, about 90 seconds. Add sunflower seeds and pulse 5 times.

3. Remove from work bowl and place on a floured surface. Knead until dough is smooth and elastic, 3 to 5 minutes. Shape into a ball. Transfer to a large oiled bowl and turn to coat all over. Cover loosely with plastic wrap. Let dough rise in a warm, draft-free place until doubled in volume, 45 to 90 minutes, depending on the humidity and heat factors.

4. Preheat the oven to 350°F (180°C). Punch down dough and form into two round loaves. Place on prepared baking sheet, at least 2 inches (5 cm) apart. Cover with a towel and let rest in a warm, draft-free place until they rise slightly, 20 to 30 minutes. Bake in preheated oven until light brown, 30 to 40 minutes. Let cool on wire rack.

Variation

Add ¼ tsp (1 mL) ground cardamom to the flour mixture.

Walnut Orange Bread

Serves 8

Vegetarian Friendly

Pair this bread with other citrus breads for a luncheon or tea.

Tip

To toast walnuts: Preheat oven to 350°F (180°C). Spread walnuts on a baking sheet and bake, shaking the pan several times, until fragrant and toasted; 6 to 9 minutes for walnut halves; 4 to 7 minutes for chopped walnuts.

- Preheat oven to 375°F (190°C)
- 9- by 5-inch (23 by 12.5 cm) loaf pan, sprayed with nonstick spray

1/4 cup	toasted walnuts (see Tip, left)	60 mL
1 1/2 cups	all-purpose flour	375 mL
1 tsp	baking powder	5 mL
1/2 tsp	salt	2 mL
1 cup	granulated sugar	250 mL
1/2 cup	unsalted butter, softened	125 mL
2	eggs	2
1/2 cup	whole milk	125 mL
1 tbsp	grated orange zest	15 mL

Icing

2 tbsp	frozen orange juice concentrate, thawed	30 mL
1/4 cup	confectioner's (icing) sugar	60 mL

1. In work bowl fitted with metal blade, pulse walnuts a few times just to chop coarsely. Transfer to a bowl.

2. In another bowl, combine flour, baking powder and salt. Set aside.

3. In same work bowl, process sugar and butter until smooth, for 10 seconds. With processor running, add eggs, milk and orange zest through feed tube. Add flour mixture and process just until incorporated, for 10 seconds. Transfer to a large bowl and fold in walnuts.

4. Transfer to prepared baking pan, smoothing top. Bake in preheated oven until a toothpick inserted in the center comes out clean, 45 to 55 minutes. Let cool in loaf pan on a wire rack for 15 minutes. Transfer to rack to cool completely.

5. **Icing:** Meanwhile, blend orange juice concentrate and confectioner's sugar together. Ice top of cooled loaf.

Variation

You can use any array of citrus for this recipe. Substitute the orange zest with lemon, lime or tangerine in equal proportions.

Banana Pear Bread

Serves 16

Vegetarian Friendly

The texture of this bread is remarkable with the oatmeal in the batter. Place a slice on a plate with fresh strawberries for serving.

Tip

To toast macadamia nuts: Place nuts in a single layer on a baking sheet in a preheated 350°F (180°C) oven, stirring once or twice, for 6 to 9 minutes for whole, 4 to 7 minutes for chopped, or until fragrant and golden.

- Preheat oven to 350°F (180°C)
- 10-inch (25 cm) tube pan, sprayed with nonstick spray

1 cup	toasted macadamia nuts (see Tip, left)	250 mL
2	medium very ripe bananas, cut into smaller chunks	2
1	medium pear, peeled, cored and halved	1
¼ cup	unsalted butter, softened	60 mL
¾ cup	lightly packed brown sugar	175 mL
1	egg, beaten	1
1 cup	buttermilk	250 mL
1 cup	all-purpose flour	250 mL
1 cup	quick-cooking rolled oats	250 mL
1 tbsp	baking powder	15 mL
1½ tsp	ground cinnamon	7 mL
½ tsp	freshly grated nutmeg	2 mL
½ tsp	salt	2 mL
½ tsp	ground allspice	2 mL

1. In work bowl fitted with metal blade, pulse macadamia nuts to chop, 2 to 3 times. Transfer to a bowl. In same work bowl, pulse bananas and pear until coarsely chopped, about 10 times. Transfer to bowl with macadamia nuts. Set aside.

2. In same work bowl, process butter and brown sugar until smooth, about 10 seconds. With motor running, pour egg and buttermilk through feed tube and process for 5 seconds. Add flour, oats, baking powder, cinnamon, nutmeg, salt and allspice and process just until incorporated, about 10 seconds. Transfer to a large bowl. Fold in nuts, pear and bananas.

3. Pour into prepared pan, smoothing top. Bake until a toothpick inserted in the center comes out clean, 45 to 50 minutes. Let cool in pan on rack for 10 minutes, and then invert onto rack to cool completely.

Chocolate Oatmeal Banana Bread

Serves 8

Vegetarian Friendly

Rich chocolate chunks and moist bananas make this bread a family favorite.

- Preheat oven to 375°F (190°C)
- 9- by 5-inch (23 by 12.5 cm) loaf pan, sprayed with nonstick spray

1	medium very ripe banana, cut into chunks	1
¼ cup	unsalted butter, softened	60 mL
¾ cup	lightly packed brown sugar	175 mL
1	egg	1
1 cup	buttermilk	250 mL
1 tsp	vanilla extract	5 mL
1 cup	old-fashioned rolled oats	250 mL
¾ cup	all-purpose flour	175 mL
¼ cup	unsweetened Dutch-process cocoa powder	60 mL
1 tbsp	baking powder	15 mL
½ tsp	salt	2 mL
1 cup	semisweet chocolate chunks	250 mL

1. In work bowl fitted with metal blade, process banana until puréed, about 10 seconds. Transfer to a bowl and set aside.

2. In same work bowl, process butter and brown sugar until smooth, about 20 seconds. With motor running, pour egg, buttermilk and vanilla through feed tube. Add oats, flour, cocoa powder, baking powder and salt. Process just until incorporated, about 10 seconds. Transfer to a bowl. Fold in banana purée and chocolate chunks.

3. Pour batter into prepared baking pan, smoothing top. Bake in preheated oven until a toothpick inserted in the center comes out clean, 50 to 60 minutes. Let cool in pan on a wire rack for 15 minutes. Transfer to rack to cool completely.

Almond Bread

Vegetarian Friendly

This simple tasting bread is full of flavor. Try a slice toasted with a few fresh berries on top or a drizzle of pure maple syrup.

Tip

Purchase almond flour in small quantities because its shelf life is short compared to other flours.

- Preheat oven to 375°F (190°C)
- 9- by 5-inch (23 by 12.5 cm) loaf pan, sprayed with nonstick spray

½ cup	unsalted butter, softened	125 mL
½ cup	granulated sugar	125 mL
1	egg	1
½ cup	whole milk	125 mL
2 tsp	almond extract	10 mL
1½ cups	all-purpose flour	375 mL
½ cup	almond flour (see Tip, left)	125 mL
½ cup	sliced almonds	125 mL
2 tsp	baking powder	10 mL
1 tsp	salt	5 mL

1. In work bowl fitted with metal blade, process butter and sugar until smooth, about 20 seconds. With motor running, add egg, milk and almond extract through feed tube. Add all-purpose flour, almond flour, almonds, baking powder and salt. Pulse just until incorporated, about 10 times.

2. Pour batter into prepared loaf pan, smoothing top. Bake in preheated oven until a toothpick inserted in the center comes out clean, 50 to 60 minutes. Let cool in pan on a wire rack for 15 minutes. Transfer to rack to cool completely

Variation

Fold 1 cup (250 mL) chocolate chips into batter.

Chocolate Cherry Loaf

Vegetarian Friendly

This rich and flavorful fruitcake is unlike fruitcakes purchased at the store, which are more handy as doorstops than cakes. You'll need a week of preplanning to soak the cherries in brandy but the wait will be worth it.

Tips

If you soak the cherries for longer than 1 week you may have to replace some of the brandy, which will have evaporated.

If you can only find cherries in a 14-oz (398 mL) can, don't worry, it will be enough.

- 9- by 5-inch (23 by 12.5 cm) loaf pan, sprayed with nonstick spray

1	can (15 oz/425 g) cherries in heavy syrup, drained	1
²⁄₃ cup	brandy	150 mL
3 tbsp	lightly packed brown sugar	45 mL
2 tbsp	unsalted butter, softened	30 mL
1 tbsp	granulated sugar	15 mL
Pinch	salt	Pinch
1	egg	1
1 tbsp	liquid honey	15 mL
1 tsp	vanilla extract	5 mL
¹⁄₃ cup	all-purpose flour	75 mL
3 tbsp	unsweetened Dutch-process cocoa powder	45 mL
¾ cup	pecan halves	175 mL

1. In a covered bowl, soak cherries in brandy. Cover and refrigerate for at least 1 week or up to 2 weeks.

2. Preheat oven to 350°F (180°C). In work bowl fitted with metal blade, process brown sugar, butter, granulated sugar and salt until smooth, about 10 seconds. Add egg, honey and vanilla and process until blended, about 20 seconds. Add flour and cocoa powder and process just until incorporated, about 10 seconds. Transfer to a bowl.

3. Drain cherries, reserving brandy. Fold into batter along with pecans. Transfer to prepared loaf pan, smoothing top. Bake in preheated oven until a toothpick inserted in center comes out clean, 20 to 25 minutes. Brush hot cake with reserved brandy. Let cool completely in pan on a wire rack before serving.

Variation

You can use candied citron or candied pineapple in place of cherries. They should also be soaked in the brandy.

Cinnamon Shortcake

Vegetarian Friendly

Top this shortcake with
sautéed apple slices,
fresh peaches or fresh
berries for a summer
treat.

Tip

When reheating
shortcake, cover with
foil and place in a warm
350°F (180°C) preheated
oven until heated. Do
not microwave or it will
become tough.

- Preheat oven to 400°F (200°C)
- 9-inch (23 cm) round cake pan, sprayed with nonstick spray

2¼ cups	cake flour	550 mL
3 tbsp	granulated sugar	45 mL
1 tbsp	baking powder	15 mL
1 tbsp	ground cinnamon	15 mL
½ tsp	salt	2 mL
½ tsp	cream of tartar	2 mL
½ cup	cold unsalted butter, cut into chunks	125 mL
1	egg, beaten	1
⅓ cup	heavy or whipping (35%) cream	75 mL

1. In work bowl fitted with metal blade, process cake flour, sugar, baking powder, cinnamon, salt and cream of tartar for 15 seconds. Add butter chunks around work bowl and pulse until mixture resembles coarse crumbs, about 10 times. With motor running, add egg and cream through feed tube until it gathers. If dough is tacky, refrigerate for 5 minutes.

2. Press into prepared cake pan. Bake in preheated oven until light brown, 15 to 20 minutes. Let cool slightly in pan on a wire rack. Serve warm.

Rich Dense Pound Cake

Serves 12

Vegetarian Friendly

This perfectly balanced pound cake has lots of uses and variations. Try this cake as a base for strawberry shortcake or an English trifle.

- Preheat oven to 325°F (160°C)
- 9- by 5-inch (23 by 12.5 cm) loaf pan, sprayed with nonstick spray

1⅔ cups	granulated sugar	400 mL
1 cup	unsalted butter, softened	250 mL
2 tsp	vanilla extract	10 mL
5	eggs	5
2 cups	all-purpose flour	500 mL
½ tsp	salt	2 mL

1. In work bowl fitted with metal blade, process sugar and butter until smooth, about 20 seconds. With motor running, add vanilla and eggs through feed tube.

2. Add flour and salt and pulse just until incorporated, about 10 times, stopping and scraping down sides of the bowl once, then pulse another 5 times.

3. Transfer to prepared pan, smoothing top. Bake in preheated oven until a toothpick inserted in the center comes out clean, 85 to 90 minutes. Let cool in loaf pan on a wire rack for 15 minutes. Transfer to rack to cool completely.

Variation

You can add a variety of extracts to enhance your pound cake. Try 1 tsp (5 mL) almond flavoring or lemon or orange extract with the vanilla.

Chocolate Zucchini Cake

Vegetarian Friendly

Zucchini makes this cake moist and packed with nutrients. Don't tell anyone that it's laced with vegetables.

- Preheat oven to 350°F (180°C)
- 13- by 9-inch (33 by 23 cm) metal baking pan, sprayed with nonstick spray

1	medium zucchini, cut into smaller pieces	1
2 cups	granulated sugar	500 mL
½ cup	unsalted butter, softened	125 mL
¼ cup	oil	60 mL
3	eggs	3
1 tsp	vanilla extract	5 mL
2½ cups	all-purpose flour	625 mL
½ cup	unsweetened Dutch-process cocoa powder	125 mL
2½ tsp	baking powder	12 mL
2 tsp	ground cinnamon	10 mL
1½ tsp	baking soda	7 mL
1 tsp	salt	5 mL
¼ cup	whole milk	60 mL

1. In work bowl fitted with shredding blade, shred zucchini. Measure 2 cups (500 mL), reserving any remaining for another use. Set aside.

2. Replace shredding blade with metal blade and process sugar, butter, oil, eggs and vanilla for 10 seconds. Add flour, cocoa powder, baking powder, cinnamon, baking soda and salt and process for 20 seconds. With motor running, pour milk through feed tube. Transfer batter to a bowl. Fold in shredded zucchini.

3. Pour batter into prepared baking pan, smoothing top. Bake in preheated oven until a toothpick inserted in the center comes out clean, 50 to 60 minutes. Let cool in pan on a wire rack for 15 minutes. Transfer to rack to cool completely.

Variation
If you would like to make this as a birthday cake, Cream Cheese Icing (page 634) works well.

Zucchini Bread

Makes 1 loaf

16 slices

Vegetarian Friendly

This bread is very moist and not too sweet — a perfect choice for snacking. Toasted, it also makes a great breakfast on the run.

Tip

Peel the zucchini or leave the skin on, whichever you prefer. If using unpeeled, we recommend buying organically grown zucchini.

- Preheat oven to 350°F (180°C)
- 9- by 5-inch (23 by 12.5 cm) loaf pan, lightly greased

1	medium zucchini (see Tip, left)	1
2 oz	bittersweet chocolate	60 g
1	egg	1
¾ cup	packed brown sugar	175 mL
1 cup	milk	250 mL
2 tbsp	vegetable oil	30 mL
1 tsp	vanilla extract	5 mL
2 cups	all-purpose flour	500 mL
1 tbsp	baking powder	15 mL
1 tsp	ground cinnamon	5 mL
½ tsp	freshly grated nutmeg	2 mL
½ tsp	salt	2 mL
½ cup	chopped pecans	125 mL

1. In work bowl fitted with shredding blade, shred zucchini. Measure 1½ cups (375 mL) and transfer to a bowl. Save remainder for another use. With motor running, add chocolate to feed tube and shred. Add to zucchini. Add egg, brown sugar, milk, oil and vanilla to bowl and stir well. Set aside.

2. In a separate bowl, mix together flour, baking powder, cinnamon, nutmeg and salt. Add zucchini mixture and pecans and stir just until combined.

3. Pour batter into prepared pan, smoothing top. Bake in preheated oven until a tester inserted in center comes out clean, about 1 hour. Let cool in pan on a rack for 5 minutes, then remove from pan and cool completely.

Spicy Gingerbread Cake

Serves 16

Vegetarian Friendly

Try this gingerbread with a dollop of lightly sweetened whipped cream.

- Preheat oven to 350°F (180°C)
- 13- by 9-inch (33 by 23 cm) metal baking pan, sprayed with nonstick spray

1¼ cups	lightly packed brown sugar	300 mL
½ cup	unsalted butter, softened	125 mL
6	eggs	6
1½ cups	light (fancy) molasses	375 mL
¼ cup	water	60 mL
5 cups	all-purpose flour	1.25 L
1 tbsp	baking soda	15 mL
1 tbsp	ground ginger	15 mL
2 tsp	ground cinnamon	10 mL
1 tsp	ground cloves	5 mL
1 tsp	salt	5 mL
1 tsp	dry mustard	5 mL
1 tsp	ground white pepper	5 mL

1. In work bowl fitted with metal blade, process brown sugar and butter until smooth, about 20 seconds. With motor running, add eggs, molasses and water through feed tube.

2. Add flour, baking soda, ginger, cinnamon, cloves, salt, dry mustard and white pepper. Process just until incorporated, for 30 seconds.

3. Pour batter into prepared baking pan. Bake in preheated oven until a toothpick inserted in the center comes out clean, 50 to 60 minutes. Let cool in pan on a wire rack for 15 minutes. Transfer to rack to cool completely.

Chocolate Chip Sour Cream Cake

Serves 16

Vegetarian Friendly

This coffee cake is very moist. You can use it as a breakfast cake or ice it for a nice snack cake.

- Preheat oven to 350°F (180°C)
- 13- by 9-inch (33 by 23 cm) metal baking pan, sprayed with nonstick spray

1¾ cups	sour cream	425 mL
1 tsp	baking soda	5 mL
1 cup	granulated sugar	250 mL
¾ cup	lightly packed brown sugar	175 mL
¾ cup	unsalted butter, softened	175 mL
3	eggs	3
2 tsp	vanilla extract	10 mL
1 tsp	almond extract	5 mL
3 cups	all-purpose flour	750 mL
1½ tsp	baking powder	7 mL
½ tsp	salt	2 mL
2 cups	semisweet chocolate chips	500 mL

1. In a bowl, combine sour cream and baking soda. Set aside.

2. In work bowl fitted with metal blade, process granulated sugar, brown sugar and butter until smooth, about 20 seconds. With motor running, add eggs and vanilla and almond extracts through feed tube.

3. Add flour, baking powder and salt. Pulse just until incorporated, about 10 times. Add sour cream mixture, stopping and scraping down sides of the bowl, then pulse 5 times more. Transfer batter to a bowl. Fold in chocolate chips.

4. Pour batter into prepared baking pan, smoothing top. Bake in preheated oven until a toothpick inserted in the center comes out clean, 50 to 60 minutes. Let cool in pan on a wire rack for 15 minutes. Transfer to rack to cool completely.

Crunchy Topping Coffee Cake

Vegetarian Friendly

Breakfast cake should have a nice balance of moisture and flavor as this cake does. A delicate crunchy topping rounds off the cake.

- Preheat oven to 350°F (180°C)
- 10-inch (25 cm) tube pan, sprayed with nonstick spray

Topping

1 cup	pecans	250 mL
¾ cup	all-purpose flour	175 mL
½ cup	granulated sugar	125 mL
½ cup	lightly packed brown sugar	125 mL
¼ cup	old-fashioned rolled oats	60 mL
1½ tbsp	ground cinnamon	22 mL
1 tsp	ground nutmeg	5 mL
½ tsp	salt	2 mL
6 tbsp	unsalted butter, softened	90 mL

Cake

½ cup	unsalted butter, softened	125 mL
1½ cups	granulated sugar	375 mL
3	eggs	3
1 tbsp	vanilla extract	15 mL
2 cups	all-purpose flour	500 mL
1¼ tsp	baking powder	6 mL
½ tsp	baking soda	2 mL
½ tsp	salt	2 mL
½ tsp	ground allspice	2 mL
1¼ cups	sour cream	300 mL

1. **Topping:** In work bowl fitted with metal blade, process pecans, flour, granulated sugar, brown sugar, oats, cinnamon, nutmeg, salt and butter for 20 seconds. Sprinkle in bottom of prepared pan. Set aside.

2. **Cake:** In same work bowl, process butter and sugar for 20 seconds. With motor running, add eggs and vanilla through feed tube. Add flour, baking powder, baking soda, salt and allspice. Pulse just until incorporated, about 10 times. Add sour cream and pulse just until incorporated, about 10 times.

3. Pour batter into prepared baking pan, smoothing top. Bake in preheated oven until a toothpick inserted in the center of cake comes out clean, 45 to 55 minutes. Let cool in pan on a wire rack for 15 minutes. Invert to rack to cool completely.

Banana Pineapple Cake

Vegetarian Friendly

This is the moistest cake on earth. It was once left out uncovered and two days later it still was moist!

Tip

If you would like the texture of chunks of pecans, toss a handful in the batter prior to baking.

- Preheat oven to 325°F (160°C)
- Two 9-inch (23 cm) round cake pans, sprayed with nonstick spray

3	large very ripe bananas	3
1	can (8 oz/227 mL) crushed pineapple, drained	1
½ cup	pecan halves	125 mL
1¼ cups	vegetable oil	300 mL
1¼ cups	granulated sugar	300 mL
3	eggs	3
1½ tsp	vanilla extract	7 mL
3 cups	all-purpose flour	750 mL
1 tsp	ground cinnamon	5 mL
1 tsp	baking soda	5 mL
1 tsp	salt	5 mL
½ tsp	freshly grated nutmeg	2 mL
	Cream Cheese Icing, optional (page 634)	

1. In work bowl fitted with metal blade, process bananas, pineapple, pecans, oil, sugar, eggs and vanilla until smooth, about 10 seconds. Add flour, cinnamon, baking soda, salt and nutmeg. Process just until incorporated, about 10 seconds. Divide batter evenly between prepared pans, spreading to sides.

2. Bake in preheated oven until a toothpick inserted in center comes out clean, 25 to 32 minutes. Let cool in pans on wire racks for 10 minutes. Invert onto racks and remove pans. Let cool completely. Ice with Cream Cheese Icing, if desired.

Variation
Replace the pineapple with ½ cup (125 mL) finely chopped ripe papaya.

24 Carrot Cake

Vegetarian Friendly

This cake was once called 24 Karrot Kake by a restaurant that served it. Too cutesy we think! But no matter what it's called, this carrot cake is incredibly moist and full of flavor.

Tip

Sprinkle grated carrots on the top of the iced cake for a nice finish.

- Preheat oven to 400°F (200°C)
- Two 9-inch (23 cm) round cake pans, sprayed with nonstick spray

3	carrots, cut into 3-inch (7.5 cm) lengths	3
1 cup	pecan halves	250 mL
1¾ cups	granulated sugar	425 mL
¾ cup	vegetable oil	175 mL
3	eggs	3
1¾ cups	all-purpose flour	425 mL
1½ tsp	baking soda	7 mL
¾ tsp	ground cinnamon	3 mL
½ tsp	salt	2 mL
¾ tsp	vanilla extract	3 mL
1	can (8 oz/227 mL) crushed pineapple, drained	1
1 cup	flaked sweetened coconut	250 mL
	Cream Cheese Icing (page 634)	

1. In work bowl fitted with shredding blade, shred carrots. Transfer to a bowl.

2. Replace shredding blade with metal blade. Pulse pecans until coarsely chopped, about 10 times. Transfer to bowl with carrots.

3. In same work bowl, process sugar, oil and eggs until smooth, about 10 seconds. Add flour, baking soda, cinnamon, salt and vanilla. Process just until incorporated, about 10 seconds. Add pineapple, coconut, pecans and carrots. Process just until incorporated, about 5 seconds. Divide batter evenly between prepared pans, spreading to sides.

4. Bake in preheated oven until a toothpick inserted in center comes out clean, about 22 to 32 minutes. Let cool in pans for 10 minutes. Invert onto racks and remove pans. Let cool completely before icing.

5. Place one cake on a serving plate. Spread with about ½ cup (125 mL) Cream Cheese Icing. Top with second layer. Spread top and sides with remaining icing. Cover loosely with plastic wrap and refrigerate for at least 1 hour or for up to 2 days.

Buttermilk Buckwheat Pancakes

Makes 12 to 14 pancakes or 6 servings

Vegetarian Friendly

This is a favorite Sunday breakfast. Add a slice or two of bacon for a treat and a good portion of maple syrup. Savor every bite.

Tips

Buckwheat flour is available in natural foods stores and some well-stocked supermarkets. If you don't have it, you can make your own by processing kasha or toasted buckwheat groats in work bowl fitted with metal blade until finely ground.

You can make this batter ahead and keep, covered, in the refrigerator for up to 2 days. The batter will thicken a bit, so you may need to add a little buttermilk to thin it out. Your pancakes will not be as airy as those made immediately after mixing, but they will still be delicious.

2½ cups	buttermilk (approx.)	625 mL
2 tsp	baking powder	10 mL
1 tsp	baking soda	5 mL
½ tsp	salt	2 mL
1 tbsp	light (fancy) molasses	15 mL
1	egg	1
2 tbsp	melted butter	30 mL
2 cups	buckwheat flour (see Tips, left)	500 mL

1. In work bowl fitted with metal blade, pulse buttermilk, baking powder, baking soda and salt to blend, 2 or 3 times. Add molasses, egg and melted butter and pulse to blend, about 5 times. Add buckwheat flour and pulse just until combined, about 5 times. Set aside for 5 minutes. Mixture should be of a pourable consistency. If necessary, add more flour or buttermilk and pulse until blended.

2. Heat a lightly greased nonstick skillet over medium heat until water dropped on the surface bounces before evaporating. Add about ¼ cup (60 mL) batter per pancake and cook until bubbles appear all over the top surface, then flip and cook until bottom side is browned, about 1 minute per side. Keep warm. Continue with remaining batter.

Chocolate Chocolate Muffins

Makes 24 muffins

Vegetarian Friendly

You can have these rich and flavorful muffins in the morning or top with icing for a cupcake.

Tip

Freeze cooled muffins in a resealable plastic bag for up to 30 days.

- Preheat oven 325°F (160°C)
- Two 12-cup muffin tins, sprayed with nonstick spray.

1¾ cups	sour cream	425 mL
1 tsp	baking soda	5 mL
1¾ cups	granulated sugar	425 mL
¾ cup	unsalted butter, softened	175 mL
3	eggs	3
2 tsp	vanilla extract	10 mL
2½ cups	all-purpose flour	625 mL
½ cup	unsweetened Dutch-process cocoa powder	125 mL
1½ tsp	baking powder	7 mL
½ tsp	salt	2 mL
2 cups	semisweet chocolate chips	500 mL

1. In a bowl, combine sour cream and baking soda. Set aside.

2. In work bowl fitted with metal blade, process sugar and butter until smooth, about 20 seconds. With motor running, add eggs and vanilla through feed tube.

3. Add flour, cocoa powder, baking powder and salt. Pulse just until incorporated, about 10 times. Add sour cream mixture and pulse, stopping and scraping down the sides of the bowl once or twice, just until incorporated, about 5 times. Transfer batter to a bowl. Fold in chocolate chips.

4. Divide batter evenly into prepared muffin tins. Bake in preheated oven until a toothpick inserted in the center comes out clean, 18 to 24 minutes. Let cool in tin on a wire rack for 15 minutes. Transfer to rack to cool completely.

Variation
Chocolate Nut Muffins: Add ½ cup (125 mL) of any type of toasted nuts to the batter with the chocolate chips.

Fresh Strawberry Muffins

Makes 12 muffins

Vegetarian Friendly

When you see that first basket of spring strawberries make these for a nice breakfast.

Tips

Sometimes the sugars of the berries caramelize onto the muffin tins and stick. Make sure you use paper liners to prevent this.

Freeze cooled muffins in a resealable plastic bag for up to 30 days.

- Preheat oven to 325°F (160°C)
- 12-cup muffin tin, lined with paper liners

1 cup	fresh strawberries, sliced	250 mL
1 cup	granulated sugar	250 mL
½ cup	unsalted butter, softened	125 mL
2	eggs	2
¾ cup	heavy or whipping (35%) cream	175 mL
1 tsp	vanilla extract	5 mL
2 cups	all-purpose flour	500 mL
2½ tsp	baking powder	12 mL
½ tsp	salt	2 mL

1. In work bowl fitted with metal blade, pulse strawberries, about 5 times to coarsely chop. Pour into a bowl and set aside.

2. In same work bowl, process sugar and butter until smooth, about 20 seconds. With motor running, add eggs, cream and vanilla through feed tube. Add chopped strawberries.

3. Add flour, baking powder and salt and pulse until incorporated, about 10 times.

4. Divide batter evenly into prepared muffin tins. Bake in preheated oven until toothpick inserted in the center comes out clean, 18 to 24 minutes. Let cool in tin on a wire rack for 15 minutes. Transfer to rack to cool completely.

Variation

Almond Strawberry Muffins: Add ½ tsp (2 mL) almond extract to to the batter with the vanilla.

Lemon Poppy Seed Muffins

Makes 48 mini muffins or 24 regular-size

Vegetarian Friendly

Tart fresh lemon juice makes these great for a summer bunch.

Tip

Freeze cooled muffins in a resealable plastic bag for up to 30 days.

- Preheat oven to 350°F (180°C)
- Two 24-cup mini-muffin tins, sprayed with a nonstick spray, or two 12-cup muffin tins, sprayed with nonstick spray

3½ cups	all-purpose flour	875 mL
1½ cups	granulated sugar	375 mL
3 tbsp	poppy seeds	45 mL
2 tbsp	grated lemon zest	30 mL
1½ tsp	baking powder	7 mL
½ tsp	salt	2 mL
1½ cups	cold unsalted butter, cut into chunks	375 mL
6	eggs	6
6 tbsp	heavy or whipping (35%) cream	90 mL
2 tbsp	freshly squeezed lemon juice	30 mL

1. In work bowl fitted with metal blade, pulse flour, sugar, poppy seeds, lemon zest, baking powder and salt until combined, about 5 times. Add butter chunks around work bowl and pulse until mixture resembles coarse crumbs, about 5 times. With motor running, add eggs, cream and lemon juice through feed tube until it gathers.

2. Divide batter evenly into prepared muffin tins. Bake in preheated oven until a toothpick inserted in the center comes out clean, 16 to 26 minutes. Let cool in tin on a wire rack for 15 minutes Transfer to rack to cool completely.

Morning Muffins

Makes 12 muffins

Vegetarian Friendly

This is a breakfast muffin packed with everything you need to start your day.

Tips

If fruit is moist, sprinkle a few spoonfuls of some of the measured flour over it prior to chopping.

Freeze cooled muffins in a resealable plastic bag for up to 30 days.

- Preheat oven to 350°F (180°C)
- 12-cup muffin tin, lined with paper liners

1 cup	dried fruit, such as raisins, cranberries, apricots	250 mL
1 cup	granulated sugar	250 mL
½ cup	unsalted butter, softened	125 mL
2	eggs	2
¾ cup	whole milk	175 mL
1 tsp	vanilla extract	5 mL
1 tsp	almond extract	5 mL
2 cups	all-purpose flour	500 mL
2½ tsp	baking powder	12 mL
½ tsp	salt	2 mL
¼ cup	sunflower seeds	60 mL

1. In work bowl fitted with metal blade, pulse dried fruit 10 times to chop. Transfer to a bowl and set aside.

2. In same work bowl, process sugar and butter until smooth, about 20 seconds. With motor running, add eggs, milk, and vanilla and almond extracts through feed tube. Add flour, baking powder and salt and pulse until incorporated, about 10 times. Transfer to a large bowl. Fold in chopped dried fruit and sunflower seeds.

3. Divide batter evenly into prepared muffin tin. Bake in preheated oven until a toothpick inserted in the center comes out clean, 18 to 24 minutes. Let cool in tin on a wire rack for 15 minutes. Transfer to rack to cool completely.

Variation

Try adding an array of nuts to the batter. You can pack it with up to 1 cup (250 mL) and fold in with the fruit and seeds.

Gingerbread Muffins

Vegetarian Friendly

Spicy ginger makes this muffin a holiday treat.

Tips

This recipe can be doubled if you have a large food processor.

Freeze cooled muffins in a resealable plastic bag for up to 30 days.

- Preheat oven to 325°F (160°C)
- 24-cup mini-muffin tin, sprayed with nonstick spray, or 12-cup muffin tin, sprayed with nonstick spray

2½ cups	all-purpose flour	625 mL
1½ tsp	ground ginger	7 mL
1 tsp	ground cinnamon	5 mL
1 tsp	ground cloves	5 mL
½ cup	granulated sugar	125 mL
½ cup	unsalted butter, softened	125 mL
1 cup	light (fancy) molasses	250 mL
1 cup	boiling water	250 mL
2 tsp	baking soda	10 mL
2	eggs	2

1. In a bowl, combine flour, ginger, cinnamon and cloves. Set aside.

2. In work bowl fitted with metal blade, process sugar and butter until smooth, about 20 seconds. With motor running, add molasses through feed tube.

3. In a pourable container, combine water and baking soda. Stir to dissolve. With motor running, add water mixture and eggs through feed tube.

4. Add flour mixture and pulse just until incorporated, about 10 times, stopping and scraping sides of the bowl once, then pulse another 5 times.

5. Divide batter evenly into prepared muffin tin. Bake in preheated oven until a toothpick inserted in the center comes out clean, 16 to 26 minutes. Let cool in tin on a wire rack for 15 minutes. Transfer to rack to cool completely.

Variation

Add ¼ cup (60 mL) chopped candied ginger after incorporating flour mixture for a sweeter taste.

Blueberry Pecan Muffins

Vegetarian Friendly

Blueberry muffins are the most popular. Here you have a moist and flavorful muffin that combines the beloved blueberry with pecans for brunch or breakfast in no time.

Tips

If the berries are thawed before adding to the batter, they can turn it an unpleasant blue color.

You can use butter in place of the shortening but your muffins will not be as flaky.

Unsalted or "sweet" butter is manufactured without adding salt to preserve the butter, thus creating a fresher product. The amount of salt added varies between brands so you don't have as much control over the amount of salt in your dish. Both butters are interchangeable, but taste for salt before adding any to your recipe.

Freeze cooled muffins in a resealable plastic bag for up to 30 days.

- Preheat oven to 375°F (190°C)
- 12-cup muffin tin, sprayed with nonstick spray

½ cup	pecan halves	125 mL
1 cup	granulated sugar	250 mL
½ cup	cold shortening or unsalted butter, cut into chunks (see Tips, left)	125 mL
2	eggs	2
¾ cup	milk	175 mL
1 tsp	vanilla extract	5 mL
2½ cups	cake flour	625 mL
1 tbsp	baking powder	15 mL
½ tsp	salt	2 mL
1 cup	frozen blueberries	250 mL

1. In work bowl fitted with metal blade, pulse pecans until coarsely chopped, about 5 seconds. Transfer to a small bowl. Set aside.

2. In same work bowl, process sugar and shortening until smooth, about 30 seconds. With the motor running, add eggs, milk and vanilla through the feed tube. Remove lid and add cake flour, baking powder and salt. Cover and pulse just until incorporated, about 10 times. Transfer to a large bowl. Fold in pecans and blueberries.

3. Divide batter evenly into prepared muffin tin. Bake in preheated oven until a toothpick inserted in center comes out clean, 18 to 22 minutes. Let cool in tin on a wire rack for 15 minutes. Transfer to rack to cool completely.

Variation

You can substitute the pecans with another nut, if desired.

Honey Apple Spice Muffins

Makes 12 muffins

Vegetarian Friendly

Serve these tasty muffins for breakfast or afternoon tea.

Tips

Dust the tops of the muffins with a little sugar and cinnamon prior to baking.

Freeze cooled muffins in a resealable plastic bag for up to 30 days.

- Preheat oven to 375°F (190°C)
- 12-cup muffin tin, sprayed with nonstick spray

½	baking apple, cored, peeled and halved	½
1 cup	granulated sugar	250 mL
½ cup	cold shortening or unsalted butter, cut into chunks (see Tips, page 516)	125 mL
2	eggs	2
¾ cup	milk	175 mL
3 tbsp	liquid honey	45 mL
1 tsp	vanilla extract	5 mL
2½ cups	cake flour	625 mL
1 tbsp	baking powder	15 mL
½ tsp	salt	2 mL
½ tsp	ground cinnamon	2 mL
¼ tsp	freshly grated nutmeg	1 mL

1. In work bowl fitted with metal blade, process apple until coarsely chopped, about 20 seconds. Transfer to a bowl. Set aside.

2. In same work bowl, process sugar and shortening until smooth, about 30 seconds. With the motor running, add eggs, milk, honey and vanilla through the feed tube. Remove lid and add cake flour, baking powder, salt, cinnamon and nutmeg. Cover and pulse just until incorporated, about 10 times. Add apple chunks and pulse until mixed, about 5 times.

3. Divide batter evenly into prepared muffin tin. Bake in preheated oven until a toothpick inserted in center comes out clean, 18 to 22 minutes. Let cool in tin on a wire rack for 15 minutes. Transfer to rack to cool completely.

Variation

Add ½ cup (125 mL) chopped walnuts to the batter with apple.

Chocolate Chunk Muffins

Vegetarian Friendly

This rich chocolate muffin is very intense. Serve with afternoon tea or coffee.

Tips

Make sure you check the potency of your baking powder. Test it by placing some powder in a glass of water, it should bubble for a few seconds.

Freeze cooled muffins in a resealable plastic bag for up to 30 days.

- Preheat oven to 375°F (190°C)
- 12-cup muffin tin, sprayed with nonstick spray

1 cup	granulated sugar	250 mL
½ cup	cold unsalted butter, cut into chunks	125 mL
2	eggs	2
¾ cup	milk	175 mL
1 tsp	vanilla extract	5 mL
1½ cups	cake flour	375 mL
¾ cup	all-purpose flour	175 mL
2 tbsp	unsweetened Dutch-process cocoa powder	30 mL
1 tbsp	baking powder	15 mL
½ tsp	ground cinnamon	2 mL
½ tsp	salt	2 mL
3 oz	semisweet chocolate, cut into chunks (about ½ cup/125 mL)	90 g

1. In work bowl fitted with metal blade, process sugar and butter until smooth, about 30 seconds. With the motor running, add eggs, milk and vanilla through the feed tube. Remove lid and add cake flour, all-purpose flour, cocoa powder, baking powder, cinnamon and salt. Cover and pulse just until incorporated, about 10 times. Add chocolate chunks and pulse until mixed, about 5 times.

2. Divide batter evenly into prepared muffin tin. Bake in preheated oven until a toothpick inserted in center comes out clean, 18 to 22 minutes. Let cool in tin on a wire rack for 15 minutes. Transfer to rack to cool completely.

Variation

Use white chocolate chunks to create a black and white muffin.

Pumpkin Muffins

Vegetarian Friendly

Fall is not the same without the aroma of hot pumpkin muffins in the air.

Tips

Make sure you drain the pumpkin of any excess liquid.

Freeze cooled muffins in a resealable plastic bag for up to 30 days.

- Preheat oven to 375°F (190°C)
- 12-cup muffin tin, sprayed with nonstick spray

1 cup	granulated sugar	250 mL
½ cup	cold unsalted butter, cut into chunks	125 mL
¾ cup	Pumpkin Purée (page 472) or canned pumpkin purée (not pie filling)	175 mL
2	eggs	2
¾ cup	milk	175 mL
1 tsp	vanilla extract	5 mL
1½ cups	cake flour	375 mL
1 cup	all-purpose flour	250 mL
1 tbsp	baking powder	15 mL
½ tsp	salt	2 mL
½ tsp	ground cinnamon	2 mL
¼ tsp	freshly grated nutmeg	1 mL

1. In work bowl fitted with metal blade, process sugar and butter until smooth, about 20 seconds. With the motor running, add pumpkin, eggs, milk and vanilla through feed tube. Remove lid and add cake flour, all-purpose flour, baking powder, salt, cinnamon and nutmeg. Cover and pulse just until incorporated, about 10 times.

2. Divide batter evenly into prepared muffin tin. Bake in preheated oven until a toothpick inserted in center comes out clean, 18 to 22 minutes. Let cool in tin on a wire rack for 15 minutes. Transfer to rack to cool completely.

Variation
Add ½ cup (125 mL) chopped pecans after incorporating flour for a nutty taste.

Lemon Citrus Scones

Makes 12 scones

Vegetarian Friendly

These light scones are packed with lemon flavor. Try them with a clotted cream or berry preserves.

Tip

Unsalted or "sweet" butter is manufactured without adding salt to preserve the butter, thus creating a fresher product. The amount of salt added varies between brands so you don't have as much control over the amount of salt in your dish. Both butters are interchangeable, but taste for salt before adding any to your recipe if substituting salted for unsalted.

- Preheat oven 425°F (220°C)
- Baking sheet, lined with parchment paper or Silpat

2 cups	all-purpose flour	500 mL
2 cups	cake flour	500 mL
2/3 cup	granulated sugar	150 mL
1 tbsp	baking powder	15 mL
1 tbsp	grated lemon zest	15 mL
1 tsp	salt	5 mL
6 tbsp	cold unsalted butter, cut into chunks (see Tip, left)	90 mL
2	eggs, beaten, divided	2
1/2 cup	heavy or whipping (35%) cream	125 mL
1/4 cup	freshly squeezed lemon juice	60 mL

1. In work bowl fitted with metal blade, process all-purpose flour, cake flour, sugar, baking powder, lemon zest and salt until combined, about 10 seconds. Add butter chunks around work bowl and pulse until mixture resembles coarse crumbs, about 10 times. Set 1 tbsp (15 mL) of the beaten egg aside. With motor running, add remaining egg, cream and lemon juice through feed tube and process until mixture starts to gather. If dough is tacky, refrigerate for 5 minutes.

2. Turn dough out onto a lightly floured work surface and knead just until it holds together, about 6 times. Shape into a ball and pat into a 10-inch (25 cm) circle. Place on prepared baking sheet.

3. Using a pizza cutter or sharp knife, cut into 12 wedges. Do not separate wedges. Brush top with reserved egg. Bake in preheated oven until light brown, 18 to 22 minutes. Serve warm.

Toasted Three-Nut Scones

Makes 12 scones

Vegetarian Friendly

These scones have a nutty taste with a hint of spices. Try them with any of the homemade nut butters (pages 479 and 480).

Tips

To toast pecans or walnuts: Place nuts individually in a single layer on a baking sheet in a preheated 350°F (180°C) oven, stirring once or twice, for 6 to 9 minutes for halves, 4 to 7 minutes for chopped, or until fragrant and golden.

To toast almonds: Place nuts in a single layer on a baking sheet in a preheated 350°F (180°C) oven for 5 to 7 minutes for slivered, or until fragrant and golden, stirring once or twice.

- Preheat oven 425°F (220°C)
- Baking sheet, lined with parchment paper or Silpat

3 cups	all-purpose flour	750 mL
1 cup	cake flour	250 mL
¾ cup	granulated sugar	175 mL
1 tbsp	baking powder	15 mL
1 tsp	salt	5 mL
6 tbsp	cold unsalted butter, cut into chunks	90 mL
2	eggs, beaten, divided	2
¾ cup	whole milk	175 mL
1 tsp	vanilla extract	5 mL
½ tsp	almond extract	2 mL
½ cup	toasted chopped pecans (see Tips, left)	125 mL
¼ cup	toasted chopped walnuts	60 mL
¼ cup	toasted chopped almonds (see Tips, left)	60 mL

1. In work bowl fitted with metal blade, process all-purpose flour, cake flour, sugar, baking powder and salt until combined, about 10 seconds. Add butter chunks around work bowl and pulse until mixture resembles coarse crumbs, about 10 times. Set 1 tbsp (15 mL) of the beaten egg aside. With motor running, add remaining egg, milk, and vanilla and almond extracts, through feed tube and process until mixture starts to gather. If dough is tacky, refrigerate for 5 minutes.

2. Turn dough out onto a lightly floured work surface and knead in pecans, walnuts and almonds. Continue to knead dough just until dough holds together, about 6 times. Shape into a ball and pat into a 10-inch (25 cm) circle. Place on prepared baking sheet.

3. Using a pizza cutter or sharp knife, cut into 12 wedges. Do not separate wedges. Brush top with reserved egg. Bake in preheated oven until light brown, 18 to 22 minutes. Serve warm.

Blueberry Lemon Scones

Makes 12 scones

Vegetarian Friendly

Fresh blueberries pair nicely with the tart lemon flavor in these scones.

Tips

You can use butter in place of the shortening but your scones will not be as flaky.

Unsalted or "sweet" butter is manufactured without adding salt to preserve the butter, thus creating a fresher product. The amount of salt added varies between brands so you don't have as much control over the amount of salt in your dish. Both butters are interchangeable, but taste for salt before adding any to your recipe.

- Preheat oven to 425°F (220°C)
- Baking sheet, lined with parchment paper or Silpat

1½ cups	all-purpose flour	375 mL
1¼ cups	cake flour	300 mL
3 tbsp	granulated sugar	45 mL
1 tbsp	baking powder	15 mL
1 tsp	salt	5 mL
2 tsp	grated lemon zest	10 mL
6 tbsp	cold vegetable shortening or unsalted butter, cut into chunks (see Tips, left)	90 mL
2	eggs, beaten, divided	2
¾ cup	heavy or whipping (35%) cream	175 mL
1 tbsp	freshly squeezed lemon juice	15 mL
½ cup	blueberries, fresh or frozen	125 mL

1. In work bowl fitted with metal blade, process all-purpose flour, cake flour, sugar, baking powder, salt and zest until combined, about 10 seconds. Add shortening chunks around work bowl and pulse until mixture resembles coarse crumbs, about 10 times. Set 1 tbsp (15 mL) of the beaten egg aside. With motor running, add remaining egg, cream and lemon juice through feed tube and process just until mixture starts to gather. If dough is tacky, refrigerate for 5 minutes.

2. Turn dough out onto a lightly floured work surface and knead in blueberries. Continue to knead dough just until it holds together, about 6 times. Shape into a ball and pat into a 10-inch (25 cm) circle. Place on prepared baking sheet.

3. Using a pizza cutter or sharp knife, cut into 12 wedges. Do not separate wedges. Brush top with reserved egg. Bake in preheated oven until light brown, 18 to 22 minutes. Serve warm.

Cherry Sour Cream Scones

Vegetarian Friendly

You can use fresh and canned cherries for these scones, without your guests knowing if they were fresh or not.

- Preheat oven to 425°F (220°C)
- Baking sheet, lined with parchment paper or Silpat

2 cups	all-purpose flour	500 mL
3 tbsp	granulated sugar	45 mL
2 tsp	baking powder	10 mL
½ tsp	baking soda	2 mL
½ tsp	salt	2 mL
6 tbsp	cold unsalted butter, cut into chunks	90 mL
1	egg, beaten, divided	1
1 cup	sour cream	250 mL
1 tsp	vanilla extract	5 mL
½ cup	fresh or canned sour cherries, pitted and drained	125 mL

1. In work bowl fitted with metal blade, process flour, sugar, baking powder, baking soda and salt until combined, about 10 seconds. Add butter chunks around work bowl and pulse until mixture resembles coarse crumbs, about 10 times. Set 1 tbsp (15 mL) of the beaten egg aside. With motor running, add remaining egg, sour cream and vanilla through feed tube and process just until mixture starts to gather. If dough is tacky, refrigerate for 5 minutes.

2. Turn dough out onto a lightly floured work surface and knead in cherries. Continue to knead dough just until it holds together, about 6 times. Shape into a ball and pat into a 10-inch (25 cm) circle. Place on prepared baking sheet.

3. Using a pizza cutter or sharp knife, cut into 12 wedges. Do not separate wedges. Brush with reserved egg. Bake in preheated oven until light brown, 18 to 22 minutes. Serve warm.

Apricot Buttermilk Scones

Makes 12 scones

Vegetarian Friendly

Many tea shops in London serve scones. Here you can create your own.

- Preheat oven to 425°F (220°C)
- Baking sheet, lined with parchment paper or Silpat

½ cup	dried apricots, finely chopped	125 mL
¼ cup	water	60 mL
2½ cups	all-purpose flour	625 mL
2 tbsp	granulated sugar	30 mL
2 tsp	baking powder	10 mL
½ tsp	salt	2 mL
½ cup	cold unsalted butter, cut into chunks	125 mL
1	egg, beaten, divided	1
¾ cup	buttermilk	175 mL

1. In a small saucepan, bring apricots and water to a simmer over medium heat, about 4 minutes. Remove from heat and set aside.

2. In work bowl fitted with metal blade, process all-purpose flour, sugar, baking powder and salt until combined, about 10 seconds. Add butter chunks around work bowl and pulse until mixture resembles coarse crumbs, about 10 times. Set 1 tbsp (15 mL) of the beaten egg aside. With motor running, add remaining egg and the buttermilk through feed tube and process just until mixture starts to gather. If dough is tacky, refrigerate for 5 minutes.

3. Turn dough out onto a lightly floured work surface. Drain apricots and knead into dough. Continue to knead dough just until it holds together, about 6 times. Shape into a ball and pat into a 10-inch (25 cm) circle. Place on prepared baking sheet.

4. Using a pizza cutter or sharp knife, cut into 12 wedges. Do not separate wedges. Brush top with reserved egg. Bake in preheated oven until light brown, 18 to 22 minutes. Serve warm.

Cranberry Orange English Scones

Makes 12 scones

Vegetarian Friendly

True English-style scones should have a tender, heavy crumb and a slightly crusty top.

- Preheat oven to 425°F (220°C)
- Baking sheet, lined with parchment paper or Silpat

1½ cups	all-purpose flour	375 mL
1¼ cups	cake flour	300 mL
3 tbsp	granulated sugar	45 mL
1 tbsp	baking powder	15 mL
1 tsp	salt	5 mL
1½ tsp	grated orange zest	7 mL
6 tbsp	cold unsalted butter, cut into chunks	90 mL
2	eggs, beaten, divided	2
¾ cup	milk, preferably whole	175 mL
1 tbsp	frozen orange juice concentrate, thawed	15 mL
½ cup	dried cranberries	125 mL

1. In work bowl fitted with metal blade, process all-purpose flour, cake flour, sugar, baking powder, salt and orange zest until combined, about 10 seconds. Add butter chunks around work bowl and pulse until mixture resembles coarse crumbs, about 10 times. Set 1 tbsp (15 mL) of the beaten egg aside. With motor running, add remaining egg, milk and orange juice concentrate through feed tube and process just until mixture starts to gather. If dough is tacky, refrigerate for 5 minutes.

2. Turn dough out onto a lightly floured work surface and knead in cranberries. Continue to knead dough just until it holds together, about 6 times. Shape into a ball and pat into a 10-inch (25 cm) circle. Place on prepared baking sheet.

3. Using a pizza cutter or sharp knife, cut into 12 wedges. Do not separate wedges. Brush with reserved egg. Bake in preheated oven until light brown, 18 to 22 minutes. Serve warm.

Fresh Blueberry Ginger Scones

Makes 12 scones

Vegetarian Friendly

Tart blueberries and ginger make a perfect balance of flavors.

- Preheat oven to 425°F (220°C)
- Baking sheet, lined with parchment paper or Silpat

3 cups	all-purpose flour	750 mL
3 tbsp	granulated sugar	45 mL
1 tbsp	baking powder	15 mL
1 tsp	salt	5 mL
1 tsp	grated lemon zest	5 mL
1/2 tsp	ground ginger	2 mL
6 tbsp	cold unsalted butter, cut into chunks	90 mL
2	eggs, beaten, divided	2
3/4 cup	milk, preferably whole	175 mL
1/4 cup	fresh blueberries	60 mL

1. In work bowl fitted with metal blade, process flour, sugar, baking powder, salt, lemon zest and ginger until combined, about 10 seconds. Add butter chunks around work bowl and pulse until mixture resembles coarse crumbs, about 10 times. Set 1 tbsp (15 mL) of the beaten egg aside. With motor running, add remaining egg and milk through feed tube and process just until mixture starts to gather. If dough is tacky, refrigerate for 5 minutes.

2. Turn dough out onto a lightly floured work surface and knead in blueberries. Continue to knead dough just until it holds together, about 6 times. Shape into a ball and pat into a 10-inch (25 cm) circle. Place on prepared baking sheet.

3. Using a pizza cutter or sharp knife, cut into 12 wedges. Do not separate wedges. Brush with reserved egg. Bake in preheated oven until light brown, 18 to 22 minutes. Serve warm.

Fresh Raspberry Scones

Makes 12 scones

Vegetarian Friendly

These scones are full of red raspberries that turn them a light pink. Perfect for Valentine's Day or a baby shower.

- Preheat oven to 425°F (220°C)
- Baking sheet, lined with parchment paper or Silpat

3 cups	all-purpose flour	750 mL
3 tbsp	granulated sugar	45 mL
1 tbsp	baking powder	15 mL
1 tsp	salt	5 mL
6 tbsp	cold vegetable shortening or unsalted butter, cut into chunks	90 mL
2	eggs, beaten, divided	2
¾ cup	milk, preferably whole	175 mL
½ cup	raspberries, cut into small pieces	125 mL

1. In work bowl fitted with metal blade, process flour, sugar, baking powder and salt until combined, about 10 seconds. Add shortening chunks around work bowl and pulse until mixture resembles coarse crumbs, about 10 times. Set 1 tbsp (15 mL) of the beaten egg aside. With motor running, add remaining egg and milk through feed tube and process just until mixture starts to gather. If dough is tacky, refrigerate for 5 minutes.

2. Turn dough out onto a lightly floured work surface and knead in raspberries. Continue to knead dough just until it holds together, about 6 times. Shape into a ball and pat into a 10-inch (25 cm) circle. Place on prepared baking sheet.

3. Using a pizza cutter or sharp knife, cut into 12 wedges. Do not separate wedges. Brush with reserved egg. Bake in preheated oven until light brown, 18 to 22 minutes. Serve warm.

White Chocolate Pecan Scones

Makes 18 scones

Vegetarian Friendly

Nutty scones with a hit of sweet chocolate.

- Preheat oven to 425°F (220°C)
- Baking sheet, lined with parchment paper or Silpat

4 cups	all-purpose flour	1 L
⅔ cup	granulated sugar	150 mL
1 tbsp	baking powder	15 mL
1 tsp	salt	5 mL
½ cup	cold unsalted butter, cut into chunks	125 mL
2	eggs, beaten, divided	2
1½ cups	heavy or whipping (35%) cream	375 mL
1 tbsp	vanilla extract	15 mL
2 cups	white chocolate chips	500 mL
1 cup	pecans, chopped and toasted	250 mL

1. In work bowl fitted with metal blade, process flour, sugar, baking powder and salt until combined, about 10 seconds. Add butter chunks around work bowl and pulse until mixture resembles coarse crumbs, about 10 times. Set 1 tbsp (15 mL) of the beaten egg aside. With motor running, add remaining egg, cream and vanilla through feed tube and process just until mixture starts to gather. If dough is tacky, refrigerate for 5 minutes.

2. Turn dough out onto a lightly floured work surface and knead in chocolate chips and pecans. Continue to knead dough just until it holds together, about 6 times. Shape into a ball and pat into a 10-inch (25 cm) circle. Place on prepared baking sheet.

3. Using a pizza cutter or sharp knife, cut into 18 wedges. Do not separate wedges. Brush with reserved egg. Bake in preheated oven until light brown, 18 to 22 minutes. Serve warm.

Lemon Currant Scones

Makes 12 scones

Vegetarian Friendly

These scones are filled
with sweet currants.

- Preheat oven to 425°F (220°C)
- Baking sheet, lined with parchment paper or Silpat

½ cup	currants	125 mL
¼ cup	hot water	60 mL
1½ cups	all-purpose flour	375 mL
1¼ cups	cake flour	300 mL
3 tbsp	granulated sugar	45 mL
1 tbsp	baking powder	15 mL
2 tsp	grated lemon zest	10 mL
1 tsp	salt	5 mL
6 tbsp	cold vegetable shortening or unsalted butter, cut into chunks	90 mL
2	eggs, beaten, divided	2
¾ cup	heavy or whipping (35%) cream	175 mL
1 tbsp	freshly squeezed lemon juice	15 mL

1. In a small saucepan, bring currants and water to a simmer over medium heat, about 4 minutes. Set aside.

2. In work bowl fitted with metal blade, process all-purpose flour, cake flour, sugar, baking powder, lemon zest and salt until combined, about 10 seconds. Add shortening chunks around work bowl and pulse until mixture resembles coarse crumbs, about 10 times. Set 1 tbsp (15 mL) of the beaten egg aside. With motor running, add remaining egg, cream and lemon juice through feed tube and process just until mixture starts to gather. If dough is tacky, refrigerate for 5 minutes.

3. Turn dough out onto a lightly floured work surface. Drain currants and knead into dough. Continue to knead dough just until it holds together, about 6 times. Shape into a ball and pat into a 10-inch (25 cm) circle. Place on prepared baking sheet.

4. Using a pizza cutter or sharp knife, cut into 12 wedges. Do not separate wedges. Brush with reserved egg. Bake in preheated oven until light brown, 18 to 22 minutes. Serve warm.

Variation
Lemon Zest Scones: Omit currants and hot water and increase lemon zest to 1 tbsp (15 mL).

Orange White Chocolate Scones

Makes 12 scones

Vegetarian Friendly

The sweet taste of chocolate and hint of citrus make this a perfect scone for spring.

Tips

You can use butter in place of the shortening but your scones will not be as flaky.

Unsalted or "sweet" butter is manufactured without adding salt to preserve the butter, thus creating a fresher product. The amount of salt added varies between brands so you don't have as much control over the amount of salt in your dish. Both butters are interchangeable, but taste for salt before adding any to your recipe.

- Preheat oven to 425°F (220°C)
- Baking sheet, lined with parchment paper or Silpat

1½ cups	all-purpose flour	375 mL
1¼ cups	cake flour	300 mL
3 tbsp	granulated sugar	45 mL
1 tbsp	baking powder	15 mL
2 tsp	grated orange zest	10 mL
1 tsp	salt	5 mL
6 tbsp	cold vegetable shortening or unsalted butter, cut into chunks (see Tips, left)	90 mL
2	eggs, beaten, divided	2
¾ cup	milk, preferably whole	175 mL
1 tbsp	freshly squeezed orange juice	15 mL
1 cup	white chocolate chips	250 mL

1. In work bowl fitted with metal blade, process all-purpose flour, cake flour, sugar, baking powder, orange zest and salt until combined, about 10 seconds. Add shortening chunks around work bowl and pulse until mixture resembles coarse crumbs, about 10 times. Set 1 tbsp (15 mL) of the beaten egg aside. With motor running, add remaining egg, milk and orange juice through feed tube and process just until mixture starts to gather. If dough is tacky, refrigerate for 5 minutes.

2. Turn dough out onto a lightly floured work surface and knead in chocolate chips. Continue to knead dough just until it holds together, about 6 times. Shape into a ball and pat into a 10-inch (25 cm) circle. Place on prepared baking sheet. If dough is tacky, refrigerate for 5 minutes.

3. Using a pizza cutter or sharp knife, cut into 12 wedges. Do not separate wedges. Brush with reserved egg. Bake in preheated oven until light brown, 18 to 22 minutes. Serve warm.

Peach Scones

Makes 18 scones

Vegetarian Friendly

Use fresh ripe peaches for these scones for the most flavor.

Tip

If the mixture seems a bit wet from the peaches you can add up to an additional ½ cup (125 mL) cake flour.

- Preheat oven to 425°F (220°C)
- Baking sheet, lined with parchment paper or Silpat

1	peach, pitted and quartered	1
3¼ cups	cake flour	800 mL
¼ cup	lightly packed brown sugar	60 mL
4 tsp	baking powder	20 mL
1 tsp	ground cinnamon	5 mL
1 tsp	salt	5 mL
6 tbsp	cold unsalted butter, cut into chunks	90 mL
2	eggs, beaten	2
¾ cup	milk, preferably whole	175 mL

1. In work bowl fitted with metal blade, pulse peach quarters until coarsely chopped. Transfer to a bowl.

2. In same work bowl, process flour, brown sugar, baking powder, cinnamon and salt until combined, about 10 seconds. Add butter chunks around work bowl and pulse until mixture resembles coarse crumbs, about 10 times. With motor running, add beaten egg and milk through feed tube and process just until mixture starts to gather. If dough is tacky, refrigerate for 5 minutes.

3. Turn dough out onto a lightly floured work surface and knead in peaches. Continue to knead dough just until it holds together, about 6 times. Shape into a ball and pat into a 10-inch (25 cm) circle. Place on prepared baking sheet.

4. Using a pizza cutter or sharp knife, cut into 18 wedges. Do not separate wedges. Bake in preheated oven until light brown, 18 to 22 minutes. Serve warm.

Variation

You may add up to ½ cup (125 mL) chopped pecans or walnuts to the scones with the peaches.

Pumpkin Raisin Scones

Makes 12 scones

Vegetarian Friendly

These scones have a beautiful orange color, just like fall leaves.

Tips

You can use butter in place of the shortening but your scones will not be as flaky.

Unsalted or "sweet" butter is manufactured without adding salt to preserve the butter, thus creating a fresher product. The amount of salt added varies between brands so you don't have as much control over the amount of salt in your dish. Both butters are interchangeable, but taste for salt before adding any to your recipe.

- Preheat oven to 425°F (220°C)
- Baking sheet, lined with parchment paper or Silpat

1½ cups	all-purpose flour	375 mL
1¼ cups	cake flour	300 mL
3 tbsp	granulated sugar	45 mL
1 tbsp	baking powder	15 mL
1 tsp	salt	5 mL
1 tsp	ground cinnamon	5 mL
½ tsp	freshly grated nutmeg	2 mL
¼ tsp	ground allspice	1 mL
¼ tsp	ground cloves	1 mL
6 tbsp	cold vegetable shortening or unsalted butter, cut into chunks (see Tips, left)	90 mL
2	eggs, beaten, divided	2
¼ cup	pumpkin purée (not pie filling)	60 mL
½ cup	milk, preferably whole	125 mL
1 tbsp	freshly squeezed lemon juice	15 mL
½ cup	golden raisins	125 mL

1. In work bowl fitted with metal blade, process all-purpose flour, cake flour, sugar, baking powder, salt, cinnamon, nutmeg, allspice and cloves until combined, about 10 seconds. Add shortening chunks around work bowl and pulse until mixture resembles coarse crumbs, about 10 times. Set 1 tbsp (15 mL) of the beaten egg aside. With motor running, add remaining egg, pumpkin, milk and lemon juice through feed tube and process just until mixture starts to gather. If dough is tacky, refrigerate for 5 minutes.

2. Turn dough out onto a lightly floured work surface and knead in raisins. Continue to knead dough just until it holds together, about 6 times. Shape into a ball and pat into a 10-inch (25 cm) circle. Place on prepared baking sheet.

3. Using a pizza cutter or sharp knife, cut into 12 wedges. Do not separate wedges. Brush with reserved egg. Bake in preheated oven until light brown, 18 to 22 minutes. Serve warm.

Pecan Scones

Vegetarian Friendly

Crunchy, nutty and full of flavor. Perfect when you do not want a fruit-based scone.

Tip

To make pecan flour: In a work bowl with metal blade, process 2 cups (500 mL) pecan halves and ¼ cup (60 mL) all-purpose flour just until fine and powdery, about 1 minute. Store, covered, in the refrigerator for up to 3 months.

- Preheat oven to 425°F (220°C)
- Baking sheet, lined with parchment paper or Silpat

2 cups	all-purpose flour	500 mL
1¼ cups	pecan flour (see Tip, left)	300 mL
3 tbsp	granulated sugar	45 mL
1 tbsp	baking powder	15 mL
1 tsp	salt	5 mL
6 tbsp	cold unsalted butter, cut into chunks	90 mL
2	eggs, beaten, divided	2
¾ cup	milk, preferably whole	175 mL
2 tsp	vanilla extract	10 mL
½ cup	chopped pecans	125 mL

1. In work bowl fitted with metal blade, process all-purpose flour, pecan flour, sugar, baking powder and salt until combined, about 10 seconds. Add butter chunks around work bowl and pulse until mixture resembles coarse crumbs, about 10 times. With motor running, add three-quarters of the beaten egg, milk and vanilla through feed tube and process just until mixture starts to gather. If dough is tacky, refrigerate for 5 minutes.

2. Turn dough out onto a lightly floured work surface and knead in pecans. Continue to knead dough just until it holds together, about 6 times. Shape into a ball and pat into a 10-inch (25 cm) circle. Place on prepared baking sheet.

3. Using a pizza cutter or sharp knife, cut into 12 wedges. Do not separate wedges. Brush with remaining beaten egg. Bake in preheated oven until light brown, 12 to 16 minutes. Serve warm.

Fresh Savory Herb Scones

Makes 18 scones

Vegetarian Friendly

Scones are not all sweet. Serve savory scones on the side of a nice soup or stew.

Tip
Once scones are baked, keep the wedges in the circle after cutting so you have a nice display for your guests.

- Preheat oven to 450°F (230°C)
- Baking sheet, lined with parchment paper

6 tbsp	shortening or butter (see Tips, page 532)	90 mL
2¼ cups	cake flour	550 mL
1 cup	all-purpose flour	250 mL
¼ cup	granulated sugar	60 mL
4 tsp	baking powder	20 mL
1 tsp	salt	5 mL
1 tsp	grated lemon zest	5 mL
1 tsp	loosely packed fresh dill fronds	5 mL
1 tsp	loosely packed fresh tarragon leaves	5 mL
2	eggs	2
¾ cup	milk	175 mL
1 tsp	freshly squeezed lemon juice	5 mL

1. In work bowl fitted with metal blade, process shortening, cake flour, all-purpose flour, sugar, baking powder, salt, lemon zest, dill and tarragon until mixture resembles fine crumbs, about 15 seconds. With the motor running, add eggs, milk and lemon juice through the feed tube just until the mixture starts to gather.

2. Scrape dough onto prepared baking sheet and spread out to a 10-inch (25 cm) circle. With a pizza cutter or sharp knife, cut into 18 wedges. Do not separate wedges. Bake in preheated oven until golden brown, 12 to 18 minutes. Serve warm.

Variation
You can use an array of fresh herbs such as chives, rosemary or thyme in place of the dill and tarragon.

Almond Poppy Seed Scones

Vegetarian Friendly

These scones look great on a spring buffet table.

Tip

Toasting the almonds prior to processing provides a stronger taste. *To toast almonds:* Preheat oven to 350°F (180°C). Spread almonds on a baking sheet and bake, shaking the pan several times, until fragrant and toasted; 5 to 7 minutes for chopped almonds; 6 to 9 minutes for whole almonds; 4 to 7 minutes for sliced and slivered almonds.

- Preheat oven to 450°F (230°C)
- Baking sheet, lined with parchment paper

½ cup	slivered almonds, toasted	125 mL
6 tbsp	cold unsalted butter, cut into chunks	90 mL
2¾ cups	all-purpose flour	675 mL
¼ cup	lightly packed brown sugar	60 mL
4 tsp	baking powder	20 mL
1 tsp	poppy seeds	5 mL
1 tsp	salt	5 mL
2	eggs	2
¾ cup	milk	175 mL

1. In work bowl fitted with metal blade, process almonds until finely ground. Transfer to a bowl. Set aside.

2. In same work bowl, process butter, flour, brown sugar, baking powder, poppy seeds and salt until mixture resembles fine crumbs, about 15 seconds. Remove lid and add almonds and pulse until incorporated, about 5 times. With the motor running, add eggs and milk through the feed tube just until mixture starts to gather.

3. Scrape dough onto prepared baking sheet and spread out to a 10-inch (25 cm) circle. With a pizza cutter or sharp knife, cut into 18 wedges. Do not separate wedges. Bake in preheated oven until golden brown, 12 to 18 minutes. Serve warm.

Variation

You can scoop the dough by spoonfuls into 12 greased muffin tins for larger portions. Bake in a preheated 425°F (220°C) oven for 16 to 20 minutes.

Chocolate Chip Scones

Vegetarian Friendly

Serve these scones to your family either as a dessert or a breakfast item.

Tip

To check for doneness, just lightly touch scones on top; they should be slightly firm.

- Preheat oven to 450°F (230°C)
- Baking sheet, lined with parchment paper

6 tbsp	cold unsalted butter, cut into chunks	90 mL
3 cups	all-purpose flour	750 mL
1/4 cup	granulated sugar	60 mL
4 tsp	baking powder	20 mL
1 tsp	salt	5 mL
2	eggs, beaten	2
3/4 cup	heavy or whipping (35%) cream	175 mL
1 tsp	vanilla extract	5 mL
1 cup	semisweet chocolate chips	250 mL

1. In work bowl fitted with metal blade, process butter, flour, sugar, baking powder and salt until mixture resembles fine crumbs, about 15 seconds. With the motor running, add eggs, cream and vanilla through the feed tube. Add chocolate chips through the feed tube just until mixture starts to gather.

2. Scrape dough onto prepared baking sheet and spread out to a 10-inch (25 cm) circle. With a pizza cutter or sharp knife, cut into 18 wedges. Do not separate wedges. Bake in preheated oven until golden brown, 12 to 18 minutes. Serve warm.

Variation

Replace 1/3 cup (75 mL) flour with unsweetened Dutch-process cocoa powder for a double chocolate scone.

Cookies, Bars, Squares and Brownies

Almond Raspberry Kiss Cookies

Makes about 24 cookies

Vegetarian Friendly

The flavors of raspberry, chocolate and almond make this an all-time favorite.

Tip

Make sure the candies are unwrapped so you don't waste time while the cookie is hot. You want to place the candies on a hot cookie. The candies will not stick to a cooled cookie.

- Preheat oven to 350°F (180°C)
- Baking sheets, lined with parchment paper or Silpats
- #40 disher or scoop

2¼ cups	all-purpose flour	550 mL
1 tsp	baking soda	5 mL
¼ tsp	salt	1 mL
½ cup	unsalted butter, softened	125 mL
½ cup	vegetable shortening	125 mL
½ cup	granulated sugar	125 mL
½ cup	packed brown sugar	125 mL
1	egg	1
1 tsp	almond extract	5 mL
1 tsp	vanilla extract	5 mL
24	almond-filled Hershey Kisses, unwrapped (see Tip, left)	24
¼ cup	raspberry preserves	60 mL
1 tbsp	corn syrup	15 mL

1. In a bowl, whisk together flour, baking soda and salt. Set aside.

2. In work bowl fitted with metal blade, process butter, shortening, granulated sugar and brown sugar until fluffy, for 20 seconds. With motor running, add egg and almond and vanilla extracts through feed tube and process for 10 seconds. Add flour mixture and process until blended, for 10 seconds.

3. Using disher, scoop dough and place on prepared baking sheets, about 2 inches (5 cm) apart. Press down with palm of your hand. Bake in preheated oven until light brown, 7 to 12 minutes. Immediately top each cookie with an almond-filled kiss, pressing down gently. Let cool on baking sheets for 10 minutes before transferring to a wire rack to cool completely.

4. In a small bowl, combine raspberry preserves and corn syrup. Drizzle over cooled cookies.

Variation

Replace almond-filled Hershey Kisses with the peanut butter and dark chocolate varieties.

Almond Cookies

**Makes about
24 cookies**

Vegetarian Friendly

These little cookies are
perfect with a strong
espresso or caffé
Americano.

Tip

If the almond paste is hard
and dried out, place in the
food processor with the
granulated sugar called
for in the recipe. Process
until smooth.

- Preheat oven to 350°F (180°C)
- Baking sheets, lined with parchment paper or Silpats
- #60 disher or scoop

½ cup	unsalted butter, softened	125 mL
1 cup	granulated sugar	250 mL
7 oz	almond paste, cut into small pieces (see Tip, left)	210 g
1	egg	1
1 cup	all-purpose flour	250 mL
½ cup	almond flour	125 mL
½ tsp	baking powder	2 mL
½ tsp	baking soda	2 mL
2	drops almond extract	2
Pinch	salt	Pinch
24	whole blanched almonds (approx.)	24

1. In work bowl fitted with metal blade, process butter, sugar and almond paste until smooth, about 2 minutes. With motor running, add egg through feed tube and process for 10 seconds. Add all-purpose flour, almond flour, baking powder, baking soda, almond extract and salt. Process for 30 seconds or until blended.

2. Using disher, scoop dough and place on prepared baking sheets, about 2 inches (5 cm) apart. Press down with palm of your hand. Place an almond on each cookie. Bake in preheated oven until light brown, 9 to 12 minutes. Let cool on baking sheets for 10 minutes before transferring to a wire rack to cool completely.

Amish Cookies

Vegetarian Friendly

Bakeries in Amish
communities all have
their versions of tender
little butter cookies.
They're so good you
can't eat just one.
Here is a perfect recipe
for them.

Tip

You can freeze the logs
for up to 3 months. That
way you will always have
cookies ready for baking.

- Preheat oven to 375°F (190°C)
- Baking sheets, lined with parchment paper or Silpats

4½ cups	all-purpose flour	1.125 L
1 tsp	baking soda	5 mL
1 tsp	cream of tartar	5 mL
1 cup	unsalted butter, softened	250 mL
1 cup	vegetable oil	250 mL
1 cup	granulated sugar	250 mL
1 cup	confectioner's (icing) sugar	250 mL
2	eggs	2
1 tsp	vanilla extract	5 mL

1. In a large bowl, whisk together flour, baking soda and cream of tartar. Set aside.

2. In work bowl fitted with metal blade, process butter, oil, granulated sugar and confectioner's sugar until blended, for 10 seconds. With motor running, add eggs and vanilla though feed tube and process until blended, for 10 seconds. Add flour mixture and process just until combined, for 1 minute.

3. Divide dough into quarters. Roll each quarter into logs about 1 inch (2.5 cm) in diameter and wrap in plastic wrap, then foil. Chill for 2 hours or freeze for 45 minutes.

4. With a sharp knife, cut each log into about 12 equal portions and place on prepared baking sheets, about 2 inches (5 cm) apart. Bake in preheated oven until light brown, 8 to 10 minutes. Let cool on baking sheets for 10 minutes before transferring to a wire rack to cool completely.

Variation

Sandwich cookies with a filling of Cream Cheese Icing (page 634).

Blue Ribbon Double Chocolate Cookies

Vegetarian Friendly

You will win a blue
ribbon with your family
when you make these
award-winning cookies.

- Preheat oven to 350°F (180°C)
- Baking sheets, lined with parchment paper or Silpats
- #24 disher or scoop

3¾ cups	all-purpose flour	925 mL
1 tsp	baking soda	5 mL
½ tsp	salt	2 mL
1¼ cups	unsalted butter, softened	300 mL
2 cups	granulated sugar	500 mL
2	eggs	2
2 tsp	vanilla extract	10 mL
2 cups	white chocolate chips	500 mL
1 cup	semisweet chocolate chips	250 mL

1. In a bowl, whisk together flour, baking soda and salt. Set aside.

2. In work bowl fitted with metal blade, process butter and sugar until combined, for 1 minute. With motor running, add eggs through feed tube and process until blended, for 10 seconds. Add vanilla. Add flour mixture and process until combined, about 20 seconds. Transfer to a bowl and stir in white and semisweet chocolate chips by hand.

3. Using a disher, scoop dough and place on prepared baking sheets, about 2 inches (5 cm) apart. Press down with palm of your hand. Bake in preheated oven until light brown, 12 to 16 minutes. Let cool on baking sheets for 10 minutes before transferring to a wire rack to cool completely.

Variation

You can use an array of chips that are available these days. Try butterscotch or milk chocolate chips in place of the white and semisweet.

Belgian Dandoy Spice Cookies

Makes 24 to 48 cookies

Vegetarian Friendly

Brussels has a long-standing relationship with this cookie. The best place to witness this is the Dandoy shop in the old city, run by the Dandoy family since 1829.

Tip

You can freeze the logs for up to 3 months. That way you will always have cookies ready for baking.

- Preheat oven to 350°F (180°C)
- Baking sheets, lined with parchment paper or Silpats
- Blending fork

1 cup	packed dark brown sugar	250 mL
3 tbsp	milk, preferably whole, or almond or soy milk	45 mL
3 cups	all-purpose flour	750 mL
1½ tsp	each ground cloves and cinnamon	7 mL
¾ tsp	each ground ginger and nutmeg	3 mL
Pinch	baking powder	Pinch
Pinch	salt	Pinch
1¼ cups	unsalted butter, softened and cut into small pieces	300 mL
¼ cup	slivered blanched almonds	60 mL

1. In a small bowl, combine brown sugar and milk and stir until smooth. Set aside.

2. In work bowl fitted with metal blade, process flour, cloves, cinnamon, ginger, nutmeg, baking powder and salt until combined, for 10 seconds. Add butter around work bowl and pulse 20 times until crumbly. Add brown sugar mixture and process until dough holds together, about 15 seconds. Transfer dough to a large bowl and blend almonds into dough by hand. Wrap in foil or plastic wrap and refrigerate overnight. (Shape into two logs if you do not have wooden molds.)

3. **If using a wooden mold:** Brush carvings in mold well with a stiff brush, but do not wash. (You should never grease or wash carved moulds. The wood will warp.) Dust well with flour. Press enough chilled dough into the mold to fill it completely. With a small knife, cut around the edge of the pattern, removing the trimmings. Carefully invert filled mold onto baking sheets. Tap lightly to release the dough onto baking sheets. Repeat until baking sheet is full, leaving 1 inch (2.5 cm) between cookies. Bake in preheated oven until light brown, 15 to 25 minutes, depending on the mold size.

4. **Without a mold:** On a lightly floured surface, cut each log into ¼-inch (0.5 cm) slices and place on prepared baking sheets, about 2 inches (5 cm) apart. Bake in preheated oven until edges are light brown, 9 to 12 minutes.

Boysenberry Chews

Vegetarian Friendly

The boysenberry was created in Buena Park, California, as a hybrid of the raspberry, blackberry and loganberry. This is a great cookie using boysenberry preserves.

Tip

Make sure the melted chocolate mixture has cooled to the touch prior to adding to the butter mixture or it will curdle.

- Preheat oven to 375°F (190°C)
- Baking sheets, lined with parchment paper or Silpats
- #60 disher or scoop

4 oz	unsweetened chocolate, chopped	125 g
½ cup	milk, preferably whole	125 mL
½ cup	unsalted butter, softened	125 mL
2 cups	granulated sugar	500 mL
1	egg	1
2 cups	all-purpose flour	500 mL
½ tsp	baking soda	2 mL
1½ cups	sweetened flaked coconut	375 mL
1 cup	boysenberry preserves	250 mL
½ cup	chopped pecans	125 mL

1. In a saucepan on low heat, melt chocolate and milk together, stirring until chocolate is melted. Set aside.

2. In work bowl fitted with metal blade, process butter and sugar until light and creamy, about 10 seconds. With motor running, add egg and melted chocolate mixture through feed tube and process until combined, about 10 seconds. Add flour and baking soda and process for 10 seconds or until blended. Transfer to a large bowl. Fold in coconut, boysenberry preserves and chopped nuts by hand. If batter is too soft, refrigerate for 15 minutes.

3. Using disher, scoop dough and place on prepared sheets, about 2 inches (5 cm) apart. Press down with palm of your hand. Bake in preheated oven until light brown, 10 to 12 minutes. Let cool on baking sheets for 10 minutes before transferring to a wire rack to cool completely.

Variation

If boysenberry preserves are difficult to locate you can use raspberry or strawberry.

Butter Crispy Cookies

Makes 30 cookies

Vegetarian Friendly

These are the best butter cookies you could make. We love the crunch of these cookies.

Tip

Make sure you slowly add the sugar into the butter or the cookies will not be as crunchy as they should be.

- Preheat oven to 325°F (160°C)
- Baking sheets, lined with parchment paper or Silpats
- #50 disher or scoop

1 cup	unsalted butter, softened	250 mL
10 tbsp	granulated sugar, divided	150 mL
	Grated zest of 1 lemon	
2 cups	all-purpose flour	500 mL
½ tsp	salt	2 mL
¼ cup	granulated sugar	60 mL

1. In work bowl fitted with metal blade, process butter for 15 seconds. With motor running, add 10 tbsp (150 mL) sugar, 1 tbsp (15 mL) at a time, through feed tube and process until incorporated. Add lemon zest, flour and salt and process until well blended, for 3 minutes. Refrigerate for 35 minutes.

2. Place ¼ cup (60 mL) granulated sugar in a shallow dish. Using disher, scoop dough and roll in sugar. Place on prepared baking sheets, about 2 inches (5 cm) apart. Press down with palm of your hand. Bake in preheated oven until light brown, 12 to 16 minutes. Let cool on baking sheets for 10 minutes before transferring to a wire rack to cool completely.

Variation
Roll the dough in colored sugars for holiday-themed cookies.

Cashew Butter Cookies

**Makes about
48 cookies**

Vegetarian Friendly

If you love peanut butter cookies, you will really love the richness of these cashew butter cookies.

Tip

This large recipe will need to be baked in batches. After cooling cookies as instructed, let baking sheets cool down completely before re-using to bake more cookies. Also, between batches keep your dough cool in refrigerator if your kitchen is warm.

- Preheat oven to 350°F (180°C)
- Baking sheets, lined with parchment paper or Silpats (see Tip, left)
- #60 disher or scoop

1¾ cups	all-purpose flour	425 mL
1 tsp	baking soda	5 mL
½ tsp	salt	2 mL
½ cup	vegetable shortening	125 mL
½ cup	cashew butter	125 mL
¾ cup	granulated sugar, divided	175 mL
½ cup	packed brown sugar	125 mL
1	egg	1
2 tbsp	milk, preferably whole	30 mL
1 tsp	vanilla extract	5 mL
1 cup	whole roasted cashews (approx.)	250 mL

1. In work bowl fitted with metal blade, process flour, baking soda, salt, shortening, cashew butter, ½ cup (125 mL) of the granulated sugar, brown sugar, egg, milk and vanilla until light and creamy, about 2 minutes. Refrigerate dough for 20 minutes.

2. Place remaining ¼ cup (60 mL) of granulated sugar in a shallow dish. Using disher, scoop dough and roll in sugar. Place on prepared baking sheets, about 2 inches (5 cm) apart. Press down with palm of your hand. Place 2 cashews on top of each cookie. Bake in preheated oven until golden brown, 10 to 12 minutes. Let cool on baking sheets for 10 minutes before transferring to a wire rack to cool completely.

Variation
Cashew Chocolate Chip Cookies: Stir in 1 cup (250 mL) semisweet chocolate chips to dough by hand.

Butter Pecan Shortbread Cookies

Vegetarian Friendly

These fast cookies have only four ingredients. They're perfect when you're out of eggs.

Tip

Toast and cool pecans prior to adding to dough or the taste will not be nutty. *To toast pecans:* Place chopped pecans in a single layer on a baking sheet. Bake at 350°F (180°C) for about 4 to 7 minutes or until fragrant.

- Preheat oven to 350°F (180°C)
- Baking sheets, lined with parchment paper or Silpats
- #70 disher or scoop

¾ cup	unsalted butter, softened	175 mL
½ cup	granulated sugar	125 mL
1½ cups	all-purpose flour	375 mL
½ cup	chopped pecans, toasted (see Tip, left)	125 mL

1. In work bowl fitted with metal blade, process butter and sugar until smooth, for 10 seconds. Add flour and process until blended, about 10 seconds. Transfer dough to a bowl and fold in pecans by hand. Refrigerate for 20 minutes or until firm.

2. Using disher, scoop dough and place on prepared baking sheets, about 2 inches (5 cm) apart. Press down with palm of your hand. Bake in preheated oven until edges are light brown, 12 to 16 minutes. Let cool on baking sheets for 10 minutes before transferring to a wire rack to cool completely.

Variation
Replace pecans with ⅔ cup (150 mL) chocolate chips.

Candied Ginger Cookies

**Makes about
24 cookies**

Vegetarian Friendly

Candied ginger nibs
make this cookie a little
special and out of the
ordinary. Expect many
requests for the recipe.

Tip

Ginger nibs are small
pieces or nibs of candied
ginger. If you don't
have ginger nibs, use
candied ginger and cut
into small pieces.

- Preheat oven to 325°F (160°C)
- Baking sheets, lined with parchment paper or Silpats
- #50 disher or scoop

1 cup	unsalted butter, softened	250 mL
⅔ cup	granulated sugar	150 mL
2 cups	all-purpose flour	500 mL
1 tsp	ground cinnamon	5 mL
1 tsp	ground ginger	5 mL
½ tsp	salt	2 mL
2 tsp	vanilla extract	10 mL
1 tbsp	candied ginger nibs (see Tip, left)	15 mL

1. In work bowl fitted with metal blade, process butter and
   sugar until fluffy, for 15 seconds. Add flour, cinnamon,
   ground ginger, salt and vanilla and process until
   incorporated, for 10 seconds. Refrigerate for 20 minutes.

2. Using disher, scoop dough and place on prepared baking
   sheets, about 2 inches (5 cm) apart. Press down with
   palm of your hand. Place a ginger nib on each. Bake in
   preheated oven until golden brown, 14 to 16 minutes. Let
   cool on baking sheets for 10 minutes before transferring
   to a wire rack to cool completely.

Chinese Almond Cookies

Makes about 30 cookies

Vegetarian Friendly

No need to buy Chinese almond cookies when making them is so easy and they taste even better than store-bought!

- Preheat oven to 325°F (160°C)
- Baking sheets, lined with parchment paper or Silpats
- #60 disher or scoop

1 cup	unsalted butter, softened	250 mL
1 cup	granulated sugar	250 mL
2	eggs	2
1 tbsp	almond extract	15 mL
2½ cups	all-purpose flour	625 mL
⅛ tsp	salt	0.5 mL
½ tsp	baking soda	2 mL
1	egg yolk	1
2 tsp	warm water	10 mL
30	whole blanched almonds (approx.)	30

1. In work bowl fitted with metal blade, process butter and sugar until creamy, for 1 minute. With motor running, add eggs and almond extract through feed tube and process until well blended, for 10 seconds. Add flour, salt and baking soda and process until a soft dough forms, for 20 seconds. Refrigerate for 20 minutes.

2. Using disher, scoop dough and place on prepared baking sheets, about 2 inches (5 cm) apart. Press down with palm of your hand. In a small bowl, whisk egg yolk and warm water. Brush egg wash over each cookie. Place an almond on each cookie. Bake in preheated oven until light brown and egg wash is shiny, 20 to 22 minutes. Let cool on baking sheets for 10 minutes before transferring to a wire rack to cool completely.

Variation
Replace ½ cup (125 mL) all-purpose flour with same amount of finely ground almonds for a crunchy cookie.

Chocolate Chunk Cookies

Makes about 36 large cookies

Vegetarian Friendly

Sometimes we like making chocolate cookies with chunks of chocolate in them instead of the traditional chips.

- Preheat oven to 325°F (160°C)
- 2 baking sheets, lined with parchment paper or Silpats
- #24 disher or scoop

4¼ cups	all-purpose flour	1.05 L
1 tsp	salt	5 mL
1 tsp	baking soda	5 mL
1½ cups	unsalted butter, melted and cooled	375 mL
1 cup	packed brown sugar	250 mL
1 cup	granulated sugar	250 mL
2	eggs	2
1 tbsp	vanilla extract	15 mL
2 cups	semisweet or milk chocolate chunks (12 oz/375 g)	500 mL

1. In a large bowl, whisk together flour, salt and baking soda. Set aside.

2. In work bowl fitted with metal blade, process butter, brown sugar and granulated sugar until blended, for 15 seconds. With motor running, add eggs and vanilla through feed tube and process until incorporated, for 10 seconds. Add flour mixture and process until a soft dough forms, for 20 seconds. Transfer dough to a large bowl and fold in chocolate chunks by hand. Refrigerate for 20 minutes.

3. Using disher, scoop dough and place on prepared baking sheets, about 2 inches (5 cm) apart. Press down with palm of your hand. Bake in preheated oven until light brown, 14 to 18 minutes. Let cool on baking sheets for 10 minutes before transferring to a wire rack to cool completely.

Chocolate Snowballs

Makes about 38 cookies

Vegetarian Friendly

Rich and a reminder of winter! These snowball cookies look great on a brunch table.

- Preheat oven to 350°F (180°C)
- Baking pans sheets, lined with parchments paper or Silpats
- #40 disher or scoop

1¼ cups	unsalted butter, softened	300 mL
⅔ cup	granulated sugar	150 mL
1 tsp	vanilla extract	5 mL
2 cups	all-purpose flour	500 mL
½ cup	unsweetened Dutch-process cocoa powder, sifted	125 mL
1 cup	hazelnuts, chopped and toasted	250 mL
1 cup	semisweet chocolate chips	250 mL
½ cup	confectioner's (icing) sugar	125 mL

1. In work bowl fitted with metal blade, process butter, sugar and vanilla until blended, for 20 seconds. Add flour and cocoa powder and process until incorporated, 3 minutes. Transfer dough to a bowl and fold nuts and chips into batter. Refrigerate for 1 hour.

2. Using disher, scoop dough and roll into perfect balls. Place on prepared baking sheets, about 2 inches (5 cm) apart. Bake in preheated oven until slightly firm, 16 to 18 minutes. Let cool on baking sheets for 10 minutes before transferring to a wire rack to cool completely. Place confectioner's sugar in a shallow dish and roll the cooled chocolate balls.

French Chocolate Cookies

Vegetarian Friendly

These small and elegant cookies are perfect to serve with cappuccino.

Tip

After cookies have cooled, refrigerate and then dip in chocolate so they firm up faster.

- Preheat oven to 350°F (180°C)
- Baking sheets, lined with parchment paper or Silpats
- #70 disher or scoop

¾ cup	unsalted butter, softened	175 mL
½ cup	granulated sugar	125 mL
1¼ cups	all-purpose flour	300 mL
½ cup	unsweetened Dutch-process cocoa powder, sifted	125 mL
4 oz	bittersweet chocolate, melted and cooled	125 g
1 cup	pecans, finely chopped and toasted (see Tip, page 546)	250 mL

1. In work bowl fitted with metal blade, process butter and sugar until fluffy, about 2 minutes. Add flour and cocoa powder and process until incorporated, for 1 minute. Refrigerate for 20 minutes.

2. Using disher, scoop dough and place on prepared baking sheets, about 2 inches (5 cm) apart. Press down with palm of your hand. Bake in preheated oven until edges start to firm, 18 to 20 minutes.

3. Let cool completely on baking sheets. Dip half of each cookie into melted chocolate and then pecans. Let cool on parchment paper until chocolate is set.

Variation
You can use any kind of chopped and toasted nuts for decoration.

Gingersnaps

Vegetarian Friendly

This is the best gingersnap cookie recipe invented. The four different spices work in unison to create the crunchiest, snappiest, most flavorful ginger cookie ever! You'd be wise to make a double batch of these cookies. They'll go fast.

- Preheat oven to 375°F (190°C)
- Baking sheets, lined with parchment paper or Silpats
- #40 disher or scoop

2¼ cups	all-purpose flour	550 mL
2 tsp	baking soda	10 mL
1 tsp	ground cinnamon	5 mL
1 tsp	ground ginger	5 mL
½ tsp	salt	2 mL
½ tsp	ground cloves	2 mL
¼ tsp	ground allspice	1 mL
¼ cup	unsalted butter, softened	60 mL
1 cup	packed light brown sugar	250 mL
1	egg	1
¼ cup	dark (cooking) molasses	60 mL
¼ cup	granulated sugar	60 mL

1. In a large bowl, whisk together flour, baking soda, cinnamon, ginger, salt, cloves and allspice. Set aside.

2. In work bowl fitted with metal blade, process butter and brown sugar until blended, for 10 seconds. With motor running, add egg and molasses through feed tube and process until incorporated, for 10 seconds. Add flour mixture and process until blended, for 10 seconds. Refrigerate for 20 minutes.

3. Place granulated sugar in a shallow dish. Using disher, scoop dough and roll in sugar. Place on prepared baking sheets, about 2 inches (5 cm) apart. Press down with palm of your hand. Bake in preheated oven until tops start to crack a bit, 8 to 10 minutes. Let cool on baking sheets for 10 minutes before transferring to a wire rack to cool completely.

Greek Butter Cookies

Vegetarian Friendly

Little bites of Greek
cookies are perfect for
a cookie tray.

Tip

If you don't have pastry
flour, substitute ¾ cup
(175 mL) each all-purpose
flour and cake flour.

- Preheat oven to 350°F (180°C)
- Baking sheets, lined with parchment paper or Silpats
- #70 disher or scoop

½ cup	unsalted butter, softened	125 mL
¾ cup	confectioner's (icing) sugar, divided	175 mL
1	egg yolk	1
1½ cups	pastry flour (see Tip, left)	375 mL
¼ tsp	ground nutmeg	1 mL

1. In work bowl fitted with metal blade, process butter, ¼ cup (60 mL) of the confectioner's sugar, egg yolk, pastry flour and nutmeg until blended, for 1 minute. Refrigerate for 20 minutes or until firm.

2. Using disher, scoop dough into rounds and roll between your palms. Place dough balls on prepared baking sheets, about 2 inches (5 cm) apart. Bake in preheated oven until light brown, 18 to 20 minutes. Let cool on baking sheets for 10 minutes before transferring to a wire rack to cool completely. Place remaining ½ cup (125 mL) confectioner's sugar in a shallow dish and roll cooled cookies.

Lemon Shortbread Cookies

**Makes about
30 cookies**

Vegetarian Friendly

You can have a batch
of these fast and easy
shortbreads ready in less
than 20 minutes.

Tip

If lemon oil is not
available, increase the
lemon zest to 2 medium
lemons.

- Preheat oven to 300°F (150°C)
- Baking sheets, lined with parchment paper or Silpats
- #50 disher or scoop

1 cup	unsalted butter, softened	250 mL
½ cup	confectioner's (icing) sugar	125 mL
1 tsp	vanilla extract	5 mL
2 cups	all-purpose flour	500 mL
	Grated zest of 1 lemon	
1 tsp	lemon oil (see Tip, left)	5 mL
¼ tsp	salt	1 mL

1. In work bowl fitted with metal blade, process butter
   and confectioner's sugar until fluffy, for 30 seconds. Add
   vanilla, flour, zest, oil and salt and process just until
   incorporated, for 20 seconds. Refrigerate for 15 minutes.

2. Using disher, scoop dough and place on prepared baking
   sheets, about 2 inches (5 cm) apart. Press down with
   palm of your hand. Bake in preheated oven until firm but
   not yet starting to brown, 20 to 22 minutes. Let cool on
   baking sheets for 10 minutes before transferring to a wire
   rack to cool completely.

Lavender Snap Tea Cookies

Vegetarian Friendly

The slight hint of lavender in these cookies is perfect for tea.

Tip

If you can't find lavender sugar you can make your own. Purchase ¼ cup (60 mL) dried lavender at a health food or specialty food store (make sure it is not treated with preservatives) and process with 2 cups (500 mL) granulated sugar in work bowl of food processor with metal blade for 30 seconds.

- Preheat oven to 325°F (160°C)
- Baking sheets, lined with parchment paper or Silpats
- #50 disher or scoop

1 cup	unsalted butter, softened	250 mL
5 tbsp	granulated sugar, divided	75 mL
5 tbsp	lavender sugar, divided (see Tip, left)	75 mL
2 cups	all-purpose flour	500 mL
½ tsp	salt	2 mL
¼ cup	granulated sugar	60 mL
30	dried lavender flowers	30

1. In work bowl fitted with metal blade, process butter until creamy, for 15 seconds. With motor running, add 5 tbsp (75 mL) granulated sugar and lavender sugar, 1 tbsp (15 mL) at a time, through feed tube and process until incorporated. Add flour and salt and process until well blended, for 30 seconds. Refrigerate for 35 minutes.

2. Place ¼ cup (60 mL) granulated sugar in a shallow dish. Using disher, scoop dough and roll in sugar. Place on prepared baking sheets, about 2 inches (5 cm) apart. Press down with palm of your hand. Lightly press a lavender flower on top of each unbaked cookie. Bake in preheated oven until light brown, 12 to 16 minutes. Let cool on baking sheets for 10 minutes before transferring to a wire rack to cool completely.

Macadamia Crunch Cookies

**Makes about
24 large cookies**

Vegetarian Friendly

Macadamia nuts are so
rich it's best to eat only
one of these delicious
cookies.

- Preheat oven to 325°F (160°C)
- Baking sheets, lined with parchment paper or Silpats
- #24 disher or scoop

2 cups	all-purpose flour	500 mL
½ cup	old-fashioned rolled oats	125 mL
1 tsp	baking soda	5 mL
½ tsp	ground nutmeg	2 mL
1 cup	unsalted butter, softened	250 mL
¾ cup	granulated sugar	175 mL
½ cup	packed brown sugar	125 mL
2	eggs	2
2 tbsp	milk, preferably whole	30 mL
2 tsp	vanilla extract	10 mL
2 cups	macadamia nuts, finely chopped	500 mL

1. In a bowl, whisk together flour, oats, baking soda and nutmeg. Set aside.

2. In work bowl fitted with metal blade, process butter, granulated sugar and brown sugar until fluffy, for 10 seconds. With motor running, add eggs, milk and vanilla through feed tube and process until blended, for 10 seconds. Add flour mixture and process just until incorporated, for 10 seconds. Transfer to a bowl and fold in macadamia nuts by hand.

3. Using disher, scoop dough and place on prepared baking sheets, about 2 inches (5 cm) apart. Press down with palm of your hand. Bake in preheated oven until light brown, 10 to 14 minutes. Let cool on baking sheets for 10 minutes before transferring to a wire rack to cool completely.

Maple Sugar Cookies

Makes 60 cookies

Vegetarian Friendly

These cookies are great served with Lavender Snap Tea Cookies (page 555) and Vanilla Rose Cookies with Rose Crème Filling (page 581) for a great trio of flavors.

Tip

Maple sugar is available at specialty gourmet stores and health food and well-stocked grocery stores.

- Preheat oven to 325°F (160°C)
- Baking sheets, lined with parchment paper or Silpats (see Tip, page 545)
- #50 disher or scoop

2 cups	unsalted butter, softened	500 mL
10 tbsp	granulated sugar	150 mL
10 tbsp	granulated maple sugar (see Tip, left)	150 mL
4 cups	all-purpose flour	1 L
1 tsp	salt	5 mL
½ cup	granulated sugar	125 mL

1. In work bowl fitted with metal blade, process butter until creamy, for 15 seconds. With motor running, add 10 tbsp (150 mL) granulated sugar and maple sugar, 1 tbsp (15 mL) at a time, through feed tube and process until incorporated. Add flour and salt and mix until blended, for 30 seconds. Refrigerate for 35 minutes.

2. Place ½ cup (125 mL) granulated sugar in a shallow dish. Using disher, scoop dough and roll in sugar. Place on prepared baking sheets, about 2 inches (5 cm) apart. Press down with palm of your hand. Bake in preheated oven until light brown, 12 to 16 minutes. Let cool on baking sheets for 10 minutes before transferring to a wire rack to cool completely.

Mexican Wedding Cakes

Makes about 48 cookies

Vegetarian Friendly

Similar to Russian tea cakes, these buttery cookies (also known as Mexican Wedding Cookies) were first made in the mid-1950s.

Tip

Make sure cookies are cooled before rolling in confectioner's sugar. If the cookies are hot the sugar will just dissolve into cookies.

- Preheat oven to 325°F (160°C)
- Baking sheets, lined with parchment paper or Silpats
- #70 disher or scoop

½ cup	unsalted butter, softened	125 mL
½ cup	granulated sugar	125 mL
1⅓ cups	all-purpose flour	325 mL
1 cup	pecans, finely chopped	250 mL
¼ tsp	vanilla extract	1 mL
Pinch	salt	Pinch
¼ cup	confectioner's (icing) sugar, sifted	60 mL

1. In work bowl fitted with metal blade, process butter, granulated sugar, flour, pecans, vanilla and salt until smooth, for 2 minutes. Refrigerate for 20 minutes.

2. Using disher, scoop dough and roll into balls between your palms. Place on prepared baking sheets, about 2 inches (5 cm) apart. Bake in preheated oven until light brown, 12 to 15 minutes.

3. Let cool on baking sheets for 10 minutes before transferring to a wire rack to cool completely. Place confectioner's sugar in a shallow dish and roll cooled cookies in sugar.

Oatmeal Raisin Cookies

**Makes about
46 large cookies**

Vegetarian Friendly

Plump raisins make this
a wonderful soft and
moist cookie.

- Preheat oven to 375°F (190°C)
- Baking sheets, lined with parchment paper or Silpats
- #24 disher or scoop

2⅓ cups	all-purpose flour	575 mL
2¼ tsp	baking powder	11 mL
1½ tsp	ground cinnamon	7 mL
1¼ tsp	salt	6 mL
½ tsp	baking soda	2 mL
1½ cups	vegetable shortening	375 mL
1⅓ cups	packed light brown sugar	325 mL
1 cup	granulated sugar	250 mL
2	eggs	2
2 tbsp	water	30 mL
2 tsp	vanilla extract	10 mL
4½ cups	quick-cooking rolled oats	1.125 L
2 cups	golden raisins	500 mL

1. In a bowl, whisk together flour, baking powder, cinnamon, salt and baking soda. Set aside.

2. In work bowl fitted with metal blade, process shortening, brown sugar, granulated sugar, eggs, water and vanilla until creamy, for 2 minutes. Add flour mixture and process until incorporated, for 10 seconds. Fold in oats and raisins. Refrigerate for 20 minutes.

3. Using disher, scoop dough and place on prepared baking sheets, about 2 inches (5 cm) apart. Press down with palm of your hand. Bake in preheated oven until light brown, 10 to 12 minutes. Let cool on baking sheets for 10 minutes before transferring to a wire rack to cool completely.

Orange Cranberry Cookies

Vegetarian Friendly

The sweet citrus taste
of orange and tart
cranberry complement
each other in this cookie.

Tip

If your cranberries are
hard, pour hot water over
them to soften. Drain off
water and pat dry.

- Preheat oven to 325°F (160°C)
- Baking sheets, lined with parchment paper or Silpats
- #40 disher or scoop

1½ cups	all-purpose flour	375 mL
1 tsp	cream of tartar	5 mL
½ tsp	baking soda	2 mL
½ cup	unsalted butter, softened	125 mL
1 cup	packed brown sugar	250 mL
2	eggs	2
2 tsp	grated orange zest	10 mL
1 tsp	orange-flavored liqueur	5 mL
½ cup	dried cranberries (see Tip, left)	125 mL

1. In a bowl, whisk together flour, cream of tartar and baking soda. Set aside.

2. In work bowl fitted with metal blade, process butter, brown sugar, eggs, orange zest and liqueur until blended, for 20 seconds. Add flour mixture and process until blended, for 10 seconds. Transfer to a bowl and fold in cranberries by hand. Refrigerate for 30 minutes.

3. Using disher, scoop dough and place on prepared baking sheets, about 2 inches (5 cm) apart. Press down with palm of your hand. Bake in preheated oven until light brown, 10 to 12 minutes. Let cool on baking sheets for 10 minutes before transferring to a wire rack to cool completely.

Variation
Try golden raisins in place of cranberries.

Orange Butter Cookies

Makes about 48 cookies

Vegetarian Friendly

The aroma of fresh orange blossoms when these cookies are baking is wonderfully enticing.

- Preheat oven to 350°F (180°C)
- Baking sheets, lined with parchment paper or Silpats (see Tip, page 545)
- #60 disher or scoop

4½ cups	all-purpose flour	1.125 L
1½ tsp	baking soda	7 mL
1½ tsp	cream of tartar	7 mL
1 tsp	salt	5 mL
¾ cup	unsalted butter, softened	175 mL
¾ cup	vegetable oil	175 mL
1¾ cups	granulated sugar, divided	425 mL
2	eggs	2
1 tsp	vanilla extract	5 mL
1 tsp	orange extract	5 mL
	Grated zest of 1 orange	

1. In a large bowl, whisk together flour, baking soda, cream of tartar and salt. Set aside.

2. In work bowl fitted with metal blade, process butter, oil, 1½ cups (375 mL) of the sugar, eggs, vanilla, orange extract and orange zest until blended, for 20 seconds. Add flour mixture and process until blended, for 10 seconds. Refrigerate for 30 minutes.

3. Place remaining ¼ cup (60 mL) of sugar in a shallow dish. Using disher, scoop dough and roll in sugar. Place on prepared baking sheets, about 2 inches (5 cm) apart. Press dough down with palm of your hand. Bake in preheated oven until light brown, 10 to 12 minutes. Let cool on baking sheets for 10 minutes before transferring to a wire rack to cool completely.

Peanut Butter Cookies

Vegetarian Friendly

Packed with nutty taste, peanut butter cookies are a favorite.

Tip
This large recipe will need to be baked in batches. After cooling cookies as instructed, let baking sheets cool down completely before re-using to bake more cookies. Also, between batches keep your dough cool in refrigerator if your kitchen is warm.

- Preheat oven to 350°F (180°C)
- Baking sheets, lined with parchment paper or Silpats (see Tip, left)
- #40 disher or scoop

3 cups	all-purpose flour	750 mL
1½ cups	granulated sugar, divided	375 mL
1 cup	packed brown sugar	250 mL
2 tsp	baking soda	10 mL
1 tsp	salt	5 mL
1 cup	vegetable shortening	250 mL
1 cup	creamy peanut butter	250 mL
¼ cup	milk, preferably whole	60 mL
1½ tsp	vanilla extract	7 mL
2	eggs	2
1 cup	finely chopped peanuts	250 mL

1. In work bowl fitted with metal blade, process flour, 1 cup (250 mL) of the granulated sugar, brown sugar, baking soda, salt, vegetable shortening, peanut butter, milk, vanilla and eggs until light and creamy, about 20 seconds. Refrigerate for 20 minutes.

2. Place remaining ½ cup (125 mL) of granulated sugar in a shallow dish. Using disher, scoop dough and roll in sugar. Then roll in chopped peanuts. Place on prepared baking sheets, about 2 inches (5 cm) apart. Press down with palm of your hand. Bake in preheated oven until golden brown, 10 to 12 minutes. Let cool on baking sheets for 10 minutes before transferring to a wire rack to cool completely.

Variation
Peanut Chocolate Chip Cookies: Stir 1 cup (250 mL) semisweet chocolate chips into dough by hand.

Pineapple Island Cookies

**Makes about
24 cookies**

Vegetarian Friendly

Crushed pineapple
makes these cookies so
moist and packed with
flavor.

- Preheat oven to 350°F (180°C)
- Baking sheets, lined with parchment paper or Silpats
- #40 disher or scoop

2 cups	all-purpose flour	500 mL
1 tsp	baking soda	5 mL
1 tsp	baking powder	5 mL
1 tsp	salt	5 mL
½ cup	unsalted butter, softened	125 mL
1 cup	granulated sugar	250 mL
1	egg	1
½ cup	crushed pineapple, drained	125 mL
1 tbsp	rum	15 mL

1. In a bowl, whisk together flour, baking soda, baking powder and salt. Set aside.

2. In work bowl fitted with metal blade, process butter and sugar until creamy, for 10 seconds. Add egg, pineapple and rum and process until blended, for 10 seconds. Add flour mixture and process until incorporated, for 10 seconds. Refrigerate for 20 minutes.

3. Using disher, scoop dough and place on prepared baking sheets, about 2 inches (5 cm) apart. Press down with palm of your hand. Bake in preheated oven until light brown, 12 to 14 minutes. Let cool on baking sheets for 10 minutes before transferring to a wire rack to cool completely.

Quadruple Chocolate Chunk Cookies

Makes 50 cookies

Vegetarian Friendly

If two chocolates in a cookie are great, four is even better. Make sure you have a glass of cold milk close by.

Tips

Purchase new baking soda when you haven't baked for a few months. Do not use soda kept in the refrigerator or freezer as a deodorizer because it may take on the taste of fish or other items.

Store cookies in an airtight container for up to 4 days. You can also freeze them in resealable plastic bags for up to 1 month.

- Preheat oven to 350°F (180°C)
- 2 baking sheets, lined with parchment paper

2 cups	granulated sugar	500 mL
1¼ cups	unsalted butter, softened	300 mL
2	eggs	2
2 tsp	vanilla extract	10 mL
3 cups	all-purpose flour	750 mL
¾ cup	unsweetened Dutch-process cocoa powder, sifted	175 mL
1 tsp	baking soda	5 mL
½ tsp	salt	2 mL
2 cups	white chocolate chips	500 mL
1 cup	semisweet chocolate chips	250 mL
1 cup	milk chocolate chips	250 mL

1. In work bowl fitted with metal blade, process sugar and butter until creamy, about 10 seconds. With motor running, add eggs and vanilla through feed tube and process until incorporated, stopping and scraping down sides of bowl as necessary. Add flour, cocoa powder, baking soda and salt and process just until combined, about 1 minute. Transfer to a large bowl. Add white, semisweet and milk chocolate chips. If dough is very soft, refrigerate until firm, about 20 minutes.

2. Scoop dough by heaping tablespoonfuls (15 mL) and squeeze into a ball. Place on prepared baking sheets, about 2 inches (5 cm) apart. Slightly flatten each cookie by pressing down with the palm of your hand or the bottom of a drinking glass. Bake in preheated oven until edges are firm, 12 to 18 minutes. Let cool on baking sheets for 10 minutes before transferring to a wire rack to cool completely.

Variations

Try some of the mint or peanut butter chips in place of the other varieties in this recipe.

For larger cookies, scoop by level ¼ cup (60 mL) to yield 32 cookies.

Thumbprint Jam Cookies

Makes about 24 cookies

Vegetarian Friendly

You can make an array of flavors with this basic thumbprint cookie.

Tip

Make sure you use a thick preserve or jam because a jelly does not have enough fruit and will spread as the cookie bakes.

- Preheat oven to 300°F (150°C)
- Baking sheets, lined with parchment paper or Silpats
- #40 disher or scoop

1 cup	unsalted butter, softened	250 mL
¾ cup	granulated sugar	175 mL
2 tsp	vanilla extract	10 mL
1 tsp	almond extract	5 mL
2¼ cups	all-purpose flour	550 mL
½ cup	finely chopped nuts, such as almonds or other nuts	125 mL
⅓ cup	preserves, such as raspberry or your favorite (see Tip, left)	75 mL

1. In work bowl fitted with metal blade, process butter, sugar and vanilla and almond extracts until creamy, for 10 seconds. Add flour and process just until incorporated, for 20 seconds. If dough is soft, refrigerate until firm, about 20 minutes.

2. Using disher, scoop dough and roll in chopped nuts. Place dough on prepared baking sheets, about 2 inches (5 cm) apart. Press down and make a little well in center with your finger or thumb. Fill each well with about ½ tsp (2 mL) of preserves. Bake in preheated oven until light brown, 18 to 24 minutes. Let cool on baking sheets for 10 minutes before transferring to a wire rack to cool completely.

Moist Pumpkin Cookies

**Makes about
36 cookies**

Vegetarian Friendly

You can use fresh or
canned pumpkin to
make this autumn
cookie.

- Preheat oven to 350°F (180°C)
- Baking sheets, lined with parchment paper or Silpats
- #60 disher or scoop

2½ cups	all-purpose flour	625 mL
2 tsp	ground cinnamon	10 mL
1 tsp	baking powder	5 mL
1 tsp	baking soda	5 mL
1 tsp	ground nutmeg	5 mL
½ tsp	salt	2 mL
½ cup	unsalted butter, softened	125 mL
1½ cups	granulated sugar	375 mL
1	egg	1
1 cup	canned or fresh pumpkin purée (not pie filling)	250 mL
1 tsp	vanilla extract	5 mL
1 cup	semisweet chocolate chips	250 mL

1. In a large bowl, whisk together flour, cinnamon, baking powder, baking soda, nutmeg and salt. Set aside.

2. In work bowl fitted with metal blade, process butter and sugar until creamy, for 10 seconds. Add egg, pumpkin and vanilla and process until blended, for 20 seconds. Add flour mixture and process until well blended, for 20 seconds. Transfer to a bowl and fold in chocolate chips by hand. Refrigerate for 20 minutes.

3. Using disher, scoop dough and place on prepared baking sheets, leaving dough in mounds. Bake in preheated oven until light brown, 12 to 15 minutes. Let cool on sheets for 10 minutes before transferring to a rack to cool completely.

Snickerdoodles

Vegetarian Friendly

The name alone makes
you smile. A simple
cookie packed with
flavor that's very soft.

- Preheat oven to 375°F (190°C)
- Baking sheets, lined with parchment paper or Silpats
- #20 disher or scoop

2¾ cups	all-purpose flour	675 mL
2 tsp	cream of tartar	10 mL
1 tsp	baking soda	5 mL
½ tsp	salt	2 mL
1 cup	unsalted butter, softened	250 mL
1¾ cups	granulated sugar, divided	425 mL
2	eggs	2
2 tsp	ground cinnamon	10 mL

1. In a large bowl, whisk together flour, cream of tartar, baking soda and salt. Set aside.

2. In work bowl fitted with metal blade, process butter and 1½ cups (375 mL) of the sugar until creamy, for 10 seconds. With motor running, add eggs, one at a time, through feed tube and process until incorporated, for 10 seconds. Add flour mixture and process until blended, for 20 seconds. Refrigerate for 20 minutes.

3. In a shallow dish, combine remaining ¼ cup (60 mL) of sugar and cinnamon. Using disher, scoop dough and roll in sugar mixture. Place on prepared baking sheets, about 2 inches (5 cm) apart. Press down with palm of your hand. Bake in preheated oven until light brown, 8 to 10 minutes. Let cool on baking sheets for 10 minutes before transferring to a wire rack to cool completely.

Sugar Cinnamon Cookies

Makes about 40 cookies

Vegetarian Friendly

Make these as one-bite cookies so you can get the entire flavor of the cookie in one bite.

- Preheat oven to 350°F (180°C)
- Baking sheets, lined with parchment paper or Silpats
- #60 disher or scoop

1¾ cups	all-purpose flour	425 mL
3 tsp	ground cinnamon, divided	15 mL
2 tsp	baking powder	10 mL
1½ tsp	ground nutmeg, divided	7 mL
¼ tsp	salt	1 mL
½ cup	unsalted butter, softened	125 mL
1¼ cups	granulated sugar, divided	300 mL
1 tbsp	freshly squeezed lemon juice	15 mL
1	egg	1
2 tbsp	milk, preferably whole	30 mL

1. In a bowl, combine flour, 2 tsp (10 mL) of the cinnamon, baking powder, 1 tsp (5 mL) of the nutmeg and salt. Set aside.

2. In work bowl fitted with metal blade, process butter and 1 cup (250 mL) of sugar until creamy, for 10 seconds. With motor running, add lemon juice, egg and milk through feed tube and process until incorporated, for 10 seconds. Add flour mixture and process until blended, for 30 seconds. Refrigerate for 20 minutes.

3. In a shallow dish, combine remaining ¼ cup (60 mL) of sugar, 1 tsp (5 mL) of cinnamon and ½ tsp (2 mL) of nutmeg. Using disher, scoop dough and roll in sugar mixture. Place on prepared baking sheets, about 2 inches (5 cm) apart. Press down with palm of your hand. Bake in preheated oven until light brown, 10 to 12 minutes. Let cool on baking sheets for 10 minutes before transferring to a wire rack to cool completely.

Sugar Cookies

**Makes about
24 large cookies**

Vegetarian Friendly

Take two cookies and
sandwich ice cream
between them for a very
special treat.

- Preheat oven to 350°F (180°C)
- Baking sheets, lined with parchment paper or Silpats
- #24 disher or scoop

1¼ cups	all-purpose flour	300 mL
2 tsp	baking powder	10 mL
¼ tsp	salt	1 mL
½ cup	unsalted butter, softened	125 mL
1¼ cups	granulated sugar, divided	300 mL
1	egg	1
1 tsp	vanilla extract	5 mL

1. In a bowl, combine flour, baking powder and salt. Set aside.

2. In work bowl fitted with metal blade, process butter and
   1 cup (250 mL) of the sugar until creamy, for 10 seconds.
   With motor running, add egg and vanilla through feed
   tube and process until incorporated, for 10 seconds. Add
   flour mixture and process until blended, about 30 seconds.
   Refrigerate for 20 minutes.

3. Place remaining sugar in a shallow dish. Using disher,
   scoop dough and roll in sugar. Place on prepared baking
   sheets, about 2 inches (5 cm) apart. Press down with
   palm of your hand. Bake in preheated oven until light
   brown, 10 to 12 minutes. Let cool on baking sheets
   for 10 minutes before transferring to a wire rack to
   cool completely.

Tangy Lemon Butter Cookies

**Makes about
24 cookies**

Vegetarian Friendly

This is a great "pucker
up" cookie for a summer
tea or brunch.

- Preheat oven to 325°F (160°C)
- Baking sheets, lined with parchment paper or Silpats
- #40 disher or scoop

3 cups	all-purpose flour	750 mL
1 tsp	baking soda	5 mL
1 tsp	cream of tartar	5 mL
Pinch	salt	Pinch
½ cup	unsalted butter, softened	125 mL
½ cup	vegetable oil	125 mL
1 cup	granulated sugar	250 mL
1	egg	1
½ tsp	vanilla extract	2 mL
½ tsp	lemon extract	2 mL
1 tsp	grated lemon zest	5 mL

1. In a bowl, combine flour, baking soda, cream of tartar and salt. Set aside.

2. In work bowl fitted with metal blade, process butter, oil, sugar, egg, vanilla and lemon extracts and zest until creamy, for 20 seconds. Add flour mixture and process until blended for 30 seconds. Refrigerate for 30 minutes.

3. Using disher, scoop dough and place on prepared baking sheet, about 2 inches (5 cm) apart. Press down with palm of your hand. Bake in preheated oven until light brown, 10 to 12 minutes. Let cool on baking sheets for 10 minutes before transferring to a wire rack to cool completely.

All-Rich Butter Cookies

Makes about 36 cookies

Vegetarian Friendly

Every European country feels that they have created the butter cookie. You can keep them simple or add any of the Variations below for your own signature butter cookie.

Tips

Be careful not to overprocess once you have added flour to the mixture.

If you don't have vanilla sugar, mix together ¾ cup (175 mL) granulated sugar and 1 tbsp (15 mL) vanilla instead.

Store cookies in an airtight container for up to 4 days. You can also freeze them in resealable plastic bags for up to 1 month.

- Preheat oven to 350°F (180°C)
- 2 baking sheets, lined with parchment paper

1 cup	unsalted butter, softened	250 mL
¾ cup	vanilla sugar (see Tips, left, and page 472)	175 mL
3 cups	all-purpose flour	750 mL

1. In work bowl fitted with metal blade, process butter until light and creamy, about 10 seconds. Add vanilla sugar and process until incorporated, about 30 seconds, stopping and scraping down sides of bowl as necessary. Add flour and process just until combined, about 10 seconds. If dough is very soft, transfer to a bowl and refrigerate until firm, about 20 minutes.

2. Scoop dough by heaping tablespoonfuls (15 mL) and squeeze into a ball. Place on prepared baking sheets, about 2 inches (5 cm) apart. Slightly flatten each cookie by pressing down with the palm of your hand or the bottom of a drinking glass. Bake in preheated oven until edges are firm and without color, 12 to 18 minutes. Let cool on baking sheets for 10 minutes before transferring to a wire rack to cool completely.

Variations

After you have made the dough you may stir in ½ cup (125 mL) chopped and toasted nuts, such as cashews, peanuts, walnuts or almonds, or ½ cup (125 mL) chopped milk chocolate.

Lemon Citrus Cookies

Vegetarian Friendly

We like how these cookies burst with lemon. Perfect to cool you down on a warm summer day.

Tips

If you don't have lemon oil you can use ½ tsp (2 mL) lemon extract. Both are available at specialty food stores and some well-stocked grocery stores.

If you have a disher or small ice cream scoop, use it to scoop the cookie dough, packing as you scoop; that way you can avoid the need to squeeze the dough into a ball.

Store cookies in an airtight container for up to 4 days. You can also freeze them in resealable plastic bags for up to 1 month.

- Preheat oven to 350°F (180°C)
- 2 baking sheets, lined with parchment paper

1½ cups	unsalted butter, softened	375 mL
1 cup	granulated sugar	250 mL
1 tbsp	grated lemon zest	15 mL
1 tsp	lemon oil (see Tips, left)	5 mL
3 cups	all-purpose flour	750 mL
1 cup	cake flour	250 mL

1. In work bowl fitted with metal blade, process butter until light and creamy, about 10 seconds. Add sugar, lemon zest and lemon oil and process until incorporated, about 30 seconds, stopping and scraping down sides of the bowl as necessary. Add all-purpose flour and cake flour and process just until combined, about 10 seconds. If dough is very soft, transfer to a bowl and refrigerate until firm, about 20 minutes.

2. Scoop dough by heaping tablespoonfuls (15 mL) and squeeze into a ball (see Tips, left). Place on prepared baking sheets, about 2 inches (5 cm) apart. Slightly flatten each cookie by pressing down with the palm of your hand or the bottom of a drinking glass. Bake in preheated oven until edges are very light brown, 12 to 18 minutes. Let cool on baking sheets for 10 minutes before transferring to a wire rack to cool completely.

Variation

Try orange or grapefruit zest in place of the lemon zest.

Orange Zest Cookies

**Makes about
48 cookies**

Vegetarian Friendly

Simple butter cookies
like these can be so
flavorful with little work.

Tips

Use a zester with five
holes to create long
strands of zest for the
decorating. Just cut the
strands of zest a few times
so they are not too long.

Store cookies in an
airtight container for up to
4 days. You can also freeze
them in resealable plastic
bags for up to 1 month.

- Preheat oven to 350°F (180°C)
- 2 baking sheets, lined with parchment paper

1½ cups	unsalted butter, softened	375 mL
1 cup	packed light brown sugar	250 mL
1 tbsp	orange zest, divided (see Tips, left)	15 mL
4 cups	all-purpose flour	1 L

1. In work bowl fitted with metal blade, process butter until light and creamy, about 10 seconds. Add brown sugar and 1½ tsp (7 mL) of the orange zest and process until incorporated, about 30 seconds, stopping and scraping down sides of the bowl as necessary. Add flour and process just until combined, about 10 seconds. If dough is very soft, transfer to a bowl and refrigerate until firm, about 20 minutes.

2. Scoop dough by heaping tablespoonfuls (15 mL) and squeeze into a ball. Place on prepared baking sheets, about 2 inches (5 cm) apart. Slightly flatten each cookie by pressing down with the palm of your hand or the bottom of a drinking glass. Place a small amount of the remaining orange zest on each cookie. Bake in preheated oven until edges are very light brown, 12 to 18 minutes. Let cool on baking sheets for 10 minutes before transferring to a wire rack to cool completely.

Strawberry Almond Cookies

Makes about 36 cookies

Vegetarian Friendly

We love how these cookies use dried strawberries, which you can find year round at health food stores and some large supermarkets.

Tips

To toast almonds: Place almonds on a baking sheet and toast, stirring partway through, in a preheated 350°F (180°C) oven for 6 to 9 minutes.

Store cookies in an airtight container for up to 4 days. You can also freeze them in resealable plastic bags for up to 1 month.

- Preheat oven to 350°F (180°C)
- 2 baking sheets, lined with parchment paper

4 oz	dried strawberries	125 g
4 oz	hot water	125 g
1½ cups	unsalted butter, softened	375 mL
1 cup	granulated sugar	250 mL
1 tsp	almond extract	5 mL
4 cups	all-purpose flour	1 L
½ cup	whole unblanched almonds, toasted (see Tips, left)	125 mL

1. In a small bowl, combine dried strawberries and hot water. Let soak until berries are soft, about 10 minutes. Drain and set aside.

2. In work bowl fitted with metal blade, process butter until light and creamy, about 10 seconds. Add sugar and almond extract and process until incorporated, about 30 seconds, stopping and scraping down sides of the bowl as necessary. Add flour and almonds and process just until combined, about 10 seconds. With motor running, add strawberries through feed tube and process until chopped and incorporated. If dough is very soft, transfer to a bowl and refrigerate until firm, about 20 minutes.

3. Scoop dough by heaping tablespoonfuls (15 mL) and squeeze into a ball. Place on prepared baking sheets, about 2 inches (5 cm) apart. Slightly flatten each cookie by pressing down with the palm of your hand or the bottom of a drinking glass. Bake in preheated oven until edges are light brown, 12 to 18 minutes. Let cool on baking sheets for 10 minutes before transferring to a wire rack to cool completely.

Variation
If dried strawberries are difficult to locate, use dried cranberries, raisins or dried blueberries instead.

Pecan Pumpkin Harvest Cookies

Makes about 40 cookies

Vegetarian Friendly

These cookies have all the flavors of fall with the addition of chocolate, but you'll love them any time of the year.

Tips

If you have an extra chocolate bar on hand, chop that up into chunks and use instead of the chocolate chips.

Store cookies in an airtight container for up to 4 days. You can also freeze them in resealable plastic bags for up to 1 month.

- Preheat oven to 350°F (180°C)
- 2 baking sheets, lined with parchment paper

1½ cups	granulated sugar	375 mL
1 cup	Pumpkin Purée (page 472) or canned pumpkin purée (not pie filling)	250 mL
½ cup	unsalted butter, softened	125 mL
1	egg	1
1 tsp	vanilla extract	5 mL
2½ cups	all-purpose flour	625 mL
2 tsp	ground cinnamon	10 mL
1 tsp	ground nutmeg	5 mL
1 tsp	baking powder	5 mL
1 tsp	baking soda	5 mL
½ tsp	salt	2 mL
1 cup	semisweet chocolate chips	250 mL
1 cup	chopped and toasted pecans (see Tip, page 546)	250 mL

1. In work bowl fitted with metal blade, process sugar, pumpkin, butter, egg and vanilla until light and creamy, about 30 seconds, stopping and scraping down sides of the bowl as necessary. Add flour, cinnamon, nutmeg, baking powder, baking soda and salt and process just until combined, about 10 seconds. Transfer to a large bowl. Fold in chocolate chips and pecans. If dough is very soft, refrigerate until firm, about 20 minutes.

2. Scoop dough by heaping tablespoonfuls (15 mL) and place on prepared baking sheets, about 2 inches (5 cm) apart. Bake in preheated oven until edges are light brown, 12 to 18 minutes. Let cool on baking sheets for 10 minutes before transferring to a wire rack to cool completely.

Variation
Try hazelnuts in place of the pecans.

Oatmeal Cinnamon Raisin Cookies

Vegetarian Friendly

We like how these cookies stay soft and moist even days after baking.

Tips

There is no need to soak the raisins if they are soft and fresh.

Store cookies in an airtight container for up to 4 days. You can also freeze them in resealable plastic bags for up to 1 month.

- Preheat oven to 350°F (180°C)
- 2 baking sheets, lined with parchment paper

1 cup	golden raisins (see Tips, left)	250 mL
1/4 cup	hot water	60 mL
1 cup	unsalted butter, softened	250 mL
3/4 cup	granulated sugar	175 mL
3/4 cup	packed light brown sugar	175 mL
1 tsp	vanilla extract	5 mL
1	egg	1
3 cups	old-fashioned rolled oats	750 mL
2 cups	all-purpose flour	500 mL
1 tsp	ground cinnamon	5 mL
1/2 tsp	baking soda	2 mL
1/2 tsp	salt	2 mL

1. In a small bowl, combine raisins and hot water. Let soak until raisins are soft, about 10 minutes. Drain. Set aside.

2. In work bowl fitted with metal blade, process butter until light and creamy, about 10 seconds. Add granulated sugar, brown sugar and vanilla. Process until incorporated, about 30 seconds. Add egg and process until incorporated, about 5 seconds, stopping and scraping down sides of the bowl as necessary. Add rolled oats, flour, cinnamon, baking soda and salt and process just until combined, about 10 seconds. With motor running, add raisins through feed tube and process until incorporated. If dough is very soft, transfer to a bowl and refrigerate until firm, about 20 minutes.

3. Scoop dough by heaping tablespoonfuls (15 mL) and squeeze into a ball. Place on prepared baking sheets, about 2 inches (5 cm) apart. Slightly flatten each cookie by pressing down with the palm of your hand or the bottom of a drinking glass. Bake in preheated oven until edges are light brown, 12 to 18 minutes. Let cool on baking sheets for 10 minutes before transferring to a wire rack to cool completely.

Variation

Replace raisins with dried cranberries during the holidays for a red festive look to your cookies. Dried cranberries are available at specialty food stores and supermarkets.

Peanut Sandwich Cookies

Makes 24 cookies

Vegetarian Friendly

If you like peanuts, you'll start craving these cookies long after they are all eaten. They are soft yet firm.

Tips

These cookies are best eaten within a few days.

If the filling is too wet, add additional sugar; if too dry, add a few drops of milk.

- Preheat oven to 375°F (190°C)
- 2 baking sheets, lined with parchment paper

Filling

8 oz	cream cheese, cubed and softened	250 g
½ cup	confectioner's (icing) sugar	125 mL
¼ cup	creamy peanut butter	60 mL

Cookie Dough

1¾ cups	all-purpose flour	425 mL
1 cup	granulated sugar, divided	250 mL
½ cup	packed light brown sugar	125 mL
½ cup	shortening	125 mL
½ cup	creamy peanut butter	125 mL
1	egg	1
2 tbsp	milk	30 mL
1 tsp	baking soda	5 mL
1 tsp	vanilla extract	5 mL
½ tsp	salt	2 mL

1. **Filling:** In work bowl fitted with metal blade, process cream cheese, confectioner's sugar and peanut butter until smooth, about 1 minute. Transfer to a small bowl. Set aside.

2. **Cookie Dough:** In clean work bowl fitted with metal blade, process flour, ½ cup (125 mL) of the granulated sugar, brown sugar, shortening, peanut butter, egg, milk, baking soda, vanilla and salt until smooth, about 2 minutes. Transfer to a bowl and refrigerate until firm, about 25 minutes.

3. Shape dough into 48 1-inch (2.5 cm) balls. Roll in remaining granulated sugar. Place on prepared baking sheets, about 2 inches (5 cm) apart. Slightly flatten each cookie by pressing down with the palm of your hand or the bottom of a drinking glass. Bake in preheated oven until edges are light brown, 10 to 14 minutes. Let cool on baking sheets for 20 minutes before transferring to a wire rack to cool completely.

4. Spread half of the cookies with 2 tsp (10 mL) each of the filling. Top with remaining cookies to form sandwiches.

Cinnamon Apple Shortbread

Makes about 36 cookies

Vegetarian Friendly

Here's a shortbread that has a crisp apple taste in every bite.

Tips

The apple needs to be cored and quartered first; otherwise it may just spin around the work bowl.

Store cookies in an airtight container for up to 4 days. You can also freeze them in resealable plastic bags for up to 1 month.

- Preheat oven to 350°F (180°C)
- 2 baking sheets, lined with parchment paper

1	baking apple, such as Granny Smith, cored, peeled and quartered (see Tips, left)	1
1 cup	unsalted butter, softened	250 mL
¾ cup	granulated sugar	175 mL
1 tbsp	vanilla extract	15 mL
3¼ cups	all-purpose flour	800 mL
2 tsp	ground cinnamon	10 mL

1. In work bowl fitted with metal blade, pulse apple until finely chopped, about 20 times. Add butter, sugar and vanilla and process until light and creamy, about 10 seconds, stopping and scraping down sides of the bowl as necessary. Add flour and cinnamon and process just until combined, about 10 seconds. If dough is very soft, transfer to a bowl and refrigerate until firm, about 20 minutes.

2. Scoop dough by heaping tablespoonfuls (15 mL) and squeeze into a ball. Place on prepared baking sheets, about 2 inches (5 cm) apart. Slightly flatten each cookie by pressing down with the palm of your hand or the bottom of a drinking glass. Bake in preheated oven until edges are light brown, 12 to 18 minutes. Let cool on baking sheets for 10 minutes before transferring to a wire rack to cool completely.

Variation
Try using a ripe pear in place of the apple.

Sugar and Spice Cookies

Vegetarian Friendly

These cookies are great
with strong coffee on a
cold, snowy day.

Tips

If your brown sugar is
hard, soften it in the
microwave on High for
10 to 20 seconds.

Store cookies in an
airtight container for up to
4 days. You can also freeze
them in resealable plastic
bags for up to 1 month.

- Preheat oven to 350°F (180°C)
- 2 baking sheets, lined with parchment paper

1 cup	unsalted butter, softened	250 mL
¾ cup	packed light brown sugar	175 mL
1 tbsp	vanilla extract	15 mL
3 cups	all-purpose flour	750 mL
1 tsp	ground cinnamon	5 mL
½ tsp	ground nutmeg	2 mL
¼ tsp	ground cloves	1 mL
¼ tsp	ground cardamom	1 mL
¼ tsp	ground mace	1 mL

1. In work bowl fitted with metal blade, process butter until light and creamy, about 10 seconds. Add brown sugar and vanilla and process until incorporated, about 30 seconds, stopping and scraping down sides of the bowl as necessary. Add flour, cinnamon, nutmeg, cloves, cardamom and mace and process just until combined, about 10 seconds. If dough is very soft, transfer to a bowl and refrigerate until firm, about 20 minutes.

2. Scoop dough by heaping tablespoonfuls (15 mL) and squeeze into a ball. Place on prepared baking sheets, about 2 inches (5 cm) apart. Slightly flatten each cookie by pressing down with the palm of your hand or the bottom of a drinking glass. Bake in preheated oven until edges are light brown, 12 to 18 minutes. Let cool on baking sheets for 10 minutes before transferring to a wire rack to cool completely.

Variations

Instead of cinnamon, nutmeg, cloves, cardamom and mace use 2¼ tsp (11 mL) pumpkin pie spice.

Fruitcake Cookies

Vegetarian Friendly

Colorful and filled with dried fruits and nuts. Most people dislike fruitcake, but so many flavors are packed into this cookie, you're bound to change minds!

Tip

Make sure you take dough out of food processor and add the fruit and nuts by hand or they will become pulverized and make the cookies very sticky.

- Preheat oven to 325°F (160°C)
- Baking sheets, lined with parchment paper or Silpats
- #24 disher or scoop

2¼ cups	all-purpose flour	550 mL
½ tsp	salt	2 mL
½ tsp	baking soda	2 mL
¾ cup	unsalted butter, melted and cooled	175 mL
1 cup	packed brown sugar	250 mL
1	egg	1
2 tsp	vanilla extract	10 mL
2 cups	chopped candied fruit	500 mL
1 cup	toasted chopped pecans	250 mL

1. In a medium bowl, whisk together flour, salt and baking soda. Set aside.

2. In work bowl fitted with metal blade, process melted butter and brown sugar for 15 seconds. With processor running, add egg and vanilla through feed tube and process for 10 seconds. Add flour mixture and process until blended, about 20 seconds. Transfer dough to a large bowl and fold in candied fruit and pecans by hand. Refrigerate dough for 20 minutes.

3. Using disher, scoop dough onto prepared baking sheets, at least 2 inches (5 cm) apart. Press down with palm of your hand. Bake in preheated oven until light brown around the edges, 14 to 18 minutes.

Vanilla Rose Cookies with Rose Crème Filling

Vegetarian Friendly

The slight hints of rose petals and vanilla enhance this sandwiched cookie.

Tips

If you can't find vanilla rose sugar, use the same amount of granulated sugar with a few drops of rose water.

Rose water is a liquid distilled from rose petals. It is available at Asian, Middle Eastern and specialty food stores, as well as cake decorating shops.

If filling is too thick, you can add drops of milk until it is spreadable.

- Preheat oven to 325°F (160°C)
- Baking sheets, lined with parchment paper or Silpats
- #50 disher or scoop

2 cups	unsalted butter, softened	500 mL
10 tbsp	granulated sugar	150 mL
10 tbsp	vanilla rose sugar (see Tips, left)	150 mL
4 cups	all-purpose flour	1 L
1 tsp	salt	5 mL
½ cup	granulated sugar	125 mL
8 oz	cream cheese, softened	250 g
1½ cups	confectioner's (icing) sugar	375 mL
1 tsp	rose water (see Tips, left)	5 mL
	Milk, if necessary (see Tips, left)	

1. In work bowl fitted with metal blade, process butter until creamy, for 15 seconds. With motor running, add 10 tbsp (150 mL) sugar and vanilla rose sugar, 1 tbsp (15 mL) at a time, through feed tube and process until incorporated. Add flour and salt and mix for 30 seconds. Refrigerate for 35 minutes.

2. Place ½ cup (125 mL) granulated sugar in a shallow dish. Using disher, scoop dough and roll in sugar. (You should have 60 cookies.) Place on prepared baking sheets, about 2 inches (5 cm) apart. Bake in preheated oven until light brown, 12 to 16 minutes. Let cool on baking sheets for 10 minutes before transferring to a wire rack to cool completely.

3. In a clean work bowl fitted with metal blade, process cream cheese, confectioner's sugar and rose water until creamy, for 15 seconds. Place 2 tsp (10 mL) crème on bottom half of cooled cookies and sandwich two together.

Almond Pumpkin Bars

Makes about 24 bars

Vegetarian Friendly

These bars are just like small pumpkin cheesecakes. We love them in the fall.

Tip

You can use 2 tsp (10 mL) pumpkin pie spice in place of cinnamon, nutmeg, cloves and allspice.

- Preheat oven to 350°F (180°C)
- 13- by 9-inch (33 by 23 cm) metal baking pan, lined with foil, sprayed with nonstick spray, then lined with parchment paper

Crust

2½ cups	gingersnap cookie crumbs (page 552) or store-bought	625 mL
½ cup	unsalted butter, melted	125 mL

Filling

3	packages (each 8 oz/250 g) cream cheese, cubed and softened	3
1	package (8 oz/250 g) small curd cottage cheese	1
¾ cup	granulated sugar	175 mL
4	eggs	4
½ cup	pumpkin purée (not pie filling)	125 mL
1 tsp	almond-flavored liqueur	5 mL
1 tsp	ground cinnamon	5 mL
½ tsp	ground nutmeg	2 mL
¼ tsp	ground cloves	1 mL
¼ tsp	ground allspice	1 mL
½ cup	slivered almonds	125 mL

1. **Crust:** In a bowl, combine gingersnap crumbs and butter. Press into bottom of prepared pan and freeze until batter is ready.

2. **Filling:** In work bowl fitted with metal blade, process cream cheese and cottage cheese until creamy, for 30 seconds. Add sugar and process until blended, for 10 seconds. With motor running, add eggs, one at a time, through feed tube and process for 10 seconds. Add pumpkin, almond liqueur, cinnamon, nutmeg, cloves and allspice and process until incorporated, for 10 seconds.

3. Pour filling over crust. Sprinkle almonds over top. Bake in preheated oven until firm, 25 to 30 minutes. Let cool completely in baking pan before cutting into bars.

Variations
Try chopped pecans in place of almonds.

Buttermilk Brownie Muffins

Makes 12 brownie muffins

Vegetarian Friendly

These brownies make perfect single-size servings for lunches or children's parties.

Tip

Make a double batch and freeze brownies in single-serving sizes.

- Preheat oven to 375°F (190°C)
- 12-cup muffin tin, lined with paper cups

⅔ cup	unsalted butter, softened	150 mL
⅔ cup	water	150 mL
¼ cup	unsweetened Dutch-process cocoa powder	60 mL
1⅓ cups	all-purpose flour	325 mL
1⅓ cups	granulated sugar	325 mL
¾ tsp	baking soda	3 mL
½ tsp	salt	2 mL
1	egg	1
⅓ cup	buttermilk	75 mL
1 tsp	vanilla extract	5 mL

1. In a small saucepan over medium heat, melt butter, water and cocoa powder. Whisk until fully melted, about 2 minutes. Remove from heat and let cool.

2. In work bowl fitted with metal blade, process flour, sugar, baking soda and salt until combined, for 10 seconds. With motor running, add egg, buttermilk and vanilla through feed tube and process until blended, for 10 seconds. Add cocoa mixture and process until incorporated, for 10 seconds.

3. Divide batter evenly into prepared muffin tin. Bake in preheated oven until a toothpick inserted in center comes out with a few moist crumbs, 18 to 20 minutes. Let cool in muffin tin on wire rack for 20 minutes before transferring to a wire rack to cool completely.

Variation
Add 1 cup (250 mL) chocolate chips into batter.

Key Lime Bars

Vegetarian Friendly

Key limes from Florida make this a pucker-up bar.

Tip

If Key limes are not available, you can use bottled Key lime juice and regular lime zest.

- Preheat oven to 350°F (180°C)
- 13- by 9-inch (33 by 23 cm) metal baking pan, lined with foil, sprayed with nonstick spray, then lined with parchment paper

Crust

2¼ cups	all-purpose flour	550 mL
½ cup	granulated sugar	125 mL
1 cup	unsalted butter, softened	250 mL
1 tbsp	grated Key lime zest	15 mL
1 tbsp	Key lime juice (see Tip, left)	15 mL

Filling

4	eggs	4
2 cups	granulated sugar	500 mL
¼ cup	all-purpose flour	60 mL
½ tsp	baking powder	2 mL
1 tbsp	grated Key lime zest	15 mL
¼ cup	Key lime juice	60 mL

1. **Crust:** In a large bowl, combine flour and sugar. Stir in butter, lime zest and lime juice until blended. Pat into bottom of prepared baking pan. Bake in preheated oven until golden brown, 20 to 24 minutes.

2. **Filling:** In work bowl fitted with metal blade, process eggs, sugar, flour, baking powder, lime zest and juice until well combined, for 10 seconds. Pour over top of hot crust.

3. Return to preheated oven and bake until set and sides are light brown, 25 to 30 minutes. Let cool completely in baking pan before cutting into bars.

Variation

After pouring filling over crust, swirl 2 oz (60 g) cooled melted semisweet chocolate into the Key lime batter.

Lemon Oatmeal Bars

Makes about 24 bars

Vegetarian Friendly

Make these with fresh lemons so you get a really tart-tasting bar!

Tip

Make sure the butter is cut into small pieces so it will incorporate well.

- Preheat oven to 375°F (190°C)
- 13- by 9-inch (33 by 23 cm) metal baking pan, lined with foil, sprayed with nonstick spray, then lined with parchment paper

1¼ cups	all purpose flour	300 mL
1 cup	unsalted butter, softened, cut into small pieces (see Tip, left)	250 mL
¾ cup	quick-cooking rolled oats	175 mL
⅔ cup	granulated sugar	150 mL
½ cup	milk, preferably whole	125 mL
1	egg	1
2 tbsp	grated lemon zest, divided	30 mL
1 tsp	baking soda	5 mL
1 tsp	vanilla extract	5 mL
1 cup	confectioner's (icing) sugar	250 mL
2 tbsp	freshly squeezed lemon juice	30 mL

1. In work bowl fitted with metal blade, combine flour, butter, oats, sugar, milk, egg, 1 tbsp (15 mL) of the lemon zest, baking soda and vanilla. Pulse until smooth, 30 times. Press into prepared baking pan. Bake in preheated oven until firm and light brown, 18 to 22 minutes. Let cool completely in baking pan.

2. In a small bowl, whisk together confectioner's sugar, lemon juice and remaining zest until smooth, about 3 minutes. Drizzle over cooled bars. Cut into bars.

Variation

You can add ½ cup (125 mL) fresh berries chopped into mixture to create berry bars. Fold berries by hand into batter after adding vanilla.

Lemon Raspberry Nut Bars

Vegetarian Friendly

Tart, sweet and nutty —
all these flavors in one
cookie bar.

Tip

If you're make the filling
prior to the crust being
baked completely, make
sure you whisk the filling
before pouring over
the crust.

- Preheat oven to 350°F (180°C)
- 13- by 9-inch (33 by 23 cm) metal baking pan, lined with foil, sprayed with nonstick spray, then lined with parchment paper

Crust

2 cups	all-purpose flour	500 mL
1/4 cup	pecans, finely chopped	60 mL
1/2 cup	granulated sugar	125 mL
1 cup	unsalted butter, softened	250 mL
1 tbsp	grated lemon zest	15 mL

Filling

4	eggs	4
2 cups	granulated sugar	500 mL
2 tbsp	all-purpose flour	30 mL
1/2 tsp	baking powder	2 mL
1 tbsp	grated lemon zest	15 mL
1/4 cup	freshly squeezed lemon juice	60 mL
1/2 cup	raspberries, cut into small pieces	125 mL

1. **Crust:** In work bowl fitted with metal blade, pulse flour, pecans and sugar until combined, about 10 times. Add butter and lemon zest and process until blended, for 10 seconds. Pat into bottom of prepared baking pan. Bake in preheated oven until golden brown, 20 to 24 minutes.

2. **Filling:** In work bowl fitted with metal blade, process eggs, sugar, flour, baking powder, lemon zest and juice until well combined, about 10 seconds. Pour over hot crust. Sprinkle raspberries over top. Return to preheated oven and bake until set, 25 to 30 minutes. Let cool completely in baking pan before cutting.

Variation
Try blackberries in place of the raspberries.

Peanut Butter Chocolate Bars

Makes about 24 bars

Vegetarian Friendly

Peanut butter and chocolate go so well together. Try making these for a kid's party or family outing — they pack well.

Tip

Make sure the butter is soft before blending with peanut butter. If cold, it won't blend with the peanut butter.

- Preheat oven to 350°F (180°C)
- 13- by 9-inch (33 by 23 cm) metal baking pan, lined with foil, sprayed with nonstick spray, then lined with parchment paper

2⅔ cups	all-purpose flour	650 mL
1 cup	unsweetened Dutch-process cocoa powder, sifted	250 mL
1 tsp	baking powder	5 mL
⅔ cup	creamy peanut butter	150 mL
½ cup	unsalted butter, softened (see Tip, left)	125 mL
1½ cups	packed brown sugar	375 mL
1½ cups	granulated sugar	375 mL
2	eggs	2
2 tsp	vanilla extract	10 mL
1¼ cups	chopped peanuts	300 mL

1. In a bowl, combine flour, cocoa powder and baking powder. Set aside.

2. In work bowl fitted with metal blade, process peanut butter and butter until creamy, for 15 seconds. Add brown sugar, granulated sugar, eggs and vanilla and process until smooth, about 30 seconds. Add flour mixture and process until incorporated for 20 seconds. Transfer to a bowl and fold in peanuts by hand.

3. Spread into prepared pan. Bake in preheated oven until the top is firm, 28 to 32 minutes. Let cool completely in baking pan before cutting into bars.

Variation

Try using chunky peanut butter for a more crunchy texture.

Peanut Butter and Jelly Bars

Makes about 24 bars

Vegetarian Friendly

You will think back to your childhood days with this moist and flavorful cookie bar.

Tip

Sometimes the batter may need more time in the freezer to firm up.

- Preheat oven to 375°F (190°C)
- 13- by 9-inch (33 by 23 cm) metal baking pan, lined with foil, sprayed with nonstick spray, then lined with parchment paper

2½ cups	all-purpose flour	625 mL
1½ tsp	baking powder	7 mL
1 cup	packed brown sugar	250 mL
1 cup	unsalted butter, softened, cut into small pieces	250 mL
2	eggs	2
1 tsp	vanilla extract	5 mL
½ cup	chunky peanut butter	125 mL
½ cup	jelly, such as raspberry or strawberry	125 mL

1. In work bowl fitted with metal blade, pulse flour, baking powder and brown sugar until blended, about 5 times. With motor running, add butter, a few pieces at a time, until it resembles coarse meal. Add eggs and vanilla thorough feed tube and process until well blended, about 15 seconds.

2. Smooth half of batter into prepared baking pan. Place in freezer for 15 minutes to firm up.

3. Dollop peanut butter and jelly over top of firm batter. Drop remaining batter by spoonfuls over top, leaving areas of the jelly-peanut butter mixture exposed. Bake in preheated oven until light brown, 28 to 32 minutes. Let cool completely in baking pan before cutting into bars.

Variation

Add 2 tsp (10 mL) almond extract to the batter for a rich almond bar.

The Perfect Fudgey Brownie

Makes 24 brownies

Vegetarian Friendly

This brownie is so rich and fast to prepare that it deserves its name — it is the perfect brownie.

Tips

Make sure the chocolate is cool to the touch prior to adding it to the other ingredients.

Store brownies wrapped in plastic wrap for up to 5 days. You can also freeze them wrapped in foil for up to 1 month.

- Preheat oven to 350°F (180°C)
- 13- by 9-inch (33 by 23 cm) metal baking pan, lined with foil and sprayed with nonstick spray or lined with parchment paper

1½ lbs	semisweet chocolate, chopped	750 g
1½ cups	almonds	375 mL
½ cup	all-purpose flour	125 mL
2 cups	Traditional Mayonnaise (page 437) or store-bought	500 mL
8	eggs	8
1½ cups	granulated sugar	375 mL
6 oz	milk chocolate, cut into chunks	175 g
¼ cup	confectioner's (icing) sugar	60 mL

1. In a double boiler over hot, not boiling water, melt semisweet chocolate. Set aside and let cool slightly.

2. In work bowl fitted with metal blade, process almonds and flour until very finely ground, about 1 minute. Add mayonnaise, eggs, sugar and melted chocolate and process until well blended, about 1 minute. Fold milk chocolate chunks into batter.

3. Spread mixture into prepared pan. Bake in preheated oven until a toothpick inserted into center comes out with loose crumbs and top is firm, 30 to 35 minutes. Let cool on a wire rack. Sprinkle with confectioner's sugar. Cut into squares.

Variation
After the brownies are baked and still hot, brush the top with ¼ cup (60 mL) coffee-flavored liqueur for an adult brownie.

Chocolate Raspberry Brownies

Makes 24 brownies

Vegetarian Friendly

Raspberries are the perfect fruit to accompany this rich chocolate brownie.

Tips

If the raspberries are large, cut them into smaller pieces.

Store brownies wrapped in plastic wrap for up to 5 days. You can also freeze them wrapped in foil for up to 1 month.

- Preheat oven to 350°F (180°C)
- 13- by 9-inch (33 by 23 cm) metal baking pan, lined with foil and sprayed with nonstick spray or lined with parchment paper

1¼ cups	granulated sugar	300 mL
¾ cup	unsalted butter, melted	175 mL
2	eggs	2
1 tsp	vanilla extract	5 mL
1½ cups	all-purpose flour	375 mL
½ cup	unsweetened Dutch-process cocoa powder, sifted	125 mL
1 tsp	baking powder	5 mL
¼ tsp	baking soda	1 mL
1 cup	milk, at room temperature	250 mL
1 cup	fresh or frozen raspberries, thawed and drained if frozen	250 mL
	Bittersweet Fudge Frosting (optional) (page 634)	

1. In work bowl fitted with metal blade, process sugar, butter, eggs and vanilla until combined, about 20 seconds. Add flour, cocoa powder, baking powder and baking soda and process until it begins to gather, 20 to 30 seconds. With motor running, add milk in a steady stream through feed tube until incorporated.

2. Transfer mixture to a bowl and carefully fold in raspberries. Transfer to prepared baking pan. Bake in preheated oven until a toothpick inserted into the center comes out with loose crumbs and top is firm, 25 to 35 minutes. Let cool on a wire rack before cutting into squares.

3. Frost with Bittersweet Fudge Frosting, if desired.

Variation

You can use 1 cup (250 mL) seedless raspberry preserves in place of the raspberries.

Oatmeal Shortbread Squares

Makes 25 cookies

Vegetarian Friendly

Made with rolled oats and half whole wheat flour, these crisp cookies are very nutritious. They make a great accompaniment to fresh berries or, with a glass of cold milk, a refreshing snack. They are rich and delicious. One will certainly be enough.

Tip

Store shortbread at room temperature in an airtight container, between layers of waxed paper, for up to 1 week.

- Preheat oven to 350°F (180°C)
- 9-inch (23 cm) square cake pan, ungreased

2 cups	old-fashioned (large flake) rolled oats	500 mL
½ cup	all-purpose flour	125 mL
½ cup	whole wheat flour	125 mL
¾ cup	packed brown sugar, such as Demerara or other raw cane sugar	175 mL
½ tsp	baking soda	2 mL
½ tsp	salt	2 mL
1 cup	cold butter, cubed	250 mL
1 tsp	vanilla extract	5 mL

1. In work bowl fitted with metal blade, process oats, all-purpose flour, whole wheat flour, brown sugar, baking soda and salt for 30 seconds to blend and grind sugar. Add butter and process until mixture resembles coarse crumbs. Sprinkle vanilla over top and pulse until blended. Transfer to a clean work surface and, using your hands, knead to form a smooth dough.

2. Press dough evenly into pan and bake in preheated oven until edges begin to brown, about 25 minutes. Place pan on a wire rack. Using a serrated knife, score the top to form 25 squares. Let cool completely in pan on rack. Recut and remove squares from pan.

Gingery Shortbread

**Makes about
24 cookies**

Vegetarian Friendly

Whole-grain brown rice
and barley flour add
wholesome nutrition
to this shortbread,
which has an appealing
gingery flavor and
crumbly texture. It's
delicious with a cup of
tea, as a complement to
fresh berries, or anytime
only a cookie will do.

Tip

Store shortbread at room
temperature in an airtight
container, between layers
of waxed paper, for up to
1 week.

- Baking sheets, ungreased

1 cup	brown rice flour	250 mL
1/2 cup	whole barley flour	125 mL
1/2 cup	all-purpose flour	125 mL
1/2 cup	packed brown sugar, such as Demerara or other raw cane sugar	125 mL
1 tsp	ground ginger	5 mL
1/4 tsp	baking powder	1 mL
1/4 tsp	salt	1 mL
1 cup	cold butter, cubed	250 mL
1/3 cup	chopped crystallized ginger	75 mL
1 tsp	vanilla extract	5 mL

1. In work bowl fitted with metal blade, process brown rice flour, barley flour, all-purpose flour, brown sugar, ground ginger, baking powder and salt for 30 seconds to blend and grind sugar.

2. Add butter and process until integrated. Add crystallized ginger and vanilla and process until crumbly. Transfer to a clean work surface and shape into 2 logs, each about 6 inches (15 cm) long. Wrap in plastic wrap and refrigerate until firm enough to slice, about 30 minutes.

3. Preheat oven to 325°F (160°C). Slice into cookies about 1/4 inch (0.5 cm) thick and place on baking sheets, about 2 inches (5 cm) apart. Bake, in batches if necessary, in preheated oven until edges are golden, about 20 minutes. Let cool on sheet on a wire rack, then transfer to rack to cool completely.

Desserts and Dessert Toppings

Ginger Strawberry Fool

Serves 4

Vegetarian Friendly

Fools, which are basically puréed fruit mixed with cream, are an old English dessert. They are delicious and very easy to make. For a great finishing touch, serve this with homemade Gingersnaps (page 552) or Gingery Shortbread (page 592).

Tip

You can also use stem ginger in syrup, available in many specialty stores. Use the same quantity of ginger and substitute 2 tbsp (30 mL) of the syrup for the frozen orange juice concentrate.

- 4 parfait or wine glasses

1	package (10 oz/300 g) frozen strawberries, thawed, or 1½ cups (375 mL) hulled strawberries	1
2 tbsp	finely chopped candied ginger (see Tip, left)	30 mL
2 tbsp	frozen orange juice concentrate or orange-flavored liqueur, such as Cointreau	30 mL
1 cup	heavy or whipping (35%) cream	250 mL
¼ cup	confectioner's (icing) sugar	60 mL
	Mint sprigs, optional	

1. In work bowl fitted with metal blade, process strawberries, ginger and orange juice concentrate until mixture is the consistency of well-mashed fruit. (It should not be smooth.)

2. In a large bowl, using an electric mixer or balloon whisk, whip cream with confectioner's sugar until soft peaks form. Gently fold in strawberry mixture. Spoon into parfait glasses and refrigerate until well chilled, about 1 hour. Garnish with a sprig of fresh mint just before serving, if using.

Variation

Strawberry Orange Fool: Substitute 1 tsp (5 mL) grated orange zest or 2 tbsp (30 mL) chopped candied orange peel for the ginger.

Rhubarb Fool

Vegetarian Friendly

If you grow rhubarb in your garden, you'll welcome this recipe. It's an easy way of transforming those juicy bitter stems into a luscious dessert. If you don't grow rhubarb, you can also make this using frozen packaged rhubarb. Don't even defrost it. Simply add the sugar and bake. Serve this with shortbread or wafers alongside.

- Preheat oven to 300°F (150°C)
- 4 cup (1 L) covered baking dish

4 cups	sliced (½ inch/1 cm) rhubarb (about 1 lb/500 g)	1 L
¾ cup	packed brown sugar, such as Demerara or evaporated cane juice	175 mL
2 tbsp	orange-flavored liqueur, such as Cointreau, optional	30 mL
¾ cup	heavy or whipping (35%) cream	175 mL

1. In baking dish, combine rhubarb and brown sugar. Stir well. Cover and bake in preheated oven until rhubarb is soft and tender, about 1 hour. Transfer to a strainer and strain off liquid. Add solids to work bowl fitted with metal blade and add liqueur, if using. Process until smooth, about 30 seconds. Cover and refrigerate until very cold, at least 4 hours or overnight.

2. In a large bowl, using an electric mixer or balloon whisk, whip cream. Gently fold cold rhubarb mixture into whipped cream, until evenly blended. Serve immediately or cover and refrigerate for up to 2 hours.

Variation

If you are not adding the orange liqueur, add 1 tsp (5 mL) cinnamon to rhubarb along with the sugar.

Candied Ginger Applesauce with Yogurt

Serves 6

Vegan Friendly

If you're fond of applesauce but would enjoy a more sophisticated spin on it, try this version. It's as easy to make as the original, but has intriguing flavor notes ranging from deliciously sweet to spicy and tart. We like to serve this with homemade Gingersnaps (page 552).

6	apples, peeled, cored and cut into quarters	6
2 tbsp	granulated sugar	30 mL
1 tbsp	freshly squeezed lemon juice	15 mL
2	pieces stem ginger in syrup, quartered	2
2 tbsp	syrup from stem ginger	30 mL
½ cup	plain yogurt, preferably Greek-style (pressed) (see Tip, page 311) or soy yogurt	125 mL
⅓ cup	liquid honey or pure maple syrup	75 mL

1. In a saucepan, combine apples, ¼ cup (60 mL) water, sugar and lemon juice. Bring to a boil over medium heat. Cover, reduce heat and simmer until apples are very soft, about 15 minutes. Let cool slightly.

2. Transfer to work bowl fitted with metal blade. Add ginger, ginger syrup, yogurt and honey. Purée until smooth, about 1 minute. Cover and chill thoroughly, for at least 3 hours, before serving.

Raspberry-Studded Mango Parfait

Serves 4

Vegan Friendly

If you're looking for a dessert that is simple to make, healthy and light, yet delicious, look no further. When mangos are in season, use lusciously ripe specimens to make this tasty combination. If you don't feel like using a tall glass, spread the mango purée over the bottom of a shallow dessert bowl and scatter the raspberries on top.

- 4 tall thin glasses

2	ripe mangos, peeled and sliced	2
1 tbsp	freshly squeezed lime juice	15 mL
1 tbsp	liquid honey or pure maple syrup	15 mL
1 cup	fresh raspberries	250 mL
1 tbsp	almond-flavored liqueur, such as Amaretto	15 mL
	Whipped cream, optional	
	Toasted chopped almonds, optional	

1. In work bowl fitted with metal blade, purée mangos, lime juice and honey.

2. In a bowl, gently toss together raspberries and liqueur. In tall thin glasses, alternate layers of mango mixture and raspberries, finishing with a layer of raspberries. Top with a small dollop of whipped cream and sprinkle with toasted almonds, if using.

Quince Parfait

Vegetarian Friendly

Quinces taste a bit like apples but are richer and denser.

Tips

When quartering quinces, cut a piece off the bottom to make it flat and, using a chef's knife, cut around the core to make 4 quarters.

It is important to steam the quinces for this recipe. If you simmer them in water, the purée is likely to be too wet to support the whipped cream.

- Vegetable steamer
- 6 parfait or wine glasses or champagne flutes (each about 6 oz/175 mL)

	Freshly squeezed juice of 1 lemon	
3	small quinces (about 12 oz/375 g total)	3
1/3 cup	granulated sugar (approx.)	75 mL
1/2 tsp	ground cinnamon	2 mL
1 cup	heavy or whipping (35 %) cream	250 mL
1/2 tsp	vanilla extract	2 mL
	Finely chopped pecans	

1. Place lemon juice in a shallow bowl. Peel quinces and cut into quarters, dipping them in lemon juice to prevent browning. Place in steamer and steam until soft and tender, about 1 hour. Transfer to work bowl fitted with metal blade and add sugar and cinnamon. Process until smooth, about 1 minute. Cover and chill thoroughly.

2. When you're ready to serve, whip cream until soft peaks form. Add vanilla and sugar to taste, and beat until stiff peaks form. Spoon a dollop of quince purée into the bottom of a parfait glass. Add a dollop of whipped cream. Repeat until glass is filled, ending with whipped cream. Sprinkle pecans over top. Repeat with remaining glasses.

Lemon-Spiked Quince with Honey

Serves 4 to 6

Vegan Friendly

Quinces make a delightfully different variation on the theme of applesauce.

Tip

To prevent browning, place peeled quince slices in a bowl of acidulated water (see Tips, page 117).

4	quinces, peeled, cored and sliced (about 2 lbs (1 kg) (see Tip, left)	4
1	piece (about 2 inches/5 cm) cinnamon stick	1
1 tbsp	freshly squeezed lemon juice	15 mL
1/4 cup	liquid honey or pure maple syrup, or to taste	60 mL
	Cream or soy creamer, optional	

1. In a saucepan, combine quinces, cinnamon stick, lemon juice and water to cover. Cover, place over low heat and simmer until fruit is tender, about 1 hour. Drain. Discard cinnamon and transfer to work bowl fitted with metal blade. Add honey. Pulse until consistency of applesauce. Serve warm or chilled. Drizzle with cream, if using.

Ginger-Spiked Apricot Whip with Amaretto

Serves 6 to 8

Vegetarian Friendly

Easy to make from ingredients you're likely to have on hand, this lovely dessert has intriguingly delicious flavors that will keep your guests guessing as to what it contains. Serve this in small (4 oz/125 mL) glasses layered like a parfait, or in fruit nappies, in which case swirl to create a marbled top. Serve with homemade Gingersnaps (page 552) for a perfect finish.

- 4-cup (1 L) covered baking dish

1 cup	dried apricots	250 mL
1	piece stem ginger in syrup	1
1 tbsp	syrup from stem ginger	15 mL
1½ cups	heavy or whipping (35%) cream	375 mL
1 tbsp	granulated sugar	15 mL
3 tbsp	almond-flavored liqueur, such as Amaretto	45 mL
	Toasted slivered almonds	

1. In baking dish, combine apricots with water to cover. Cover and set aside to soak for at least 2 hours or overnight. Preheat oven to 325°F (160°C). Bake in preheated oven until apricots are tender, about 1 hour. Let stand, uncovered, for 30 minutes to cool.

2. Transfer apricots with liquid to work bowl fitted with metal blade. Add stem ginger and syrup and process until smooth, about 30 seconds.

3. In a large bowl, using an electric mixer or balloon whisk, whip cream until soft peaks form. Add sugar and almond liqueur and beat until stiff peaks form.

4. **To makes parfaits:** Place alternate layers of whipped cream and apricot mixture in glasses, beginning and ending with cream. Sprinkle toasted almonds liberally over top. If using fruit nappies, place a generous layer of whipped cream on bottom, a generous layer of apricot mixture on top and finish with a layer of whipped cream. Using a kitchen knife swirl the mixture to create a marble effect. Sprinkle liberally with toasted almonds.

Cherry Clafouti

Serves 4

Vegetarian Friendly

This is a particularly easy-to-make version of clafouti, which is basically a fruit pancake that is often served as a dessert in French bistros. Eaten warm it is comforting and delicious.

Tip

A 9-inch (23 cm) square baking or gratin dish (about 2 inches/5 cm deep) works perfectly for this recipe. If your baking dish is smaller, increase the baking time accordingly.

- Preheat oven to 375°F (190°C)
- 6-cup (1.5 L) baking or gratin dish (about 2 inches/5 cm deep) or a small glass pie plate, greased

1	can (14 oz/398 mL) pitted cherries in syrup, drained (about 1⅓ cups/325 mL)	1
2	eggs	2
½ cup	milk	125 mL
¼ cup	granulated sugar	60 mL
3 tbsp	all-purpose flour	45 mL
2 tbsp	butter, melted	30 mL
1 tsp	grated lemon zest	5 mL
1 tsp	almond extract	5 mL
Pinch	salt	Pinch
	Confectioner's (icing) sugar	

1. Spread cherries over bottom of prepared dish.

2. In work bowl fitted with metal blade, process eggs, milk, sugar, flour, butter, lemon zest, almond extract and salt until smooth, about 1 minute. Pour over cherries.

3. Bake in preheated oven until puffed and golden, about 25 minutes. Serve warm. Dust with confectioner's sugar just before serving.

Variations

Brandied Cherry Clafouti: Use brandied cherries instead of cherries in syrup. Use 2 tbsp (30 mL) of the brandy in the batter and reduce the quantity of milk by an equal amount.

Blueberry Clafouti: Substitute an equal quantity of blueberries for the cherries.

Overloaded Blueberry Raspberry Clafouti

Vegetarian Friendly

Overloaded with luscious berries and made with cream and an abundance of eggs, this is the *ne plus ultra* of clafouti. It is rich and delicious — the perfect dish for late summer when berries are abundant and at their best.

Tip

Watch carefully after placing the clafouti under the broiler. Once the sugar starts to caramelize, it will quickly move toward burning.

- Preheat oven to 350°F (180°C)
- 10-inch (25 cm) deep-dish pie plate, greased

2 cups	raspberries	500 mL
2 cups	blueberries	500 mL
½ cup + 2 tbsp	granulated sugar + extra for dusting, divided	125 mL + 30 mL
5	eggs	5
½ cup	heavy or whipping (35%) cream	125 mL
⅓ cup	melted butter	75 mL
⅓ cup	all-purpose flour	75 mL
2 tsp	finely grated lemon zest	10 mL

1. Arrange raspberries and blueberries over bottom of prepared dish. Dust lightly with sugar.

2. In work bowl fitted with a metal blade, process eggs, cream, ½ cup (125 mL) of the sugar, melted butter, flour and lemon zest until smooth, about 30 seconds. Pour over fruit.

3. Bake in preheated oven until edges are set and center is slightly jiggly, about 50 minutes. Remove from oven and preheat broiler. Sprinkle remaining 2 tbsp (30 mL) sugar over top. Place under broiler until sugar is golden. Serve warm.

Orange-Spiked Apple Charlotte

Serves 4 to 6

Vegan Friendly

This old-fashioned version of Apple Charlotte — applesauce flavored with marmalade — encased in grilled bread is true comfort food. The end result resembles a winter version of summer pudding. Add a dollop of vanilla ice cream for a perfect finish.

- Preheat oven to 350°F (180°C)
- 4 cup (1 L) baking dish, greased

8	cooking apples, peeled, cored and quartered	8
1/3 cup	granulated sugar	75 mL
2 tbsp	butter or vegan alternative	30 mL
1 tbsp	freshly squeezed lemon juice	15 mL
3 tbsp	orange marmalade	45 mL
	Softened butter or vegan alternative	
5	slices white bread, crusts removed (approx.)	5

Cinnamon Sugar

2 tbsp	granulated sugar	30 mL
1/2 tsp	ground cinnamon	2 mL
	Ice cream or whipped cream, optional	

1. In a saucepan over low heat, combine apples, sugar, butter, 2 tbsp (30 mL) water and lemon juice. Cover and cook until apples are very soft, about 25 minutes. Transfer to work bowl fitted with a metal blade. Add marmalade and process until apples are the consistency of sauce and mixture is blended, about 30 seconds. Set aside.

2. Butter bread on both sides. In a skillet over medium-high heat, sauté bread, in batches, turning once, until nicely browned. As completed, transfer to a cutting board. Cut bread to fit tightly over the bottom of prepared baking dish, then cut strips to fit around the sides, overlapping slightly. (You don't want any gaps. If you need to brown additional bread, do so.) Add apple mixture. Place final pieces of bread over top. Bake in preheated oven for 30 minutes, then remove from oven and preheat broiler.

3. **Cinnamon Sugar:** In a small bowl, combine sugar and cinnamon. Sprinkle over top of pudding and place under broiler until sugar is caramelized. Serve warm or cooled with ice cream or whipped cream, if desired.

Peaches with Raspberry Coulis and Passion Fruit Sorbet

Serves 6

Vegan Friendly

This dessert is so good — and all you do is turn on the food processor and assemble it.

Tips

If you prefer a seedless coulis, put the mixture through a fine sieve after processing.

Use canned peach halves, drained; frozen peaches, thawed; or fresh freestone peaches, in season.

- **6 dessert dishes**

¾ cup	fresh raspberries or ½ package (10 oz/300 g) unsweetened frozen raspberries, thawed	175 mL
¼ cup	granulated sugar	60 mL
1 tbsp	freshly squeezed lemon juice	15 mL
6	large scoops passion fruit or lemon sorbet	6
6	peach halves (see Tips, left)	6

1. In work bowl fitted with metal blade, process raspberries, sugar and lemon juice until smooth, about 1 minute. Refrigerate until ready to use.

2. Place 1 scoop sorbet in a dessert dish. Top with a peach half and drizzle with raspberry coulis. Serve immediately.

Cranberry Pear Gingersnap Betty

Serves 4 to 6

Vegetarian Friendly

Flavorful fruit baked in a sweetened crumb mixture is a perfect finish to any meal.

- Preheat oven to 375°F (190°C)
- 8-cup (2 L) baking dish, greased

8 oz	gingersnap cookies	250 g
2 tbsp	granulated sugar	30 mL
1 tsp	ground ginger	5 mL
¼ cup	butter, melted	60 mL
2	cans (each 14 oz/398 mL) pear halves, drained, ½ cup (125 mL) syrup reserved	2
½ cup	dried cranberries	125 mL
1 tbsp	freshly squeezed lemon juice	15 mL

1. In work bowl fitted with metal blade, process gingersnaps until they are fine crumbs, about 1 minute. Add sugar and ginger and pulse to blend. Add butter and process until blended.

2. Spread one-third of the crumb mixture in bottom of prepared dish. Lay half of the pears over the crumbs and sprinkle with cranberries. Spoon 2 tbsp (30 mL) of the reserved pear syrup over fruit. Repeat layers. Top with remaining crumbs.

3. Mix together remaining pear syrup and lemon juice and pour over top. Bake in preheated oven until top is golden and mixture is bubbling, about 25 minutes.

Variations

Cherry Pear Gingersnap Betty: Substitute ½ cup (125 mL) dried cherries for the cranberries.

Cranberry Pear Brown Betty: Substitute 2 cups (500 mL) fine bread crumbs for the gingersnap crumbs and 1 tsp (5 mL) ground cinnamon for the ginger. Add 2 tbsp (30 mL) granulated sugar to the mixture.

Indian Banana Pudding

Serves 8

Vegan Friendly

This traditional Indian pudding has an unusual thickener: dried split peas. Exotic and delicious, it has a light banana flavor enhanced with sweet dates and the texture of crunchy toasted almonds.

Tips

To toast almonds: Place nuts in a single layer on a baking sheet in a preheated 350°F (180°C) oven for 5 to 7 minutes for slivered, or until fragrant and golden, stirring once or twice.

This pudding is best eaten the day it is prepared. Refrigerating the bananas causes them to lose color.

- 8-cup (2 L) covered baking dish, greased

½ cup	yellow split peas	125 mL
2 tbsp	coarsely chopped peeled gingerroot	30 mL
¼ cup	packed brown sugar, such as Demerara or evaporated cane juice sugar	60 mL
1	can (14 oz/400 mL) coconut milk	1
½ tsp	almond extract	2 mL
1 tsp	ground cardamom	5 mL
2	ripe bananas, peeled and chopped	2
¼ cup	finely chopped pitted soft dates, preferably Medjool	60 mL
½ cup	toasted slivered almonds, divided	125 mL
	Whipped cream, optional	

1. In a large deep saucepan, combine split peas and 3 cups (750 mL) water. Cover and bring to a boil. Boil for 3 minutes. Turn off heat and soak for 1 hour. Drain and rinse thoroughly under cold water.

2. Preheat oven to 350°F (180°C). In work bowl fitted with metal blade, process soaked peas, ginger, brown sugar and ½ cup (125 mL) of the coconut milk until puréed, about 1 minute. Add remaining coconut milk, almond extract and cardamom and process until smooth. Pour into prepared baking dish.

3. Cover and bake in preheated oven until peas are tender and mixture begins to thicken, about 45 minutes. Stir in bananas. Replace cover and bake for 15 minutes. Remove from oven and, using a wooden spoon, beat mixture vigorously. Fold in dates and half the almonds. Transfer to a serving bowl. Cover and refrigerate until thoroughly chilled, about 1½ hours. Garnish with remaining almonds and serve with a dollop of whipped cream, if using.

Persimmon Pudding

Serves 6 to 8

Vegetarian Friendly

With their bright orange color, persimmons, which arrive in markets in the late fall, are a welcome treat. This dessert, which resembles a pudding cake, is a classic southern recipe, often served as the finale for Thanksgiving dinner.

Tips

Persimmons must be fully ripe and quite soft. Otherwise they are likely to be unpleasantly bitter.

Depending on where you live, you may be able to buy frozen or prepared persimmon pulp. You'll need about 1½ cups (375 mL) persimmon flesh for this recipe.

When baking, the pudding will puff up over the sides of the pan, but it will be solid enough not to drip so don't worry about it.

- Preheat oven to 325°F (160°C)
- 8-inch (2 L) square baking pan, greased

1 cup	all-purpose flour	250 mL
2 tsp	baking powder	10 mL
1 tsp	ground cinnamon	5 mL
1 tsp	freshly grated nutmeg	5 mL
½ tsp	salt	2 mL
4	ripe persimmons (see Tips, left)	4
1 cup	packed brown sugar	250 mL
1 cup	buttermilk	250 mL
2	eggs	2
1 tsp	vanilla extract	5 mL
1 cup	milk, divided	250 mL
½ cup	chopped walnuts	125 mL
¼ cup	melted butter	60 mL
	Whipped cream or ice cream	

1. In a bowl, combine flour, baking powder, cinnamon, nutmeg and salt. Mix well and set aside.

2. Slice off stem end of persimmons, cut in half vertically and, using a grapefruit spoon, scoop out the flesh and discard skins. Transfer to work bowl fitted with metal blade. Add brown sugar and buttermilk to work bowl. Process until smooth, about 30 seconds. Add eggs and vanilla and process until blended, about 15 minutes.

3. Remove lid and add half the flour mixture to work bowl. Replace lid and process for 10 seconds. With motor running, add half of the milk through feed tube and process until smooth. Remove lid and add remaining flour mixture. Replace lid and process until thick and smooth, about 10 seconds. With motor running, add remaining milk through feed tube in a steady stream until incorporated. Add walnuts and melted butter and pulse just to incorporate, about 5 times.

4. Pour into prepared pan, spreading to edges and smoothing top. Bake in preheated oven until a tester inserted in the center comes out clean, about 1 hour. Let cool slightly. Serve lukewarm with whipped cream or ice cream.

Down-Home Sweet Potato Pudding

Vegetarian Friendly

This old-fashioned pudding is a favorite comfort food dessert. Using canned sweet potatoes dramatically reduces the preparation time for this southern classic, but if you prefer, you can peel and cook fresh sweet potatoes yourself. If you like a hint of orange flavor, add the orange zest. Serve this with a dollop of whipped cream.

- Preheat oven to 350°F (180°C)
- 6-cup (1.5 L) baking dish, greased

1	can (19 oz/540 mL) sliced sweet potatoes, drained (about 2 medium, peeled sliced and cooked)	1
1	can (12 oz/370 mL) evaporated milk	1
1 cup	packed brown sugar	250 mL
3	eggs	3
2 tbsp	butter, melted	30 mL
2 tbsp	dark rum or 1 tsp (5 mL) vanilla extract	30 mL
1 tsp	grated orange zest, optional	5 mL
½ tsp	freshly grated nutmeg	2 mL
½ tsp	ground cinnamon	2 mL
	Whipped cream, optional	

1. In work bowl fitted with metal blade, process sweet potatoes, evaporated milk, brown sugar, eggs and butter until smooth, about 1 minute. Add rum, orange zest, if using, nutmeg and cinnamon and pulse until blended, about 5 times.

2. Pour mixture into prepared dish. Bake in preheated oven until set, about 45 minutes. Spoon into bowls and top with whipped cream, if using.

Variation

For a bit of crunch, sprinkle ½ cup (125 mL) chopped pecans evenly over the pudding before baking.

Lemon Pots de Crème

Vegetarian Friendly

If you're a fan of creamy
puddings but are
looking for something
that is lighter than
most, try this. It's a great
combination of lemon
flavor mellowed with
gentle cream. Serve with
elegant wafers.

Tip

If you prefer, make this
in eight 4-oz (125 mL)
ramekins. Reduce the
cooking time to about
25 minutes.

- Preheat oven to 325°F (160°C)
- Six 6-oz (175 mL) ramekins (see Tip, left)

2 cups	half-and-half (10%) cream	500 mL
2 tbsp	grated lemon zest	30 mL
½ cup	freshly squeezed lemon juice (about 2 lemons)	125 mL
½ cup	granulated sugar	125 mL
4	eggs	4

1. In a saucepan over medium heat, heat cream until bubbles form around the edges. Set aside.

2. Meanwhile, in work bowl fitted with metal blade, process lemon zest and juice and sugar until zest is very finely minced, about 30 seconds. Add eggs and process until blended. Add ½ cup (125 mL) of the warm cream and pulse until well combined. With motor running, add remainder down feed tube.

3. Place a fine-mesh sieve over a 4-cup (1 L) measuring cup or bowl with a pouring spout and strain lemon mixture. Pour strained mixture into ramekins and cover tightly with foil. (Secure with string or silicone ties.) Fill a baking dish big enough to hold the ramekins with hot water that comes two-thirds up their sides. Bake until center is slightly jiggly, about 35 minutes. (Baking time will vary depending upon the configuration of the ramekins.) Let cool on a rack for 1 hour. Transfer to refrigerator and chill thoroughly for at least 3 hours.

Chocolate Fudge Cake

Serves 8 to 10

Vegetarian Friendly

Chocoholics rejoice! Get a cold glass of milk for this decadent chocolate overload cake.

- Preheat oven to 350°F (180°C)
- 13- by 9-inch (33 by 23 cm) metal baking pan, sprayed with nonstick spray

3 cups	cake flour	750 mL
1 cup	unsweetened Dutch-process cocoa powder	250 mL
2½ tsp	baking powder	12 mL
¾ tsp	baking soda	3 mL
½ tsp	salt	2 mL
1 cup	unsalted butter, softened	250 mL
2 cups	lightly packed brown sugar	500 mL
1½ cups	whole milk	375 mL
3	eggs	3
½ tsp	vanilla extract	2 mL
½ tsp	rum extract	2 mL
	Chocolate Cream Cheese Icing (page 633)	

1. In a bowl, combine flour, cocoa powder, baking powder, baking soda and salt. Set aside.

2. In work bowl fitted with metal blade, process butter and brown sugar until smooth, about 30 seconds. Remove lid and add flour mixture. Process until incorporated, about 20 seconds. With motor running, add milk, eggs and vanilla and rum extracts through feed tube and process until smooth, about 30 seconds.

3. Pour batter into prepared pan, smoothing out to the sides. Bake in preheated oven until a tester inserted in the center comes out clean, 26 to 32 minutes. Let cool in pan on a wire rack for 10 minutes before transferring to a rack to cool completely. When cool, ice with Chocolate Cream Cheese Icing.

White Cake

Serves 12

Vegetarian Friendly

This simple, yet tasty cake is perfect for any occasion. Frost with either Bittersweet Fudge Frosting (page 634) or Buttercream Frosting (page 633).

Tip

If the milk is room temperature it incorporates more easily.

- Preheat oven to 350°F (180°C)
- 13- by 9-inch (33 by 23 cm) metal baking pan, sprayed with nonstick spray

1¼ cups	unsalted butter, softened	300 mL
2 cups	granulated sugar	500 mL
6	egg whites	6
2 tsp	vanilla extract	10 mL
3½ cups	cake flour	875 mL
1 tbsp	baking powder	15 mL
½ tsp	salt	2 mL
1 cup	whole milk, at room temperature, divided (see Tip, left)	250 mL

1. In work bowl fitted with metal blade, process butter and sugar until creamy, about 20 seconds. With motor running, pour egg whites through feed tube in a steady stream until incorporated, about 30 seconds. Add vanilla through feed tube.

2. In a bowl, blend together cake flour, baking powder and salt. Remove the lid and add half of the flour mixture to work bowl. Replace lid and process for 20 seconds.

3. With motor running, add half of the milk through feed tube and process until smooth, about 20 seconds. Remove the lid and add remaining flour mixture. Replace lid and process until thick and smooth, about 20 seconds. With motor running, add remaining milk through feed tube in a steady stream until incorporated, about 20 seconds. Scrape down bowl. Process just to incorporate, 5 seconds more. Pour into prepared pan, spreading to edges and smoothing top. Bake in preheated oven until golden brown and a toothpick inserted into the center comes out clean, 32 to 38 minutes. Let cool completely in pan on a rack.

Variation

You can substitute 2 whole eggs and 3 egg whites for the 6 egg whites to make a yellow cake.

French Apple Cheesecake

Serves 10 to 12

Vegetarian Friendly

Light crisp apples with a crunchy topping make this creamy cheesecake a decadent dessert for fall.

Tip

If using graham cracker crumbs, you'll need 1½ cups (375 mL) for this recipe.

- Preheat oven to 350°F (180°C)
- 9-inch (23 cm) cheesecake pan, or spingform pan with 3-inch (7.5 cm) sides, lined with parchment paper

Crust

6 oz	graham crackers (about 24 crackers) (see Tip, left)	175 g
¼ cup	unsalted butter, melted	60 mL

Topping

½ cup	pecans	125 mL
½ cup	lightly packed brown sugar	125 mL
¼ cup	unsalted butter, softened	60 mL
¼ cup	all-purpose flour	60 mL
¼ cup	old-fashioned rolled oats	60 mL
1½ tsp	ground cinnamon	7 mL
½ tsp	ground nutmeg	2 mL
½ tsp	salt	2 mL
2	baking apples, such as Rome, Jonathan, peeled, cored and quartered	2

Filling

4	packages (each 8 oz/250 g) cream cheese, cubed and softened	4
¼ cup	sour cream	60 mL
1¼ cups	lightly packed brown sugar	300 mL
4	eggs	4
2 tsp	vanilla extract	10 mL
2 tsp	freshly squeezed lemon juice	10 mL

1. **Crust:** In work bowl fitted with metal blade, process crackers until finely ground. Transfer to a bowl and mix in butter. Press into bottom of cheesecake pan and freeze until filling is ready.

2. **Topping:** In work bowl fitted with metal blade, process pecans, brown sugar, butter, flour, oats, cinnamon, nutmeg and salt for 20 seconds. Transfer to a large bowl. Set aside. Replace metal blade with slicing blade and slice apples. Add to bowl and toss to coat with pecan mixture. Set aside.

3. **Filling:** In clean work bowl with metal blade, process cream cheese, sour cream and brown sugar for 1 minute. With motor running, add eggs, vanilla and lemon juice through feed tube and process until blended. Pour batter over frozen crust, smoothing out to sides of pan. Sprinkle apple topping on top to create an even layer.

4. Bake in preheated oven until cake starts to pull away from sides of pan but is still loose in center and look puffy, 75 to 90 minutes. Let cool in pan on a wire rack for 2 hours. Cover with plastic wrap and refrigerate for at least 2 hours before serving.

Variation
Try sliced pears in place of apples.

New York Cheesecake

Serves 12 to 14

Vegetarian Friendly

The empire state claims they started the cheesecake craze. Here is a typical dense cake, tall and high.

Tip

If using graham cracker crumbs, you'll need 1½ cups (375 mL) for this recipe.

- Preheat oven to 500°F (260°C)
- 9-inch (23 cm) cheesecake pan, or spingform pan with 3-inch (7.5 cm) sides, lined with parchment paper
- Large 14-cup food processor

Crust

6 oz	graham crackers (about 24 crackers) (see Tip, left)	175 g
¼ cup	butter, melted	60 mL

Filling

5	packages (each 8 oz/250 g) cream cheese, cubed and softened	5
¼ cup	sour cream	60 mL
1¼ cups	granulated sugar	300 mL
¼ cup	all-purpose flour	60 mL
1½ tsp	grated lemon zest	7 mL
1½ tsp	grated orange zest	7 mL
5	eggs	5
2	egg yolks	2
¼ cup	heavy or whipping (35%) cream	60 mL
2 tsp	vanilla extract	10 mL

1. **Crust:** In work bowl fitted with metal blade, process crackers until finely ground. Transfer to a bowl and mix in butter. Press into bottom of cheesecake pan and freeze until filling is ready.

2. **Filling:** In clean work bowl fitted with metal blade, process cream cheese, sour cream, sugar, flour and lemon and orange zests for 2 minutes. With motor running, add eggs, egg yolks, cream and vanilla through feed tube and process until blended. Pour batter over frozen crust, smoothing out to sides of pan.

3. Bake in preheated oven for only 10 minutes. Reduce heat to 200°F (100°C). Bake for 60 minutes more. The top should be puffy like a soufflé with a light golden color. Let cool in pan on a wire rack for 2 hours. Cover with plastic wrap and refrigerate for at least 6 hours prior to serving.

Deep Dark Chocolate Fudge Cheesecake

Serves 6 to 8

Vegetarian Friendly

Here's a chocolate fudge cheesecake that's so rich you'll need a glass of milk to wash it down!

Tip

Make sure the chocolate is cooled to room temperature after melting; otherwise you'll get strange chunks in your batter.

- Preheat oven to 325°F (160°C)
- 6-inch (15 cm) cheesecake pan, or springform pan with 3-inch (7.5 cm) sides, lined with parchment paper

Crust

7	chocolate sandwich cookies (about 3 oz/90 g)	7
2 tbsp	butter, melted	30 mL

Filling

4 oz	unsweetened chocolate, chopped	125 g
2	packages (each 8 oz/250 g) cream cheese, cubed and softened	2
¾ cup	granulated sugar	175 mL
2	eggs	2
1 tsp	vanilla extract	5 mL
¼ cup	semisweet chocolate chips	60 mL

1. **Crust:** In work bowl fitted with metal blade, process cookies until finely ground, about 20 seconds. You should have ¾ cup (175 mL). Transfer to a bowl and mix in butter. Press into bottom of cheesecake pan and freeze until filling is ready.

2. **Filling:** In a microwave-safe bowl, microwave unsweetened chocolate on Medium, stirring every 30 seconds, until soft and almost melted, 1 to 1½ minutes. Stir until completely melted and smooth. Let cool slightly.

3. In clean work bowl fitted with metal blade, process cream cheese and sugar until smooth, about 20 seconds. With motor running, add melted chocolate, eggs and vanilla through feed tube and process until blended.

4. Pour over frozen crust, smoothing out to sides of pan. Sprinkle chocolate chips over top. Bake in preheated oven until it starts to pull away from sides of pan and center has a slight jiggle to it, 35 to 45 minutes. Let cool on a wire rack for 2 hours. Cover with plastic wrap and refrigerate for at least 2 hours before serving.

Lemon Mist Cheesecake

Serves 10 to 12

Vegetarian Friendly

Tart yet tangy, lemon cheesecake is refreshing with iced tea on a lazy afternoon.

Tip

To make the lemons easier to juice, roll them firmly on your counter to break up the membranes of the fruit.

- Preheat oven to 325°F (160°C)
- 9-inch (23 cm) cheesecake pan, or springform pan with 3-inch (7.5 cm) sides, lined with parchment paper

Crust

14	lemon cookies (about 6 oz/175 g)	14
¼ cup	butter, melted	60 mL

Filling

4	packages (each 8 oz/250 g) cream cheese, cubed and softened	4
1 cup	granulated sugar	250 mL
3	eggs	3
2 tbsp	grated lemon zest	30 mL
¼ cup	freshly squeezed lemon juice	60 mL
1 tsp	vanilla extract	5 mL

1. **Crust:** In work bowl fitted with metal blade, process cookies until finely ground. You should have 1½ cups (375 mL). Transfer to a bowl and mix in butter. Press into bottom of cheesecake pan and freeze until filling is ready.

2. **Filling:** In clean work bowl fitted with metal blade, process cream cheese and sugar until smooth, about 20 seconds. With motor running, add eggs, lemon zest and juice and vanilla through feed tube and process until blended. Pour batter over frozen crust, smoothing out to sides of pan.

3. Bake in preheated oven until it starts to pull away from sides of pan but is still a bit loose in center and looks puffy, 45 to 55 minutes. Let cool in pan on a wire rack for 2 hours. Cover with plastic wrap and refrigerate for at least 2 hours before serving.

Variation

Add ½ tsp (2 mL) grated lemon zest to a graham cracker crust if you can't find lemon cookies.

Citrus Bliss Cheesecake

Serves 10 to 12

Vegetarian Friendly

Tangy orange and lemon flavors come together in one sublime cheesecake.

Tip

The orange juice concentrate packs a powerful orange flavor while the orange juice alone does not.

- Preheat oven to 325°F (160°C)
- 9-inch (23 cm) cheesecake pan, or springform pan with 3-inch (7.5 cm) sides, lined with parchment paper

Crust

14	butter cookies (6 oz/175 g)	14
¼ cup	butter, melted	60 mL

Filling

3	packages (each 8 oz/250 g) cream cheese, cubed and softened	3
1 cup	sour cream	250 mL
1 cup	granulated sugar	250 mL
4	eggs	4
1 tbsp	grated lemon zest	15 mL
1 tbsp	grated orange zest	15 mL
2 tbsp	freshly squeezed lemon juice	30 mL
2 tbsp	orange juice concentrate (see Tip, left)	30 mL
2 tsp	vanilla extract	10 mL

1. **Crust:** In work bowl fitted with metal blade, process cookies until finely ground, about 20 seconds. You should have 1½ cups (375 mL). Transfer to a bowl and mix in butter. Press into bottom of cheesecake pan and freeze until filling is ready.

2. **Filling:** In clean work bowl fitted with metal blade, process cream cheese, sour cream and sugar until smooth, about 20 seconds. With motor running, add eggs, lemon and orange zests, lemon juice, orange juice concentrate and vanilla through feed tube and process until blended. Pour batter over frozen crust, smoothing out to sides of pan.

3. Bake in preheated oven until it starts to pull away from sides of pan but is still a bit loose in center and looks puffy, 45 to 55 minutes. Let cool on a wire rack for 2 hours. Cover with plastic wrap and refrigerate for at least 2 hours before serving.

Variation

Add 1 tsp (5 mL) ground cinnamon for a spiced cheesecake.

Three-Nut Cheesecake

Serves 10 to 12

Vegetarian Friendly

A rich nutty taste permeates this creamy cheesecake.

Tip

If you process nuts alone you may get nut butter; adding a little flour to the nuts prevents this by drying the oils.

- Preheat oven to 350°F (180°C)
- 9-inch (23 cm) cheesecake pan, or springform pan with 3-inch (7.5 cm) sides, lined with parchment paper

Crust

1½ cups	pecan halves	375 mL
¼ cup	all-purpose flour	60 mL
¼ cup	unsalted butter, melted	60 mL

Filling

1 cup	walnut halves	250 mL
¾ cup	cashews, unsalted	175 mL
2 tsp	all-purpose flour	10 mL
4	packages (each 8 oz/250 g) cream cheese, cubed and softened	4
1⅓ cups	granulated sugar	325 mL
4	eggs	4
1 tbsp	grated lemon zest	15 mL
2 tbsp	freshly squeezed lemon juice	30 mL
1 tsp	vanilla extract	5 mL
¼ tsp	maple flavoring	1 mL

1. **Crust:** In work bowl fitted with metal blade, process pecans and flour until finely ground, about 20 seconds. Transfer to a bowl and mix in butter. Press into bottom of cheesecake pan. Bake in preheated oven until nuts are toasted, about 10 minutes.

2. **Filling:** In work bowl, pulse walnuts, cashews and flour until coarsely chopped, about 15 times. Transfer to a bowl. Set aside.

3. In clean work bowl, process cream cheese and sugar until smooth, about 20 seconds. With motor running, add eggs, lemon zest and juice, vanilla and maple flavoring through feed tube and process until blended. Pour half of the batter over crust, smoothing out to sides of pan. Sprinkle half of the chopped nuts over top. Spoon remaining batter over nuts. Sprinkle remaining nuts over top.

4. Bake in preheated oven until it starts to pull away from sides of pan but is still a bit loose in center and looks puffy, 45 to 55 minutes. Let cool in pan on a wire rack for 2 hours. Cover with plastic wrap and refrigerate for at least 2 hours before serving.

Cherry Almond Crème Tarts

Makes 12 tarts

Vegetarian Friendly

These tarts are perfect to have on hand in the freezer in case of a dessert emergency!

- Preheat oven to 350°F (180°C)
- Twelve 3-inch (7.5 cm) tart pans with removable bottoms

1	recipe Buttery Tart Pastry Dough (page 477)	1
7 oz	almond paste, cut into small chunks	210 g
¾ cup	granulated sugar	175 mL
½ cup	slivered almonds, divided	125 mL
⅓ cup	unsalted butter, softened	75 mL
3	eggs	3
1 tsp	vanilla extract	5 mL
1 tsp	almond extract	5 mL
¾ cup	cake flour	175 mL
12 oz	prepared cherry pie filling (about 1½ cups/375 mL)	375 g

1. Press dough into tart shells. Set aside.

2. In work bowl fitted with metal blade, process almond paste, sugar and ¼ cup (60 mL) of the almonds until softened, about 30 seconds. Add butter and process until incorporated. With motor running, add eggs, vanilla and almond extracts through feed tube, processing until well incorporated, about 20 seconds. Remove lid and add flour and process until smooth, about 20 seconds. Divide mixture evenly between tart shells.

3. Spoon pie filling into a sieve set over a bowl and drain off most of the thick liquid (discard liquid or reserve for another use). Divide drained cherries evenly on top of almond filling and sprinkle with remaining almonds, just pressing slightly into the almond cream.

4. Place tart pans on baking sheet. Bake in preheated oven until crust is light brown and filling is set, 30 to 35 minutes. Let cool on a wire rack completely before removing from tins.

Banana Cupcakes

Makes 24 cupcakes

Vegetarian Friendly

Bananas tend to make the moistest cupcakes that you can imagine. Top with a fluffy icing, such as Cream Cheese Icing.

- Preheat oven to 350°F (180°C)
- Two 12-cup muffin tins, lined with paper liners

3 cups	cake flour	750 mL
1 tsp	baking soda	5 mL
½ tsp	baking powder	2 mL
½ tsp	salt	2 mL
½ cup	pecans	125 mL
1 cup	unsalted butter, softened	250 mL
2 cups	granulated sugar	500 mL
1½ cups	mashed ripe bananas (about 4)	375 mL
3	eggs	3
6 tbsp	buttermilk	90 mL
2 tsp	vanilla extract	10 mL
	Cream Cheese Icing (page 634)	

1. In a bowl, combine flour, baking soda, baking powder and salt. Set aside.

2. In work bowl fitted with metal blade, pulse pecans about 10 times to chop. Transfer to another bowl.

3. In same work bowl, process butter, sugar and bananas until smooth, about 30 seconds. With motor running, add eggs, buttermilk and vanilla through feed tube. Add flour mixture. Process until incorporated, about 20 seconds. Fold in pecans.

4. Divide evenly in prepared muffin tins. Bake in preheated oven until a tester inserted in the center comes out clean, 18 to 22 minutes. Let cool in tins for 10 minutes prior to removing and placing on a wire rack to cool completely. Ice cooled cupcakes with Cream Cheese Icing.

Hummingbird Cupcakes

Makes 24 cupcakes

Vegetarian Friendly

These cupcakes are full of moist textures and flavor. They're so good you can eat them without a frosting.

- Preheat oven to 325°F (160°C)
- Two 12-cup muffin tins, lined with paper liners

3 cups	all-purpose flour	750 mL
1 tsp	ground cinnamon	5 mL
1 tsp	baking soda	5 mL
1 tsp	salt	5 mL
½ tsp	freshly grated nutmeg	2 mL
½ cup	pecans	125 mL
2 cups	granulated sugar	500 mL
2¼ cups	mashed ripe bananas (about 6)	550 mL
1¼ cups	oil	300 mL
3	eggs	3
1½ tsp	vanilla extract	7 mL
1	can (8 oz/227 mL) crushed pineapple, drained	1

1. In a bowl, combine flour, cinnamon, baking soda, salt and nutmeg. Set aside.

2. In work bowl fitted with metal blade, pulse pecans about 10 times to chop. Transfer to another bowl.

3. In same work bowl, process sugar and bananas until smooth, about 30 seconds. With motor running add oil, eggs and vanilla through feed tube. Remove lid and add flour mixture and pineapple. Process until incorporated, about 20 seconds. Fold in pecans.

4. Divide evenly in prepared muffin tins. Bake in preheated oven until a tester inserted into center comes out clean, 18 to 22 minutes. Let cool in tins for 10 minutes prior to removing and placing on a wire rack to cool completely.

Cinnamon Pecan Cupcakes

Makes 12 cupcakes

Vegetarian Friendly

These are perfect cupcakes to serve for brunch or afternoon coffee.

Tips

If butter and cream cheese are not softened prior to use, place in small chunks in the work bowl and process until smooth. Then add sugar.

Double the recipe if desired for 24 cupcakes. Rotate tins during baking to prevent burning on the edges.

- Preheat oven to 375°F (190°C)
- 12-cup muffin tin, lined with paper liners or sprayed with nonstick spray

½ cup	pecan halves	125 mL
1½ cups	granulated sugar	375 mL
¾ cup	unsalted butter, softened	175 mL
4 oz	cream cheese, cubed and softened	125 g
3	eggs	3
1½ tsp	freshly squeezed lemon juice	7 mL
1 tsp	vanilla extract	5 mL
1⅓ cups	cake flour	325 mL
1½ tsp	ground cinnamon	7 mL
Pinch	salt	Pinch

1. In work bowl fitted with metal blade, process pecans until finely chopped. Transfer to a bowl.

2. In same work bowl, process sugar, butter and cream cheese until smooth, about 30 seconds. With motor running, add eggs, lemon juice and vanilla through feed tube and process until blended. Remove lid and add cake flour, cinnamon and salt. Cover and process just until incorporated, about 15 seconds. Add pecans and process for 5 seconds.

3. Divide batter evenly into prepared muffin tin. Bake in preheated oven until a toothpick inserted in center comes out clean, 22 to 26 minutes. Let cool in tin for 10 minutes on a wire rack. Transfer to rack to cool completely.

Variation

You can also bake this recipe in a parchment-lined 9- by 5-inch (23 by 12.5 cm) metal loaf pan. Increase baking time to 40 to 45 minutes.

Blueberry Crisp

Serves 8 to 10

Vegan Friendly

Rich blueberries make this a perfect crisp when berries are plentiful.

- Preheat oven to 400°F (200°C)
- 13- by 9-inch (33 by 23 cm) glass baking dish, buttered or sprayed with nonstick spray

Topping

1 cup	all-purpose flour	250 mL
1 cup	packed light brown sugar	250 mL
2/3 cup	old-fashioned rolled oats	150 mL
1/2 tsp	ground cinnamon	2 mL
1/4 tsp	salt	1 mL
2/3 cup	cold unsalted butter, cut into small chunks, or vegan alternative	150 mL

Filling

3 1/2 cups	fresh or frozen blueberries (1 1/2 lbs/750 g)	875 mL
1/2 cup	granulated sugar	125 mL
	Finely grated zest and juice of 1 lemon	
3 tbsp	all-purpose flour	45 mL

1. **Topping:** In a food processor fitted with metal blade, process flour, brown sugar, oats, cinnamon and salt for 5 seconds. Remove lid and distribute butter evenly over top. Cover and pulse until mixture resembles coarse crumbs, about 20 times. Set aside.

2. **Filling:** In a large bowl, combine blueberries, sugar, lemon zest and juice and flour. Stir to coat berries evenly. Transfer to prepared baking dish. Crumble topping over berries. Bake in preheated oven until bubbling around sides, 28 to 32 minutes. Serve warm.

Mixed Fruit Buckle

Serves 12 to 16

Vegetarian Friendly

A buckle is a cake that is laced with large pieces of fruit. This is a good one for summer picnics.

- Preheat oven to 375°F (190°C)
- 13- by 9-inch (33 by 23 cm) glass baking dish, buttered or sprayed with nonstick spray

Streusel Topping

1⅔ cups	all-purpose flour	400 mL
½ cup	granulated sugar	125 mL
2 tsp	ground cinnamon	10 mL
¼ tsp	salt	1 mL
½ cup	cold unsalted butter, cut in small chunks	125 mL

Cake

¾ cup	unsalted butter, softened	175 mL
2 cups	granulated sugar	500 mL
6	eggs	6
1 tbsp	vanilla extract	15 mL
1 tsp	almond extract	5 mL
2⅔ cups	all-purpose flour	650 mL
1 tbsp	baking powder	15 mL
1 tsp	salt	5 mL
8 cups	chopped peeled stone fruit, such as peaches, plums and nectarines, divided	2 L

1. **Streusel Topping:** In a food processor fitted with metal blade, process flour, sugar, cinnamon and salt for 10 seconds. Remove lid and distribute butter evenly over top. Cover and pulse until mixture resembles coarse crumbs, about 20 times. Set aside.

2. **Cake:** In a mixer bowl fitted with paddle attachment, beat butter and sugar until smooth, about 3 minutes. Add eggs, one at a time, beating well between each addition. Beat in vanilla and almond extracts. Using a wooden spoon, gradually stir in flour, baking powder and salt just until incorporated. Add half the fruit to batter and fold in gently with a large rubber spatula. Spread batter into prepared dish and top evenly with rest of fruit. Sprinkle with Streusel Topping.

3. Bake in preheated oven until cake springs back in center when lightly pressed and toothpick comes out clean, 45 to 50 minutes. Let cool on a rack. Serve warm.

Apple Crisp with Crumb Topping

Vegan Friendly

When you have an abundance of apples and want a fast dessert try this instead of pie.

Tips

Make sure the butter is cold from the refrigerator or topping will not be crumbly.

Use a food processor with a slicing blade to make quick work of slicing the apples. You don't even need to clean the bowl after making the topping.

- Preheat oven to 350°F (180°C)
- 13- by 9-inch (33 by 23 cm) glass baking dish, buttered

Topping

1½ cups	all-purpose flour	375 mL
½ cup	lightly packed light brown sugar	125 mL
2 tbsp	granulated sugar	30 mL
½ tsp	ground cinnamon	2 mL
¼ tsp	salt	1 mL
½ cup	cold unsalted butter, cut into small chunks, or vegan alternative	125 mL

Filling

1 cup	granulated sugar	250 mL
2 tbsp	all-purpose flour	30 mL
1 tsp	ground cinnamon	5 mL
½ tsp	freshly grated nutmeg	2 mL
¼ tsp	ground cloves	1 mL
6	large baking apples, peeled and thinly sliced	6

1. **Topping:** In a food processor fitted with metal blade, pulse flour, brown and granulated sugars, cinnamon and salt until combined, about 5 times. Remove lid and distribute butter evenly over top. Cover and pulse until mixture resembles coarse crumbs, about 20 times. Transfer to a bowl. Set aside.

2. **Filling:** In a large bowl, combine sugar, flour, cinnamon, nutmeg and cloves. Add apples and toss to evenly coat. Transfer to prepared baking dish. Crumble topping over apples. Bake in preheated oven until brown and bubbling, 35 to 40 minutes. Serve warm.

Variation
You can add ¼ cup (60 mL) nuts to the topping when processing flour mixture.

Pear Pandowdy

Serves 16

Vegan Friendly

A pandowdy is an old-fashioned dessert often made with apples. Here we've used pears. The dough is placed on top of the fruit prior to baking to form a crisp crumbly topping. Serve warm with vanilla ice cream, if desired.

Tip

Pears do not have to be peeled; just core and process.

- Preheat oven to 375°F (190°C)
- 13- by 9-inch (33 by 23 cm) metal baking pan, buttered

Topping

¾ cup	cake flour	175 mL
¾ cup	all-purpose flour	175 mL
2 tsp	granulated sugar	10 mL
¼ tsp	salt	1 mL
½ cup	cold unsalted butter, cut into chunks, or vegan alternative	125 mL
¼ cup	cold water	60 mL

Filling

1 cup	granulated sugar	250 mL
3 tbsp	all-purpose flour	45 mL
1½ tsp	ground cinnamon	7 mL
½ tsp	freshly ground nutmeg	2 mL
8	pears, cored and quartered, such as Anjou or Bartlett (see Tip, left)	8
2 tbsp	unsalted butter, melted, or vegan alternative	30 mL
2 tbsp	apple cider or apple juice	30 mL

1. **Topping:** In work bowl fitted with metal blade, process cake and all-purpose flours, sugar and salt until combined, about 5 seconds. Remove lid and distribute butter evenly over top. Cover and pulse until mixture resembles coarse crumbs, about 20 times. The mixture should be in small pieces. With motor running, add water through feed tube until dough begins to gather. Remove dough and pat into a ball. If it is sticky at this point you can cover and place in the refrigerator until firm, 5 to 10 minutes. Roll out to 13- by 9-inch (32.5 by 23 cm) rectangle, ¼-inch (0.5 cm) thick. Cut into squares. Set aside.

2. **Filling:** In a large bowl, blend together sugar, flour, cinnamon and nutmeg. Set aside.

3. Replace metal blade with slicing blade and slice pears. Add pears to sugar mixture and toss to fully coat. Transfer to prepared baking dish. Slowly drizzle butter and apple cider over top. Place dough squares over top. Bake in preheated oven until pears are tender and top is golden brown, 45 to 55 minutes.

Apple Pockets

Vegetarian Friendly

Keep these pockets on hand in the freezer in case of company.

Tips

If you have a smaller package of puff pastry, the pastry may be thinner but will still work.

You can use 3 different types of baking apples in these pockets. Good baking apples are McIntosh, Jonagold, Granny Smith and Pippin.

You can freeze the apple pockets for up to 1 month. Cover with foil and reheat in a preheated 350°F (180°C) oven for 10 minutes.

- Preheat oven to 425°F (220°C)
- Baking sheet, lined with parchment paper

3	large baking apples (about 1½ lbs/750 g) (see Tips, left)	3
2 tbsp	freshly squeezed lemon juice	30 mL
½ cup	lightly packed brown sugar	125 mL
1½ tbsp	all-purpose flour	22 mL
1 tsp	ground cinnamon	5 mL
½ tsp	freshly ground nutmeg	2 mL
1	package (18 oz/540 g) puff pastry, thawed (see Tips, left)	1
2 tsp	water	10 mL
2 tsp	coarse sugar	10 mL

1. Peel, quarter and core apples. In work bowl fitted with slicing blade, slice apples. Transfer to a large bowl filled with enough water to cover apple slices and lemon juice. Set aside.

2. In another large bowl, blend together brown sugar, flour, cinnamon and nutmeg. Drain apples well and add to sugar mixture. Toss to fully coat apple pieces. Set aside.

3. Working with one half of pastry, on a lightly floured board, roll one sheet of pastry into a 12-inch (30 cm) square. Using a pizza cutter, cut equally, horizontally and vertically, so you end up with 3 strips by 3 strips to make 9 squares.

4. Place about ¼ cup (60 mL) of the sliced apple mixture into center of each square of pastry. Working with one square at a time, starting with two opposite corners, fold into the center and press to seal over the apple filling. Repeat with third and fourth corners, meeting over top first ones to resemble an envelope and press to seal edges. If pastry seems dry, lightly brush edges with water before folding to ensure a good seal. Transfer to prepared baking sheet, about 2 inches (5 cm) apart. Brush each with a little water and sprinkle with coarse sugar. Repeat with remaining pastry and filling to make 18 pockets. Bake in preheated oven until golden brown and puffed up, 18 to 24 minutes. Serve hot.

Pumpkin Pecan Pie

Serves 6 to 8

Vegetarian Friendly

Who doesn't love both pumpkin and pecan pies? Here they are together in one pie.

Tip

Check your pie at 40 minutes. If a knife comes out runny with a few firm pieces attached, the pie needs 10 minutes more; if you see only firm pieces but the knife is still not clean, it needs 5 additional minutes. You never want the knife to come out completely clean the first time because it might be overbaked at this point.

- Preheat oven to 375°F (190°C)
- 9-inch (23 cm) pie plate

½	recipe Spiced Pie Pastry Dough (page 476)	½
½ cup	pecan halves	125 mL
1½ cups	pumpkin purée (not pie filling)	375 mL
¾ cup	packed light brown sugar	175 mL
2 tsp	ground cinnamon	10 mL
1 tsp	ground ginger	5 mL
½ tsp	ground cloves	2 mL
½ tsp	salt	2 mL
½ tsp	freshly grated nutmeg	2 mL
3	eggs, beaten	3
1¼ cups	milk, preferably whole	300 mL
¾ cup	evaporated milk	175 mL

1. On a lightly floured surface, roll out dough and fit into bottom of pie pan. Set aside.

2. In a food processor fitted with metal blade, pulse pecans until finely chopped, about 15 times. Do not overprocess or you will get pecan butter. Spread pecans over pastry.

3. In same work bowl, process pumpkin, brown sugar, cinnamon, ginger, cloves, salt and nutmeg until smooth, about 30 seconds. With motor running, add eggs through feed tube. Then pour in milk and evaporated milk in a steady stream and process until incorporated.

4. Pour mixture over pecans in prepared pie shell. Bake in preheated oven until crust is firm and light brown and a knife inserted into the center of filling comes out clean, 40 to 50 minutes (see Tip, left). Let cool on a wire rack for at least 1 hour prior to cutting.

Variation
Reduce milk by ¼ cup (60 mL) and use coffee-flavored liqueur instead.

Apple Spice Pie

Vegetarian Friendly

You can create this pie faster than going to the store or bakery and purchasing one.

Tip

Use a mixture of three different types of baking apples in your pie.

- Preheat oven to 400°F (200°C)
- 9-inch (23 cm) pie plate

1	recipe Spiced Pie Pastry Dough (page 476)	1
6	large baking apples, peeled, cored and quartered (see Tip, left)	6
¼ cup	freshly squeezed lemon juice	60 mL
1 cup	granulated sugar	250 mL
3 tbsp	all-purpose flour	45 mL
1½ tsp	ground cinnamon	7 mL
½ tsp	freshly grated nutmeg	2 mL
2 tbsp	butter, melted	30 mL
2 tsp	water	10 mL
2 tsp	coarse sugar	10 mL

1. On a lightly floured surface, roll out half of the dough and fit into bottom of pie pan. Roll the remaining half into a ¼-inch (0.5 cm) thick circle for the top. Set aside.

2. In a food processor fitted with slicing blade and with motor running, slice apples. Transfer to a bowl filled with enough water to cover apple slices and lemon juice. Set aside.

3. In a large bowl, blend together sugar, flour, cinnamon and nutmeg until fully incorporated. Drain apples and add to sugar mixture. Toss to fully coat apple slices. Fill bottom crust with apple mixture. Drizzle butter over top. Place top pastry crust over filling. Seal and crimp edges, trimming off any excess dough. Using a knife, make several slits in the top of the dough, or use a small cookie cutter to cut a design from the center of the pie for steam to escape.

4. Brush top with water and sprinkle with coarse sugar. Bake in preheated oven until light brown and filling is bubbling, 40 to 55 minutes. Let cool on a wire rack for at least 1 hour before cutting.

Pear Almond Crème Tarts

Makes 2 tarts

Vegetarian Friendly

These are the beautiful tarts that you see in French pastry shop windows. It's amazing at how expensive they are when they're so simple to make.

Tip

You can make the cream a few days prior to use. Cover and refrigerate and then stir before using.

- Preheat oven to 375°F (190°C)
- Two 8-inch (20 cm) metal tart pans with removable bottoms

1	recipe Buttery Tart Pastry Dough (page 477)	1
7 oz	almond paste, cut into chunks	210 g
¾ cup	granulated sugar	175 mL
⅓ cup	unsalted butter, softened	75 mL
3	eggs	3
1 tsp	vanilla extract	5 mL
¾ cup	cake flour	175 mL
12	small canned pear halves, drained	12

1. Press dough into tart pans. Set aside.

2. In a food processor fitted with metal blade, process almond paste and sugar until softened, about 30 seconds. Add butter and process until incorporated. With motor running, add eggs and vanilla through feed tube until well incorporated, about 20 seconds. Add flour and process until smooth, about 30 seconds.

3. Divide mixture evenly between tart shells. Slice each pear half vertically into 6 to 8 slices, trying to keep the pear looking like it's still intact. Place sliced pear over almond cream, pressing to fan pear. Do this five more times around the tart so you have 6 pear halves on each tart. Bake in preheated oven until crust is light brown and filling is set, 45 to 60 minutes.

Variation

Try using 6 fresh peaches, peeled, pitted and cut in half, or 1 cup (250 mL) canned peaches or cherries, drained, in place of the pears for each tart.

Caramel Chocolate Tarts

Vegetarian Friendly

This chocolate-rich tart is filled with a sweet caramel chocolate cream.

Tip

Make sure the chocolate is cool prior to adding it to the milk or it may turn into chocolate chips.

- Instant-read thermometer

1	recipe Chocolate Tart Dough (page 478), baked	1
4 oz	unsweetened chocolate, chopped	125 g
1 cup	granulated sugar	250 mL
1/3 cup	all-purpose flour	75 mL
1 tbsp	cornstarch	15 mL
1 tsp	instant coffee granules	5 mL
Pinch	salt	Pinch
4 oz	soft caramels, cut into small pieces (about 12)	125 g
2 cups	milk	500 mL
5	egg yolks, beaten	5
1 tsp	vanilla extract	5 mL
	Whipped cream	

1. Set aside prepared baked tart shells until filling is ready.

2. In a microwave-safe bowl, microwave chocolate on Medium, stirring every 30 seconds, until soft and almost melted, 1 to 1½ minutes. Stir until completely melted and smooth. Let cool slightly.

3. Meanwhile, in work bowl fitted with metal blade, process sugar, flour, cornstarch, coffee granules and salt until combined, about 10 seconds. Add caramels to work bowl. Set aside.

4. In a saucepan over medium heat, bring milk, chocolate and eggs yolks to a simmer, stirring, until an instant-read thermometer registers 160°F (71°C) and mixture is thick enough to coat the back of a spoon. Add vanilla. With motor running, add to sugar mixture through feed tube until blended and caramels are chopped.

5. Divide mixture evenly between tart shells. Refrigerate, covered, until set, at least 1 to 2 hours or for up to 4 hours. Serve with whipped cream.

Variation
Add ½ cup (125 mL) hazelnuts to the mixture for a nutty taste.

Cherry Almond Tart

Vegetarian Friendly

Bright red cherries encased by the almond cream make this a delight for any holiday pastry table in spring or winter.

Tips

Make sure almond paste is cut into smaller pieces prior to placing into food processor.

To use up leftover dough, add a little lemon zest and make small rounds the size of a large marble. Place on a lined baking sheet and bake in 350°F (180°C) oven until golden, for 8 to 10 minutes. Roll warm cookies in sugar.

- Preheat oven to 375°F (190°C)
- 10-inch (25 cm), metal tart pan with removable bottom

1	recipe Buttery Tart Pastry Dough (page 477)	1
7 oz	almond paste, cut into chunks	210 g
¾ cup	packed light brown sugar	175 mL
⅓ cup	unsalted butter, softened	75 mL
3	eggs	3
1 tsp	vanilla extract	5 mL
1 tsp	almond extract	5 mL
¾ cup	cake flour	175 mL
¾ cup	drained sour cherries (jarred or thawed frozen)	175 mL

1. Press dough into tart pan and set aside. (You will not need all of the dough. See Tips, left.)

2. In a food processor fitted with metal blade, process almond paste and brown sugar until softened, about 30 seconds. Add butter and process until incorporated. With motor running, add eggs, and vanilla and almond extracts through feed tube until well incorporated, about 20 seconds. Add flour and process until smooth, about 30 seconds.

3. Pour mixture into prepared tart shell. Arrange cherries on top. Bake in preheated oven until crust is light brown and filling is set, 45 to 60 minutes.

Hard Whiskey Sauce

**Makes 2 cups
(500 mL)**

Vegetarian Friendly

This thick sauce is
perfect for bread
pudding or topping
ice cream.

Tip

Store sauce, covered and
refrigerated, for up to
2 weeks. Serve warm.

½ cup	unsalted butter, melted	125 mL
1½ cups	confectioner's (icing) sugar	375 mL
½ cup	whiskey	125 mL

1. In a saucepan, melt butter over low heat.

2. In work bowl fitted with metal blade, process sugar and
   melted butter. With motor running, add whiskey through
   feed tube until combined. Serve.

Spicy Applesauce

**Makes 3 cups
(750 mL)**

Vegan Friendly

This is not your typical
applesauce. It's hot,
flavorful and spicy.

7	baking apples, such as McIntosh, Rome, Granny Smith, peeled and quartered	7
1¼ cups	granulated sugar	300 mL
¼ cup	liquid honey or pure maple syrup	60 mL
2 tbsp	freshly squeezed lemon juice	30 mL
1 tsp	freshly grated nutmeg	5 mL
1 tsp	ground cinnamon	5 mL
¼ tsp	cayenne pepper	1 mL

1. In work bowl fitted with slicing blade, slice apples.

2. In a medium saucepan over medium heat, combine
   apple slices, sugar, honey, lemon juice, nutmeg, cinnamon
   and cayenne. Reduce heat to low and cook, stirring
   occasionally, until apples are tender and softened, about
   8 minutes.

3. Transfer mixture to work bowl fitted with a metal blade
   and pulse about 10 times just to chop finely. Serve warm
   or let cool completely before refrigerating, about 1 hour.

Raspberry Sauce

Makes 1½ cups (375 mL)

Vegan Friendly

Use this sauce in the Macadamia-Crusted Salmon (page 269) or spoon over ice cream or a vegan alternative for a wonderful treat.

Tips

Store sauce, cooled completely, covered and refrigerated, for up to 5 days.

1	bag (10 oz/300 g) frozen raspberries, thawed (about 2 cups/500 mL)	1
1 cup	granulated sugar	250 mL
¼ cup	cornstarch	60 mL
2 tsp	freshly squeezed lemon juice	10 mL

1. In work bowl fitted with metal blade, process raspberries, sugar, cornstarch and lemon juice until smooth, about 1 minute.

2. Transfer mixture to a saucepan over medium heat. Heat mixture, stirring constantly, until it starts to boil and thicken, about 10 minutes. Place in a bowl.

Variation

You can use a bag of mixed berries, about 2 cups (500 mL) in place of the raspberries.

Apple Raisin Sauce

Makes 2 cups (500 mL)

Vegan Friendly

Serve this lovely sauce with scones or over ice cream.

Tips

If the apples are not baking apples they may break down too much and create applesauce. Cortland and Granny Smith are good choices for baking apples.

Store sauce, cooled completely, covered and refrigerated for up to 3 days.

3	baking apples, peeled, cored and quartered (see Tips, left)	3
½ cup	granulated sugar	125 mL
1 tsp	ground cinnamon	5 mL
½ tsp	ground nutmeg	2 mL
½ cup	golden raisins	125 mL
2 tbsp	rum, optional	30 mL

1. In work bowl fitted with slicing blade, slice apples.

2. In a saucepan over medium heat, combine apples, sugar, cinnamon and nutmeg. Cook, stirring, until the mixture starts to break down and bubbles slightly, about 5 minutes. Remove from heat and stir in raisins, and rum, if using. Serve warm or cold.

Variation

You can use the same amount of dried cranberries in place of the raisins.

Buttercream Frosting

**Makes about
2 cups (500 mL)**

Vegetarian Friendly

The food processor
makes the creamiest
and smoothest
frostings! You don't
even have to sift the
confectioner's sugar. Use
in for Banana Cupcakes
(page 618), 24 Carrot
Cake (page 509),
Cinnamon Pecan
Cupcakes (page 620) or
Hummingbird Cupcakes
(page 619).

½ cup	unsalted butter, softened, cut into cubes	125 mL
3½ cups	confectioner's (icing) sugar	875 mL
¼ cup	milk, preferably whole	60 mL
2 tsp	almond extract	10 mL

1. In work bowl with metal blade, process butter until smooth, about 30 seconds. Scrape down bowl. Add confectioner's sugar and process until it just begins to gather, about 15 seconds. With motor running, drizzle milk and almond extract through feed tube and process until smooth, about 30 seconds.

Variations
Add 1 cup (250 mL) toasted sweetened coconut flaked for a flavorful frosting.

Use the same amount of vanilla in place of almond extract for a vanilla buttercream.

Chocolate Cream Cheese Icing

**Makes about
2 cups (500 mL)**

Vegetarian Friendly

This is the richest
icing we know. Use
high-quality chocolate
for best results. Use on
a favorite cupcake or for
white cake layers.

6 oz	unsweetened chocolate, chopped	175 g
4 oz	bittersweet chocolate, chopped	125 g
4 oz	cream cheese, cubed and softened	125 g
2 cups	confectioner's (icing) sugar	500 mL
¼ cup	milk, preferably whole	60 mL
1½ tbsp	butter, softened	22 mL
1 tsp	vanilla extract	5 mL

1. In a heatproof bowl set over a saucepan of simmering water, melt unsweetened and bittersweet chocolates, stirring until smooth. Let cool slightly.

2. In work bowl fitted with metal blade, process cream cheese and melted chocolates for 10 seconds. Add confectioner's sugar and process for another 15 seconds. With motor running, add milk, butter and vanilla through feed tube and process until smooth, about 45 seconds.

3. Transfer to a bowl. If icing is too loose, chill in the refrigerator until firm enough to spread.

Bittersweet Fudge Frosting

Makes about 2¼ cups (550 mL)

Vegetarian Friendly

When you're in need of a deep rich fudge frosting to top your cakes or cupcakes, this one fits the bill perfectly.

4 oz	bittersweet chocolate, chopped	125 g
½ cup	unsalted butter, softened, cut into cubes	125 mL
4 cups	confectioner's (icing) sugar	1 L
1 tsp	rum extract	5 mL

1. In a heatproof bowl set over a saucepan of simmering water, melt chocolate, stirring until smooth. Let cool slightly.

2. In work bowl fitted with metal blade, process butter until smooth, about 30 seconds. Scrape down bowl. Add confectioner's sugar and process until it just begins to gather, about 15 seconds. With motor running, add chocolate and rum extract through feed tube and process until smooth, about 30 seconds.

Cream Cheese Icing

Makes 2 cups (500 mL), enough for one 9-inch (23 cm) cake

Vegetarian Friendly

The texture is perfect and spreads nicely.

Tip

If butter or cream cheese is not softened there will be chunks in the icing.

8 oz	cream cheese, cubed and softened	250 g
¼ cup	unsalted butter, softened, cut into cubes	60 mL
1½ tsp	vanilla extract	7 mL
2½ cups	confectioner's (icing) sugar	625 mL

1. In work bowl fitted with metal blade, process cream cheese and butter until smooth, about 20 seconds. With motor running, add vanilla through feed tube until incorporated. Scrape down bowl. Add confectioner's sugar and process until smooth, about 30 seconds.

Library and Archives Canada Cataloguing in Publication

Geary, George
    650 best food processor recipes / George Geary & Judith Finlayson; editor: Carol Sherman.

Includes index.
ISBN 978-0-7788-0250-1

1. Food processor cookery. I. Finlayson, Judith II. Title.
III. Title: Six hundred and fifty best food processor recipes.

TX840.F6G43 2010   641.5'892   C2010-903259-4

Index